VISUAL QUICKSTART GUIDE

Photoshop 6

FOR WINDOWS AND MACINTOSH

Elaine Weinmann
Peter Lourekas

Peachpit Press

In memory of Bert Weinmann,
Loving, vivacious, and courageous spirit

Visual QuickStart Guide
Photoshop 6 for Windows and Macintosh
Elaine Weinmann and Peter Lourekas

Peachpit Press
1249 Eighth Street
Berkeley, CA 94710
510/524-2178
800/283-9444
510/524-2221 (fax)

Find us on the World Wide Web at: www.peachpit.com

Visual QuickStart Guide is a trademark of Peachpit Press, a division of Addison Wesley Longman

Cover design: The Visual Group
Interior design: Elaine Weinmann
Production: Elaine Weinmann and Peter Lourekas
Illustrations: Elaine Weinmann and Peter Lourekas, except as noted

Colophon
This book was created with QuarkXPress 4.03 on a Power Macintosh 8500 and a Power PowerTower Pro 200. The primary fonts used were New Baskerville and Franklin Gothic from Adobe Systems Inc. and Anna and Gillies Gothic from Image Club Graphics, Inc.

ISBN 0-201-71309-8
9 8 7 6 5 4 3 2 1

Printed and bound in the United States of America

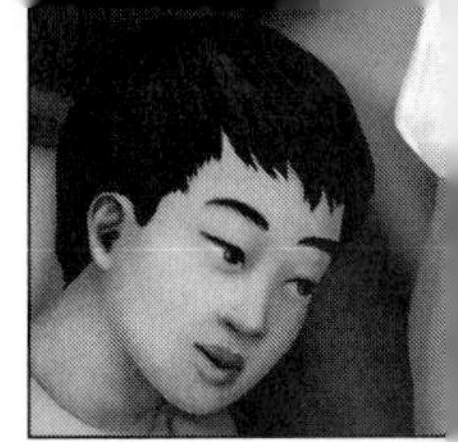

Acknowledgements

WELL, IT WAS A CLOSE RACE between us and the Supreme Court, and for quite a while it was too close to call, but the Presidential election was settled (sort of) before we finished this book. Well, at least we counted all our pixels and gave it our all, if that's any concession. If there are any errors in this book, the television set in Elaine's office is to blame.

As for whatever was done right in this book, we owe some gratitude to all of the following people:

Nancy Aldrich-Ruenzel, Publisher, Peachpit Press. She "suggested" we try to finish this book in a compressed time frame—and we fell for it! Luckily for her, Santa Claus bestowed the two newest members of our household, Poo-Chi Distraction 1 and Poo-Chi Distraction 2 (robotic interactive puppies) after we dotted the last "i."

Marjorie Baer, Executive Editor, for helping us find the help we sorely needed.

Cary Norsworthy, Editor, for answering our constant questions and requests so quickly, it borders on mindreading.

Victor Gavenda, Technical Editor at Peachpit Press, for testing this book in Windows and revising several chapters when he should have been on a tropical island recuperating from coauthorship of his awesome new book, *Real World Bryce 4* (Peachpit Press? Why, of course).

Lisa Brazieal, Production Coordinator, for getting our electronic files ready for the print shop.

Mimi Heft, for her beautiful cover design.

Gary-Paul Prince, Publicist.

Keasley Jones, Associate Publisher.

The rest of the growing family of ***Peachpitters.***

Tom Baer, Ronnie Bincer, Lisa Brenneis, Nolan Hester, Barb Obermeier, freelance writers, for revising various chapters ("delegate" is our favorite new word!).

Leona Benten, for proofreading and copy editing.

Cheryl Landes, for indexing.

Adobe Systems, Inc., for making software that's not always easy to write about, but *is* easy to get enthusiastic about. (Just do us a favor, folks—slow down the upgrade cycle. What's the Big Hurry?)

Lois Thompson and the ***crew*** at ***Malloy Lithographing,*** for not only doing a quality print job, but doing it in record time under enormous pressure.

The artists

Jeff Brice
4510 171 Avenue S.E.
Snohomish, WA 98290
Voice 360-568-7924
jb@jeffbrice.com
www.jeffbrice.com
(xxvi, color section, 516)

Alicia Buelow
150a Mississippi Street
San Francisco, CA 94107
abuelow@sirius.com
www.aliciabuelow.com
(color section)

Stephanie Dalton Cowan
Stephanie Dalton Cowan
Toll free 877-792-7096
daltoncowan@earthlink.net
www.theispot.com/artist/scowan
Stock art:
www.artville.com/cd/smblicns
(color section)

Wendy Grossman
355 West 51st Street
New York, NY 10019
Voice 949-362-1848
and 212-262-4497
wendygart@aol.com
www.rosebudstudios.com
(pages 60, 216 and color section)

David Humphrey
448 West 16th Street, 5th Fl.
New York, NY 10011
Voice 212-780-0512
aikenhump@aol.com
(page 117)

Alan Mazzetti
834 Moultrie Street
San Francisco, CA 94110
Voice 415-647-7677
maymaz@pacbell.net
www.amazzetti.com
(color section, 516)

Walter Robertson
Artesano Design Studio
10 Tamarac Place
Aliso Viego, CA 92656
Voice 949-362-1848
artesano@home.com
www.ArtesanoOnline.com
(color section)

Naomi Shea
35 Hyde Hill Road
Williamsburg, MA 01096
Voice 413-268-3407
naomi@naomishea.com
www.naomishea.com
(color section, 515)

Suling Wang
Voice 415-474-0259
Fax 801-751-4690
Suling_wang@mindspring.com
www.best.com/~sulingw/
(xxiv, xxv, color section)

WE STILL REMEMBER clearly how difficult it was to scrape a color gallery together for early editions of this book. We had to use overnight carriers to get artists' work. Then, once we got the files, they were incredibly cumbersome to store. We had to rely on the telephone for communication (so retro!), and to tell you the truth, there wasn't much great work being done yet in Photoshop. Electronic image editing was still in its infancy as an art form. Oh, what a difference a few years makes! The Internet has made viewing of artists' portfolios easy and it's easy to transmit work as e-mail attachments or on itty bitty disks. Even more important, we have an awesome selection of artwork and artists to choose from! The hardest part was narrowing down the number of works to the 32 images we decided to showcase. Luckily, thanks to Adobe and their frequent "rev" cycle, we can look forward to including new artists in future editions of this book.

PHOTO CREDITS

Nadine Markova *(Mexico City), pages 25, 157*

Paul Petroff *(Seattle, Washington), pages 87, 116, 156, 157, 329*

John Stuart *(NY, NY), page 383*

Cara Wood *(Poughkeepsie, NY), page 252*

PhotoDisc, *pages v, 6, 28, 30, 47, 57, 74, 76, 79, 83, 88, 89, 96, 99, 122, 146, 147, 148, 155, 171, 176, 177, 183, 185, 189, 190, 206, 217, 218, 225, 237, 258, 304, 312, 317, 359, 410, 412, 428*

Corel Professional Photos, *pages 56, 108, 205, 241, 397*

All other images are owned by the authors.

TABLE OF CONTENTS

Note: New or substantially changed features are listed in boldface.

Table of Contents

Suling Wang, ©2000 Harper Collins Publishers

Suling Wang, ©2000 Harper Collins Publishers

a = 30°
r = 0.60
a = -27°
r = 0.67
km
29 October
STOCKPORT
5 November

©Jeff Brice

THE BASICS 1

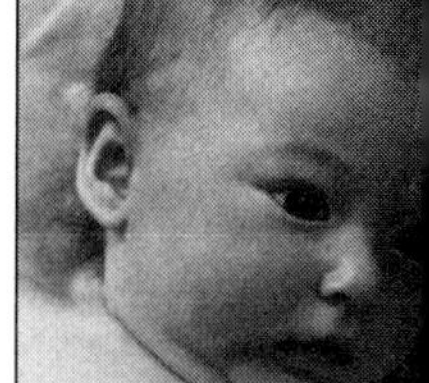

Tool tips

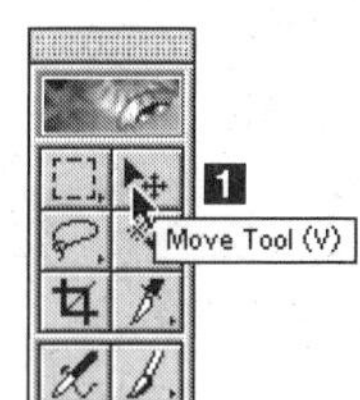

Rest the pointer on a tool icon—without clicking or pressing the mouse button—to learn that tool's name or shortcut **1**. Use the same method to learn the function of a palette or options bar setting **3**. (Check the **Show Tool Tips** box in Edit menu > Preferences > General to enable this feature.)

Tool shortcuts

Hide/show the Toolbox and all open palettes	Tab
Cycle through hidden, related tools on the same pop-out menu	Shift and shortcut key or Alt-click/Option-click the currently visible tool icon
Cycle through blending modes for the current tool or layer	Shift + or Shift -

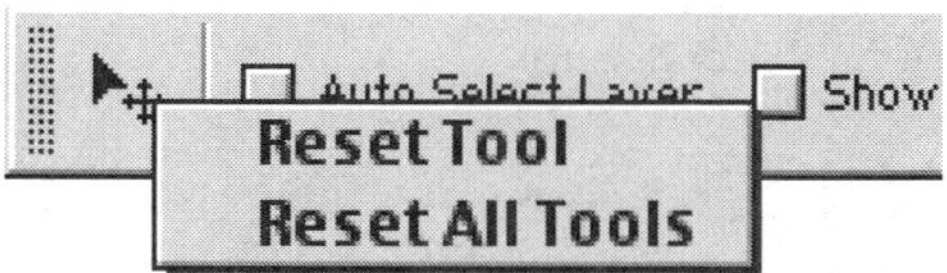

2 *To access the **Reset Tool** command for an individual tool or the **Reset All Tools** for all tools, click the tool icon on the options bar.*

Using the Toolbox

To **choose** a tool whose icon is currently visible, click once on its icon. Click the tiny arrowhead next to a tool icon to choose a related tool from a pop-out palette.

Or even better, choose a tool using its shortcut (memorize the boldface letters on the next three pages). If you forget a tool's shortcut, just leave the cursor over the tool icon for a moment, and the tool tip will remind you **1**. Press **Shift** and the same shortcut key to cycle through hidden, related tools, or Alt-click/Option-click the currently visible tool.

Attributes are chosen for each tool (e.g., blending mode, opacity percentage) from the new **options bar** at the top of your screen (read more about the options bar on page 5) **3**. The options on the bar change depending on which tool is selected. *6.0!*

Options bar settings remain in effect for an individual tool until they are changed or the tool is reset. To reset a tool to its defaults, click the tool icon on the options bar, then choose **Reset Tool** **2**. To reset all tools, choose **Reset All Tools** from the same menu or click Reset All Tools in Edit menu > Preferences > General. *6.0!*

TIP Choose whether a tool **pointer** looks like its Toolbox icon or a crosshair in Edit menu > Preferences > Display & Cursors.

If you try to use a tool **incorrectly**, a cancel icon will appear ⊘. Click with the tool in the image window to make an explanation appear.

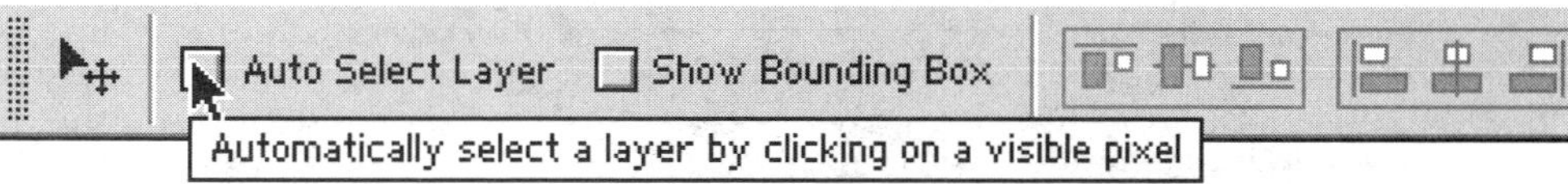

3 *Choose options for the current tool from the **options bar** at the top of your screen.*

The Toolbox 6.0!

Press **Shift** and a shortcut key to cycle through related tools on the same pop-out palette.

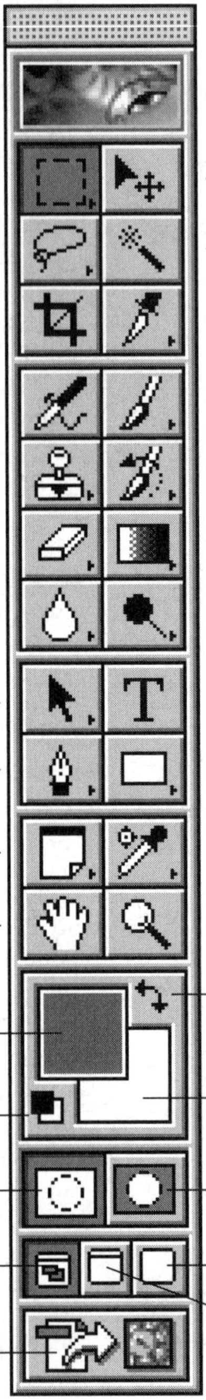

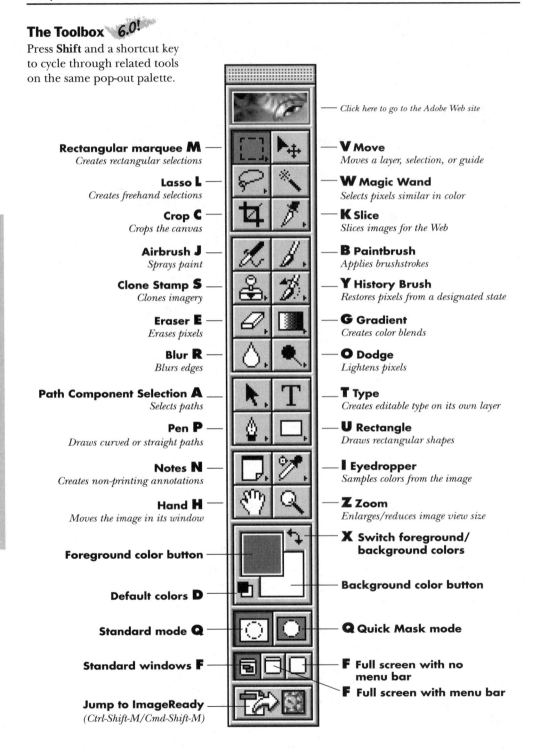

Click here to go to the Adobe Web site

Rectangular marquee M
Creates rectangular selections

V Move
Moves a layer, selection, or guide

Lasso L
Creates freehand selections

W Magic Wand
Selects pixels similar in color

Crop C
Crops the canvas

K Slice
Slices images for the Web

Airbrush J
Sprays paint

B Paintbrush
Applies brushstrokes

Clone Stamp S
Clones imagery

Y History Brush
Restores pixels from a designated state

Eraser E
Erases pixels

G Gradient
Creates color blends

Blur R
Blurs edges

O Dodge
Lightens pixels

Path Component Selection A
Selects paths

T Type
Creates editable type on its own layer

Pen P
Draws curved or straight paths

U Rectangle
Draws rectangular shapes

Notes N
Creates non-printing annotations

I Eyedropper
Samples colors from the image

Hand H
Moves the image in its window

Z Zoom
Enlarges/reduces image view size

X Switch foreground/background colors

Foreground color button

Background color button

Default colors D

Standard mode Q

Q Quick Mask mode

Standard windows F

F Full screen with no menu bar

F Full screen with menu bar

Jump to ImageReady
(Ctrl-Shift-M/Cmd-Shift-M)

The Toolbox

6.0!

M Elliptical Marquee
Creates oval selections

Single row
Creates 1-pixel high selections

Single column
Creates 1-pixel wide selections

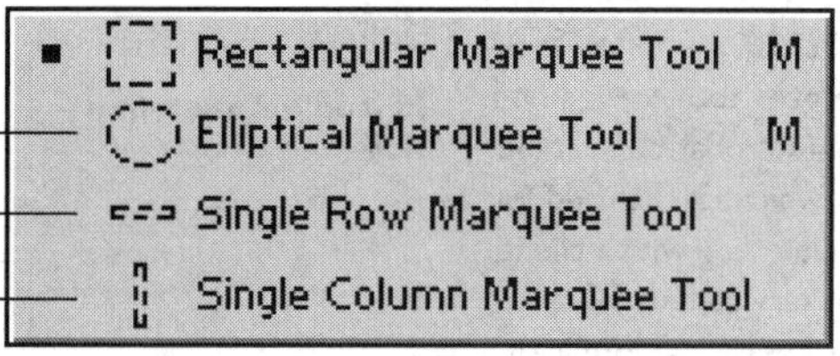
Rectangular Marquee Tool M
Elliptical Marquee Tool M
Single Row Marquee Tool
Single Column Marquee Tool

L Polygonal Lasso
Creates polygonal selections

L Magnetic Lasso
Creates snap-to freehand selections

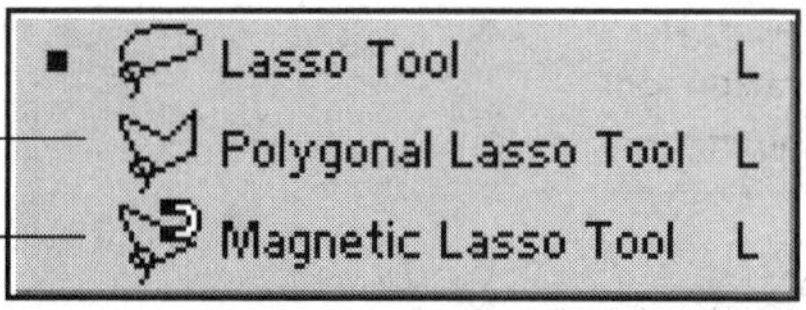
Lasso Tool L
Polygonal Lasso Tool L
Magnetic Lasso Tool L

S Pattern Stamp
Applies patterns

Clone Stamp Tool S
Pattern Stamp Tool S

E Background Eraser
Erases sampled color to transparency

E Magic Eraser
Erases areas of color by clicking

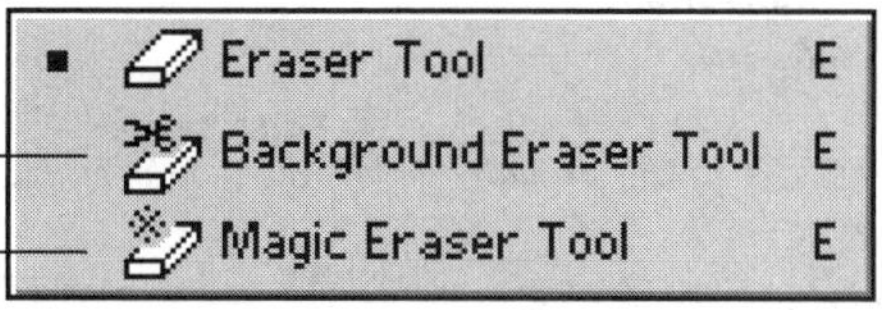
Eraser Tool E
Background Eraser Tool E
Magic Eraser Tool E

R Sharpen
Sharpens pixels

R Smudge
Smudges pixels

Blur Tool R
Sharpen Tool R
Smudge Tool R

A Direct Selection
Selects segments and points of a path

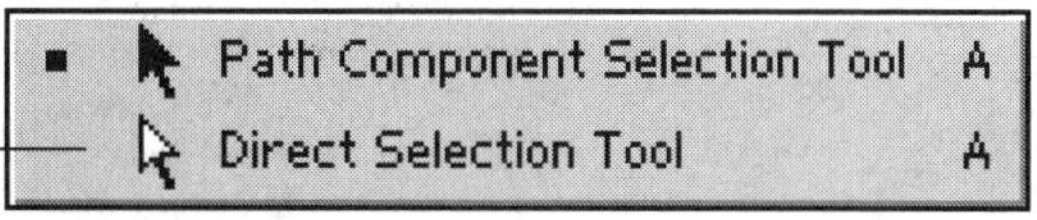
Path Component Selection Tool A
Direct Selection Tool A

P Freeform Pen
Draws freehand paths

Add-anchor-point
Adds points to a path

Delete-anchor-point
Deletes points from a path

Convert-point
Converts corner points into curve points, and vice versa

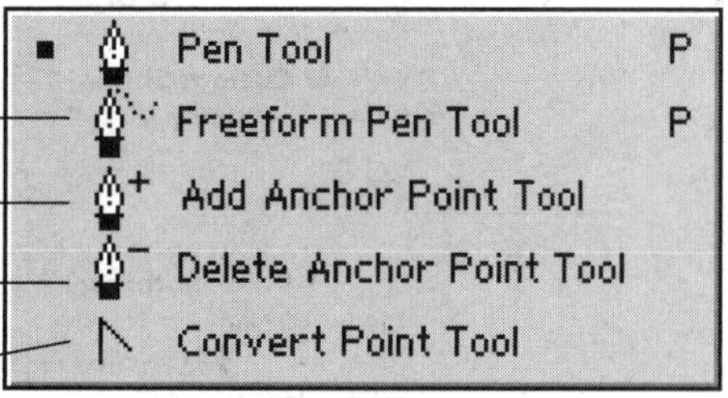
Pen Tool P
Freeform Pen Tool P
Add Anchor Point Tool
Delete Anchor Point Tool
Convert Point Tool

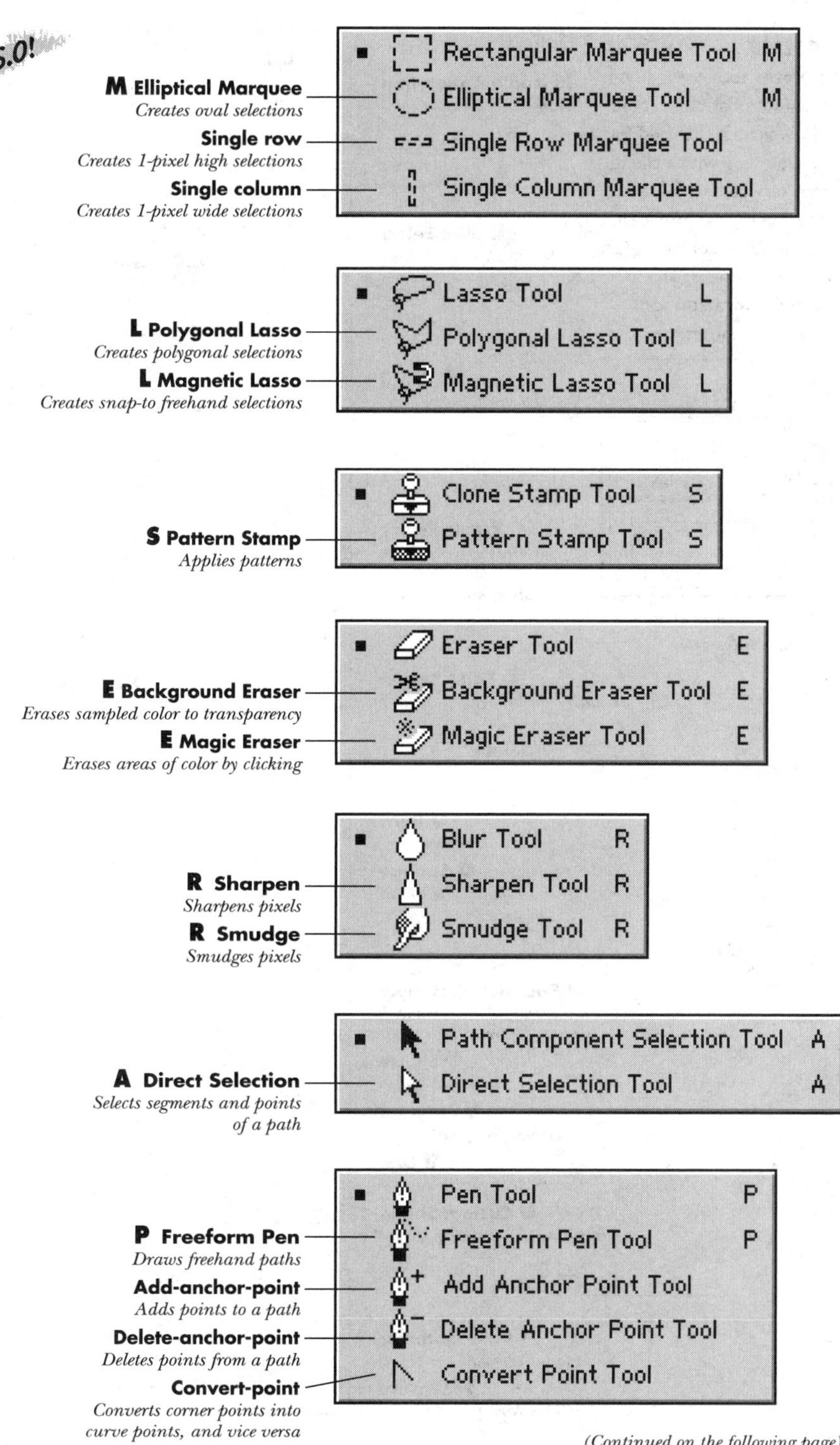

(Continued on the following page)

Annotate

The **Notes** tool creates non-printing Acrobat-compatible notes, which can be used for communicating with a client, output service, etc. **1** When you click a note icon, a note window containing the message opens. The **Audio Annotation** tool creates audio notes.

1 *An* ***annotation*** *created using the* ***Notes*** *tool.*

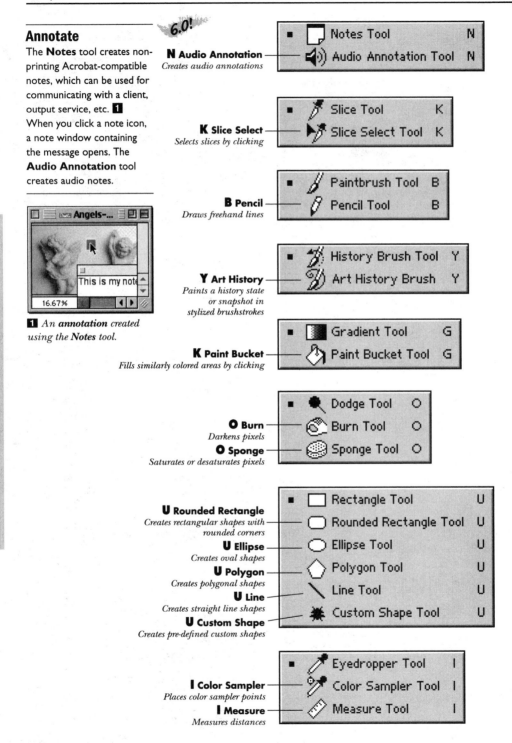

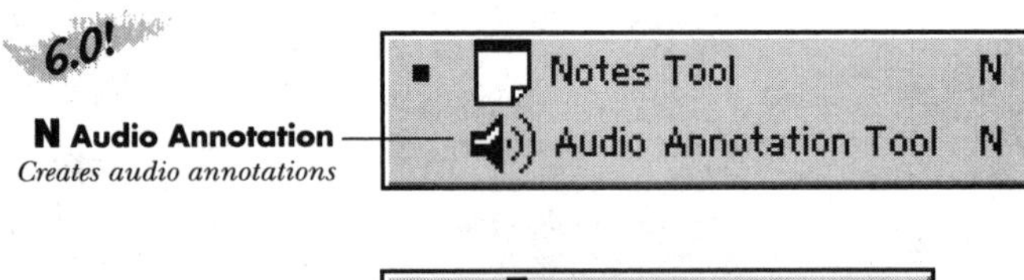

N Audio Annotation
Creates audio annotations

K Slice Select
Selects slices by clicking

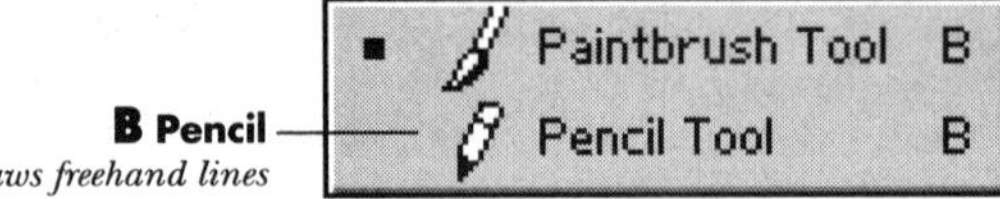

B Pencil
Draws freehand lines

Y Art History
Paints a history state or snapshot in stylized brushstrokes

K Paint Bucket
Fills similarly colored areas by clicking

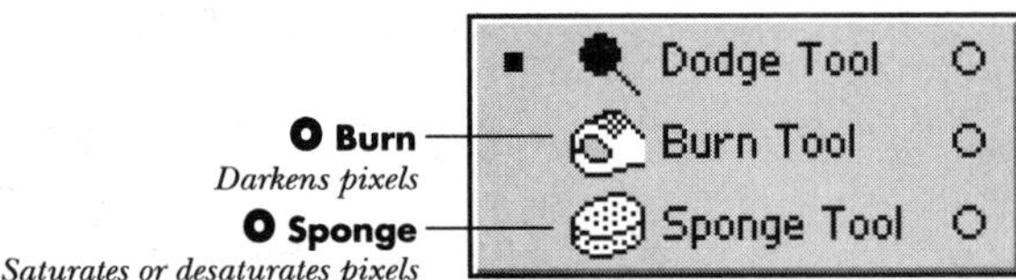

O Burn
Darkens pixels

O Sponge
Saturates or desaturates pixels

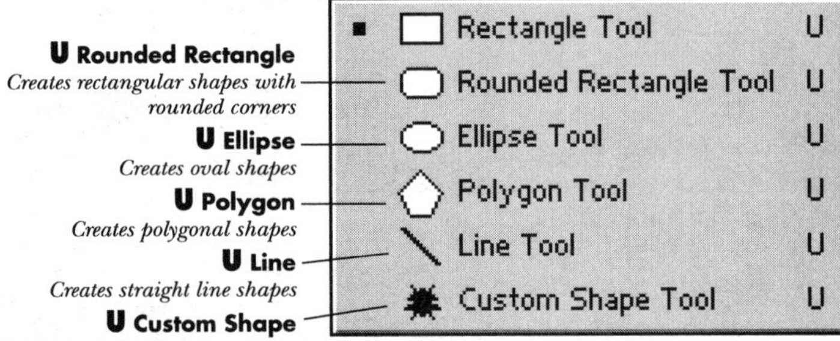

U Rounded Rectangle
Creates rectangular shapes with rounded corners

U Ellipse
Creates oval shapes

U Polygon
Creates polygonal shapes

U Line
Creates straight line shapes

U Custom Shape
Creates pre-defined custom shapes

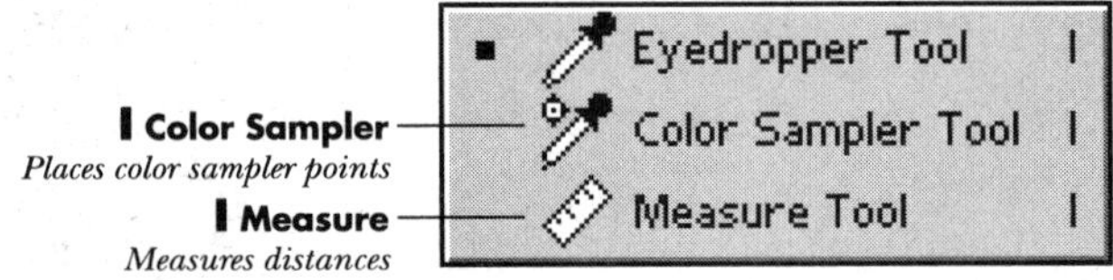

I Color Sampler
Places color sampler points

I Measure
Measures distances

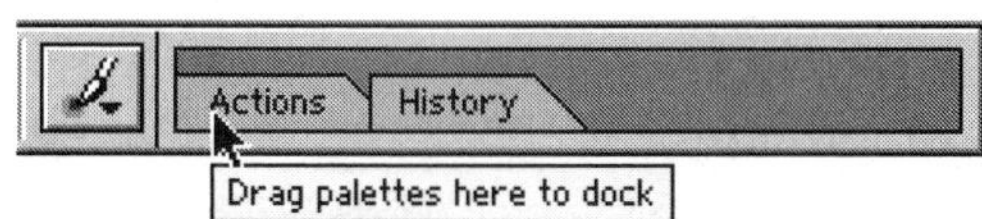

On the right side of the options bar is an area called the ***palette well*** *that you can dock (store) palettes in.*

Options bar 6.0!

The options bar is used to choose settings for each tool (e.g., opacity, fade distance, blending mode). Options on the bar change depending on which tool is currently chosen, and your choices will remain in effect until you change them. Like the palettes, the options bar can be dragged to a different part of your screen.

Click the ***Painting Brush*** *arrowhead to open the* ***picker***.

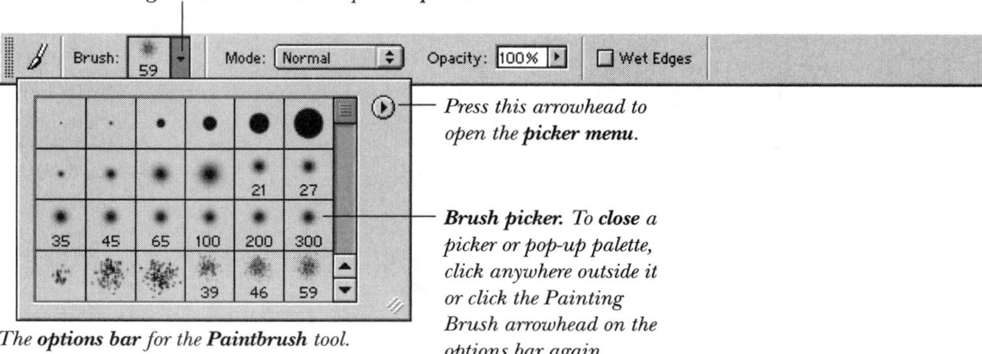

Press this arrowhead to open the ***picker menu***.

Brush picker. *To* ***close*** *a picker or pop-up palette, click anywhere outside it or click the Painting Brush arrowhead on the options bar again.*

The ***options bar*** *for the* ***Paintbrush*** *tool.*

The ***options bar*** *for the* ***Rectangular Marquee*** *tool.*

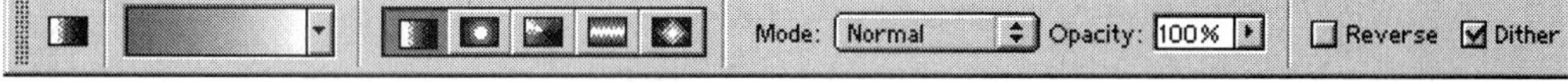

The ***options bar*** *for the* ***Gradient*** *tool.*

The ***options bar*** *for the* ***Pen*** *tool.*

The ***options bar*** *for the* ***Rectangle*** *tool.*

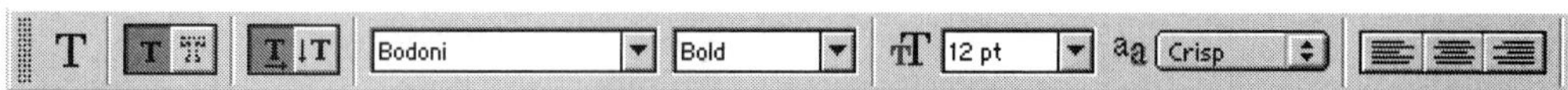

The ***options bar*** *for the* ***Type*** *tool.*

Options Bar

The Photoshop screen: Mac OS

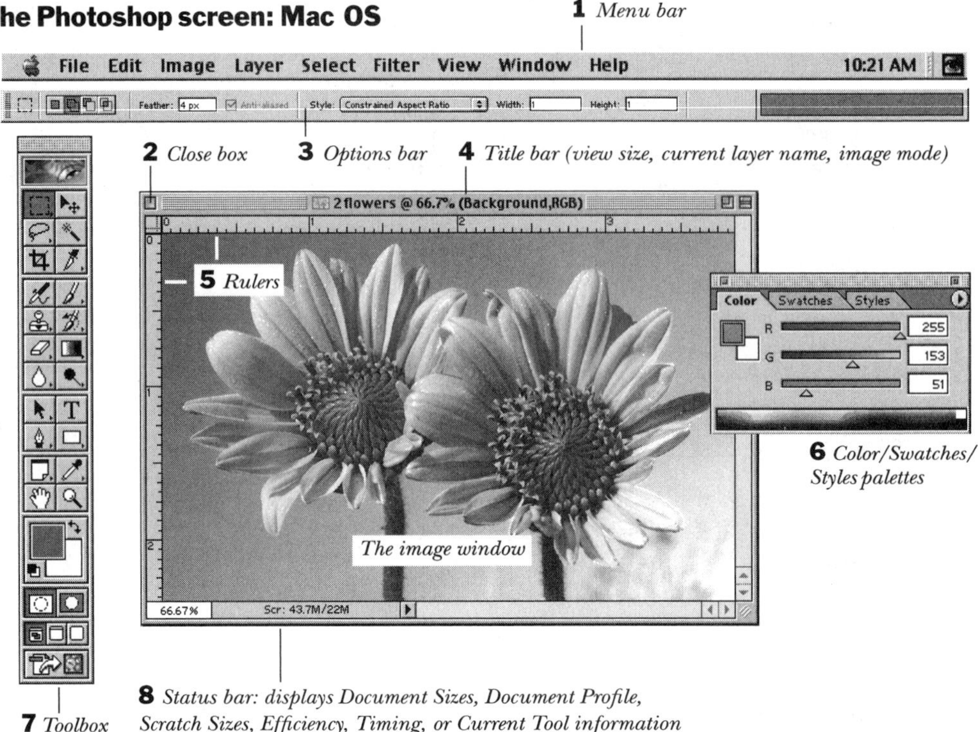

Key to the Photoshop screen: Mac OS and Windows

1 ***Menu bar***
Press any menu heading to access dialog boxes, submenus, and commands.

2 ***Close box*** *(Mac OS)*
To close an image or a palette, click its close box.

3 ***Options bar***
Use to choose settings for the current tool.

4 ***Title bar*** *(view size, current layer, image mode)*
Displays the image's title, view size, current layer (or the Background), and image mode.

5 ***Rulers***
Choose View menu > Show Rulers to display rulers. The position of the pointer is indicated by a mark on each ruler. Choose ruler units in Edit menu > Preferences > Units & Rulers.

6 ***Palettes***
There are 12 moveable palettes. Their default groupings can be changed. Click a tab (palette name) in a palette group to bring that palette to the front of its group.

7 ***Toolbox***
Press Tab to show/hide the Toolbox and all open palettes.

8 ***Status bar***
The status bar displays Document Sizes, Document Profile, Scratch Sizes (the amount of RAM currently available to Photoshop), Efficiency (the percentage of RAM being used), Timing, or Current Tool (the name of the current tool) information. Press and hold on the status bar to display the page preview, which is a thumbnail of the image relative to the paper size. Alt-press/Option-press on the status bar to display the image's dimensions, number of channels, mode, and resolution. To reset the timer, choose Timing with Alt/Option held down.

The Photoshop screen: Windows

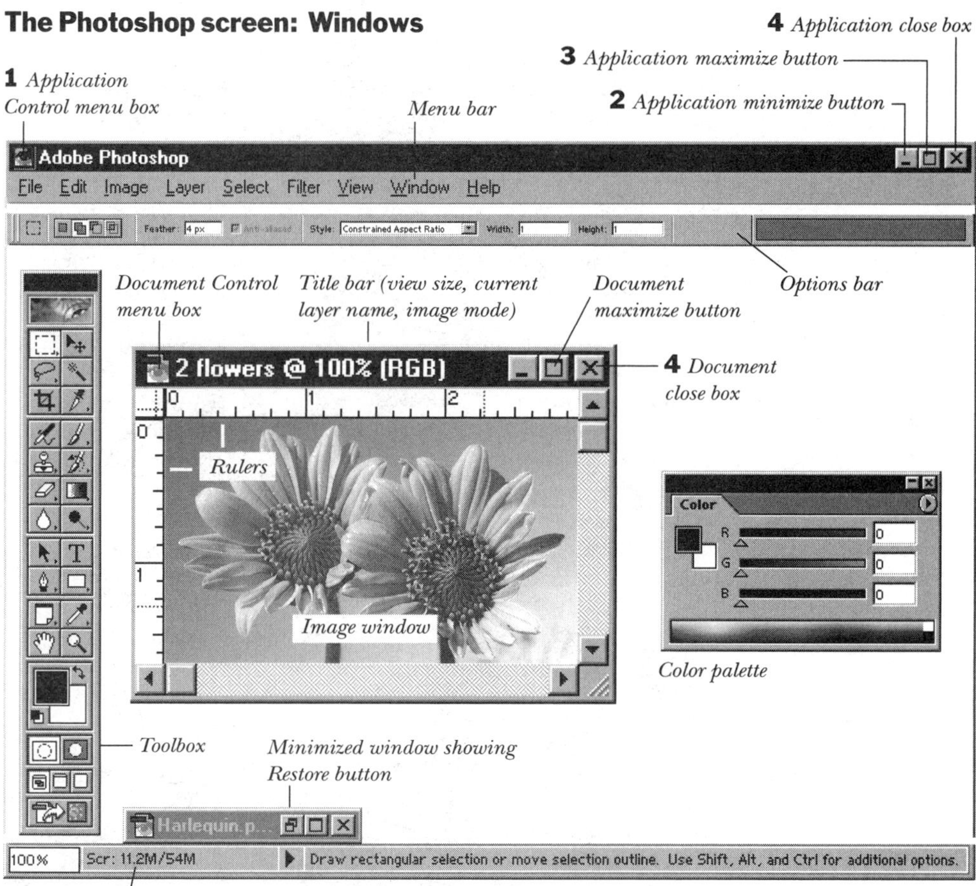

Status bar: displays Document Sizes, Scratch Sizes, Efficiency, or Timing information

Key to the Photoshop screen: Windows only

1 ***Application (or Document) Control menu box***
The Application Control menu box commands are Restore, Move, Size, Minimize, Maximize, and Close. The Document Control menu box commands are Restore, Move, Size, Minimize, Maximize, Close, and Next.

2 ***Application (or Document) minimize button***
Click the Application Minimize button to shrink the document to an icon in the Taskbar. Click the icon on the Taskbar to restore the application window to its previous size.

Click the Document Minimize button to shrink the document to an icon at the lower left corner of the application window. Click the Restore button to restore the document window to its previous size.

3 ***Application (or Document) maximize/restore button***
Click the Application or Document Maximize button to enlarge a window to its largest possible size. Click the Restore button to restore a window to its previous size. When a window is at the restored size, the Restore button turns into the Maximize button.

4 ***Application (or Document) close box***
Closes the application (or image).

The menus 

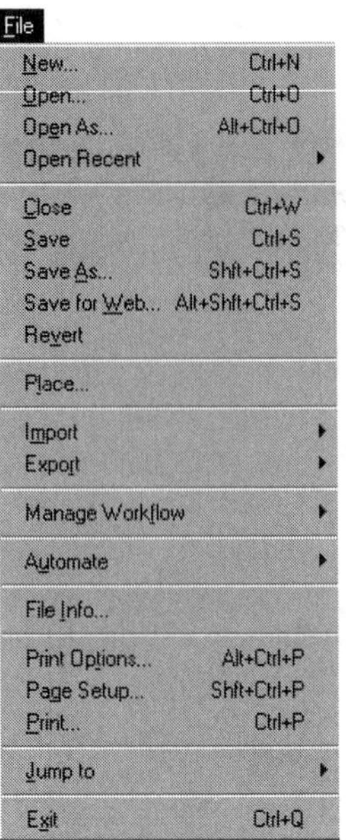

File menu

File menu commands are used to create, open, place, close, save, scan, import, export, or print an image, manage workflows, automate operations, and exit/quit Photoshop. Use the File menu > Jump to submenu to switch to helper applications, such as Adobe ImageReady or GoLive.

Edit
Undo State Change ⌘Z
Step Forward ⇧⌘Z
Step Backward ⌥⌘Z
Fade... ⇧⌘F
Cut ⌘X
Copy ⌘C
Copy Merged ⇧⌘C
Paste ⌘V
Paste Into ⇧⌘V
Clear
Fill...
Stroke...
Free Transform ⌘T
Transform
Define Brush...
Define Pattern...
Define Custom Shape...
Purge
Color Settings... ⇧⌘K
Preset Manager...
Preferences

Edit menu

Edit menu is a storehouse of image editing commands for copying, transforming, pasting, and recoloring imagery, and for creating custom brushes, patterns, and shapes. Fade lessens the effect of most operations (e.g., the last applied filter, adjust command, or tool stroke). The Purge commands free up memory. Color Settings, the Preset Manager, and Preferences are also accessed here.

Image menu

An image can be converted to any of eight image (color) modes via the Mode submenu. The Adjust commands modify an image's hue, saturation, brightness, or contrast. The Image Size command modifies an image's file size, dimensions, or resolution. The Canvas Size dialog box is used to add or subtract from an image's editable canvas area. The Extract command allows you to make complex selections. And Liquify pushes pixels around.

Layer menu

Layer menu commands add, duplicate, delete, modify, add masks to, group, arrange, align, distribute, merge, and flatten layers. Some of these commands can be accessed more quickly via the Layers palette menu.

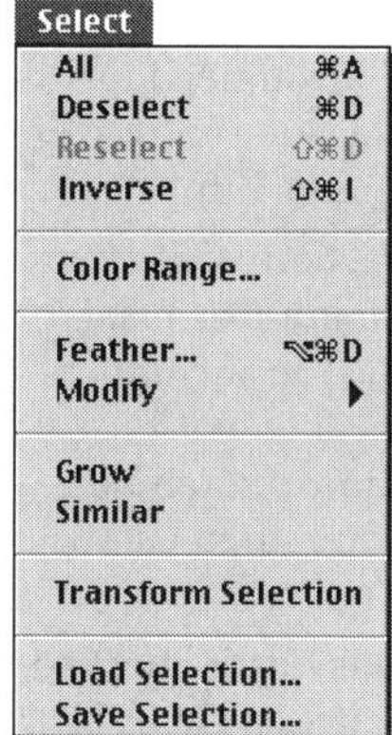

Select menu

The All command on the Select menu selects an entire layer. The Deselect command deselects all selections. The Reselect command restores the last deselected selection. The Color Range command creates a selection based on color. Other Select menu commands enlarge, contract, smooth, or feather selection edges, and save selections to and from channels.

View menu

The View menu commands control what does and doesn't display on screen. The Gamut Warning highlights colors that won't print on a four-color press. The Proof Setup commands allow you to see how your image will look in different output color spaces. The New View command displays the same image in a second window. Other View menu commands control view sizes and the display of rulers, grids, guides, and slices.

Filter menu

Filters, which perform a wide range of image editing functions, are organized into submenu groups. The Digimarc filter embeds a copyright watermark into an image.

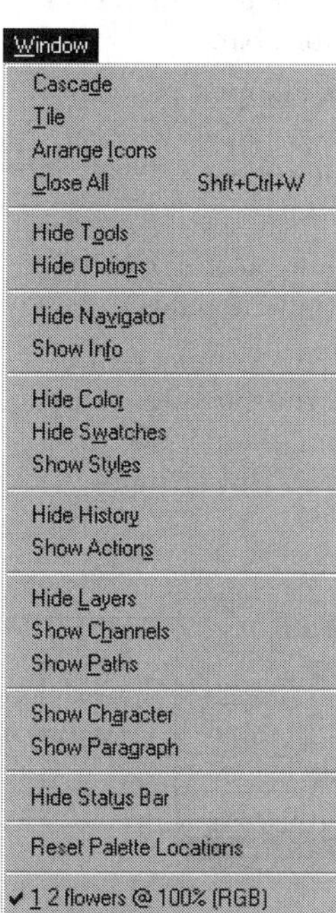

Window menu

Window menu commands show and hide the palettes. Open images are also listed and can be activated via this menu.

Windows: You can also arrange image windows or hide/show the status bar via Window menu commands.

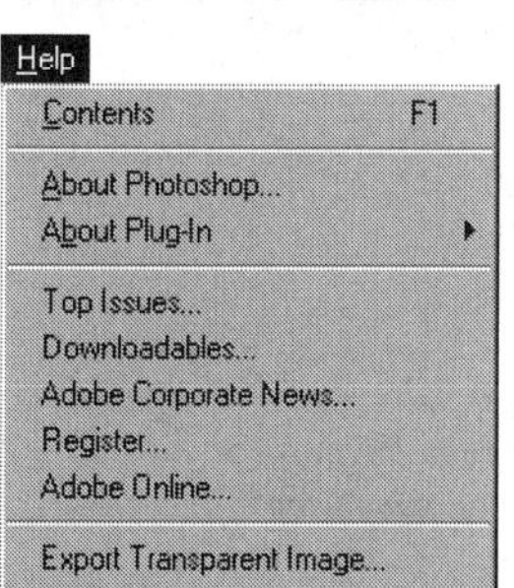

Help menu

Use the Help menu commands to access the Photoshop manual online, get the latest news from Adobe, connect to Adobe Online, or to perform automated tasks via on-screen prompts.

The palettes

How to use the palettes

Many of the operations that you will perform in Photoshop will be accomplished via moveable palettes. To save screen space, the palettes are joined into these default groups: **Navigator/Info**, **Color/Swatches/Styles**, **History/Actions**, **Layers/Channels/Paths**, **Character/Paragraph**, and the **Toolbox**.

To **open** a palette, choose Window menu > Show [palette name]. The palette will appear in front within its group.

TIP To open the Character/Paragraph group, choose the Type tool, then click Palettes on the options bar. 6.0!

Press Tab to **show/hide** all open palettes, including the Toolbox. Press Shift-Tab to show/hide all open palettes except the Toolbox.

To **display** an open palette at the front of its group, click its tab (palette name).

You can **separate** a palette from its group by dragging its tab **1**–**2**. You can **add** a palette to any group by dragging the tab over the group. Use the **resize** box (lower right corner) to widen a palette if you need to make additional tabs visible. You can resize any palette other than Color or Info.

To **shrink/expand** a palette, double-click its tab or click the palette minimize/maximize (Win)/zoom box (Mac) in the upper right corner. If the palette is not at its default size, click the minimize/zoom box once to restore its default size, then click a second time to shrink the palette.

If the **Save Palette Locations** box is checked in the Edit menu > Preferences > General dialog box, palettes that are open when you exit/quit Photoshop will reappear in their same location when you re-launch.

To restore the palettes' default groupings at any time, choose Window menu > **Reset Palette Locations**. 6.0!

TIP Quick-change: Click in a field on a palette (or in a dialog box), then press the up or down arrow on the keyboard to change that value incrementally.

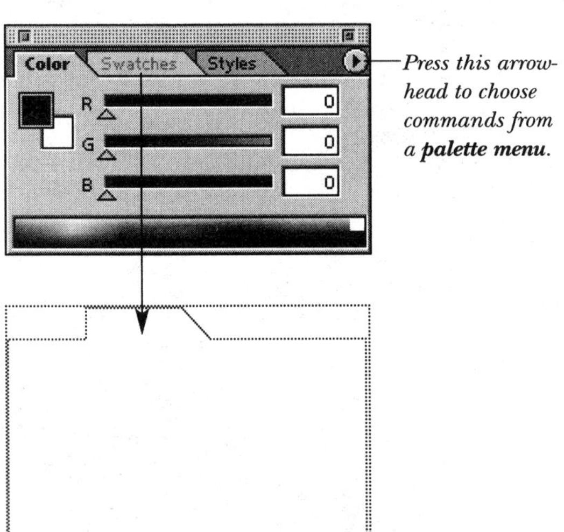

*Press this arrowhead to choose commands from a **palette menu**.*

1 *To **separate** a palette from its group, drag the tab (palette name) away from the palette group.*

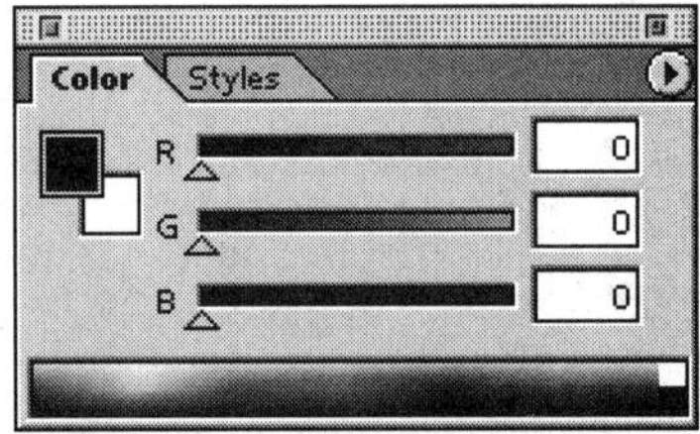

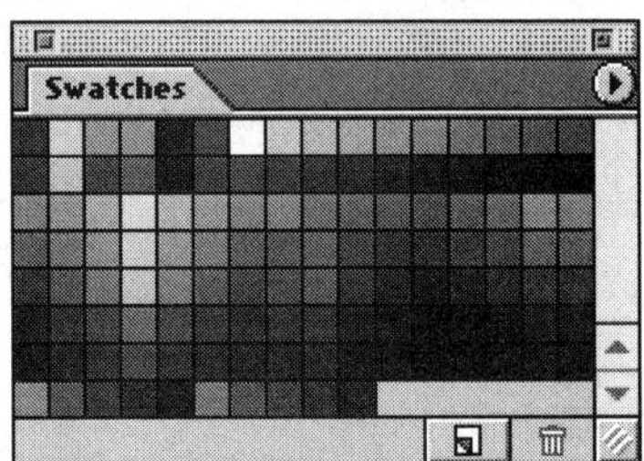

2 *The Swatches palette is now on its own.*

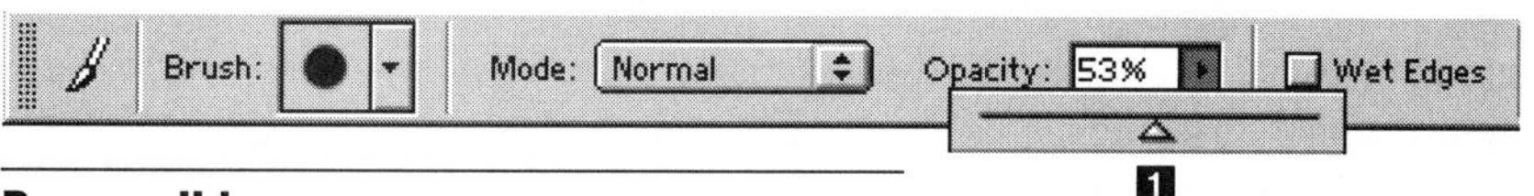

Pop-up sliders

There are two ways to use a pop-up slider **1**: Press an arrowhead and drag the slider in one movement or click the arrowhead and then drag the slider. To close a slider, click anywhere outside it or press Enter/Return. If you click the arrowhead to open a slider, you can press Esc while the slider is open to restore its last setting.

Color palette

The Color palette is used for mixing and choosing colors. Colors are applied using a painting or editing tool or using a command, such as Fill or Canvas Size. Choose a color model for the palette from the palette menu. Mix a color using the sliders or quick-select a color by clicking on the color bar at the bottom of the Color palette.

To open the Color Picker, from which you can also choose a color, click once on the Foreground or Background color square if it's already active or double-click the square it it's not active.

__Foreground__ color square. The currently active square has a white border.

__Background__ color square.

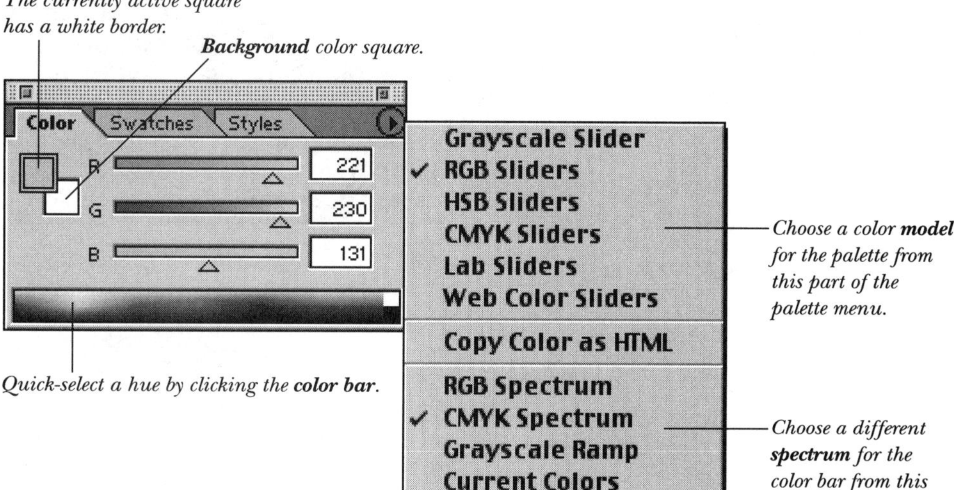

Quick-select a hue by clicking the __color bar__.

Choose a color __model__ for the palette from this part of the palette menu.

Choose a different __spectrum__ for the color bar from this part of the menu.

Swatches palette

The Swatches palette is used for choosing already mixed colors. Individual swatches can be added to or deleted from the palette. Custom swatch palettes can also be loaded, appended, and saved using Swatches palette menu commands.

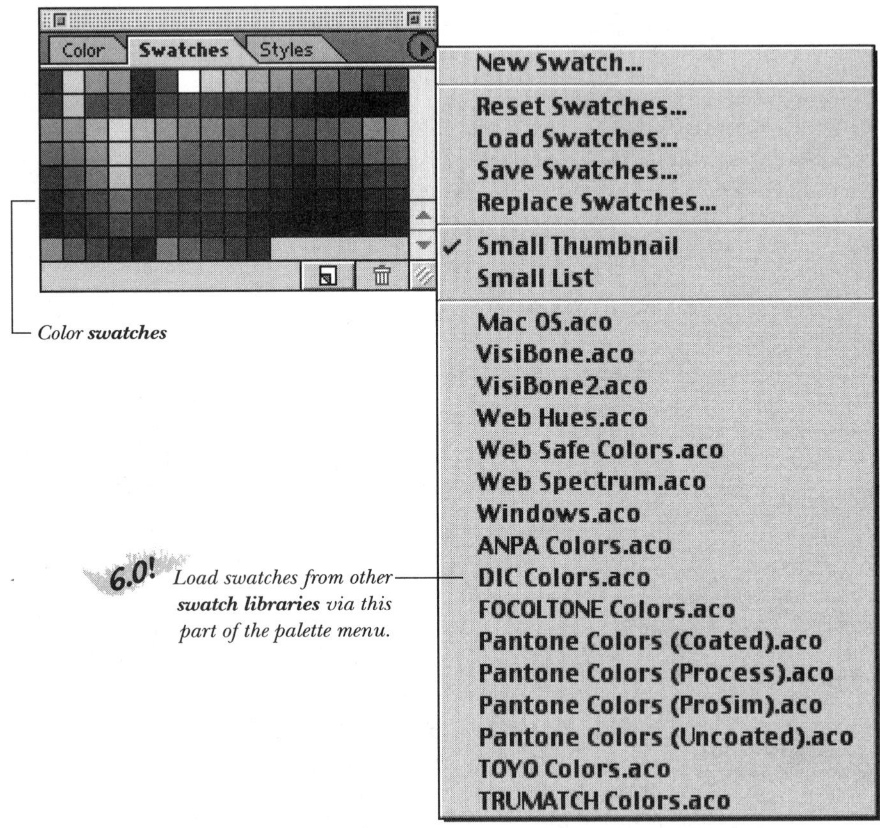

Color ***swatches***

Load swatches from other ***swatch libraries*** *via this part of the palette menu.*

Styles palette 6.0!

The Styles palette is used to apply previously saved individual effects or combinations of effects. Originally part of ImageReady, the Styles palette is now part of Photoshop.

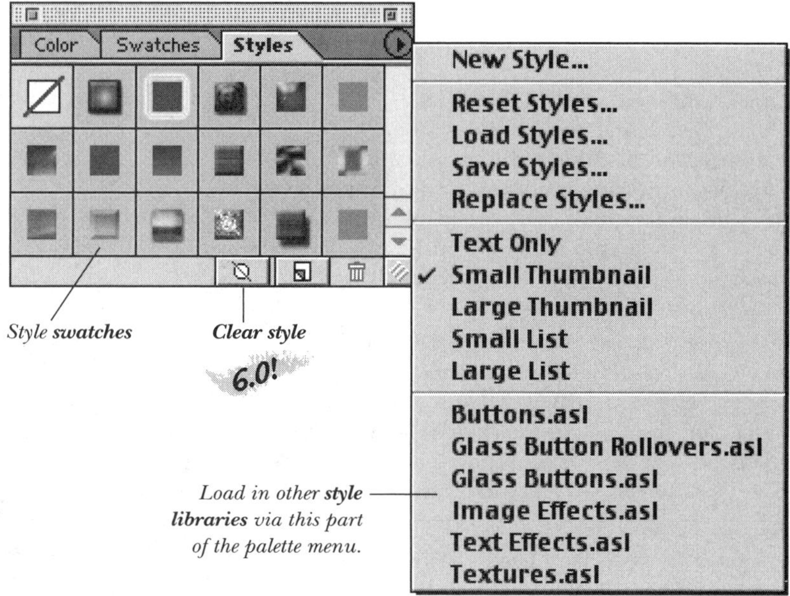

Style ***swatches***

Clear style 6.0!

Load in other ***style libraries*** *via this part of the palette menu.*

Navigator palette

The Navigator palette is used for moving an image in its window or for changing an image's view size.

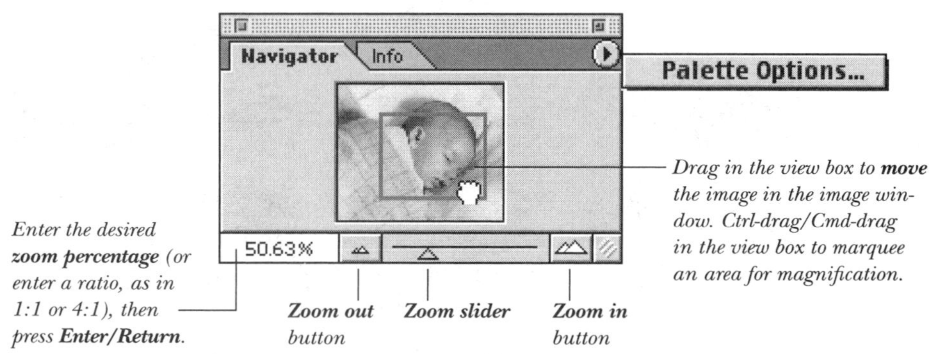

Drag in the view box to ***move*** *the image in the image window. Ctrl-drag/Cmd-drag in the view box to marquee an area for magnification.*

Enter the desired ***zoom percentage*** *(or enter a ratio, as in 1:1 or 4:1), then press* ***Enter/Return****.*

Zoom out *button*

Zoom slider

Zoom in *button*

Styles Palette; Navigator Palette

Info palette

The Info palette displays a color breakdown of the pixel currently under the pointer. The palette will also show readouts for up to four color samplers, if they are placed on the image. If a color adjustment dialog box is open, the palette will display before and after color readouts. The Info palette also shows the *x/y* position of the pointer on the image.

Other information may display on the palette, depending on which tool is being used (such as the distance between points when a selection is moved, a shape is drawn, or the Measure tool is used; the dimensions of a selection or crop marquee; or the width, height, and angle of a selection as it's transformed).

Press an arrowhead to choose a mode for a readout: Actual Color (the current image mode), Grayscale, RGB, Web, HSB, CMYK, Lab Color, Total Ink, or the current layer Opacity. The palette color mode can be different from the current image mode.

TIP If an exclamation point appears next to a color readout, it means that color is outside the printable, CMYK gamut.

TIP You can also change a color readout mode or unit of measurement by choosing Palette Options from the Info palette menu and making your choices in the Info Options dialog box.

__Color breakdown__ for the pixel currently under the pointer.

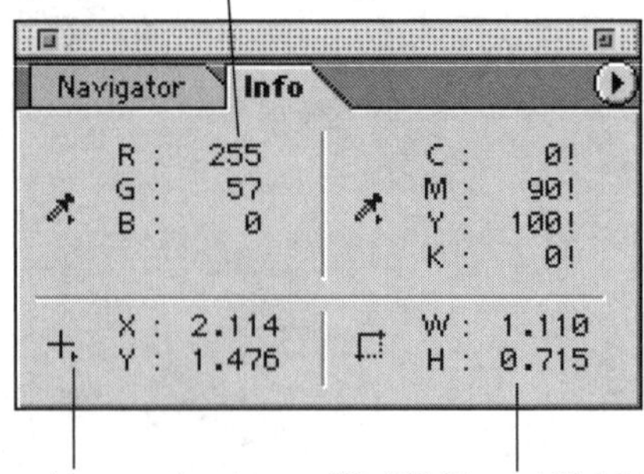

Press this arrowhead to choose a different __unit of measurement__ for the palette (and the rulers).

The __Width__ and __Height__ of an active __selection__.

During a __transform__ operation, the width (W), height (H), angle (A), and horizontal skew (H) or vertical skew (V) of the transformed layer, selection, or path is shown in this area.

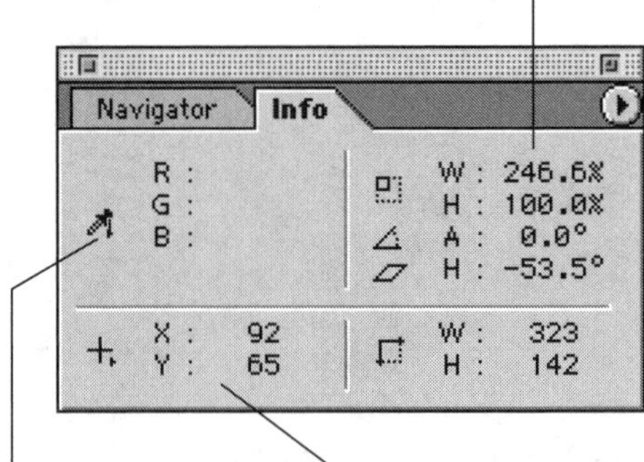

Press an arrowhead to choose a different __color mode__ for that readout.

The x/y __location__ of the pointer on the image.

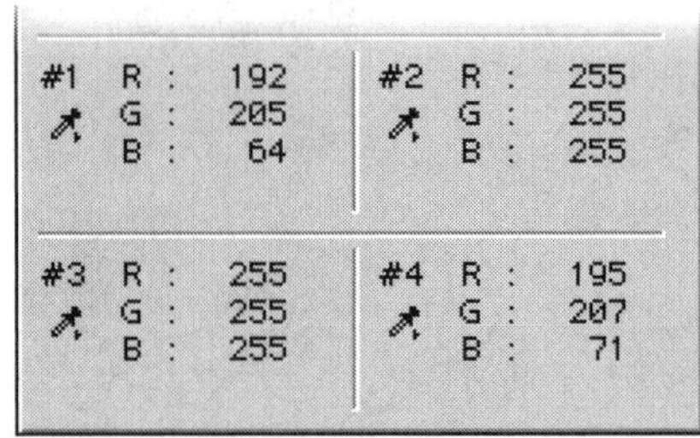

__#1, #2, #3,__ and __#4__ color readouts from four __color samplers__ that were placed on the image.

Info Palette

Layers palette 6.0!

Normally, when you create a new image, it will have an opaque Background. Using the Layers palette, you can add, delete, show/hide, duplicate, group, link, and restack layers on top of the Background. Each layer can be assigned its own blending mode and opacity and can be edited separately without changing the other layers. You can also attach a **mask** to a layer.

In addition to standard layers, you can also create two other kinds of layers in Photoshop: **adjustment layers**, which are used for applying temporary color or tonal adjustments to the layers below it, and **editable type layers**, which are created automatically when the Type or Vertical Type tool is used. If you apply a **layer effect** to a layer (e.g., Inner Glow, Drop Shadow), a layer effect icon and pop-up menu will appear next to the layer name.

Only the current layer (also called the "chosen" or "active" layer), can be edited. To **choose** a layer, click its name on the Layers palette.

Starting out transparent

Click **Contents: Transparent** in the File menu > New dialog box to have the bottommost tier of a new image be a layer with transparency instead of an opaque Background.

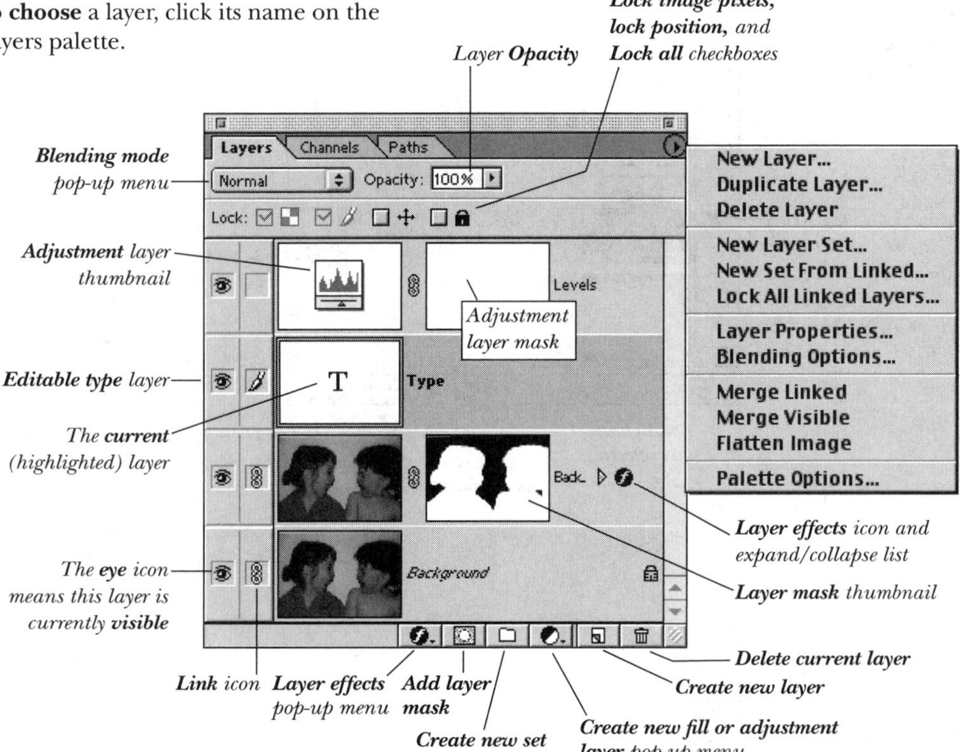

Layers Palette

Channels palette

The Channels palette is used to display one or more of the channels that make up an image. It is also used for creating and displaying alpha channels, which are used for saving selections, and spot color channels, which are used for producing spot color plates.

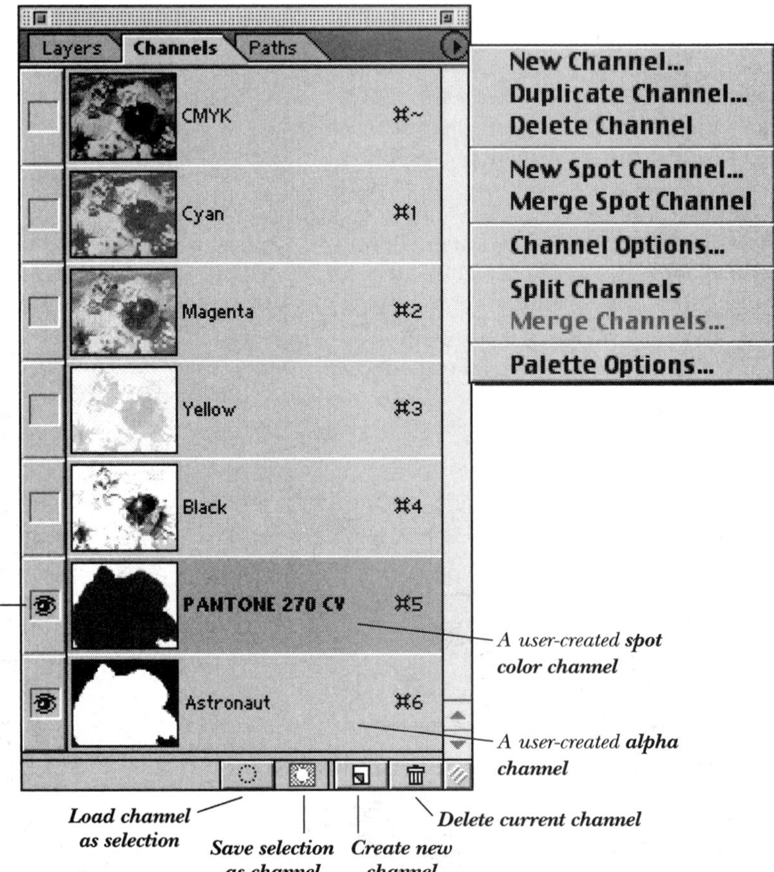

The ***eye*** *icon means this channel is currently* ***displayed****. To display a channel, click its name or use the keystroke that's listed on the palette.*

A user-created ***spot color channel***

A user-created ***alpha channel***

Load channel as selection

Save selection as channel

Create new channel

Delete current channel

Paths palette

A path is a shape that is composed of curved and straight line segments connected by anchor points. A path can be drawn directly with a shape tool or a Pen tool or you can start by creating a selection and then convert the selection into a path. A path can be filled or stroked. To create a precisely-drawn selection, you can draw a path and then convert it into a selection. The Pen tool and its relatives, the Add-anchor-point, Delete-anchor-point, and Convert-point tools, can be used to reshape a path. Paths are saved and accessed via the Paths palette.

TIP While a shape layer, or an image layer that is masked by a layer clipping path, is selected, the clipping path will be listed on the Paths palette.

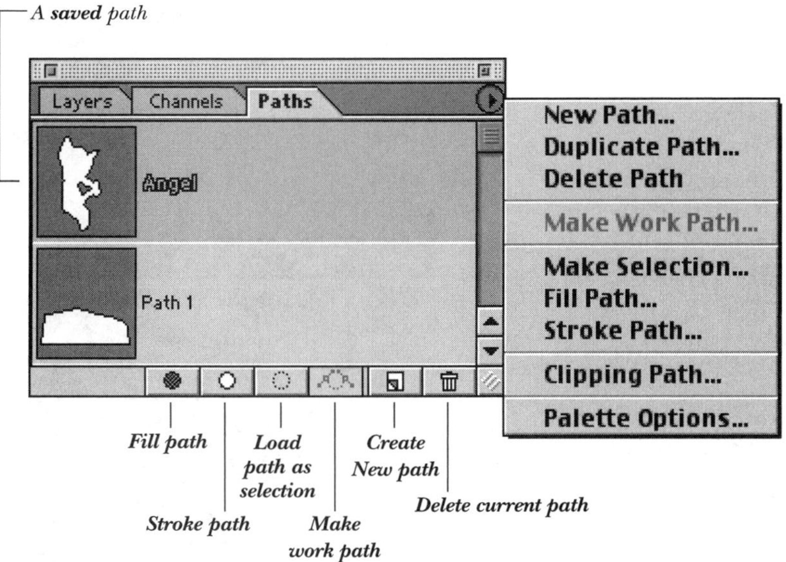

History Palette; Actions Palette

History palette

The History palette is used to selectively undo one or more previous steps in the image-editing process. Each brushstroke, filter application, or other operation is listed as a separate state on the palette, with the bottommost state being the most recent. Clicking on a prior state restores the document to that stage of the editing process. What happens to the document when you click on a prior state depends on whether the palette is in linear or non-linear mode.

In linear mode, if you click back on and then delete a state or resume image-editing from an earlier state, all subsequent states (dimmed, on the palette) will be deleted. In non-linear mode, you can click back on an earlier edit state or delete a state without losing subsequent states. This option is turned on or off via the Allow Non-Linear History box in the History Options dialog box (choose History Options from the palette menu). You can switch between linear and non-linear mode at any time during editing.

The History Brush tool restores an image to a designated prior state where the brush is dragged in the image window. The Art History Brush does the same thing in stylized strokes.

Actions palette

The main purpose for the Actions palette is to automate image processing. You can use it to record a series of commands and then replay those commands on one image or on a batch of images. The palette can also be used to create and access keyboard shortcuts.

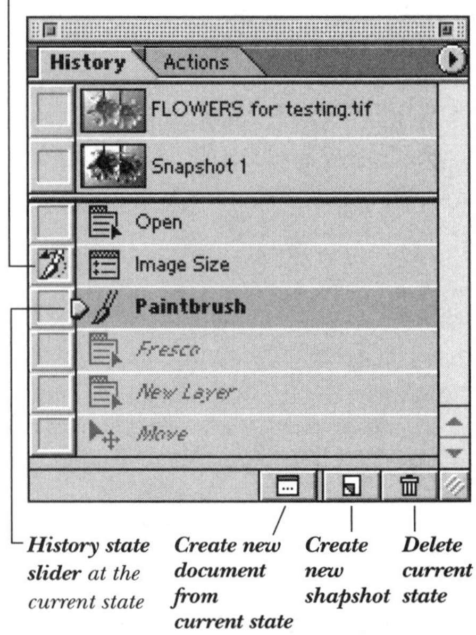

*This is the **History** palette in **linear** mode. Note that some steps are grayed out.*

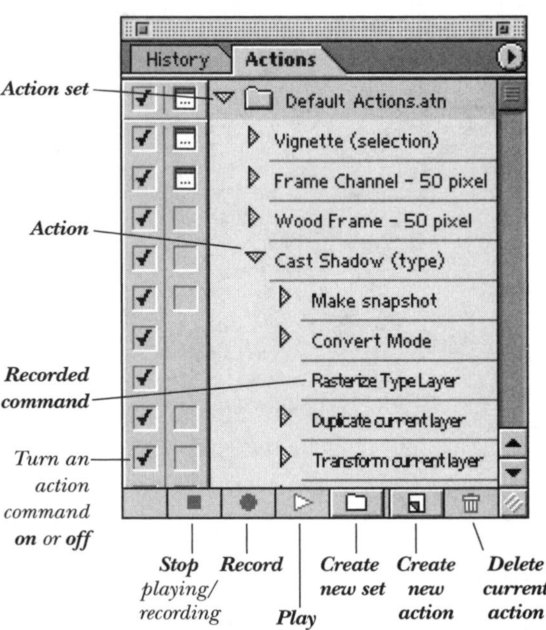

Character palette *6.0!*

Type in Photoshop is no longer created via a dialog box. Instead, it is accomplished via the new Character palette. Character attributes can also be chosen from the Type tool options bar.

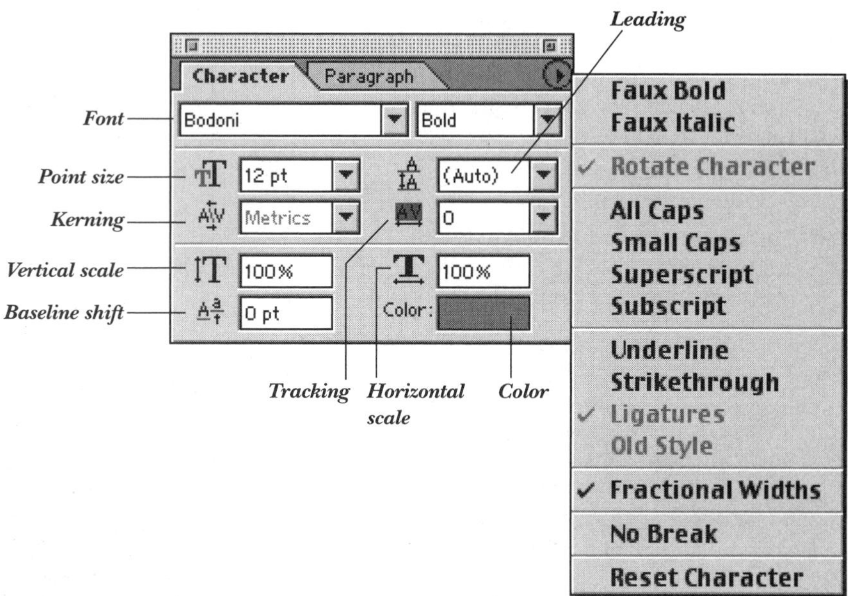

Paragraph palette *6.0!*

The paragraph palette is used to apply paragraph-wide attributes to type, including indentation and space before.

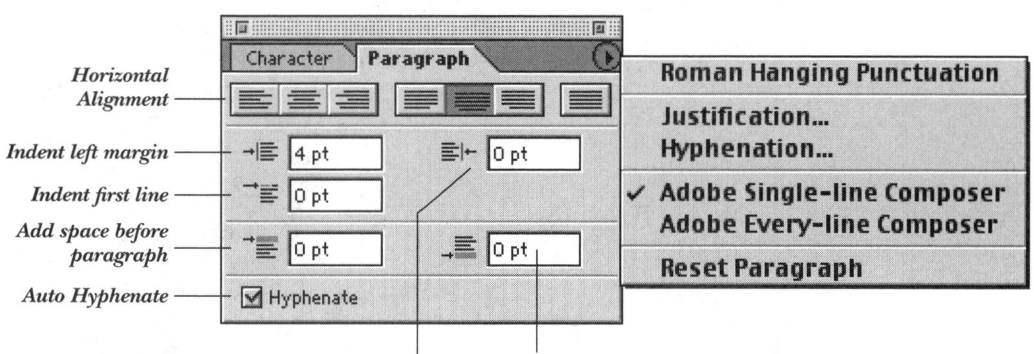

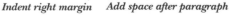

Choosing brushes 6.0!

Brush tips for painting and editing tools are no longer chosen from a standalone palette. Instead, a brush picker opens if you click the Painting Brush arrowhead on the options bar. You can also load, append, and save brushes and brush libraries via picker menu commands (click the arrowhead in the circle on the right side of the picker). To close the picker, click outside it or click the Painting Brush arrowhead again.

TIP The numeral under a brush tip icon is the diameter of the tip in pixels.

TIP When you use a brush from the picker, you'll actually be working with a copy of the brush—not the original.

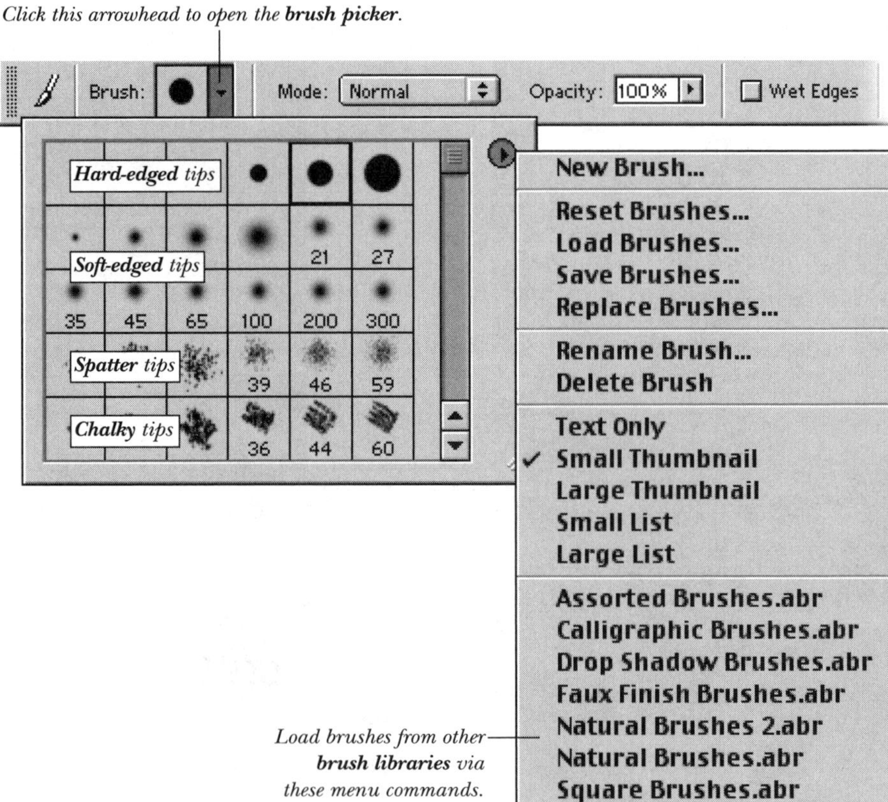

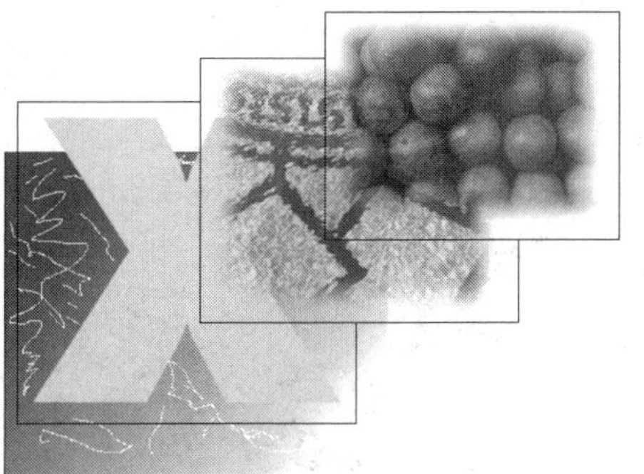

1 *Layers are like clear acetate sheets:* ***opaque*** *where there is imagery,* ***transparent*** *where there is no imagery.*

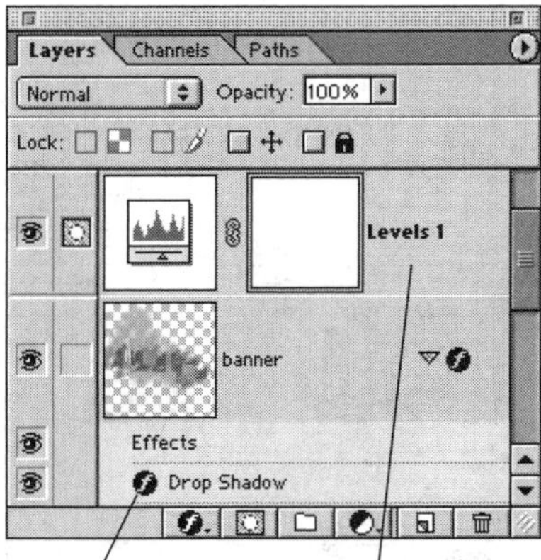

A ***layer effect***

2 *The Levels command applied via an* ***adjustment layer****.*

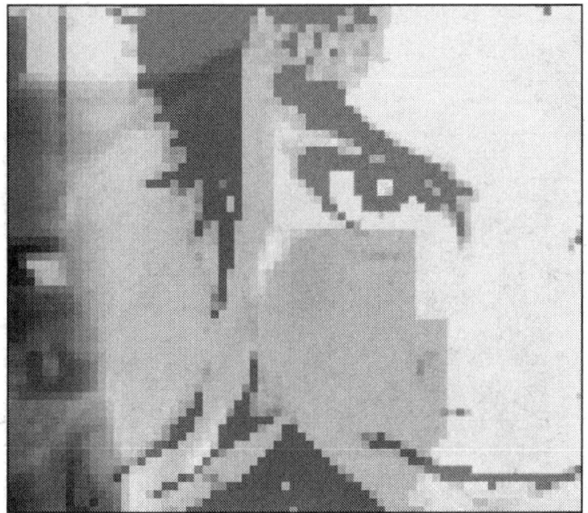

3 *Individual* ***pixels*** *are discernible in this image because it is shown at 500% view.*

Mini-glossary

Current layer and layer transparency

The currently highlighted layer on the Layers palette is the only layer that can be edited. An image can have just a Background (no layers) or you can add multiple layers to it **1**. Layers can contain layer effects, they can be restacked and moved, and they are transparent where there are no pixels, so you can see through a whole stack of them. The advantage of working with multiple layers is that you can assign image components to separate layers and edit them individually without changing other layers.

Adjustment layer

Unlike a standard layer, modifications that are made to an adjustment layer won't alter actual pixels until it is merged with the layers below it **2**. Adjustment layers are ideal for experimenting with color or tonal adjustments. An adjustment layer only affects the layers below it.

Pixels (picture elements)

The dots used to display a bitmapped image in a rectangular grid on a computer screen **3**.

Vector 6.0!

In addition to pixel imagery, in Photoshop 6 editable type and shapes automatically appear on their own mathematically defined vector layers **4**. The overall file resolution can be kept at a level that's suitable for the pixel imagery; the vector elements will print at the printer resolution.

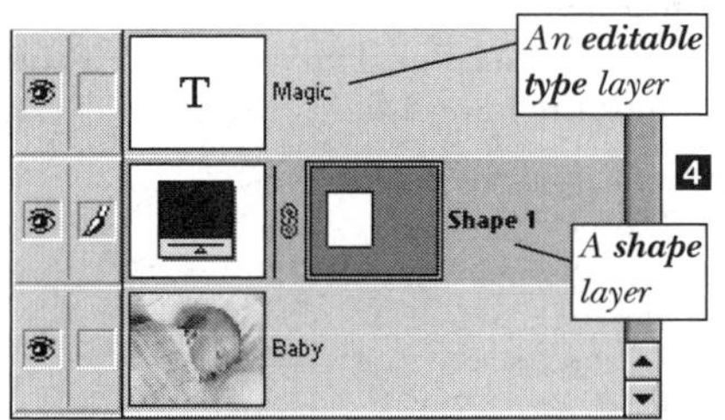

4

Mini-Glossary

Selection
A selection is an area of an image that is isolated via a special marquee so it can be modified while the rest of the image is protected **1**. A moving marquee marks the boundary of a selection. If you move a selection that contains pixels, the cutout area that's left behind is filled automatically with the current Background color if the selection is on the Background, or with transparency if the selection is on a layer. A selection can be created using a selection tool (e.g., Lasso or Magic Wand) or a selection command (e.g., Color Range). You can also convert a path into a selection or load an alpha channel mask as a selection.

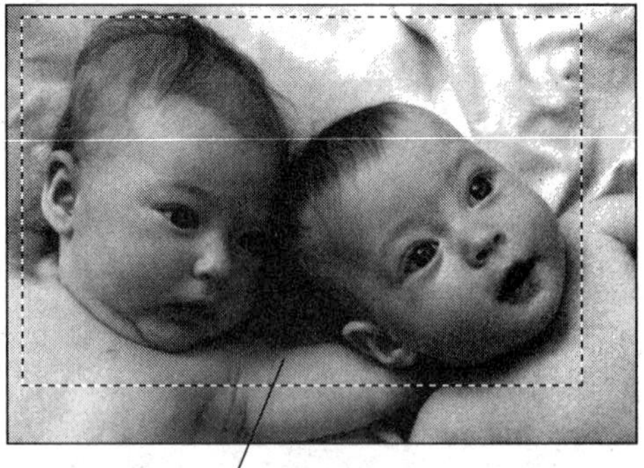

1 *A **selected** area of an image.*

Resolution
Image resolution is the number of pixels an image contains, and it is measured in pixels per inch **2**. The monitor's resolution is also measured in pixels per inch. Output devices also have their own resolution, which is measured in dots per inch.

File size
The file size of an image, which is measured in bytes, kilobytes, megabytes, or gigabytes.

Dimensions
The width and height of an image.

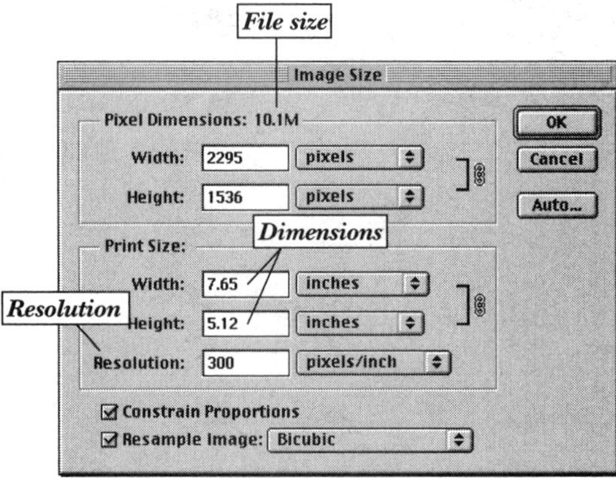

2 *The **Image Size** dialog box is used to change an image's **dimensions** or **resolution**.*

Brightness
The lightness (luminance) of a color **3**.

Hue
The wavelength of light that gives a color its name—such as red or blue—irrespective of its brightness and saturation.

Saturation
The purity of a color. The more gray a color contains, the lower is its saturation.

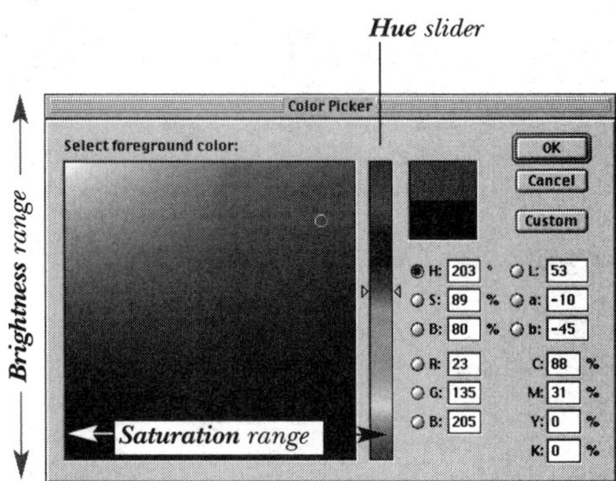

3 *The Photoshop **Color Picker**.*

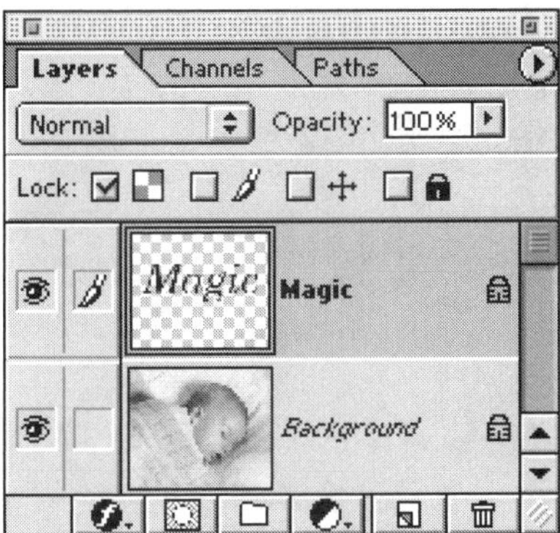

Build your image using layers

You can work on one layer at a time without affecting the other layers, and discard any layers you don't need. To conserve memory if you're working on a large image, merge two or more layers together periodically.

Using a **layer mask** or a layer **clipping path**, you can temporarily hide pixels on an individual layer so you can experiment with different compositions. When you're finished using a layer mask, you can discard it or permanently apply the effect to the layer.

Quick on the redraw

To speed performance, choose Palette Options from the Layers, Channels, or Paths palette menu, then click **Thumbnail Size**: None or the smallest thumbnail option.

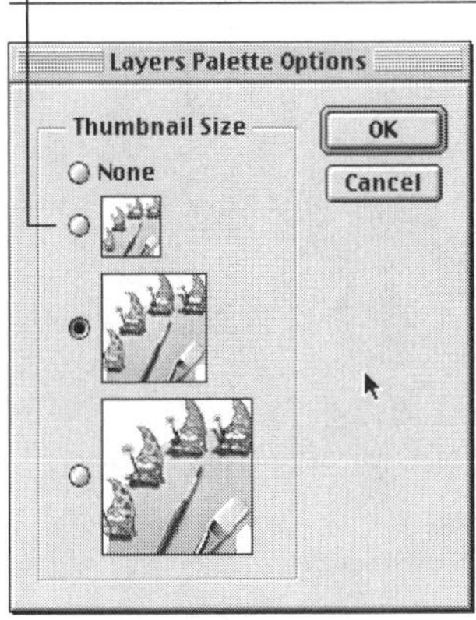

Production techniques

- To undo the last modification, choose Edit menu > **Undo** (Ctrl-Z/Cmd-Z) (some commands can't be undone). To undo multiple steps, click a prior state on the **History** palette or use the **History Brush** tool to restore selective areas.
- Periodically click the "Create new snapshot button" on the History palette to save temporary versions of the image. Click a **snapshot** thumbnail to revert to that version of the image.
- Use an **adjustment layer** to try out tonal and color adjustments, and then merge the adjustment layer downward to apply the effect, or discard the adjustment layer. Use the Layers palette Opacity slider to lessen the effect of an adjustment layer. Create a clipping group with the layer directly below an adjustment layer to limit the adjustment effect to that layer.
- Use Edit menu > **Fade** (Ctrl-Shift-F/Cmd-Shift-F) to lessen the last applied filter, adjust command, or tool edit without having to undo and redo—and choose a blending mode or opacity for the operation while you're at it.
- **Interrupt screen redraw** after executing a command or applying a filter by choosing a different tool or command. (To cancel a command while a progress bar is displaying, press Esc.)
- Choose the lowest possible **resolution** and **dimensions** for your image, given your output requirements. You can create a practice image at a low resolution, saving the commands you use in an **action**, and then replay the action on a higher resolution version. Remember also that vector layers (editable type and shapes) print at the printer resolution—not at the document resolution.
- Display your image in **two windows** simultaneously, one in a larger view size than

(Continued on the following page)

Production Techniques

the other, so you don't have to change view sizes constantly.

- Save a complex selection to a special grayscale channel called an **alpha channel**, which can be loaded and reused on any image whenever you like. Or create a **path** or a layer **clipping path**, which occupies significantly less storage space than an alpha channel, and can be converted into a selection.
- Use **Quick Mask** mode to turn a selection into a mask, which will cover the protected areas of the image with transparent color and leave the unprotected area as a cutout, and then modify the mask contour using a painting tool. Turn off Quick Mask mode to convert the cutout area back into a selection.
- Since CMYK files process more slowly than RGB files, use Proof Setup > **Working CMYK** to preview your image as CMYK Color mode, then convert it to the real CMYK Color mode when it's completed.
- Memorize as many **keyboard shortcuts** as you can. Start by learning the shortcuts for choosing tools (see pages 2–4). Use on-screen tool tips to refresh your memory or refer to our shortcuts list. Shortcuts are included in most of the instructions in this book.
- Try to allot at least 60 MB of **RAM** to Photoshop, or four times an image's RAM document size.
- Choose Edit menu > **Purge** submenu commands periodically to regain RAM that was used for the Clipboard, the Undo command, the History palette, or All of the above 4. The Purge commands can't be undone.

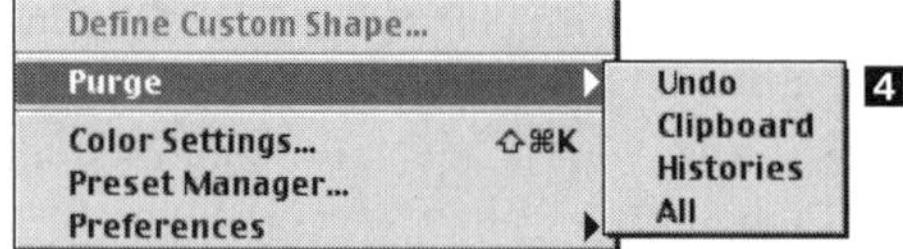

Context menus save time

To choose from an on-screen **context menu**, Right-click/Control-click on a Layers, Channels, or Paths palette thumbnail, name, or feature 1. Or, choose a tool, then Right-click/Control-click with the pointer over the image window to choose commands or options for that tool 2–3.

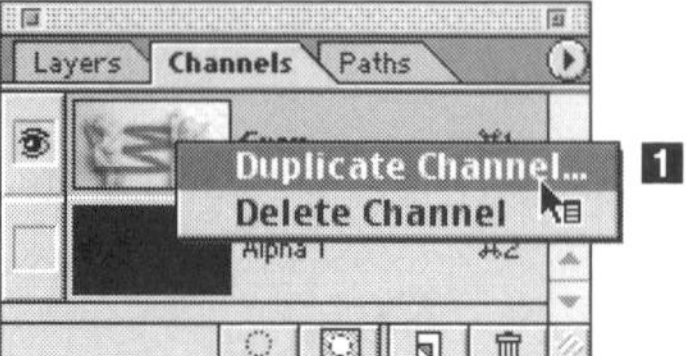

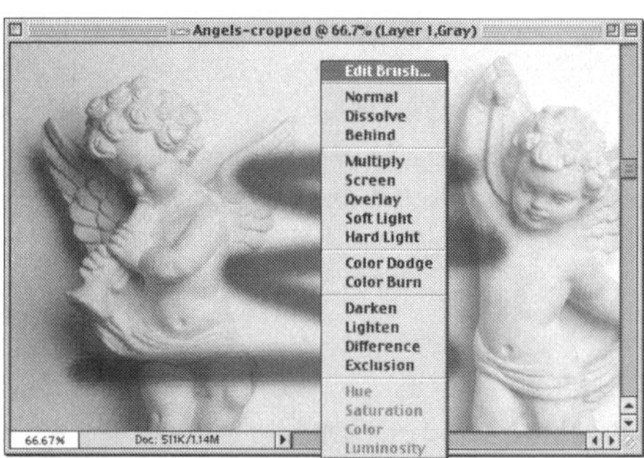

2 *Right-click/Control-click with a* ***painting*** *tool to choose from a list of* ***blending modes.***

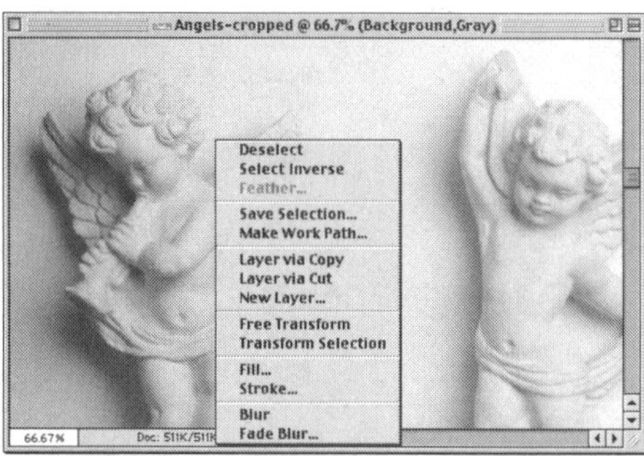

3 *Right-click/Control-click with a* ***selection*** *tool to choose from a list of* ***commands.***

PHOTOSHOP COLOR 2

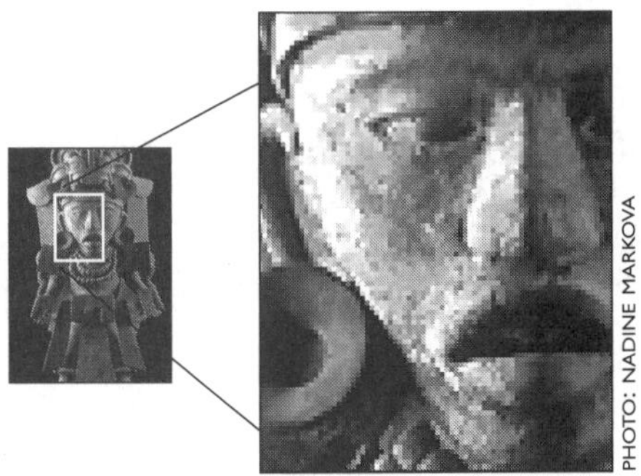

1 *A close-up of an image, showing individual pixels.*

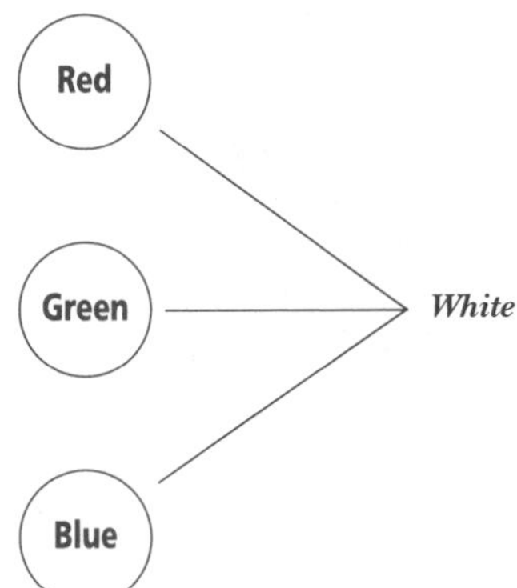

2 *The **additive primaries** on a computer monitor.*

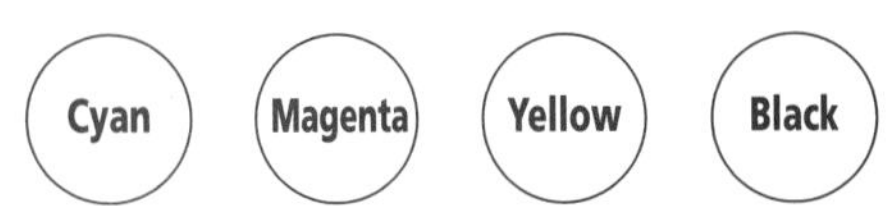

3 *The **subtractive primaries**—printing inks.*

THIS CHAPTER consists of an introduction to color basics (color models, image modes, and blending modes) and to Photoshop's color management features.

Color basics

Pixels

The screen image in Photoshop is a bitmap, which is a geometric arrangement (mapping) of a layer of dots of different shades or colors on a rectangular grid. Each dot, called a pixel, represents a color or shade. By magnifying an area of an image, you can edit pixels individually **1**. Every Photoshop image is a bitmap, whether it originates from a scan, from another application, or entirely within the application using painting and editing tools. (Don't confuse Bitmap image mode with the term "bitmap.") Bitmap programs are ideal for producing painterly, photographic, or photorealistic images that contain subtle gradations of color. If you drag with a painting tool across an area of a layer, pixels under the pointer are recolored.

RGB vs. CMYK color

Red, green, and blue (RGB) light are used to display a color image on a monitor. When these additive primaries in their purest form are combined, they produce white light **2**.

The three subtractive primary inks used in four-color process printing are cyan (C), magenta (M), and yellow (Y) **3**. When they are combined, a dark, muddy color is produced. To produce a rich black, printers usually mix black (K) ink with small quantities of cyan, magenta, and/or yellow ink.

The display of color on a computer monitor is highly variable and subject to the whims of ambient lighting, monitor temperature, and room color. In addition, many colors that are seen in nature cannot be printed, some colors that can be displayed on screen cannot be printed, and some printable colors can't be displayed on screen. All monitors display color using the RGB model—CMYK colors are merely simulated. You don't need to bother with a RGB-to-CMYK conversion if your image is going to be output to the Web or to a film recorder.

An exclamation point will appear on the Color palette if you choose a non-printable (out of gamut) color **1**. Exclamation points will also display on the Info palette if the color currently under the pointer is out of gamut **2**. Using Photoshop's Gamut Warning command, you can display non-printable colors in your image in gray, and then, using the Sponge tool, you can desaturate them to bring them into gamut.

You can use the grayscale, RGB (red-green-blue), HSB (hue-saturation-brightness), CMYK (cyan-magenta-yellow-black), or Lab (lightness-a, axis-b axis) color model when you choose colors in Photoshop via the Color Picker or Color palette.

Channels

Every Photoshop image is a composite of one or more semi-transparent, colored-light overlays called channels. For example, an image in RGB Color mode is composed of the red, green, and blue channels. To illustrate, open a color image, then click Red, Green, or Blue on the Channels palette to display only that channel. Click RGB (Ctrl-~/Cmd ~) to restore the full channel display. (If the channels don't display in color, check the Color Channels in Color box in Edit menu > Preferences > Display & Cursors.)

Color adjustments can be made to an individual channel, but normally modifications are made and displayed in the multichannel, composite image (the topmost channel name on the Channels palette), and affect all of an image's channels at once. Special

Web graphics

If you're creating an image for a Web site, use the RGB color model. Bear in mind that RGB colors—or colors from any other color model, for that matter—may not match the color palette of your Web browser (see page 408). For the best results, load one of the Web or Visibone palettes onto the Swatches palette and use the Web Color Sliders and Make Ramp Web Safe options on the Color palette.

Default number of channels for each image mode

One	Three	Four
Bitmap	RGB	CMYK
Grayscale	Lab	
Duotone	Multichannel	
Indexed Color		

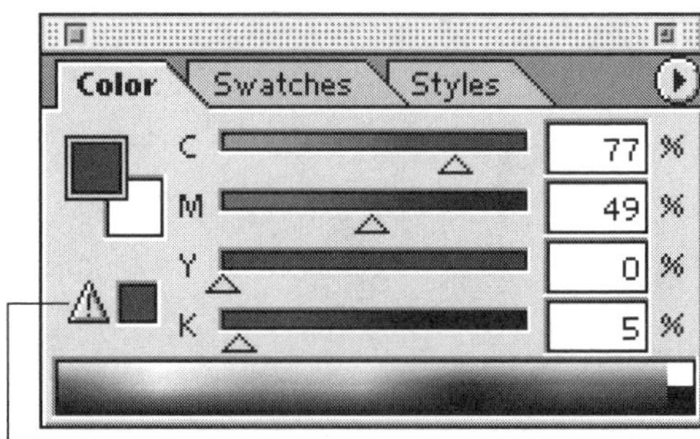

1 ***Out of gamut*** *indicator.*

2 ***Out of gamut*** *indicator.*

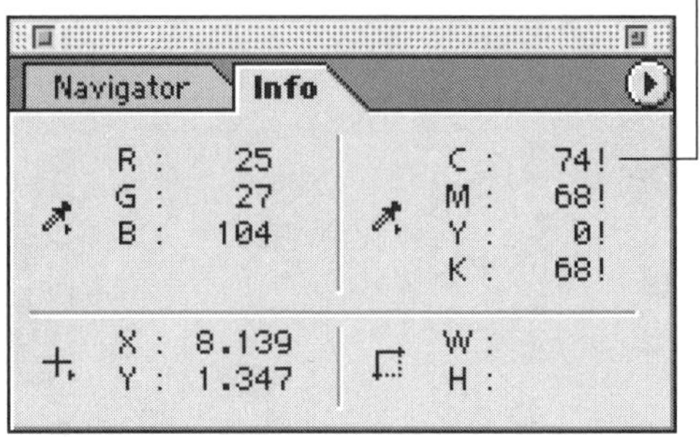

Channels

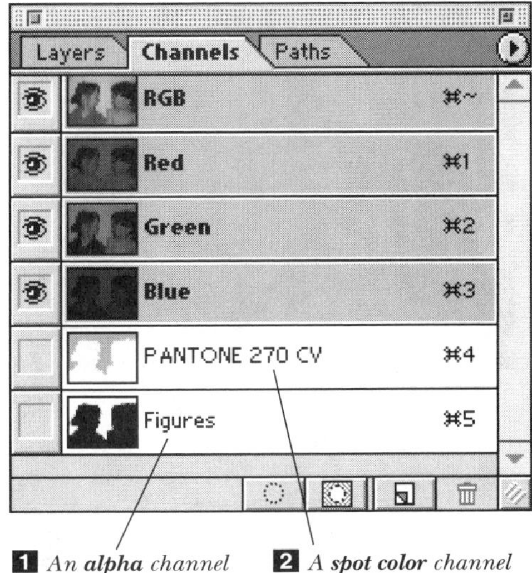

1 *An **alpha** channel* **2** *A **spot color** channel*

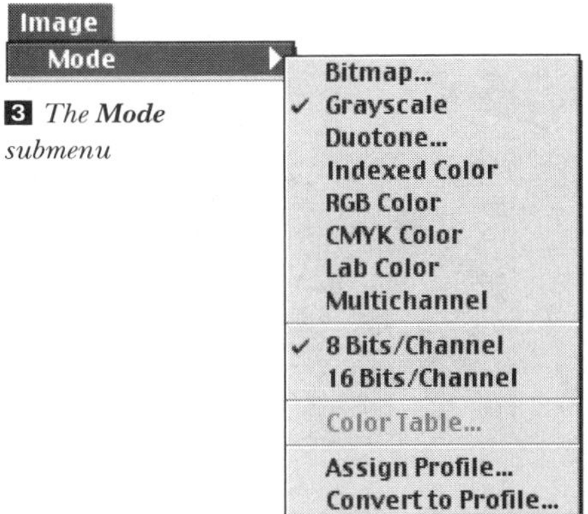

3 *The **Mode** submenu*

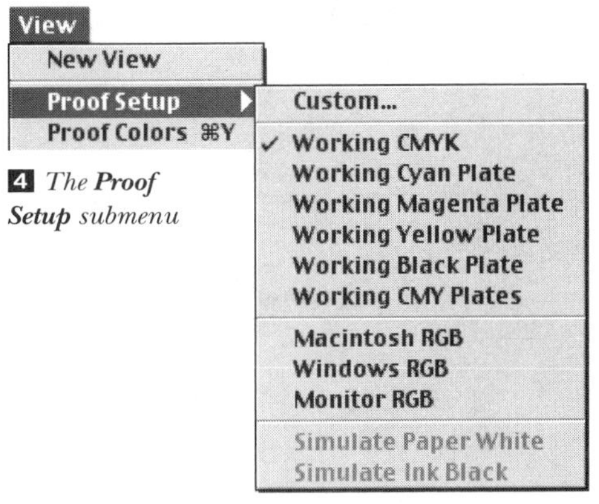

4 *The **Proof Setup** submenu*

grayscale channels that are used for saving selections as masks, called alpha channels, can be added to an image **1**. You can also add spot color channels **2**. Only the currently highlighted channels can be edited.

The more channels an image contains, the larger is its file storage size. The storage size of an image in RGB Color mode, which has three channels (Red, Green, and Blue), will be three times larger than the same image in Grayscale mode, which has one channel. The same image in CMYK Color mode will have four channels (Cyan, Magenta, Yellow, and Black), and will be even larger.

Image modes

An image can be converted to, displayed in, and edited in any one of eight image modes: Bitmap, Grayscale, Duotone, Indexed Color, RGB Color, CMYK Color, Lab Color, and Multichannel. Simply choose the mode you want from the Image menu > Mode submenu **3**. To access a mode that is unavailable (whose name is dimmed), you must first convert your image to a different mode. For example, to convert an image to Indexed Color mode, it must be in RGB Color or Grayscale mode.

Some mode conversions cause noticeable color shifts; others cause subtle color shifts. Very dramatic changes may occur if an image is converted from RGB Color mode to CMYK Color mode, because printable colors will be substituted for rich, glowing RGB colors. Color accuracy may diminish if an image is converted back and forth between RGB and CMYK Color modes too many times.

Medium to low-end scanners usually produce RGB scans. If you're creating an image that's going to be printed, for faster editing and to access all the filters, edit it in RGB Color mode and then convert it to CMYK Color mode when you're ready to imageset it. You can use View menu > Proof Setup **4** in conjunction with View menu > Proof Colors (Ctrl-Y/Cmd-Y) to preview an image in CMYK Color mode without actually changing its mode. You can CMYK-preview your image in one window and open a second window to display the same image without the CMYK preview.

Some conversions will cause layers to be flattened, such as a conversion to Indexed Color, Multichannel, or Bitmap mode. For other conversions, you'll have the option to click Don't Flatten if you want to preserve layers.

High-end scanners usually produce CMYK scans, and these images should be kept in CMYK Color mode to preserve their color data. If you find working on such large files to be cumbersome, you can work out your image-editing scheme on a low resolution version of an image, save the commands using the Actions palette, and then apply the action to the high resolution, CMYK version. You will still, however, have to perform some operations manually, like adding strokes with the Paintbrush tool.

Some output devices require that an image be saved in a particular image mode. The availability of some commands and tool options in Photoshop may also change depending on an image's current mode.

These are the image modes, in brief:

In **Bitmap** mode **1**, pixels are 100% black or 100% white only, and layers, filters, and Adjust commands are unavailable, except for the Invert command. An image must be in Grayscale mode before it can be converted to Bitmap mode.

In **Grayscale** mode **2**, pixels are black, white, or up to 254 shades of gray. If an image is converted from a color mode to Grayscale mode and then saved and closed, its luminosity (light and dark) values will remain intact, but its color information will be deleted and cannot be restored.

An image in **Indexed Color** mode has one channel and a color table containing a maximum of 256 colors or shades (8-bit color). This is the maximum number of colors available in such Web-friendly formats as GIF and

1 ***Bitmap*** *mode, Method: Diffusion Dither*

2 ***Grayscale*** *mode*

The ***Channels*** *palette for an image in various modes:*

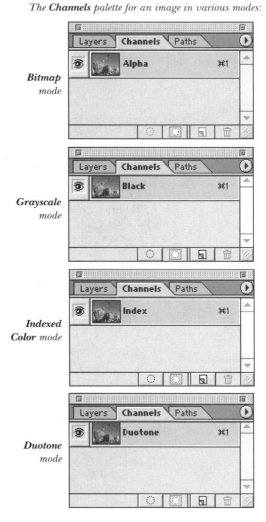

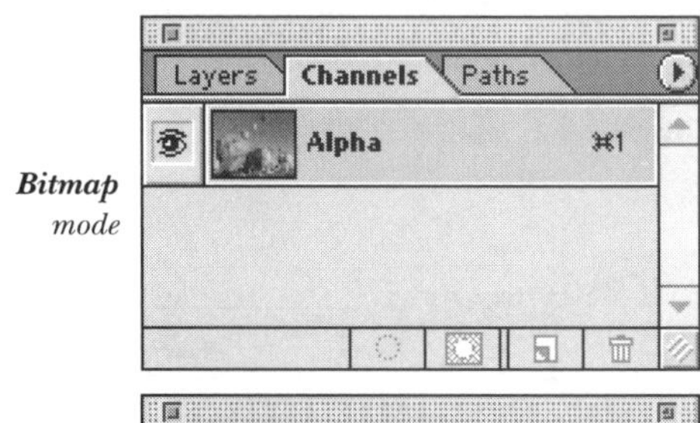

Bitmap *mode*

Grayscale *mode*

Indexed Color *mode*

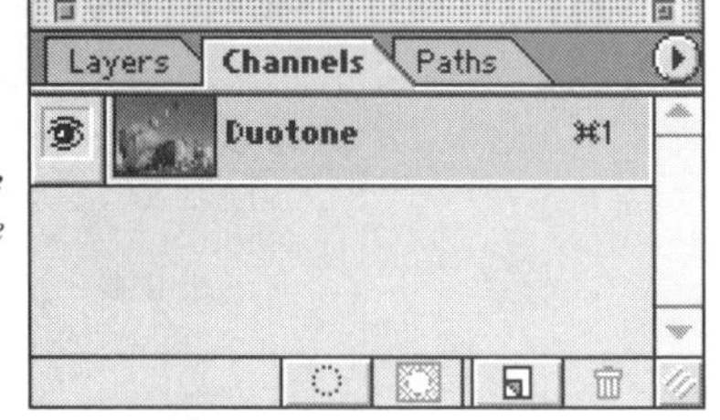

Duotone *mode*

*The **Channels** palette for an image in various modes:*

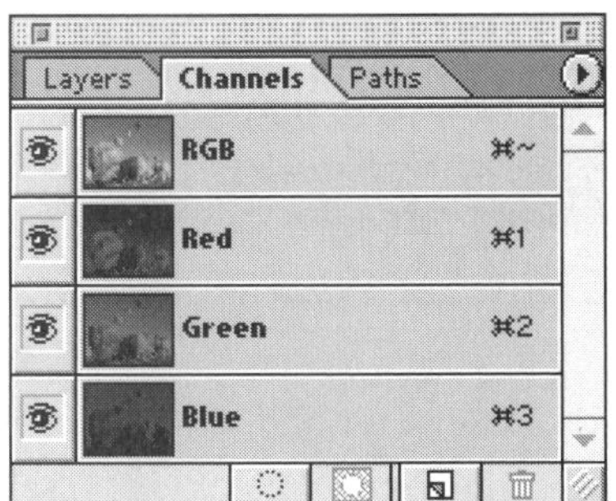

***RGB Color** mode*

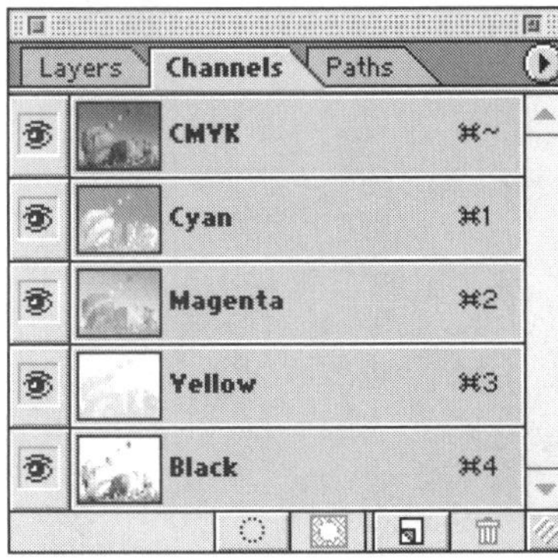

***CMYK Color** mode*

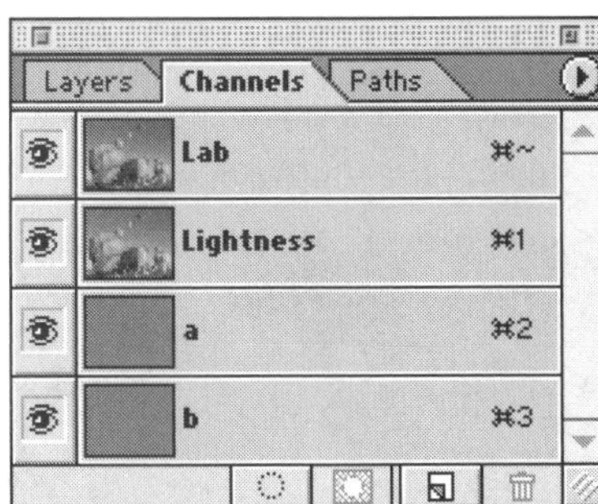

***Lab Color** mode*

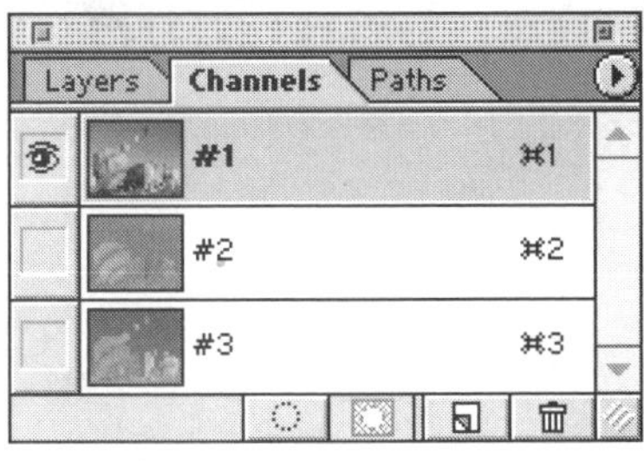

***Multichannel** mode*

PNG-8, although in Photoshop 6 it's best to use the Save for Web command to prepare graphics for display in Web browsers. It is often helpful to reduce images to 8-bit color for use in multimedia applications. You can also convert an image to Indexed Color mode to create arty color effects.

RGB Color is the most versatile mode because it is the only mode in which all of Photoshop's tool options and filters are accessible. Some video and multimedia applications can import an RGB image in the Photoshop file format.

Photoshop is one of few programs in which images can be displayed and edited in **CMYK Color** mode. You can convert an image to CMYK Color mode when you're ready to output it on a color printer or color separate it.

Lab Color is a three-channel mode that was developed for the purpose of achieving consistency among various devices, such as printers and monitors. The channels represent lightness, the colors green-to-red, and the colors blue-to-yellow. Photo CD images can be converted to Lab Color mode or RGB Color mode in Photoshop. Sometimes files are saved in Lab color mode for export to other operating systems.

A **Duotone** is a printing method in which two or more plates are used to add richness and tonal depth to a grayscale image.

A **Multichannel** image is composed of multiple, 256-level grayscale channels. This mode is used for certain grayscale printing situations. You could use multichannel mode to assemble individual channels from several images before converting the new image to a color mode. Spot color channels are preserved if you convert an image to Multichannel mode. If you convert an image from RGB Color to Multichannel mode, the Red, Green, and Blue channels will be converted to Cyan, Magenta, and Yellow. The image may become lighter as a result, but otherwise it won't change significantly.

The blending modes

You can select from an assortment of blending modes on the options bar, the Layers palette, or the Fill, Stroke, Fade, or Fill Path dialog box. The mode you choose for a tool or a layer affects how that tool or layer modifies underlying pixels, which in the following text is called the "base color." The "blend layer" is the layer for which a mode is chosen.

TIP To cycle through blending modes for the currently selected tool, press Shift + or Shift -.

Note: If the Lock transparent pixels box is checked on the Layers palette for the target layer, only pixels—not transparent areas—can be recolored or otherwise edited.

Opacities add up

When you choose a mode and an opacity for a **tool**, be sure to factor in the mode and opacity of the current **layer** you're working on. If you choose 60% opacity for the Paintbrush tool on a layer that has a 50% opacity, for example, your resulting brush stroke will have an opacity of 30%.

NORMAL
All base colors are modified. *Note:* For an image in Bitmap or Indexed Color mode, Normal mode is called Threshold.

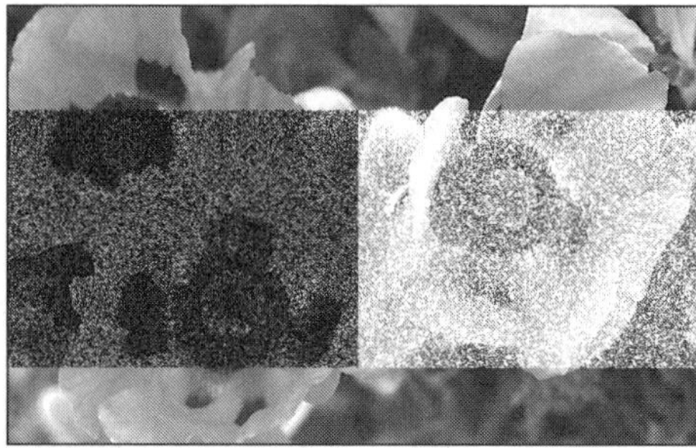

DISSOLVE
Creates a chalky, dry brush texture with the paint or blend layer color. The higher the pressure or opacity, the more solid the stroke.

BEHIND
Not available for layers. Only transparent areas are modified, not existing base color pixels (turn off "Lock transparent pixels"). The effect is like painting on the reverse side of clear acetate. Good for creating shadows. Cannot be used on the Background.

CLEAR
Not available for layers. Makes the base color transparent where strokes are applied (turn off "Lock transparent pixels"). Available only for a multi-layer image when using the Paint Bucket tool, the Line tool (with the Fill Region option chosen), or the Fill, Stroke, Fill Path, or Stroke Path command. Cannot be used on the Background.

MULTIPLY
A dark paint or blend layer color removes the lighter parts of the base color to produce a darker base color. A light paint or blend layer color darkens the base color less. Good for creating semi-transparent shadows.

SCREEN

A light paint or blend layer color removes the darker parts of the base color to produce a lighter, bleached base color. A dark paint or blend layer lightens the base color less.

OVERLAY

Multiplies (darkens) dark areas and screens (lightens) light base colors. Preserves luminosity (light and dark) values. Black and white aren't changed, so detail is maintained.

SOFT LIGHT

Lightens the base color if the paint or blend layer color is light. Darkens the base color if the paint or blend layer color is dark. Preserves luminosity values in the base color. Creates a soft, subtle lighting effect.

HARD LIGHT

Screens (lightens) the base color if the paint or blend layer color is light. Multiplies (darkens) the base color if the paint or blend layer color is dark. Greater contrast is created in the base color and layer color. Good for painting glowing highlights and creating composite effects.

COLOR DODGE

Lightens the base color where the paint or blend layer color is light. A dark paint or blend layer color tints the base color slightly.

COLOR BURN

A dark paint or blend layer color darkens the base color. A light paint or blend layer color tints the base color slightly.

DARKEN

Base colors that are lighter than the paint or blend layer color are modified, base colors that are darker than the paint or blend layer color are not. Use with a paint color that is darker than the base colors you want to modify.

LIGHTEN

Base colors that are darker than the paint or blend layer color are modified, base colors that are lighter than the paint or blend layer color are not. Use with a paint color that is lighter than the base colors you want to modify.

DIFFERENCE

Creates a color negative effect on the base color. When the paint or blend layer color is light, the negative (or invert) effect is more pronounced. Produces noticeable color shifts.

EXCLUSION

Grays out the base color where the paint or blend layer color is dark. Inverts the base color where the paint or blend layer color is light.

HUE

The blend color's hue is applied. Saturation and luminosity values are not modified in the base color.

SATURATION

The blend color's saturation is applied. Hue and luminosity values are not modified in the base color.

COLOR

The blend color's saturation and hue are applied. The base color's light and dark (luminosity) values aren't changed, so detail is maintained. Good for tinting.

LUMINOSITY

The base color's luminosity values are replaced by tone (luminosity) values from the paint or blend layer color. Hue and saturation are not affected in the base color.

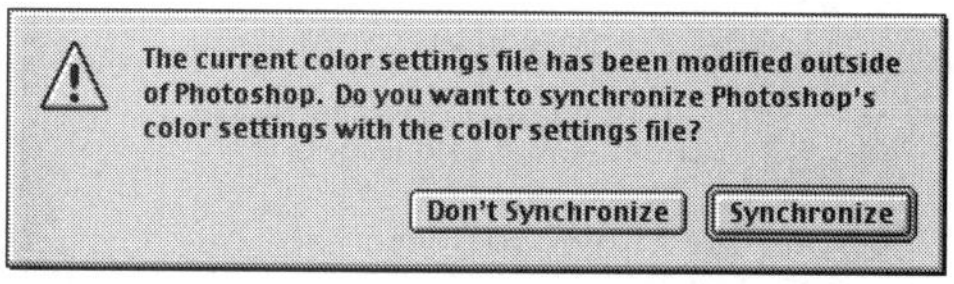

The current color settings file has been modified outside of Photoshop. Do you want to synchronize Photoshop's color settings with the color settings file?

Don't Synchronize | Synchronize

*The Synchronize alert box may open when Photoshop 6 is launched if the current color settings have been modified in another Adobe program (e.g., Illustrator 9). Click **Synchronize** to have Photoshop's Color Settings match (be in sync with) the Color Settings from the other program.*

Color management

Problems with color can creep up on you when various hardware devices and software packages you use treat color differently. For example, if you open a graphic in several different imaging programs and in a Web browser, the colors in your image might look completely different in each case. And none of those programs may match the color of the picture you originally scanned in on your scanner. Print the image, and you will probably find that your results are different again. In some cases, you might find these differences slight and unobjectionable. But in other circumstances, such color changes can wreak havoc with your design and turn a project into a disaster.

A color management system can solve most of these problems by acting as a color interpreter. A good system knows how each device and program understands color, and it can help you move your graphics between them all by adjusting color so that it appears the same in every program and device. A color profile is a mathematical description of a device's color space. Both Illustrator 9.0 and Photoshop 6 use ICC (International Color Consortium) profiles to tell your color management system how particular devices use color.

You can find most of Photoshop's color management controls in the Color Settings dialog box under the Edit menu. This dialog box includes a list of predefined management settings for various publishing situations, including prepress output and Web output.

Photoshop 6 also supports color management policies for RGB and CMYK color files, for files using spot colors, and for grayscale files. These color management policies govern how Photoshop deals with color when opening graphics that do or do not have an attached color profile.

TIP Consult with your prepress service provider, if you are using one, about color management. Make sure your color management workflows will work together.

TIP If you're planning to use the same graphics for different purposes, such as for the Web and for printed material, you may benefit from using color management.

Calibration

The first step toward achieving color consistency is to calibrate your monitor. In this procedure, you will define the RGB color space your monitor can display using the Adobe Gamma control panel, which is installed automatically with Photoshop and some other Adobe applications. You will adjust the contrast and brightness, gamma, color balance, and white point of your monitor.

The Adobe Gamma Control Panel creates an ICC profile, which Photoshop can use as its working RGB space to display the colors in your artwork accurately.

Note: You have to calibrate your monitor and save the settings as an ICC profile only once for all applications.

To calibrate your monitor:

1. Give the monitor 30 minutes to warm up and the display to stabilize, and establish a level of room lighting that will remain constant.
2. Make the desktop pattern light gray.
3. **Mac OS:* Choose Apple menu > Control Panels > Adobe Gamma.

   **Windows 98:* Choose Start menu > Settings > Control Panels, then open the Adobe Gamma utility.

   Windows NT: Run the Adobe Gamma.cpl utility from C:\Program Files\Common Files\ Adobe\Calibration or double-click the utility's alias in the Photoshop 6\ Goodies\Calibration folder.
4. Click Step by Step (Wizard) (Windows)/ Step-by-Step (Assistant) (Mac OS), which will walk you through the process **1**.
   or
   Click Control Panel to choose settings from a single dialog box with no

1 *This is the* ***Adobe Gamma*** *dialog box set for the* ***Step by Step*** *calibration method.*

Calibration

*Gamma utility location in Photoshop

Macintosh: Choose Apple menu > Control Panels > Adobe Gamma.

Windows NT: Run the Adobe Gamma.cpl utility from C:\Program Files\Common Files\Adobe\Calibration or double-click the utility's alias in the Control Panels folder, reached from the Start menu.

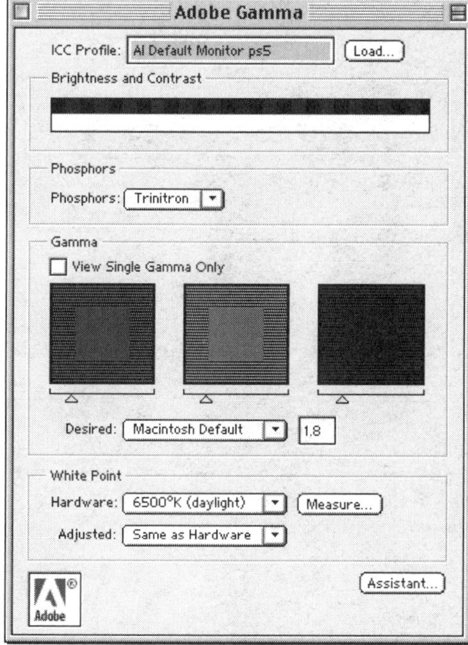

1 *This* ***Adobe Gamma*** *dialog box will open if you choose the Control Panel option. With* ***View Single Gamma Only*** *unchecked, adjustments can be made to the individual Red, Green, and Blue components.*

explanation. (If the Adobe Gamma dialog opens directly, you can skip this step.)

Note: Click Next. If you're using the Assistant, click Next between dialogs.

5. Leave the default monitor ICC profile.
   or
   Click Load and choose a profile that more closely matches your monitor **1**.
6. Turn up your monitor's brightness and contrast settings; leave the contrast at the maximum; and adjust the brightness to make the alternating gray squares in the top bar as dark as possible, but not black, while keeping the lower bar bright white.
7. For Phosphors, select your monitor type or choose Custom and enter the Red, Green, and Blue chromaticity coordinates specified by your monitor's manufacturer.
8. The gray square represents a combined grayscale reading of your monitor. Adjust the gamma using this slider until the smaller, solid color box matches the outer, stripey box. It helps to squint. You might find it easier to deselect the View Single Gamma Only box and make separate adjustments based on the readings for Red, Green, and Blue.
9. For Desired, choose the default for your system: 1.8 (Mac OS) or 2.2 (Windows), if this option is available.
10. For Hardware, choose the white point the monitor manufacturer specifies or click Measure and follow the instructions.
11. For Adjusted, choose Same as Hardware, or, if you know the color temperature at which your image will ultimately be viewed, you can choose it from the pop-up menu or choose Custom and enter it here. *Note:* This option is not available for all monitors.
12. Close the Adobe Gamma window and save the profile. *Mac OS:* Save it in the System Folder > ColorSync Profiles folder. *Windows:* Save it in Windows > System > Color (extension, .icm). Photoshop can use this profile as its

working RGB space in the Color Settings dialog box (see the next page).

Note: If you change your monitor's brightness and contrast settings or change the room lighting, you should recalibrate your monitor. Also, keep in mind that this method is just a start. Professional-level calibration requires more precise monitor measurement using expensive hardware devices such as a colorimeter and a spectrophotometer.

To choose a predefined color management setting

1. Choose Edit menu > Color Settings.
2. Choose a configuration Option from the Settings pop-up menu:

   Color Management Off emulates the behavior of applications that do not support color management. This is a good choice for projects destined for video or onscreen presentation.

   ColorSync Workflow (Mac OS only) manages color using the ColorSync 3.0 color management system. Profiles are based on those in the ColorSync control panel (including the monitor profile you may have created using the Adobe Gamma).

   Emulate Photoshop 4 uses the same color workflow used by the Mac OS version of Photoshop 4 and earlier versions. This option does not recognize or save color profiles.

   U.S. Prepress Defaults manages color using settings based on common press conditions in the U.S. In the European or Japanese Prepress setting, the CMYK Work Space is changed to a press standard for that region.

   Photoshop 5 Default Spaces uses the same working spaces as the default settings in Photoshop 5.

   Web Graphics Defaults manages color for content that will be published on the Web. Uses the RGB profile.

Point and learn

The Color Settings dialog box **1** provides a Description area **2** that displays valuable information on options the pointer is currently over. Make use of this great feature!

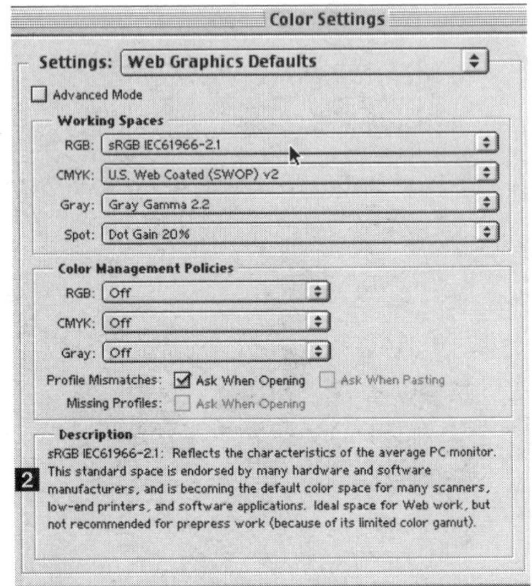

1 *The* ***Color Settings*** *dialog box with the* ***Web Graphics Defaults*** *setting chosen.*

Document-specific color

Photoshop 6 supports **document specific color**, which means each open document keeps its own profile for controlling how the document previews and manages color on output. The current working space is used to create previews for documents that have no embedded profile. Photoshop no longer forces all open documents into the current working space in order to preview color accurately. This is a dramatic improvement in desktop color management.

Bruce Fraser's RGB

Gamma = 2.2

White point = 6500K

Primaries = Custom

		x	y
red	=	0.6400	0.3300
green	=	0.2800	0.6500
blue	=	0.1500	0.0600

Choosing individual work space settings

You can choose color working spaces, which define how RGB and CMYK color will be treated in your document. For CMYK settings, you should check with your service provider. You can also specify dot gain for grayscale images and spot color or gamma for grayscale images. The following choices are available for RGB settings:

Adobe RGB (1998)

This color space produces a wide range of colors, and is useful if you will be converting RGB images to CMYK images. This is not a good choice for Web work.

sRGB IEC61966-2.1

This is a good choice for Web work, as it reflects the settings on the average computer monitor. Many hardware and software manufacturers are using it as the default space for scanners, low-end printers, and software. sRGB IEC61966-2.1 should not be used for prepress work—Apple RGB or ColorMatch RGB should be used instead.

Apple RGB

This space is useful for files that you plan to display on Mac monitors, as it reflects the characteristics of the older standard Apple 13-inch monitors. It also is a good choice for working with older desktop publishing files, such as Adobe Photoshop 4.0 and earlier.

ColorMatch RGB

This space produces a smaller range of color than the Adobe RGB (1998) model, but it matches the color space of Radius Pressview monitors and is useful for print production work.

Monitor RGB

This choice sets the RGB working space to your monitor's profile. This is a useful setting if you know that other applications you will be using for your project do not support color management. Keep in mind that if

(Continued on the following page)

you share this configuration with another user, the configuration will use that user's monitor profile as the RGB working space, and color consistency may be lost.

ColorSync RGB (Mac only)

Use this color space to match Photoshop's RGB space to the space specified in the Apple ColorSync 3.0 (or later) control panel. This can be the profile you created using Adobe Gamma. If you share this configuration with another user, it will utilize the ColorSync space specified by that user.

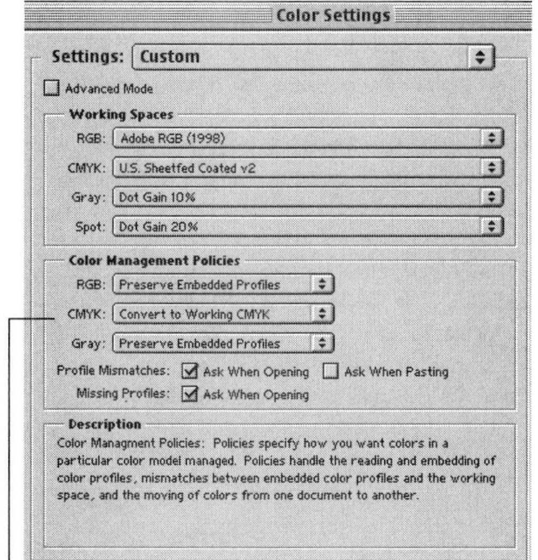

1 *Color Management Policies options are chosen from the middle portion of the* ***Color Settings*** *dialog box.*

You can choose a customized color management policy that will tell Photoshop how to deal with artwork that doesn't match your current color settings.

To customize your color management policies:

1. Choose Edit menu > Color Settings.
2. Choose any predefined setting from the Settings pop-up menu other than Emulate Photoshop 4.
3. Choose a color management policy:

   If you choose **Off**, Photoshop will not color manage imported or opened color files.

   Choose **Preserve Embedded Profiles** if you think you're going to be working with both color managed and non color managed documents. This will tie each color file's profile to the individual file. Remember, in Photoshop 6, each open document can have its own profile.

   Choose **Convert to Working Space** if you want all your documents to reflect the same color working space. This is usually the best choice for Web work.

   For Profile Mismatches, check **Ask When Opening** to have Photoshop display a message if the color profile in a file you are opening does not match your selected working space. If you choose this option, you can override your color management policy when opening documents.

   Check **Ask When Pasting** to have Photoshop display a message when color profile mismatches occur as you paste color data into your document. If you choose this option, you can override your color management policy when pasting.

   For files with Missing Profiles, check **Ask When Opening** to have Photoshop display a message offering you the opportunity to assign a profile.
4. Click OK.

To customize your conversion options:

1. Choose Edit menu > Color Settings.
2. Check the Advanced Mode box **1**.
3. Under Conversion Options, choose a color management Engine that will be used to convert colors between color spaces: Adobe (ACE) uses Adobe's color management system and color engine; Apple ColorSync or Apple CMM uses Apple's color management system; and Microsoft ICM uses the system provided in the Windows 98 and Windows 2000 systems. Other CMMs can be chosen to fit into color workflows that use specific output devices.
4. Choose a rendering Intent to determine how colors will be changed as they are moved from one color space to another:

   Perceptual changes colors in a way that seems natural to the human eye, even though the color values actually do change; good for continuous tone images.

   Saturation changes colors with the intent of preserving vivid colors, although it compromises the accuracy of the color; good for charts and business graphics.

   Absolute Colorimetric keeps colors that are inside the destination color gamut unchanged, but the relationships between colors outside this gamut are changed in an attempt to preserve a color.

   Relative Colorimetric, the default intent for all predefined settings options, is the same as Absolute Colorimetric, except it compares the white point, or extreme highlight, of the source color space to the destination color space and shifts all colors accordingly. The accuracy of this intent depends on the accuracy of white point information in an image's profile.

   Note: Differences between rendering intents are visible only on a printout or a conversion to a different working space.

Save your settings

To save your custom settings for later use, click **Save** in the Color Settings dialog box. If you want your custom file to display on the Settings pop-up menu, in Windows, save it in the Settings folder in the default location: deeply nested in the Program Files folder. On Mac OS, save it in the System Folder > Application Support > Adobe > Color > Settings folder. When you're ready to reuse the saved settings, choose the file name from the Settings pop-up menu. To locate a settings file that isn't saved in the Settings folder (and thus isn't on the Settings menu), click **Load** in the Custom Settings dialog box.

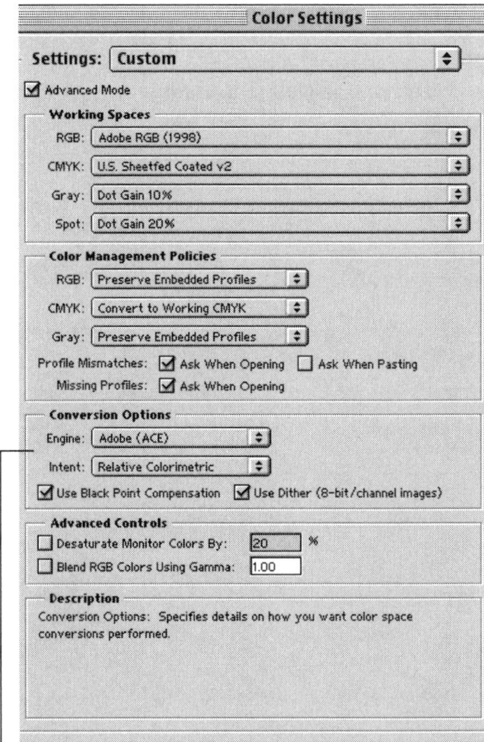

1 *When the **Advanced Mode** box is checked in the **Color Settings** dialog box, the **Conversion Options** become available.*

Check **Use Black Point Compensation** if you would like to adjust for differences in black points between color spaces. When this option is chosen, the full dynamic range of the source color space is mapped into the full dynamic range of the destination color space. If you don't select this option, your blacks may appear as grays.

We recommend you check Use Black Point Compensation for RGB to CMYK , but consult your print shop before checking it for a CMYK to CMYK conversion.

Check **Use Dither** if you want Photoshop to dither colors when converting 8-bits-per-channel images between color spaces. Sometimes when an image is converted from one color space to another, colors that don't exist in the destination space are lost, resulting in banding or other color artifacts. When this option is checked, Photoshop will mix blocks of similar colors to substitute for the missing color, giving a smoother appearance. The file size may increase, however.

We recommend keeping the Use Dither box checked when converting between RGB and CMYK spaces for print, but turning it off when preparing graphics for the Web. The Save for Web dialog box provides more precise controls for dithering images.

5. Click OK.

TIP When you save a file in a format that supports embedded profiles (e.g., the native Photoshop or PDF formats), you can check the Embed ICC Profile option to save the profile in the document.

(Continued on the following page)

You may decide later that you want to change the color profile of a document or remove a profile from a document. For example, you may want to prepare a document for a specific output purpose, and you may need to adjust the profile accordingly. You also may want to use this option if you change your mind about your color management settings. The Assign Profile command reinterprets the color data directly in the color space of the new profile (or lack thereof), and visible shifting of colors can be the result. When you use the Convert Profile command, however, the color numbers are recalculated before the new profile is applied in an effort to preserve the document's appearance. In either case, keep the Preview box checked so you know what you're getting into.

To change or delete a document's color profile:

1. Choose Image menu > Mode > Assign Profile **1**.
2. Click Don't Color Manage This Document to remove the color profile.
   or
   Click Working [plus the document color mode and name of the working space you are using] to assign that particular working space to a document that uses no profile or that uses a profile that is different from the working space.
   or
   Click Profile to reassign a different profile to a color managed document. Choose a profile from the pop-up menu.
3. Click OK.

   Note: If you save a file in (or export a file to) a format that supports embedded profiles, you will have the choice to select or deselect the Embed ICC Profile option. You should keep this option chosen (checked) unless you have a specific reason to uncheck it.

Where you'll see it

The assigned profile is listed as the **Source Space** in the Adobe Photoshop 6 section of the File menu > Print dialog box. And if you choose **Document Profile** from the status bar pop-up menu at the bottom of the application/document window, the profile will appear on the status bar.

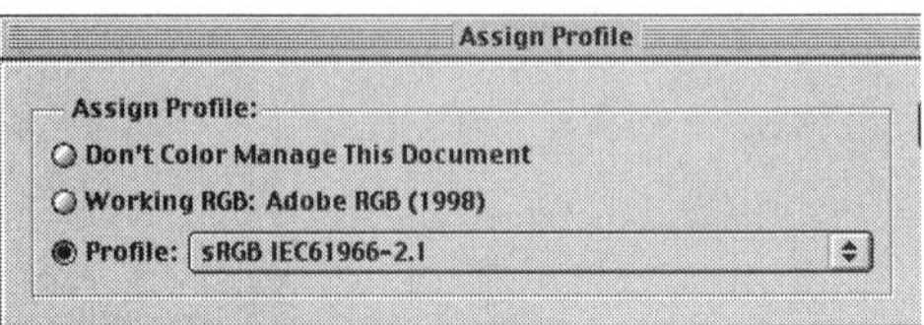

1 *The **Assign Profile** dialog box.*

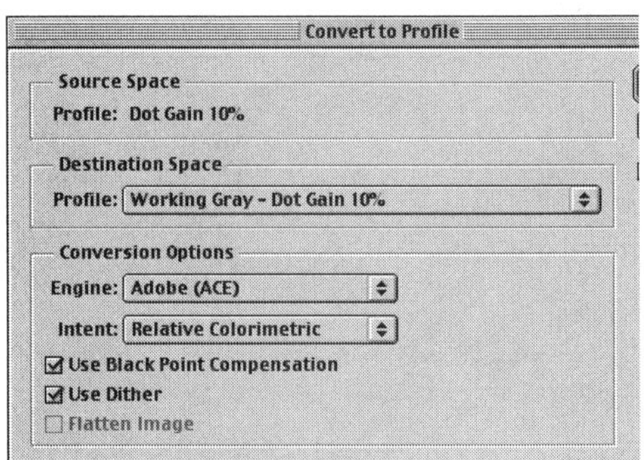

2 *The **Convert to Profile** dialog box.*

Assign Profile

If Preserve Color Numbers is gray

The **Preserve Color Numbers** option is available only when the color mode of the current file is the same as that of the output device profile currently chosen in the Proof Setup dialog box. For example, if the document color mode is RGB and the chosen proofing profile is an RGB profile, then the Preserve Color Numbers option will be available.

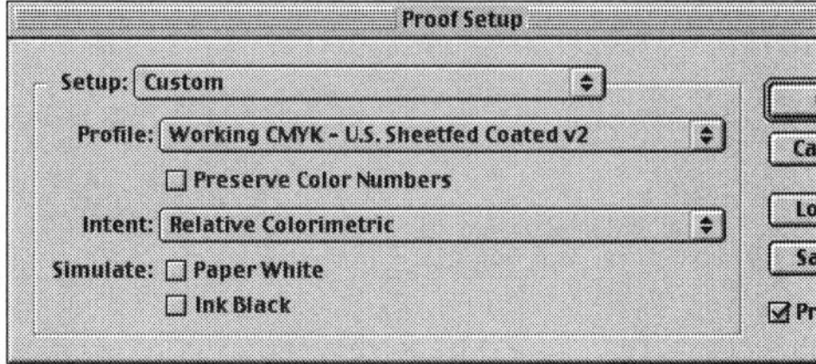

1 *The **Proof Setup** dialog box.*

To convert a document's color profile:

1. Choose Image menu > Mode > Convert to Profile.
2. Choose the space that you want to convert the document to from the Destination Space pop-up menu. It doesn't have to be the current working space.

   For information on the Conversion Options, see "To customize your conversion options" on page 40.

Specifying a color management setup is all well and good, but sometimes all you want is to know how a document will look when it is printed out or viewed on a Windows or Mac monitor as part of a Web page. To do this, you can soft proof your colors. While this method is less accurate than actually making a print or viewing your Web artwork on different monitors, it can give you a general idea of how your work will look with different settings.

To proof your colors:

1. From the View menu > Proof Setup submenu, choose which type of output display you want to simulate.

   Custom will allow you to create a proofing model for a specific output device using the Proof Setup dialog box **1**. To do this, choose the color profile for your desired output device from the Profile pop-up menu, then check or uncheck Preserve Color Numbers, if this option is available. If you check this option, Photoshop will simulate how the colors will appear if they're not converted to the proofing space. If you uncheck this option, Photoshop will simulate how the colors will appear if they are converted, and you will need to specify a rendering intent as described on page 40 ("customize your conversion options").

(Continued on the following page)

Check the **Simulate Paper White** box to preview the shade of white of the print medium defined in the document's profile.

Check **Simulate Ink Black** to preview the full range of gray values defined in the document's profile.
or
Choose **Working CMYK** to soft proof colors using the CMYK working space as defined in the Color Settings dialog box.
or
Choose **Working Cyan Plate**, **Working Magenta Plate, Working Yellow Plate**, **Working Black Plate**, or **Working CMY** to soft-proof various ink colors as defined in the current CMYK working space.
or
Choose **Macintosh RGB** or **Windows RGB** to soft proof colors using a Mac or Windows monitor profile as the proofing space you want to simulate.
or
Choose **Monitor RGB** to use your monitor profile as the space for proofing.

2. View menu > Proof Colors will be checked automatically so the soft proof can be previewed. Uncheck this option to turn off proofing.

TIP Click the Save button to save a custom proof setup. Saved proof setups are listed at the bottom of the Proof Setup submenu.

TIP For instructions on how to use the color management features in the Print Options and Print dialog boxes, see pages 376–379 and 381.

STARTUP 3

1 *Click **Adobe Photoshop 6**.*

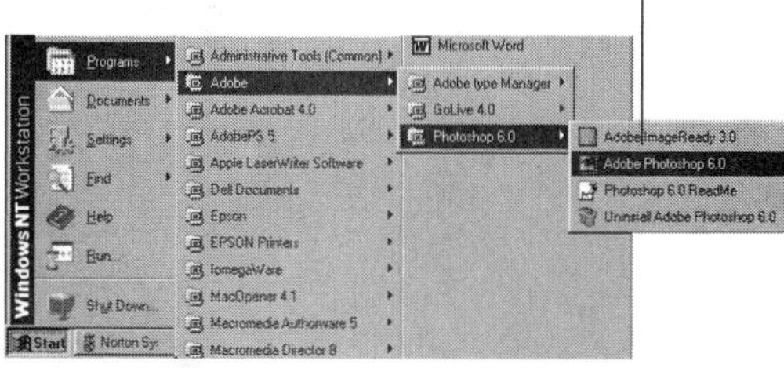

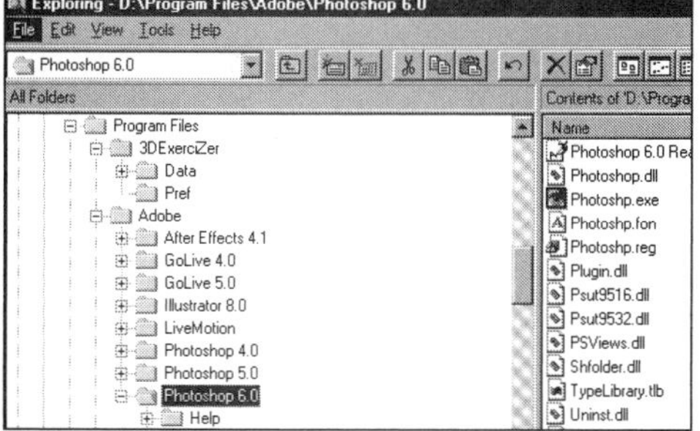

2

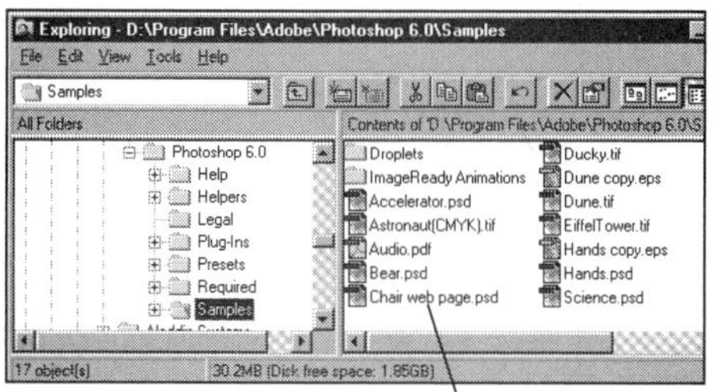

3 *Double-click a **Photoshop** file in **Windows Explorer**.*

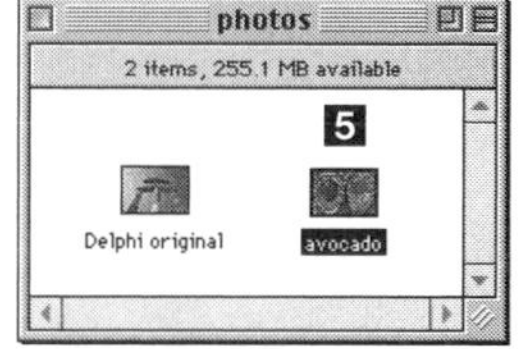

IN THIS CHAPTER you will learn how to get started: launch the application, scan an image, create a new image, open an existing image, and place an image into Photoshop. You'll also learn how to change an image's dimensions, resolution, or file storage size; apply the Unsharp Mask filter to resharpen an image after resampling; enlarge an image's canvas size; and crop, flip, rotate, save, copy, and close an image. And finally, you learn how to change the view size of an image, move an image in its window, and switch screen display modes.

To launch Photoshop (Windows):

In Windows 95, 98, or NT, click the Start button on the Taskbar, choose Programs, choose Adobe, choose Photoshop 6.0, then click Adobe Photoshop 6.0 **1**. (If you don't yet have an icon for Photoshop on your desktop, open the Adobe Photoshop folder, then drag the Photoshop application icon to the desktop.)

or

Open the Adobe Photoshop folder in My Computer, then double-click the Photoshop application icon **2**.

or

Double-click a Photoshop file icon **3**.

To launch Photoshop (Mac OS):

If you're using System 8.5 or later, click once on the Photoshop icon in the Launcher **4**. (If you don't yet have an icon for Photoshop in the Launcher, open the Adobe Photoshop 6 folder in the Finder, then drag the Photoshop application icon into the Launcher window.)

or

Open the Adobe Photoshop 6 folder in the Finder, then double-click the Photoshop application icon.

or

Double-click a Photoshop file icon **5**.

Where images come from

An image can be created, opened, edited, and saved in over a dozen different file formats in Photoshop **1**. Of these, you might use only a few, such as TIFF, GIF, JPEG, EPS, and the native Photoshop file format. Because Photoshop accepts so many formats, an image can be gathered from any number of sources: scanners, drawing applications, PhotoCDs, still images, video captures, or even other operating systems. You can also create an image entirely within Photoshop.

✓ Photoshop document
Photoshop
Photoshop 2.0
BMP
CompuServe GIF
Photoshop EPS
JPEG
PCX
Photoshop PDF
PICT File
PICT Resource
Pixar
PNG
Raw
Scitex CT
Targa
TIFF
Photoshop DCS 1.0
Photoshop DCS 2.0

1 *These are the* ***formats*** *that are available in Photoshop on Mac OS.*

Scanning

Using a scanning device and scanning software, a slide, flat artwork, or a photograph can be digitized (translated into numbers) so it can be read, displayed, edited, and printed by a computer. You can scan directly into Photoshop or you can use other scanning software and save the scan in a file format that Photoshop opens.

To produce a high-quality scan for print output, start with as high quality an original as possible. Some scanners will compress an image's dynamic range and increase its contrast, so choose a photograph with good tonal balance. If you're going to scan it yourself, set the scanning parameters carefully.

The quality of a scan will partially depend on the type of scanner you use. If you're going to dramatically transform the image in Photoshop (e.g., apply filter effects or add a lot of brushstrokes), you can use an inexpensive flat-bed scanner, which will produce an RGB scan. For more accurate color and crisper details, use a slide scanner to scan a transparency.

For professional-quality output, have your artwork scanned by a service bureau on a high-resolution CCD scanner, such as a Scitex Smart-Scanner, or on a drum scanner. A high-end scanner can capture a wide dynamic range of color and shade and can optically distinguish subtle differences in luminosity, even in shadow areas. High-end scanners usually produce CMYK scans, which

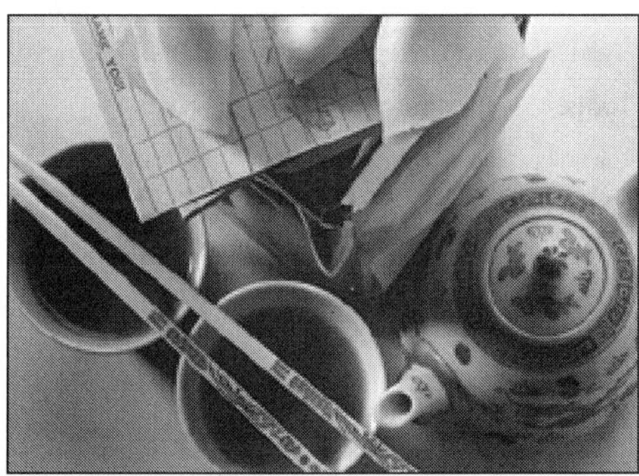

1 *72 ppi.*

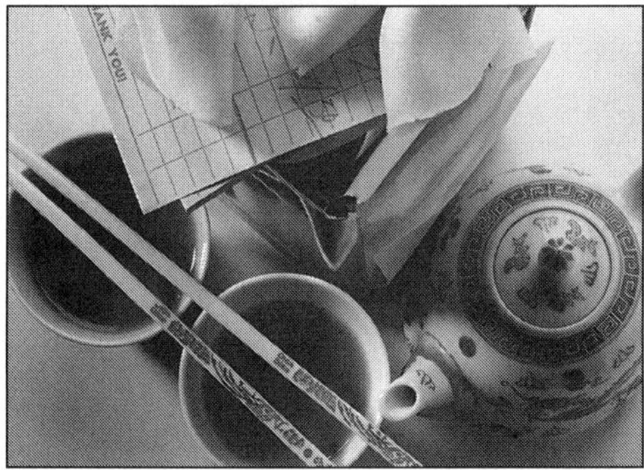

2 *150 ppi.*

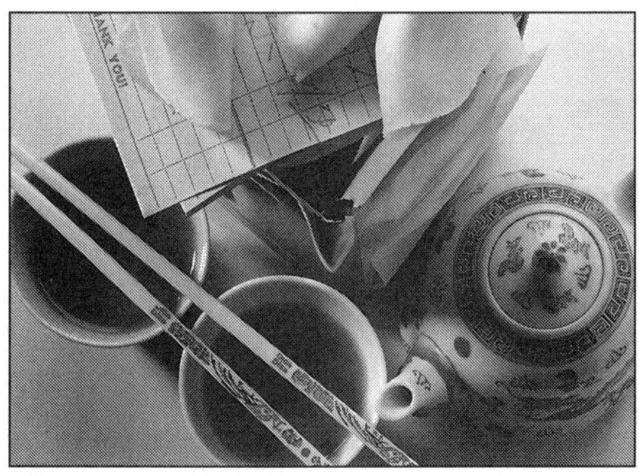

3 *300 ppi.*

are usually large in file size.

Desktop scanning software basics

Scanning software usually offers most of the options that are discussed below, although terms may vary. The quality and file storage size of a scan are partially determined by the mode, resolution, and scale you specify, and whether you crop the image.

Preview: Place the art in the scanner, then click Preview or PreScan.

Scan mode: Choose Black-and-White Line Art (no grays), Grayscale, or Color (choose millions of colors, if available). An image scanned in Color will be approximately three times larger in file size than the same image scanned in Grayscale.

Resolution: Scan resolution is measured in pixels per inch (ppi) **1**–**3**. The higher the resolution of an image, the more pixels it contains, and thus the more information for detail, but the larger will be its file size. Choose the minimum resolution necessary to obtain the desired output quality from your final output device. But don't choose a higher resolution than you really need—the image will be larger in storage size than necessary, it will take longer to render on screen, display on the Web, or print, and there will be no improvement in output quality. On the other hand, too low a resolution will cause a printed image to look coarse and jagged, and its details will be lost.

Before selecting a resolution for print output, ask your print shop what printer or imagesetter resolution and halftone screen frequency they plan to use. (The scan resolution is different from the resolution of the output device.)

As a general rule, for a grayscale image, you should choose a resolution that is one-and-a-half times the halftone screen frequency (lines per inch) of your final output device, or twice the halftone screen frequency for a color image. Use a high scanning resolution (600 ppi or higher) for line art. For example, if your print shop is going to use a

133-line screen for black-and-white printing, you should use 200 ppi as your scan resolution. If your prepress shop is going to use an imagesetter that doesn't have halftoning technology, ask them to recommend an appropriate scan resolution. To calculate the appropriate file size for a scan, see the instructions on page 51.

Cropping: If you're planning to use only part of an image, reposition the handles of the box in the preview area to reduce the scan area. Cropping can significantly reduce the storage size of a scan.

Scale: To enlarge an image's dimensions, choose a scale percentage above 100%. Enlarging an image or increasing its resolution in Photoshop or any other software program may cause it to blur, because the program uses mathematical "guesswork" (interpolation) to fill in additional information. An image's original information is only recorded at the time of scanning!

Scan: Click Scan and choose a location in which to save the file.

16-bits per channel mode

An average-quality scanner can capture 10 bits of accurate data per channel from an image. A high-end scanner can capture up to 16 bits of accurate data per channel. If the 16-bit scanner also has a wide dynamic color range and good optical density (at least 3.3), then those extra pixels of data will capture even finer details of color and shade—even in shadow areas. Photoshop can open a CMYK file containing 16 bits per channel (a 64-bit total for four channels). All the image's original pixel information is preserved, and the image can be edited and adjusted. You have to convert a 16-bit image down to 8-bit before printing, however (Image menu > Mode > 8 Bits/Channel).

There are two restrictions to keep in mind. First, a 16-bit image can only have *one* layer. And second, not every Photoshop edit command can be used on it.

Available in 16-bits per channel mode

Tools	Adjust submenu commands	Other
Marquee	Levels	Canvas Size
Lasso	Auto Levels	Histogram
Measure	Auto Contrast	Duplicate
Zoom	Curves	Image Size
Hand	Color Balance	Rotate Canvas
Eyedropper	Brightness/Contrast	some filters
Slice	Hue/Saturation	
Color Sample	Channel Mixer	
Crop	Gradient Map	
Clone Stamp	Invert	
History Brush	Equalize	
Pen tools		

ImageReady info

The first time you choose a scanning module from the File > Import submenu, choose Twain_32 Source (Win) or Twain Select (Mac OS), choose a Twain device (the scanner), then choose Twain_32 (Win) or Twain Acquire (Mac OS). Thereafter, to access the scanning software, just choose File menu > Import > Twain_32 (Win) or Twain Acquire (Mac OS). (See the Photoshop documentation for information about scanning modules.)

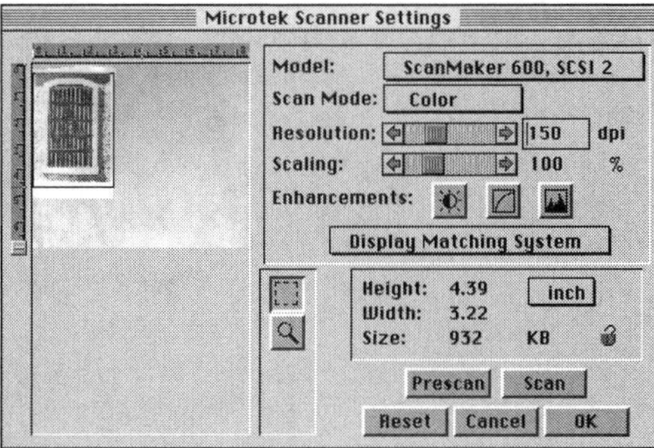

1 *Note how the file* ***Size*** *changes as you change the mode, resolution, and scale settings.*

Note: To scan into Photoshop, the scanner's plug-in or Twain module must be in the Import-Export folder inside the Adobe Photoshop > Plug-Ins folder.

If your scanner doesn't have a Photoshop-compatible scanner driver, scan your image outside Photoshop, save it as a TIFF, then open it in Photoshop as you would any other image.

To calculate the proper resolution for a scan, follow the instructions on the next page.

To scan into Photoshop:

1. Choose a scanning module or choose File menu > Import > Twain_32 (Win) or Twain Acquire (Mac OS).
2. Click Prescan **1**.
3. Following the guidelines outlined on the previous two pages, choose a Scan Mode and Resolution.
4. *Optional:* Choose a different Scaling percentage and/or crop the image preview.
5. Click Scan. The scanned image will appear in a new, untitled window.
6. Save the image (see pages 61–63). If it requires color correction, see pages 394–398. If it needs to be straightened out, see the tip on page 82.

The resolution of a Photoshop image, like any bitmapped image, is independent of the monitor's resolution, so it can be customized for a particular output device, with or without modifying its file storage size.

TIP An image whose resolution is greater than the monitor's resolution will appear larger than its print size when it's displayed in Photoshop at 100% view.

Note: It's always best to scan an image at the outset at the final size and resolution that are required for your final output device.

To calculate the proper resolution for a scan or for an existing image:

1. Create a new RGB document (File menu > New), enter the final Width and Height dimensions, choose 72 ppi for the image Resolution, then click OK. (The Resolution will be readjusted in step 5).
2. Choose Image menu > Image Size.
3. Click the Auto button on the right side of the dialog box.
4. Enter the Screen frequency of your final output device (the lpi, or lines per inch setting that your print shop will be using) **1**.
5. Click Quality: Draft (1x screen frequency), Good (1½ x screen frequency), or Best (2 x screen frequency).
6. Click OK.
7. Jot down the Document Size: Resolution value, which is the proper value to enter when you scan your image.

   Note: If you're going to scale the final image up or down in Photoshop, you should multiply the resolution by that scale factor to arrive at the proper resolution for the scan. You don't need to multiply the resolution if you scale the original image when you scan it.
8. Click OK. The image now has the correct resolution.

Resolution for Web graphics

When creating an image which will be output to the Web, first decide how large your user's browser's window is likely to be, and then figure out how much of the window you want your image to cover. Begin by determining what monitor resolution your viewers are most likely to use. These days, according to Websites like websnapshot.com which track such things, more than half of all browsers are running on monitors set to 800x600 pixel resolution. When you subtract the space taken up by menu bars, scroll bars, and other controls that are part of the browser interface, you're left with a "canvas" of about 740x460 at the most. Given that most viewers won't fill their entire screen with the browser window, you shouldn't count on much more room than 660x420.

You might find it useful to create a blank document at 660x420 resolution, 72 pixels per inch, to use as a template. Keep it in the background while you work, so as you create the actual images for your Web page you can see what portion of the screen they'll cover. (Don't fret over the inch equivalent for pixels. Onscreen imagery is measured in pixels.)

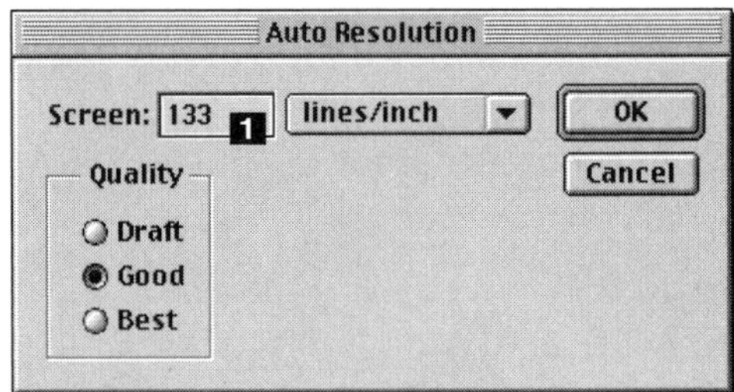

Calculate Resolution

File storage sizes of scanned images

Size (In inches)	PPI (Resolution)	Black/White 1-Bit	Grayscale 8-Bit	CMYK Color 24-Bit
2 x 3	150	17 K	132 K	528 K
	300	67 K	528 K	2.06 MB
4 x 5	150	56 K	440 K	1.72 MB
	300	221 K	1.72 MB	6.87 MB
8 x 10	150	220 K	1.72 MB	6.87 MB
	300	879 K	6.87 MB	27.50 MB

Note: *File storage sizes are for a one-layer TIFF file with no alpha channels.*

Potential gray levels at various output resolutions and screen frequencies

	Output Resolution (DPI)	Screen Frequency (LPI) 60	85	100	133	150
Laser printers	**300**	26	13			
	600	101	51	37	21	
Image-setters	**1270**	256*	224	162	92	72
	2540		256*	256*	256*	256*

Note: *Ask your print shop what screen frequency (lpi) you will need to specify when image-setting your file. Also ask your prepress shop what resolution (dpi) to use for imagesetting. Some imagesetters can achieve resolutions above 2540 dpi. Note that as the line screen frequency (lpi) goes up at a constant dpi, the number of gray levels goes down.*

**PostScript Level 2 printers produce a maximum of 256 gray levels. PostScript Level 3 printers can produce a greater number of gray levels.*

Using the status bar

Windows: Choose Window menu > Show Status Bar to display the status bar or Hide Status Bar to hide it.

Windows and Mac OS:

When **Document Sizes** is chosen from the status bar pop-up menu at the bottom of the application/image window, the status bar displays the file storage size for a flattened file (the first amount) and the file storage size for a layered file (the second amount) **1**.

When **Document Profile** is chosen, the embedded color profile is listed; the word "Untagged" appears when there is no profile.

When **Scratch Sizes** is chosen, the bar displays the amount of storage space Photoshop is using for all currently open pictures (on the left) and the amount of RAM currently available to Photoshop (on the right). When the first amount is greater than the second amount, Photoshop is using virtual memory on the scratch disk.

When **Efficiency** is chosen, the bar displays the percentage of process time devoted to actual program operations in RAM. A percentage below 100 indicates the scratch disk is being used.

When **Current Tool** is chosen, the name of the current tool displays.

And finally, press and hold on the status bar to display the page **preview**, which is a thumbnail of the image relative to the paper size (including custom printing marks, if any).

Storage size

Windows: To view the actual storage size of an image, use Windows Explorer to open the folder that contains the file you're interested in, and look in the Size column **2**. Or for an even more accurate figure, Right-click the file icon and click Properties.

Mac OS: To view the actual storage size of an image, look at the file information in the Finder. Or for an even more accurate figure, click once on the file icon in the Finder, then choose File menu > Get Info (Cmd-I) **3**.

Do this any time

Regardless of which option is chosen from the status bar pop-up menu, you can always Alt-press/Option-press on the status bar to display the image's **dimensions**, number of **channels**, **mode**, and **resolution**.

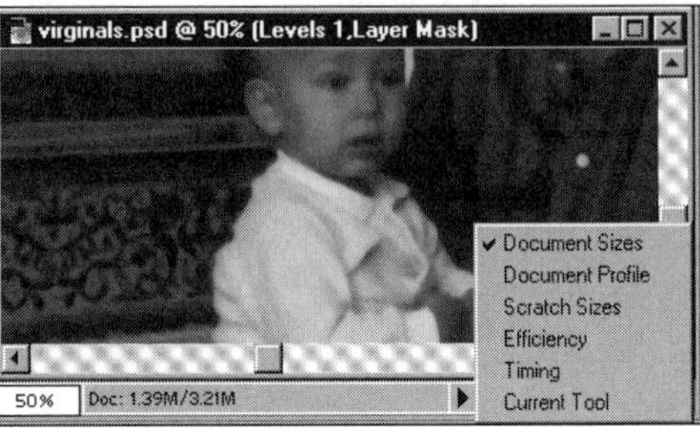

1 *The status bar with **Document Sizes** chosen. The figure on the left is the **RAM** required for the **flattened** image with no extra channels; the figure on the right is the **RAM** required for the image with **layers** and **extra channels**, if any.*

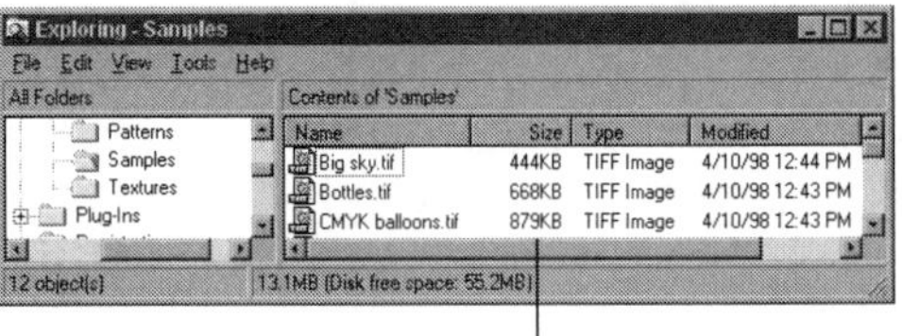

2 *Windows: The storage size of an image is listed in the **Size** column.*

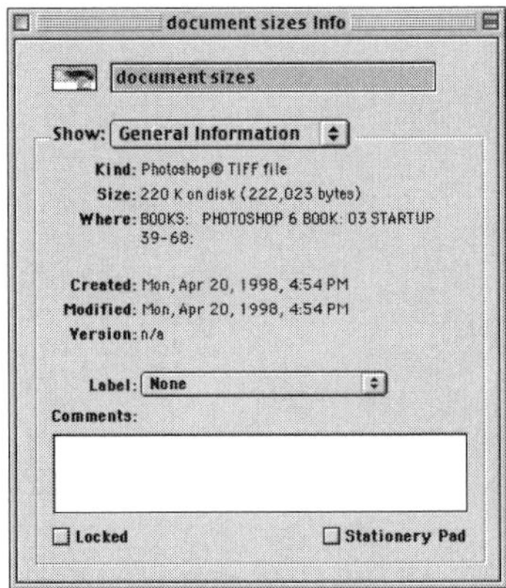

3 *Mac OS: For the actual **storage size** of an image, use Get Info (Cmd-I).*

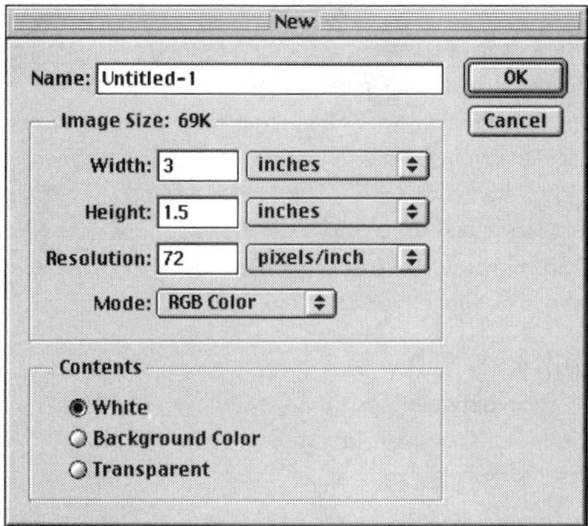

1 *In the* ***New*** *dialog box, enter a* ***Name*** *and enter* ***Width, Height,*** *and* ***Resolution*** *values. Also choose an image* ***Mode*** *and click a* ***Contents*** *type for the Background.*

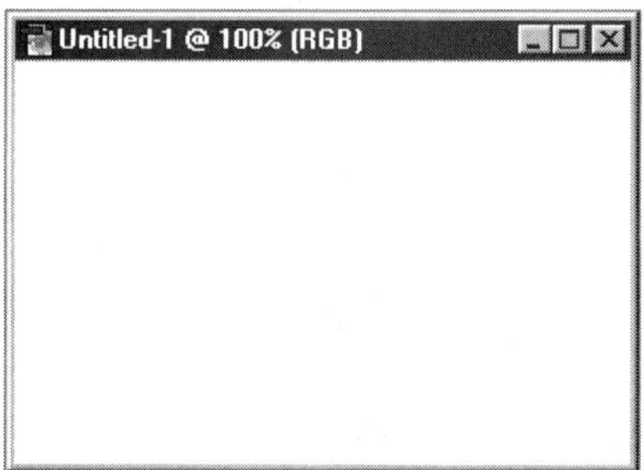

2 *A* ***new,*** *untitled image window (Windows).*

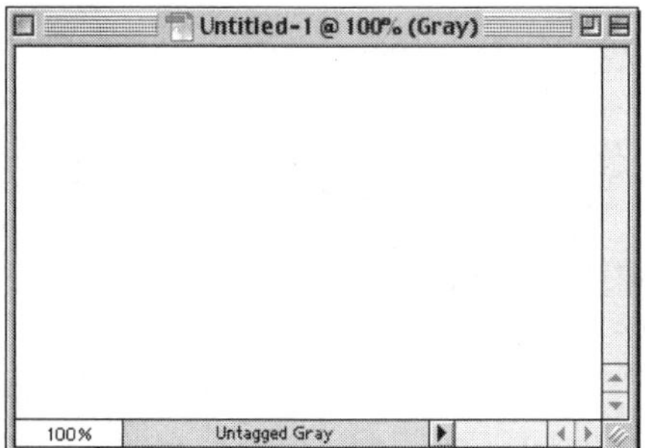

3 *A* ***new,*** *untitled image window (Mac OS).*

To create a new image:

1. Choose File menu > New (Ctrl-N/ Cmd-N).
2. Enter a name in the Name field **1**.
3. Choose a unit of measure from the pop-up menus next to the Width and Height fields.
4. Enter Width and Height values.
5. Enter the Resolution required for your final output device—whether it's an imagesetter or the Web (resolution issues are discussed on pages 47–50).
6. Choose an image mode from the Mode pop-up menu. You can convert the image to a different mode later (see "Image modes" on pages 27–29).
7. Click Contents: White or Background Color for the Background. To choose a Background color, see pages 165–169. Or choose the Transparent option if you want the background to be a layer.

   Note: An image that contains one or more layers can only be saved in the Photoshop, PDF, or Advanced TIFF file format. If you're going to export the file to another application, though, you'll need to save a flattened copy of it in another format, since few applications can read Photoshop's layer transparency. (More about layers and transparency in Chapters 7 and 14.)
8. Click OK (Enter/Return). An image window will appear (Win)**2**/(Mac OS)**3**.

TIP If you want the New dialog box settings to match those of another open document, with the New dialog box open, choose the name of the image that has the desired dimensions from the bottom of the Window menu.

TIP If there is an image on the Clipboard from Photoshop or from Illustrator, the New dialog box will automatically display its dimensions. To prevent those dimensions from displaying, hold down Alt/ Option as you choose File menu > New.

Note: To open an Adobe Illustrator file, follow the instructions on page 58 or 60.

To open an image within Photoshop:

1. Choose File menu > Open (Ctrl-O/ Cmd-O).

2. Locate the file you want to open (Win) **1**/(Mac OS) **2**. If the image was saved with a thumbnail preview, click Show Preview to display it.

Windows: To view files in all formats, choose All Formats from the Files of type drop-down menu.

Mac OS: To view files in all formats, choose Show: All Documents.

Once it's opened, an image can be saved in any format that Photoshop reads.

Mac OS: To search for a file, click Find, type the file name, then click Find again.

Note: If the name of the file you want to open doesn't appear on the scroll list, it means the plug-in module for its format isn't installed in the Photoshop Plug-Ins folder. Install the plug-in.

3. Highlight the file name, then click Open.
or
Double-click the file name.

Got a Profile Mismatch? See page 39.

For some file formats, a further dialog box will open. For example, if you open an EPS, Adobe Illustrator, or PDF file that hasn't yet been rasterized (converted from object-oriented to bitmap), the Rasterize Generic Format dialog box will open. Follow steps 4–9 on pages 58–59.

TIP Special plug-in modules must be used to open an image in some file formats, such as Scitex CT or PICT Resource (access them via File menu > Import).

Pick-n-choose

Windows: To specify a particular **file format** when opening a file, choose File menu > Open As, choose the necessary format from the Open as drop-down menu, then click Open. This is useful for Mac OS files that lack extensions. *Mac OS:* Choose Show: All Documents, choose a file name, choose a format, then click Open.

Quick switch

To cycle between open image windows, use the **Ctrl-Tab/Control-Tab** shortcut.

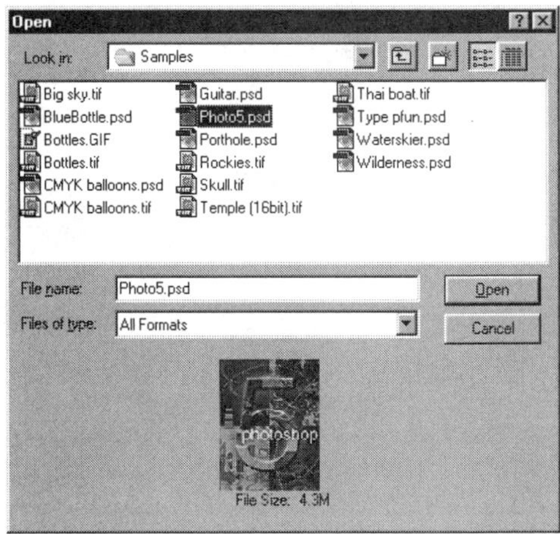

1 ***Windows:*** *Double-click a file name.*

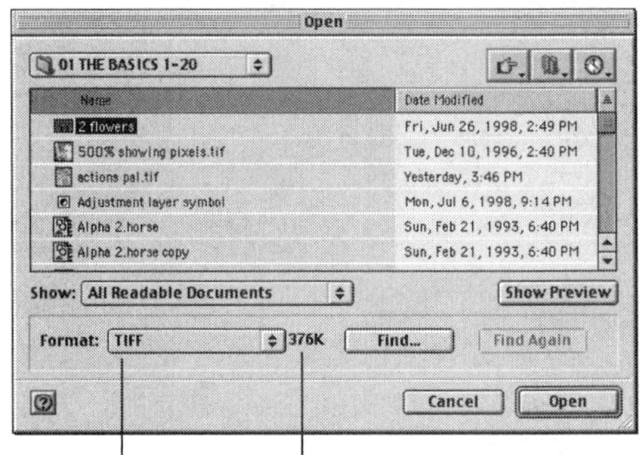

2 ***Mac OS:*** *Double-click a file name.*

Do it again 6.0!

To reopen a file that was closed recently, choose that file name from the File menu > **Open Recent** submenu.

To open a Photoshop image from Windows Explorer:

Double-click a Photoshop image file icon in Windows Explorer 1. Photoshop will launch if it hasn't already been launched.

To open a Photoshop image from the Finder (Mac OS):

Double-click a Photoshop image file icon in the Finder 2. Photoshop will launch if it hasn't already been launched.

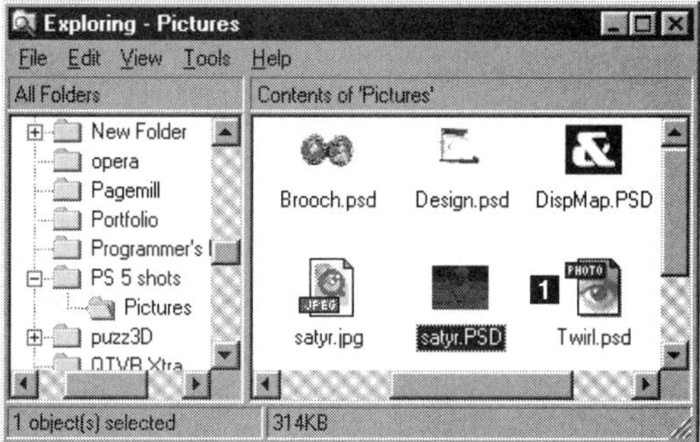

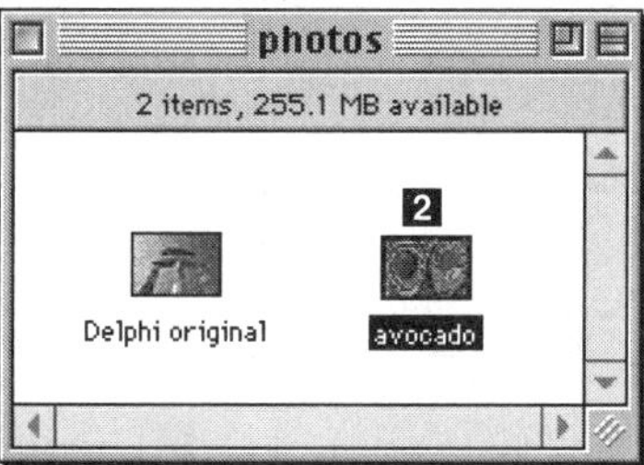

***Double-click** a Photoshop **file icon**.*

Thumbnails

Windows: To create image icons for Windows Explorer that will show when the Views menu is set to Large Icon, click the Save Thumbnail checkbox for individual files as you save them. To create thumbnails of all subsequently saved images for display in the Open dialog box, choose Edit menu > Preferences > Saving Files, then choose Image Previews: Always Save 3. A thumbnail icon will only appear for an image that has a PSD, JPG, PDF, or TIF file extension.

Mac OS: To create image icons for the Finder, choose Edit menu > Preferences > Saving Files, choose Image Previews: Always Save, then check the Icon box 4. To choose icons for individual files as you save them instead, choose Image Previews: Ask When Saving. Saving a multi-megabyte image with a preview could increase its file storage size. To create thumbnail icons of all subsequently saved images for display in the Open dialog box, check the Macintosh and/or Windows Thumbnail box 5. To access this feature, the Apple QuickTime extension must be in the System Folder > Extensions folder (it's usually installed as part of the System software).

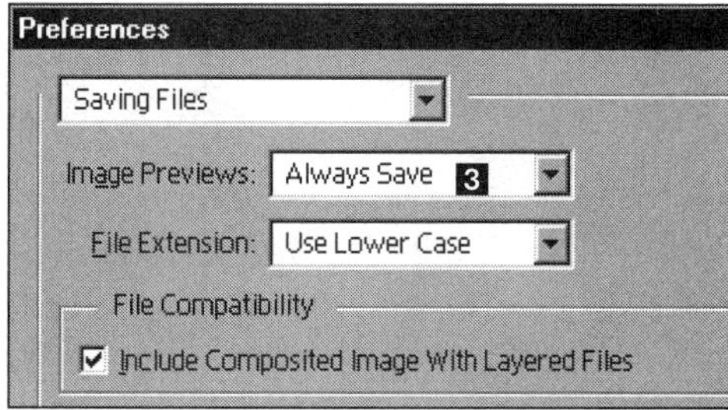

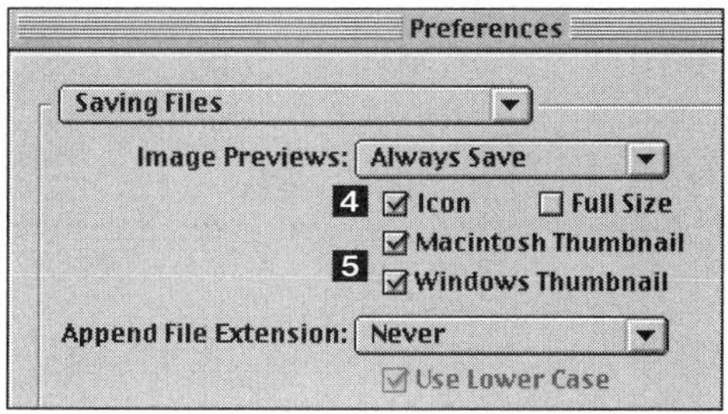

6.0! You can open Kodak Photo CD files in Photoshop via the Kodak PCD Format dialog box. An image in Photo CD format can be converted to Photoshop's RGB Color or Lab Color mode.

To open a Kodak Photo CD file:

1. Choose File menu > Open (Ctrl-O/ Cmd-O).
2. Locate and double-click the Photo CD file name.
   or
   Highlight the Photo CD file name and click Open.
3. Under Source Image 1–2:
   Choose a Resolution (Win)/Pixel size (Mac). A size of 768 by 512 pixels will produce an image that is approximately 10.5 by 7 inches. The image width, followed by height, will appear on the Resolution/Pixel pop-up menu.
   Choose a device profile (film and scanner type) from the Profile pop-up menu (see the sidebar on the next page). Use the Image Info area to see the source image's film and scanner type.
4. Under Destination Image:
   Choose a resolution for the opened image. This choice, combined with the pixel size choice, will determine the on-screen size of the image.
   Choose a Color Space (RGB or Lab) for the opened image.
   Click an orientation option.
5. Click OK. The image will open in Photoshop.

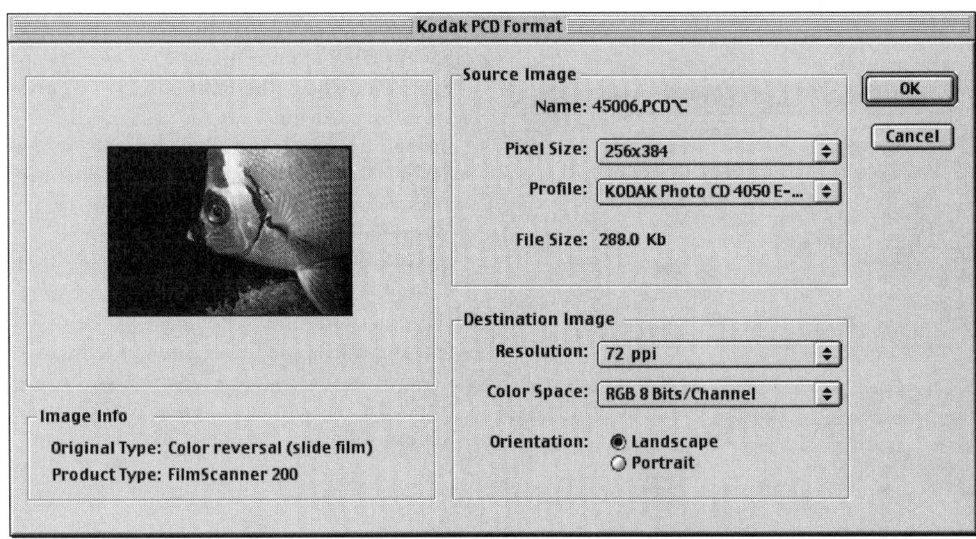

1 *The **Kodak PCD Format** dialog box (Mac OS)*

Kodak profiles

Kodak uses the 4045 and 4050 model film scanners and has also upgraded its PhotoCD transform profiles to version 3.4. The Photo CD device profiles are as follows:

Photo CD 4050E-6 V3.4	Ektachrome scanned on 4050 model
Photo CD 4050K-14 V3.4	Kodachrome scanned on 4050 model
Photo CD Color Negative V3.0	Color negative scanned on older or unspecified scanner
Photo CD Universal E-6 V3.2	Universal Ektachrome scanned on older or unspecified scanner
Photo CD Universal K-14 V3.2	Universal Kodachrome scanned on older or unspecified scanner

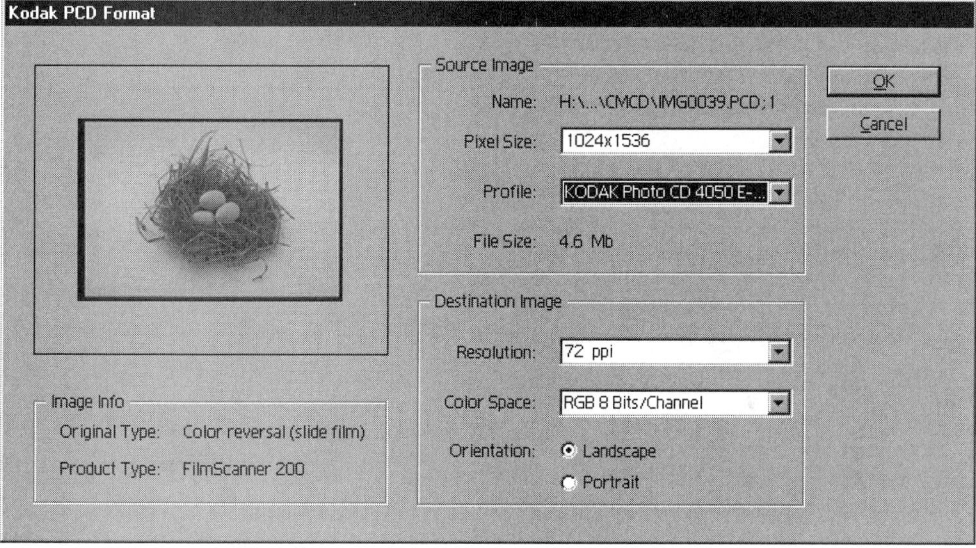

2 *The* ***Kodak PCD Format*** *dialog box (Windows).*

6.0!

When an EPS or Adobe Illustrator file is opened or placed in Photoshop, it is rasterized, which means it's converted from its native object-oriented format into Photoshop's pixel format. Follow these instructions to open an EPS or Illustrator file as a new file. Or follow the instructions on page 5x to place an EPS file into an existing Photoshop file.

Note: To open a single-page PDF file in Photoshop, you can use the Open command (this page) or the Place command (page 60). To open a multi-page PDF as multiple images in Photoshop format, choose File menu > Automate > Multi-Page PDF to PSD (see page 357).

In Photoshop 6, Illustrator 9 files are listed as generic PDF format (not EPS).

To open an EPS, PDF, or Illustrator file as a new image:

1. Choose File menu > Open (Ctrl-O/ Cmd-O).
2. If the file name isn't listed, *Windows:* Choose All Formats from the Files of type drop-down menu; *Mac OS:* Choose Show: All Documents.
3. Locate and highlight the file to be opened, then click Open.
   or
   Double-click a file name.

   Note: If you're opening a PDF that contains more than one page, another dialog box will open **1**. Click the left or right arrow to locate the page that you want to open, then click OK. Or click "Go to page," enter a page number **2**, then click OK twice.
4. *Optional:* In the Rasterize Generic EPS (or PDF) format dialog box, check the Constrain Proportions box to preserve the file's height and width ratio **3**–**4**.
5. *Optional:* Choose a unit of measure from the drop-down menus next to the Height and Width fields, and enter new dimensions.

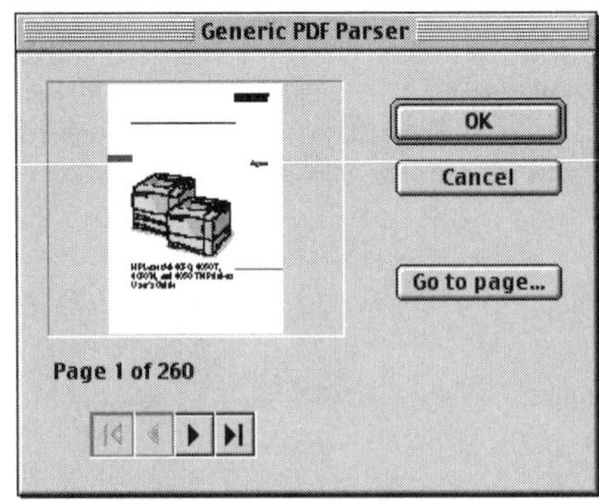

1 *For a **PDF** file, click the right or left arrow to locate the page you want to open...*

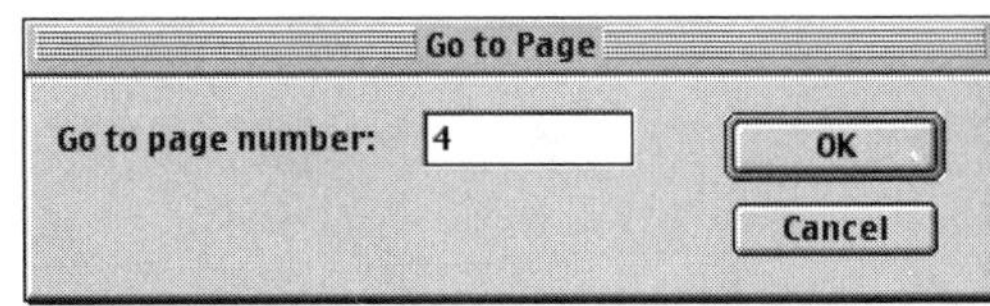

2 *...or enter the number of the page that you want to open.*

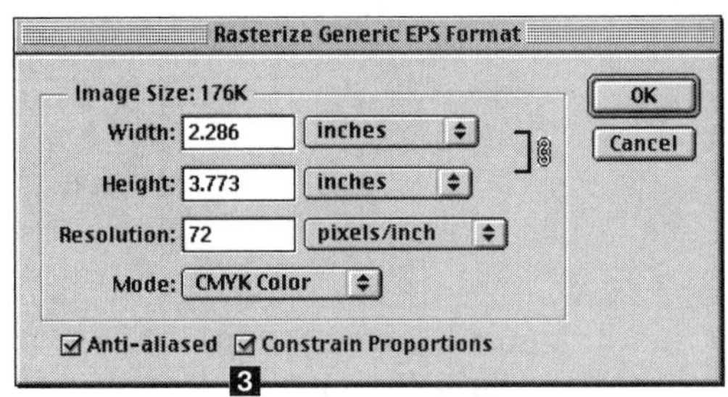

3

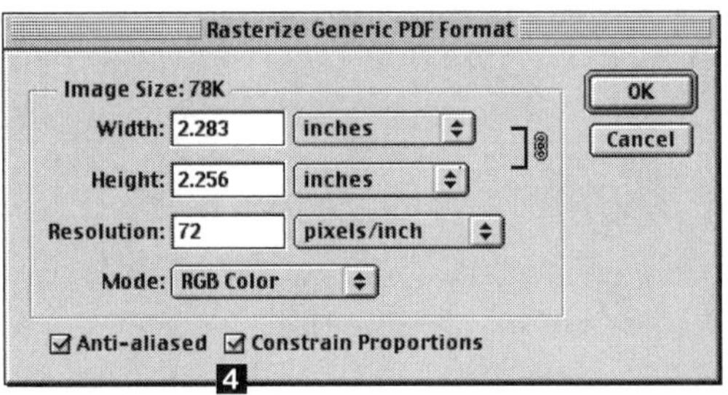

4

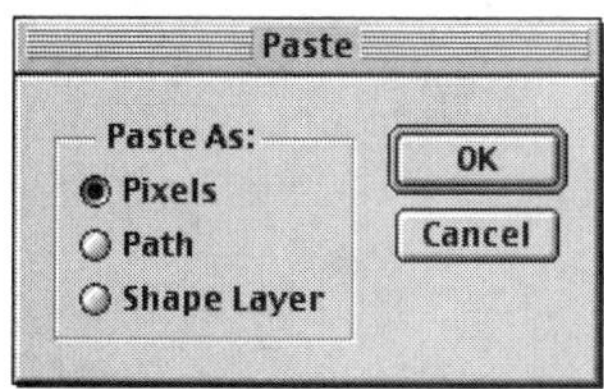

1

6. Enter the final resolution required for your image in the Resolution field. Entering the correct final resolution before rasterizing will produce the best rendering of the image.
7. Choose an image mode from the Mode pop-up menu. (See "Image modes" on pages 27–29.)
8. Check the Anti-aliased box to reduce jaggies and soften edge transitions.
9. Click OK.

TIP If the PDF contains security settings, those settings must be disabled via Acrobat Exchange before the file can be opened.

TIP PDF and EPS files open with a transparent background. To create a white background, create a new layer, set the Background color to white (or whatever color you want), then choose Layer menu > New > Background From Layer.

6.0!

Pixel paste

You can copy an object in Illustrator and paste it into a Photoshop image, where the Paste dialog box will open automatically. Click Paste As: Pixels, Path, or Shape Layer 1 (shapes are discussed in Chapter 16). The Shape Layer paste option provides more flexibility than opening or placing a vector object, because the vector shape will be editable in Photoshop.

When you place an object-oriented (vector) image into a Photoshop image, it becomes bitmapped and it is rendered in the resolution of the Photoshop image. The higher the resolution of the Photoshop image, the better the rendering.

Note: You can also drag a path from an Illustrator image window into a Photoshop image window—it will appear on a new layer.

To place an EPS, PDF, or Adobe Illustrator image into an existing Photoshop image:

1. Open a Photoshop image.
2. Choose File menu > Place.
3. Locate and highlight the file that you want to open **1**. To place a PDF that contains multiple pages, choose a page, then click OK (see page 58).
4. Click Place. A box will appear on top of the image. Pause, if necessary, to allow the image to draw inside it **2**.
5. *Perform any of these optional steps (use the Undo command to undo any of them):*

   To resize the placed image, drag a handle of the bounding box. Shift-drag to preserve the proportions of the placed image as you resize it.

   To move the placed image, drag inside the bounding box.

   To rotate the placed image, position the pointer outside the bounding box, then drag. You can move the center point to rotate from a different axis.
6. To accept the placed image, press Enter/Return or double-click inside the bounding box. The placed image will appear on a new layer.

TIP To remove the placed image, press Esc before or while it's rendering. If the image is already rendered, drag its layer into the trash on the Layers palette.

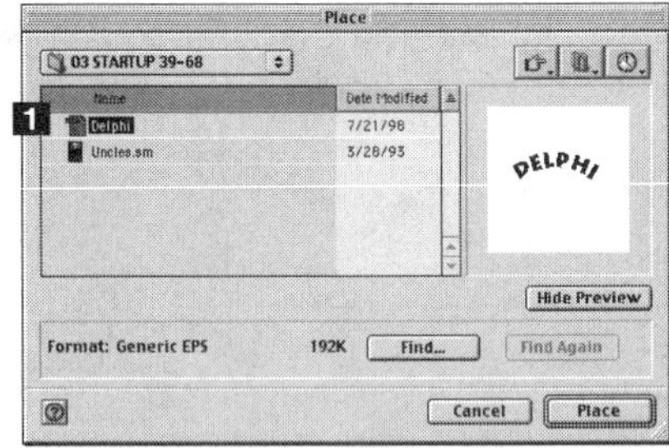

2 *The word "Delphi" was created in Adobe Illustrator and then placed into a Photoshop file.*

*To produce this image, artist **Wendy Grossman** created the musical notes and other shapes in Illustrator and then imported them into Photoshop.*

Place an EPS, PDF, or Illustrator Image

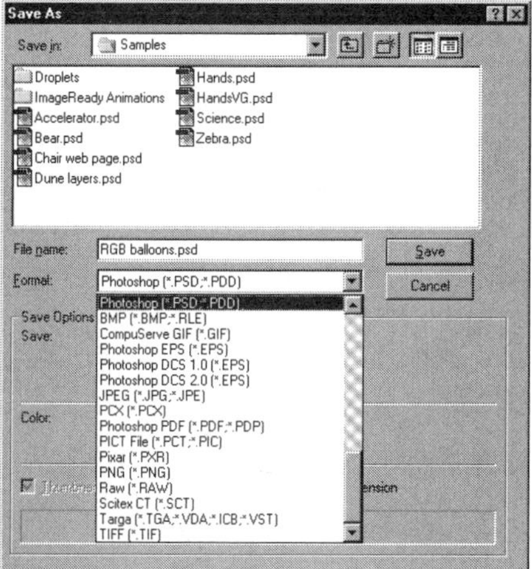

1 *Windows: **Save** dialog box.*

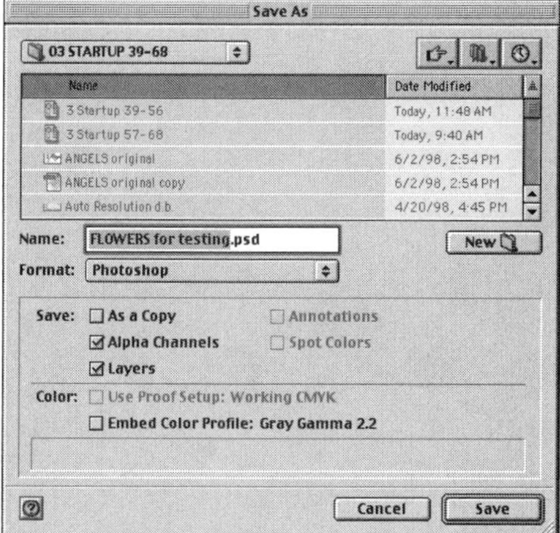

2 *Mac OS: **Save As** dialog box.*

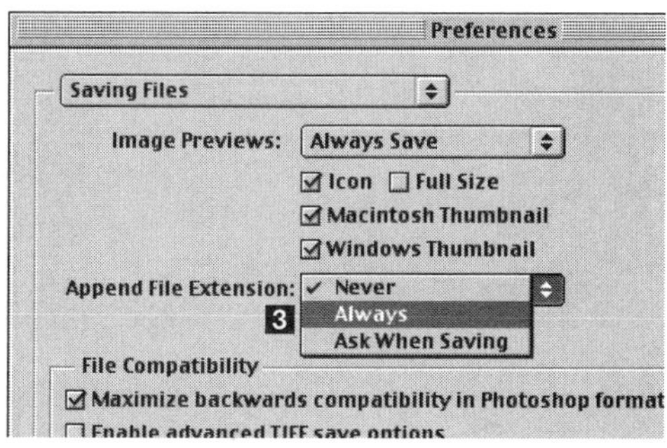

Saving files

Special instructions for saving in the EPS, DCS, PICT, and TIFF file formats are in Chapter 22. The GIF and JPEG formats are covered in Chapter 23.

To save a new image: 6.0!

1. Choose File menu > Save (Ctrl-S/ Cmd-S).
2. Type a name in the File name (Win) **1**/ Name (Mac OS) **2** field.
3. Choose a location for the file.

   Windows: To locate another folder or drive, click the drop-down menu at the top of the dialog box.

   Mac OS: To locate a drive, choose from the pointing hand menu, then double-click a folder to save the file in or create a new folder by clicking New.
4. Choose a file format from the Save As (Win)/Format (Mac OS) pop-up menu. Only the native Photoshop, Advanced TIFF, and Photoshop PDF formats can save files containing multiple layers.
5. Check any options in the Save area of the dialog box; you can also check Color: Embed Color Profile... if the file contains an embedded profile and the format you are saving to supports embedded profiles (see page 42).
6. Click Save.

TIP *Mac OS:* Choose Append File Extension: Always or Ask When Saving in File menu > Preferences > Saving Files if you want a three-character file extension to be appended automatically to your files. This is essential for Windows export **3**.

Also check the "Maximize backwards compatibility in Photoshop format" box if you want a non-layered version of every image to be saved automatically with each layered version. This is useful if the image is going to be exported to another application.

6.0!

Saving layers, vectors, and effects

Photoshop, Advanced TIFF, and **Photoshop PDF** are the only formats in which the following image elements are preserved:

- multiple layers and layer transparency
- adjustment layers
- editable type layers
- layer effects
- grids and guides
- ICC color management profiles (the PICT, JPEG, DCS, and EPS formats also preserve profiles)
- Lab Color image mode (the EPS and DCS formats also preserve this mode)

Note: An image in Duotone color mode can't be saved in Advanced TIFF format.

TIP Flatten a copy of any layered image instead of the original so you'll have the option to rework it (see page 63).

The prior version of a file is overwritten when the Save command is chosen.

To save an existing image:

Choose File menu > Save (Ctrl-S/Cmd-S).

The simple Revert command (instructions here) restores a document to its last-saved version. The History palette, which is discussed in Chapter 8, is a full-service, multiple-undo feature. Its partner, the History Brush tool, is used to selectively revert a portion of an image. Revert does show up as a state on the History palette, so you can undo it, if need be, by clicking an earlier history state.

To revert to the last saved version:

Choose File menu > Revert.

What is the Duplicate command?

The Image menu > Duplicate command copies an image and all its layers, layer masks, and channels into currently available memory. A permanent copy of the file is ***not*** saved to disk unless you then choose File > Save. An advantage of the Duplicate command is that you can use the duplicate to try out variations without altering the original file. HOWEVER, Duplicate should be used with caution, because if an application freeze or a system crash occurs, you'll lose whatever's currently in memory, including your duplicate image!

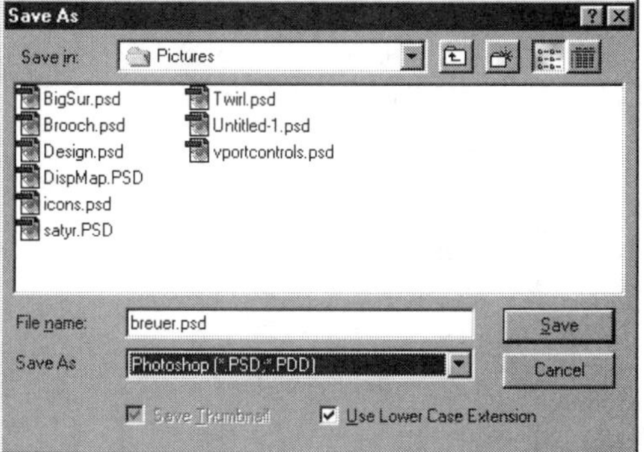

1 *Windows:* ***Save As*** *dialog box. Check* ***Use Lower Case Extension*** *to list the file's extension in lower case style.*

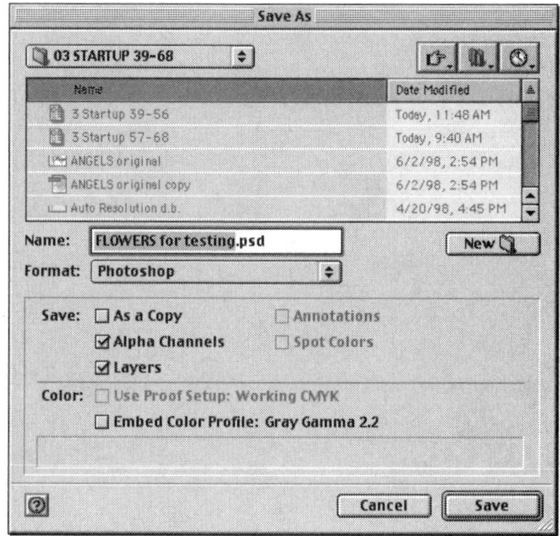

2 *Mac OS:* ***Save As*** *dialog box.*

Using the Save As command, you can save a copy of an image in a different image mode or use the copy for a design variation. You could save a version of an image in CMYK Color mode, for example, and keep the original version in RGB Color mode.

To save a new version of an image:

1. Choose File menu > Save As (Ctrl-Shift-S/Cmd-Shift-S).
2. Enter a new name or modify the existing name in the File name field (Win) **1**/ Name (Mac OS) **2** field.
3. Choose a location in which to save the new version.
4. Choose a different file format from the Save As (Win)/Format (Mac) pop-up menu. Only those formats that are available for the current image (color) mode will be available.

   Beware! If the chosen format cannot support multiple layers, the Layers option will automatically become unavailable and the saved file will be flattened.
5. Check available Save: options as desired, and also check Embed Color Profile... if that option is available (see page 42).

   TIP Check As a Copy to copy the file and continue working on the original.
6. Click Save. For an EPS file, follow the instructions on page 387. For a TIFF or PICT file, follow instructions on pages 390–391. Consult the Adobe Photoshop User Guide for other formats. The new version will remain open; the original file will close automatically.

TIP If you don't change the file name and you click Save, a warning prompt will appear. Click Replace to save over the original file or click Cancel to return to the Save As dialog box.

Navigating

In this section you'll learn how to change the view size of an image, move an image in its window, switch screen display modes, display an image in two windows simultaneously, and recolor the work canvas.

You can display an entire image in its window or magnify part of an image to work on a small detail. The view size is indicated as a percentage in three locations: on the image window title bar, in the lower left corner of the application/image window, and in the lower left corner of the Navigator palette. The view size of an image has no affect on its printout size.

A portion of an image is ***magnified****.*

To change the view size using the Navigator palette:

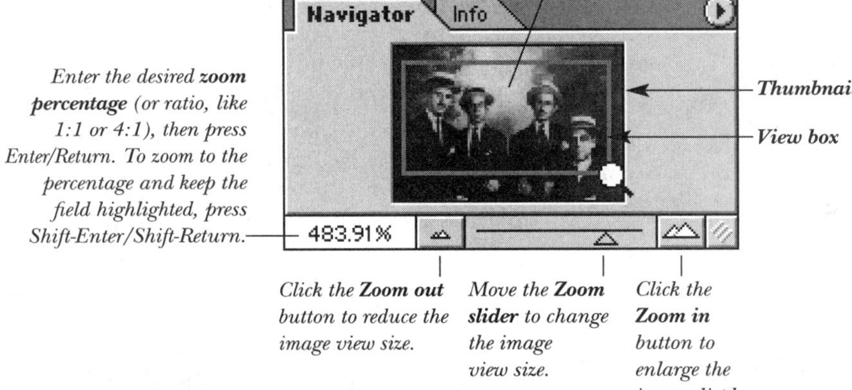

Drag the view box on the thumbnail to ***move*** *the image in the image window. Ctrl-drag/Cmd-drag across part of the thumbnail (as in this illustration) to marquee the area you want to* ***magnify****.*

Enter the desired ***zoom percentage*** *(or ratio, like 1:1 or 4:1), then press Enter/Return. To zoom to the percentage and keep the field highlighted, press Shift-Enter/Shift-Return.*

Thumbnail

View box

Click the ***Zoom out*** *button to reduce the image view size.*

Move the ***Zoom slider*** *to change the image view size.*

Click the ***Zoom in*** *button to enlarge the image display.*

TIP You can also change the view size by double-clicking the zoom percentage box in the lower left corner of the application/image window, typing the desired zoom percentage, and then pressing Enter/Return.

TIP To change the edge color of the view box on the Navigator palette, choose Palette Options from the palette menu, then choose a preset color from the Color pop-up menu or click the color swatch and choose a color from the Color Picker.

View size shortcuts

WINDOWS

Zoom in (window doesn't resize)	Ctrl +
Zoom out (window doesn't resize)	Ctrl –
Zoom in (window resizes)	Ctrl Alt +
Zoom Out (window resizes)	Ctrl Alt –
Actual pixels/100% view	Ctrl Alt 0
Fit on screen	Ctrl 0 (zero)

MACINTOSH

Zoom in (window resizes)	Cmd +
Zoom Out (window resizes)	Cmd –
Zoom in (window doesn't resize)	Cmd Option +
Zoom out (window doesn't resize)	Cmd Option –
Actual pixels/100% view	Cmd Option 0
Fit on screen	Cmd 0 (zero)

1 ***Click*** *on the image with the Zoom tool to* ***enlarge*** *the view size. Note the plus sign in the pointer.*

2 ***Alt-click/Option-click*** *on the image with the Zoom tool to* ***reduce*** *the view size. Note the minus sign in the pointer.*

To change the view size using the Zoom tool:

6.0!

1. Choose the Zoom tool (Z).
2. On the Zoom options bar, uncheck the **Resize Windows To Fit** box to prevent the image window from resizing as you change the view size **3**. Check the **Ignore Palettes** box to allow the image window to be enlarged all the way to the edge of your screen.
3. To **magnify** the image, click in the image window **1** or drag a marquee across an area to magnify that area.
   or
   To **reduce** the view size, Alt-click/ Option-click in the image window **2**.
   or
   To view the image at actual pixel size, click **Actual Pixels** on the options bar.
   Note: The view size will equal the actual print size only when the display ratio is 100% and the image resolution and monitor resolution are the same.
   or
   To display the entire image in the largest possible size that will fit on your screen/ application window, click **Fit On Screen** on the options bar (Ctrl-0/Cmd-0).
   or
   Click **Print Size** on the options bar to display the image at its print size.

TIP Ctrl-Spacebar/Cmd-Spacebar click or drag to zoom in when another tool is selected or a dialog box with a Preview option is open. Alt-Spacebar-click/ Option-Spacebar-click to zoom out. To have the window resize automatically when the view size is changed using keyboard shortcuts, check Keyboard Zoom Resizes Windows in Edit > Preferences > General.

TIP If you like to take the slow, leisurely approach, you can change the view size by choosing View menu > Zoom In or Zoom Out.

3

Note: If the scroll bars aren't active, the entire image is displayed, and there is no need to move it.

To move a magnified image in its window:

Click outside, or drag, the view box on the Navigator palette **1**.

or

Click the up or down scroll arrow on the image window. Drag a scroll box to move the image more quickly.

or

Choose the Hand tool (H), then drag in the image window **2**.

TIP See other shortcuts for moving an image in its window in the shortcuts section.

To change the screen display mode:

Click the Standard screen mode button in the lower left corner of the Toolbox (F) **3** to display the image, menu bar, palettes, and scroll bars on the image window. This is the standard mode.

or

Click the Full screen mode with menu bar (middle) button (F) **4**, **6** to display the image at full size without scroll bars, with the menu bar and palettes visible. The area around the image will be gray. Nice way to see an image in its full glory.

or

Click the Full screen mode button in the lower right corner of the Toolbox (F) **5** to display the full size image and palettes without the menu bar or scroll bars. The area around the image will be dramatic black.

TIP Press Tab to show/hide the Toolbox and any open palettes. Or press Shift-Tab to show/hide just the palettes, leaving keep the Toolbox open.

TIP Use the Hand tool (H) to move the image in its window when the scroll bars are hidden and the image is magnified, or use the Navigator palette. Hold down Spacebar to use the Hand tool while another tool is selected.

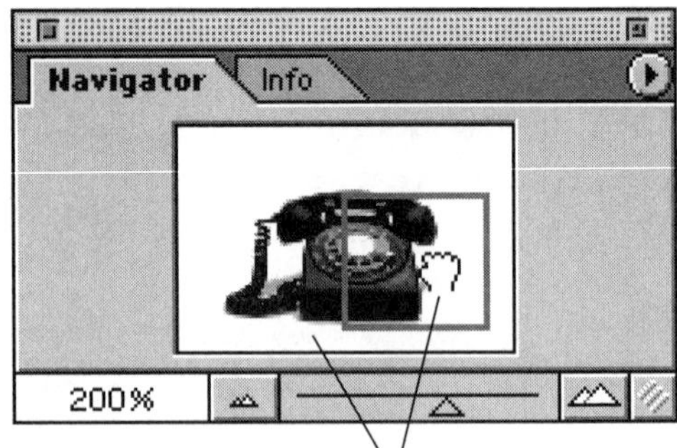

1 *Click outside of, or drag, the view box on the **Navigator** palette to move an image in its window.*

2 *Or move an image in its window using the **Hand** tool.*

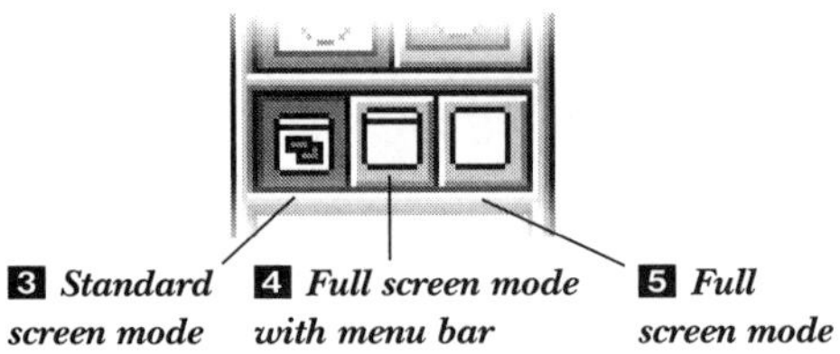

3 ***Standard screen mode*** **4** ***Full screen mode with menu bar*** **5** ***Full screen mode***

6 ***Full screen mode with menu bar.***

Move Image in Window; Screen Modes

1 *An image displayed in **two windows** simultaneously: one in a small view size for previewing, the other in a larger view size for editing.*

2 *To **recolor** the **work canvas**, choose the Paint Bucket tool and a Foreground color, then Shift-click on the work canvas.*

The number of images that can be open at a time depends on available RAM and scratch disk space. You can open the same image in two windows simultaneously: one in a large view size, such as 400%, to edit a detail and the other in a smaller view size, such as 100%, to view the whole image. Or, leave the image in RGB Color mode in one image window and choose View menu > Proof Setup > Working CMYK for the same image in a second window. The History palette will be identical for both windows.

To display one image in two windows:

1. With an image open, choose View menu > New View. The same image will appear in a second window **1**.
2. *Optional:* Move either window by dragging its title bar, and/or resize either window.

Note: The work canvas color will be the same for all open images.

To recolor the work canvas:

1. Enlarge the image window, if necessary, so at least some portion of the work canvas is visible.
2. Choose a Foreground color (see pages 165–169).
3. Choose the Paint Bucket tool (G or Shift-G).
4. Shift-click on the work canvas **2**. You can't undo this. To restore the default gray, choose 20% gray as the Foreground color from the Color palette, then Shift-click the work canvas again.

Ending a work session

To close an image:

Click the close box in the upper right corner of the image window (Win) **1**/upper left corner of the image window **2** (Mac).

or

Choose File menu > Close (Ctrl-W/Cmd-W).

If you attempt to close an image that was modified since it was last saved, a warning prompt will appear **3**. Click Don't Save to close the file without saving, or click Save to save the file before closing, or click Cancel to cancel the close operation.

To exit/quit Photoshop:

Windows: Choose File menu > Exit (Ctrl-Q) or click the application windows's close box.

Mac OS: Choose File menu > Quit (Cmd-Q).

All open Photoshop files will close. If changes were made to an open file since it was saved, a prompt will appear **4**. Click Don't Save to close the file without saving, or click Save to save the file before exiting/quitting, or click Cancel to cancel the exit/quit operation altogether.

1 *Windows: Click the* ***close*** *box in the upper* ***right*** *corner of the image window.*

2 *Mac OS: Click the* ***close*** *box in the upper* ***left*** *corner of the image window.*

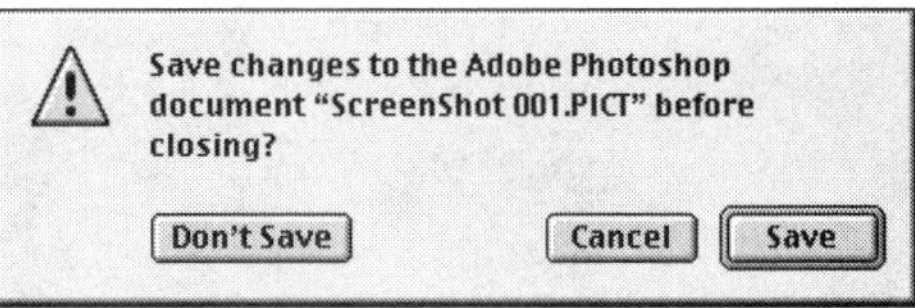

3 *If you attempt to close an image that was modified since it was last saved, this prompt will appear.*

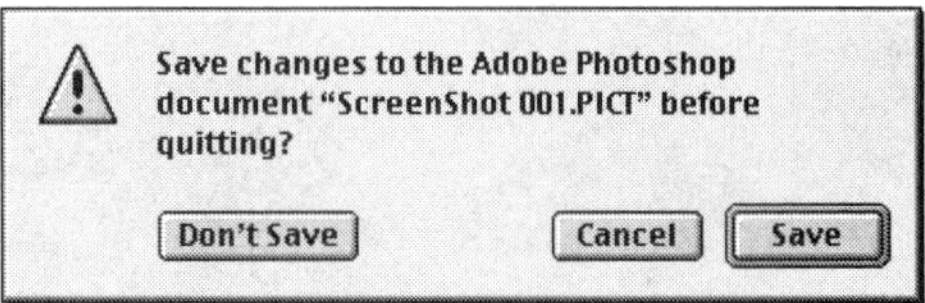

4 *If changes were made to an open file since it was saved, this prompt will appear.*

PIXEL BASICS 4

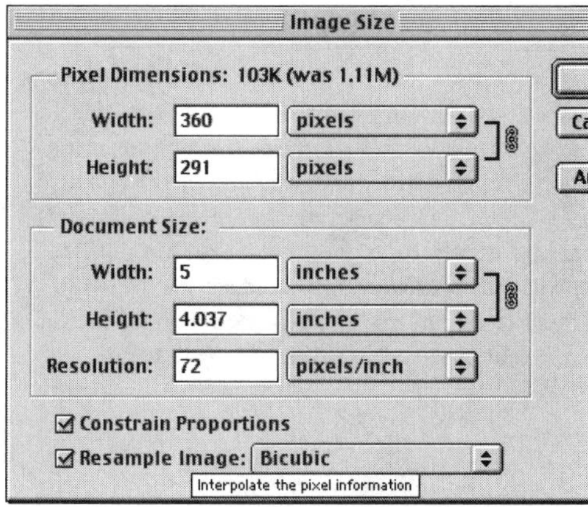

1 *For Mac OS, enter a* ***Resolution*** *of* ***72 pixels/inch*** *in the* ***Image Size*** *dialog box.*

IN THIS CHAPTER you'll learn how to change an image's overall dimensions or resolution; sharpen the image afterwards; change an image's canvas size; crop an image; flip an image; and rotate an image.

Note: Changing an image's dimensions in Photoshop while preserving its current resolution (leaving the Resample Image box checked) causes resampling, which degrades image quality. That's why it's always best to scan or create an image at the desired size. If you have to resample, apply the Unsharp Mask filter afterward to resharpen (see pages 74–75).

Changing dimensions and resolution

To change an image's pixel dimensions for on-screen output:

1. Choose Image menu > Image Size.
2. Make sure the Resample Image box is checked **1**.
3. To preserve the image's width-to-height ratio, leave the Constrain Proportions box checked.
4. Set the Resolution to 72 ppi.
5. Enter new values in the Pixel Dimensions: Width and/or Height fields.
6. Click OK.

To change an image's dimensions for print output:

1. Choose Image menu > Image Size.
2. To preserve the image's width-to-height ratio, check the Constrain Proportions box **1**. To modify the image's width independently of its height, uncheck the Constrain Proportions box.
3. *Optional:* To preserve the image's resolution, check the Resample Image box **2** and choose Nearest Neighbor, Bilinear, or Bicubic as the interpolation method. Bicubic causes the least degradation in image quality.
4. Choose a unit of measure from the pop-up menu next to the Print Size: Width and Height fields.
5. Enter new numbers in the Width and/or Height fields. The Resolution will change if the Resample Image box is unchecked.
6. Click OK.

TIP To restore the original Image Size dialog box settings, Alt-click/Option-click Reset.

TIP File menu > Print Options can also be used to resize and rescale print dimensions, but it won't preserve the image resolution.

Previewing the print

To see the image size relative to the paper size, press and hold on the status bar at the bottom of the image window or use File menu > Print Options. To display the image on screen at the size it will print, choose View menu > **Print Size**.

Note: At 100% view on a Macintosh monitor, the on-screen display size will match the print size only if the image resolution is the same as the monitor resolution (72 ppi). On a Windows monitor (96 ppi) at 100% view, a Mac-generated image will look slightly smaller than actual size. What if you're in a cross-platform workgroup? You could set the Windows monitor screen area and the Mac's monitor resolution to a similar pixel dimension.

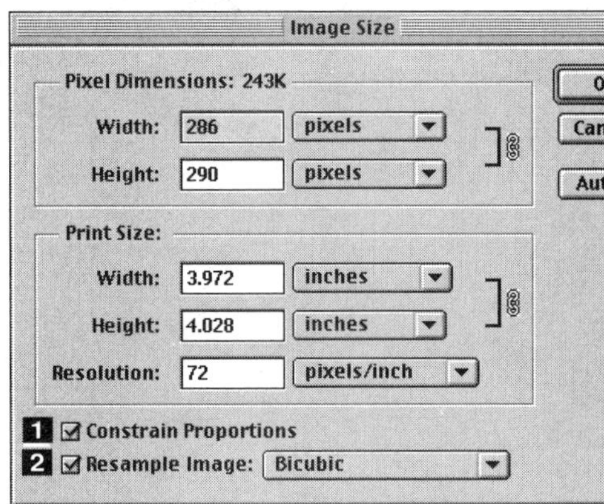

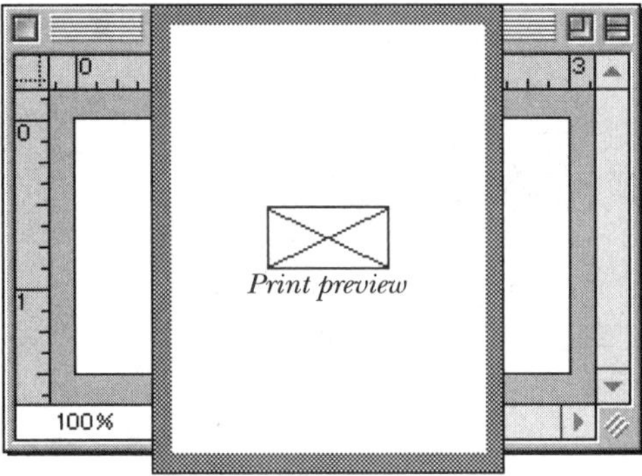

Print preview

Cash in on a high resolution

An image contains a given number of pixels after scanning, and its print dimensions and resolution are interdependent. If an image's resolution or dimensions are changed with the Resample Image box unchecked in Image menu > Image Size, the file's total pixel count is preserved. Increasing an image's pixels per inch resolution will shrink its print (physical) dimensions; lowering an image's pixels per inch resolution will enlarge its print dimensions.

If your file has a higher resolution than needed (more than twice the screen frequency), you can allocate the extra resolution to the print size dimensions by unchecking the Resample Image box (the width, height, and resolution are now interdependent), and then lowering the resolution to twice the screen frequency. The width and height values will automatically increase, and the file storage size and pixel dimensions will remain constant—no pixels will be added or deleted from the image.

If you must further enlarge the image's dimensions, click in the Width field, check the Resample Image box, and enter a new Width value. The Height will change proportionately, and the file storage size and pixel dimensions will increase, but you'll be resampling, so after clicking OK, apply the Unsharp Mask filter to resharpen (see pages 74–75).

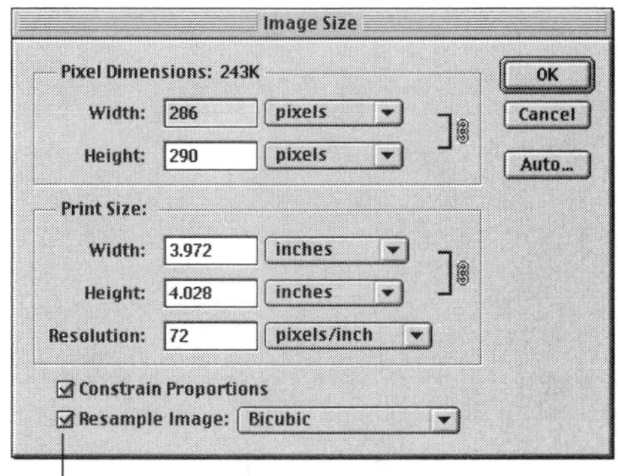

1 *Check the* ***Resample Image*** *box, and the image will be resampled; uncheck Resample Image to avoid resampling.*

Note: If you increase an image's resolution (resample up) with the Resample Image box checked, pixels will be added and the image's file storage size will increase, but its sharpness will diminish. If you decrease an image's resolution (downsample), information will be deleted from the file, and it can only be retrieved using the History palette before the image is closed. Blurriness caused by resampling may only be evident when the image is printed; it may not be discernible on screen. That's why it's always best to scan or create an image at the proper resolution. Follow the instructions on page 74 to resharpen a resampled image. (See also pages 47 and 50.)

To change an image's resolution:

1. Choose Image menu > Image Size.
2. To preserve the image's dimensions (Width and Height), check the Resample Image box **1**.
   or
   To preserve the image's total pixel count, uncheck Resample Image. The Width and Height dimensions will change to preserve the current pixel count.
3. Enter a number in the Resolution field.
4. Click OK.

TIP The History Brush won't work on a resampled image. You will only be able to set the source for the History Brush from the current state forward.

The Fit Image command has no effect on an image's resolution—it only changes its physical dimensions. Use it to make an image smaller.

To resize an image to fit a specific width or height:

1. Chose File menu > Automate > Fit Image **1**.
2. Enter a Width or Height value in pixels. The other field will automatically adjust *after* you click OK, so the width-to-height ratio will stay the same.
3. Click OK.

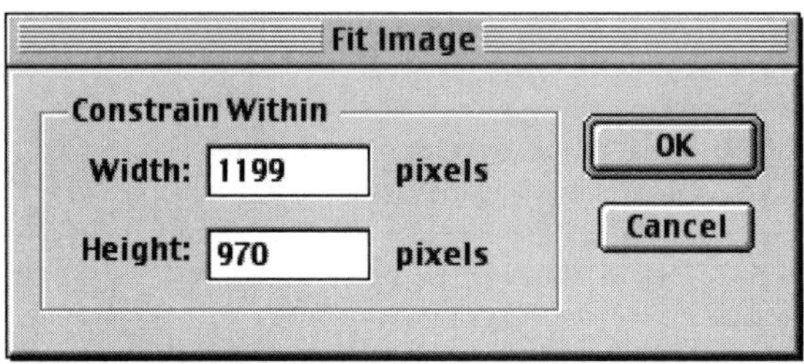

1 *Use the* ***Fit Image*** *command to change an image's* ***dimensions*** *without changing its resolution.*

The Resize Image command duplicates an image and resizes the duplicate automatically. All you have to do is respond to a sequence of dialog boxes—Photoshop will figure out the math for you.

To resize an image automatically:

1. Choose Help menu > Resize Image.
2. Click Print or Online **1**, then click Next.
3. Enter the desired output size **2**, then click Next. If you chose Online in the previous step, click Finish now. For print output, follow the remaining steps.
4. Click or enter the lpi as per your print shop's instructions **3**, then click Next.
5. Move the Quality slider **4**, then note the final image size in the Results box. If there's a message below the Results box, read that as well. If you want to proceed, click Next.
6. Click Finish **5**, and then save the resized image. (Or click Cancel.)

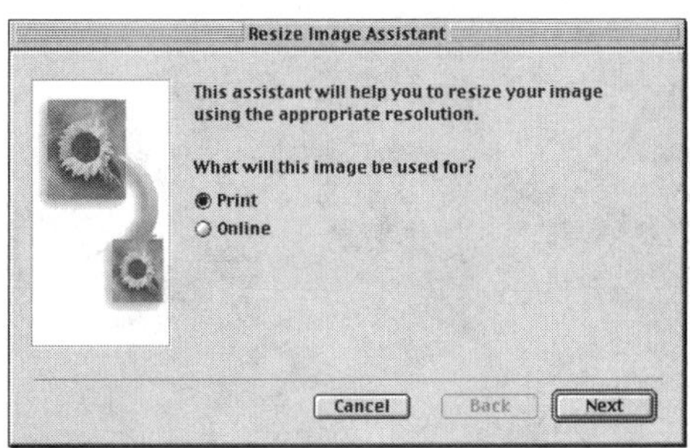

1 *Click **Print** or **Online**.*

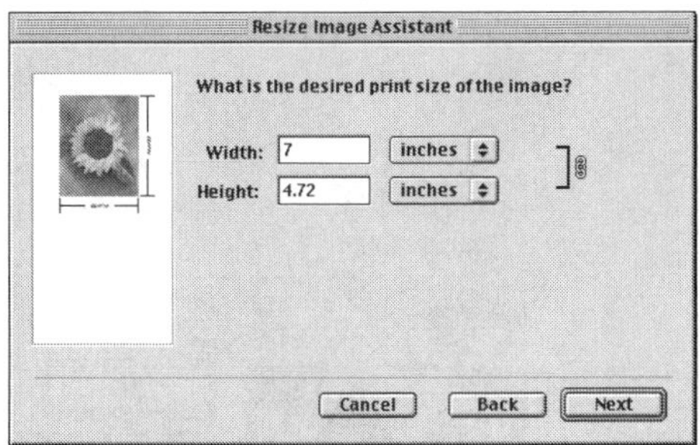

2 *Enter the desired **print size**.*

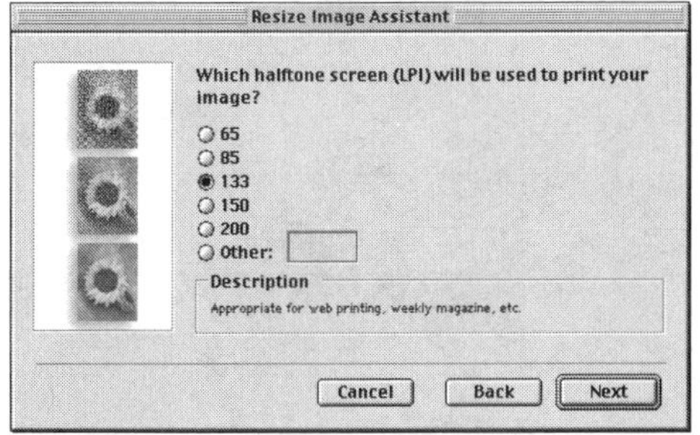

3 *Click or enter the **lpi** that your print shop specifies.*

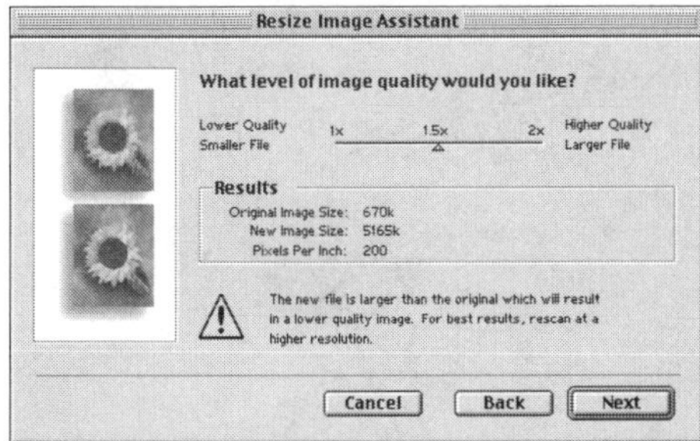

4 *Move the slider to the desired image **quality**.*

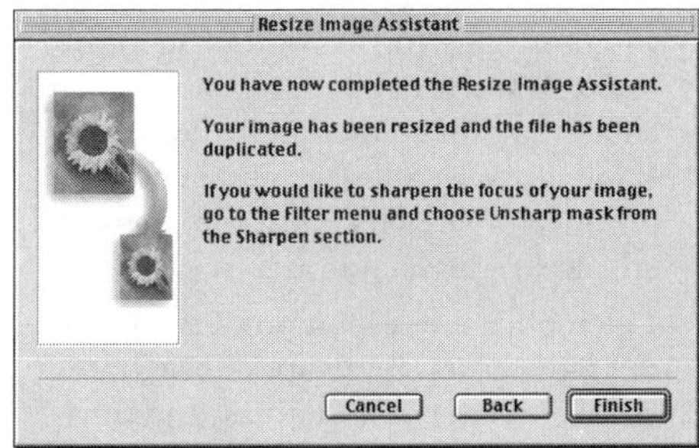

5 *Click **Finish**.*

If you change an image's dimensions or resolution with the Resample Image box checked, convert it to CMYK Color mode, or transform it, blurring may occur due to the resampling process. Despite its name, the Unsharp Mask filter has a focusing effect. It increases contrast between adjacent pixels that already have some contrast. You can specify the amount of contrast to be added (Amount), the number of surrounding pixels that will be modified around each pixel that requires more contrast (Radius), and determine which pixels the filter effects or ignores by specifying the minimum degree of existing contrast (Threshold).

Note: The Unsharp Mask effect may be more noticeable on screen than on high-resolution print output.

To apply the Unsharp Mask filter:

1. Choose Filter menu > Sharpen > Unsharp Mask **1**.
2. Choose an Amount for the percentage increase in contrast between pixels **2**. Use a low setting (below 50) for figures or natural objects; use a higher setting if the image contains sharp-edged objects. Too high a setting will produce obvious halos around high contrast areas. The larger the image, the less sharpening may be required. For a high-resolution image, use an Amount between 150 and 200%.
3. To choose an appropriate Radius value, which is a little trickier, you need to factor in the final size, the resolution, and the subject matter of the image. Choose a Radius value (0.1–250) for the number of pixels surrounding high contrast edges that will be modified. Try between 1 and 2 pixels. A higher value could produce too much contrast in areas that are already high contrast.

   The higher the resolution of the image, the more pixels there are on the border between high contrast areas, and thus the higher the Radius setting is required.

1 *The original image, a bit blurry.*

If you click on the image, that area will display here in the preview window.

2 *When using the* ***Unsharp Mask*** *dialog box, start with conservative* ***Amount, Radius,*** *and* ***Threshold*** *settings.*

After Unsharp Masking with a high Amount (160%). Radius 1.5, Threshold 0. Notice the halos around the edges and the centers of the flowers.

After Unsharp Masking with a high Radius (6.0). Amount of 130, Threshold of 0. The soft gradations have become choppy and the image has an unnatural contrast and sharpness.

After Unsharp Masking with a high Threshold (15). Amount of 160, Radius of 1.5. Even with the same Amount setting as in the top image, the soft gradations in the petals and the background are preserved.

Try a high Radius setting for a low contrast image, and a lower Radius setting for an intricate, high contrast image.

Note: The higher the Radius setting, the lower the Amount setting can be, and vice versa.

4. Choose a Threshold value (0–255) for the minimum amount of contrast an area must have before it will be modified. At a Threshold of 0, the filter will be applied to the entire image. A Threshold value above 0 will cause sharpening along already high-contrast edges, less so in low contrast areas. If you raise the Threshold, you can then increase the Amount and Radius values to sharpen the edges without over-sharpening areas that don't require it. To prevent noise from distorting skin tones, specify a Threshold between 8 and 20.
5. Click OK.

TIP To soften a grainy scan, apply the Filter menu > Blur > Gaussian Blur filter at a low setting (below 1) and then apply the Filter menu > Sharpen > Sharpen Edges once or twice afterward to resharpen.

TIP To avoid waiting for the full screen Unsharp Mask preview on a large image, first get close to the desired settings using just the preview window with Preview unchecked, then check the Preview box to preview the results on the full screen, and finally, readjust the settings, if needed.

TIP Try applying the Unsharp Mask filter to one or two individual color channels (for example, just the Red or Green channel in an RGB image). If you sharpen two separate channels, use the same Radius value for both. You can also convert an image to Lab Color mode then apply the filter to the L channel to sharpen luminosity without affecting color pixels.

Changing the canvas

The Canvas Size command changes the live, editable image area.

Note: If you want to enlarge the canvas area manually, right on the image, use the Crop tool (see page 79). You can also use the Crop command to reduce the image size.

1 *The original image.*

To change the canvas size:

1. If the image has a Background, choose a Background color (see pages 165–169) **1**.
2. Choose Image menu > Canvas Size **2**.
3. *Optional:* Choose a different unit of measure from either pop-up menu. If you choose "columns," the current Column Size: Width in Edit menu > Preferences > Units & Rulers will be used as the increment.
4. Enter new numbers in the Width and/or Height fields. Changing one dimension has no effect on the other dimension.
5. *Optional:* To reposition the image on its new canvas, click an unoccupied Anchor square. The dark gray square represents the existing image area.
6. Click OK. Any added areas will automatically be filled with the current Background color (unless the background is a layer with transparency, in which case added canvas areas will be transparent) **3**.

*Note the **New** and **Current** file **Sizes** as you change the canvas size.*

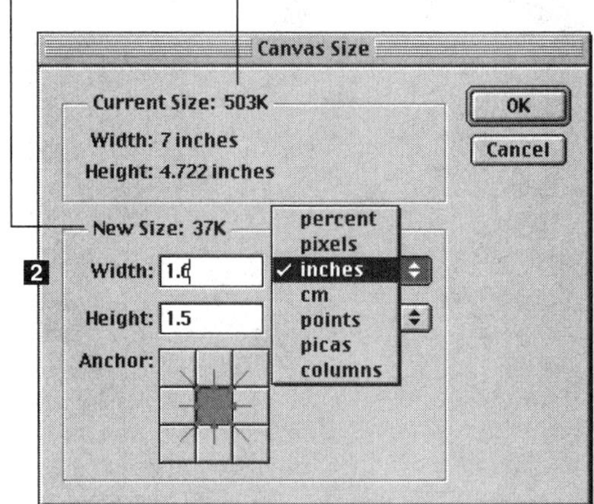

2

3 *The same image with **added canvas** pixels.*

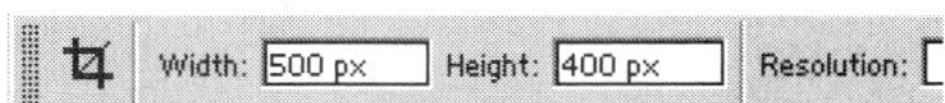

1 *The left side of the* ***Crop*** *options bar* ***after*** *drawing a marquee with the tool.*

2 *The right side of the* ***Crop*** *options bar after drawing a marquee with the tool.*

3 *Marquee the portion of the image you want to* ***keep****.*

4 *The* ***cropped*** *image.*

6.0!

A whole image can be cropped using the crop tool, the Crop command, or the Trim command. Photoshop 6 includes a number of new options for the Crop tool.

To crop an image using a marquee:

1. Choose the Crop tool (C).
2. Drag a marquee over the portion of the image that you want to keep **3**.
3. Do any of the following on the Crop options bar:

   Check the **Shield cropped area** box if you want the area outside the crop marquee to be darkened by a cropping shield (it helps you see what's left). Click the **Color** swatch if you want to change the color for the darkened area, and choose an **Opacity** for the shield color.

   If you're cropping a layer, click **Cropped Area: Delete** to have the cropped out areas be deleted or click **Hide** to have them be saved with the file and extend beyond the edge of the current image area. Use the Move tool to reposition any hidden layer pixels that extend off the edge. This isn't available for the Background.

   For the **Perspective** option, see online Help.
4. *Do any of these optional steps:*

   To resize the marquee, drag any handle (double-arrow pointer). Shift-drag to preserve the marquee's proportions. Alt-drag/Option-drag to resize the marquee from its center.

   To reposition the marquee, position the pointer inside the marquee, then drag.

   To rotate the marquee, position the cursor outside it (curved arrow pointer), then drag in a circular direction. To change the axis point around which the marquee rotates, drag the circle away from the center of the marquee before

(Continued on the following page)

rotating. (The crop marquee can't be rotated for an image in Bitmap mode.)

5. Press Enter/Return **4**.
   or
   Double-click inside the marquee. If you rotated the marquee, the rotated image will be squared off in the image window.
   or
   Click the ☑ on the options bar.

TIP To cancel the cropping process before accepting it, press Esc, or click the ☒ on the options bar.

TIP To resharpen an image after cropping, apply the Unsharp Mask filter (see pages 74–75).

To specify dimensions and resolution as you crop an image:

1. Choose the Crop tool (C).
2. On the Crop options bar, enter values in the **Width** and/or **Height** fields **1**.
   or
   Click **Front Image** **2** to insert the current image's Width, Height, and Resolution values into those fields. Use this option if you want to crop one open image to the dimensions of another open image.

   Note: The crop marquee will match this width-to-height ratio.
3. *Optional:* Modify the **Resolution**. If, after clicking Front Image, you raise the current resolution and then crop, the print size will decrease. If you lower the current resolution and then crop, the print size will increase. In both cases, the pixel count will remain unchanged.

   To clear the Width, Height, and Resolution fields, click **Clear**.
4. Drag a crop marquee on the image, then double-click inside the marquee or press Enter/Return.

No snap?

Normally, the crop marquee will snap to the edge of the image. To override this snap function (let's say you want to crop slightly inside the edge of the image), start drawing the marquee, then hold down Ctrl-Shift-/Cmd-Shift as you drag the marquee near the edge of the image.

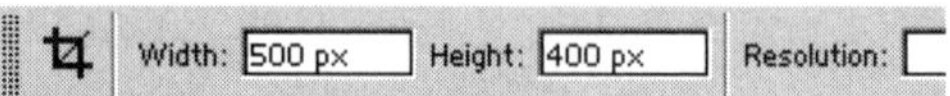

1 *The left side of the **Crop** options bar **before** drawing a marquee with the tool.*

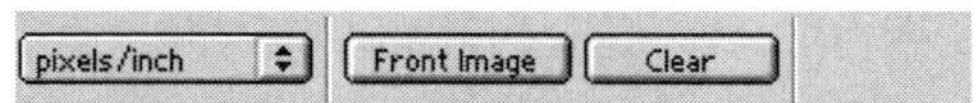

2 *The right side of the **Crop** options bar before drawing a marquee with the tool.*

To crop one image to fit exactly inside another image

Open both images, activate the destination image, choose the Crop tool, click **Front Image** on the Crop options bar, activate the image you want to crop, then draw a marquee. After cropping, Shift-drag-and-drop the layer or copy-and-paste the layer onto the destination image. The resolution will adjust automatically.

1 *Drag any of the crop marquee handles* ***outside*** *the canvas area into the work canvas.*

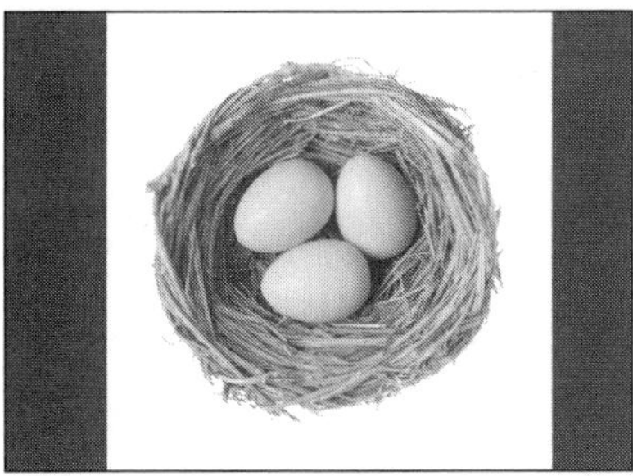

2 *The newly* ***cropped*** *image has different proportions. In our example, the added pixels filled automatically with the current Background color (dark gray) because the default Background wasn't changed (Layers palette).*

Cropping with a marquee that's larger than the image will effectively increase the image's canvas size.

To enlarge an image's canvas area using the Crop tool:

1. Enlarge the image window so the work canvas (the gray area) around the image is showing.
2. Choose the Crop tool (C).
3. Draw a crop marquee within the image.
4. Drag any of the handles of the marquee into the work canvas **1**–**2**. If areas of the image originally extended outside the canvas border, those areas can now be included.
5. Double-click inside the marquee or press Enter/Return. If there were no hidden pixels, the added canvas area will fill with the current Background color if the bottommost layer is the Background or with transparency if the bottommost layer is a layer.

The Crop command is simple and straightforward, but it's only useful if you don't need any of the options that the Crop tool provides. You start by drawing a selection marquee.

To crop an image using the Crop command:

1. Choose the Rectangular Marquee tool (M).
2. Draw a marquee over the part of the image you want to keep.
   or
   To control the size of the marquee, use the Style: Fixed Size or Constrained Ratio features on the Rectangular Marquee options bar, then click on the image.
3. Choose Image menu > Crop.

6.0!

To quickly trim away excess transparent or color areas from around an image, use the Trim command.

To crop an image using the Trim command:

1. Choose Image menu > Trim.
2. Choose a Based On option **1**:

   Transparent Pixels to trim away any extra transparency at the edges of the image, while preserving all image pixels.

   Top Left Pixel Color to remove any border areas that match the color of the upper left pixel from the image.

   Bottom Right Pixel Color to remove any border areas that match the color of the lower right pixel from the image.
3. Choose which areas of the image you want to be trimmed: **Top, Bottom, Left,** or **Right**.
4. Click OK.

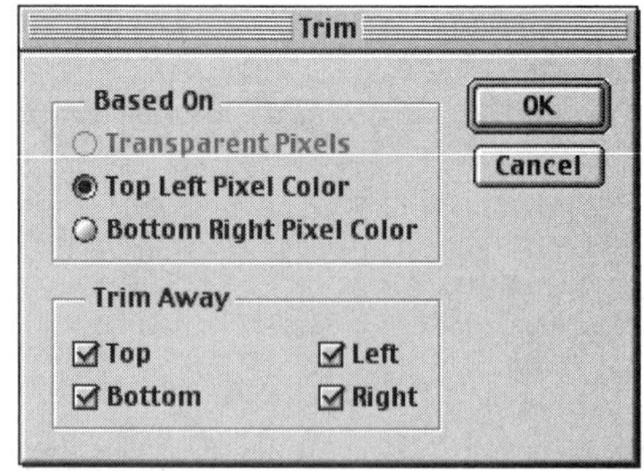

1 *The **Trim** command removes excess transparent areas or color areas, depending on which **Based On** option you choose.*

1 *The original image.*

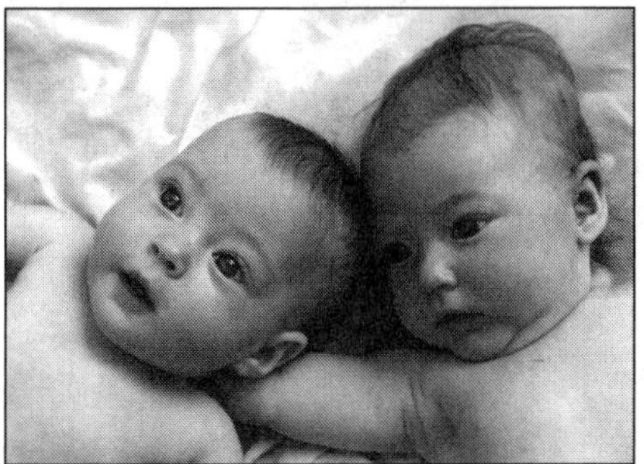

2 *The image* ***flipped horizontally****.*

3 *The original image* ***flipped vertically****.*

Note: The Rotate Canvas > Flip Horizontal and Flip Vertical commands, discussed below, flip all the layers in an image. If you want to flip one layer at a time, use Edit menu > Transform > Flip Horizontal or Flip Vertical instead.

To flip an image:

To flip the image left to right, choose Image menu > Rotate Canvas > Flip Horizontal **1**–**2**.

or

To flip the image upside-down to produce a mirror image, choose Image menu > Rotate Canvas > Flip Vertical **3**.

Note: The Rotate Canvas commands rotate all the layers in an image. To rotate one layer at a time, use a rotate command from the Edit menu > Transform submenu.

To rotate an image by a preset amount:

Choose Image Menu > Rotate Canvas > 180°, 90° CW (clockwise), or 90° CCW (counterclockwise).

To rotate an image by specifying a number:

1. Choose Image Menu > Rotate Canvas > Arbitrary.
2. Enter a number between -359.99° and 359.99° in the Angle field **1**.

   TIP To straighten out a crooked scan, measure the angle using the Measure tool, then enter that angle.
3. Click °CW (clockwise) or °CCW (counterclockwise)
4. Click OK **2**.

1

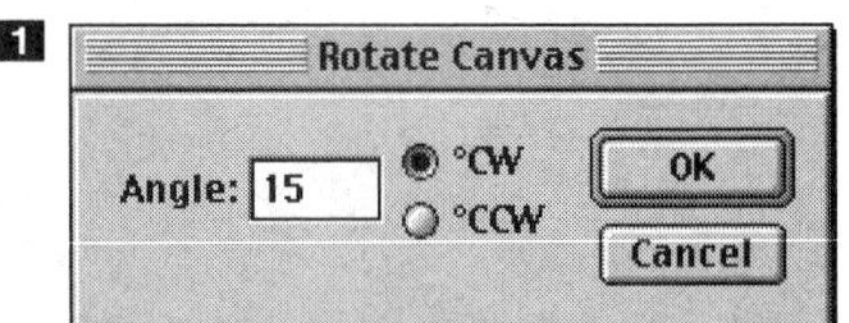

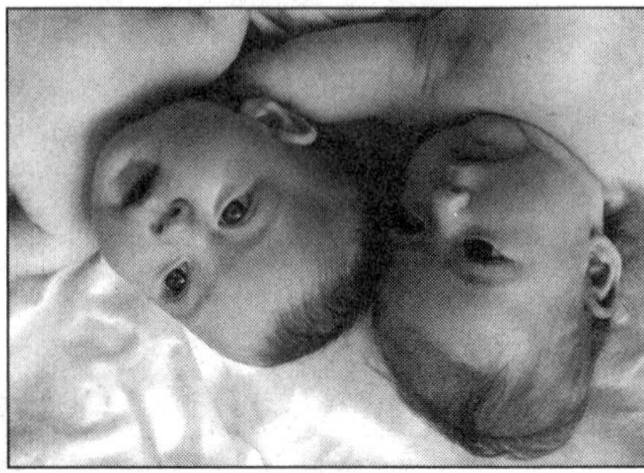

2 *After* ***rotating*** *an image 180°. Compare with the flipped images, above.*

SELECT 5

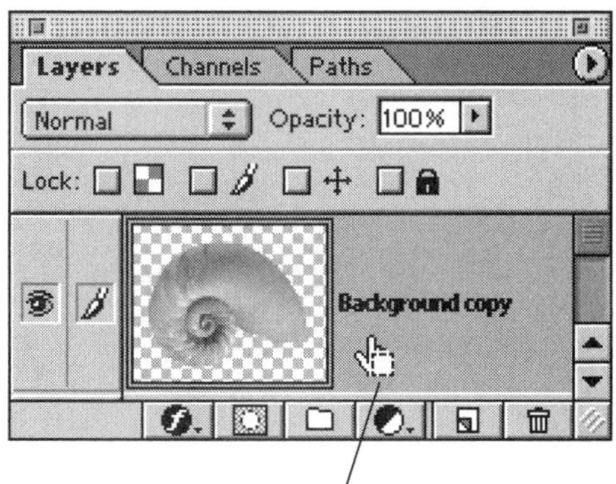

1 ***Ctrl-click/Cmd-click*** *a layer name to* ***select*** *all the opaque pixels on that layer.*

2 ***Opaque pixels—not*** *transparent areas—are selected on a layer.*

WHEN A SELECTION is active on an image, only that area is editable—the rest of the image is protected. A selection border has a moving marquee. This chapter covers the creation of selections using the Rectangular Marquee, Elliptical Marquee, Lasso, Polygonal Lasso, Magic Wand, and Magnetic Lasso tools, as well as the Color Range and Extract commands. You will also learn how to create selections of various shapes; how to select by color; how to deselect, reselect, inverse, or delete a selection; how to move or hide a selection marquee; how to transform, add to, or subtract from a selection; and how to create a vignette.

A selection contains pixels from whichever layer is currently active. If the Move tool is used to move a selection on the Background of an image, the current Background color will be applied automatically to the exposed area. If a selection is moved on a layer using the Move tool, on the other hand, the exposed area will become transparent. (Read more about layers in Chapter 7.)

TIP A selection can be converted into a path for precise reshaping, and then converted back into a selection (see pages 260 and 270). Quick Masks, which function like selections, but can be painted on an image, are covered in Chapter 15.

To select an entire layer:

Choose a layer, then choose Select menu > All (Ctrl-A/Cmd-A). A marquee will surround the **entire** layer.

To select only **opaque pixels**—not the transparent areas—on a layer, Ctrl-click/Cmd-click the layer name on the Layers palette **1**–**2**. Or Right-click/Control-click a layer thumbnail and choose Select Layer Transparency from the context menu.

To create a rectangular or elliptical selection:

1. Choose a layer.
2. Choose the Rectangular Marquee **1** or Elliptical Marquee tool (M or Shift-M).
3. *Optional:* To specify the exact dimensions of the selection, with the Rectangular or Elliptical Marquee tool highlighted, choose Fixed Size from the Style pop-up menu on the options bar **2**, then enter Width and Height values. Remember, though, you're counting pixels based on the file's resolution, not the monitor's resolution, so the same Fixed Size marquee will appear larger in a low resolution file than in a high resolution file.

   To specify the width-to-height ratio of the selection (3-to-1, for example), choose Constrained Aspect Ratio from the Style pop-up menu, then enter Width and Height values. Enter the same number in both fields to create a circle or a square.
4. *Optional:* To soften the edges of the selection before it's created, enter a Feather value above zero on the options bar **3**. The Anti-aliased option can be turned on or off for the Elliptical Marquee tool.
5. If you specified Fixed Size values (or are using the Single Row or Single Column tool), click on the image. For any other Style, drag diagonally **4**–**5**. A marquee will appear. To create a square or a circular selection for the Normal Style, start dragging, then finish the marquee with Shift held down.

   Hold down Spacebar to move the marquee while drawing it. To move the marquee after releasing the mouse, drag inside it.

TIP As you drag the mouse, the dimensions of the selection will be indicated in the W and H area on the Info palette.

TIP To add to or subtract from a selection, see page 96.

1

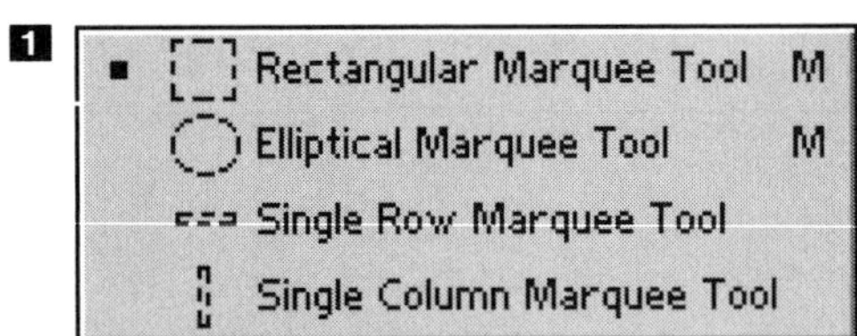

2 *Instead of drawing the marquee manually, you can choose **Fixed Size** from the **Style** pop-up menu, and enter exact **Width** and **Height** dimensions.*

3 *Enter a **Feather** value to soften the edges of the selection.*

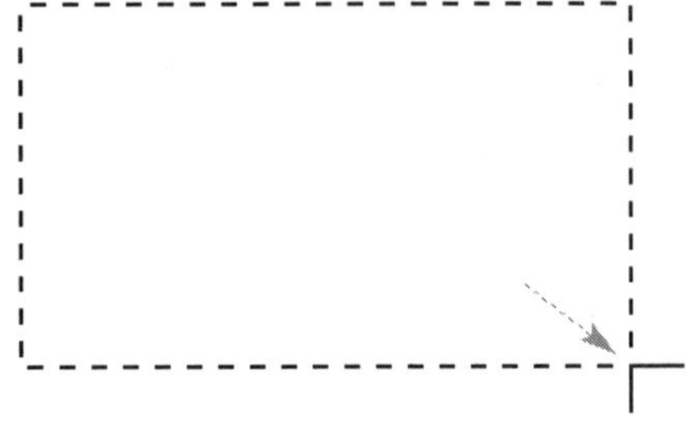

4 *Drag diagonally to create a **rectangular** selection...*

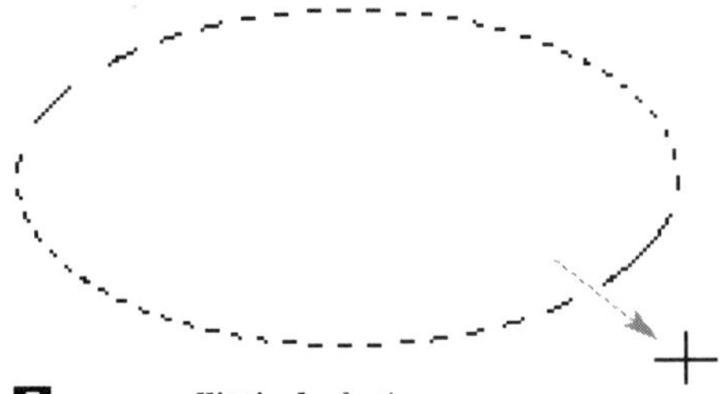

5 *...or an **elliptical** selection.*

Anti-aliasing

Check the **Anti-aliased** box on the options bar before using a selection tool to create a selection with a softened edge that steps to transparency. Uncheck Anti-aliased to create a crisp, hard-edged selection.

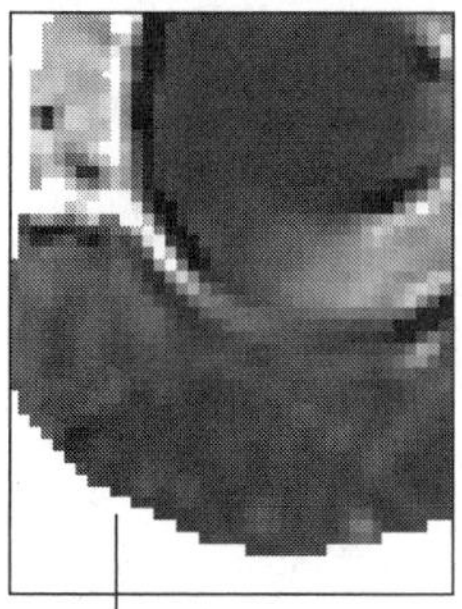

Aliased

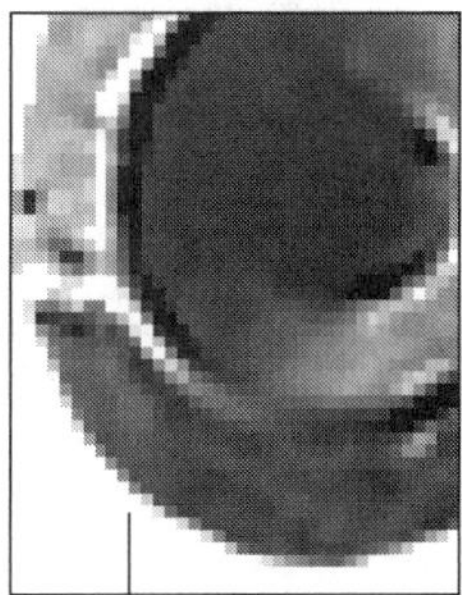

Anti-aliased

1 *A curved **Lasso** tool selection.*

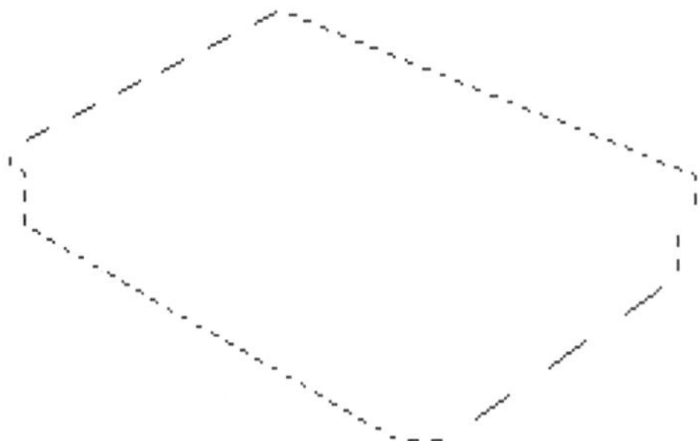

2 *A straight-edged **Polygon Lasso** tool selection.*

Deleting polygon lasso corners

Press **Delete** to erase the last-created corner. Hold down Delete to erase multiple corners.

Note: Since it's difficult to precisely reselect an area (unless you save the selection in an alpha channel or as a path), try to refine your selection before you deselect it.

TIP If the shape you want to select isn't too complex, use the Pen or Freeform Pen tool to trace it (and then convert the path into a selection) instead of using the Lasso—you'll get a smoother selection. You can also convert a selection into a path for precise reshaping.

To create a freeform selection:

1. Choose a layer.
2. Choose the Lasso tool (L or Shift-L).
3. *Optional:* Enter a Feather value on the Lasso options bar to soften the edges of the selection.
4. Drag around an area of the layer **1**. When you release the mouse, the open ends of the selection will join automatically.

TIP To feather a selection after it's created, use the Select menu > Feather command (Ctrl-Alt-D/Cmd-Option-D).

TIP To create a straight side using the Lasso tool, with the mouse button still down, press Alt/Option, and click to create corners. Drag, then release Alt/Option to resume drawing a freehand selection.

To create a polygonal selection:

1. Choose a layer.
2. Choose the Polygon Lasso tool (L or Shift-L).
3. To create straight sides, click to create points **2**. To join the open ends of the selection, click on the starting point (a small circle will appear next to the pointer). Or Ctrl-click/Cmd-click or double-click anywhere on the image to close the selection automatically.

   Alt-drag/Option-drag to create a curved segment as you draw a polygonal selection. Release Alt/Option to resume drawing straight sides.

If you click on a layer pixel with the Magic Wand tool, a selection will be created that includes adjacent pixels of a similar shade, color, or transparency level. You can then add similarly colored, non-adjacent pixels to the selection using the Similar command or add non-similar colors by Shift-clicking.

To select by color (Magic Wand):

1. Choose a layer.
2. Choose the Magic Wand tool (W).
3. With the **Contiguous** box checked on the Magic Wand options bar **1**, the selection will be limited to areas that are connected to the first pixel you click on. Uncheck this option to select non-contiguous areas.
4. On the Magic Wand options bar, check the **Use All Layers** box to sample from colors in all the currently displayed layers to create the selection. Only pixels on the current layer can be edited, but you can apply changes within the same selection marquee through successive layers.

   or

   Uncheck the **Use All Layers** box to sample colors only on the current layer.

   Also, check the **Anti-aliased** box for a smoother selection edge.
5. Click on a shade or color in the image window.
6. *Do any of these optional steps:*

   To enlarge the selection based on the current Tolerance setting on the Magic Wand options bar, choose Select menu > **Grow** as many times as you like (use a low Tolerance). You can also access this command by Right-clicking/Ctrl-clicking in the image window.

   To select additional, non-contiguous areas of similar color or shade based on the current Tolerance setting on the Magic Wand options bar, choose Select menu > **Similar**.

   To change the range of shades or colors within which the Magic Wand tool

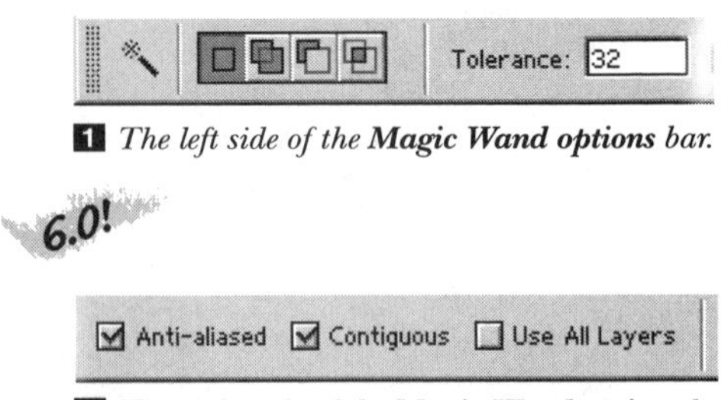

1 *The left side of the* ***Magic Wand options*** *bar.*

2 *The right side of the* ***Magic Wand options*** *bar.*

*A **Magic Wand** selection using a **Tolerance** of **10**.*

*A **Magic Wand** selection using a **Tolerance** of **40**. At a higher Tolerance, more pixels are selected.*

selects, enter a number between 0 and 255 in the **Tolerance** field on the Magic Wand options bar **2**, then click on the image again. At a Tolerance of 32, the Magic Wand will select within a range of 16 shades below and 16 shades above the shade on which it is clicked. Enter 0 to select only one color or shade. To gradually expand or narrow the range of shades or colors the Magic Wand tool selects, modify the Tolerance value between clicks. The higher the Tolerance, the broader the range of colors the wand selects.

TIP Choose Edit > Undo (Ctrl-Z/Cmd-Z) to deselect the last created selection area.

TIP To quickly select all the opaque pixels on a layer (not the Background or fully transparent areas), Ctrl-click/Cmd-click the layer name.

TIP To add to or subtract from the selection, see page 96.

TIP To Expand or Contract a selection by a specified number of pixels, choose either command from the Select menu > Modify submenu.

TIP To remove a flat-color background from around a shape, first select the background of the image using the Magic Wand tool, then press Backspace/Delete.

In creating the Magnetic Lasso tool (and the Extract command, discussed on page 98), Adobe has attempted to make the difficult task of selecting irregular shapes and furry, fuzzy, or complex edges a little easier (a little less cursing). Neither technique solves the problem completely, but they're useful tools nevertheless.

The Magnetic Lasso tool creates a freeform selection automatically as you move or drag the mouse. It snaps to the nearest distinct shade or color that defines the edge of a shape. *Note:* This tool utilizes a lot of processor time and RAM. If you move or drag the mouse quickly, the tool may not keep pace with you.

To select using the Magnetic Lasso:

1. Choose a layer.
2. Choose the Magnetic Lasso tool (L or Shift-L).
3. *Optional:* Change any of the tool's options bar settings. See "The Magnetic Lasso options" on the next page.
4. Click to establish a fastening point. Move the mouse, with or without pressing the mouse button, along the edge of the shape that you want to select **1**. As you move or drag, the selection line will snap to the edge of the shape. The temporary points that appear will disappear when you close the selection.
5. If the selection line starts to follow adjacent shapes that you don't want to select, click on the edge of the shape that you *do* want to select to add a fastening point manually. Continue to move or drag to complete the selection.
6. To close the selection line: **2**

   Double-click the mouse anywhere over the shape.
   or
   Click on the starting point (a small circle will appear next to the Magnetic Lasso tool pointer).
   or

Make your life easier

To temporarily heighten contrast in an image to enhance the Magnetic Lasso tool's effectiveness, choose **Brightness/Contrast** from the "Create new fill or adjustment layer" pop-up menu at the bottom of the Layers palette, and move the Contrast slider to the right. Delete the adjustment layer when you're done using the Magnetic Lasso.

1 *Move the mouse **slowly** around a shape.*

2 *After **closing** the selection.*

Magnetic Lasso

Scrap it

Press **Esc** to cancel a partial selection line (then you can start again). Press **Delete** to erase the last drawn fastening points in succession.

1 *Choose a **Feather** value from the left side of the **Magnetic Lasso** options bar.*

6.0!

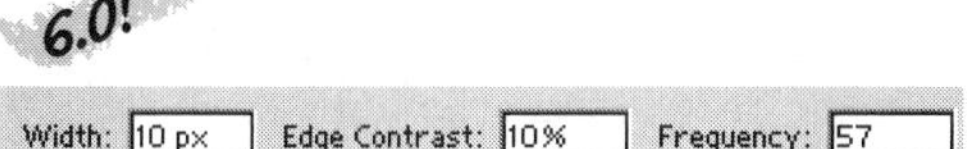

2 *Choose **Width, Edge Contrast,** and **Frequency** values from the right side of the **Magnetic Lasso** options bar.*

*When **Other Cursors: Precise** is chosen in Edit menu > Preferences > **Display & Cursors**, the pointer will be a circle with a crosshair in the center, and its diameter will be the current Lasso Width. To use a temporary Precise pointer, press Caps Lock.*

Press Enter/Return.
or
Ctrl-click/Cmd-click.
or
Alt-double-click/Option-double-click to close with a straight segment.

TIP Alt-click/Option-click to use the Polygon Lasso tool temporarily while the Magnetic Lasso is selected. Alt-drag/Option-drag to use the Lasso tool.

Magnetic Lasso options bar settings 6.0!

The **Feather** amount is the softness of the edges of the selection **1**.

The **Width** (1–40) is the size of the area in pixels under the pointer that the tool considers when it places a selection line **2**. Use a wide Width for a high contrast image with strong edges. Use a narrow Width for an image that has subtle contrast changes or small shapes that are close together; the selection will be more precise and the line won't flip-flop back and forth across the edge.

TIP To decrease the Width setting by one pixel as you create a selection, press "[". To increase it, press "]".

Edge Contrast (1–100) is the degree of contrast needed between shapes for an edge to be discerned. Use a low Edge Contrast for a low contrast image.

TIP If you enter a low or high Width, do the same for the Edge Contrast.

Frequency (0–100) controls how often fastening points are placed as a selection is made. The lower the Frequency, the less frequently points are placed. Use a high Frequency to select an irregular contour.

Using the Color Range command, you can select areas based on colors in the image or based on a luminosity or hue range.

To select by color (Color Range):

1. Choose a layer. The Color Range command samples colors from all the currently visible layers, but only the current layer will be available for editing. You can limit the selection range by first creating a selection.
2. Choose Select menu > Color Range.
3. Choose from the Select pop-up menu. You can limit the selection to a preset color range (e.g., Reds, Yellows), to a luminosity range (Highlights, Midtones, or Shadows), or to Sampled Colors (shades or colors you'll click on with the Color Range eyedropper). The Out of Gamut option can be used on an image only in Lab Color or RGB Color mode. If you choose a preset color range and the image contains only light saturations of that color, an alert box will warn you that the selection marquee will be present, but invisible.
4. Choose a Selection Preview option for previewing selection areas on the image.
5. To preview the selection, click the Selection button; to redisplay the whole image, click the Image button. Or, hold down Ctrl/Cmd with either option chosen to toggle between the two. If the image extends beyond the edges of the image window, use the Image option—the entire image will be displayed in the preview box to facilitate sampling.
6. If you chose Sampled Colors in step 3, click or drag in the preview box or in the image window with the eyedropper cursor to sample colors in the image.
7. *Optional:* Move the Fuzziness slider to the right to expand the range of colors or shades selected or move it to the left to narrow the range.
8. *Optional:* If you chose Sampled Colors for step 3, Shift-click in the image window or in the preview box to add more colors or shades to the selection. Alt-click/Option-click to remove colors or shades from the selection. Or click the "+" or "-" eyedropper icon button in the Color Range dialog box, then click on the image or in the preview box without holding down Shift or Alt/Option.
9. Click OK.

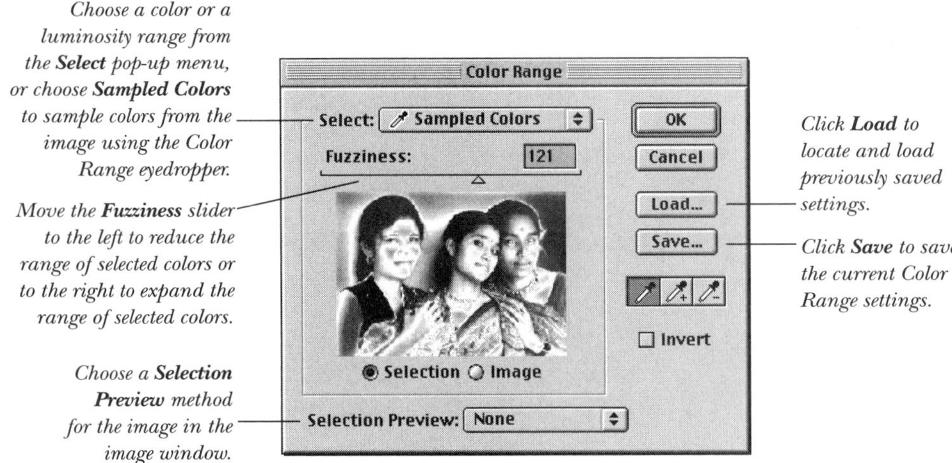

*Choose a color or a luminosity range from the **Select** pop-up menu, or choose **Sampled Colors** to sample colors from the image using the Color Range eyedropper.*

*Move the **Fuzziness** slider to the left to reduce the range of selected colors or to the right to expand the range of selected colors.*

*Choose a **Selection Preview** method for the image in the image window.*

*Click **Load** to locate and load previously saved settings.*

*Click **Save** to save the current Color Range settings.*

■1 A *frame* selection created using the Rectangular Marquee tool.

■2 *Here's another option. The Marquee tool was used to select the center area, then the Inverse command was used to reverse the selected and non-selected areas so the outer area became the selection. The Levels command was used to screen back the selected area.*

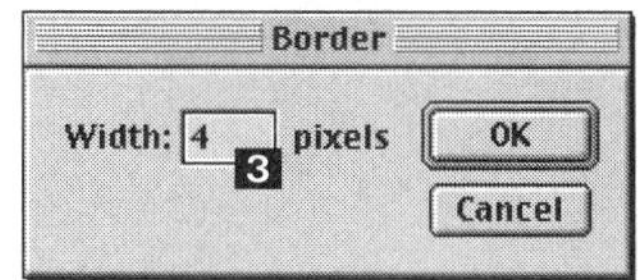

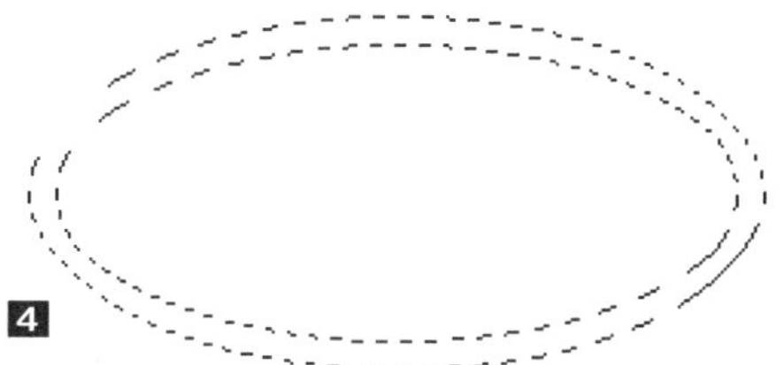

■4

To create a frame selection:

1. Choose a layer.
2. Choose the Rectangular or Elliptical Marquee tool (M or Shift-M), then drag to create a selection, or choose Select menu > Select All (Ctrl-A/Cmd-A).
3. Alt-drag/Option-drag a smaller selection inside the first selection ■1. To subtract from a selection using another method, see page 96.

To select a narrow border around a selection:

1. Create a selection.
2. Choose Select menu > Modify > Border.
3. Enter the desired Width (1–64) of the border in pixels ■3.
4. Click OK. The new selection will evenly straddle the edge of the original selection ■4.

To deselect a selection:

With any tool selected, choose Select menu > Deselect (Ctrl-D/Cmd-D).

or

Click inside the selection with any selection tool **1**.

Note: If you click *outside* the selection with the Magic Wand, Polygon Lasso, or Magnetic Lasso tool, you will create a new selection.

TIP It's difficult to reselect the same area twice, so deselect a selection only when you're sure you've finished using it. If you unintentionally deselect, choose Undo immediately. If you think you might want to reuse a selection, save it as a path or in an alpha channel.

To reselect the last selection:

Choose Select menu > Reselect (Ctrl-Shift-D/Cmd-Shift-D).

TIP If you click a prior state on the History palette that involved a selection, the Reselect command will reselect the selection from that prior state.

If you delete a selection from a layer, the original selection area will become transparent **2**. If you delete a selection from the Background, the selection area will fill with the current Background color **3**.

To delete a selection:

Press Backspace/Delete.

or

Choose Edit menu > Clear.

or

Choose Edit menu > Cut (Ctrl-X/Cmd-X) to place the selection on the Clipboard.

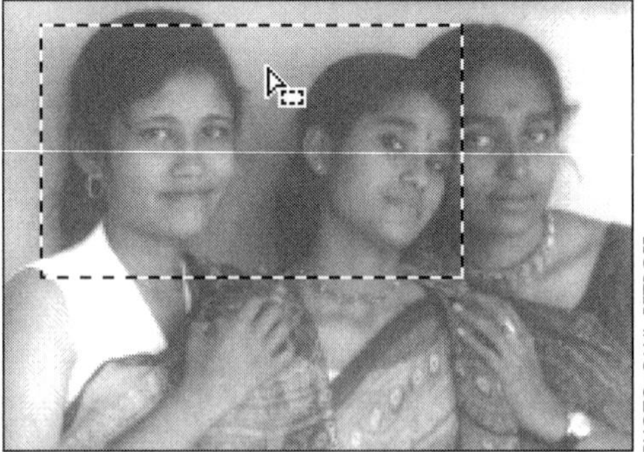

1 *Click **inside** a selection to **deselect** it.*

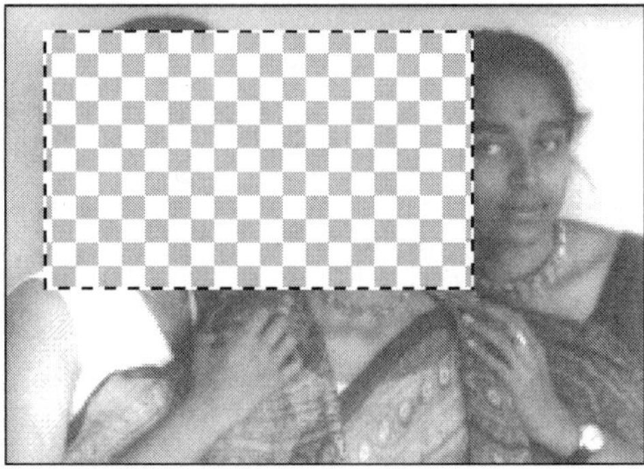

2 *A selection deleted from a **layer**.*

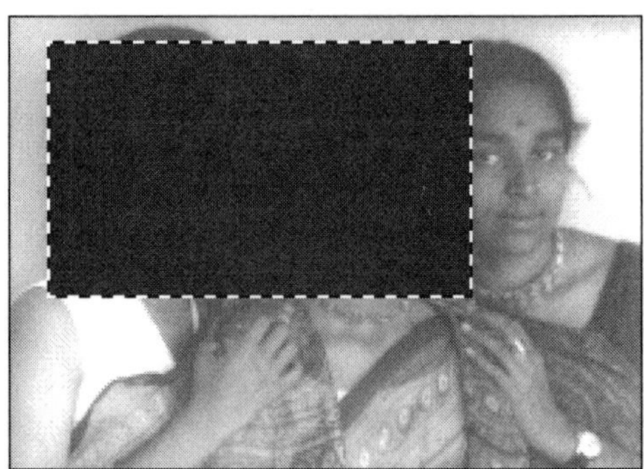

3 *A selection deleted from the **Background**.*

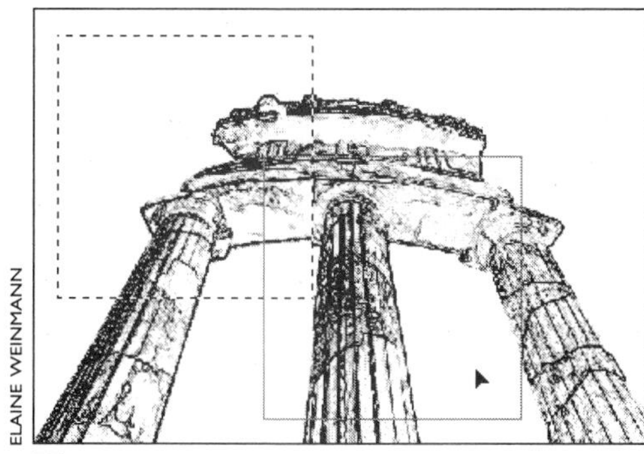

1 ***Moving** a marquee.*

Follow these instructions to move only the selection marquee—**not** its contents.

To move a selection marquee:

1. *Optional:* To aid in positioning the marquee, choose View menu > Show > Grid or drag a guide or guides from the horizontal or vertical ruler. Also, turn on View menu > Snap To > Guides and/or View menu > Snap To > Grid.
2. Choose any selection tool.
3. Drag inside the selection **1**. Hold down Shift after you start dragging to constrain movement to a multiple of 45°.
   or
   Press any arrow key to move the marquee one pixel at a time.

TIP You can drag a selection marquee from one image window into another image window using a selection tool.

TIP If you drag a selection on a **layer** using the Move tool, the selection's pixel contents will be cut from that layer and the empty space will be replaced by layer **transparency**. If a selection is moved on the **Background**, on the other hand, the empty space will be filled with the current **Background color**.

To switch the selected and unselected areas:

Choose Select menu > Inverse (Ctrl-Shift-I/ Cmd-Shift-I) 1–2.

TIP Choose Inverse again (or use the same shortcut) to switch back to the original selection.

TIP It's easy to select a shape on a flat color background: Choose the Magic Wand tool, enter 5 or less in the Tolerance field on the Magic Wand options bar, click on the flat color background to select it entirely, then choose Select menu > Inverse.

1 *The original selection—the* ***angels*** *are selected.*

2 *The selection is* ***inverted****—now the* ***background*** *is selected.*

Sometimes selection edges ("marching ants") can be annoying or distracting. To hide them temporarily, follow the instructions below. You can even hide selection edges while some Image menu and Filter menu dialog boxes are open.

To hide a selection marquee: 6.0!

Choose View menu > Show > **Selection Edges** to uncheck the command. The selection will remain active.

To redisplay the selection marquee, choose View menu > Show > Selection Edges to check the command.

The Ctrl-H/Cmd-H shortcut hides/shows whichever options are currently available on the Show submenu. The **Show Extras Options** dialog box 3 (View menu > Show > Show Extras Options) controls what options are listed on the Show submenu.

TIP To verify that a selection is still active, press on the Select menu. Most commands will be available if a selection is active.

6.0!

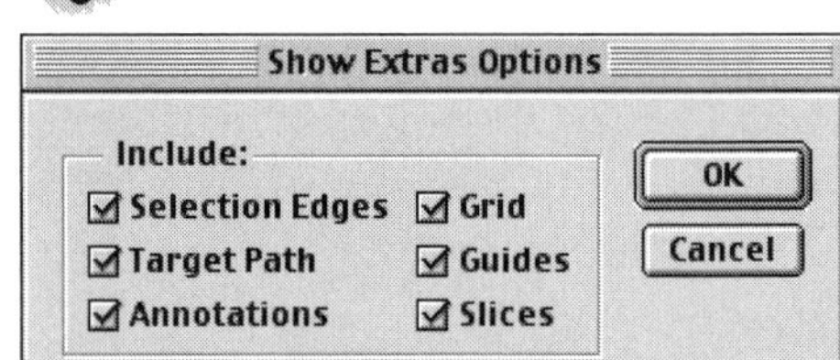

3 *In the* ***Show Extras Options*** *dialog box, check or uncheck the on-screen features you want to show/hide using the Ctrl-H/Cmd-H shortcut.*

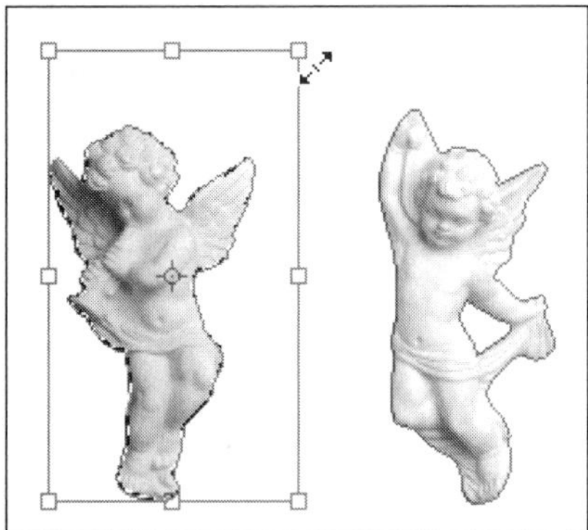

1 *Scaling a selection marquee.*

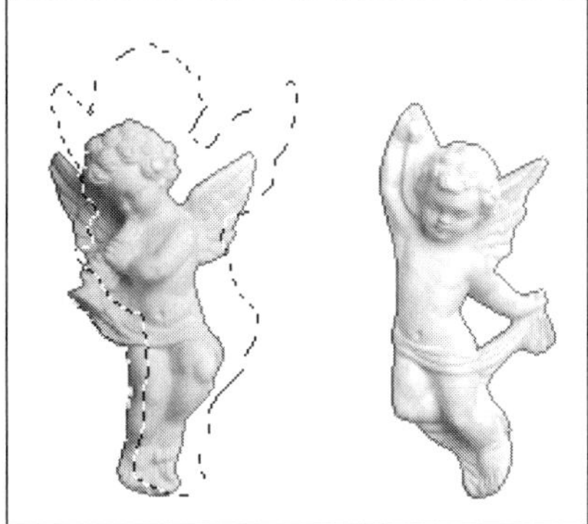

2 *The marquee is enlarged—**not** its contents.*

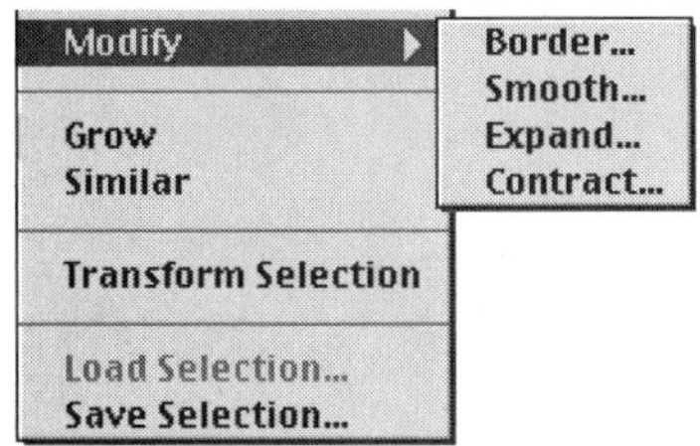

3 *You can use the **Select** menu > **Modify** submenu commands to modify an existing selection.*

Note: The Transform Selection command (discussed below) affects only the selection marquee—not its contents. To transform pixel contents, you can either use a command on the Edit menu > Transform submenu or in Photoshop 6 or later, you can transform selection contents using its bounding box (see page 124).

To transform a selection marquee:

Choose Select menu > Transform Selection, then follow the instructions on pages 123–127 to flip, rotate, scale, etc. **1**–**2**

TIP Right-click/Control-click on the image, then choose a transform command from the context menu.

To modify a selection marquee via a menu command:

Choose Select menu > Modify > Smooth (see page 118) **3** or Select menu > Modify > Expand or Contract, enter a value, then click OK.

or

Choose Select menu > Grow or Similar. These two commands use the current Magic Wand Tolerance setting (see page 86). You can repeat either command to expand the selection further.

To add to a selection:

Choose any selection tool other than the Magic Wand, click the "Add to selection" button on the options bar **1**, choose other options bar settings for the tool, if desired, then drag across the area to be added **2**–**3**. (to bypass the "Add to selection" button, position the cursor over the selection, then Shift-drag over the area to be added).

or

Click the Magic Wand tool, click the "Add to selection" button on the options bar, then click outside the selection. (To bypass the "Add to selection" button, Shift-click outside the selection.)

TIP If the additional selection overlaps the original selection, it will become part of the new, larger selection. If the addition does not overlap the original selection, a second, separate selection will be created.

To subtract from a selection:

Choose any selection tool other than the Magic Wand, click the "Subtract from selection button" on the options bar **1**, choose other options bar settings, if desired, then drag around the area to be subtracted. (To bypass the "Subtract from selection" button, Alt-drag/Option-drag around the area to be subtracted.)

or

Click the Magic Wand tool, click the "Subtract from selection" button on the options bar, then click inside the selection. (To bypass the "Subtract from selection" button, Shift-click inside the selection.)

6.0!

To select the intersection of two selections:

1. With a selection present, choose a selection tool.
2. Click the Intersect with selection button on the options bar **1**, then create a new selection that overlaps the current selection **4**–**5**. (To bypass the button, Alt-Shift-drag/Option-Shift-drag.)

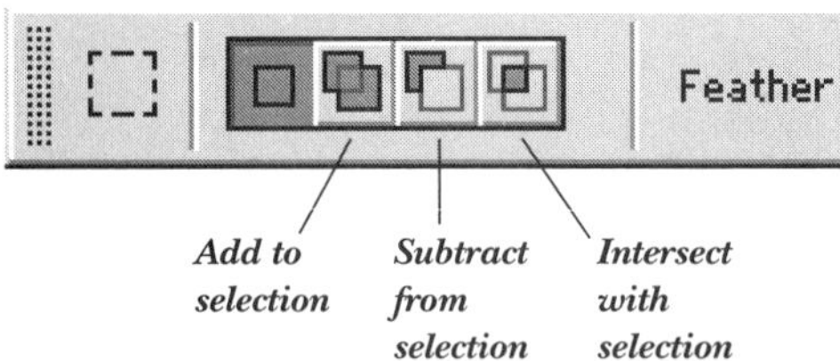

1 *Use these buttons on the* ***options bar*** *to amend a selection.*

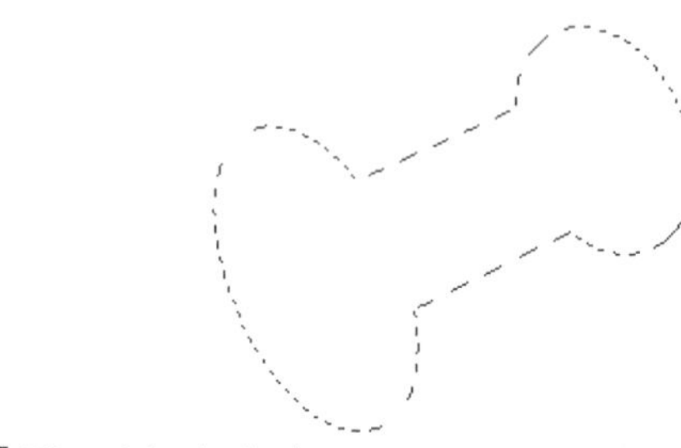

2 *The original selection.*

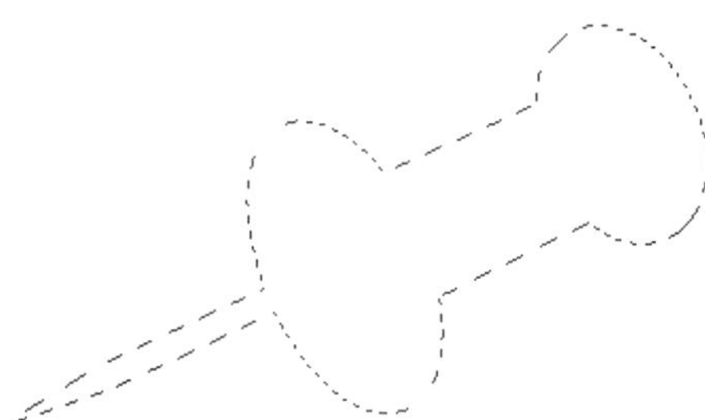

3 *After adding an additional selection area.*

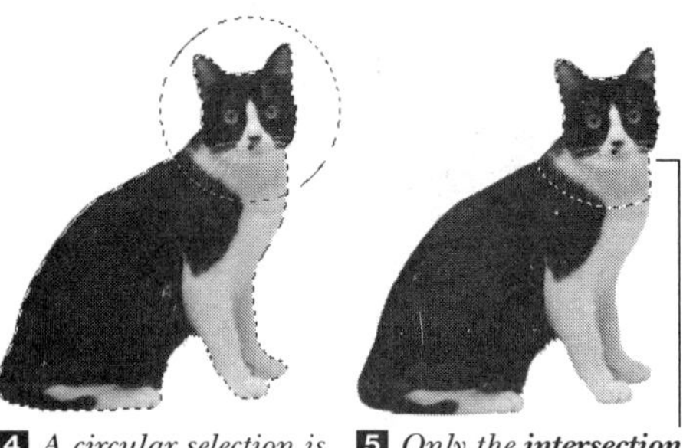

4 *A circular selection is drawn over an existing selection with* ***Alt/Option*** *and* ***Shift*** *held down.*

5 *Only the* ***intersection*** *of the two selections remains selected.*

1 *First create a **feathered**-edge selection.*

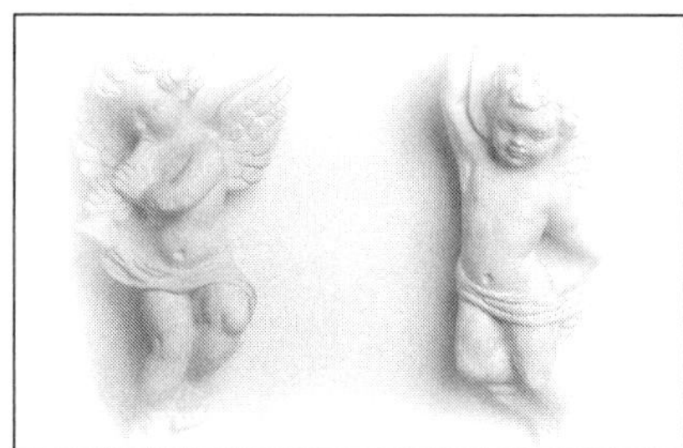

2 *The **vignette**.*

3 *The original image (Peter's relatives—no kidding).*

4 *The **vignette**.*

To vignette an image:

1. For a multi-layer image, choose a layer, and uncheck the "Lock transparent pixels" box. The vignette you create is going to appear to fade into the layer or layers below it.

   For an image with a Background only, choose a Background color (see pages 165–169) for the area around the vignette.
2. Choose the Rectangular Marquee or Elliptical Marquee tool (M or Shift-M), or the Lasso tool (L or Shift-L).
3. Enter 15 or 20 px in the Feather field on the options bar. Alternatively, you can feather the selection after it's created (after step 4) using Select menu > Feather.
4. Create a selection **1**.
5. Choose Select menu > Inverse (Ctrl-Shift-I/Cmd-Shift-I).
6. Press Backspace/Delete.
7. Deselect (Ctrl-D/Cmd-D) **2**–**5**.

5 *For this illustration, we applied the Glass filter for step 6.*

If you've ever torn your hair out trying to mask a shape with an irregular edge (a figure with curly hair or an animal in a landscape), you'll appreciate the Extract command. The nicest part about this feature is that you'll create the mask on a full-size preview right in the dialog box **1**, so you can tweak it until you're certain you've got it just right. When you click OK, the masked area will be preserved; the remaining areas will be erased to transparency.

1 *After outlining the chimp with the* ***Highlight marker*** *and filling the interior of the chimp with the* ***Paint bucket****.*

To mask a shape using the Extract command:

1. *Note:* For safety's sake, work on a copy of the image—or at least on a duplicate layer. You could also make a snapshot of the original image.

   Choose the layer from which you want to extract imagery.
2. Choose Image menu > Extract (Ctrl-Alt-X/Cmd-Option-X). A full-screen, resizable dialog box will open.
3. You'll use the Edge Highlighter to mask the object border first, and then click on the interior with the Fill tool to define the fill.

   Choose the **Edge Highlighter** tool from the toolbox in the dialog box (B) **2**.
   and
   In the Tool Options area **3**, enter or choose a **Brush Size** in pixels for the marker. The sharper the edge of the object you're going to extract, the smaller the brush you can use. Use a large brush if the shape has wide, choppy edges.
   and
   Choose Red, Green, or Blue as the **Highlight** color for the mask. Or choose Other and choose a color from the Color Picker.
4. *Optional:* If you're going to trace a crisp-edged shape (e.g., a geometric shape), check the **Smart Highlighting** box. The highlight will be the minimum width

6.0!

6.0!

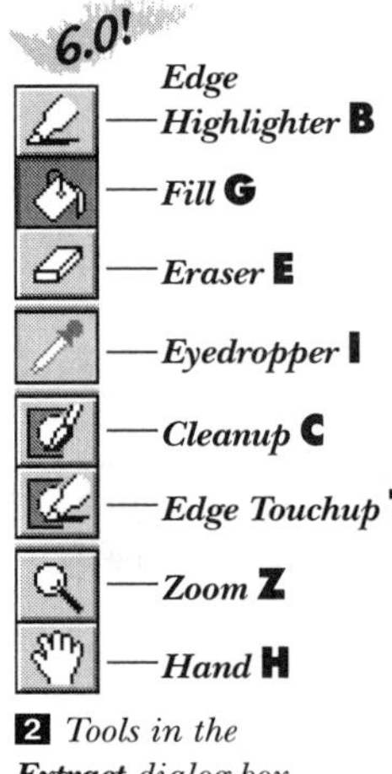

2 *Tools in the* ***Extract*** *dialog box.*

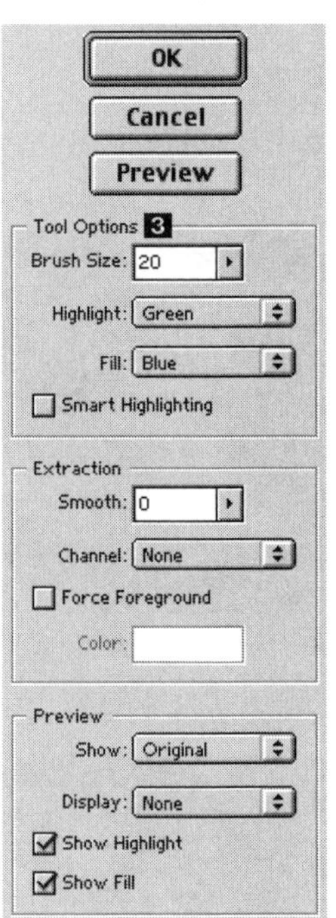

The **Extract** command overdid it in these areas.

1 *After extracting (chimp not in the mist!).*

2 *After using the **Art History Brush** to restore areas of the chimp's face and arm.*

necessary to cover the edge of the shape, regardless of the current brush size.

5. Drag around the border of the area of the image you want to extract. Complete the loop to make a closed shape. Drag right along the object's border so as to catch any frizz or fringe. You don't need to drag along the edge of the canvas area if the imagery extends that far.
6. *Optional:* Raise the Extraction: **Smooth** value to eliminate extraneous pixels.
7. Choose the **Fill** (second) tool (G) from the toolbox in the dialog box.
   and
   Choose Red, Green, or Blue as the **Fill** color for the mask. Or choose Other and choose a color from the Color Picker.
   and
   Click on the area of the image that you want to extract. (Click again to un-fill.)

   Note: To extract pixels of one color, instead of using the Fill tool, check the Force Foreground box, choose the Eyedropper tool in the dialog box (I), then click a color in the preview window. Or click the Color swatch and choose a color from the Color Picker.
8. Use the **Eraser** tool (E) from the dialog box if you need to un-mask any masked areas. Choose a Brush Size for the Eraser in the Tool Options area of the dialog box.

   TIP To zoom in on the preview, use the Ctrl-+/Cmd-+ shortcut. To zoom out, Ctrl--/Cmd--. You could also use the Zoom tool in the dialog box (Alt-click/Option-click to reduce the view).

   TIP If the preview is at larger than 100% view, you can use the Hand tool from the dialog box (H) to move it around (press Spacebar to access the Hand tool temporarily).

(Continued on the following page)

Extract

9. Click **Preview**, then in the Preview area of the dialog box, do any of the following:

Check the **Show Highlight** and/or **Show Fill** boxes.

Choose Show: **Extracted** to toggle to the extracted image view; choose **Original** to toggle back to the original image.

Choose Display: **None** to display the background as transparent; choose **Black Matte, Gray Matte,** or **White Matte** to display the extracted shape on a background of black, gray, or white, respectively; choose **Other** to choose a custom color; or choose **Mask** to display the discarded area as black and the protected area as white.

10. To refine the mask further, do any of the following:

6.0! Use the **Cleanup** tool (C), which gradually subtracts opacity. (Alt-drag/ Option-drag to restore opacity.)

6.0! Use the **Edge Touchup** tool (T), which gradually sharpens edges.

Change the **Smooth** value.

11. Click OK. After clicking OK, if you want to restore lost areas, use the History Brush tool (see page 146). Or to erase further by hand, use the Background Eraser (see page 206).

Channel it

To make the marker highlight conform to the shape of a selection, create a selection, choose Select menu > Modify > **Border** (Width about 9 pixels), then click OK. **Inverse** the selection, and save the selection in an **alpha channel**. Choose Image menu > **Extract**, then choose that alpha channel from the Extraction: **Channel** pop-up menu. Finally, click with the **Fill** tool (G) inside the highlighted area.

COMPOSITING 6

1 *Moving a selection on a* ***layer****...*

2 *...a* ***transparent*** *hole is left behind.*

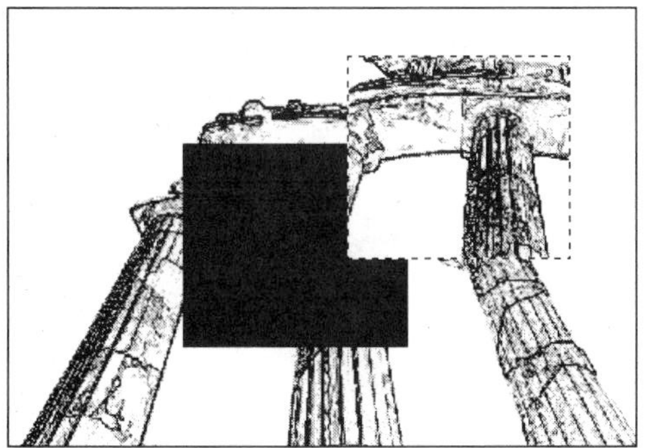

3 *Moving a selection on the* ***Background****: the exposed area fills with the current* ***Background color****.*

THIS CHAPTER covers methods for composing image elements: the Clipboard (Cut, Copy, Paste, and Paste Into), drag-and-drop, cloning, and pattern stamping. Also covered are techniques for precisely positioning and aligning image elements and smoothing the seams between them.

Moving

In these instructions and in the "drag-copy" instructions on the next page, you'll be moving actual image pixels. (To move just a selection marquee without moving its contents, see page 93.)

To move a selection's contents:

1. *Optional:* To help you position the selection, choose View menu > Show > Grid (Ctrl-Alt-'/Cmd-Option-') or drag a guide or guides from either ruler. Also, turn on View menu > Snap To > Guides and Snap To > Grid.
2. If the selection is on the Background, choose a Background color. The area exposed by the moved selection will fill with this color automatically. If the selection is on a layer, the exposed area will fill with transparency.
3. Choose the Move tool (V). (You can use Ctrl/Cmd to access the Move tool when most other tools are chosen.)
4. Position the pointer over the selection (the pointer will have a scissors icon), then drag. The selection marquee and its contents will move together **1**–**3**.

   Beware! When you deselect the selection, its pixel contents will drop back into its original layer, in its new location, regardless of which layer is currently active.

TIP Press an arrow key to move a selection marquee in 1-pixel increments.

Drag-Copy Selection; Align Layer to Marquee

To drag-copy a selection:

1. Choose the Move tool (V). (You can use Ctrl/Cmd to access the Move tool when most other tools are chosen.)
2. Alt-drag/Option-drag the selection you want to copy (release the mouse first, then Alt/Option). The copied pixels will remain selected 1–2.

TIP Press Alt-arrow/Option-arrow to offset a copy of a selection one pixel from the original. Press Alt-Shift-arrow/Option-Shift-arrow to offset a copy by ten pixels.

1 *Alt-dragging/Option-dragging a selection.*

The Align to Selection commands align layer pixels to a currently active selection marquee. If you need to align objects from different layers, you can align each one individually to the same marquee or you can link them first (see page 249) and then align them all at once.

To align a layer or layers to a selection marquee:

1. Create a selection.
2. Choose a layer or one layer in a set of linked layers.
3. Choose the Move tool, click an align button on the Move options bar 3. 6.0!
   or
   Choose Layer menu > Align To Selection > Top Edges, Vertical Centers, Bottom Edges, Left Edges, Horizontal Centers, or Right Edges.

   The layer pixels will align to the edges or center of the selection marquee, depending on which alignment option you choose.

2 *A* ***copy*** *of the* ***selected pixels*** *is moved.*

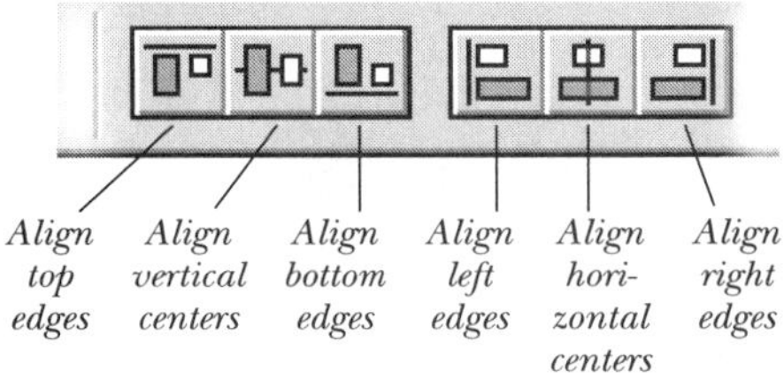

3 *The* ***align*** *buttons on the* ***Move*** *options bar.*

Purge thy Clipboard

If the Clipboard imagery is large, the remaining available memory for other processing functions will be reduced. To **empty** the Clipboard and reclaim memory, choose Edit menu > **Purge** > **Clipboard**. This can't be undone.

Clipboard basics

You can use the Edit menu > **Cut** or **Copy** command to save a selection to a temporary storage area called the **Clipboard**, and then use Edit menu > **Paste** or **Paste Into** to paste the Clipboard pixels onto another layer in the same image or in another image. The Cut, Copy, and Paste Into commands are available only while a selection is active.

If you create a selection and choose Edit menu > **Cut**, the selection will be placed on the Clipboard. (The **Clear** command doesn't use the Clipboard.) If you Cut or Clear a selection from the Background, the exposed area will be filled with the current Background color. If you remove a selection from a layer, the area left behind will be transparent.

TIP For a soft transition between pasted imagery and a layer, check the **Anti-aliased** box on the options bar for your selection tool before you use it.

The Edit menu > **Paste** command pastes the Clipboard contents into a new layer, all the while preserving any pasted pixels that extend beyond the image window. You can move the entire layer to reveal the extended pixels. If you then save your document, the extended areas will save with it. If you subsequently crop the layer, however, click **Cropped Area: Hide** on the Crop options bar if you don't want the extended pixels to be discarded.

The same Clipboard contents can be pasted an unlimited number of times. If the **Export Clipboard** box is checked in Edit menu > Preferences > General, the Clipboard contents will be stored in temporary system memory even if you exit/quit Photoshop. The Clipboard can contain only one selection at a time, however, and the Clipboard contents are replaced each time the Cut or Copy command is chosen.

TIP The dimensions in the **New** dialog box automatically match the dimensions of imagery currently on the Clipboard.

Copying

Before using either the Clipboard commands or the drag-and-drop method to copy imagery, compare the **dimensions** of the source image with the dimensions of the destination image. If the imagery being copied is larger than the destination image, some of the copied pixels will extend beyond the image window when they're pasted or dropped, and they will be hidden from view. Move the layer using the Move tool if you want to reveal the out-of-view pixels.

The size of a selection may also change when it's pasted or dropped for another reason: it is rendered in the **resolution** of the destination image. If the resolution of the destination image is higher than that of the source imagery, the copied image will appear smaller when it's pasted or dropped. Conversely, if the resolution of the destination image is lower than that of the source image, the source imagery will look larger when it's pasted or dropped.

TIP If you want the imagery to stay the same size, before copying it, standardize the resolution (and dimensions, if desired) of the source and destination images using Image menu > Image Size. To paste into a smaller image, see page 107.

To copy and paste a selection:

1. Select an area on a layer or on the Background. To feather the selection, choose Select menu>Feather, and enter a value.
2. Choose Edit menu > Copy **1** (Ctrl-C/Cmd-C) (or choose Edit menu > Cut to cut the selection).
3. Choose a layer for pasting.
4. Choose Edit menu > Paste (Ctrl-V/Cmd-V) **2**.
5. *Optional:* Restack, move, or defringe the new layer.

TIP To turn a selection into a new layer, choose Layer menu > New > Layer Via Copy or Layer Via Cut (see page 121).

1 *An area of the Background is placed on the* ***Clipboard*** *via Edit menu >* ***Copy****.*

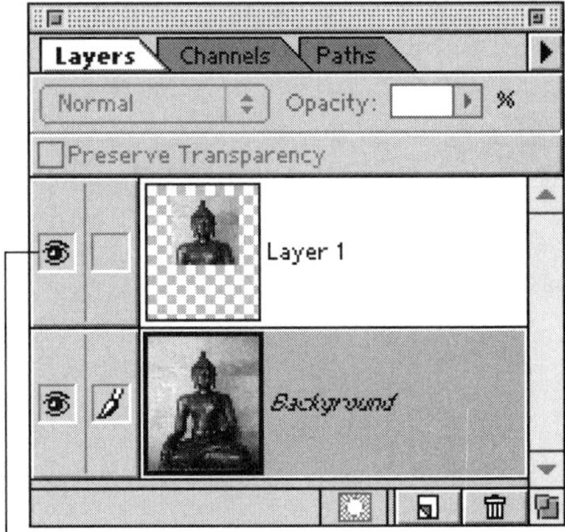

2 *The* ***pasted*** *imagery appears on a new layer.*

1 *A selection is dragged from the* ***Background****. The exposed area* ***temporarily*** *fills with the Background color.*

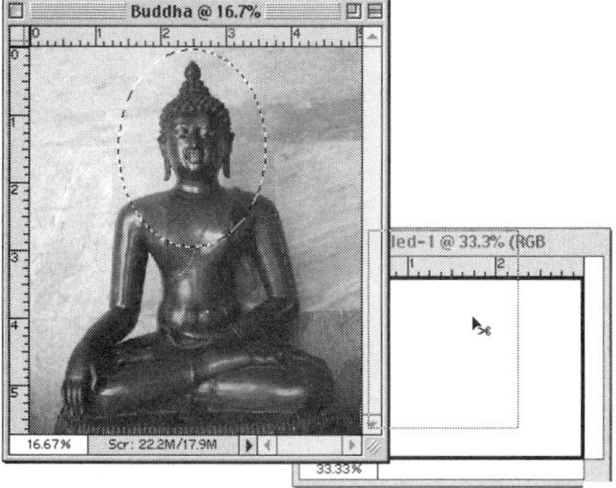

2 *A* ***dark border*** *appears in the destination image window.*

3 *The mouse is released, and the copied pixels appear in the* ***destination*** *image window. The source image is unchanged.*

If you drag selected pixels from one image to another, presto, those selected pixels will be copied onto a new layer in the destination image. This drag-and-drop method bypasses the Clipboard, so it saves memory and preserves the current Clipboard contents. If your monitor is too small to display two image windows simultaneously, use the copy-and-paste method instead.

To drag-and-drop a selection between images:

1. Open the source and destination images, and arrange them so their windows don't completely overlap.
2. In the source image, select an area on a layer or on the Background.
3. Choose the Move tool (V). (You can use Ctrl/Cmd to access the Move tool when most other tools are chosen.)
4. Check Show Bounding Box on the Move options bar, if desired, to make the selection's bounding box visible. *6.0!*
5. Drag the selection into the destination image window, and release the mouse where you want the pixels to be dropped **1**–**3**. The copied imagery will appear on a new layer. You can reposition the imagery using the Move tool.

TIP Shift-drag to drop the selection in the exact center of the destination image automatically. You can release the mouse when the pointer is anywhere inside the destination image window.

TIP To drag-and-drop a whole layer to another image, see pages 135–136.

TIP Drag-and-drop is the only way to copy a shape layer from one document to another. Ctrl-click/Cmd-click the shape layer to select it.

If you use the Paste Into command to paste the Clipboard contents inside a selection, a new layer will be created automatically and the active marquee will become a layer mask. The pasted imagery can then be repositioned within the layer mask or the mask itself can also be reshaped so it reveals more or reveals less.

To paste into a selection:

1. Select an area of a layer. If you want to feather the selection, choose Select menu > Feather and enter a value.
2. Choose Edit menu > Copy to copy pixels only from the active layer, or choose Edit menu > Copy Merged (Ctrl-Shift-C/ Cmd-Shift-C) to copy pixels within the selection area from all the currently visible layers.
3. Leave the same layer active, or choose a different layer, or choose a layer in another image.
4. Select the area (or areas) that you want to paste the Clipboard contents into.
5. Choose Edit menu > Paste Into (Ctrl-Shift-V/Cmd-Shift-V). A new layer and layer mask will be created **1**–**3**.
6. *More options:*

   The entire Clipboard contents were pasted onto the layer, but the layer mask is probably hiding some of them. To **move** the **layer mask** relative to the layer, choose the Move tool, click the layer mask thumbnail (the thumbnail on the right), then drag in the image window. To **move** the **layer contents**, click the layer thumbnail, then drag in the image window.

   Paint on the layer mask in the image window with white to **expose** more of the image or with black to **hide** more of the image.

   To move the layer and layer mask in unison, click between the layer and layer mask thumbnails to link the two layer components together (reclick the link icon to unlink), then drag in the image window using the Move tool.

1 *To create this effect in one image, a music layer was selected and copied. In another image, the type layer was Ctrl-clicked/Cmd-clicked, then Edit menu > Paste Into was chosen. A new layer resulted.*

2 *The layer contents can be repositioned within the layer mask, since the two thumbnails aren't linked together. For this image, the music layer thumbnail was activated and then the layer contents were moved upward using the Move tool.*

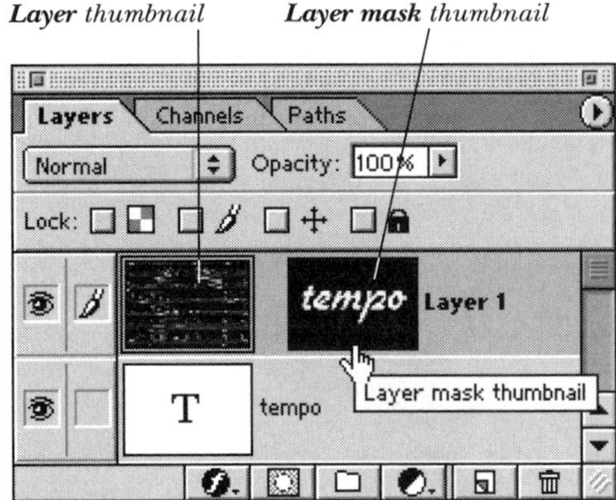

3 *The pasted image appears on a new layer via* ***Paste Into****, and a layer mask is created automatically. The pasted image (the music) is only visible within the white areas in the* ***layer mask*** *(the letter shapes).*

Off the edge?

- To **remove** pixels that extend beyond the edge of a layer, make sure the layer is active, choose Edit menu > Select All, then choose Image menu > Crop. Trimming off the extra pixels will reduce the file's storage size.
- If you apply an image editing command, such as a filter, to a whole layer, any pixels beyond the edge of the layer will also be modified. To **include** these pixels by making them visible in the image window, enlarge the canvas size (Image menu > Canvas Size).
- To **select** pixels that extend beyond the edge of a layer, **Ctrl-click/Cmd-click** the layer name on the Layers palette—don't use Edit menu > Select All.

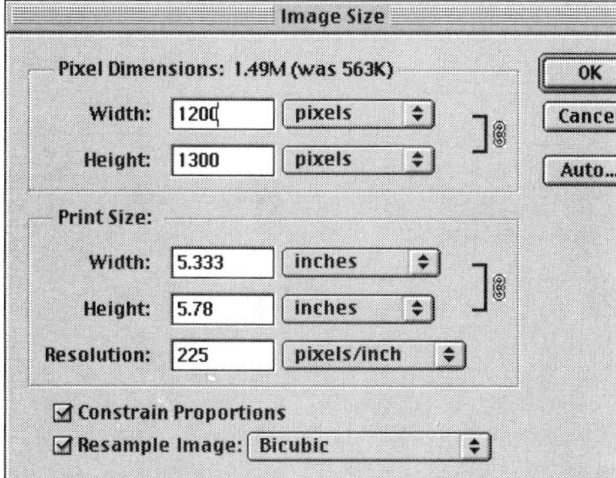

1 *Use the* ***Image Size*** *dialog box to change an image's* ***resolution*** *and* ***dimensions****.*

Normally, in Photoshop, if you move a large selection or layer, or paste into another image, all the current or pasted pixels on a layer are preserved, even if they extend beyond the visible edge of the layer. If you want to trim the pasted imagery as it's pasted, follow these instructions, but read "Copying" on page 104 before you proceed.

To paste into a smaller image:

1. Click in the destination image window, then Alt-press/Option-press and hold on the Status bar at the bottom of the image window. With your other hand, jot down the image's width, height, and resolution on a piece of paper (yes, paper, as in from a tree).
2. Click in the source image window, choose Image menu > Duplicate, then click OK.
3. With the duplicate image window active, choose Image menu > Image Size.
4. Check the Resample Image box, and change the resolution to the same value as that of the destination image **1**. In the Print Size: Width or Height field, enter a smaller number than the dimensions that you jotted down for step 1, then click OK.
5. Choose the layer you want to copy.
6. Choose Select menu > All to select the layer, choose Edit menu > Copy, click in the destination image, then choose Edit menu > Paste.
   or
   Shift-drag the source layer name into the destination image window.
7. Close the duplicate image. Save the original image, if desired.

TIP In lieu of steps 3 and 4 above, you can choose File menu > Automate > Fit Image and enter the desired pixel dimensions for the width or the height (from step 1). Fit Image won't change the image resolution; the copied or dragged layer will take on the resolution of the destination file.

Sharpening and blurring

The Blur tool decreases contrast between pixels. Use it to soften edges between shapes. The Sharpen tool increases contrast between pixels. Use it to delineate edges between shapes. Neither tool can be used on a image in Bitmap or Indexed Color mode.

To sharpen or blur edges:

1. Choose the Blur tool or the Sharpen tool (R or Shift-R). Each tool keeps its own options bar settings.
2. 6.0! On the Sharpen or Blur options bar **1**:

   Click the **Painting Brush** arrowhead, then click a hard-edged or soft-edged tip.
   and
   Choose a blending **Mode**. Normal sharpens/blurs pixels of any shade or color. Darken only sharpens/blurs pixels that are darker than the Foreground color. Lighten only sharpens/blurs pixels that are lighter than the Foreground color. Hue or Color mode will cause a slight buildup of complementary colors. Saturation mode will cause a buildup of existing colors. Luminosity mode will intensify the existing luminosity. (The blending modes are described on pages 30–32.) You'll see a greater distinction between modes with the Sharpen tool than with the Blur tool.

   TIP Right-click/Control-click on the image to choose a blending mode.

   Choose a **Pressure** percentage. Try a low setting at first (oh, say, around 30%).
3. *Optional:* Check the Use All Layers box on the options bar to pick up pixels from other visible layers under the pointer to place onto the active layer.
4. Drag across an area in the image window to sharpen or blur **2**–**3**. To intensify the effect, stroke again.

TIP To avoid creating an overly grainy texture, use the Sharpen tool with a medium Pressure setting and stroke only once on the same area.

Use everything you've got 6.0!

With the **Use All Layers** box unchecked on the options bar for the Magic Wand, Smudge, Sharpen, Blur, or Clone Stamp tool, you will sharpen, blur, etc. using pixels from only the currently chosen layer. With the Use All Layers box checked, you will sharpen, blur, etc. using sampled data from all the currently visible layers under the pointer. With the Use All Layers option on, try applying pixels onto a new layer.

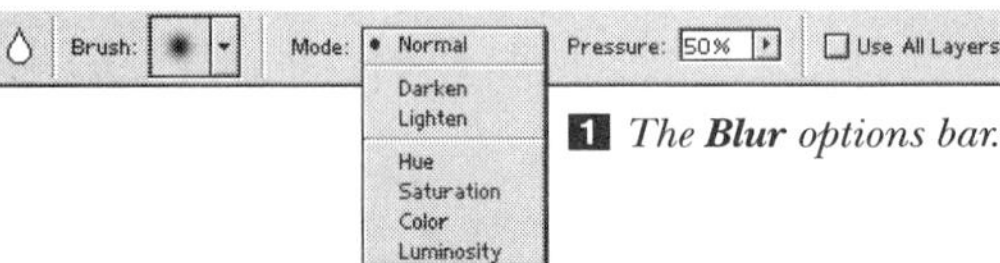

1 *The **Blur** options bar.*

2 *The original image.*

3 *After using the **Sharpen** tool on the strawberry in the center, and the **Blur** tool on the rest of the image.*

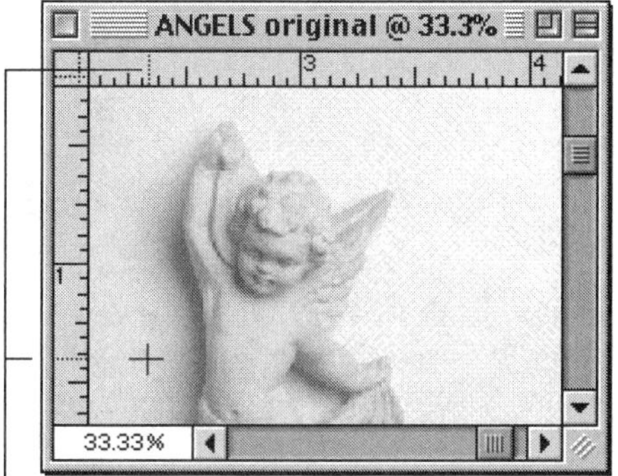

1 *The position of the pointer is indicated by a dotted marker on each ruler.*

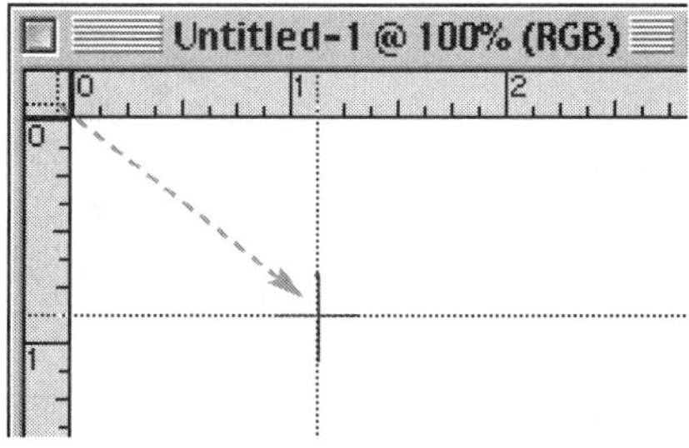

2 *Dragging the* ***ruler origin.***

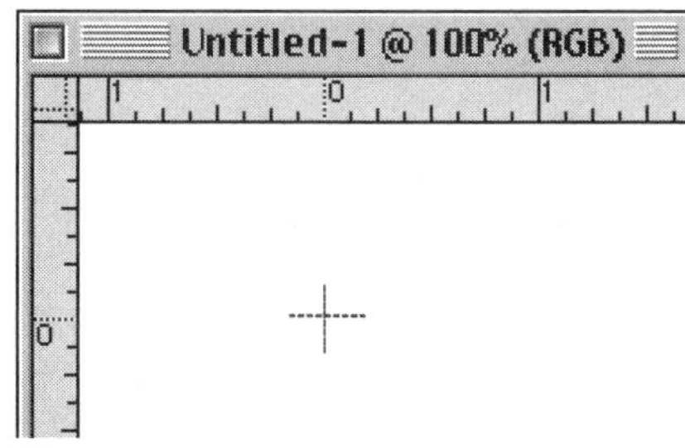

3 *The* ***new ruler origin.***

Using rulers and guides

Grids, rulers, and guides can help you position objects precisely.

To hide or show rulers:

Choose View menu > Show Rulers (Ctrl-R/ Cmd-R). Rulers will appear on the top and left sides of the image window, and the current position of the pointer will be indicated by a dotted marker on each ruler **1**. To hide the rulers, choose View menu > Hide Rulers.

TIP To quickly access the Units & Rulers Preferences dialog box to change the ruler units, double-click either ruler.

The ruler origin is the point from which an object's location is measured.

To change the rulers' zero origin:

6.0!

1. *Optional:* To make the new ruler origin snap to a gridline, first display the grid by choosing View menu > Show > Grid (Ctrl-Alt-'/Cmd-Option-'). Then you can choose View menu > Snap To > Grid.

   To make the ruler origin snap to a guide, choose View menu > Snap To > Guides, then drag a guide into the image window, if you haven't already done so.

   See also "To use the Snap feature" on the following page.
2. Drag from the intersection of the rulers in the upper left corner of the image window diagonally into the image **2**–**3**. Note where the zeros are now located on the rulers.

TIP To reset the ruler origin, double-click the square where the rulers intersect in the upper left corner of the image window.

Rulers

The Snap feature works like an electronic "tug." When View menu > Snap is on, as you move a selection border, slice, drawing tool pointer, path, or shape, that item will snap to the nearest guide, grid, slice, or document edge, depending on which of those options is chosen on the View menu > Snap To submenu.

To use the Snap feature:

6.0!

1. Choose View menu > Snap To > Guides, Grid, Slices, Document Bounds, All [of the above], or None.

   Note: To turn on the Snap To > Grid function, the grid must be showing (View menu > Show > Grid).
2. Make sure View menu > Snap is on (has a check mark) (Ctrl-;/Cmd-;).

The grid is a non-printing framework that can be used to align image elements. Guides are individual guidelines that you drag into the image window yourself. With View menu > Snap To > Guides turned on, a selection or tool pointer will snap to a guide if it's moved within 8 screen pixels of the guide. Ditto for View menu > Snap To > Grid.

To hide or show the grid:

6.0!

Choose View menu > Show > Grid (Ctrl-Alt-'/Cmd-Option-') **3**. To hide the grid, choose the command again. The grid can be turned on or off for individual files.

Show or snap it all 6.0!

Show or hide Selection Edges, the Target Path, Grid, Guides, Slices, Annotations, or all of the above via the View menu > **Show** submenu **1**. The **Show Extras** command shows/hides only the currently enabled items on the Show submenu.

Turn on the snap feature for Guides, Grid, Slices, Documents Bounds, or all of the above via the View menu > **Snap To** submenu **2**. The **Snap** command turns all of the current chosen Snap To options on and off.

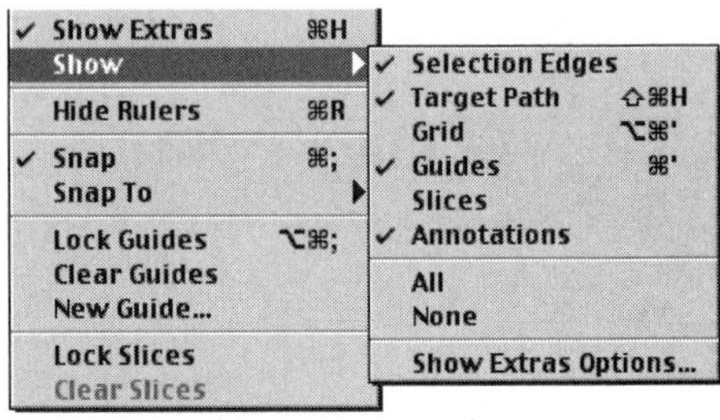

1 *The **Show Extras** command shows/hides the currently enabled items on the **Show** submenu.*

2 *The **Snap** command turns the currently enabled commands on the **Snap To** submenu on or off.*

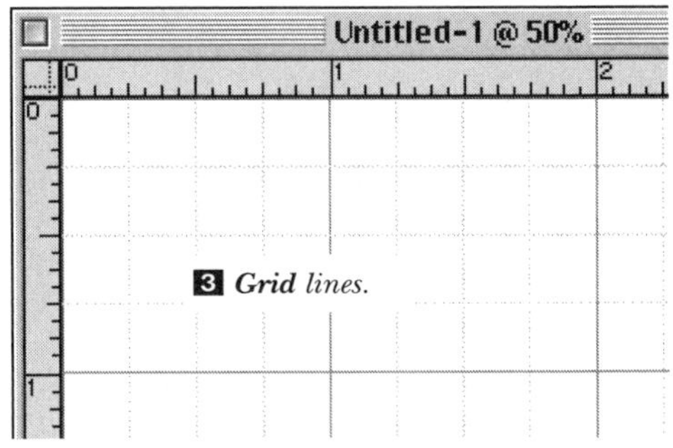

3 *Grid lines.*

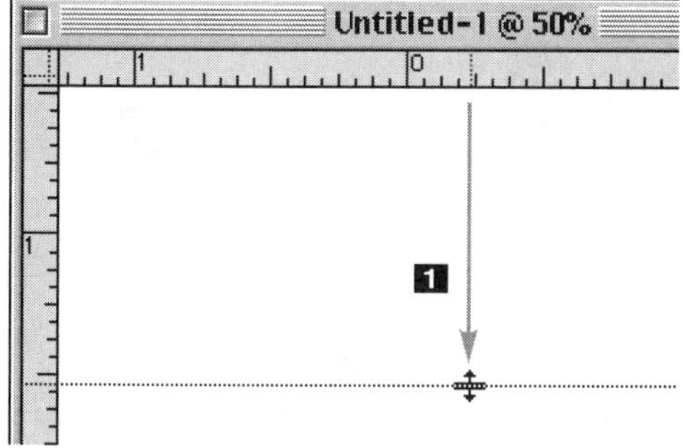

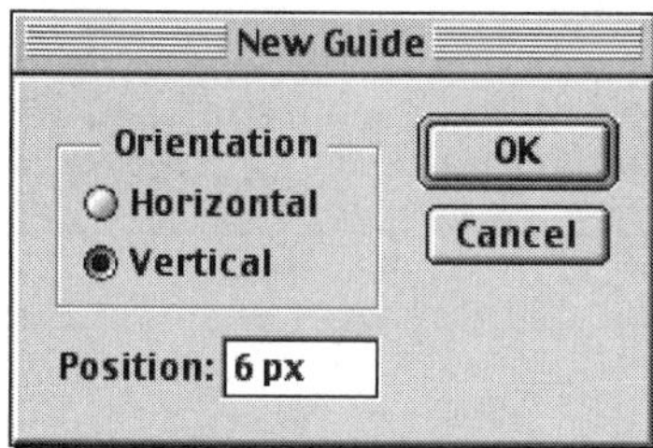

2 *Use the **New Guide** dialog box to place a new guide at a specified location.*

To create a guide:

Make sure the rulers are displayed, then drag from the horizontal or vertical ruler into the image window **1**. With Snap checked, Shift-drag to snap the guide to a ruler increment. If the grid is displayed and View menu > Snap To > Grid is turned on, the guide can be snapped to a grid line. A guide can also be snapped to a selection marquee.

TIP To **lock** all guides so they can't be moved using the Move tool, choose View menu > Lock Guides (Ctrl-Alt-;/Cmd-Option-;).

TIP Alt-drag/Option-drag as you create a guide to **switch** it from vertical to horizontal (or vice versa).

TIP To **move** an existing guide, drag it using the Move tool (make sure the guides aren't locked). Guides will keep their relative positions if you resize the image, provided they're not locked.

TIP You can choose a new guide **color** or **style** in Edit menu > Preferences > Guides & Grid. Double-click a guide with the Move tool to quickly open that dialog box.

To place a guide at a specified location: 6.0!

1. Choose View menu > New Guide.
2. Click Horizontal or Vertical **2**.
3. Enter a Position in any measurement unit.
4. Click OK.

To remove guides:

To remove one guide, drag it out of the image window using the Move tool.
or
To remove all guides, choose View menu > Clear Guides.

To use the Measure tool:

1. Choose the Measure tool (I or Shift-I; it's on the Eyedropper tool pop-out palette—new location).
2. Drag in the image window **1**. The angle (A) and distance (D) of the measure line will be displayed on the Info palette **2**. Shift-drag to constrain the angle to a multiple of 45°.
3. *Optional:* After dragging with the Measure tool, Alt-drag/Option-drag from either end of the line to create a protractor **3**. The angle formed by the two lines will display on the Info palette **4**. You can readjust the angle at any time by dragging either end of the line.
4. Choose another tool when you're finished using the Measure tool. If you reselect it, the measure line will redisplay. To remove a measure line, drag it off the image using the Measure tool.

TIP You can drag a measure line or protractor to another area of the image using the Measure tool. Drag any part of the line except an endpoint, unless you want to change its angle.

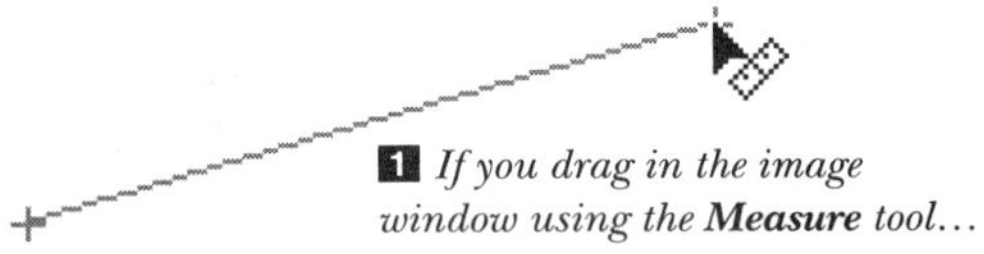

1 *If you drag in the image window using the **Measure** tool...*

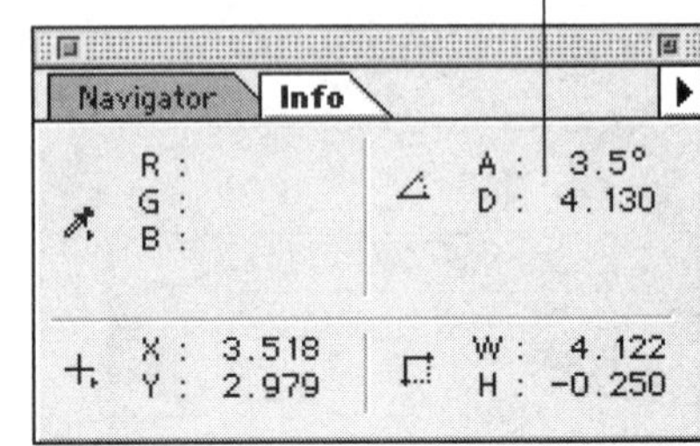

2 *...**Angle** (A) and **distance** (D) readouts will appear on the **Info** palette.*

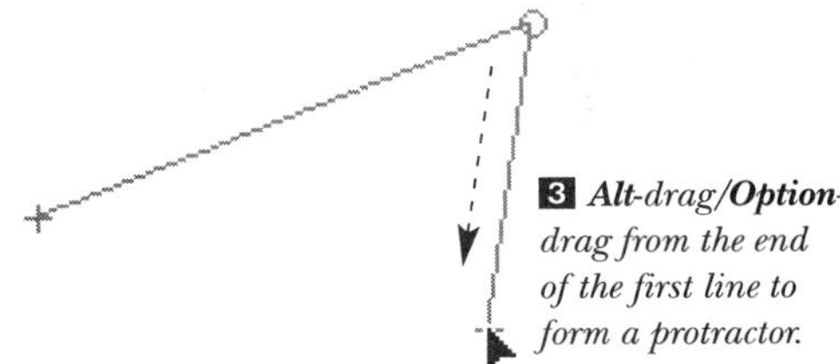

3 ***Alt**-drag/**Option**-drag from the end of the first line to form a protractor.*

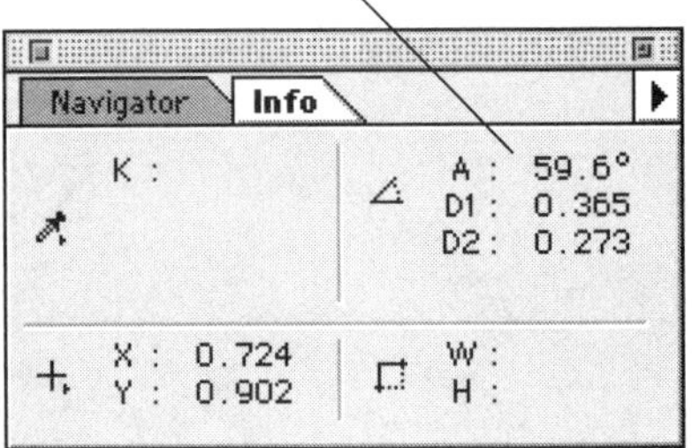

4 *If you create a **protractor**, its **angle** (A) and the distance (length) of each line from its starting point (**D1** and **D2**) will be displayed on the **Info** palette.*

1 *The left side of the* ***Clone Stamp*** *options bar.*

2 *The right side of the* ***Clone Stamp*** *options bar.*

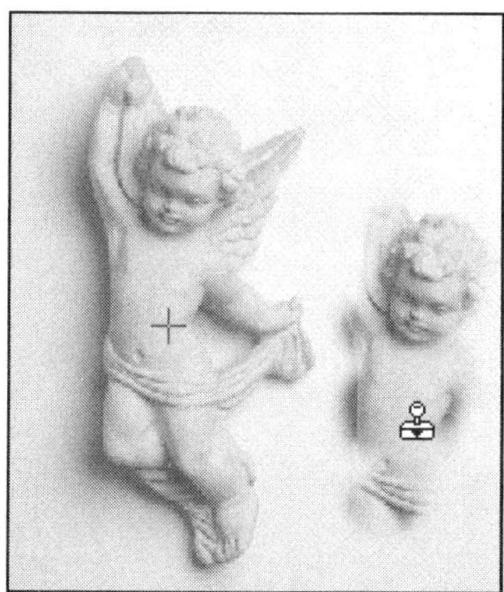

3 *Drag the mouse where you want the clone to appear. To produce this illustration, the* ***Aligned*** *option was turned* ***on*** *for the Clone Stamp tool.*

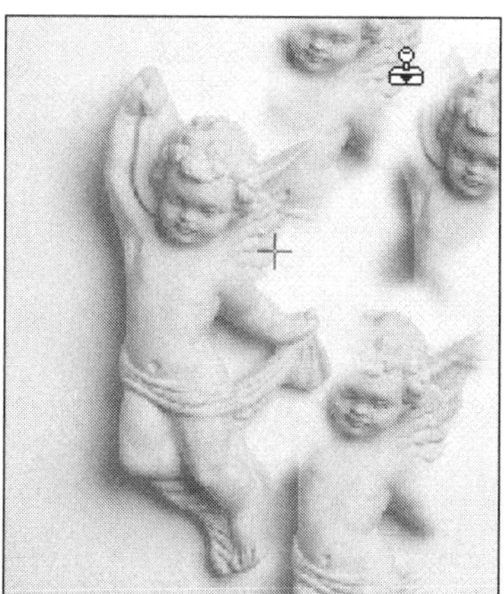

4 ***Uncheck*** *the* ***Aligned*** *option for the Clone Stamp tool to create multiple clones from the same source point.*

The Clone Stamp tool (formerly called the Rubber Stamp tool) is used to clone imagery from one layer to another within the same image or to clone imagery from one image to another.

To clone areas in the same image:

1. Choose the Clone Stamp tool (S or Shift-S).
2. On the Clone Stamp options bar **1**–**2**: 6.0!

   Click the **Painting Brush** arrowhead, then click a tip size that's appropriate for the area you want to clone.
   and
   Choose a blending **Mode**.
   and
   Choose an **Opacity** percentage.
   and
   Check the **Aligned** box to create a single, uninterrupted clone from the same source point. You can release the mouse and drag in another area, or even switch modes or brushes between strokes **3**. Uncheck Aligned to create repetitive clones from the same source point. The crosshair pointer will return to the same source point each time you release the mouse **4**.
   and
   Check the **Use All Layers** box to sample pixels from all currently visible layers that you Alt-click/Option-click over. Uncheck Use All Layers to sample pixels from only the current layer.
3. On the Layers palette, choose the layer that you want to clone from.
4. In the image window, Alt-click/Option-click the area of the layer you want to clone from, to establish a source point. Don't click a transparent part of a layer—there will be nothing to clone.
5. On the same layer, drag the mouse back and forth where you want the clone to appear.
   or

(Continued on the following page)

Choose or create another layer, then drag the mouse. Two pointers will appear on the screen: a crosshair pointer over the source point and a Clone Stamp pointer (or Brush Size pointer) where you drag the mouse. Imagery from the source point will appear where the mouse is dragged, and it will replace any underlying pixels.

Note: If the "Lock transparent pixels" box is checked on the Layers palette, the cloned imagery will only appear where the layer isn't transparent.

6. *Optional:* To establish a new source point to clone from, Alt-click/Option-click a different area in the source image.

TIP You can change options bar settings for the Clone Stamp tool between strokes. To create a "double exposure" effect, choose a low Opacity percentage so the underlying pixels will partially show through the cloned pixels **1**.

TIP To paint areas from earlier stages of the same editing session, use the History Brush tool.

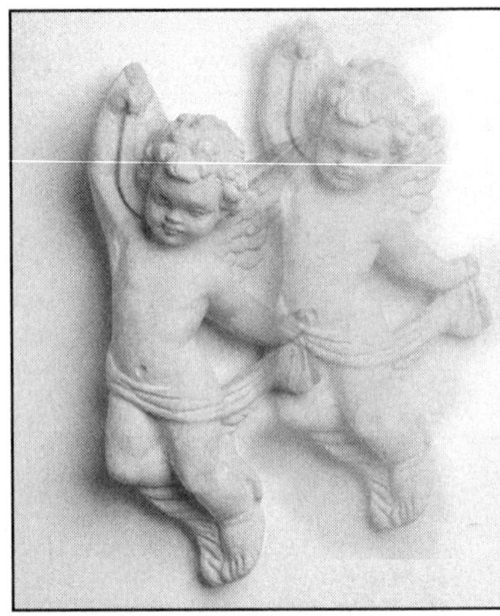

1 *An **Opacity** of 50% was chosen for the Clone Stamp tool to create this double exposure effect.*

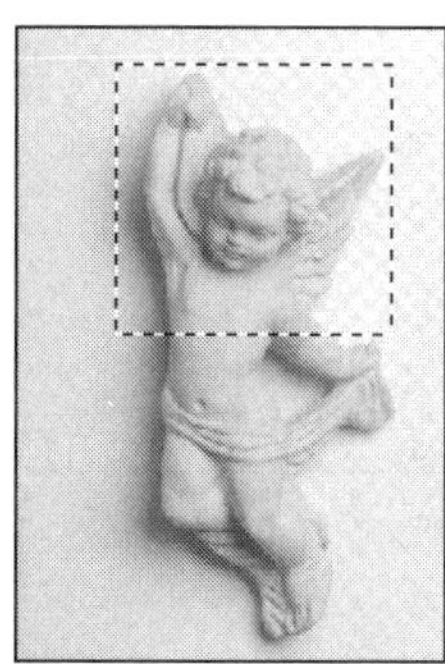

1 *Select an area of an image, then choose Edit menu >* ***Define Pattern****.*

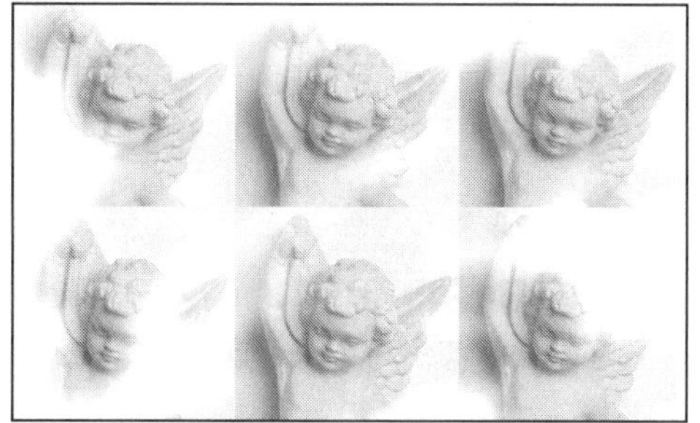

2 *The pattern is then applied in another image using various opacities for the* ***Pattern Stamp*** *tool.*

To use the Pattern Stamp tool:

1. To create a custom pattern, choose the Rectangular Marquee tool, select an area of an image for the tile **1**, choose Edit menu > Define Pattern, type a Name, click OK, then deselect (Ctrl-D/Cmd-D).
2. Choose the Pattern Stamp tool (S or Shift-S). 6.0!
3. On the Pattern Stamp options bar, choose options as per step 2 on the previous page. Check the Aligned box to stamp pattern tiles in a perfect grid, regardless of how many separate strokes you use; uncheck Aligned if you don't want the tiles to align.

   Click the Pattern arrowhead, then click a pattern on the picker **3**. Your custom pattern, from step 1, should be the last pattern listed.
4. Drag on a layer in the same image or in another image to stamp the pattern **2**. No source point is required for this tool.

TIP Right-click/Control-click in the image window to choose a blending mode.

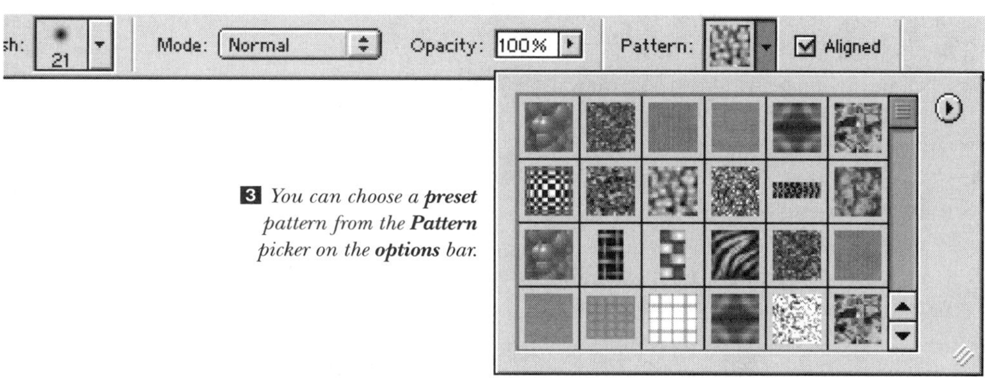

3 *You can choose a* ***preset*** *pattern from the* ***Pattern*** *picker on the* ***options*** *bar.*

Pattern Stamp

You can use the Clone Stamp tool to clone imagery from one image to another. Try using it to gather imagery from different open images into one final image. To create a brushstroke version of an image or images, clone to a new document that has a white or solid-colored background using a soft brush.

To clone from image to image:

1. Open two images, and position the two windows side by side.
2. If both images are color, choose the same image mode for both. You can also clone between a color image and a grayscale image. *Note:* Choose the Don't Flatten option to preserve layers.
3. Choose the Clone Stamp tool (S or Shift S).
4. On the Clone Stamp options bar 1–2:
   6.0! Click the **Painting Brush** arrowhead, then click a brush tip.
   and
   Choose a blending **Mode**.
   and
   Choose an **Opacity**.
   and
   Check the **Aligned** box to reproduce a continuous area from the source point or uncheck the Aligned box to produce multiple clones from the source point.
5. Click in the image window that you want to clone to, and choose a layer for the clone.
6. Alt-click/Option-click the area of the source (non-active) image that you want to clone from 3–4.
7. Drag back and forth on the destination (active) image to make the clone appear.

1 *The left side of the **Clone Stamp** options bar.*

2 *The right side of the **Clone Stamp** options bar.*

***Source** image.*

***Destination** image.*

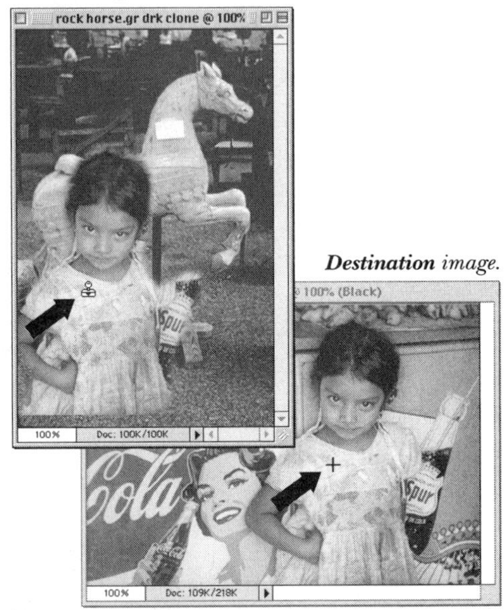

3 ***Alt-click/Option-click** on the **non-active** image to establish a **source** point, then drag back and forth in short strokes on the **active** (destination) image to make the **clone** appear.*

4 *To create this effect, an image was cloned to a new document with a white background.*

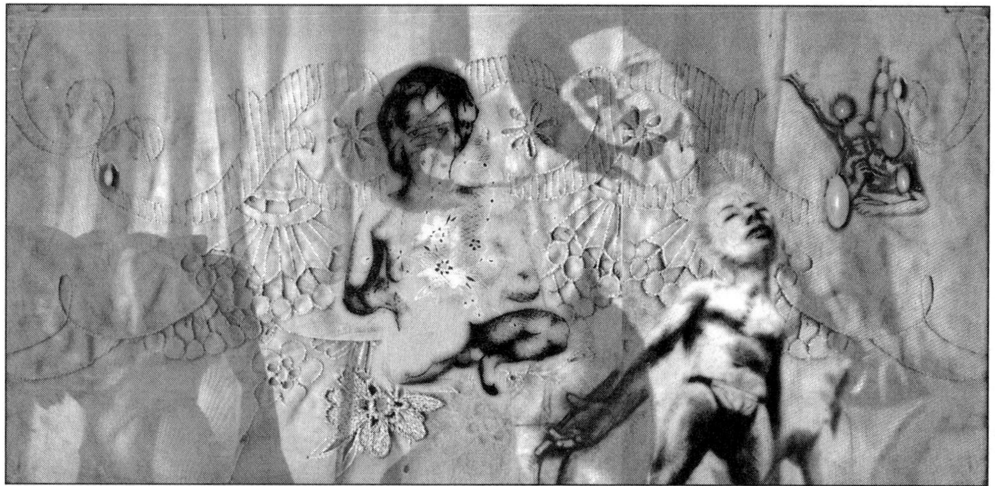

***Physique Medley**, David Humphrey. To produce this image, Humphrey composited scanned embroidery and his own charcoal drawings and photographs, among other things. He adjusted luminosity levels of the various components on individual layers using blending modes (Darken, Multiply) and the Eraser and Burn tools.*

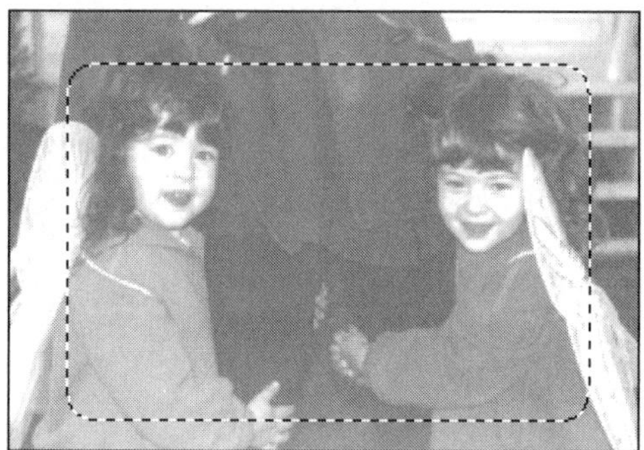

1 *The original image, with a **feathered** selection.*

2 *After inversing the selection and pressing Delete.*

Apply the Feather command to fade the edge of a selection by a specified number of pixels inward and outward from the marquee. A feather radius of 5, for example, would create a feather area 10 pixels wide.

Note: The feather won't be visible until the selection is modified with a painting tool, copied/pasted, moved, or filled, or a filter or Image menu command is applied to it.

To feather an existing selection:

1. Choose Select menu > Feather (Ctrl-Alt-D/Cmd-Option-D).
2. Enter a number up to 250 in the Feather Radius field. The width of the feather is affected by the image resolution. The higher the image resolution, the wider you need to make the feather Radius.
3. Click OK (Enter/Return) **1**–**2**. *Note:* If the feather radius is too wide for the selection area, the message "No pixels are more than 50% selected" will appear.

TIP To specify a feather radius for a selection before it's created, choose a Marquee or Lasso tool and enter a Feather value on the options bar.

To eliminate a noticeable seam after pasting or moving layer pixels, use the Defringe command. It recolors pixels on the edge of the selection with pixel colors from just inside the edge within a specified radius.

Note: If the imagery you moved or pasted was originally on a black background and was anti-aliased, you can try using Select menu > Matting > Remove Black Matte command to remove unwanted remnants from the black background. Choose Select menu > Matting > Remove White Matte command if the imagery was originally on a white background.

To defringe a layer:

1. With the paste layer chosen, choose Layer menu > Matting > Defringe.
2. Enter a Width for the Defringe area **1**. Try a low number first (1, 2, or 3 pixels) so your edges don't lose definition. Some non-edge areas may also be affected.
3. Click OK.

The Smooth command adds unselected pixels to, or removes unselected pixels from, a selection from within a specified radius. It's a good way to eliminate extraneous selection areas, particularly after using the Magic Wand tool.

To smooth a selection edge:

1. Choose Select menu > Modify > Smooth.
2. Enter a Sample Radius value (1–100 pixels) **2**. If most pixels within the specified radius are selected, any unselected pixels in that radius will be added to the selection; if most pixels are unselected within the specified radius, any selected pixels will be removed from the selection.
3. Click OK **3**–**4**.

1 *Use the* ***Defringe*** *command to make montaged imagery look more seamless.*

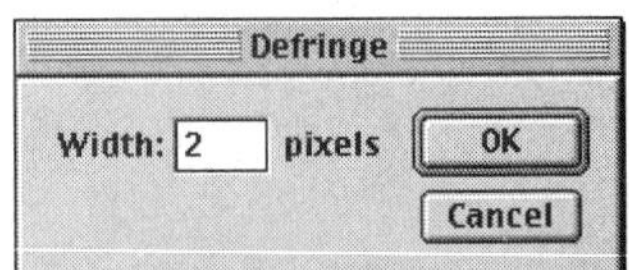

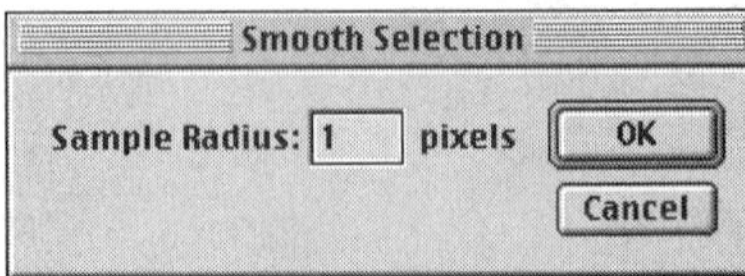

1 *Use the* ***Smooth Selection*** *command to clean up selections.*

3 *The original Magic Wand tool selection.*

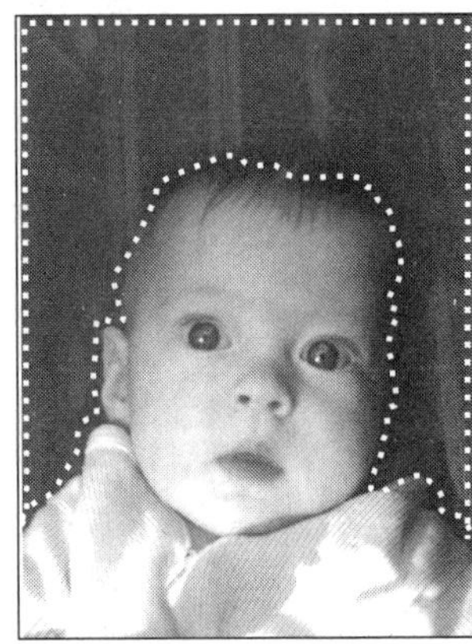

4 *After applying the* ***Smooth*** *command, Sample Radius of 3.*

LAYERS 7

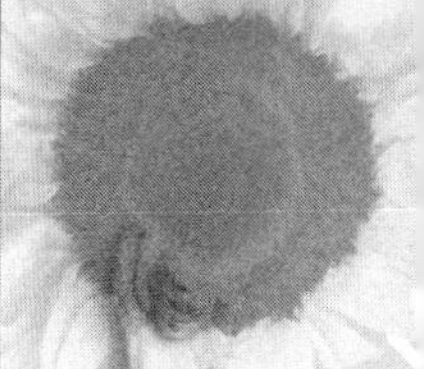

Chapter topics

Create a new layer
Turn a selection into a layer
Duplicate a layer
Hide/show layers
Flip a layer
Delete a layer
Transform a layer
Restack a layer
Convert the Background into a layer
Create a Background for an image
Move a layer
Create a layer set
Lock a layer
Create a new fill layer
Drag-and-drop/copy a layer to another file
Merge or flatten layers

For additional layer topics, see Chapter 14

LAYERS ARE LIKE clear acetate sheets: opaque where there is imagery and transparent where there is no imagery. To each layer, you can assign a different opacity and mode to control how that layer blends with the layers below it. You can change the stacking order of layers, and you can also assign a layer mask to any layer. Only one layer can be edited at a time, which means you can easily modify one part of an image without disturbing the other layers.

If you choose Contents: White or Background Color for a new image (File menu > New), the bottommost area of the image will be the Background, which is not a layer. If you choose Contents: Transparent, the bottommost component of the image will be a layer. More layers can be added to an image at any time.

Layers are listed on the Layers palette from topmost to bottommost, with the Background, of course, at the bottom of the list. The layer that is currently highlighted (active) on the palette is the only layer that can be edited. Click a layer name to activate that layer. The name of the currently active layer (or the Background) is listed on the image window title bar.

The currently ***active*** *layer (note the brush icon)*

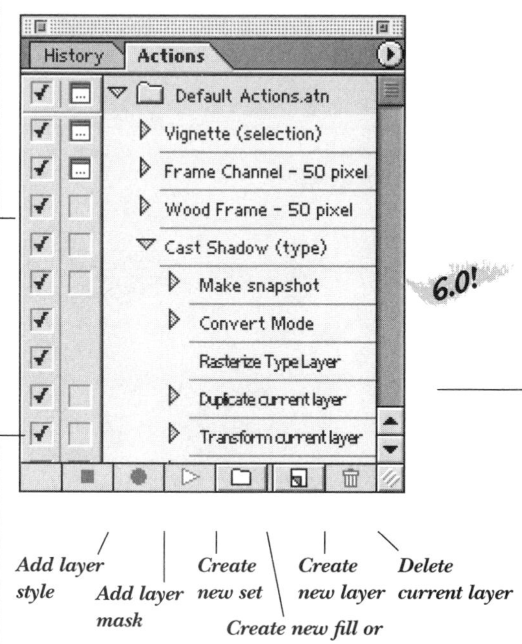

Add layer style ***Add layer mask*** ***Create new set*** ***Create new fill or adjustment layer*** ***Create new layer*** ***Delete current layer***

Show/hide layer

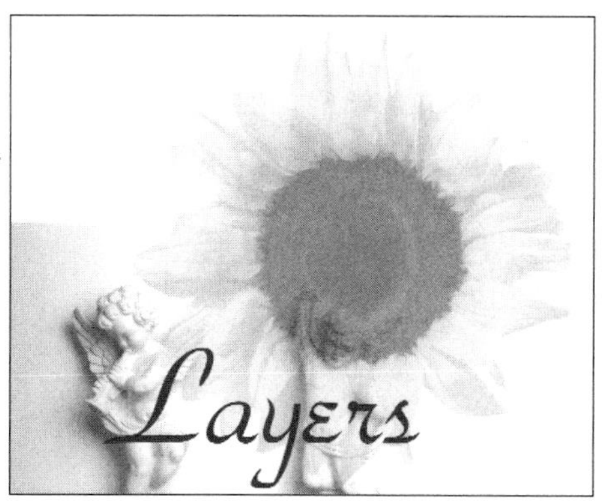

Layers Palette

If you've already learned how to paste a selection or create type, you know that both operations create a new layer automatically. And in Chapter 9, you'll learn about a special variety of layers called adjustment layers, which are used to preview color adjustment effects on underlying layers. In this chapter, you'll learn the layer basics.

Beware! If you save your image in any file format except Photoshop (.psd) or advanced TIFF (.tif), all layers will be flattened and any transparency in the bottommost layer will become opaque white. Also, if you change image modes (e.g., from RGB to CMYK), click Don't Flatten or Don't Merge if you want to preserve layers.

Note: An image can contain as many layers as available memory and storage allow, but since the pixel areas on a layer occupy storage space, when you finish a large image, you can merge or flatten its layers together to reduce its storage size **1**.

To create a new layer:

1. To create a layer with 100% opacity and Normal mode, click the Create new layer button at the bottom of the Layers palette **2** and skip the remaining steps.
   or
   To choose options for the new layer as it's created, choose New Layer from the Layers palette command menu or Alt-click/Option-click the Create new layer button at the bottom of the palette **2**, then follow the remaining steps.
2. *Do any of the following optional steps:*

   Enter a new name for the layer in the Name field **3**.

   Click the Group With Previous Layer box to make the new layer a part of a clipping group (see page 247).

   6.0! Choose a color for the area on the Layers palette behind the layer's eye and brush/link icons.

   Choose a different blending Mode or Opacity (both can be changed later).

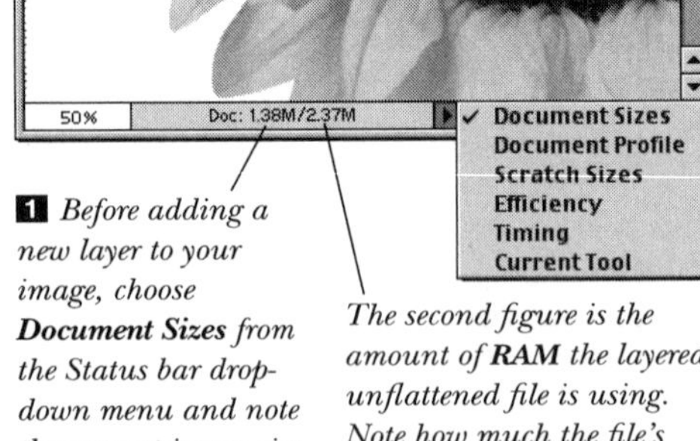

1 *Before adding a new layer to your image, choose **Document Sizes** from the Status bar drop-down menu and note the current image size.*

*The second figure is the amount of **RAM** the layered, unflattened file is using. Note how much the file's storage size increases when you add a new layer. The image in this illustration contains two layers.*

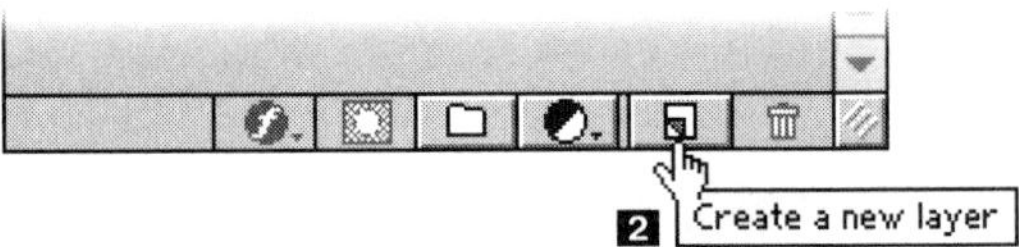

2

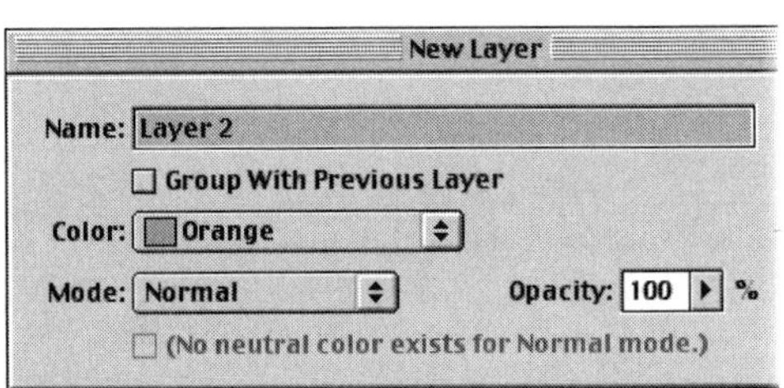

3 *Enter a name and choose options for a layer in the **New Layer** dialog box.*

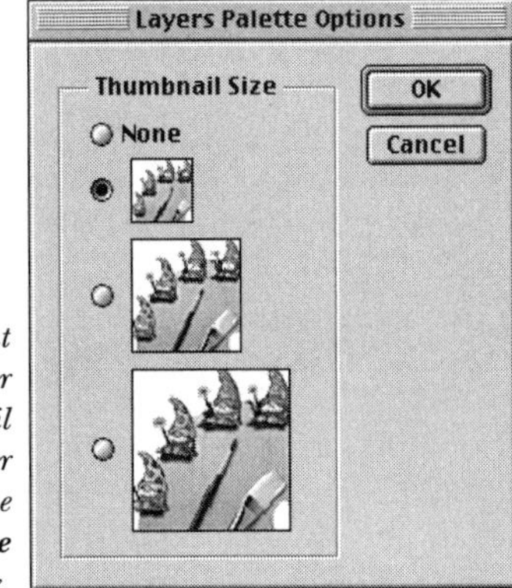

4 *Click a different **Thumbnail Size** or turn off thumbnail display altogether (None) in the **Layers Palette Options** dialog box.*

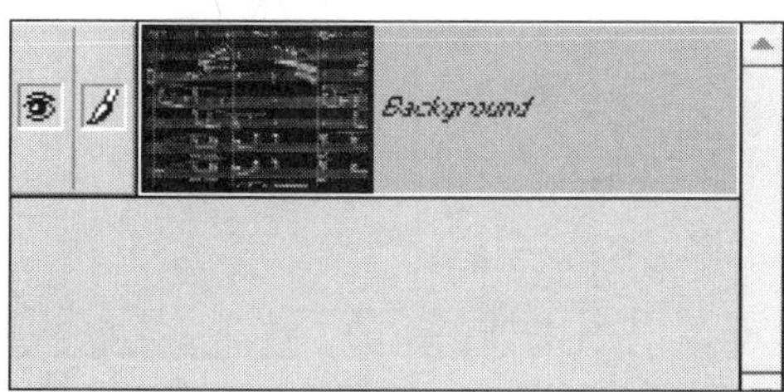

1 *A detail of the Layers palette, showing the original **Background**.*

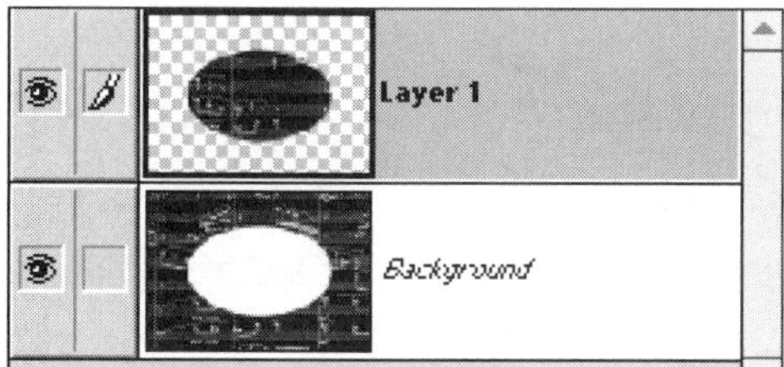

2 *After choosing the **Layer Via Cut**, a selection is cut from the Background and placed on its own layer.*

3 ***Right-click/Control-click**, then choose **Duplicate Layer** from the context menu.*

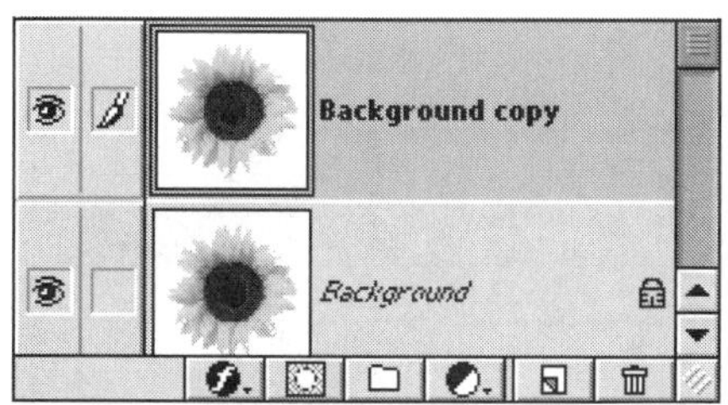

4 *The **duplicate** layer appears on the palette.*

3. Click OK. The new layer will appear directly above the previously active layer.

TIP To improve Photoshop's performance if you're working on a large file, choose Palette Options from the Layers palette menu, then click the smallest thumbnail size (**4**, previous page).

To turn a selection into a layer:

1. Create a selection.
2. To place a **copy** of the selected pixels on a new layer and leave the original layer untouched, choose Layer menu > New > Layer Via Copy (Ctrl-J/Cmd-J).
   or
   To place the selected pixels on a new layer and **remove** them from the original layer, choose Layer menu > New > Layer Via Cut (Ctrl-Shift-J/Cmd-Shift-J) **1**–**2**.
3. *Optional:* Click the eye icon for the original layer to temporarily hide it from view.

To duplicate a layer in the same image:

To create a new layer with a generic name, drag the name of the layer you want to duplicate over the Create new layer button at the bottom of the Layers palette. The duplicate layer will appear above the original layer, and it will be the active layer.
or
To name the duplicate as you create it, Right-click/Control-click the name of the layer you want to duplicate and choose Duplicate Layer or Alt-drag/Option-drag the layer over the Create new layer button. Type a name for the duplicate layer in the "As" field, then click OK **3**–**4**.

We can think of at least two reasons to hide the layers you're not currently working on. One, to remove them as a visual distraction and two, to improve Photoshop's performance.

Note: If you're going to be printing your image, remember that only visible layers will print. Ditto for merging layers: Only visible layers can be merged (you'll learn about merging and flattening at the end of this chapter). Be especially careful when using the Flatten Image command—it discards hidden layers.

To hide or show layers:

Click the eye icon on the Layers palette for any individual layer you want to hide **1**–**3**. Click in the eye column again to redisplay the layer.

or

Drag in the eye column to hide or show multiple layers.

or

Alt-click/Option-click an eye icon to hide all other layers except the one you click on (including the Background). Alt-click/Option-click again to redisplay all layers.

or

Right-click/Control-click in the eye column and choose "Show/Hide all other layers" from the context menu **4**.

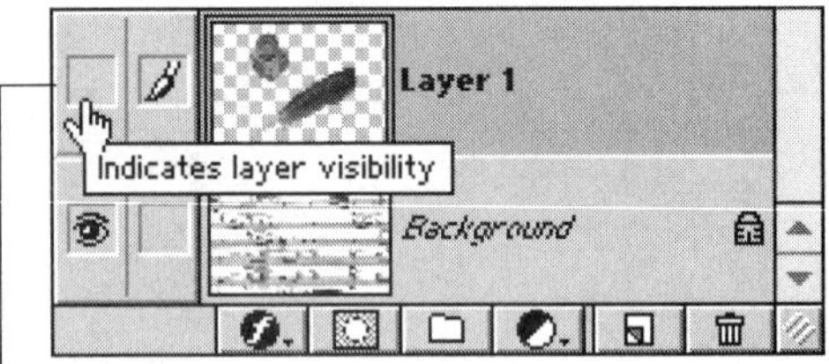

1 *Click the **eye** icon to **hide** a layer. Click again to **redisplay** it.*

2 *Layer 1 **hidden**.*

3 *Layer 1 redisplayed.*

4 *Choose a command from a **context** menu.*

Hide/Show Layers

1 *The original image.*

2 *Layer 1* ***flipped*** *horizontally.*

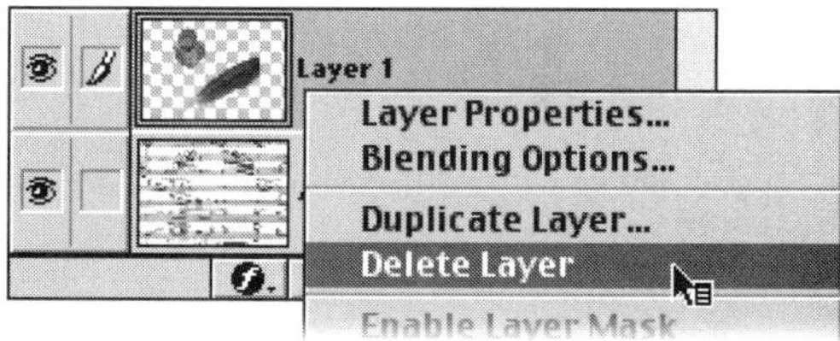

3 *Deleting Layer 1 via the context menu.*

4 *After* ***deleting*** *Layer 1.*

To flip a layer:

1. On the Layers palette, choose the layer that you want to flip. Any layers that are linked to the active layer will also flip.
2. Choose Edit menu > Transform > Flip Horizontal **1**–**2** or Flip Vertical.

To delete a layer:

On the Layers palette, click the name of the layer you want to delete. Then click the trash button and click Yes or Alt-click/Option-click the trash button to bypass the prompt.

or

Right-click/Control-click the name of the layer you want to delete, choose Delete Layer from the context menu, then click Yes **3**–**4**.

TIP Change your mind? No problem. Choose Edit menu > Undo or click a prior state on the History palette.

To transform (scale, rotate, skew, distort, or apply perspective to) a layer by dragging:

1. On the Layers palette, activate the layer you want to transform. Any layers that are linked to the active layer will also transform. You can't transform a 16 bits/channel image.

   Optional: Create a selection to limit the transformation to those pixels.

2. Choose Edit menu > Transform > Scale, Rotate, Skew, Distort, or Perspective. A solid bounding box will appear around the opaque part of the layer.

3. *Optional:* To transform the layer or selection from a location in other than its center, move the reference point **1**. You can even move it outside the bounding box.

4. *Note:* If you're going to perform multiple transformations, to save time and preserve image quality, after performing this step for the first command, choose and then perform additional transform commands, and then accept them all at once (step 5).

   To **Scale** the layer horizontally and vertically, drag a corner handle **1**. To scale only the horizontal or vertical dimension, drag a side handle. Shift-drag to scale proportionately. Alt-drag/Option-drag to scale from the reference point.

   For **Rotate**, position the pointer near a bounding box handle, either inside or outside the box (the pointer will become a double-headed arrow), then drag in a circular direction **2**. Shift-drag to constrain the rotation to a multiple of 15°.

   For **Skew**, drag a corner handle to reposition just that handle or drag a side handle to skew along the current horizontal or vertical axis. Alt-drag/Option-drag to skew symmetrically from the center of the layer.

   For **Distort** **3**, drag a corner handle to freely reposition just that handle or drag

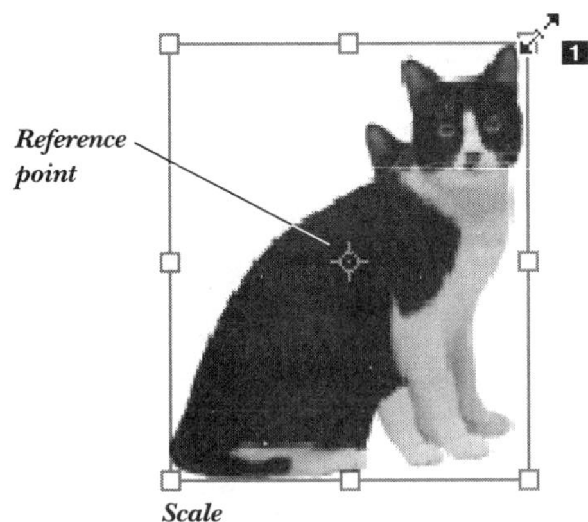

Scale

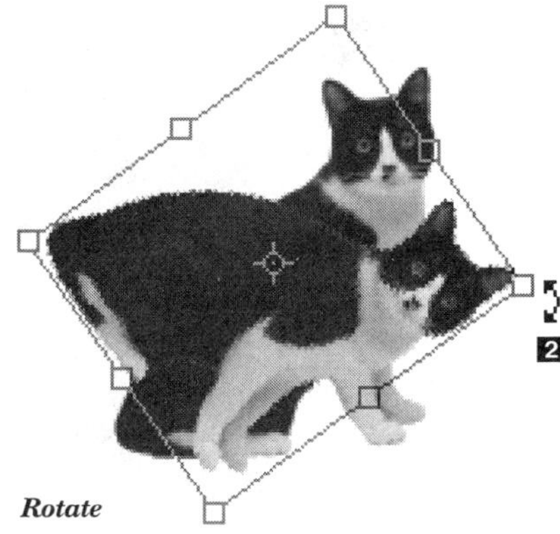

Rotate

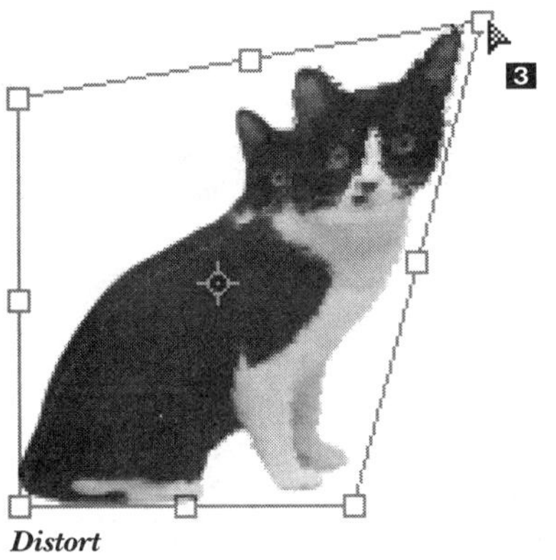

Distort

Transform Commands

General information

Choose an **interpolation** method for the transform commands in Edit menu > Preferences > General (Ctrl-K/Cmd-K). Bicubic (Better)—the slowest method—causes the least degradation to the image.

To **repeat** the last transformation, choose Edit menu > Transform > Again (Ctrl-Shift-T/Cmd-Shift-T).

To transform a **duplicate** of a selection, hold down Alt/Option as you choose the command or use this shortcut: Ctrl-Alt-T/Cmd-Option-T.

In addition to transforming a layer, you can also transform an **alpha channel**, a **selection border** (see page 95), a **path** (see page 265), or an unlinked, active **layer mask**.

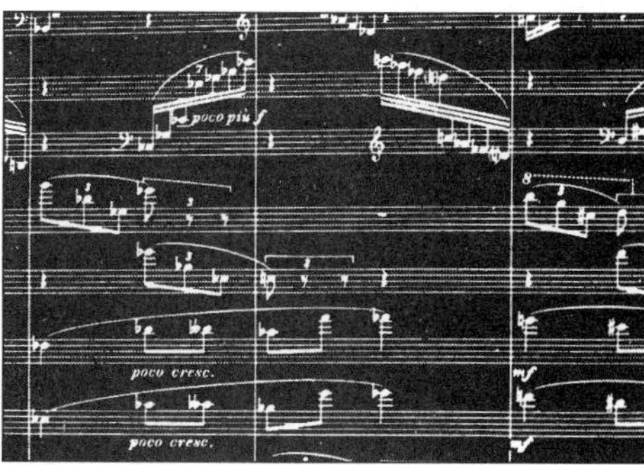

1 *The original image.*

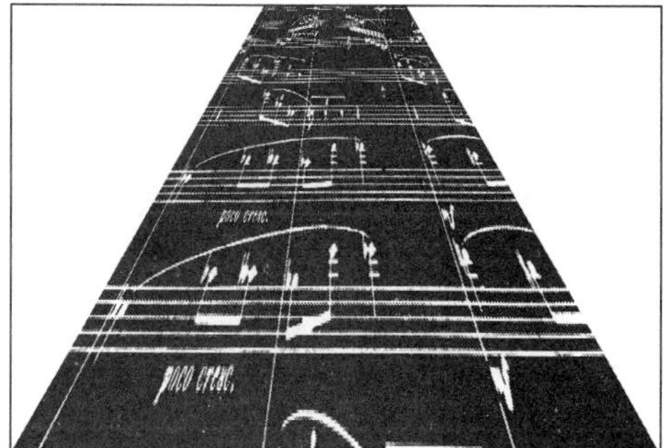

2 *A **perspective** transformation.*

a side handle to distort the side of the bounding box along the horizontal and/or vertical axis. Alt-drag/Option-drag to distort symmetrically from the center of the layer. Distort can be more drastic than Skew.

For **Perspective**, drag a corner handle along the horizontal or vertical axis to create one-point perspective along that axis **1**–**2**. The adjacent corner will move in unison. Or drag a side handle to skew along the current horizontal or vertical axis.

5. To accept the transformation, double-click inside the bounding box or click the ✓ on the options bar (Enter/Return). To cancel the transformation, click the ✕ (Esc).

TIP To undo the last handle modification, choose Edit menu > Undo.

TIP To move the entire layer (or selection), drag inside the transform bounding box.

Once you're acquainted with the individual Transform commands, you'll probably want to start using the Free Transform command, especially if you want to perform a series of transformations. With Free Transform, the various commands are accessed using keyboard shortcuts—you don't have to choose each command individually from a menu. And best of all, image data is resampled only once: when you accept the changes.

To free transform:

1. On the Layers palette, activate the layer you want to transform. Any layers that are linked to the active layer will also transform. You can't transform a 16-bits/channel image.

   Optional: Create a selection to limit the transformation to those pixels.

2. Choose Edit menu > Free Transform (Ctrl-T/Cmd-T).
   or
   Choose the Move tool and check Show Bounding Box on the option bar.
   6.0! *Note:* This option can interfere with the Auto Select Layer option (see page 130).

3. Follow step 4 on the previous page, with these exceptions:

   To **Skew**, Ctrl-Shift-drag/Cmd-Shift-drag.

   To **Distort**, Ctrl-drag/Cmd-drag.

   To apply **Perspective**, Ctrl-Alt-Shift-drag/ Cmd-Option-Shift-drag a corner handle.

   The transformation will automatically occur from the center of the layer image.

5. To accept the transformation, double-click inside the bounding box or click the ✓ on the options bar (Enter/Return). To cancel the transformation, click the ✕ (Esc). You must accept or cancel to return to normal editing.

TIP As you transform a layer or a selection, note the width (W), height (H), rotation angle (A), and horizontal skew (H), or vertical skew (V) readout(s) on the options bar or the Info palette.

What's left?

If you transform a **layer** (or a selection on a layer), any empty space remaining after the transformation will be replaced by layer **transparency**. If you transform a selection on the **Background**, any remaining empty space will be filled with the current **Background color**.

Free Transform

6.0!

1 *Sections of the options bar with the* ***Free Transform*** *command chosen:*

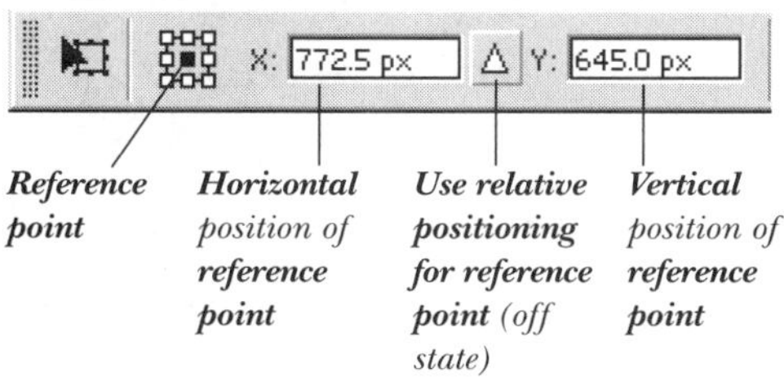

2

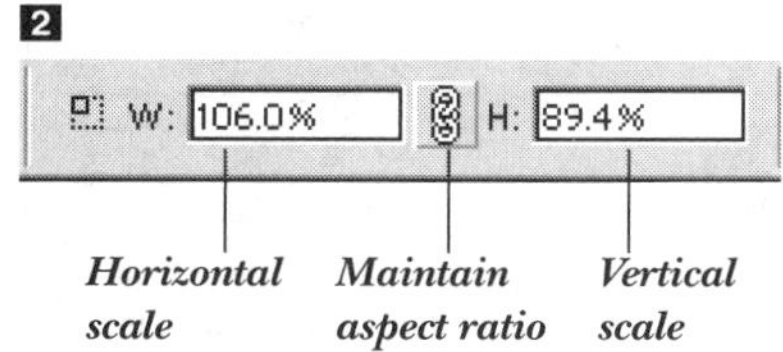

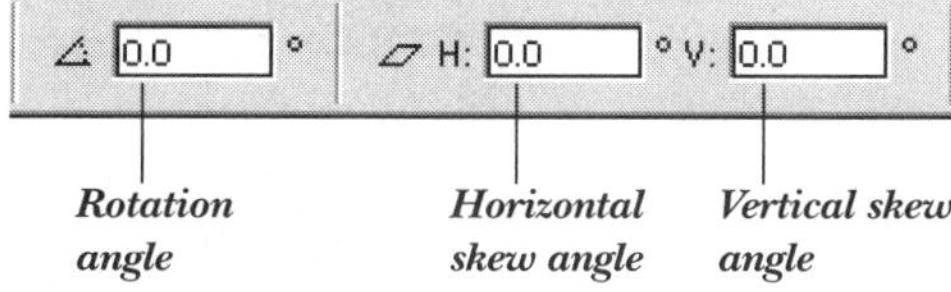

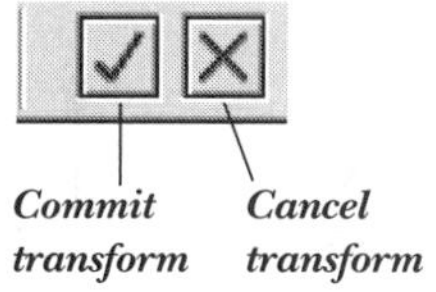

Follow these instructions if you'd rather transform a layer by entering exact numeric values than by dragging the mouse. The controls for numeric transforms display on the options bar whenever a transform function is chosen. 6.0!

To transform a layer by entering numeric values:

1. On the Layers palette, activate the layer that you want to transform. Any layers that are linked to it will also transform.
2. Choose Edit menu > Free Transform (Ctrl-T/Cmd-T).
3. On the options bar, choose the reference point location for the move, rotate, and flip transformations by clicking one of the nine little reference point squares.

   or

   In the document window, drag the reference point to the desired location.

   or

   Click the "Use relative positioning for reference point" button to set the X and Y fields to 0; otherwise those values will reflect the absolute position of the reference point as measured from the upper left corner of the layer. (Click the icon again to turn off the option. To change the units, Right-click/Control-click either value.)
4. Do any of the following:

   To **move** the layer, enter new X and Y Position values **1**.

   Note: To move a layer or selection numerically, you must first set a reference point using the Reference point location icon. Otherwise the reference point, not the image, will move.

   To **rotate** the layer, enter a rotation angle.

   To **scale** the layer, enter W (width) and/or H (height) values **2**. (Right-click/Control-click either value to choose different units from the pop-up menu.) Click the Maintain Aspect Ratio

(Continued on the following page)

button to preserve the current width-to-height ratio.

To **skew** the layer, enter a Horizontal and/or Vertical Skew angle (the amount of slant) **3**.

5. To accept the transformation, double-click inside the bounding box or click the ✓ on the options bar (Enter/Return). To cancel the transformation, click the ✕ (Esc).

TIP Choose the Measure tool (Shift-I), drag in the image window to define an angle, then with the Measure tool still selected, choose Edit menu > Transform > Rotate. The layer will rotate automatically along the angle you defined.

To restack a layer:

1. On the Layers palette, click the name of the layer you want to restack.
2. Drag the layer name upward or downward on the palette, and release the mouse when a dark horizontal line appears in the desired location **1**–**4**.

TIP You can also restack an active layer by choosing Layer menu > Arrange > Bring to Front, Bring Forward, Send Backward, or Send to Back (see the shortcuts below). A layer can't be stacked below the Background.

TIP To move the Background upward on the list, it must first be converted into a layer (see page 129).

Restack an active layer

Windows		Macintosh	
Bring Forward	Ctrl]	Bring Forward	Cmd]
Bring to Front	Ctrl Shift]	Bring to Front	Cmd Shift]
Send Backward	Ctrl [	Send Backward	Cmd [
Send to Back	Ctrl Shift [	Send to Back	Cmd Shift [

1 *The original image.*

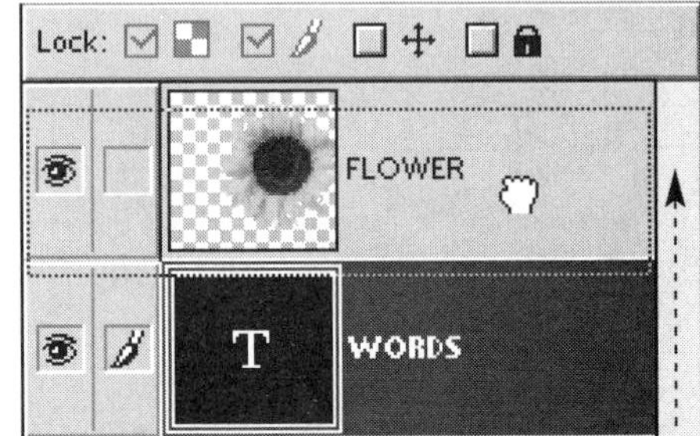

2 *Dragging the WORDS layer* ***upward****.*

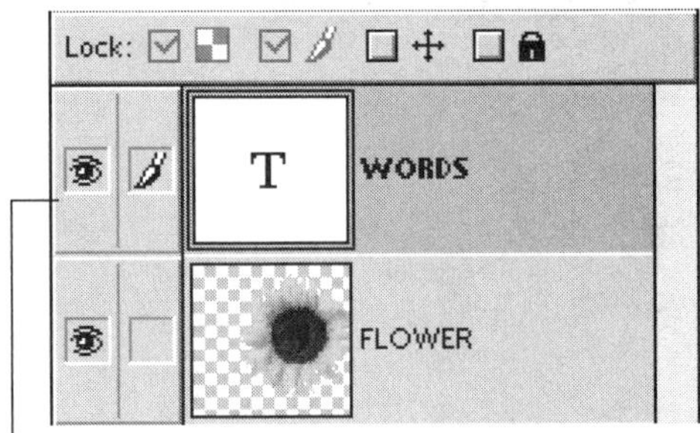

3 *Now the WORDS layer is above the FLOWER layer.*

4 *Here's how it looks.*

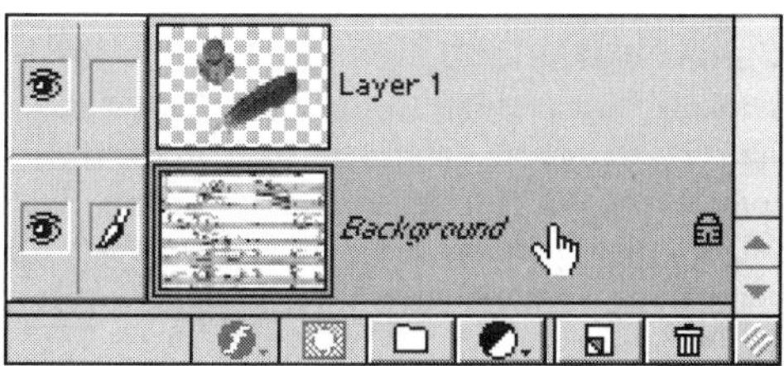

1 *Double-click the* ***Background****.*

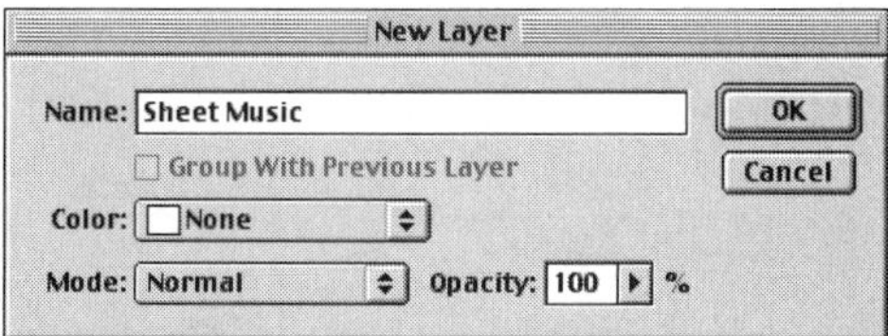

2 ***Name*** *the layer.*

3 *The former Background is now a* ***layer****.*

The standard things that you can do to a layer (e.g., move it upward or downward in the layer stack, choose a blending mode or opacity for it, or create a layer mask for it) can't be done to the Background—unless you first convert it into a layer.

To convert the Background into a layer:

Double-click the Background on the Layers palette **1**, type a new Name **2**, and choose a Mode and Opacity for the layer, then click OK **3**.

or

Alt-double-click/Option-double-click the Background on the Layers palette to bypass the dialog box. *6.0!*

If you need to create a Background for a file that doesn't have one, you can convert an existing layer into the Background (new to Photoshop 6.0).

To convert a layer into the Background: *6.0!*

1. Choose a layer.
2. Choose Layer menu > New > Background From Layer (at the top of the Layer menu). The new Background will be placed at the bottom of the stack on the Layers palette.

To move multiple layers in unison, see page 249.

To move a layer:

1. On the Layers palette, choose the layer you want to move.
2. Choose the Move tool (V) or hold down Ctrl/Cmd.
3. Drag in the image window. The entire layer will move 2–3.

TIP Press an arrow key with the Move tool chosen to move an active layer one pixel at a time. Press Shift-arrow to move a layer 10 screen pixels at a time. (Don't use Alt/Option arrow—that shortcut duplicates the layer.)

TIP If pixels are moved beyond the existing edge of the image, don't worry—they'll be saved with the image.

TIP If the Auto Select Layer box is checked (options bar), you can quickly select a layer by clicking any visible pixels in that layer with the Move tool. However, if this option is on, you may not be able to drag any area of a chosen layer that has an opacity below 50%.

TIP For faster previewing if high resolution images when using the Move tool, choose Edit menu > Preferences > Display & Cursors, then check the Use Pixel Doubling box. Pixels will temporarily double in size while you drag (they'll be half their normal resolution).

Quick layer select

With the Move tool chosen, Right-click/Control-click in the image window and choose a layer from the context menu 1. (Ctrl-right-click/Cmd-Control-click with any other tool selected.) Only layers containing non-transparent pixels under the pointer will appear on the menu.

With the Move tool chosen, Ctrl-click/Cmd-click an object in the image window to quickly activate that object's layer. (*Mac OS:* Cmd-Option-Control-click with any other tool selected.)

1 *Choosing a layer from a context menu.*

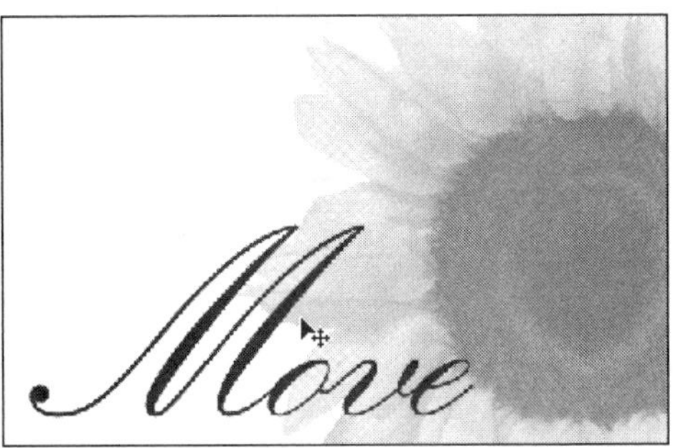

2 *The original image.*

3 *After **moving** the type layer with the **Move** tool.*

Out, set, Out!

To move a layer out of its set, drag the layer name over the current set name or over another set name or above or below a layer name outside the set.

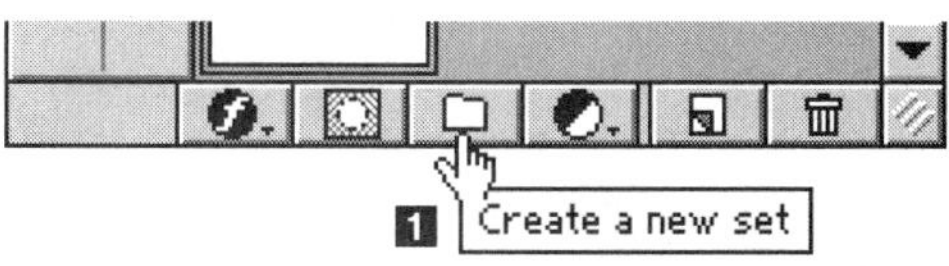

1

Click the triangle to expand or contract the layer set list.

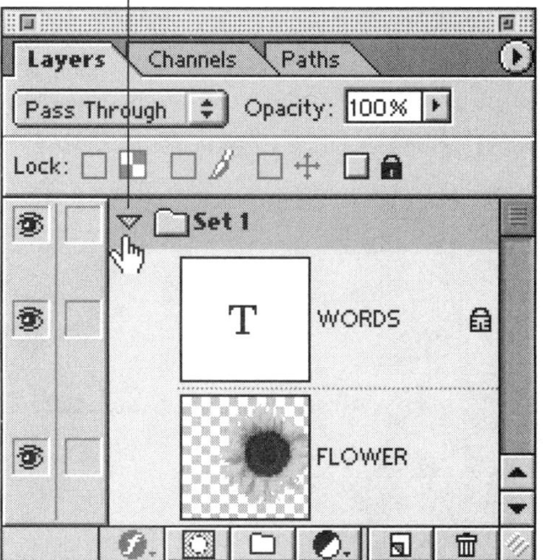

2 *The WORDS and FLOWER layers were dragged into the **Set 1** folder.*

Lock position *Lock all*

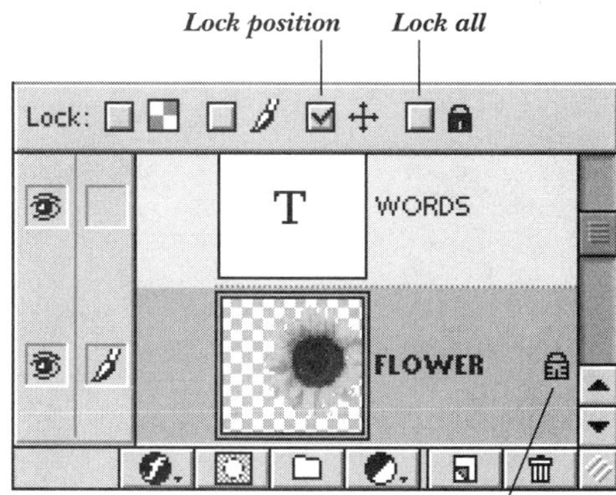

3 *The lock icon appears next to the layer **name.***

Photoshop 6 introduces a very useful organization tool: layer sets. Once layers are organized into a set, you can display just the name of the set on the Layers palette or you can click the arrow to reveal all the layer names within the set **2**. Sets make the Layers palette easier to work with, particularly for images that contain many layers.

The adjustment layers and the blending modes of layers within a set affect only the layers within that set. So another good reason to use sets is to limit the effect of blending modes and adjustment layers to a group of layers. Furthermore, like any individual layer, a whole set can be modified by a layer mask. With the exception of Pass Through blending mode (the default mode for a set), a layer set behaves as though all the layers in the set were merged into one.

To create a layer set: 6.0!

1. Click the Create new set button at the bottom of the Layers palette **1**.
   or
   Choose Layer menu > New > Layer Set, change the Name, Color, blending Mode, or Opacity setting for the new set, if desired, then click OK.
3. On the Layers palette, drag each layer you want to include in the set onto the set's folder icon **2**.

The new Lock feature in Photoshop 6 helps to prevent inadvertent edits.

To lock a layer: 6.0!

1. On the Layers palette, choose the layer you want to lock.
2. Check the "Lock position" box to lock only the layer's location **3**. Now the layer can't be moved, but its pixels can still be edited.
   or
   Check the "Lock all" box to protect the layer from any and all edits.

TIP To lock transparent pixels or image pixels (the first two checkboxes), see page 133.

Layer Sets; Lock a Layer

6.0!

A fill layer works like an adjustment layer, except in this case it contains a solid color, gradient, or pattern. Like an adjustment layer, a fill layer can be edited or removed without affecting any other layers. (Read about adjustment layers on pages 151–155.)

To create a new Fill layer:

1. On the Layers palette, activate the layer that you want the fill layer to appear above (you can restack it later).
1. Choose Solid Color, Gradient, or Pattern from the "Create new fill or adjustment layer" pop-up menu at the bottom of the Layers palette **1**.
   or
   To choose options for the Layer as you create it, choose Layer menu > New Fill Layer > Solid Color, Gradient, or Pattern, then do any of the following: Enter a Name for the layer; choose a Color for the area on the Layers palette behind the layer's eye and brush/link icons; choose a different Opacity or Mode; or click the Group With Previous Layer box to make the new layer a part of a clipping group (see page 247). Click OK. All of these options can be changed later.
2. For a **Solid Color** layer, choose a color from the Color Picker, then click OK.

   For a **Gradient** layer, choose from the gradient picker and set its Style, Angle, and Scale. (For the Reverse, Dither, or Align with Layer options, see page 212).

   For a **Pattern** layer, choose from the pattern picker and choose a Scale percentage (1–1000) **2**. *Optional:* Uncheck the Link with Layer box to keep the pattern stationary if the layer is moved; click Snap to Origin to make the pattern snap to the current ruler origin (the location where the zeros on the horizontal and vertical rulers meet (see page 233); or click the "Create new preset" button to create a preset.
3. Click OK.

TIP Adjust the mode or opacity of the fill layer using the Layers palette.

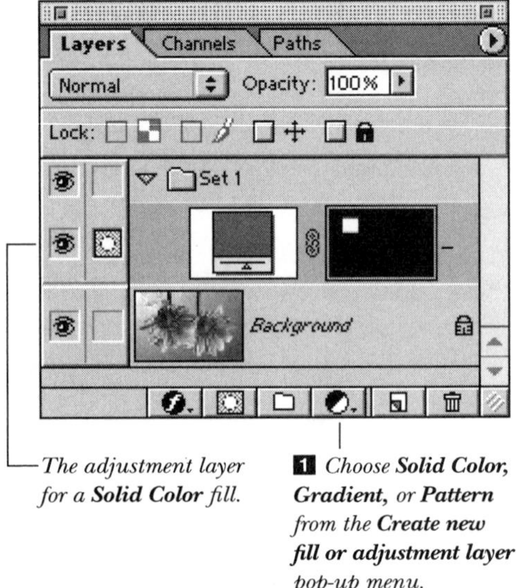

*The adjustment layer for a **Solid Color** fill.*

1 *Choose **Solid Color, Gradient,** or **Pattern** from the **Create new fill or adjustment layer** pop-up menu.*

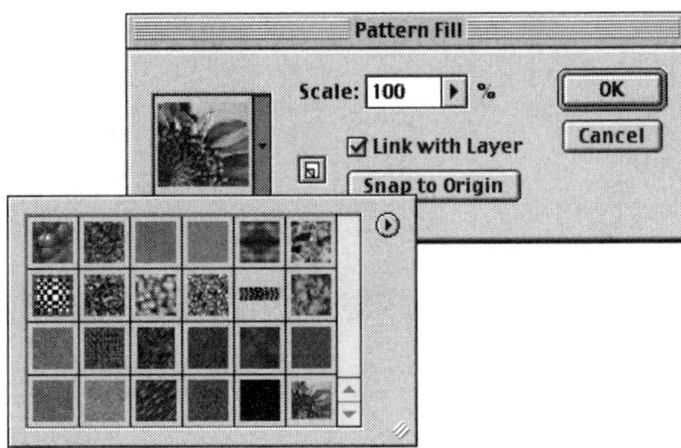

2 *Choose options for a pattern fill layer in the **Pattern Fill** dialog box.*

New Fill Layer

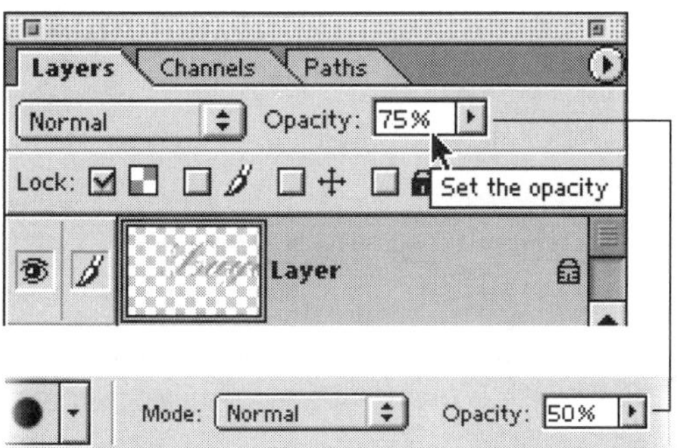

1 *This* ***layer's*** *opacity is 75% (Layers palette) and the Paintbrush* ***tool*** *opacity is 50% (options bar); the opacity of the resulting stroke will be 37%.*

2 *A rendered type layer is recolored with* ***Lock transparent pixels*** *turned* ***on.***

3 *Only the* ***type*** *is recolored—not the transparent pixels.*

Tools and layers

You can use any painting or editing tool to edit pixels on the currently active layer, but keep in mind that in addition to the blending Mode and Opacity settings chosen for each **tool** from the options bar, the blending Mode and Opacity of the currently active **layer** also contribute to a tool's effect **1**. For example, if a layer has a 60% opacity, a painting or editing tool with an opacity of 100% will work at a maximum opacity of 60% on that layer; at an even lower opacity if the tool opacity is below 100%.

Lock transparent pixels 6.0!

With **Lock transparent pixels** checked on the Layers palette, only **non-transparent** pixels on a layer can be edited or recolored **2–3**; blank areas will remain transparent (this replaces Preserve Transparency from Photoshop 5). Turn this option off if you want to **create visible pixels**. It can be turned on or off for individual layers.

Note: Lock transparent pixels is in a fixed "on" position for a non-rendered type layer. It can be turned on or off for a rendered type layer.

If you use the Eraser tool with "Lock transparent pixels" checked, you will recolor visible pixels with the current background color rather than remove them.

TIP Press / to toggle the "Lock transparent pixels" option on/off.

You can change the size or color of the checkerboard pattern that is used to indicate transparent areas on a layer or turn off the checkerboard pattern altogether in Edit menu > Preferences > Transparency & Gamut (Ctrl-K/Cmd-K, then Ctrl-4/Cmd-4).

Use all layers

With **Use All Layers** checked on the options bar for the Blur, Sharpen, Smudge, Paint Bucket, Magic Eraser, or Magic Wand tool, the tool will sample pixels from all the currently visible layers. Regardless of whether Use All Layers is on or off, pixels can only be altered on the currently active layer.

Let's say you're about to perform an operation that requires or causes your file to become flattened, such as converting it to Indexed Color mode (which does not support multiple layers) or saving it to a format other than Photoshop. If you want to preserve a copy of a few individual layers from the file before it's flattened, the following instructions will come in handy. You can save individual layers to a new document or to an existing, open document.

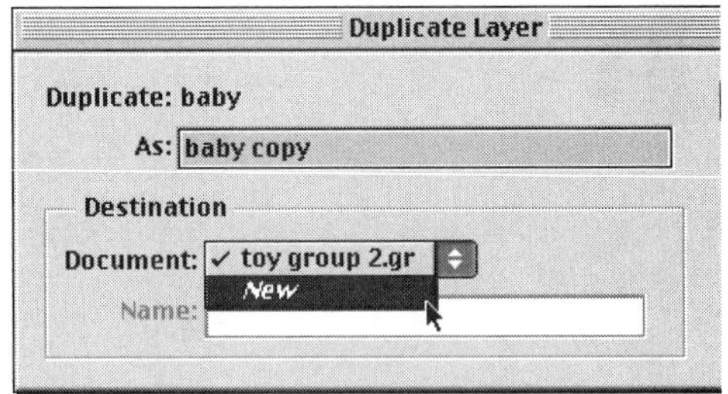

1 *Choose a* ***Destination Document*** *in the* ***Duplicate Layer*** *dialog box.*

To save a copy of a layer in a new file:

1. On the Layers palette, choose the layer that you want to save a copy of.
2. Right-click/Control-click that layer, and choose Duplicate Layer from the context menu.
3. Choose Destination Document: New **1**.
4. In the As field, enter a name for the layer to appear in the new file.
5. In the Destination: Name field, enter a name for the new file.
6. Click OK, and save the new document.

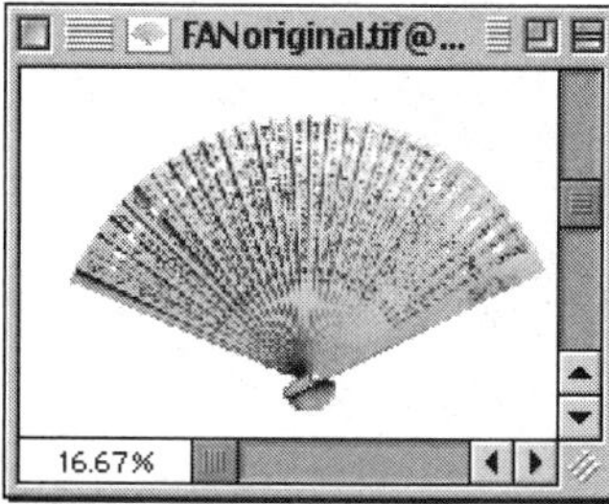

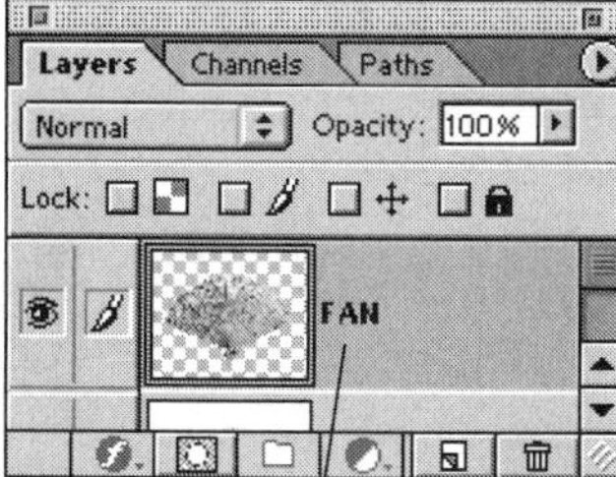

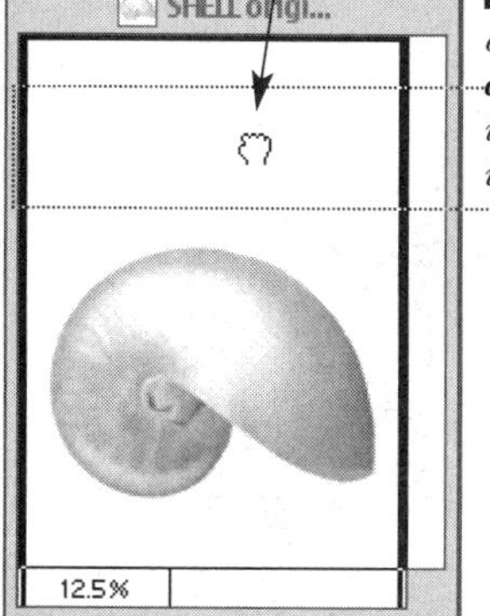

1 *Choose a layer in a **source** image, then **drag** the layer name into the **destination** image window.*

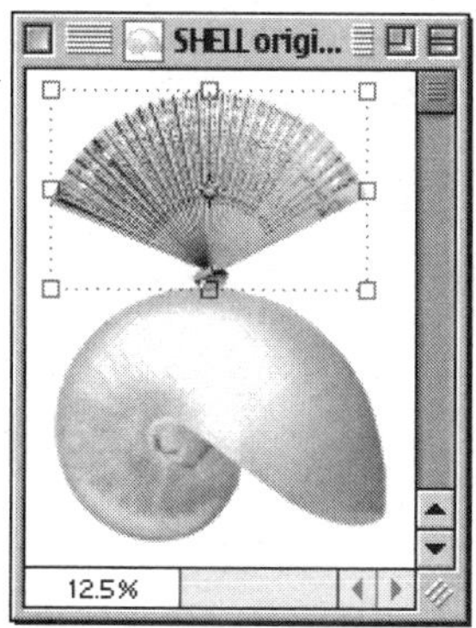

2 *This is the destination image after the SHELL layer was added.*

There are two methods for drag-copying layers between images. Choose your method based on how much of each layer you need to copy (area wise) and whether you want to copy linked layers. If you drag a layer name from the Layers palette to the destination image window, any areas that extend beyond the edge of the image boundary will be copied along with it. This method is described in the instructions below. If, on the other hand, you want to trim any overhanging areas from the layer as you copy it, use the method described on the next page instead; the latter method is the only way to copy linked layers.

To drag-and-drop a layer to another image (Layers palette):

1. Open both the image that contains the layer you want to copy and the image the layer will be copied to (the "destination image"), and make sure the two windows don't completely overlap.
2. Click in the source image window.
3. On the Layers palette, click the name of the layer you want to copy **1**. Any tool can be selected.
4. Drag the layer name from the Layers palette into the destination image window, and release the mouse when the darkened border is in the desired spot. The added layer will be stacked above the previously active layer in the destination image **2**.

TIP Shift-drag to place the layer in the center of the destination image.

Use this method to copy individual layers or a series of linked layers from one file to another.

To drag-and-drop a layer to another image (Move tool):

1. Open the image that contains the layer that you want to copy (the "source" image) and the image to which the layer is to be copied (the "destination" image).
2. On the Layers palette, click the name of the layer that you want to copy.
   or
   To move multiple layers, make sure they're linked (see page 249).
3. *Optional:* Click in the destination image window, then click the name of the layer on the Layers palette above which you want the added layer to appear.
4. Choose the Move tool (V).
5. Click in the source image window. Drag the active layer(s) from the source image window into the destination image window **1**. The new layer(s) will be positioned where you release the mouse, above the currently active layer in that file **2**.
6. *Optional:* Use the Move tool to reposition the layer in the destination image window.
7. *Optional:* Restack the new layer or layers (drag them upward or downward on the Layers palette).

TIP To copy a layer into the center of another image, start dragging the layer, hold down Shift, then continue to drag.

1 *The flower layer is dragged from the* ***source image window*** *into the* ***destination image window.***

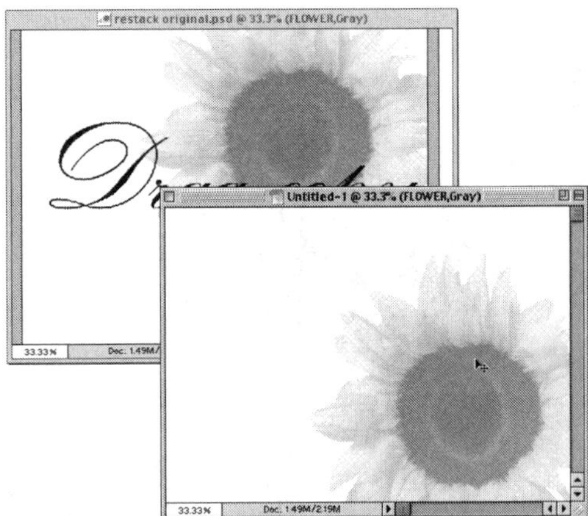

2 *The new layer appears in the* ***destination*** *image.*

Drag-and-Drop a Layer

Why does it look smaller!?

When you copy-and-paste or drag-and-drop imagery between files, it is rendered in the resolution of the destination image. If the resolution of the destination file is **higher** than that of the source file, the layer will look **smaller** when it's pasted or dropped.

Conversely, if the resolution of the destination file is **lower** than that of source file, the layer will look **larger** when it's pasted or dropped. If the pasted or dropped imagery extends beyond the edge of the live canvas area in the destination file, you can use the Move tool to move the hidden parts into view. The hidden pixels will save with the image.

Use the Clipboard (Copy and Paste commands) if you want to copy only the visible portion of a layer (when displayed at 100% view) and you don't want to copy any pixels that may extend beyond the layer's edge.

To copy and paste only the visible part of a layer to another image:

1. On the Layers palette, activate the layer you want to copy.
2. Choose Select menu > All (Ctrl-A/Cmd-A). The selection will not include any areas that extend beyond the edge of the canvas area.
3. Choose Edit menu > Copy (Ctrl-C/Cmd-C).
4. Click in the destination image window.
5. Choose Edit menu > Paste (Ctrl-V/Cmd-V). The pasted pixels will appear on a new layer. The layer can be restacked using the Layers palette.
6. Click back in the original image window, then choose Select menu > Deselect (Ctrl-D/Cmd-D) to deactivate the selection.

Merging and flattening

The sad truth is, most file formats other than Photoshop (.psd), Photoshop PDF (.pdf) and advanced TIFF (.tif) don't support multiple layers. In order to export your file to another application, it's going to have to get flattened. We think the best way to do this is to save a flattened copy of it using File menu > **Save as** with the **As a Copy** box checked (the layered version will remain open). This way, the layered version will be preserved forever and for all time so you can overwork it to death at some later date.

If you're the cocky sort and you're positive your image is totally and completely done, finis, you can flatten it yourself down into the Background using the **Flatten Image** command (see page 140). Actually, since flattened files are smaller than layered files, flattening the stuff you're done is a good way to free up storage space—if you happen to need storage space. (That reminds us how times have changed. We had to save our first book, QuarkXPress layout, illustrations, and all, onto twelve floppy disks!)

Whereas the Flatten Image command is used when a file is complete, the two merge commands, **Merge Down** and **Merge Visible**, are normally used as an image is being edited. Using either of these commands, you can merge two or more layers together on a case by case basis, while leaving the remaining layers intact.

To merge two layers together:

1. Activate the topmost layer of the two layers you want to merge. The layer can't have a layer mask. If you choose a layer set, all the layers in the set will be merged into one layer.
2. Choose Merge Down (Ctrl-E/Cmd-E) from the Layers palette menu. The active layer will merge into the layer directly below it **1**–**2**. For a layer set, choose Merge Layer Set.

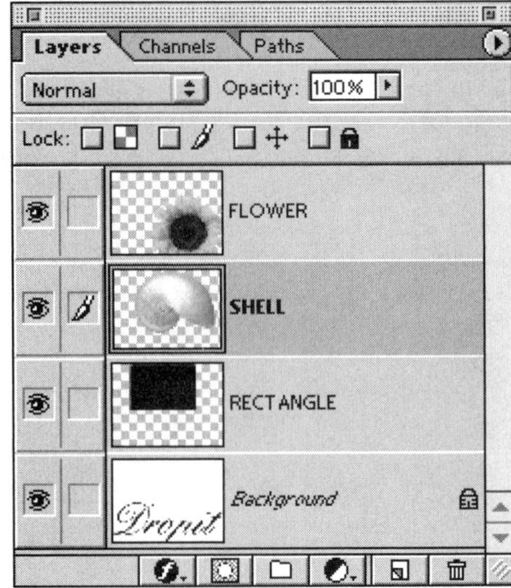

1 *The SHELL layer is chosen.*

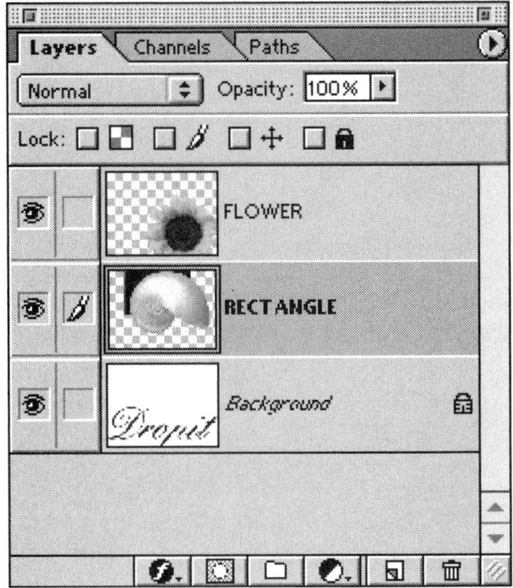

2 *After choosing the* ***Merge Down*** *command.*

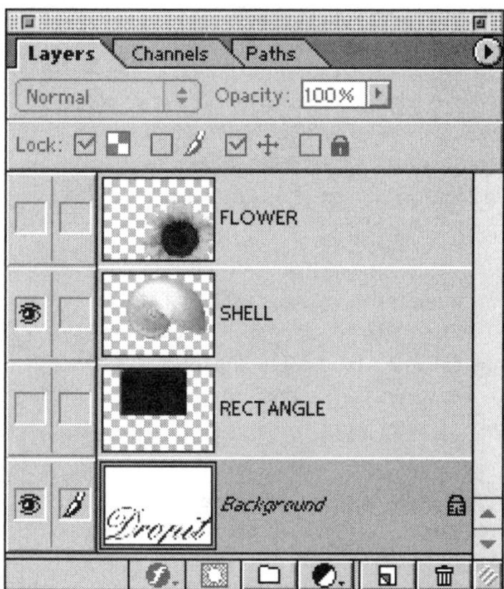

1 *The SHELL layer and background are visible and the Background is chosen; the FLOWER and RECTANGLE layers are hidden.*

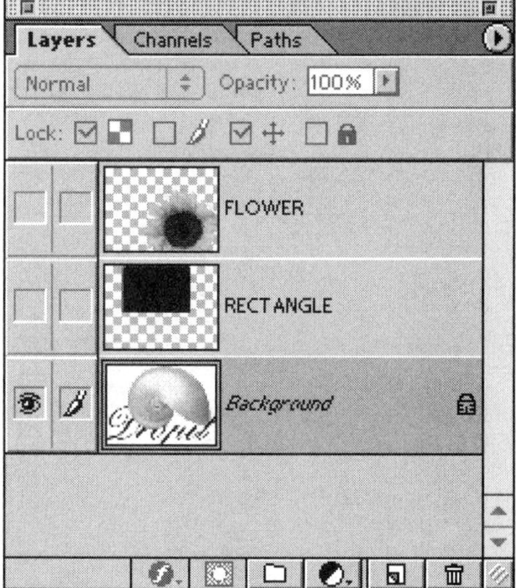

2 *After choosing the* ***Merge Visible*** *command, the SHELL layer merges into the Background. The FLOWER and RECTANGLE layers stay as they are.*

The Merge Visible command merges all the currently visible layers into the bottommost visible layer and **preserves** hidden layers.

To merge multiple layers:

1. Make sure only the layers you want to merge are visible (all should have eye icons on the Layers palette) and **hide** any layers you **don't** want to merge. They don't have to be consecutive. Hide the Background if you don't want to merge layers into it.
2. Activate any one of the layers to be merged. *Beware!* If you merge an editable type layer or an adjustment layer, it will no longer be editable.
3. Choose Merge Visible (Ctrl-Shift-E/ Cmd-Shift-E) from the Layers palette menu **1**–**2**.

Beware! The Flatten Image command merges currently displayed layers into the bottommost visible layer and **discards hidden layers**.

To flatten layers:

1. Make sure all the layers you want to flatten are visible (have eye icons) **1**. It doesn't matter which layer is currently active.
2. Choose Flatten Image from the Layers palette menu. If the file contains any hidden layers, you'll get a warning prompt; click OK **2**. If there were any transparent areas in the bottommost layer, they will become white.

Other merge commands

To merge a **copy** of all the currently visible layers or layer sets into the bottommost visible layer (it can be a new layer that you create just for this purpose), hold down Alt/Option and choose Merge Visible from the Layer menu or the Layers palette menu.

To merge linked layers, choose **Merge Linked** from the Layers palette menu or the Layer menu. The Merge Linked command **discards** hidden, linked layers. You have to link the actual layers in a set (not the set itself) to use this command.

To merge layers in a clipping group, activate the underlined layer, then choose **Merge Group** from the Layers palette menu or the Layer menu. The Merge Group command **discards** hidden layers or hidden layers within a group.

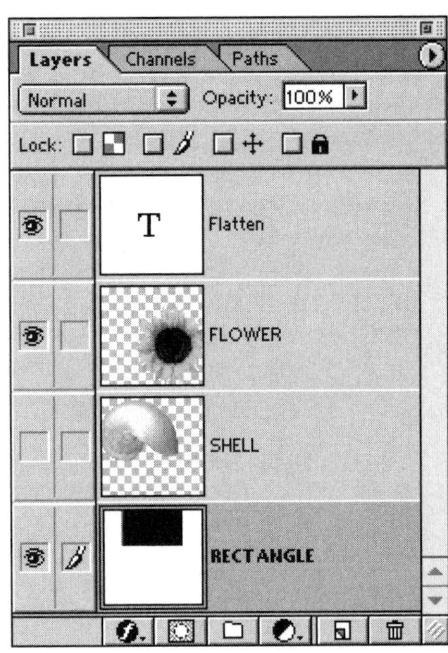

1 *Before choosing the Flatten Image command, make sure all the layers you want to merge are visible!*

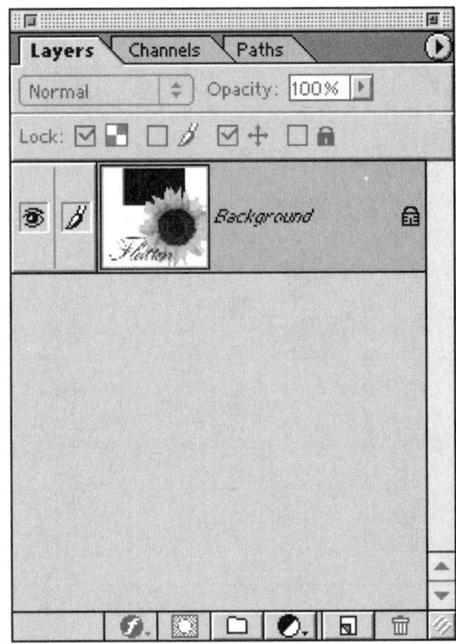

2 *After choosing the* ***Flatten Image*** *command, all the visible layers are flattened into the bottommost visible layer. Photoshop* ***discarded*** *the SHELL layer, because it was* ***hidden***.

HISTORY 8

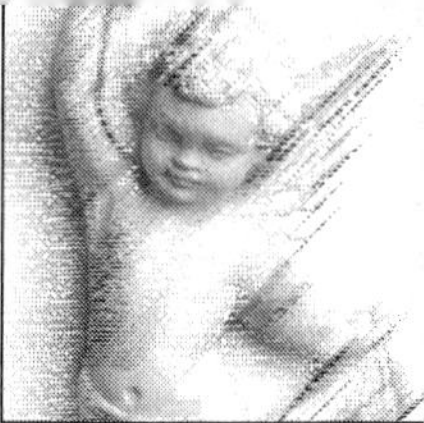

6.0!

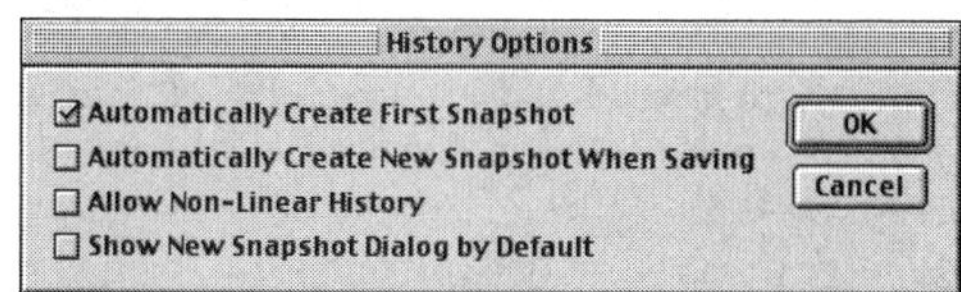

1 ***Allow Non-Linear History*** *and other options are turned on or off in the* ***History Options*** *dialog box.*

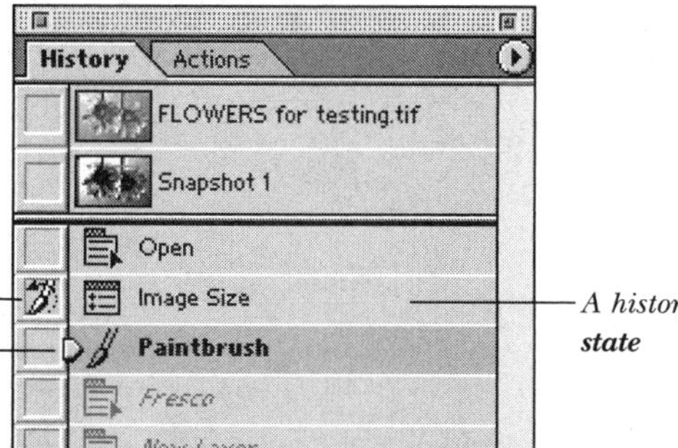

Source for the ***History Brush***

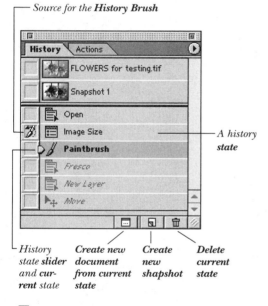

A history ***state***

History state ***slider*** *and* ***current*** *state*

Create new document from current state

Create new shapshot

Delete current state

2 *The* ***History*** *palette in* ***linear*** *mode. Note that some steps are grayed out. Figure* **2** *on page 143 shows the palette in non-linear mode.*

IN THIS CHAPTER you'll learn how to use the History palette to selectively undo up to 99 previous stages of an image-editing session, called states. You'll also learn how to restore selective areas to a prior state using the History Brush or Art History brush tool, by filling a selection with a history state, or by erasing to a history state.

The History palette displays a list of the most recent states that were applied to an image, with the bottommost state being the most recent. Clicking on a prior state restores the image to that stage of the editing process. What happens to the image when you do this depends on whether the palette is in linear or non-linear mode, so it's essential to learn the difference between the two.

Using the History palette

Linear and non-linear

There are two ways in which the History palette can be used: Linear mode or Non-Linear mode. This option is turned on/off via the **Allow Non-Linear History** box in the History Options dialog box **1** (choose History Options from the palette menu). You can switch between these two modes at any time during an editing session.

In **linear** mode, if you click back on an earlier state and resume image-editing from that state or delete it, all subsequent (dimmed) states will be deleted **2**.

In the History palette's **non-linear** mode, if you click back on or delete an earlier state, subsequent states won't be deleted (or dimmed). If you then resume image-editing while that earlier state is selected, the new edits will show up as the latest states on the palette and earlier states will be preserved. If you delete an earlier state and then click on the latest state, the deleted edits will still appear in the actual image. Non-linear is the more flexible of the two modes.

When would you want to work in non-linear mode? When you need flexibility. Let's say you apply paint strokes to a layer, try out different blending modes for that layer, and then settle on a mode that you like. If you want to reduce the number of states on the palette, you can then delete any of the other blending mode states, whether they're before or after the one you've settled on. You can pick and choose.

When would you want to work in linear mode? If you find non-linear mode confusing or disorienting or if you want the option to revert back to an earlier state with a nice, clean break.

Clearing the palette

If you close an image or choose File menu > Revert, all the history states for that image will be removed from the palette. To preserve history states as you restore an image, instead of using Revert, put the History palette into non-linear mode, then click back on a prior state or click the First Snapshot thumbnail at the top of the palette (more about snapshots on pages 144–145).

To deliberately clear the History palette for all currently open images to free up memory, choose Edit menu > Purge > **Histories**. To clear the History palette for the current document only, choose **Clear History** from the palette menu. The Purge *can't* be undone, but Clear History *can* be undone.

The max 6.0!

To specify the number of states that can be listed on the palette for an editing session, enter a number in the **Maximum History States** field (1–100) in Edit menu > Preferences > General (it was moved from the History Options dialog box to General Preferences). If you exceed that maximum during an editing session, earlier steps will automatically be **removed** to make room for the new ones. *Note:* The maximum number of states may be limited by various factors, including the image size, the kind of edits that are made to the image, and currently available memory. Each open image keeps its own list of states.

History shortcuts

Step Forward one state	Ctrl-Shift-Z/Cmd-Shift-Z
Step Backward one state	Ctrl-Alt-Z/Cmd-Option-Z

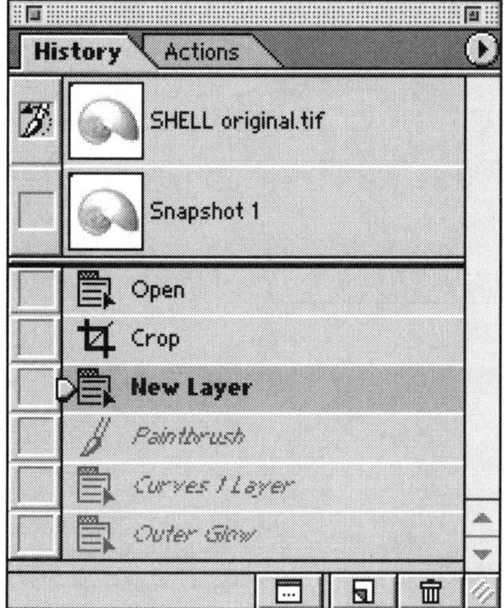

1 *Clicking on a prior state with the* ***History*** *palette in* ***linear*** *mode.*

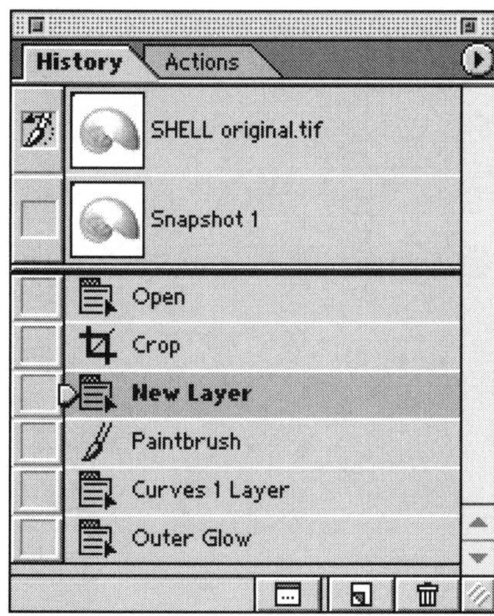

2 *Clicking on a prior state with the* ***History*** *palette in* ***non-linear*** *mode.*

Note: If the palette is in linear mode (Allow Non-Linear History is turned off), the states below the one you click on will become dimmed. If you delete the state you click on or edit the image at that state, all the dimmed states will be **deleted**. If you change your mind, choose Undo immediately to restore them. If the palette is in non-linear mode, you can restore the document to the latest stage of editing by clicking the bottommost state.

To revert to a prior history state:

Click a prior state on the History palette **1**–**2**.

or

Choose Step Forward or Step Backward from the palette menu (see the shortcuts at left).

or

Drag the slider on the left side of the palette to the desired state.

To duplicate a state:

1. Turn on Allow Non-Linear History.
2. Alt-click/Option-click a state. The duplicate will be listed as the latest (bottommost) state.

Note: If the Allow Non-Linear History option is on and you delete a state, **only** that state will be deleted. If Allow Non-Linear History is off and you delete a state, **all** subsequent states will be deleted along with it; you can choose Edit menu > Undo to restore them.

To delete a state:

Drag the name of the state that you want to delete over the Delete current state (trash) button on the History palette.

TIP Keep Alt-clicking/Option-clicking the trash button to delete a series of states from the current state backward.

Using snapshots

A snapshot is like a copy of a history state, with one major difference: unlike a state, a snapshot will stay on the palette even if the state from which it was created is deleted (due to the maximum number of history states being reached or the palette being cleared or purged). It's a good idea to create a snapshot before performing a long series of editing steps or running an action on an image. ***Beware!*** All snapshots are deleted when an image is closed.

To have a snapshot be created automatically at the beginning of every new work session, check **Automatically Create First Snapshot** in History Options. To have a snapshot be created each time a file is saved, check **Automatically Create New Snapshot When Saving**. 6.0!

To create a snapshot of a history state:

1. Click the state that you want to create a snapshot of **1**.
2. Click the Create new snapshot button **2**. If the **Show New Snapshot Dialog by Default** is checked in History Options, the New Snapshot dialog box will open; follow the remaining steps. 6.0!
   or
   To choose options for the snapshot as you create it, choose New Snapshot from the palette menu; or Alt-click/ Option-click the Create new snapshot button; or Right-click/Control-click the state and choose Create New Snapshot from the context menu.
3. Type a Name for the snapshot **3**.
4. Choose From: Full Document to make a snapshot of all the layers in the image at that state; or choose Merged Layers to create a snapshot that merges all layers in the image at that state; or choose Current Layer to make a snapshot of only the currently active layer at that state.
5. Click OK. A new snapshot thumbnail will appear near the top of the palette **4**.

1 *First click a **state** on the History palette.*

2 *Then click or Alt-click/ Option-click the **Create new snapshot** button.*

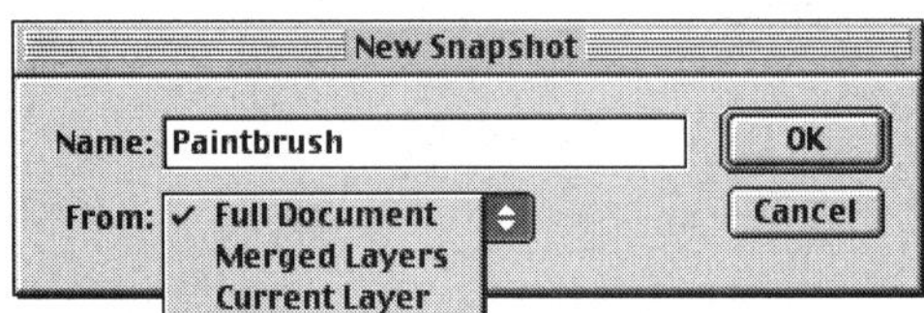

3 *Enter a **name** and choose **layer** options in the **New Snapshot** dialog box.*

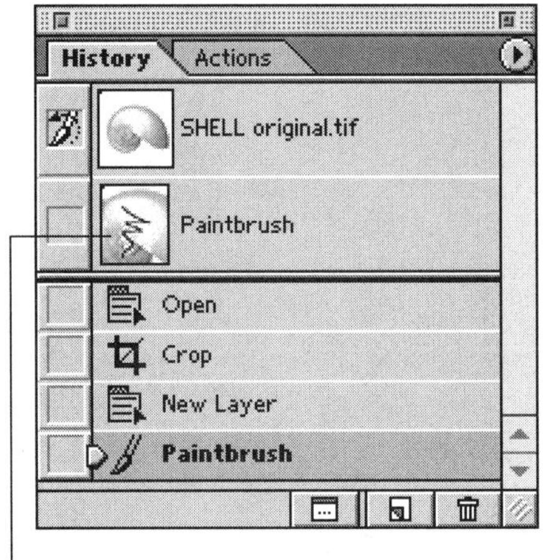

4 *A **thumbnail** for the new snapshot appears on the History palette.*

Create Snapshot

Power tip

To replace the contents of one image with a history state from another image, drag the state from the source document's history palette into the destination image window.

1 *Drag a snapshot or state over the* ***Create new document from current state*** *button.*

2 *A* ***duplicate*** *of the snapshot appears in a new document.*

To make a snapshot become the latest state:

Click a snapshot thumbnail. If the Allow Non-Linear History option is turned off and edits were made to the image since that snapshot was taken, the document will revert to the snapshot stage of editing and all the states will be dimmed. If you then resume editing, all dimmed states will be deleted. If Allow Non-Linear History was on, subsequent states will remain on the palette.

or

With either History option chosen, Alt-click/Option-click a snapshot thumbnail. The other states will remain available and that snapshot will become the latest state.

To delete a snapshot:

Click the snapshot thumbnail, choose Delete from the palette menu or click the Delete current state (trash) button, then click Yes.

or

Drag the snapshot to the Delete current state (trash) button.

If you turn a history snapshot or state into a new document, you'll have a sort of freeze insurance—something to fall back on in the event of a system or power failure. *Note:* Only one history state can be copied at a time.

To create a new document from a history state or snapshot:

Drag a snapshot or a state over the Create new document from current state button **1**.

or

Click a snapshot or a state, then click the Create new document from current state button.

or

Right-click/Control-click a snapshot or a state, then choose New Document from the context menu.

A new image window will appear, bearing the title of the state from which it was created, and "Duplicate State" will be the name of the starting state for the new image **2**. Save the new image!

Restoring and erasing

You can select any snapshot or state on the History palette to use as a source of earlier pixel data for the History Brush. Dragging with the brush restores pixels from that prior state of editing. This replaces the Rubber Stamp's From Saved option.

Note: The History Brush can't be used on an image if you've changed its pixel count since it was opened (e.g., by resampling or cropping or by changing its image mode or canvas size).

History Brush

To use the History Brush:

1. Choose the History Brush tool (Y or Shift-Y).
2. 6.0! From the History Brush options bar **1**:
   Choose a blending Mode and an Opacity.
   and
   Click the Painting Brush arrowhead, then click a brush tip on the picker.
3. On the History palette, click the blank box at the left side of the palette for the state or snapshot that you want to use as a source for the History Brush (the History Brush icon will appear where you click).
4. Choose the layer on which you want to paint the restored pixels.
5. Draw strokes on the image. Pixel data from the prior state of that layer will replace the current pixel data where you draw strokes **2**–**3**.

TIP Here's an example of how the History brush could be used to restore an earlier stage of an image. You add brushstrokes to a layer and then decide several editing steps later that you want to remove them. Clicking on the state prior to brushstrokes state could cause other edits to be deleted. Instead, click in the box next to any state prior to the state in which the strokes were added to set the source for the History Brush, click the layer on the Layers palette to which the brush strokes were added, choose the

Snapshot as History Brush source

Modify a layer (e.g., apply an Adjust command, a filter, or paint strokes), take a snapshot of the current state, and then delete that state or choose Undo. Set the History Source icon to the snapshot, then stroke with the History Brush on the layer that you modified to selectively restore it.

6.0!

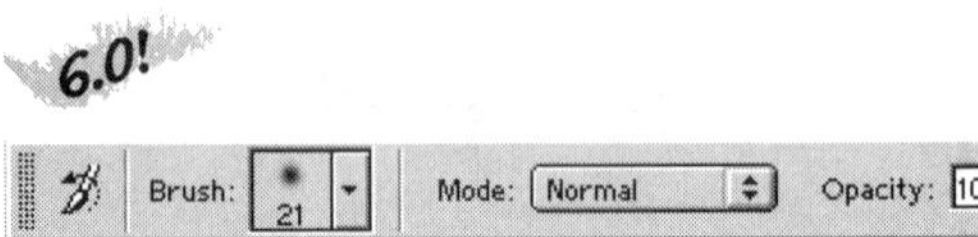

1 *Choose a blending Mode, Opacity percentage, and brush tip from the* ***History Brush*** *options bar.*

2 *The original image.*

3 *After applying the Graphic Pen filter, positioning the* ***History Source*** *icon at a prior state, and then painting across parts of the image using the* ***History Brush*** *at 95% opacity.*

1

2 *The original image.*

3 *We applied the Glass filter to a layer, selected the area around the tree, and then filled the selection with an earlier history state (**Use: History**). Try doing the same thing using the Distort > Wave or Ripple filter or an Artistic or Sketch filter.*

History Brush tool (Y), then paint out the added strokes.

TIP To paint pixel data from a later state onto an earlier state, click an earlier state, and then choose a later state as the source for the History Brush. The new data will become the most recent state.

Note: The Fill > Use: History command can't be used on an image if you've changed its pixel count since it was opened (e.g., by resampling or cropping or by changing its image mode or canvas size). Furthermore, vector data layers (type and shapes) can't be restored using the History Brush, nor can a layer clipping path on an image layer that has been modified.

To fill a selection or a layer with a history state:

1. Choose a layer that contains pixels.
2. *Optional:* Create a selection.
3. On the History palette, click in the left-most column for the state you want to use as a fill (a History Brush icon will appear where you click).
4. Choose Edit menu > Fill.
5. Choose Use: History **1**.
6. Choose a Blending Mode and an Opacity percentage.
7. Click OK **2**–**3**.

Fill with History

Using the Art History brush, you can paint a designated history state or snapshot back onto an image in an assortment of different shaped brushstrokes (actually, in our humble opinion, all the different brush choices —Tight Long, Loose Curl, etc.—look like worms). Adjacent colors are blended to produce a painterly effect, and those colors will vary depending on the current Fidelity setting for the Art History Brush. By all means use a stylus if you have one.

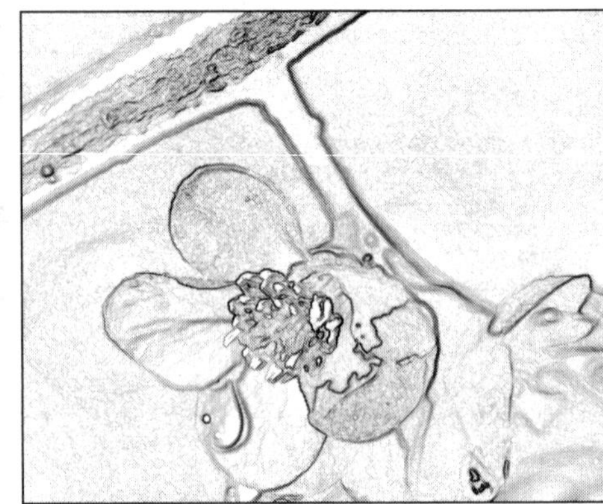

*A continuous-tone image, after applying Photoshop's **Find Edges** filter.*

To use the Art History brush:

1. Perform some edits on an image to create states on the History palette. You can then fill the image window with white.
2. On the History palette, click in the leftmost column at the state or snapshot from which you want the brushstrokes to take their pixel data. The source icon for the History Brush will appear there.
3. Choose the Art History Brush (Y or Shift-Y).
4. From the Art History Brush options bar:

   6.0! Click the Painting Brush arrowhead, then click a brush tip on the picker.

   and

   Choose a blending **Mode** and an **Opacity percentage**.

   and

   Choose a painting **Style** from the pop-up menu.

   and

   Choose a **Fidelity** (0–100%) value for the amount the paint color can vary from actual colors in the source state or snapshot. The lower the Fidelity, the more the paint color can deviate from the source color.

   and

   Choose an **Area** (0-500 pixels) for the size of the overall area the strokes can cover. The wider the area, the greater the number of strokes will be applied.

   and

   Choose a **Spacing** value (0–100%). Choose a low Spacing value to apply

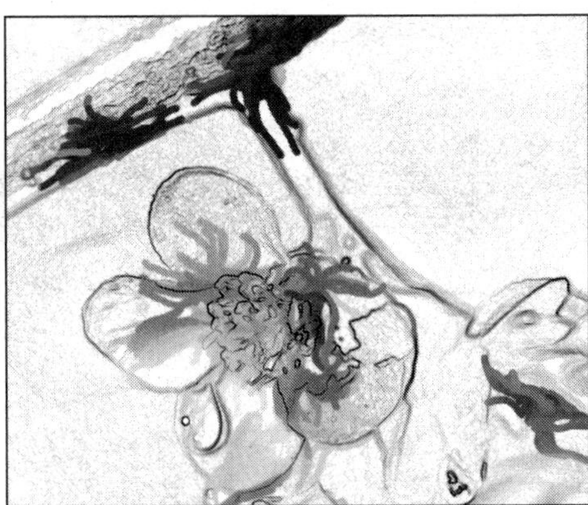

*After clicking in the leftmost column on the History palette at a prior state (the original photo), and then adding brushstrokes here and there using the **Art History Brush** (Darken mode, Loose Long, Fidelity 100%).*

Art History Brush

paint strokes only over pixels that are similar in color to those in the source state or snapshot. Choose a high Spacing value to allow strokes to be painted over pixels that differ from the source color.
and
If you're using a pressure-sensitive tablet, click the **Brush Dynamics** arrowhead, then a Stylus: Size for the area of coverage and an Opacity. If you're not using a stylus, use the palette to set Fade options for the brush. Click the arrowhead to close the palette.

5. Choose a layer, and then draw strokes in the image window. The longer you keep the mouse button down in the same spot, the more colors will blend in that area.

   Feel free to switch stroke shapes or adjust other parameters on the Art History Brush options bar between strokes, or choose different source states on the History palette. You'll achieve a less machine-made look by doing so, in fact. Another way to achieve a more personalized look with this tool is by using custom brush shapes (see pages 200–201 and 203).

You can use the Eraser tool with its Erase to History option to restore pixels from the currently active state on the History palette. An advantage of using the Eraser is that in addition to choosing an opacity and mode for the tool, you can also choose a tool type (Paintbrush, Airbrush, Pencil, or Block).

Note: The Erase to History feature can't be used on an image if you've changed its pixel count since it was opened (e.g., by resampling or cropping or by changing its image mode or canvas size).

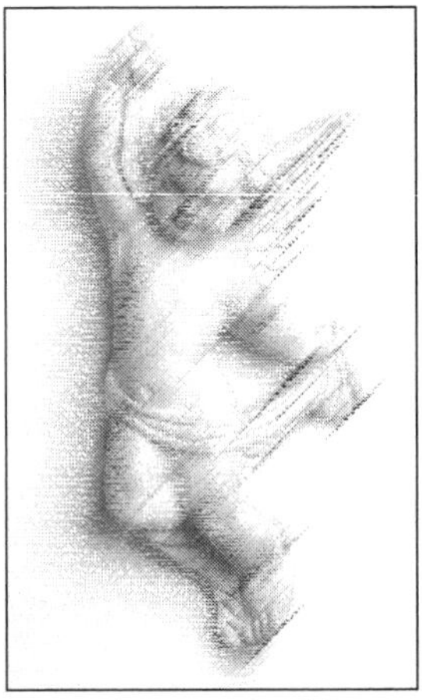

*A **snapshot** is made of the original image, then the Rough Pastels filter is applied.*

To erase to history:

1. Choose the Eraser tool (E or Shift-E).
2. Select an image layer—not a shape layer.
3. 6.0! On the Eraser options bar:
   Click the Painting Brush arrowhead, then click a brush tip in the picker.
   and
   Choose a Mode (Paintbrush, Airbrush, Pencil, or Block).
   and
   Choose an Opacity or Pressure percentage.
   and
   Check the Erase to History box.
4. *Optional:* Check the Wet Edges box to make the erasure stronger at the edges of the stroke.
5. *Optional:* Click the Brush Dynamics arrowhead and enter a number of Fade steps to make the eraser stroke fade gradually. Click the arrowhead again to close the pop-up palette.
6. Establish the History source by clicking the box next to a state or a snapshot at the far left side of the History palette.
7. Choose a layer on the Layers palette.
8. Drag in the image window.

*Then the **Eraser** tool is used with its **Erase to History** option to restore the angel's face, belly, and toes from the snapshot. (The standard painting cursor is shown in this figure.)*

Adjust Commands 9

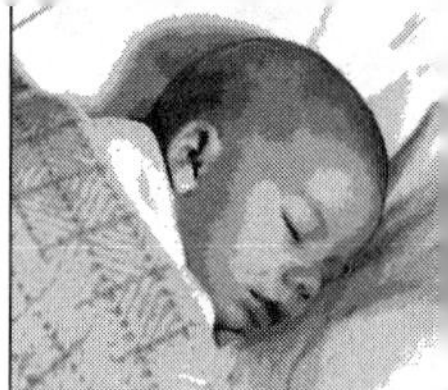

Chapter topics

Creating and using adjustment layers
Auto Contrast
Equalize
Invert
Threshold
Posterize
Brightness/Contrast
Levels
Screen back a layer
Dodge and Burn tools
Channel Mixer

To use the Hue/Saturation, Desaturate, Replace Color, and other Image menu > Adjust submenu commands to perform **color** *adjustments, see Chapter 11, Recolor.*

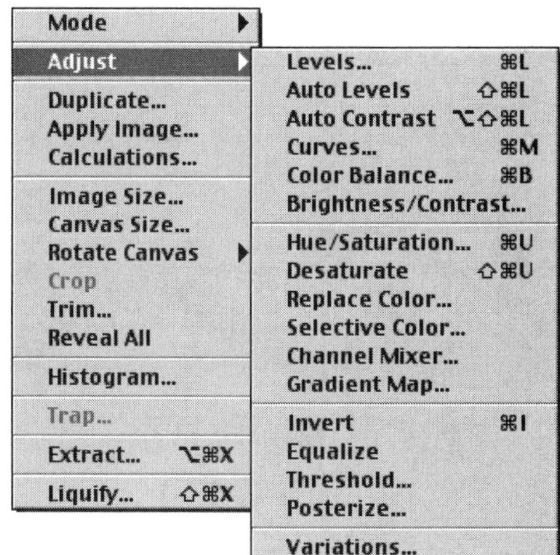

1 *The Image menu >* ***Adjust*** *submenu.*

THIS CHAPTER covers many methods for adjusting an image's light and dark values. You can make simple adjustments, like inverting a layer to make it look like a film negative or posterizing it to restrict its luminosity levels to a specified number. Or you can make more precise lightness or contrast adjustments to a layer's highlights, midtones, or shadows using such features as Levels or Curves. And you can darken smaller areas by hand using the Burn tool or lighten areas using the Dodge tool.

Adjust command basics

Here are a few pointers for applying adjust commands:

- For flexibility in editing, use **adjustment layers** (instructions begin on the following page).
- To apply any adjust command to a selected area of a layer rather than to an entire layer, create a **selection** before you choose the command.
- To **reset** the settings in a dialog box, hold down Alt/Option and click Reset.
- Use the **Preview** option in the Adjust submenu dialog boxes to see how the adjustment looks on the image. CMYK color displays more acccurately with Preview on.
- To progressively reduce an adjust command's effect in increments, use Edit menu > **Fade** (Ctrl-Shift-F/Cmd-Shift-F) —it's not just for filters any more.
- To reopen a dialog box with its **last used** settings rather than the default settings, hold down Alt/Option while choosing the command or include Alt/Option in the command shortcut.

Adjustment layers

There are two ways to apply the adjust commands. They can be applied directly to the current layer (or to a selection on the current layer) or they can be applied via an adjustment layer. We prefer the latter method because it offers the most flexibility.

Unlike normal layers, an adjustment layer affects all the visible layers below it—not just the current layer. But the beauty of an adjustment layer is that it doesn't actually change pixels until it's merged with the layer below it (Ctrl-E/Cmd-E), so you can use it to try out various effects. We think of adjustment layers as a handy way to preview color and tonal adjustments.

On this page and the following three pages we explain how to create and use adjustment layers. If you prefer, you can skip ahead and read about the individual adjust commands first (starting on page 156), and then return to these pages afterwards.

To create an adjustment layer: 6.0!

1. Choose the layer above which you want the adjustment layer to appear.
2. Choose an adjust command from the "Create new fill or adjustment layer" pop-up menu at the bottom of the Layers palette **1**–**2**.
   or
   Choose a command from the Layer menu > New Adjustment Layer submenu, then click OK.
3. Make the desired adjustments, then click OK.

To modify an adjustment layer:

1. On the Layers palette, double-click the adjustment layer thumbnail (the thumbnail on the left).
   or
   The slow way: Click the adjustment layer name, then choose Layer menu > Layer Content Options.
2. Make the desired changes in the adjust dialog box, then click OK.

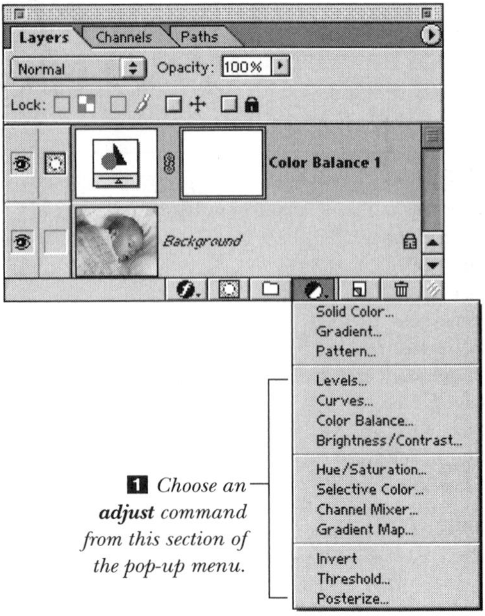

1 *Choose an* ***adjust*** *command from this section of the pop-up menu.*

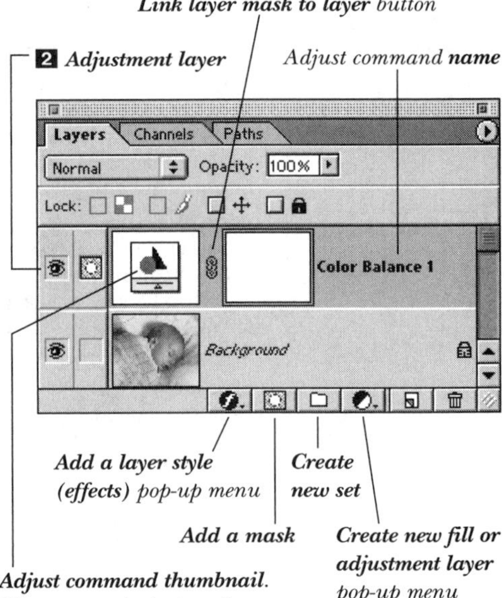

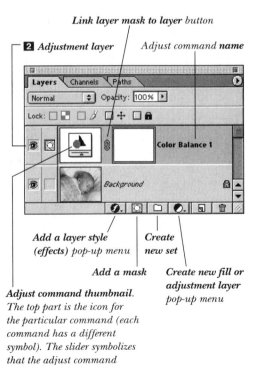

2 ***Adjustment layer***

Adjust command thumbnail. *The top part is the icon for the particular command (each command has a different symbol). The slider symbolizes that the adjust command is editable or changeable.*

From file to file

To copy an adjustment layer from one image to another, **drag-and-drop** it from the source image's Layers palette into the destination image window.

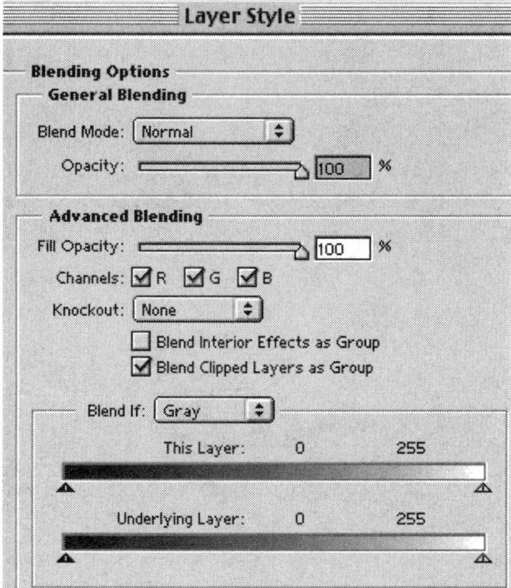

1 *Choose* ***Blending Options*** *for an adjustment layer in the* ***Layer Style*** *dialog box.*

You can control how an adjustment layer blends with underlying layers. This is accomplished via the Layer Style dialog box.

To choose blending options for an adjustment layer (or any layer): 6.0!

1. Double-click an adjustment layer (or ordinary layer) name on the Layers palette.
2. Make sure Blending Options is chosen on the left side of the Layer Style dialog box.
3. Change the **General Blending: Blend Mode** and/or **Opacity** settings **1**.
4. Change any of these **Advanced Blending** options:

   Uncheck any **Channels** you want to exclude from blending with the underlying layer. To set the blend range for each channel one at a time, choose a channel from the Blend If pop-up menu; to work on all the channels simultaneously, leave Gray as the choice on the pop-up menu. The current image mode (e.g., RGB, CMYK) determines which Channels are available.

   Move the leftmost Blend If: **This Layer** slider to the right to remove shadow areas from the active layer. Move the rightmost This Layer slider to the left to remove highlights from the active layer.

   Move the leftmost **Underlying Layer** slider to the right to restore shadow areas from the layer directly below the active layer. Move the rightmost Underlying Layer slider to the left to restore highlights from the layer directly below the active layer.

   (To read about Knockout and the two "Blend..." checkboxes, see page 239.)
5. Click OK.

6.0! You can keep an adjustment layer right where it is and change the adjust command that it contains (e.g., Levels, Curves, Brightness/Contrast).

To choose a different command for an existing adjustment layer:

1. Choose an adjustment layer on the Layers palette.
2. Choose the command you want to switch to from the Layer menu > Change Layer Content submenu.

TIP To discard an adjustment layer, drag it to the Delete layer (trash) button.

1 *An adjustment layer is chosen.*

When you merge down an adjustment layer, the adjustments become permanent for the image layer below it, so be certain you want the effect to become permanent before you perform another operation. If you change your mind, choose Edit menu > Undo or click the prior state on the History palette.

To merge an adjustment layer:

1. Choose the adjustment layer you want to merge downward **1**.
2. Choose Merge Down from the Layers palette menu (Ctrl-E/Cmd-E) **2**.

   Note: An adjustment layer cannot be merged with another adjustment layer; since they don't contain pixels, there's nothing to merge. You can, however, merge multiple adjustment layers into an image layer (or layers) using the Merge Visible or Flatten Image command (see pages 138–140).

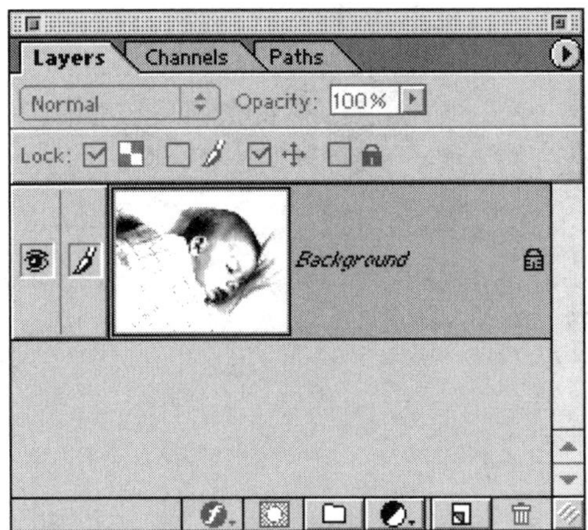

2 *After applying the* ***Merge Down*** *command, the Brightness/Contrast values from the adjustment layer are permanently applied to the layer below it (in this case, Background).*

Change Layer Content; Merge Adjust Layer

1 *Choose a **blending mode** for an adjustment layer.*

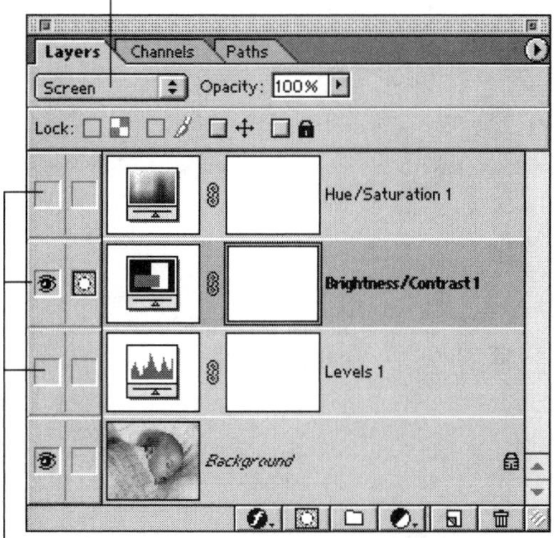

2 ***Show/hide** adjustment layers to compare their effects.*

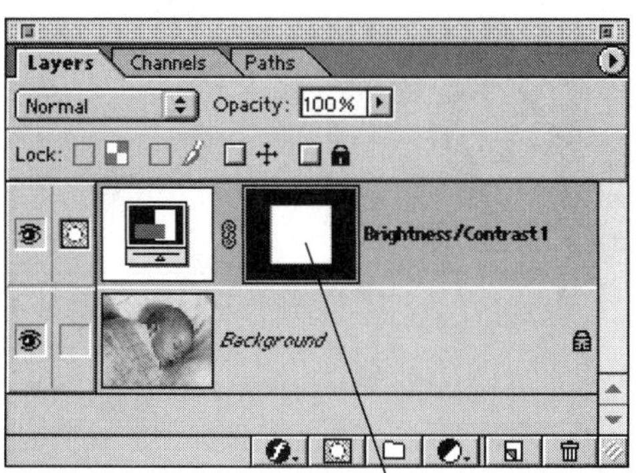

3 *A **rectangular selection** was created before the adjustment layer command was chosen.*

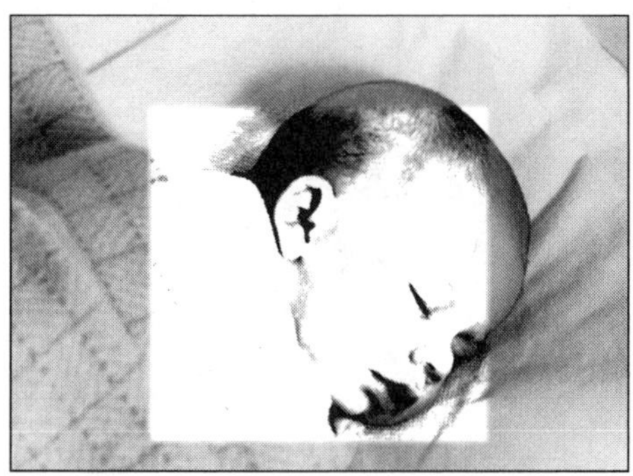

4 *The **Brightness/Contrast** adjustment only affects the **rectangular selection** area.*

Ways to use adjustment layers

Change an adjustment layer's **blending mode** (Layers palette) to produce a variety of visual effects in relationship to its underlying layers **1**. For example, try Overlay mode to heighten contrast, Multiply mode to darken the image, or Screen mode to lighten the image. You can stack several adjustment layers, then hide, or lower the opacity of, each layer to see how the underlying image is altered **2**.

To **compare** different settings for the same adjustment command, create multiples of the same adjustment layer, like Levels or Color Balance, hide all the adjustment layers, and then show/hide them one at a time. You can restack adjustment layers among themselves or place them at different locations within the overall layer stack.

To prevent an underlying layer from being affected by an adjustment layer, **restack** it so it's above the adjustment layer.

To limit the area an adjustment layer affects, create a **selection** before you create it. The selection area is shown in white on the layer mask thumbnail **3**–**4**. Or **paint** or **fill** with black on the adjustment layer to remove the adjustment effect or white to reveal the adjustment effect. The strokes will display on the layer mask thumbnail. To read more about **adjustment layer masks**, see page 163.

Normally, an adjustment layer will affect all the currently visible layers below it, but you can use a **clipping group** to limit an adjustment layer's effect to only the layer or layers it's grouped with (see step 5 on page 242). If you choose a command from the Layer menu > New Adjustment Layer submenu, you can check the Group With Previous Layer box in the New Layer dialog box.

To use the **Gradient Map** adjust command, see page 220.

Adjust commands

Next we'll show you how to use the individual Image menu > Adjust submenu commands. They can be applied to a layer directly or via an adjustment layer. Try applying the adjust commands to a grayscale image first to learn how they work, then use them on color images.

The simple, one-step Auto Contrast command turns the almost-lightest pixels in an image white and turns the almost-darkest pixels black, and then redistributes the gray levels in between.

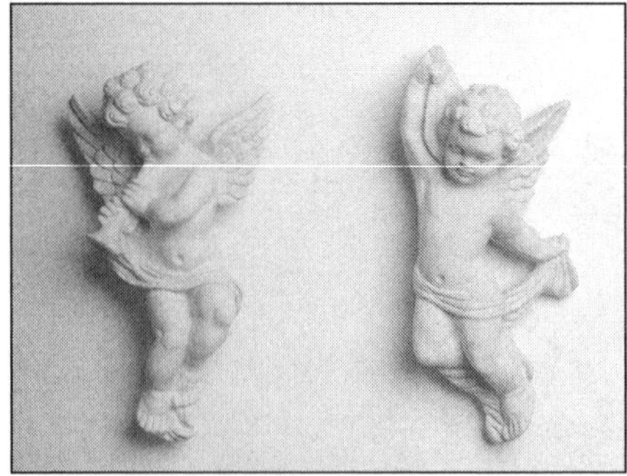

1 *The original image.*

To adjust an image using Auto Contrast:

Choose Image > Adjust > Auto Contrast (Ctrl-Alt-Shift-L/Cmd-Option-Shift-L) **1**–**2**.

2 *After applying **Auto Contrast**.*

The Equalize command redistributes the active layer's brightness values. It may improve an image that lacks contrast or is too dark.

To equalize a layer:

Choose Image menu > Adjust > Equalize. To limit the Equalize effect to part of a layer, select that area before choosing the command, then click "Equalize selected area only" in the Equalize dialog box. To equalize an entire layer based on the values within the selected area, click "Equalize entire image based on selected area." **3**–**5**

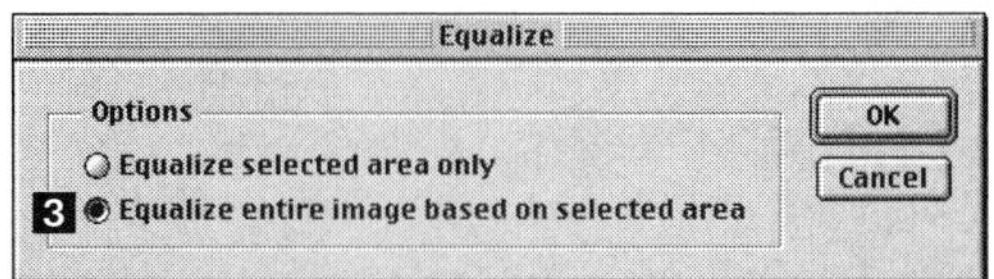

4 *The original image.*

5 *After applying the **Equalize** command.*

1 *The original image.*

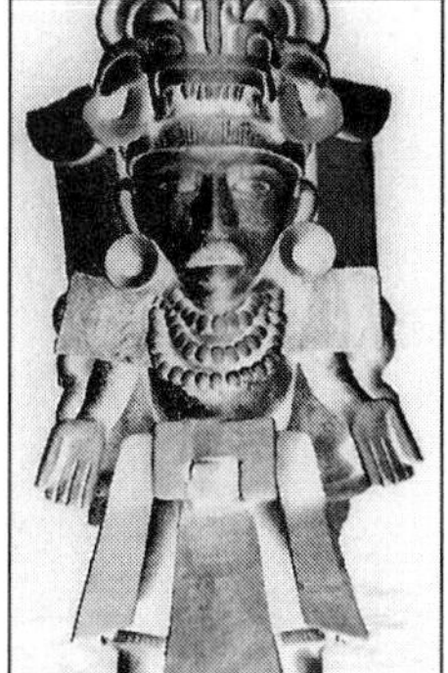

2 *The image* ***inverted****.*

3 *The original image.*

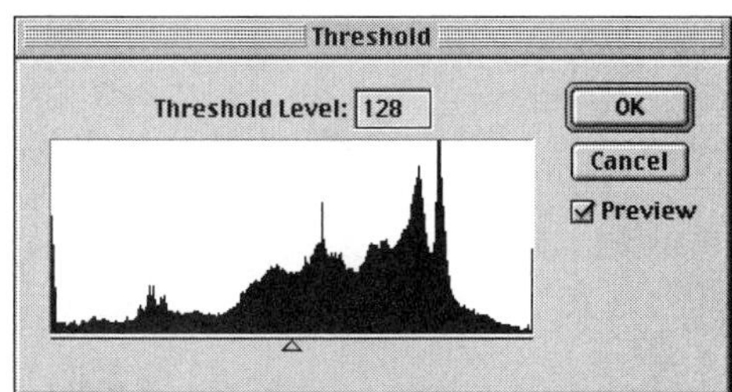

4 *Move the* ***Threshold*** *slider to control the cutoff point for black/white values.*

5 *After applying the* ***Threshold*** *command.*

Choose the Invert command to make a layer or the Background look like a film negative. You can also use this command to make a negative look like a positive, though this is not the most exacting way to do it from a photographer's point of view. Each pixel will be replaced with its opposite brightness and/or color value.

To invert lights and darks:

Choose a layer, then choose Image menu > Adjust > Invert (Ctrl-I/Cmd-I) **1**–**2**.
or
To use an adjustment layer to invert the layers below it, choose Invert from the "Create new fill or adjustment layer" pop-up menu at the bottom of the Layers palette.

The Threshold dialog box makes the current layer or the Background high contrast by converting color or gray pixels into black and white pixels.

To make a layer high contrast:

1. Choose a layer or the Background **3**, then choose Image menu > Adjust > Threshold.
   or
   To use an adjustment layer, choose Threshold from the "Create new fill or adjustment layer" pop-up menu at the bottom of the Layers palette.
2. Move the slider to the right to increase the number of black pixels **4**.
   or
   Move the slider to the left to increase the number of white pixels.
   or
   Enter a value (1–255) in the Threshold Level field. Pixels lighter than the value you choose will become white, pixels darker than the value you choose will become black.
3. Click OK **5**.

Use the Posterize command to reduce the number of color or value levels in the current layer or the Background to a specified number. We love this simple command.

To posterize:

1. Choose a layer **1**, then choose Image menu > Adjust > Posterize.
   or
   To use an adjustment layer, choose Posterize from the "Create new fill or adjustment layer" pop-up menu at the bottom of the Layers palette.
2. Make sure the Preview box is checked, then enter the desired number of Levels (2–255) **2**. To produce a poster or silkscreen effect, try a Levels value between 4 and 8.
3. Click OK **3**.

TIP If the number of shades in an image is reduced using the Posterize command (or any other tonal adjustments are made, for that matter, without using an adjustment layer), and the image is saved and closed, the original value levels data will be permanently lost.

TIP Create a gradient using two or more colors, then create a Posterize adjustment layer above the gradient layer—the gradient will have obvious color bands.

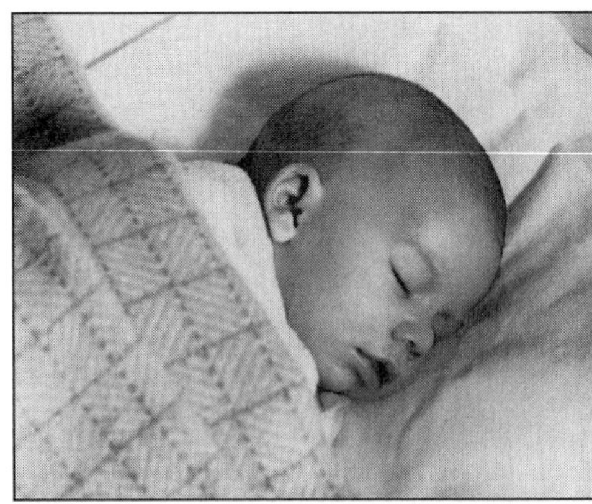

1 *The original image.*

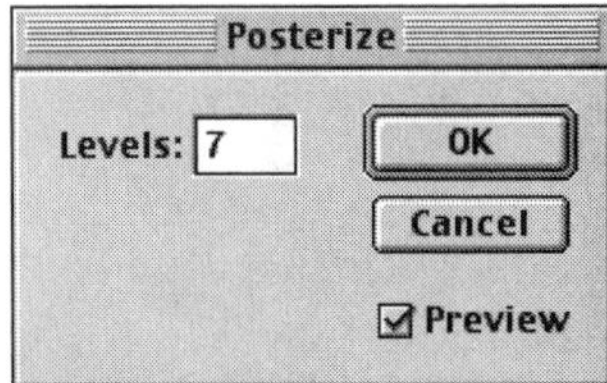

2 *Enter the desired number of color or value* ***Levels*** *in the* ***Posterize*** *dialog box.*

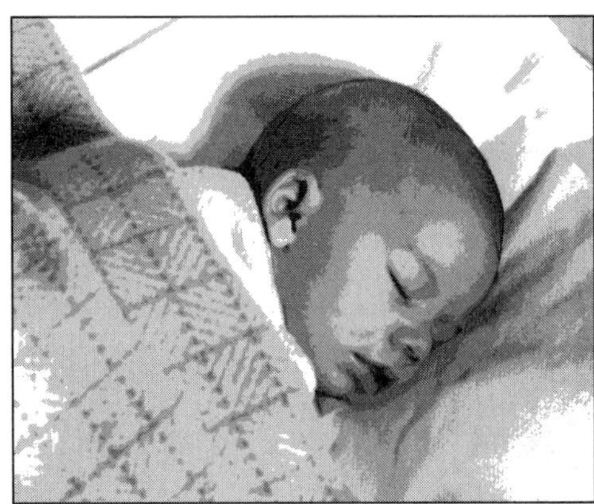

3 ***Posterized.***

PHOTO: PAUL PETROFF

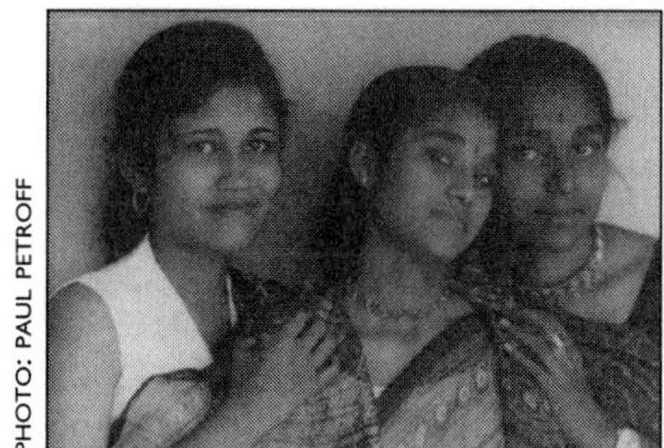

1 *The original image.*

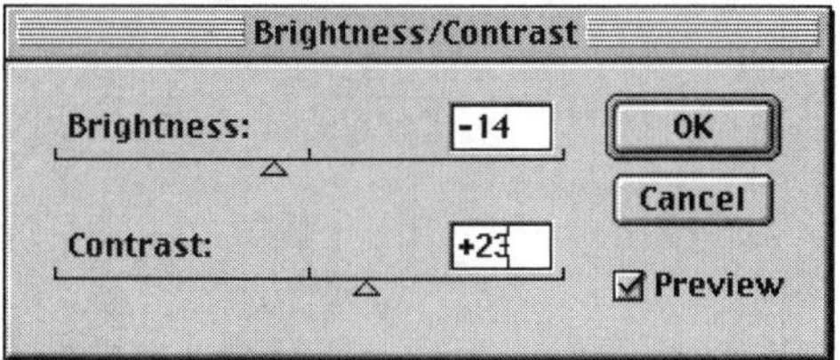

2 *Move the **Brightness** and/or **Contrast** sliders in the **Brightness/Contrast** dialog box.*

3 *The **Brightness** slider moved to the right.*

4 ***Brightness** and **contrast** adjusted.*

If you use the Levels dialog box to make tonal adjustments, you'll be able to adjust the shadows, midtones, and highlights separately and with more precision, but the Brightness/Contrast command, discussed here, is simpler to use.

To adjust brightness and contrast (Brightness/Contrast):

1. Choose a layer **1**, then choose Image menu > Adjust > Brightness/Contrast.
   or
   To use an adjustment layer, choose Brightness/Contrast from the "Create new fill or adjustment layer" pop-up menu at the bottom of the Layers palette.
2. To lighten the layer, move the brightness slider to the right **2**.
   or
   To darken the layer, move the Brightness slider to the left.
   or
   Enter a value (-100–100) in the Brightness field.
3. To intensify the contrast, move the Contrast slider to the right.
   or
   To lessen the contrast, move the Contrast slider to the left.
   or
   Enter a value (-100–100) in the Contrast field.
4. Click OK **3**–**4**.

Use the Levels dialog box to make fine adjustments to a layer's highlights, midtones, or shadows. We use this dialog box, day in and day out, for most of our image adjustments.

To adjust brightness and contrast using Levels:

1. Choose a layer **1**, then choose Image menu > Adjust > Levels (Ctrl-L/Cmd-L).
   or
   To use an adjustment layer, choose Levels from the "Create new fill or adjustment layer" pop-up menu at the bottom of the Layers palette.
2. Do any of the following **2**:
   To brighten the highlights and intensify contrast, move the **Input highlights** slider to the left. The midtones slider will move along with it. Readjust the midtones slider, if necessary.
   To darken the shadows, move the **Input shadows** slider to the right. The midtones slider will move along with it. Readjust the midtones slider, if necessary.
   To adjust the midtones independently, move the **Input midtones** slider.
   To decrease contrast and lighten the image, move the **Output shadows** slider to the right.
   To decrease contrast and darken the image, move the **Output highlights** slider to the left.
   Note: You can enter values in the Input Levels or Output Levels fields instead of moving the sliders. To save the current settings, click **Save**. Use **Load** to reapply the saved settings to other images.
3. Click OK **2**–**4**.

TIP To adjust levels automatically, choose Image menu > Adjust > **Auto Levels** (Ctrl-Shift-L/Cmd-Shift-L) or click Auto in the Levels dialog box.

TIP To intensify contrast in the image, move the Input shadows and highlights sliders closer together.

1 *The original image.*

2

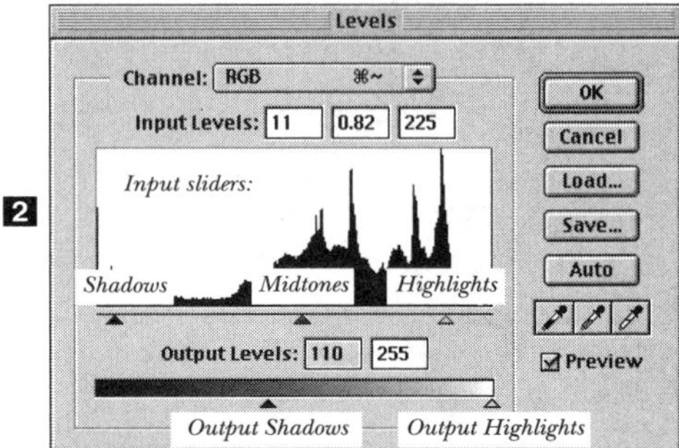

PHOTO: PAUL PETROFF

3 *After **Levels** adjustments.*

4 *To produce this image, an area of the image was selected before the Levels adjustment layer was made.*

1 *The original image.*

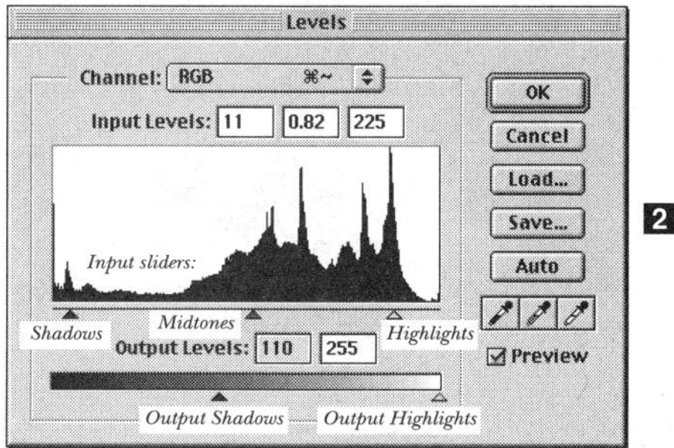

2

3 *The music layer* ***screened back.***

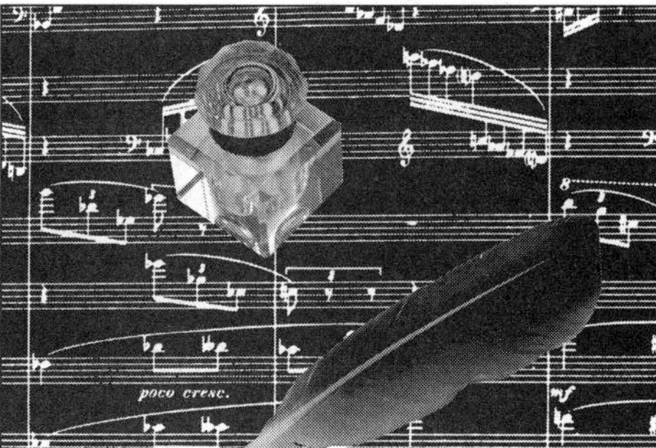

4 *The Output slider positions reversed.*

This is just another way to use the Levels command.

To screen back a layer:

1. Choose a layer or the Background **1**, then choose Image menu > Adjust > Levels (Ctrl-L/Cmd-L).
   or
   To use an adjustment layer, choose Levels from the "Create new fill or adjustment layer" pop-up menu at the bottom of the Layers palette.
2. To reduce contrast, move the Input highlights slider slightly to the left **2**.
   and
   Move the Output shadows slider to the right.
3. To lighten the midtones, move the Input midtones slider to the left.
4. Click OK **3**.

TIP To make a layer look like a film negative, reverse the position of the two Output sliders **4**. The farther apart you move the sliders, the more brightness and contrast attributes will be reversed. Try the Invert command for a similar effect.

PHOTO: PAUL PETROFF

5 *The original image.*

6 *The* ***screened back*** *version.*

To lighten pixels by hand in small areas, use the Dodge tool; to darken pixels, use the Burn tool. You can choose separate brush tips and other options bar settings for each tool.

To lighten using the Dodge tool or darken using the Burn tool:

1. Choose a layer. *Note:* The Dodge and Burn tools can't be used on a image in Bitmap or Indexed Color mode.
2. Choose the Dodge or Burn tool (O or Shift-O).
3. 6.0! On the tool's options bar **1**:

   Click the Painting Brush arrow, then click a hard-edged or soft-edged brush tip from the picker. A large, soft tip will produce the smoothest result.
   and
   Choose Shadows, Midtones, or Highlights from the Range pop-up menu to Dodge or Burn only pixels in that value range.
   and
   Choose an Exposure setting between 1% (low intensity) and 100% (high intensity). Try a low exposure first (20%-30%) so the tool won't bleach or darken areas too quickly.
4. Stroke on any area of the layer. Pause between strokes to allow the screen to redraw **2**–**3**. To dodge or burn in a straight line, click on the image, move the pointer, then Shift-click on the image again.

TIP If you Dodge or Burn an area too much, choose Edit menu > Undo or use the History palette to remove those states. Don't use the opposite tool to fix it—it will end up looking blotchy.

TIP To create a smooth, even highlight or shadow line, dodge or burn a path using the Stroke Path command with the Dodge or Burn tool chosen (see page 271).

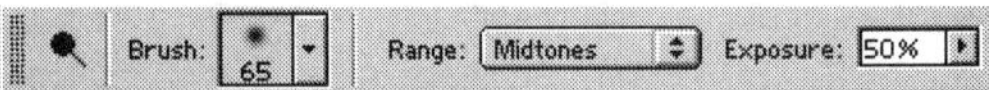

1 *Choose settings for the* ***Dodge*** *or* ***Burn*** *tool from the options bar.*

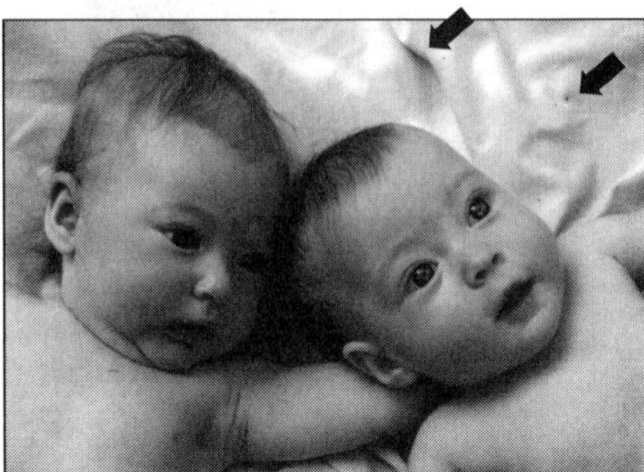

2 *The* ***Dodge*** *tool with* ***Shadows*** *chosen from the Dodge Options palette was used to eliminate dark spots in the background of this image.*

3 *After* ***dodging.***

Dodge or Burn

Layer mask shortcuts

- **Alt**-click/**Option**-click the adjustment layer mask thumbnail to **view** the mask in the image window.
- **Alt-Shift**-click/**Option-Shift**-click the adjustment layer mask thumbnail to view the mask in a rubylith color.
- **Shift**-click the adjustment layer mask thumbnail to **temporarily turn off** the mask for an adjustment layer.
- **Ctrl**-click/**Cmd**-click the adjustment layer mask thumbnail to convert the non-masked area into a **selection**.

1 *We painted with black on the left side of the* ***Threshold*** *adjustment layer. The Threshold effect is only visible in the "****unpainted****" area.*

2 *In this image, the adjustment layer's opacity was lowered to 60%, which causes the Threshold effect to blend with the overall underlying image.*

There are two ways to restrict an adjustment layer effect to a specific area of an image. One way is to create a selection before you create the adjustment layer. Another way is to create a selection or paint with black on the adjustment layer after it's created (instructions below). More about layer masks on pages 242–246.

To restrict an adjustment layer's effect using a mask: 6.0!

1. Choose an adjustment layer. Make the Foreground color Black. The Color palette will reset automatically to the Grayscale model.
3. To mask the adjustment layer effect:

   Create a selection using any selection tool (e.g., Rectangular Marquee, Lasso, or Magic Wand), choose Edit menu > Fill (Shift-Delete/Shift-Backspace), choose Use: Foreground Color, then click OK.
   or
   Choose the Paintbrush tool (B), choose Mode: Normal and Opacity 100% from the options bar, then paint on the image **1**. To partially mask the adjustment layer effect, choose a lower Opacity for the Paintbrush.
4. *More options:*

   To restore the adjustment layer effect, paint or fill with white.

   To reveal just a small area of the adjustment effect, fill the entire layer with black and then paint with white over specific areas.

   To make the adjustment effect visible on the entire image, fill the whole adjustment layer with white.

TIP To diminish the adjustment layer's effect over the entire layer by a percentage, lower the layer opacity via the Layers palette Opacity slider **2**.

TIP By default, an adjustment layer contains a pixel-based layer mask. To create a clipping path (vector mask) for an adjustment layer, see page 278.

To make a layer grayscale using the Channel Mixer:

1. Choose a layer or the Background, then choose Image menu > Adjust > Channel Mixer.
   or
   To use an adjustment layer, choose Channel Mixer from the "Create new fill or adjustment layer" pop-up menu at the bottom of the Layers palette.
2. Check the Monochrome box **1**. The layer or image will become grayscale and Gray will be the only choice on the Output Channel drop-down menu.
3. Move any Source Channels slider to modify how much that color channel is used as a source for the luminosity levels in the grayscale image. Drag a slider to the left to decrease the amount of that color in the output channel or to the right to increase the amount of that color.
4. Move the Constant slider to the left to add black or to the right to add white.
5. Click OK. The image is still in its original color mode. If you like, you can now convert it to Grayscale mode.

TIP If you applied the Channel Mixer to a layer, you can choose a different layer opacity or blending mode for the layer.

TIP To add a color tint to a layer, first check the Monochrome box in the Channel Mixer dialog box, and then uncheck it to restore the color Output Channels. Choose an Output Channel and move the Source Channel sliders to produce a different color tint. Repeat for any other Output Channel(s).

Try one of theirs

To use a **preset Channel Mixer** effect (e.g., RGB Rotate Channels, CMYK Swap Cyan & Magenta), first make sure the Channel Mixer Presets folder has been copied from the Photoshop 6.0 CD-Rom into the Adobe Photoshop 6.0 > Presets folder. To load an effect, click Load in the Channel Mixer dialog box, open the Presets > Channel Mixer Presets folder inside the application folder, open any one of the four folders there, then double-click a mixer. Windows: The abbreviated names represent Channel Swap, Grayscale, Special Effects, and YCC Color.

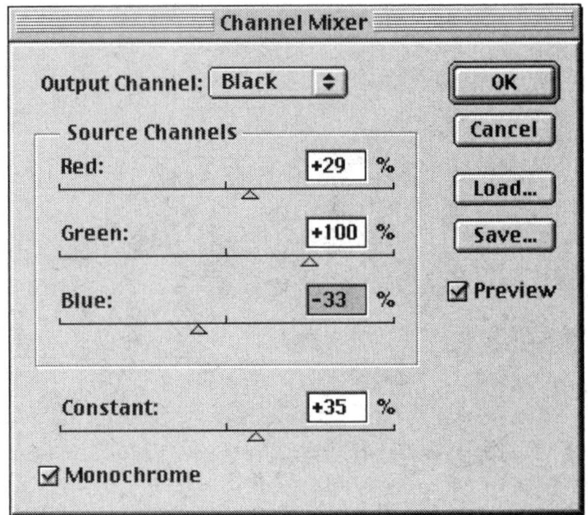

1

CHOOSE COLORS 10

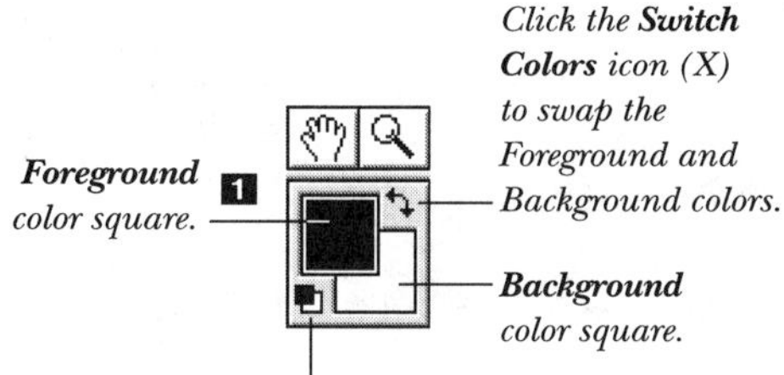

*Click the **Default Colors** icon (D) to make the Foreground color black and the Background color white.*

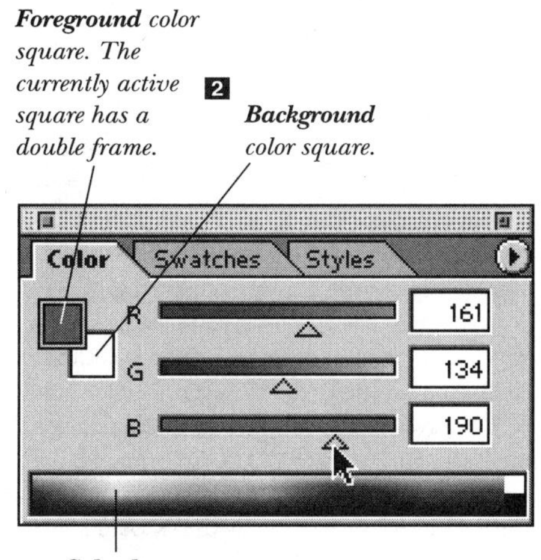

***Color bar**.*

IN THIS CHAPTER you will learn how to choose colors. Colors are applied using various painting and editing tools, as well as some commands.

What are the Foreground and Background colors?

When you use a painting tool, create type, or use the Stroke command, the current **Foreground** color is applied.

When you use the Eraser tool, increase an image's canvas size, or move a selection on the Background using the Move tool, the hole that's left behind is automatically filled with the current **Background** color. The Gradient tool can produce blends using the Foreground and/or Background colors.

The Foreground and Background colors are displayed in the Foreground and Background color squares on the Toolbox **1** and on the Color palette **2**. (When written with an uppercase "F" or "B," these terms refer to colors, not the overall foreground or background areas of a picture.)

There are several ways to choose a Foreground or Background color, and they are described on the following pages:

- Enter values in fields or click on the large color square in the **Color Picker**.
- Choose premixed matching system colors using the **Custom Colors** dialog box.
- Enter values in fields or move sliders on the **Color** palette.
- Click a swatch on the **Swatches** palette.
- Pluck a color from an image using the **Eyedropper** tool.

To choose a color using the Color Picker:

1. Click the Foreground or Background color square on the Toolbox.
   or
   Click the Foreground or Background color square on the Color palette if it is already active (has a double frame).
   or
   Double-click the Foreground or Background color square on the Color palette if it is not active.

   Note: If the color square you click on is a Custom color, the Custom Colors dialog box will open. Click Picker to open the Color Picker dialog box.
2. *Optional:* In the Photoshop Color Picker, check the Only Web Colors box to make only Web-safe colors available for online/on-screen output.
3. Click a color on the vertical color slider to choose a hue **1**, then click a variation of that hue in the large square **2**.
   or
   To choose a specific process color for print output, enter percentages from a matching guide in the C, M, Y, and K fields.
   or
   For on-screen output, enter a value (0 to 255) for the R, G, and B components. When all these components are set to 0, black is produced; when all three are set to 255, white is produced. You can also enter numbers in the HSB or Lab fields.
4. Click OK.

TIP To use the Photoshop Color Picker, choose File menu > Preferences > General (Ctrl-K/Cmd-K), then choose Color Picker: Adobe. You can choose the Windows/Apple color picker from the same pop-up menu. Only one color picker is accessible at a time.

New color. ***Old*** *color.*

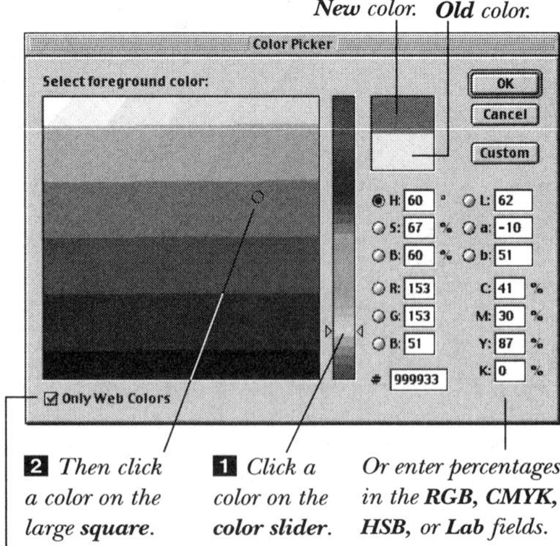

2 *Then click a color on the large* ***square****.*

1 *Click a color on the* ***color slider****.*

Or enter percentages in the ***RGB, CMYK, HSB,*** *or* ***Lab*** *fields.*

Check the ***Only Web Colors*** *box in the* ***Color Picker*** *to make only Web-safe colors available.*

Out of gamut?

An exclamation point in the Color Picker or on the Color palette indicates there is no ink combination for the color you chose—it is out of **printable gamut**. If you're planning to print your image, choose an in-gamut color or click the exclamation point to have Photoshop substitute the closest printable color (shown in the swatch below the exclamation point). If you convert your image to CMYK Color mode, the entire image will be brought into printable gamut. The out-of-gamut range is defined by the CMYK output profile currently chosen in the Color Settings dialog box.

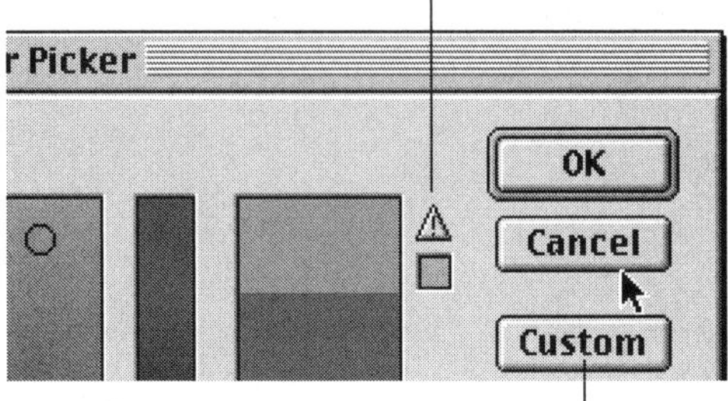

Click ***Custom*** *to choose a predefined color.*

Color separate from elsewhere

To color separate a Photoshop image that contains spot color channels using QuarkXPress, InDesign, Illustrator, or FreeHand, first convert the file to CMYK Color mode and save it in the Photoshop DCS 2.0 format (see page 389). If you use a Pantone color in a spot channel, check the **Short PANTONE Names** box in Edit menu > Preferences > General (Ctrl-K/Cmd-K) so other applications will recognize the Pantone name.

1 *Choose a matching system from the* ***Book*** *pop-up menu, then type a* ***number.***

The number you type will appear here.

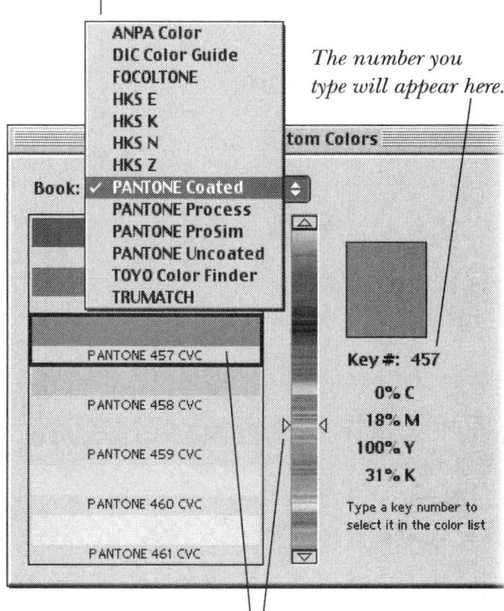

2 *Or click a color on the vertical* ***color slider,*** *then click a* ***swatch.***

Normally, Photoshop separates all colors in an image into the four process colors, regardless of whether they are process or spot colors. In order to separate a spot color to a separate plate from Photoshop, you must create a spot color channel for it (see page 193).

Note: Don't rely on your monitor to represent matching system colors accurately—you must choose them from a printed PANTONE, TRUMATCH, TOYO, DIC, FOCOLTONE, or ANPA Color swatch book. But before you do so, find out which brand of ink your printer is planning to use.

For online output, you can choose Hexadecimal colors (HKS E, HKS K, KHS N, and KHS Z).

To choose a custom color:

1. Click the Foreground or Background color square on the Toolbox.
   or
   Click the Foreground or Background color square on the Color palette if it is already active.
   or
   Double-click the Foreground or Background color square on the Color palette if it is not active.

   Note: If the color square you click on is not a Custom color, the Color Picker dialog box will open. Click Custom to open the Custom Colors dialog box.
2. Choose a matching guide system from the Book pop-up menu **1**.
3. Type a number (it will appear on the "Key #" line).
   or
   Click a color on the vertical color slider, then click a swatch **2**.
4. *Optional:* Click Picker to return to the Color Picker.
5. Click OK.

TIP To load a matching system palette onto the Swatches palette, see page 170.

To choose a color using the Color palette:

1. Click the Foreground or Background color square if it isn't already active **1**.
2. Choose a color model for the sliders from the Color palette command menu **2**.
3. Move any of the sliders **3**.
   or
   Click or drag on the color bar.
   or
   Enter values in the fields.

TIP In the RGB model, white (the presence of all colors) is produced when all the sliders are in their rightmost positions, black (the absence of all colors) is produced when all the sliders are in their leftmost positions, and gray is produced when all the sliders are vertically aligned in any other position.

TIP Right-click/Control-click the color bar to choose a different spectrum style for the color bar from a context menu.

Color palette tips

Alt-click/Option-click the color bar to choose a color for the **non-selected** color square.

The colors on the slider bars will update as you drag. To turn this feature off, uncheck the **Dynamic Color Sliders** box in Edit menu > Preferences > General.

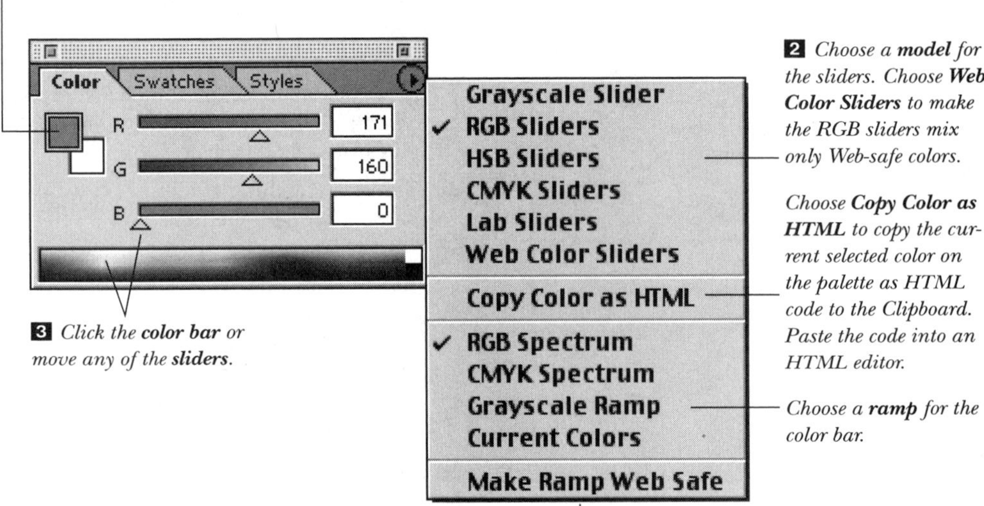

1 *Click the **Foreground** or **Background** **color** square. The currently active square will have a white border.*

2 *Choose a **model** for the sliders. Choose **Web Color Sliders** to make the RGB sliders mix only Web-safe colors.*

*Choose **Copy Color as HTML** to copy the current selected color on the palette as HTML code to the Clipboard. Paste the code into an HTML editor.*

*Choose a **ramp** for the color bar.*

3 *Click the **color bar** or move any of the **sliders**.*

*Choose **Make Ramp Web Safe** to make the color bar contain only Web-safe colors. Choose this option again to restore the normal color spectrum.*

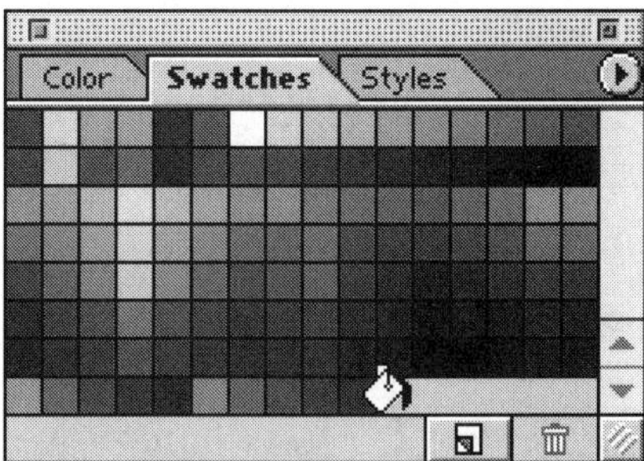

1 *Click in the white area below the swatches.*

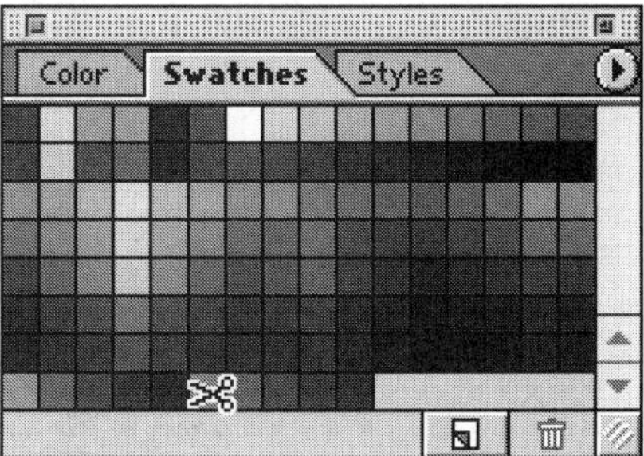

2 *Ctrl-click/Cmd-click a swatch to delete it.*

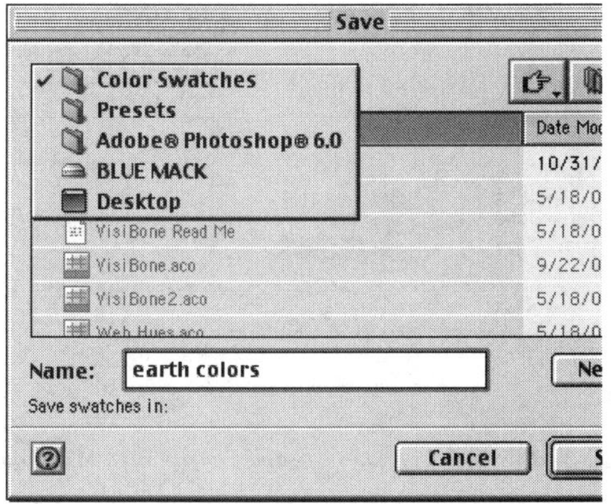

3 *Enter a **Name** and open the **Color Swatches** folder.*

To choose a color from the Swatches palette:

To choose a color for the currently active color square, click a color swatch.

To choose a color for the square that isn't currently active, Alt-click/Option-click a color swatch.

To add a color to the Swatches palette:

1. Mix a color using the Color palette.
2. Click the Swatches tab to display the Swatches palette.
3. Position the cursor in the blank area below the swatches on the palette, and click (paint bucket pointer) **1**. The new color will appear next to the last swatch.
4. Enter a Name, then click OK.

TIP To replace an existing swatch with the new color, Shift-click the color to be replaced.

To delete a color from the Swatches palette:

Ctrl-click/Cmd-click on a swatch (scissors cursor) **2**.

TIP To restore the default Swatches palette, choose Reset Swatches from the Swatches palette command menu, then click OK.

Note: If you edit the Swatches palette and then exit/quit and re-launch Photoshop, your edited palette will reopen.

To save an edited swatches library:

1. Choose Save Swatches from the Swatches palette menu.
2. Enter a name for the edited library in the Name field **3**.
3. Choose a location in which to save the library (note the default location in the screenshot at left), then click Save.

You can load any of the 16 preset color swatch libraries that are supplied with Photoshop or any preset palette that you've created onto the Swatches palette. You can either replace the existing preset library with the new one or append the new preset library to the existing preset library.

To replace or append a swatches library:

6.0!

1. Choose a library name from the bottom of the palette menu.
2. Click Append to add the new library swatches to the current palette.
   or
   Click OK to replace the current palette with the new library swatches.

TIP To enlarge the palette to display the loaded swatches, drag the palette resize box or click the palette zoom box.

To locate and open a swatches library that isn't in the default Adobe Photoshop 6.0 > Presets > Color Swatches folder or in the Adobe Photoshop Only folder within the Color Swatches folder 1–2, use the Load Swatches command.

To load a swatches library:

1. Choose Load Swatches from the Swatches palette menu.
2. Locate and highlight the swatches library you want to open.
3. Click Load (Win)/Open (Mac). The loaded swatches will appear below the existing swatches on the Swatches palette.

Back to basics

To restore the default palette, choose **Reset Swatches** from the Swatches palette menu.

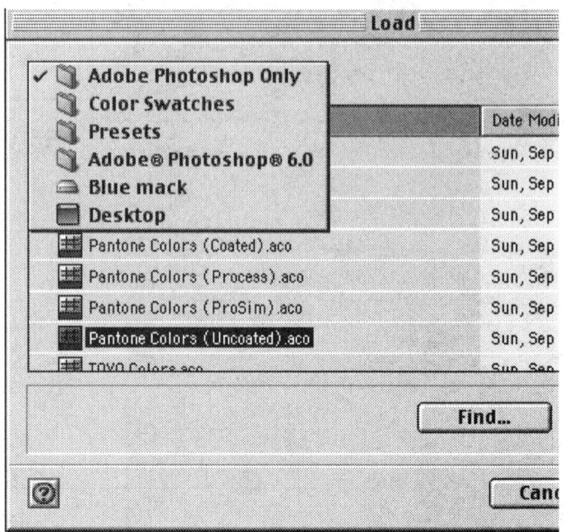

1 *Default color matching system swatches libraries are located in the Adobe Photoshop 6.0 >* ***Presets*** *>* ***Color Swatches*** *>* ***Adobe Photoshop Only folder*** *on* ***Mac OS.***

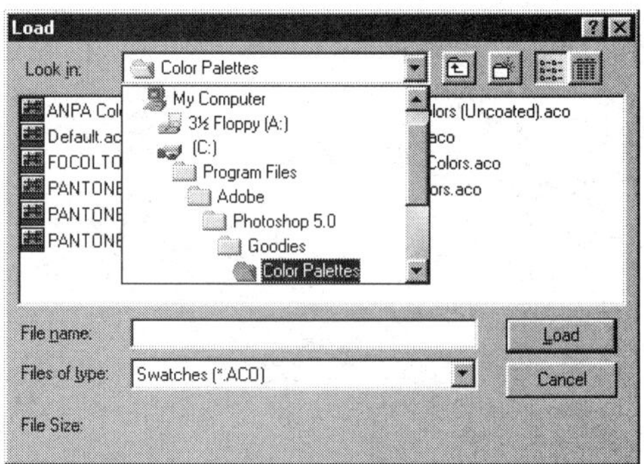

2 *The* ***default swatches libraries*** *location in* ***Windows.***

Replace or Load Swatches Set

1 ***Sampling*** *a color from an image using the* ***Eyedropper*** *tool.*

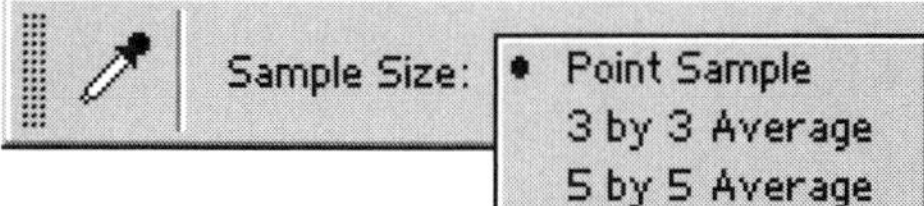

2 *Choose a* ***Sample Size*** *from the* ***Eyedropper*** *options bar.*

To choose a color from an image using the Eyedropper:

1. On the Color palette, click the Foreground or Background color square if it is *not* already active.
2. Click on a color in any open image window **1**. You can also drag over a color area to preview the colors in that area (watch the color square change on the Toolbox or the Color palette), then release the mouse when the pointer is over the desired color. A breakdown of the quantities of the chosen color's components will appear on the Info palette.

TIP To change the area within which the Eyedropper tool samples, choose Point Sample (the exact pixel that's clicked on) or 3 by 3 or 5 by 5 Average (an average within a 3 x 3 or 5 x 5 pixel square) from the Eyedropper options bar **2**. If you Right-click/Control-click on the image with the Eyedropper, you can choose any of those settings from a context menu. (For the Copy Color as HTML options, see the next page.)

TIP Alt-click/Option-click or drag in the image window with the Eyedropper tool to choose a Background color when the Foreground color square is active or a Foreground color when the Background color square is active.

Colors can be copied as hexadecimal values from a file in Photoshop or ImageReady and then pasted into an HTML file. There are two methods for copying a color.

To copy a color as a hexadecimal value:

Method 1

1. Choose the Eyedropper tool (I).
2. *Photoshop:* Right-click/Ctrl-click a color in the image window, then choose Copy Color as HTML.

   ImageReady: Click the color in the image which you want to copy (it will become the Foreground color). With the Eyedropper tool still over the image, Right-click/Control-click to choose from the Eyedropper tool context menu, then choose Copy Foreground Color as HTML from the context menu.

   The selected color will be copied to the Clipboard as a hexadecimal value.
3. To paste the color into an HTML file, display the HTML file in your HTML editing application, then choose Edit menu > Paste. You can insert the code for any HTML element that allows a color property.

Method 2

1. Choose a Foreground color via the Color palette, Color Picker, or Swatches palette.
2. *Photoshop:* Choose Copy Color As HTML from the Color palette menu.

   ImageReady: Choose Edit menu > Copy Foreground Color as HTML.

   The Foreground color will be copied to the Clipboard as a hexadecimal value.
3. To paste the color into an HTML file, open the destination application, display the HTML file, then choose Edit menu > Paste.

Recolor 11

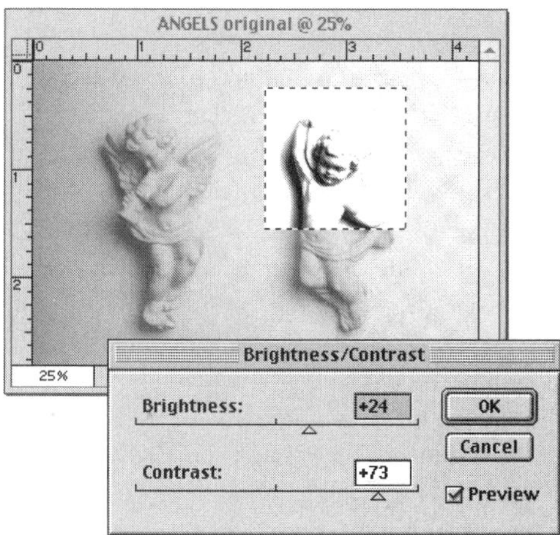

1 *Changes only preview in the image window or a selection when the **Preview** box is checked.*

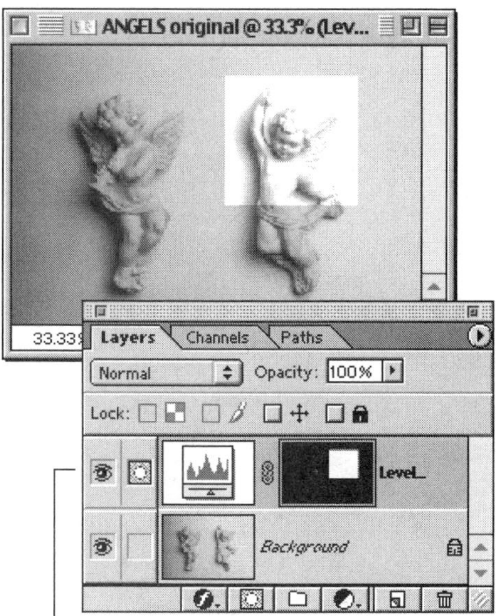

2 *For more flexibility, try out adjustments via an **adjustment layer**.*

IN THIS CHAPTER you will learn to fill a selection with color, a pattern, or imagery; apply a stroke to a selection or a layer; adjust a color image using the Hue/Saturation, Color Balance, Variations, Curves, and Levels commands; use the Color Sampler tool to get multiple color readouts; change colors using the Replace Color command; strip color from a layer; saturate or desaturate colors using the Sponge tool; blend channels using the Channel Mixer; use a neutral color layer to heighten color; tint a grayscale image; and create and print spot color channels.

Note: Make sure your monitor is calibrated before performing color adjustments (see page 34).

Adjust command basics

Every Image menu > Adjust submenu dialog box has a **Preview** box. Changes preview in the image or selection when the Preview box is checked **1**.

TIP While a dialog box is open, you can Ctrl-Spacebar-click/Cmd-Spacebar-click to **zoom in** or Alt-Spacebar-click/Option-Spacebar-click to **zoom out**, or press Spacebar to **move** the image around in the image window.

In addition to the standard method for applying Adjust submenu commands, many of those commands can be applied via an **adjustment layer** **2**. Unlike the standard method, which affects only the currently active layer, the adjustment layer affects all the currently visible layers below it. The adjustment layer, however, doesn't actually change pixels until it's merged with the layer below it. Adjustment layers are used in this chapter, but to learn how to create and

(Continued on the following page)

use them, follow the instructions on pages 152–155. Similarly, you can use a **fill layer** to apply a solid color, gradient, or pattern (see page 132).

You can use the **Save** command in the Levels, Curves, Replace Color, Selective Color, Hue/Saturation, Channel Mixer, or Variations dialog box to save color adjustment settings. You can then apply them to another layer or to another image via the **Load** button for the same command. And any Adjust submenu command can be recorded and applied via an **action**.

Some of the Adjust submenu commands, such as Variations, Color Balance, and Brightness/Contrast, produce broad, overall changes. Other commands, such as Levels, Curves, Hue/Saturation, Replace Color, Selective Color, and Channel Mixer, offer a greater degree of control, but are a little trickier to use. Which command you decide to use will depend on the kind of imagery you're working with and whether it will be color separated or output online. For example, a color cast (e.g, too much blue or too much magenta) will be most noticeable in figurative photography, so this kind of imagery would require careful color adjustment.

TIP To restore the original settings to any Adjust submenu dialog box while it is still open, Alt-click/Option-click Reset.

Fill shortcuts

Windows

Fill with Foreground color, 100% opacity	Alt-Backspace
Fill with Background color, 100% opacity	Ctrl-Backspace
Fill visible pixels (not transparent areas) with the Foreground color	Alt-Shift - Backspace
Fill visible pixels (not transparent areas) with the Background color	Ctrl-Shift-Backspace

Mac OS

Fill with Foreground color, 100% opacity	Option-Delete
Fill with Background color, 100% opacity	Cmd-Delete
Fill visible pixels (not transparent areas) with the Foreground color	Option-Shift-Delete
Fill visible pixels (not transparent areas) with the Background color	Cmd-Shift-Delete

1 *Select an area to use as a **tile** for a pattern.*

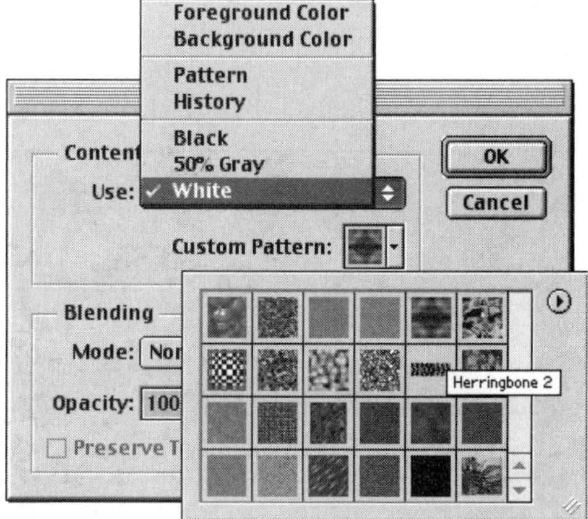

2 *The **Fill** dialog box.*

3 *The tile used as a **fill pattern** in another image.*

To fill a selection or a layer with a color, a pattern, or imagery: 6.0!

1. To fill with a flat Foreground or Background **color**, choose that color now from the Color or Swatches palette.
   or
   To fill with **history**, click in the box next to a state on the History palette to establish a source for the History Brush.
   or
   To create a tiling **pattern**, you don't need to do anything—you'll have access to the pattern presets. If you'd like to create a custom pattern now, select an area on a layer in any open image using the Rectangular Marquee tool (no feathering!) **1**, choose Edit menu > Define Pattern, enter a Name, then Deselect (Ctrl-D/Cmd-D).
2. Choose a layer. To fill the entire layer, uncheck the **Lock transparent pixels** box on the Layers palette; to fill only non-transparent areas on the layer, check the "Lock transparent pixels" box.

   To limit the fill area, create a **selection** using any selection method.
3. Choose Edit menu > Fill (Shift-Backspace/Shift-Delete).
4. From the **Use** pop-up menu, choose what you want to fill the selection or layer with: **2**

   Foreground Color, Background Color, Black, 50% Gray, or White.

   Pattern; click the Custom Pattern arrowhead, then choose a pattern from the picker.

   History to fill the selection or layer with imagery from the active layer at the state that you chose as a source.
5. Choose a blending Mode and an Opacity percentage.
6. *Optional:* If you forgot to check the "Lock transparent pixels" box on the Layers palette, you can check Preserve Transparency box here instead.

(Continued on the following page)

7. Click OK **3**.

TIP If you dislike the new fill color, choose Edit menu > Undo now so it won't blend with your next color or mode choice.

TIP To fill a layer using a layer effect, double-click the layer name, then, in Layer Style, click Color Overlay, Gradient Overlay, or Pattern Overlay. Adjust the settings, then click OK. You can apply one, two, or all three of the Overlay effects to the same layer.

6.0!

It's a pattern 6.0!

Using the **presets** feature in Photoshop 6, it's easy to save patterns for future use. To learn more about presets, see pages 371–374. Nevertheless, for safe-keeping, you should hold onto any files that contain imagery you've used as the source for a pattern tile in case the presets are accidentally deleted.

You're not limited to the Fill command to apply patterns. You can also apply a pattern using the **Pattern Stamp** tool (see page 115) or the **Paint Bucket** tool.

1 *To produce this image, the pattern layer was duplicated, the opacity of the duplicate was lowered to 43%, and its blending mode was changed to Multiply.*

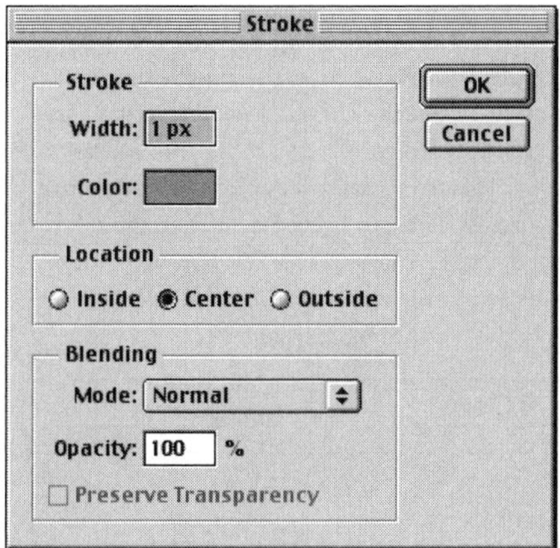

1 *Choose options in the* ***Stroke*** *dialog box.*

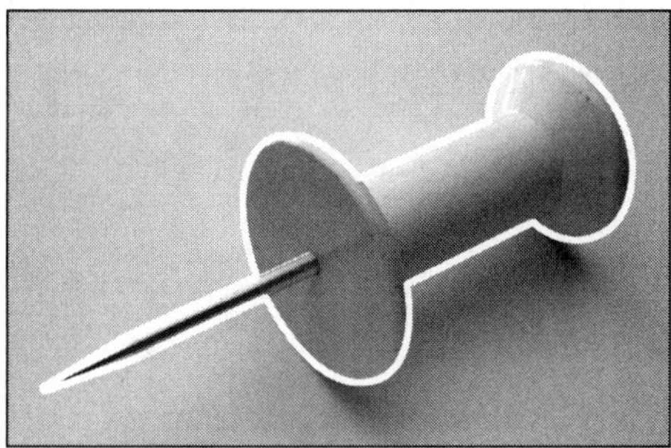

2 *A* ***white stroke*** *was applied to the pushpin.*

To apply a stroke to a selection or a layer:

1. *Optional:* If you prefer to choose a stroke color via the Color palette or Swatches palette, do it now. If you prefer to choose a color from the Color Picker, you can access it when you get to the Stroke dialog box.
2. Choose a layer. If you don't want the stroke to extend into transparent areas on the layer, check the "Lock transparent pixels" box on the Layers palette and don't choose the Location: Outside option for step 6.

   Optional: Select an area on the layer.
3. Choose Edit menu > Stroke.
4. Enter a Width (1–16) **1**.
5. If you didn't choose a stroke color for step 1, click the Color swatch, then choose a color from the Color Picker. 6.0!
6. Click Location: Inside, Center, or Outside (the position of the stroke on the edge of the selection or layer imagery).
7. Choose a blending Mode and an Opacity.
8. Click OK **2**.

TIP To stroke a path, see page 271.

TIP You can also stroke a path as a layer effect. Double-click a layer name, click Stroke in the Layer Style dialog box, adjust the settings, then click OK. 6.0!

Stroke

To adjust a color image using Hue/Saturation:

1. Choose a layer. *Optional:* Select an area of the layer to recolor only that area.
2. Choose Image menu > Adjust > Hue/ Saturation (Ctrl-U/Cmd-U).
   or
   Create an adjustment layer by choosing Hue/Saturation from the "Create new fill or adjustment layer" pop-up menu at the bottom of the Layers palette.
3. From the Edit pop-up menu, choose Master to adjust all the image colors at once or choose a preset range to adjust only colors within that range **1**.
4. Make sure the Preview box is checked.
5. Do any of the following:

   Move the **Hue** slider **2** to the left or the right to shift colors to another part of the color bar.

   Move the **Saturation** slider to the left to decrease saturation or to the right to increase saturation.

   To lighten the image or layer, move the **Lightness** slider to the right. To darken the image or layer, move it to the left.

   TIP To add Color Sampler points while the Hue/Saturation dialog is open, choose Edit: Master, then Shift-click on the image (see pages 180–181).
6. If a preset color range was chosen from the Edit pop-up menu, the adjustment slider and color selection droppers are available **3**. You can use the adjustment slider to narrow or widen the range of colors that the Hue, Saturation, and Lightness sliders will affect.

   By default, the adjustment slider covers 90° of the color bar, the gray areas to the left and right (the fall-off) occupy 30° each, and the dark gray area (the color range) occupies 30°.

   Do any of the following to the adjustment slider:

   Drag the darkest gray area in the center to reposition the whole slider, as is, to a

To colorize a color or grayscale image

Check the **Colorize** box in the Hue/Saturation dialog box to tint the current layer. Move the Hue slider to apply a different tint; move the Saturation slider to reduce/increase tint color intensity; move the Lightness slider to lighten or darken the tint (and the image or layer). The Edit pop-up menu defaults to Master when the Colorize option is on. To produce a duotone, see page 392.

To tint a grayscale image using this method, convert it to RGB Color or CMYK Color mode first.

1 *From the* ***Edit*** *pop-up menu, choose* ***Master*** *or choose a preset* ***color*** *range.*

2 *Then move the* ***Hue, Saturation,*** *or* ***Lightness*** *sliders.*

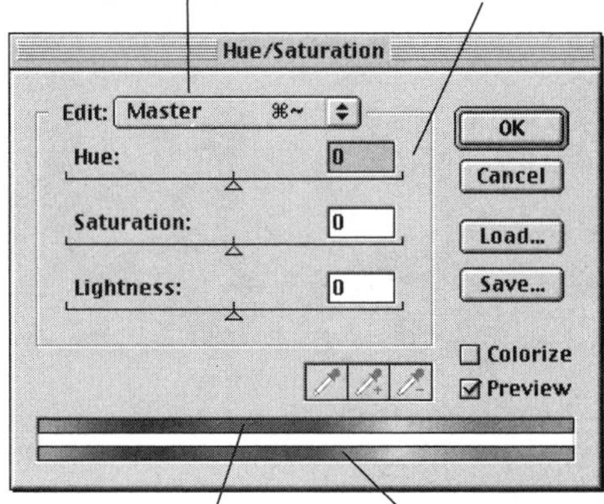

The ***reference*** *color bar won't change.*

Color ***adjustments*** *will be displayed in this color bar.*

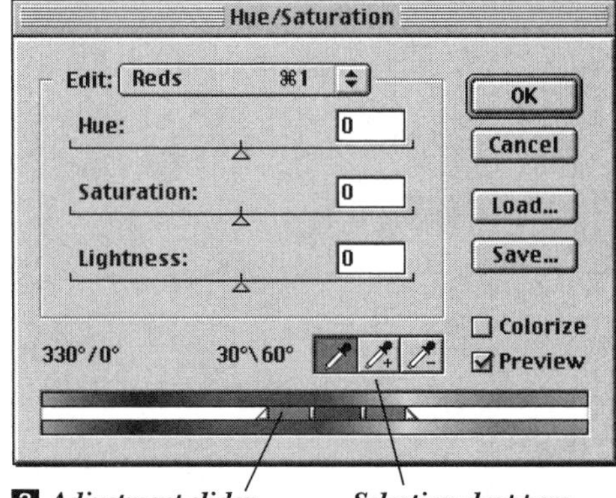

3 ***Adjustment slider.*** ***Selection droppers.***

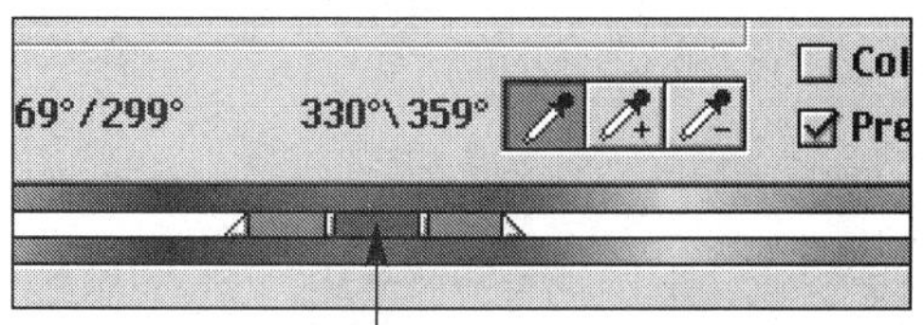

1 *The adjusment slider is moved into a different range.*

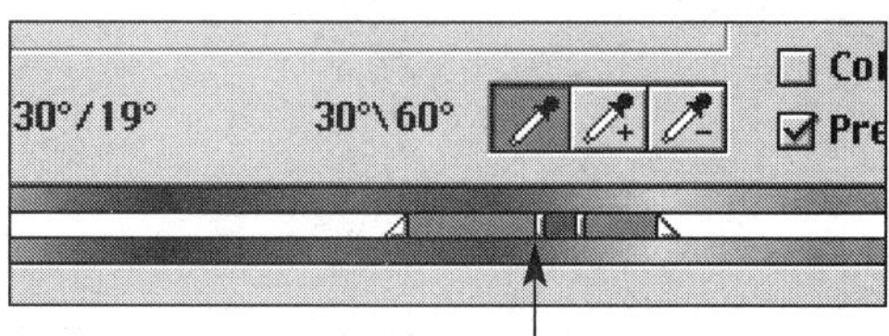

2 *The vertical white bar is moved inward to* ***narrow*** *the* ***color range****.*

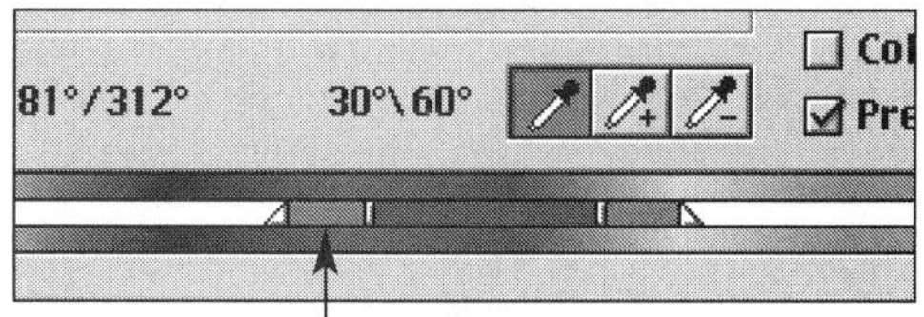

3 *The gray area (the fall-off) is moved outward to* ***widen*** *the* ***color range****. The fall-off is unchanged.*

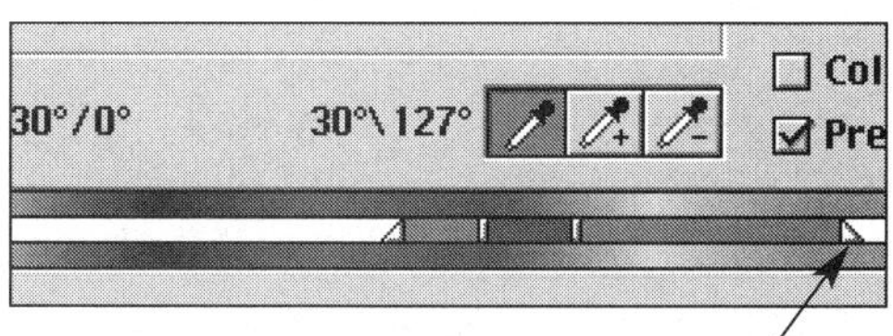

4 *The triangle moved is outward to* ***widen*** *the* ***fall-off****. The color range is unchanged.*

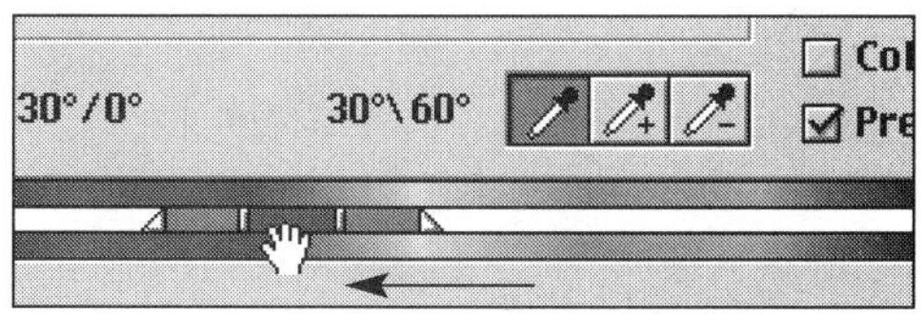

5 *Ctrl-drag/Cmd-drag to reposition the display position of the slider and the colors on the color bars.*

new spot on the color bar to shift it into a different color range **1**. The Edit pop-up menu will update to reflect the new color range choice.

Drag either or both of the vertical white bars on the slider to narrow or expand the range. Decreasing the range increases the fall-off area, and vice versa **2**.

Drag either or both of the gray areas to widen or narrow that range without altering the fall-off area **3**.

Drag the outer triangles on the slider to change how much of the current range falls off into adjacent colors **4**. Drag outward to increase fall-off or inward to decrease it. *Note:* A very short fall-off may produce dithering in the image.

Ctrl-drag/Cmd-drag either color bar to adjust where colors are displayed on the bar **5**. Colors wrap from one edge to the other. This won't affect the actual image.

If you alter the slider for any of the six preset color ranges, then that current color adjustment will become the new listing on the Edit pop-up menu. If, for example, you move the preset Reds range slider so it enters the Yellows range, then the menu will list Yellows and Yellows 2, and will no longer list Reds, since the Yellows range now includes Reds.

Click on a color in the image window—related colors will be adjusted. Or use the + or - dropper to add to or subtract from any current color range by clicking on the image. Hold down Shift while the regular dropper is selected to make it function temporarily like an add dropper; hold down Alt/Option to make the regular dropper function temporarily like a subtract dropper.

7. Click OK.

TIP To restore the original dialog box settings, Alt-click/Option-click Reset.

Instead of using the Eyedropper tool to get a color readout from one spot, you can use the Color Sampler tool to place up to four color readout markers, called color samplers, on an image. As you perform color and shade adjustments, before and after color breakdown readouts will display on the Info palette. You can also place color samplers while a color adjustment dialog box is open (Shift-click on the image). Color samplers save with the file in which they are placed.

To place color samplers on an image:

1. Choose the Color Sampler tool (I or Shift-I).
2. Click on up to four locations on the image to position color samplers **1**.

   Note: If you choose a tool other than the Color Sampler, Eyedropper, or a painting or editing tool, the samplers will disappear from view. To redisplay them, choose one of the above-mentioned tools or open an Adjust submenu dialog box. To deliberately hide them, choose Hide Color Samplers from the Info palette menu.

TIP Color samplers gather data from the topmost visible layer that contains visible pixels in the spot where the sampler is located. If you hide a layer from which a sampler is reading, the sampler will then read from the next layer down that contains visible pixels in that spot. The Info palette will update if you hide a layer from which it was reading sampler data.

TIP The samplers are located on the canvas. They won't move if a layer is transformed or flipped, but they *will* move if the whole canvas is rotated.

To move a color sampler:

Choose the Color Sampler tool (I or Shift-I), then drag a color sampler.

or

Choose the Eyedropper tool (I or Shift-I), then Ctrl-drag/Cmd-drag a color sampler.

1 *Click on an image with the* ***Color Sampler*** *tool to create up to four sampler locations.*

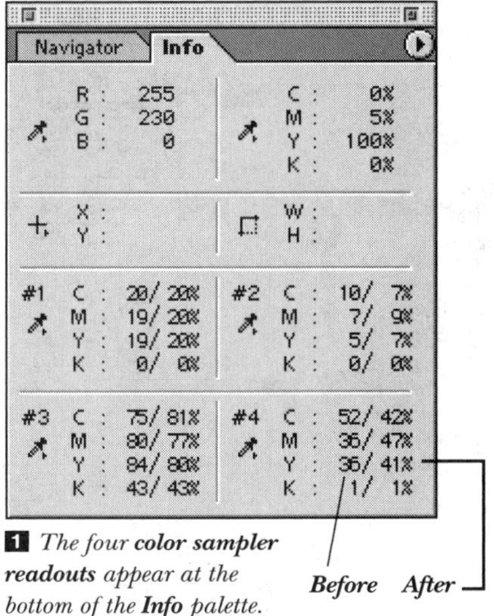

1 *The four* ***color sampler readouts*** *appear at the bottom of the* ***Info*** *palette.*

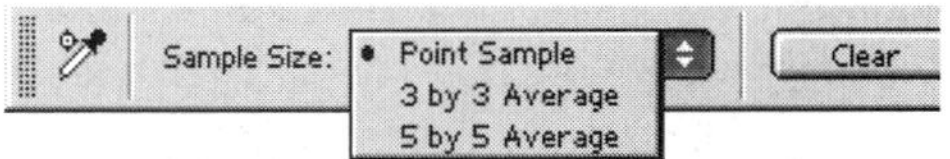

2 *Choose a* ***Sample Size*** *from the* ***Color Sampler*** *options bar.*

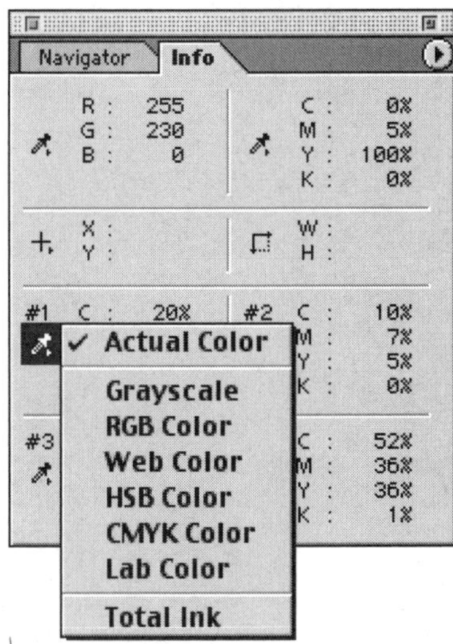

3 *You can choose a different* ***color model*** *for each color sampler.*

Using the Info palette with the Color Sampler tool

The Info palette displays before adjustment and after adjustment color breakdowns of the pixel or pixel area under each color sampler **1**. The size of the sample area depends on which **Sample Size** setting is chosen on the Color Sampler options bar **2**. 6.0! Choose Point Sample to sample only the pixel under the pointer; choose 3 by 3 Average or 5 by 5 Average to sample an average color from a 3- or 5-pixel area. If you change the Sample Size for the Color Sampler tool, that setting will also change for the Eyedropper, and vice versa.

To choose a **color model** (Grayscale, RGB Color, etc.) for a section of the Info palette, press the tiny arrowhead next to a dropper icon on the palette, then choose from the pop-up menu that opens **3**. Actual Color is the image's current color mode; Total Ink is the total percentage of CMYK under the pointer based on the current settings in CMYK Setup. The model you choose for the Info palette doesn't have to match the current image mode. (You can also choose a color model in the Info Options dialog box, which opens when you choose Palette Options from the Info palette menu.)

To remove a color sampler:

Choose the Color Sampler tool, then Alt-click/Option-click a sampler (the pointer will become a scissors icon) or drag the sampler out of the image window. That sampler's readout area will be removed from the Info palette, and the remaining samplers will be renumbered automatically.

or

Choose the Eyedropper tool, then Alt-Shift-click/Option-Shift-click a sampler.

or

Click Clear on the options bar to remove all color samplers. 6.0!

Use the Replace Color command to change colors in an image without having to first select them.

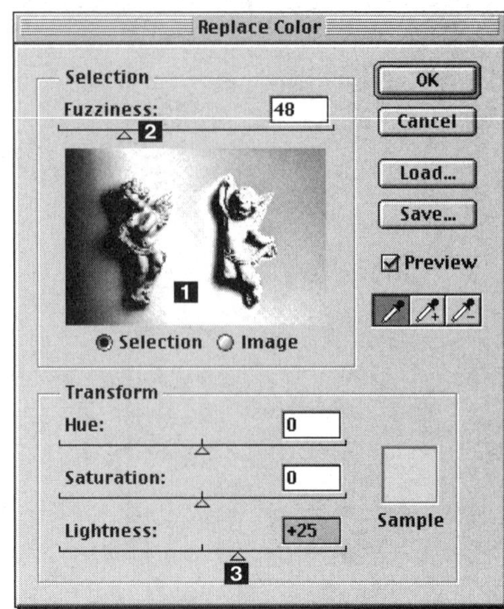

*The **white** areas in the preview window are the areas that will be modified.*

To replace colors:

6.0!

1. *Optional:* For an RGB image, choose View menu > Proof Setup > Working CMYK to see a soft proof of the actual image and modifications to it in CMYK color. (The Sample swatch in the Replace Color dialog box will continue to display in RGB.) You can choose this command even while the dialog box is open.
2. Choose a layer.
3. *Optional:* Create a selection to restrict color replacement to that area.
4. Choose Image menu > Adjust > Replace Color.
5. Click on the color you want to replace either in the preview window in the Replace Color dialog box or in the image window **1**.

   TIP Initially, the preview window is solid black. Click the Selection button to preview the selection in the preview window or click the Image button to display the entire image (*Mac OS:* press Control to toggle between the two display modes). If your image extends beyond the edges of your monitor, click Image so you'll be able to sample from the entire image preview with the eyedropper.
6. *Optional:*

   Move the Fuzziness slider to the right to add related colors to the selection **2**.

   or

   Shift-click in the preview window or the image window to add other color areas to the selection. Or choose the + eyedropper and click without holding down Shift.

   or

   Alt-click/Option-click in the preview window or in the image window to subtract color areas from the selection. Or choose the – eyedropper icon and click without holding down Shift.

Replace Color

4 *The original image.*

5 *After a **Lightness** adjustment to the background.*

7. Move the Hue, Saturation, or Lightness sliders to change the selected colors (only the Lightness slider will be available for a Grayscale image). The Sample swatch will change as you move the sliders **3**.

   The Transform sliders will stay in their current positions even if you click on a different area of the image.

8. Click OK **4**–**5**.

TIP The Sample swatch color from the Replace Color dialog box will also display in the currently active square on the Color palette, and the Color palette sliders will reflect its individual components. If the gamut alarm displays, you have produced a non-printable color using the Transform sliders. The Transform sliders won't change the amount of Black (K) in a color for an image in CMYK Color mode. That component is set by Photoshop's Black Generation function.

TIP To restore the original dialog box settings, Alt-click/Option-click Reset.

Use the Desaturate command to strip color from a layer (convert it to grayscale) without actually changing the color mode for the whole image.

To convert a layer or the Background to grayscale:

1. Choose a layer or the Background.
2. Choose Image menu > Adjust > Desaturate (Ctrl-Shift-U/Cmd-Shift-U).

Use the Color Balance dialog box to apply or correct a warm or cool cast in a layer's highlights, midtones, or shadows. Color adjustments will be easier to see in an image that has a wide tonal range.

To colorize or color correct using Color Balance:

1. Make sure the composite color image is displayed (the first channel on the Channels palette). To colorize a Grayscale image, first convert it to a color image mode.
2. Choose a layer.
3. Choose Image menu > Adjust > Color Balance (Ctrl-B/Cmd-B).
   or
   Create an adjustment layer by choosing Color Balance from the "Create new fill or adjustment layer" pop-up menu at the bottom of the Layers palette.
4. At the bottom of the dialog box, click the tonal range you want to adjust: Shadows, Midtones, or Highlights **1**.
5. *Optional:* Check the Preserve Luminosity box to preserve brightness values.
6. Move any slider toward a color you want to add more of. Cool and warm colors are paired opposite each other. Pause to preview.

   TIP Move sliders toward related colors to make an image warmer or cooler. For example, move sliders toward Cyan and Blue to produce a cool cast.
7. *Optional:* Repeat step 6 with any other Tone Balance button selected.
8. Click OK.

Hand tinting

Use the **Paintbrush** or **Airbrush** tool with a light opacity (options bar) to tint small areas manually.

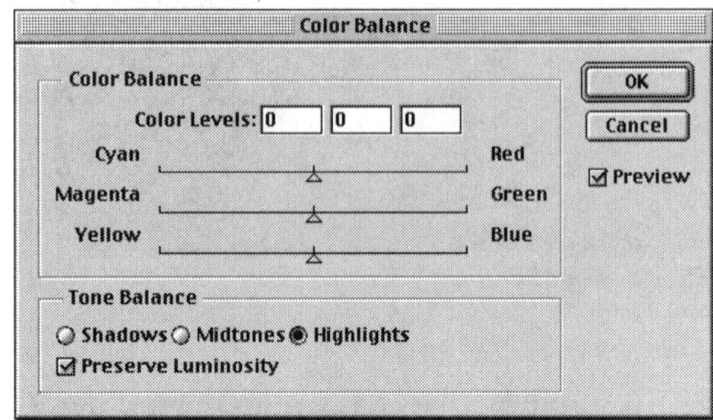

1 *Click **Tone Balance: Shadows, Midtones,** or **Highlights**, then move any of the sliders.*

Color Balance

*Click the **Original** thumbnail to restore the unmodified layer.*

1 *First click **Shadows, Midtones, Highlights,** or **Saturation**.*

2 *Move the **Fine/Coarse** slider to control the degree of adjustment.*

*The **Current Pick** thumbnail represents the modified layer.*

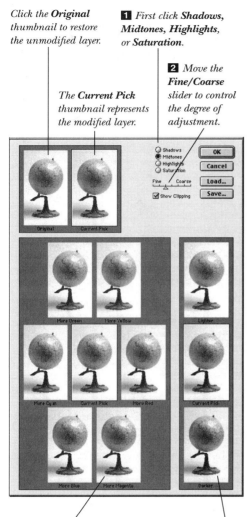

3 *Click any **More [. . .]** thumbnail to add more of that color to the layer. Click the diagonally opposite thumbnail to undo the modification.*

4 *Click **Lighter** or **Darker** to modify the luminosity without modifying the hue.*

Thumbnail previews in the Variations dialog box represent how an image will look with various color adjustments. To make more precise adjustments and preview changes in the image window, use the Color Balance or Levels dialog box.

Note: The Variations command can't be used on an Indexed Color image.

To adjust color using thumbnail Variations:

1. Choose a layer.
2. Choose Image menu > Adjust > Variations.
3. Click Shadows, Midtones, or Highlights at the top of the dialog box to modify only those areas **1**.
   or
   Click Saturation to adjust only saturation.
4. Position the Fine/Coarse slider to the right of center to make major adjustments or to the left of center to make minor adjustments **2**. Each notch to the right doubles the adjustment per click. Each notch to the left halves the adjustment per click.
5. Click any "More..." thumbnail to add more of that color to the layer **3**. Pause to preview. To lessen the amount of a color, click its diagonally opposite color.

   Note: Compare the Current Pick thumbnail, which represents the modified layer, with the Original thumbnail. Click the Original thumbnail to undo the Variations adjustment.
6. *Optional:* Click Lighter or Darker to change the luminosity without changing the hue **4**.
7. *Optional:* If you chose to adjust Shadows, Highlights, or Saturation, you can check the Show Clipping box to display neon highlights in areas that will be converted to black or white.
8. *Optional:* Repeat steps 3–6 with a different tonal range chosen.
9. Click OK.

Use the Sponge tool to make color areas on the current layer more or less saturated. (The Sponge tool is also discussed on page 397, where it's used to bring colors into printable gamut.) This tool can't be used on a Bitmap or Indexed Color image.

1 *Choose settings for the* ***Sponge*** *tool from the options bar.*

To saturate or desaturate colors using the Sponge tool:

1. Double-click the Sponge tool (O or Shift-O).

6.0!

2. On the Sponge options bar: **1**

   Click the Painting Brush arrowhead, then click a brush. A soft brush will produce the smoothest result.
   and
   Choose Mode: Desaturate or Saturate.
   and
   Choose a Pressure percentage between 1% (low intensity) and 100% (high intensity). Try a low Pressure percentage first (20%-30%) so the tool won't saturate or desaturate areas too quickly.

   TIP Press a single- or double-digit number on the keyboard to change the Pressure incrementally.

3. Choose a layer.
4. Stroke on any area of the layer **2**. Pause to allow the screen to redraw, if necessary. Stroke again to intensify the effect.

TIP If you Saturate or Desaturate an area too much, choose Edit menu > Undo or click an earlier state or snapshot on the History palette. Don't try to use the tool with its opposite setting to fix it—you'll get uneven results.

TIP You can also adjust saturation in an image using the Image menu > Adjust > Hue/Saturation or Replace Color command.

2 *Using the* ***Sponge*** *tool to desaturate colors in an image.*

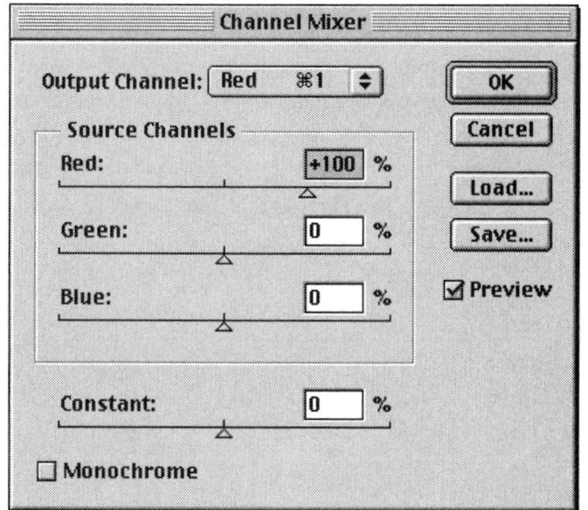

1 *In the* ***Channel Mixer*** *dialog box, choose an* ***Output Channel*** *and then move the* ***Source Channel*** *sliders.*

The Channel Mixer produces unique mixtures of RGB or CMYK channels—mixtures that may be too difficult to achieve using other commands. To use the Channel Mixer to perform a color-to-grayscale conversion or to tint a grayscale image, see page 164.

To use the Channel Mixer:

1. Choose a layer, and make sure the composite color channel is displayed (top channel on the Channels palette).
2. Choose Image menu > Adjust > Channel Mixer.
   or
   Create an adjustment layer by choosing Channel Mixer from the "Create new fill or adjustment layer" pop-up menu at the bottom of the Layers palette.
3. Choose a channel from the Output Channel pop-up menu **1**.
4. Do any of the following:

   Move whichever slider is set at 100% (the chosen output channel) below 100 to reduce the amount of that color in the channel or above 100 to increase the amount of that color.

   Move any of the other sliders to the left to add more of that color to the output channel (a negative value) or to the right to subtract more of that color (a positive value). *Note:* for a Black source channel, move it to the left to reduce or to the right to increase the amount of black.

   Bear in mind the mixing relationship between these six basic color components: Cyan to Red, Magenta to Green, and Yellow to Blue. Decreasing Cyan, for example, will result in more Red in the channel, and vice versa. If you forget these relationships, open up the Color Balance dialog box.

   Move the Constant slider to the right to add the current output channel color as a wash over the entire image. Move it to the left to subtract that color and add its related colors to the entire layer.
5. Click OK.

Curves and Levels

If you use the Curves or Levels command to make color or tonal adjustments, you should adjust the overall tone of the image first (the composite channel), and then adjust individual color channels, if necessary (a bit more cyan, a bit less magenta, etc.).

Using the Curves command, you can correct a picture's highlights, quarter tones, midtones, three-quarter tones, or shadows separately. You can even use multiple adjustment layers to do this. Use one adjustment layer for the composite channel first and then use another one for each individual channel to fine tune the color. And you can experiment with the layer opacity or use a layer mask to remove or lessen the effect in specific areas.

To adjust color or values using the Curves command:

1. *Optional:* To adjust a combination of two or more channels at the same time, Shift-click those channel names on the Channels palette now. *Note:* You can't do this for a Curves adjustment layer!
2. Choose Image menu > Adjust > Curves (Ctrl-M/Cmd-M).
   or
   Create an adjustment layer by choosing Curves from the "Create new fill or adjustment layer" pop-up menu at the bottom of the Layers palette.
3. Move the pointer over the grid. The default Input and Output readouts in the lower left corner of the dialog box are the brightness values for RGB Color mode or the percentage values for CMYK Color mode. Click the gradient bar to switch between the two readouts.
4. *Optional:* Choose a Channel to adjust it separately (this won't work if you're working on an adjustment layer). If you chose more than one channel in step 1, you can select that combo now (e.g., "RB" for the red and blue channels).
5. If the gradient on the gradient bar is white on the left side (for CMYK mode),

Changing channels

If you adjust an individual color channel, keep in mind that **color opposites** (cyan and red, magenta and green, yellow and blue) work in tandem. Lowering cyan, for example, adds more red; lowering red adds more cyan. In fact, you'll probably need to adjust more than one channel to remove an undesirable color cast. If you overzealously adjust only one channel, you'll throw off the color balance of the whole image.

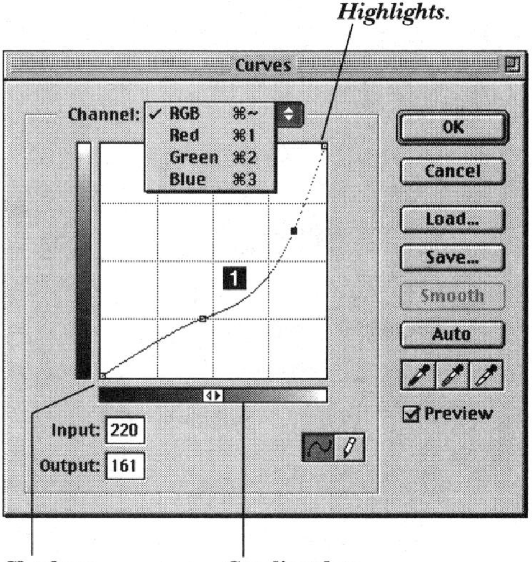

2 *The original image.*

3 *After a **Curves** adjustment.*

drag the part of the curve you want to adjust upward to darken or downward to lighten **1**. (Click the double arrow in the middle of the gradient bar to reverse the curve.) Reverse this instruction for RGB mode.

and/or

For more precise adjustments, click on the curve to create up to 14 additional points to force the curve to remain fixed, then drag between points to make subtle adjustments. (To remove a point, click on it and press Backspace/Delete; or Ctrl-click/Cmd-click on it.)

and/or

Move the extreme end of the curve to reduce absolute black to below 100%, or absolute white to above 0%.

Note: Once you've added a point, you can then enter numbers in the Input and/or Output fields for that point.

6. Click OK **2**–**3**.

TIP The Curves pencil tool tends to produce a bumpy curve, resulting in sharp color transition jumps.

TIP For an image in RGB Color mode, click on the image to see that pixel's placement on the curve. Ctrl-click/Cmd-click on the image to place that point on the curve. The pixel value will show on the individual C, M, Y, and K channels, but not on the composite CMYK channel.

TIP Alt-click/Option-click the grid in the Curves dialog box to narrow the grid spacing; Alt-click/Option-click again to widen the grid spacing.

TIP Shift-click on the image to place Color Sampler points while the Curves dialog box is open.

TIP Click the Auto button to have Photoshop set the highlight and shadow values in an image and redistribute the midrange color values. Individual channel curves will be altered.

To adjust individual color channels using Levels:

1. Display the Info palette.
2. Choose Image menu > Adjust > Levels (Ctrl-L/Cmd-L).
   or
   Create an adjustment layer by choosing Levels from the "Create new fill or adjustment layer" pop-up menu at the bottom of the Layers palette.
3. Check the Preview box.
4. If there's an obvious predominance of one color in the image (e.g., too much red or green), choose that channel from the Channel pop-up menu **1**.

   Follow any of these steps for a **CMYK** Color image (the sliders will have the **opposite** effect in an **RGB** image):

   To increase the amount of that particular color, move the black or gray Input Levels slider to the right. The black triangle affects the shadows in the image, the gray triangle affects the midtones.
   or
   To decrease the amount of that color, move the gray or white Input Levels slider to the left. The white slider affects the highlights.
   or
   To tint the image with the chosen channel color, move the white Output Levels slider to the left. To lessen the chosen channel color, move the black Output Levels slider to the right. The Output sliders are particularly effective for adjusting skin tones in a photograph.

   Repeat these steps for any other channels that need adjusting, bearing in mind that one channel adjustment may affect another.
5. Click OK.

TIP Alt-click/Option-click Reset to restore the original dialog box settings.

TIP Shift-click on the image to place Color Sampler points while the Levels dialog box is open.

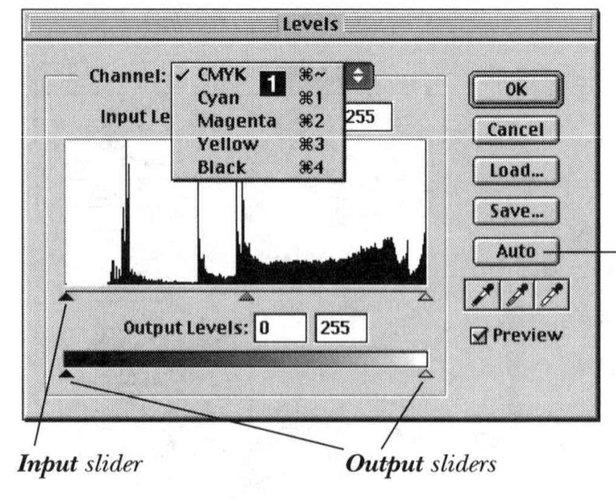

***Input** slider*

***Output** sliders*

*Click **Auto** to have Photoshop set the highlight and shadow values in an image and redistribute the midrange color values. Individual channel curves will be altered.*

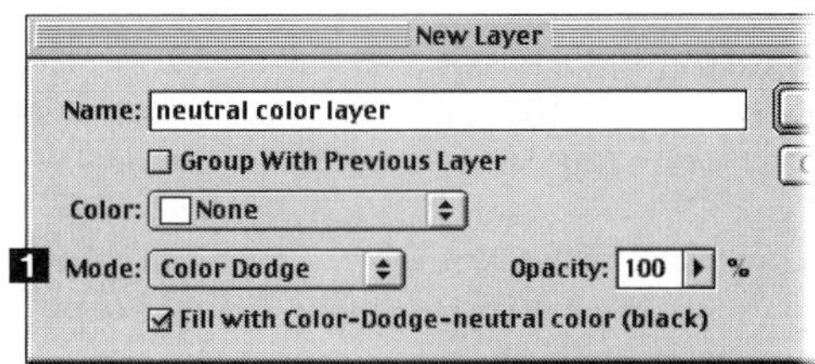

2 *The original image.*

3 *After painting on the Color Dodge mode layer, choosing Color Burn as the layer mode, and painting medium gray strokes on the Color Burn mode layer.*

4 *The original image.*

5 *After choosing Overlay mode, checking the "Fill with..." option for the neutral layer, and applying Dodge and Burn strokes to the neutral layer to heighten the highlights and shadows.*

In this exercise, you'll be painting shades of gray on a special neutral black or white layer in Color Dodge or Color Burn mode in order to heighten or lessen color in the underlying layer. You're welcome to try out other layer modes.

To heighten color or silhouette color areas on black:

1. Convert the image to RGB image mode, and activate the layer that you want to affect.
2. Alt-click/Option-click the "Create new layer" button on the Layers palette.
3. Type a name for the layer.
4. Choose a Mode. We chose Color Dodge mode for our illustration **1**, but you can choose any mode other than Normal, Dissolve, Hue, Saturation, Color, or Luminosity.
5. Check the "Fill with [mode name]-neutral color" box, then click OK. Our layer was filled with black.
6. Choose the Paintbrush tool (B or Shift-B), and choose a brush from the options bar.
7. Choose Grayscale Slider from the Color palette menu.
8. Paint with a 60-88% gray. You'll actually be changing the neutral black on the layer. Areas you stroke over will become much lighter.

   If you're displeased with the results, paint over areas or fill the entire layer again with black to remove all the changes, and start over. Repainting or refilling with black will remove any existing editing effects while preserving pixels in the underlying layers.
9. To heighten the color effect, you can choose another mode from the Layers palette. We chose Color Burn mode. Your image strokes will be silhouetted against black **2**–**5**. Paint with a medium gray if you want to restore more of the original color.

To convert a color layer to grayscale and selectively restore its color:

1. Choose a layer in a color image. Layers below this layer will be affected by the adjustment layer you're about to create.
2. Create an adjustment layer by choosing Hue/Saturation from the "Create new fill or adjustment layer" pop-up menu at the bottom of the Layers palette.
3. Move the Saturation slider all the way to the left (to -100) **1**.
4. Click OK.
5. Set the Foreground color to black.
6. With the adjustment layer chosen, paint across the image where you want to restore the original colors from the underlying layers **2**. Paint with white to restore grayscale areas.

   You can also restack a layer above the adjustment layer to fully restore that layer's color.

TIP Choose any of the following mode and opacity combinations for the adjustment layer:

Dissolve with a 40%–50% Opacity to restore color with a chalky texture.

Multiply with a 100% Opacity to restore subtle color in the darker areas of the image.

Color Dodge to lighten and intensify color or Color Burn to darken and intensify color.

TIP To limit the adjustment layer effect to just the layer directly below it, Alt-click/Option-click the line between them on the Layers palette to create a clipping group.

Hide behind a mask

Duplicate a color layer, choose Image menu > Adjust > **Desaturate** (Ctrl-Shift-U/Cmd-Shift-U), choose Layer menu > Add Layer Mask > **Hide All** to create a layer mask for that layer, and then paint with white to reveal parts of the grayscale layer above the color layer. You can gradually reshape the mask this way, alternately painting with black to add to the mask or white to remove the mask.

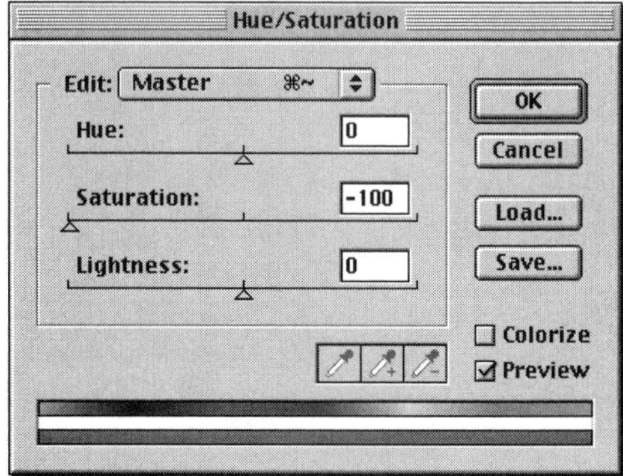

1 *In the* ***Hue/Saturation*** *dialog box, move the* ***Saturation*** *slider all the way to the left to remove color from the layer.*

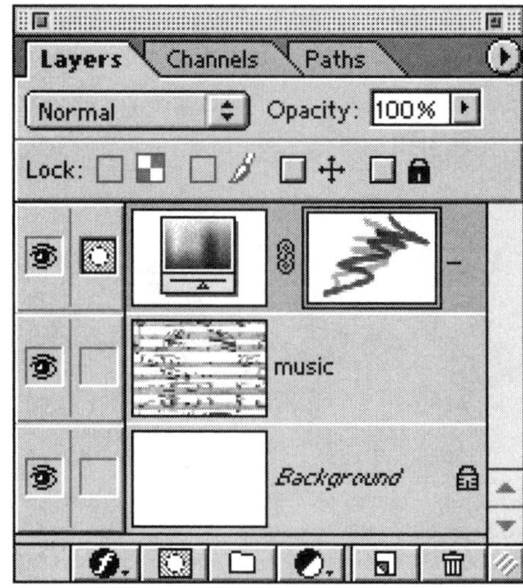

2 *Brushstrokes are applied to an* ***adjustment layer****.*

Copy to a spot color channel

To copy an image shape to a spot color channel, first make a selection on a layer. Then, with the selection active, create a new spot color channel. Or choose an existing spot color channel and fill the selection with black.

To copy an image's light and dark values to a spot color channel, first create a selection and copy it to the Clipboard. Then create or choose a spot color channel, and paste onto that channel.

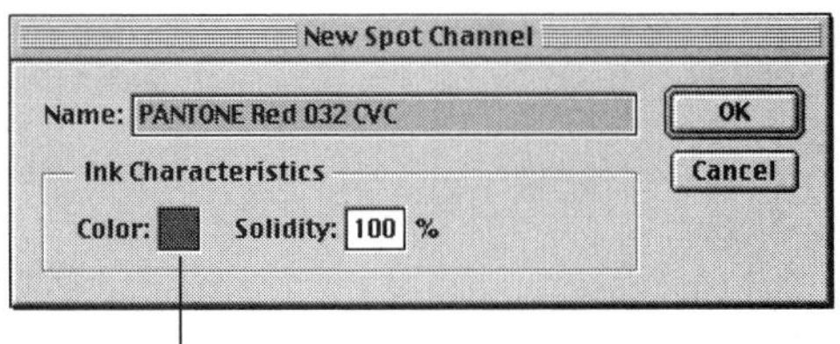

1 *Click the **Color** swatch in the **New Spot Channel** dialog box.*

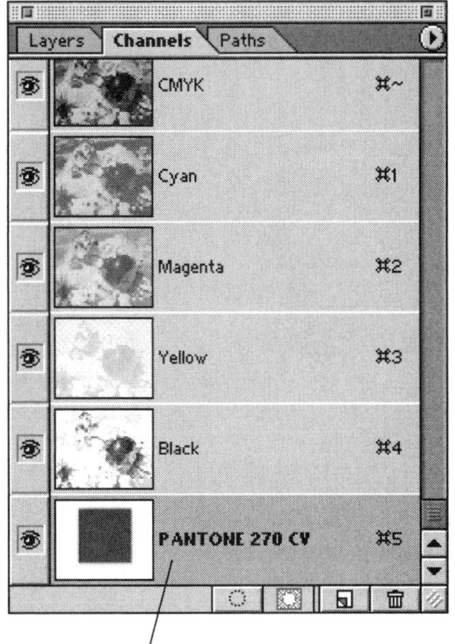

2 *The new spot channel.*

A spot color can be placed in its own separate channel. Then when the image is color separated, this spot color channel will appear on its own plate.

To create a spot color channel:

1. Display the Channels palette, and drag it away from the Layers palette so you can see both palettes at once.
2. Choose New Spot Channel from the Channels palette menu.
3. Click the Color swatch, **1** and if necessary, click Custom to open the Custom Colors dialog box.
4. Choose a Pantone or other spot color matching system name from the Book pop-up menu, choose a color, then click OK.
5. *Optional:* To change the way color in the spot channel displays on screen, enter a new Ink Characteristics: Solidity percentage. At 100%, it will display as a solid color; at a lower percentage, it will appear more transparent (as a preview for, say, a spot color varnish).
6. Click OK. The new spot channel will automatically display the name of the color you chose **2**. Any stroke that is applied or image element that is created while the spot color channel is active will appear in that color (see the following page).

TIP To **change** the spot color in a channel, double-click the channel name, then follow steps 3–6, above. The channel will automatically be renamed for the new color and all the pixels on the channel will display in that new color.

Spot Color Channel

To paint on a spot color channel:

1. Create a spot color channel (instructions on the previous page).
2. Double-click the spot color channel name, enter 100% in the Solidity field, then click OK.
3. Choose the Paintbrush tool. (The Color palette will display in grayscale mode while a spot color channel is active.) Choose black as the Foreground color.
4. On the Paintbrush options bar, choose Normal as the painting Mode and choose an Opacity percentage to establish the tint percentage for the spot color ink on the spot color plate.
5. Make sure the spot color channel is still active, then paint on the image.

Spot color channel basics

If the **eye** icon is present for both the spot color channel and the topmost (composite) channel on the Channels palette, then the spot channel will be displayed along with the other image layers. To display the spot channel by itself, hide the composite channel by clicking its eye icon.

If you want to know the **opacity** of a spot color area, choose the spot color channel, choose Actual Color mode for the readout on the Info palette, move the pointer over the image, and then note the K (grayscale percentage) on the palette.

When a spot color channel is active, the thumbnail for the most recently active **layer** will have a black border and edits will affect only the spot channel. If you click the topmost (composite) channel on the Channels palette, edits will now affect the most recently active layer, not the spot channel.

To add **type** to a spot color channel, see page 311.

If a color image with a spot color channel (or an image in Duotone mode), is converted to Multichannel mode, any spot colors in the image (or duotone) will be placed in separate spot channel(s). Preexisting

Lighten or darken a spot channel tint

Choose the spot channel on the Channels palette, then choose Image menu > Adjust > **Levels**. To darken the tint, move the black Input slider to the right; to lighten the tint, move the black Output slider to the right. Position the pointer over the image so you can get an opacity readout on the Info palette (choose Actual Color mode for the readout). Readjust either slider, if desired.

spot channels, if any, will remain after the conversion. To **tint** an entire image with a spot color, convert the image to Duotone mode and specify the desired spot color as the monotone color (see page 392).

To **export** a file that contains spot channels, save it in the DCS 2.0 format. Each spot channel will be preserved as a separate file, along with the composite DCS file. Also, let Photoshop assign the spot channel name for you. Then other applications will recognize it as a spot color. The Photoshop PDF format also supports spot colors.

Printing spot color channels

Spot channel colors **overprint** all other image colors. The stacking order of a spot channel on the Channels palette controls the order in which that color overprints. To prevent a spot color from overprinting, you must manually knock out (delete) any areas from other channels that fall beneath the spot color shapes (read more about this in the *Adobe Photoshop User Guide*). And talk with your print shop to see if this step is necessary.

Choosing **Merge Spot Channel** (Channels palette menu) merges the spot color into the existing color channels, so you can then print a composite (single-page) proof on a color printer. Otherwise, non-merged spot channels will print as separate pages. Merging a spot color channel into the other color channels will change the actual spot color, because CMYK inks can't exactly replicate spot color inks. When a spot color channel is merged into other color channels, its Solidity value will determine the merged spot color's tint percentage. The lower the Solidity, the more transparent the newly merged color will be. All image layers are flattened when spot channels are merged.

TIP Use the Solidity option in the Spot Channel Options dialog box to produce an on-screen simulation of the actual ink opacity for the spot plate. For an opaque ink, such as a metallic ink, use 100% Solidity. For a transparent, clear varnish, use 0% Solidity.

To convert an alpha channel into a spot color channel:

1. Double-click an alpha channel on the Channels palette.
2. Choose Color Indicates: Spot Color **1**.
3. Click the Color swatch, click Custom, if necessary, to open the Custom Colors dialog box, choose a spot color, then click OK.
4. Click OK. Former non-white (black or gray) areas on the channel will now display in the spot color.

TIP To reverse the spot color and white areas, choose the channel, then choose Image menu > Adjust > Invert (Ctrl-I/Cmd-I).

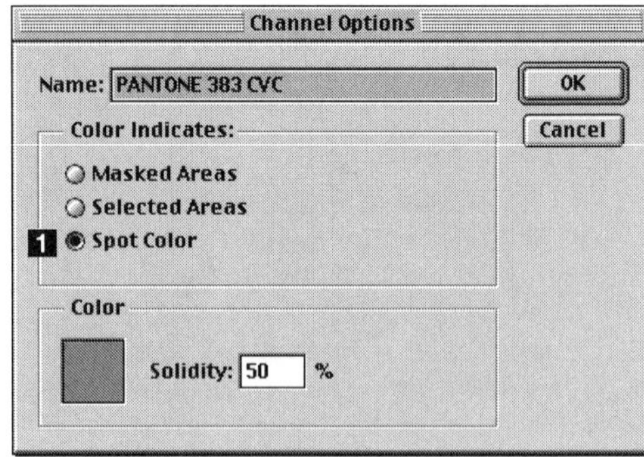

PAINT 12

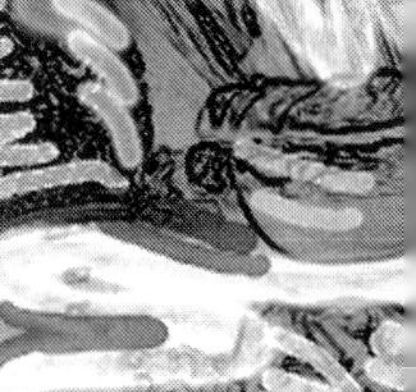

Painting tool shortcuts

Cycle through the blending Modes on the options bar	Shift + *or* Shift -
Cycle through the brushes on the Brush picker	[*or*]
Choose an Opacity level	0 through 9 (e.g., 2 = 20 %) *or* quickly type a percentage (e.g. "38")

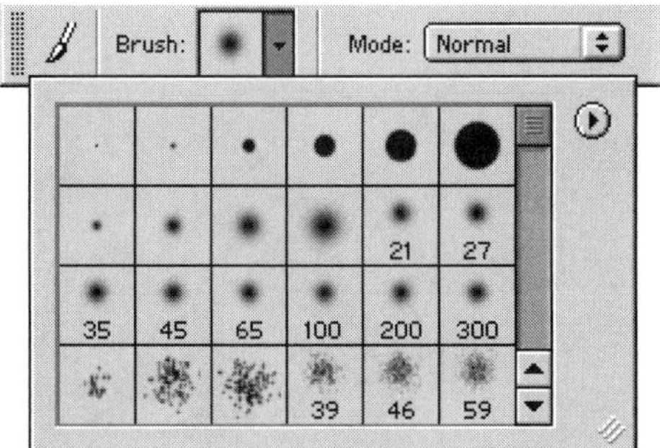

1 *Click a **brush** for the **Paintbrush** or **Airbrush** tool on the brush picker.* 6.0!

Opacity: 100% ▸ ☐ Wet Edges

2 *And choose an **Opacity** (or **Pressure**) percentage.*

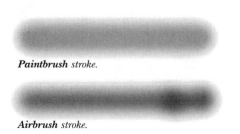

***Paintbrush** stroke.*

***Airbrush** stroke.*

IN THIS CHAPTER you will learn how to use Photoshop's Airbrush, Pencil Paintbrush, Paint Bucket, Eraser, Magic Eraser, Background Eraser, Smudge, and Gradient tools to embellish a scanned image or paint a picture from scratch. You will also learn how to create custom brush tips for the painting tools; how to save and load brush libraries; and how to choose options for individual tools, such as a blending mode and an opacity percentage.

To use the Paintbrush or Airbrush tool:

1. Choose a layer. Create a selection on the layer if you want to restrict the brushstrokes to that area.
2. Click the Paintbrush tool (B) or Airbrush tool (J).
3. Choose a Foreground color (see pages 165–169).
4. On the options bar: 6.0!
   Click the Painting Brush arrowhead, then click a brush **1**. The number under the brush icon is the brush width in pixels. If you let the pointer rest over a brush, a Tool Tip will display with the brush name and width. (To load other brush libraries onto the picker, see page 201.) Click anywhere outside the picker to close it.
   and
   Choose a blending Mode (see "Blending modes" on pages 30–32).
   and
   Choose an Opacity percentage for the Paintbrush tool or a Pressure percentage for the Airbrush tool **2**. At 100%, the stroke will completely cover underlying pixels.

(Continued on the following page)

6.0!

5. *Optional:* To create strokes that fade as they finish, click the Brush Dynamics arrowhead on the right side of the options bar, then choose Fade from any or all of the Size, Opacity, and Color pop-up menus on the Brush Dynamics pop-up palette (see 1 on the next page). Enter the desired number of steps (1–9999) in the fields to the right of the pop-up menus. The higher the number of steps, the longer the stroke will be before it fades.
6. *Optional:* Check the Wet Edges box for the Paintbrush tool to produce a stroke with a higher concentration of color at the edges, like the pooling effect in traditional watercoloring 1–4.
7. Drag across any area of the picture. If you press and hold on an area with the Airbrush tool without dragging, the paintdrop will gradually widen and become more saturated (up to the full brush width).

   Note: Check the "Lock transparent pixels" box on the Layers palette to recolor only non-transparent areas.

TIP To draw a straight stroke, click once to begin the stroke, then Shift-click a different location to complete the stroke.

TIP Alt-click/Option-click in any open image to sample a color while a painting tool is chosen (temporary Eyedropper).

TIP Each tool keeps its own options bar settings.

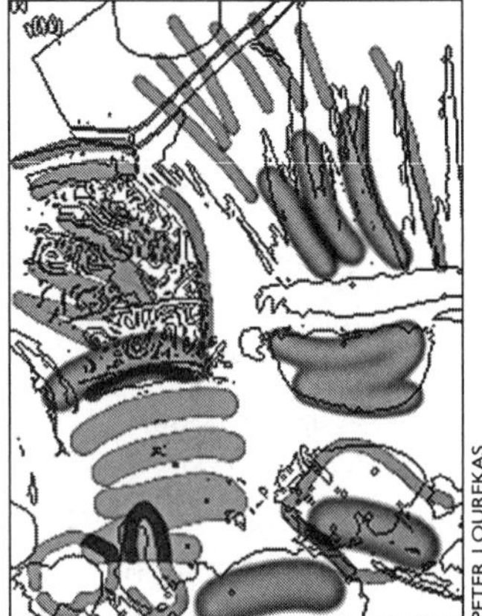

1 *Strokes created with the Paintbrush tool with the* ***Wet Edges*** *box checked on the options bar.*

2 *More* ***Wet Edges****.*

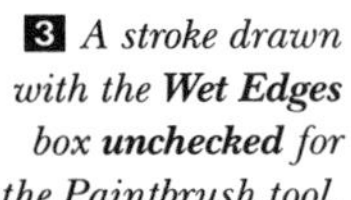

3 *A stroke drawn with the* ***Wet Edges*** *box* ***unchecked*** *for the Paintbrush tool.*

4 *A stroke drawn with the* ***Wet Edges*** *box checked.*

Paintbrush and Airbrush Tools

Where did the Line tool go?

In Photoshop 6, draw straight lines using the **shapes** tools (**Line** tool) (see page 280).

***Brush Dynamics** arrowhead.*

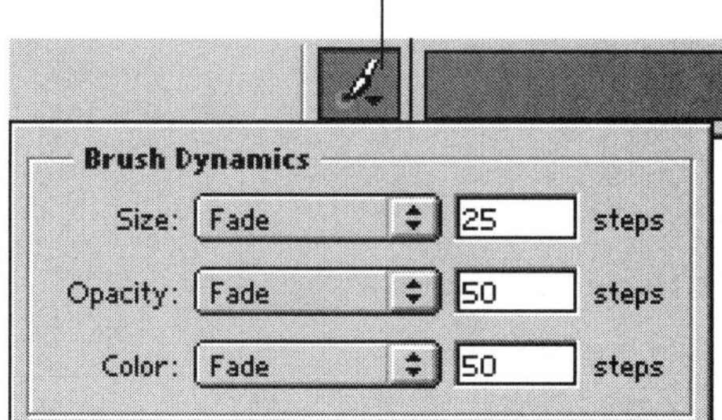

1 *To create strokes that fade as they finish, choose **Fade** from any of the pop-up menus on the **Brush Dynamics** pop-up palette.*

The Brush Dynamics pop-up palette, which you got a glimpse of in step 5 on the previous page, is where you can choose options to make a brush stroke fade in size, opacity, or color as it finishes or choose options for a stylus for use with a pressure-sensitive tablet. This pop-up palette is available for the Paintbrush, Airbrush, Pencil, History Brush, Art History Brush, Clone Stamp, Pattern Stamp, Eraser, Background Eraser, Blur, Sharpen, Smudge, Dodge, Burn, and Sponge tools.

To choose Fade options: 6.0!

1. Click the Brush Dynamics arrowhead on the options bar, then choose Fade for any or all of the following options: **1**

   Size to have the brush stroke size decrease over the length of the stroke.

   Opacity/Pressure to have the opacity decrease over the length of the stroke.

   Color to have the Foreground color shift to the Background color over the length of the stroke (available only for the Airbrush, Paintbrush, and Pencil tools).

2. Enter a Steps value (1–9999). Each step is equal to one mark of the brush tip. Click outside the pop-up palette to close it. (If your strokes fade too quickly, increase the number of steps.)

To choose options for a stylus:

1. Click the Brush Dynamics arrowhead on the options bar, then choose Stylus for any of the following options:

   Size to link stylus pressure to the width of the stroke.

   Opacity/Pressure to link stylus pressure to color opacity and intensity.

   Color to cause light stylus pressure to paint with the Background color and then transition to the Foreground color as stylus pressure increases.

2. Enter a Steps value (1–9999).

TIP Brush Dynamics settings stick when you change brushes and also when you exit/quit and restart Photoshop.

As we explain on page 201, seven brush libraries are supplied with Photoshop 6, and any brush can be customized to your liking.

To modify an existing brush:

6.0!

1. On the options bar, click the Edit Brush button **1**.
2. Move the Diameter slider or enter a value for the Diameter (width) of the stroke (1–999 pixels).
3. Move the Hardness slider or enter a Hardness value for the percentage of the diameter of the stroke that's opaque (0–100%).
4. Move the Spacing slider or enter a Spacing percentage (0–999%). The higher the Spacing, the farther apart the paintdrops will be.
   or
   Uncheck the Spacing box to have the brush respond to mouse or stylus speed. The faster the mouse or stylus is dragged, the more paintdrops will skip (see also "To choose options for a stylus" on the previous page).
   Note: For many of the default brushes, the only option that can be changed is the Spacing percentage.
5. Enter an Angle (-180–180°) or move the gray arrow in a circular direction in the left preview box.
6. Enter a Roundness value (0–100%) or reshape the brush by dragging either black dot inward or outward in the left preview box. The higher the value, the rounder the brush.

6.0!

7. The edited brush settings will be temporary unless you save them as a new preset. Click the "Create new preset" button if you want to save the edited version of the brush to the brush picker. (The new preset still isn't saved to a library, though).
8. Click the Edit Brush button again to close the window. If you open the brush picker, you'll see that the brush icon has updated.

It's a copy!

If you modify an existing preset, you are actually modifying a **copy** of the preset—not the original brush that's in the current library.

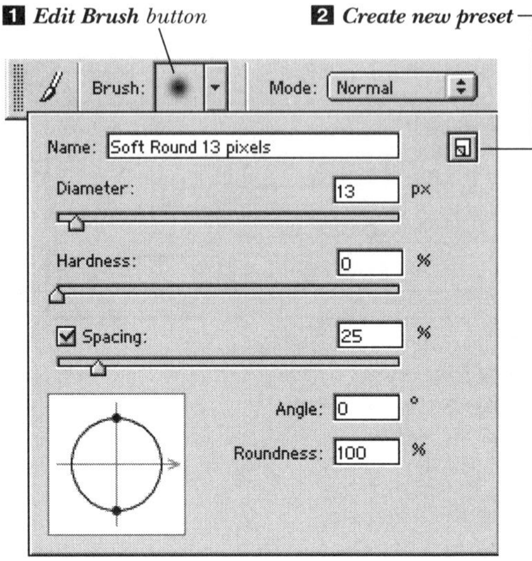

*Choose **Diameter, Hardness, Spacing, Angle,** and **Roundness** values in the edit brush window.*

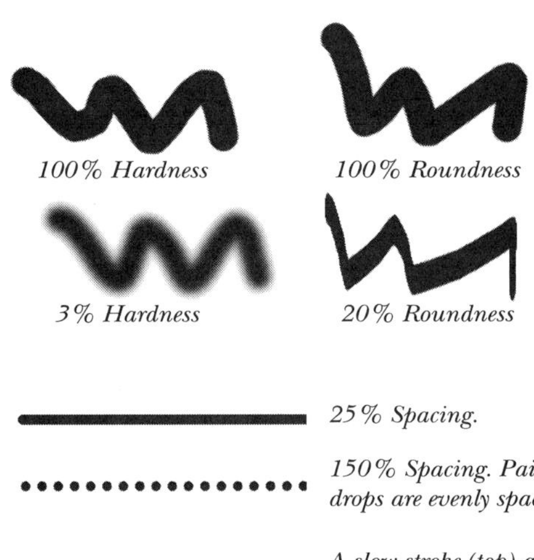

100% Hardness

100% Roundness

3% Hardness

20% Roundness

25% Spacing.

150% Spacing. Paintdrops are evenly spaced.

A slow stroke (top) and a fast stroke (bottom) with the Spacing box unchecked. Paintdrops are unevenly spaced.

Modify Brush

Restoring the default brushes

The brushes that were on the brush picker when you last exit/quit Photoshop will still be there next time you launch Photoshop. To restore the default brush library, choose **Reset Brushes** from the brush picker menu, then click OK.

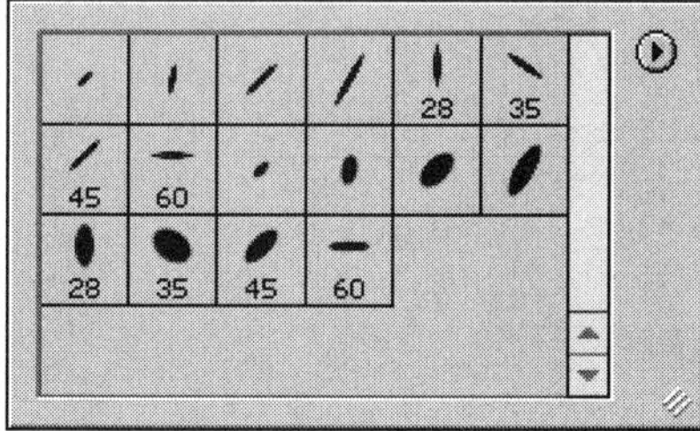

1 *Calligraphic Brushes.*

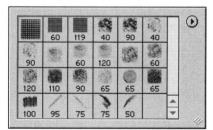

2 *Faux Finish Brushes.*

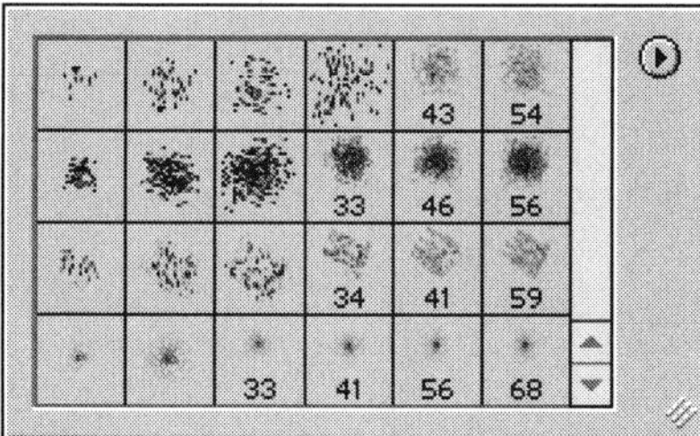

3 *Natural Brushes.*

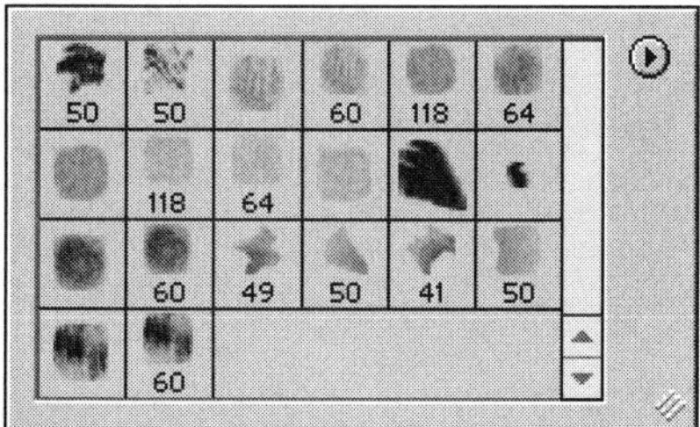

4 *Natural Brushes 2.*

To create a new brush: 6.0!

1. Click the Painting Brush arrowhead, then choose New Brush from the brush picker menu.
2. Follow steps 2–8 on the previous page to customize the brush. Type a name for the new brush, then click OK. The new brush will appear after the last brush on the brush picker. To save a brush to a library, see page 374.

To delete a brush: 6.0!

1. Open the brush picker.
2. Alt-click/Option-click the brush you want to delete. You can't undo this.
   or
   Right-click/Control-click the brush you want to delete, then choose Delete Brush from the context menu.

6.0! Seven brush libraries are supplied with Photoshop in addition to the default brushes. The Square Brushes, Drop Shadow Brushes, Natural Brushes, and Assorted Brushes are from Photoshop 5.5. The Calligraphic Brushes, Faux Finish Brushes, and Natural Brushes 2 brushes are new to Photoshop 6 **1**–**4**.

To load a brush library:

1. Open the brush picker.
2. Click the arrowhead on the right side of the picker, then choose a brush library name from the bottom of the menu.
3. Click Append to add the additional brushes to the current picker.
   or
   Click OK to replace the current brushes on the picker with those in the library.

TIP To locate and open a brush library that isn't in the default Adobe Photoshop 6 > Presets > Brushes folder, choose Load from the picker menu.

In these instructions you'll learn a nice technique for applying tints to a grayscale image. By drawing colored strokes on a separate layer, you'll have the flexibility to change the blending mode or opacity for your painting tool or for the color layer or erase or dodge here or there—all without changing the underlying gray image at all.

To apply tints to a grayscale image:

1. Open a Grayscale mode image and convert it to RGB Color mode (Image menu > Mode > RGB Color).
2. Alt-click/Option-click the "Create new layer" button at the bottom of the Layers palette to add a new layer above the grayscale imagery, choose Mode: Color for the new layer, then click OK.
3. Choose the Paintbrush tool (B) or Airbrush tool (J).
4. Choose a Foreground color.
5. From the options bar:

   Choose a brush.
   and
   Choose an Opacity/Pressure percentage below 100%. Choose a low-ish opacity for a subtle tint. You can change opacities between strokes. You can also lower the opacity of the whole layer via the Layers palette.
6. Paint strokes on the new layer **1**.
7. *Optional:* Use the Eraser tool to remove areas of unwanted color (uncheck the "Lock transparent pixels" box for this), then repaint, if desired. Or use the Dodge tool at a low Exposure percentage to gently lighten the tints.
8. *Optional:* Choose a different blending mode for the color layer. Try Multiply, Soft Light, Color Burn, or Color. You can also use the Channel Mixer to apply colors.

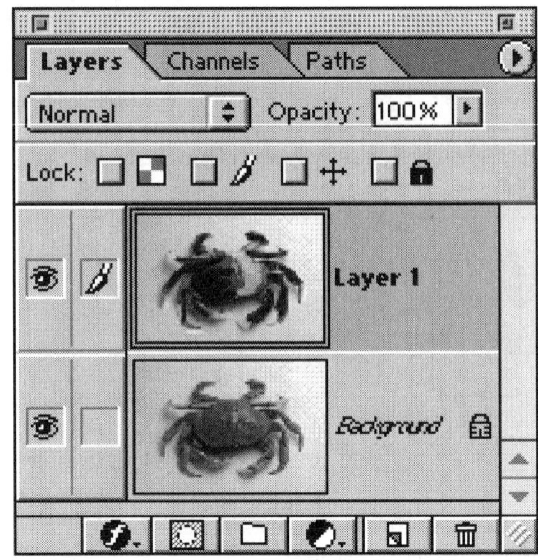

1 *The **color tints** are on Layer 1. The original Background image still looks like grayscale (even though the image is now in RGB Color mode).*

Tint a Grayscale Image

1 *Select an area of an image.*

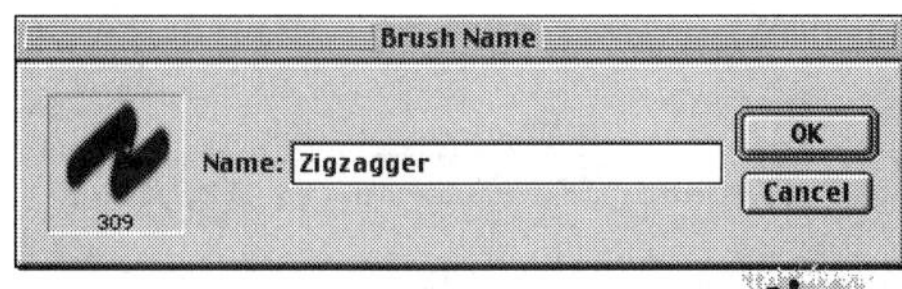

2 *Enter a* ***Name*** *for the new brush.*

3 *The* ***custom brush*** *used with the Paintbrush tool at various opacities, and with the Wet Edges box checked on the options bar.*

To create a brush from an image:

1. Choose the Rectangular Marquee tool (M or Shift-M).
2. Marquee an area of a picture (maximum 1,000 by 1,000 pixels). Try using a distinct shape on a white background **1**.
3. Choose Edit menu > Define Brush.
4. Enter a Name for the new brush, then click OK. The new brush will appear after the last brush on the picker. Use it with the Paintbrush **2** or Airbrush tool. Adjust the Spacing value for the gap between paintdrops (1–999%) on the edit brush pop-up palette.
5. Deselect the selection (Ctrl-D/Cmd-D).

Any new presets in the brush picker will be wiped out if the current brush library is 6.0! replaced or reset to the default. To preserve any new brushes you create for future use, follow these instructions to save the currrent presets to a new library.

To save brush presets as a new library:

1. Choose Save Brushes from the brush picker menu.
2. Enter a Name for the set. Leave the default extension for the brush library as is (.abr).
3. Choose a location in which to save the set, then click Save (Enter/Return).

The Paint Bucket tool replaces pixels with the Foreground color or a pattern, and fills areas of similar shade or color within a specified Tolerance range. You can use the Paint Bucket without creating a selection.

To fill an area using the Paint Bucket:

1. Choose a layer. If you don't want to fill transparent areas on the layer, check the "Lock transparent pixels" box.
   Note: The Paint Bucket tool won't work on an image in Bitmap color mode.
2. Choose the Paint Bucket tool (G). It's on the Gradient tool pop-out palette.
3. 6.0! On the Paint Bucket options bar 1–2:
   Choose Fill: **Foreground**.
   and
   Choose a blending **Mode** (Shift + or Shift - to cycle through the modes). Need a suggestion? Try Multiply, Soft Light, or Color Burn.
   and
   Choose an **Opacity** percentage.
   and
   Enter a **Tolerance** value (0–255). The higher the Tolerance value, the wider the range of colors the Paint Bucket will fill. Try a low number first.
   and
   Check the **Anti-aliased** box to smooth the edges of the fill area.
   and
   Check the **Contiguous** box to fill only areas that are contiguous to the image area you click on. Uncheck this option to fill non-contiguous areas.
   and
   Check the **All Layers** box if you want the Paint Bucket to fill areas on the active layer based on colors the tool detects on all the currently visible layers instead of just the colors it detects on the currently active layer.
4. Choose a Foreground color.
5. Click on the image 3–4. The little black spill is the part of the tool pointer that you need to watch as you click.

Apply patterns with the Paint Bucket

Choose **Fill: Pattern** from the options bar, then choose a pattern from the picker. To create a custom pattern, create a rectangular selection, choose Edit menu > Define Pattern, enter a name, click OK, then deselect. The custom pattern will be the last pattern swatch in the picker.

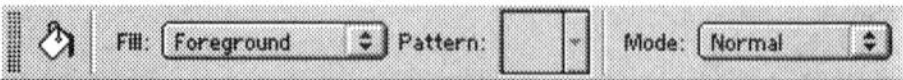

1 *The left side of the **Paint Bucket** options bar.*

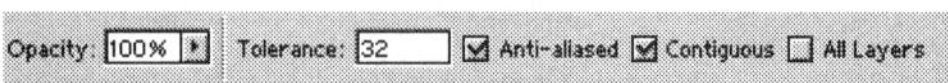

2 *The right side of the **Paint Bucket** options bar.*

PHOTO: PAUL PETROFF

3 *The original image.*

4 *After clicking with the **Paint Bucket** tool.*

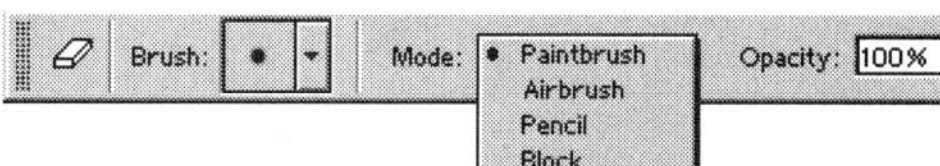

1 *The left side of the* ***Eraser*** *tool options bar.*

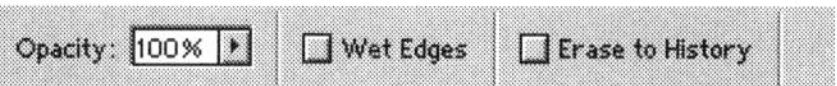

2 *The right side of the* ***Eraser*** *tool options bar.*

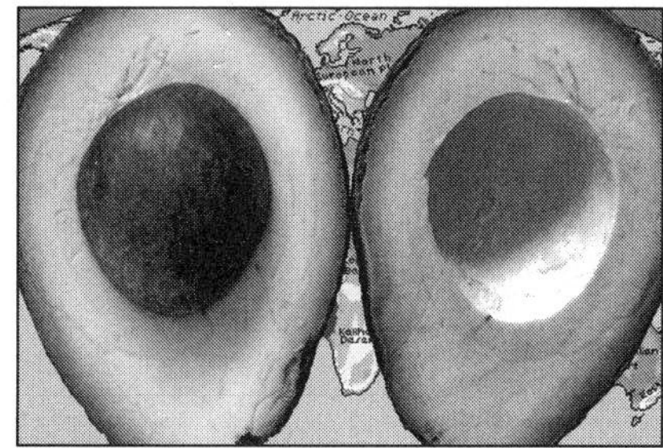

3 *The original image.*

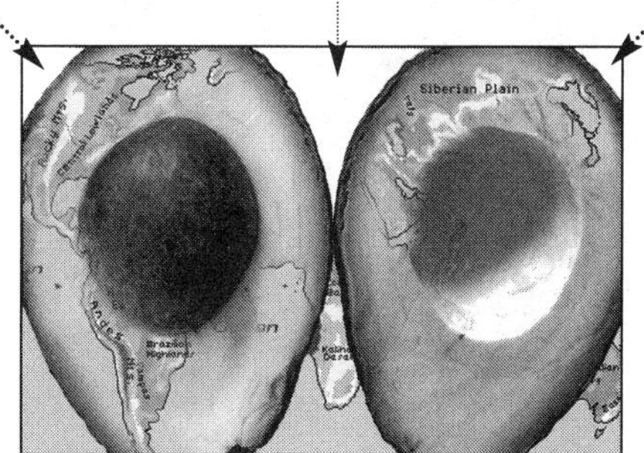

4 *After erasing part of the avocados layer to reveal the map underneath it (Airbrush option, 55% opacity), and erasing part of the map layer to white (Paintbrush option, 100% opacity).*

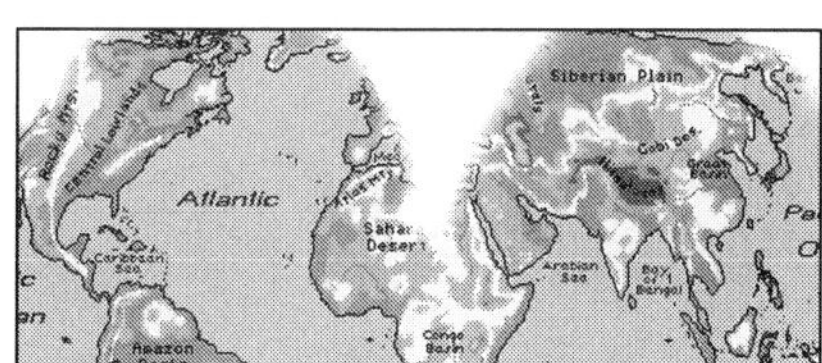

5 *A detail of the partially* ***erased*** *map layer.*

To erase part of a layer:

1. Choose a layer. If you use the Eraser tool on a layer with the "Lock transparent pixels" box checked or use it on the Background of an image, the erased area will be replaced with the current Background color. If "Lock transparent pixels" is unchecked for the layer, the erased area will be replaced with transparency.
2. Choose the Eraser tool (E or Shift-E).
3. On the Eraser options bar: 6.0!

   Click the Painting Brush arrowhead, then click a brush in the picker.
   and
   Choose Mode: Paintbrush, Airbrush, Pencil, or Block **1**–**2**. For a wet-edged eraser effect, choose Paintbrush and check the Wet Edges box.
   and
   Choose an Opacity/Pressure percentage.
4. If you're going to erase the Background of the image or if "Lock transparent pixels" is checked on the Layers palette, choose a Background color.
5. Click on or drag across the layer **3**–**5**.

TIP To restore areas on the current layer from a history state, move the History source icon to the desired state on the History palatte, then use the Eraser tool with the Erase to History box checked on the options bar (or Alt-drag/Option-drag to turn on Erase to History temporarily). The Erase to History option won't be available if you add a new layer or change the number of pixels in (resample) the file.

The Background Eraser tool erases to transparency or to the current Background color by dragging. This tool's strength is that you can control several criteria, such as whether the tool erases contiguous or non-contiguous pixels. By choosing your brush carefully, you can control the size of the area that is erased as well as the softness of the edge of the erased area.

To use the Background Eraser:

1. Choose the Background Eraser tool on the Eraser tool pop-out palette (it has a scissors icon) (E or Shift-E).
2. To control where the erasure occurs, from the Limits pop-up menu on the options bar, choose **1**:

   6.0!

   Discontiguous to erase all pixels within the current Tolerance range, whether or not they are next to one another. If you choose this option, also choose Once from the Sampling pop-up menu (step 5).
   or
   Contiguous to erase only adjacent pixels within the current Tolerance range that match the first pixel that you click on.
   or
   Find Edges to erase contiguous pixels, but preserve object edges (high contrast borders) **2**.
3. Choose a hard-edged or soft-edged brush from the brush picker.
4. Choose a Tolerance percentage. The higher the Tolerance value, the wider the range of colors similar to the first color clicked on will be erased.
5. From the Sampling pop-up menu, choose:

   Continuous to erase to transparency all the pixels you drag across within the current Tolerance range.

   Once to erase to transparency only the pixels that closely match the first pixel you drag across. To erase only one color, choose Once and make the Tolerance 1%.

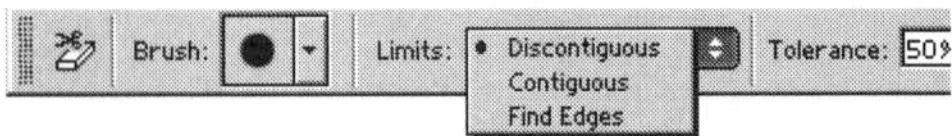

1 *The left side of the* ***Background Eraser*** *options bar.*

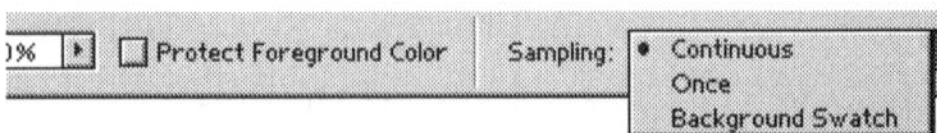

2 *The right side of the* ***Background Eraser*** *options bar.*

2 *The* ***Find Edges*** *option worked successfully to erase the background on this image.*

Background Eraser

The original image.

After using the ***Background Eraser*** *tool with various options bar settings.*

Background Swatch to erase only pixels that match the current Background color. Choose a Background color now. Use a low Tolerance with this option.

6. *Optional:* To protect a particular color from erasure, check the Protect Foreground Color box and make sure Once is chosen from the Sampling pop-up menu. Select the Foreground color square on the Color palette, hold down Alt/Option, then in the image window, click to sample the color that you want to protect. This can be anywhere on the image—the background or the foreground.
7. If you're using a pressure-sensitive tablet, choose Brush Dynamics settings from the options bar.
8. Choose the layer from which you want to erase pixels.
9. Drag across the area of the image that you want to erase. The active part of the tool is the crosshair.

   If you're unhappy with the results, undo or click on an earlier history state, change any of the parameters described in steps 2–5 on the previous page, then try again. To widen or narrow the range of colors that the tool erases, change the Tolerance value on the Background Eraser options bar.

The Magic Eraser erases by clicking with the mouse—not by dragging. It erases pixels that are similar in color to the pixel you click on within a defined Tolerance range. It works like the Paint Bucket tool, except it removes, rather than adds, pixels from a layer. Used with an Opacity setting below 100%, the Magic Eraser can be used to make target areas of a layer partially transparent.

To use the Magic Eraser:

1. Choose the Magic Eraser tool on the Eraser tool pop-out palette (Shift-E).
2. 6.0! On the Magic Eraser options bar **1**–**2**:

   Enter a **Tolerance** value. The higher the Tolerance, the wider the range of colors that will be erased. Enter a low Tolerance if you want to erase only colors that are very similar to the color you click on. Enter "0" to erase one color.
   and
   Check the **Anti-aliased** box to slightly soften the edges of the erased area.
   and
   Check the **Contiguous** box to erase only pixels that are next to one another. Uncheck this option to erase similarly colored pixels throughout the layer (**3**–**4**, this page, and **1**, next page).
   and
   Check the **Use All Layers** box to have the Magic Eraser erase areas on the active layer based on colors the tool detects on all the currently visible layers. With this option unchecked, the tool will detect only the colors on the currently active layer. In either case, only pixels on the currently active layer will be erased.
   and
   Choose an **Opacity** percentage. Enter 100% to erase to transparency or a lower opacity to erase partially.
3. Choose the layer from which you want to erase pixels.
4. In the image window, carefully position the tool's crosshair on the area that you want to erase, then click.

1 *The left side of the* ***Magic Eraser*** *options bar.*

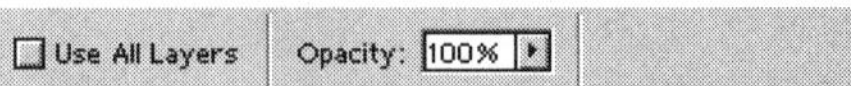

2 *The right side of the* ***Magic Eraser*** *options bar.*

3 *The original image.*

4 *After clicking on the rightmost leaf, with the* ***Contiguous*** *option turned* ***off*** *on the Magic Eraser options bar.*

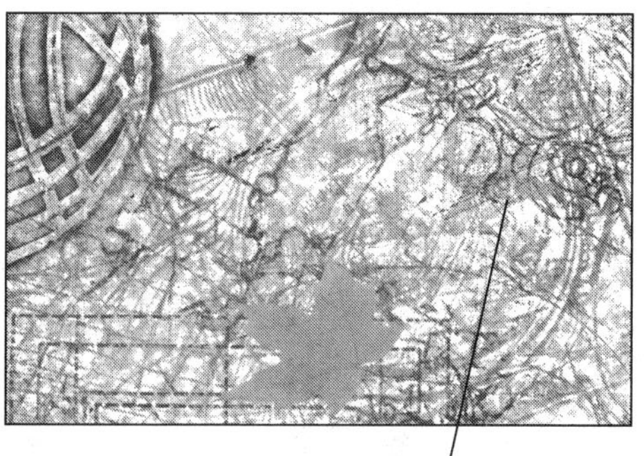

1 *After clicking on the rightmost leaf in the original image, with the **Contiguous** option turned **on**. The three dark leaves disappear.*

2 *Using the **Pencil** tool with the **Auto Erase** box checked on the options bar.*

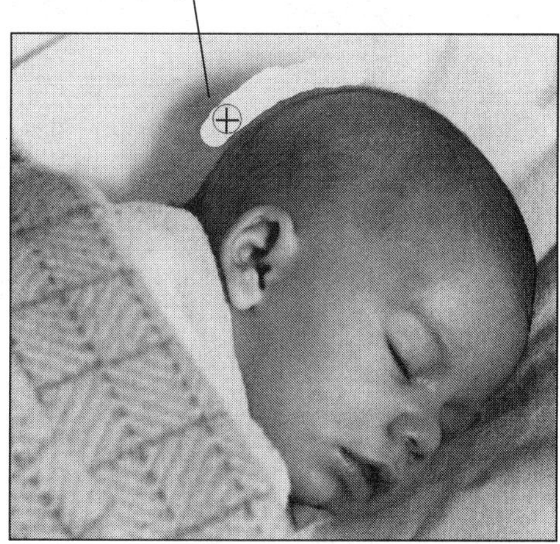

If the erasure is too large or too small, undo, change the Tolerance value on the Magic Eraser options bar, then try clicking again on the image.

The auto eraser (the Pencil tool with the Auto Erase option, actually) applies the Background color if you start dragging the mouse with the pointer over a Foreground color pixel. The tool paints the Foreground color if you begin dragging with the pointer over any other color.

To auto erase:

1. Choose a Foreground color and a Background color. You can use the Eyedropper tool to sample a color from the image.
2. Choose a layer.
3. Choose the Pencil tool (B or Shift-B).
4. Check the Auto Erase box on the Pencil options bar.
5. Draw strokes on the image **2**. Start dragging with the pointer over a Foreground color pixel (if any) to apply the Background color. Start dragging with the pointer over a non-Foreground color pixel to apply the Foreground color.

To smudge colors:

1. Choose a layer. *Note:* The Smudge tool can't be used on an image in Bitmap or Indexed Color mode.
2. Choose the Smudge tool (R or Shift-R).
3. On the Smudge options bar 1–2:

   6.0! Click the Painting Brush arrowhead, then click a brush in the brush picker.
   and
   Choose a blending Mode (see pages 30–32). Try Normal to smudge all shades or colors, or Darken to push dark colors into lighter colors, or Lighten to push light colors into darker colors.
   and
   Move the Pressure slider below 100%.
4. *Optional:* Check the Use All Layers box on the options bar to start the smudge with colors from all the currently visible layers in the image (uncheck Finger Painting if you use this option). Uncheck Use All Layers to smudge only with colors from the active layer. In either case, of course, pixels will only smudge on the currently active layer.
5. *Optional:* To start the Smudge with the Foreground color, check the Finger Painting box on the options bar. With Finger Painting turned off, the smudge will start with the color under the pointer where the stroke begins. The higher the Pressure percentage, the more Foreground color will be applied.

   Hold down Alt/Option to temporarily turn on the Finger Painting option if the Finger Painting box is unchecked.
6. Drag across an area of the image 3–6. Pause, if necessary, to allow the screen to redraw.

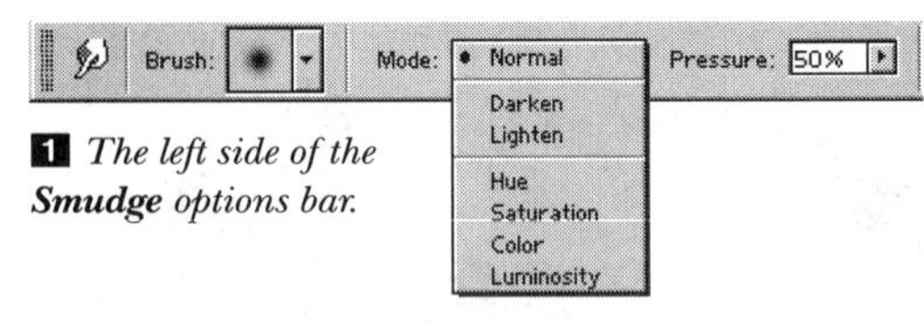

1 *The left side of the* ***Smudge*** *options bar.*

2 *The right side of the* ***Smudge*** *options bar.*

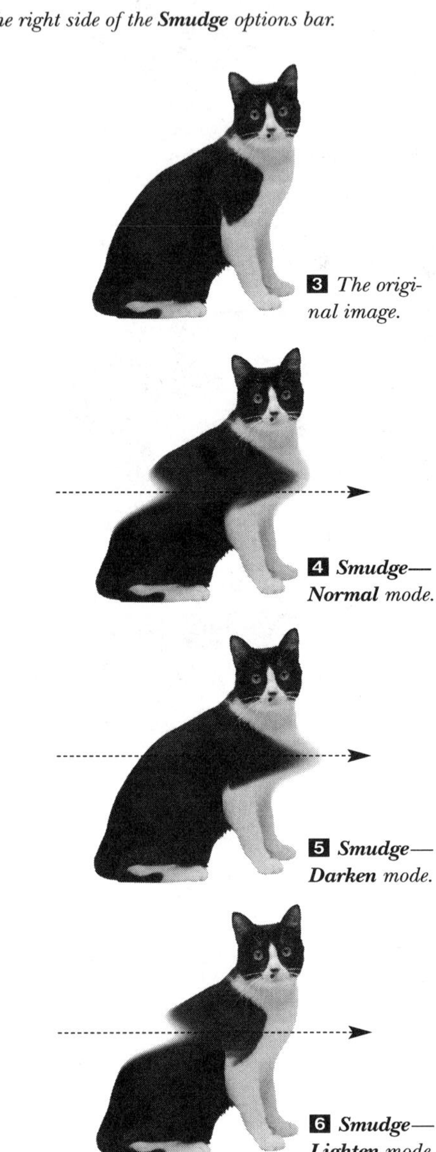

3 *The original image.*

4 ***Smudge— Normal*** *mode.*

5 ***Smudge— Darken*** *mode.*

6 ***Smudge— Lighten*** *mode.*

GRADIENTS 13

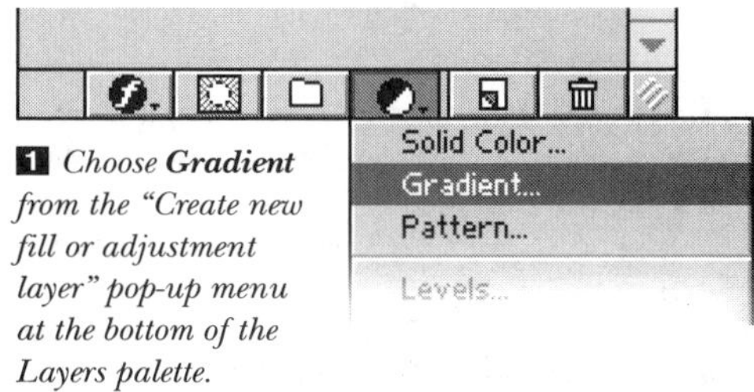

1 *Choose **Gradient** from the "Create new fill or adjustment layer" pop-up menu at the bottom of the Layers palette.*

2 *Click the gradient arrowhead, then choose from the **gradient** picker.*

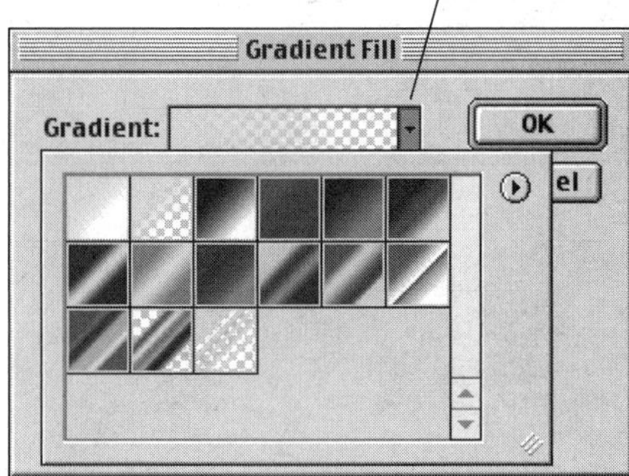

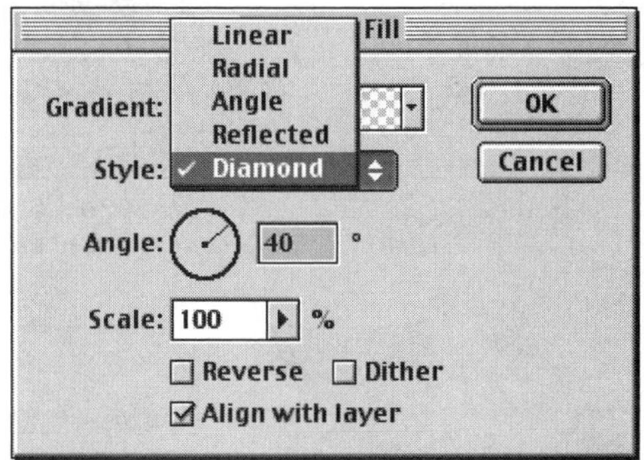

3 *Choose a gradient **Style, Angle,** and **Scale** percentage in the **Gradient Fill** dialog box.*

A GRADIENT IS A GRADUAL blend between two or more colors. Photoshop 6 offers two ways to apply a gradient. One way is to use the **Gradient tool** to apply a gradient directly to a content layer (note the tool's new location on the Toolbox). The Gradient tool would be the way to go if you want to custom fit a gradient by hand in a particular area or fill a layer mask (for any fill or adjustment layer) with a gradient for a gradual masking effect.

A second option is to use the new **gradient fill layer** feature to apply a gradient that appears in its own layer, with a layer mask that can be used to mask gradient layer pixels. This latter type of gradient is easier to edit. 6.0!

To apply a gradient as a fill layer:

1. Choose a layer. The Gradient tool can't be used on an image in Bitmap or Indexed Color mode.
2. *Optional:* Select an area of a layer to limit the gradient fill to that area (see the sidebar on the next page). Otherwise, the gradient will fill the entire layer.
3. Choose Gradient from the "Create new fill or adjustment layer" pop-up menu at the bottom of the Layers palette, **1**.
4. Click the gradient arrowhead at the top of the dialog box, then choose a preset gradient from the picker **2**.
5. Choose a gradient Style: **Linear, Radial, Angular, Reflected,** or **Diamond** **3**.
   and
   Choose an **Angle** by moving the dial or entering a value.
   and
   Use the **Scale** slider to scale the gradient relative to the layer. The higher the scale

(Continued on the following page)

value, the more gradual the transition between gradient colors.

6. *Optional:* Drag in the image window to reposition the gradient in the image. This is so cool.
7. Do any of the following:

   Check/uncheck the **Reverse** box to reverse the order of colors in the gradient.

   Check the **Dither** box to minimize banding (stripes) in the gradient.

   Check the **Align with layer** box to have the length of the gradient fill be calculated based on the dimensions of the bounding box of the layer.
8. Click OK 3–7.
9. *Optional:* Use the Layers palette to change the gradient fill layer opacity or blending mode. You can get some beautiful effects this way. If the layer imagery has transparent edges, double-click the layer name to access the Layer Style and apply an effect to the layer.

   Note: To adjust any of the gradient settings, double-click the gradient fill layer thumbnail—the Gradient Fill dialog box will reopen. This is what we meant before when we said this method offers the most flexibility.

TIP To hide a gradient fill layer, click the eye icon for the layer. To delete a gradient fill layer, drag it over the Delete layer (trash) button.

Mask a gradient fill

If you create a selection before creating a gradient fill layer, the gradient will be limited to just the area inside the selection. The former selection will be displayed as an area of white within the gradient fill layer mask 1–2.

To limit a gradient fill any time after a fill layer is created, click the layer mask thumbnail and paint on the layer mask.

Gradient fill thumbnail.

1 *A **mask** on the **gradient fill** layer limits the fill effect.*

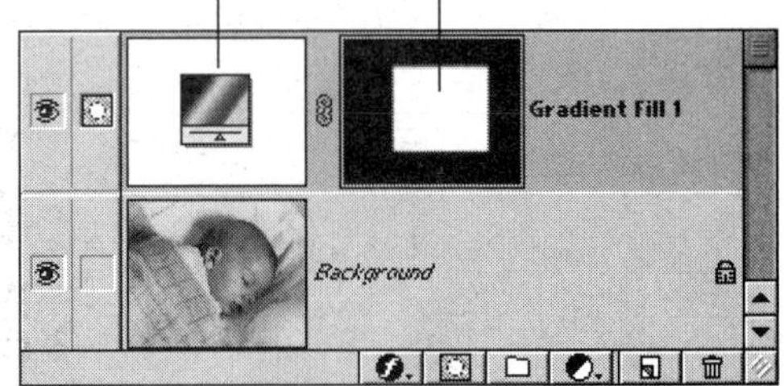

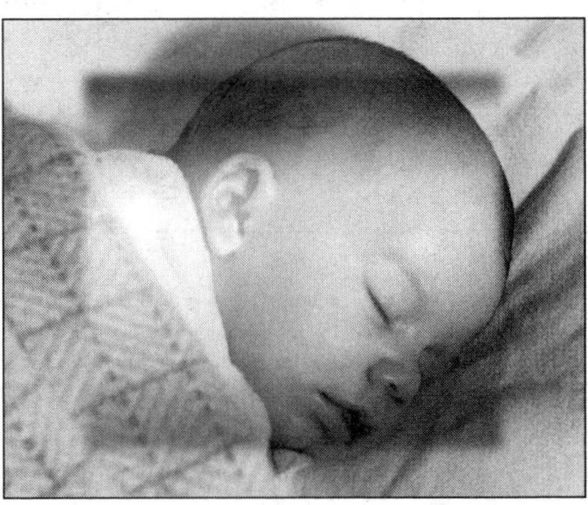

2 *The **gradient fill** is limited to the rectangular **mask**. We chose **Hard Light** blending mode for the gradient layer.*

*The five basic gradient **Styles**.*

3 ***Linear** gradient.*

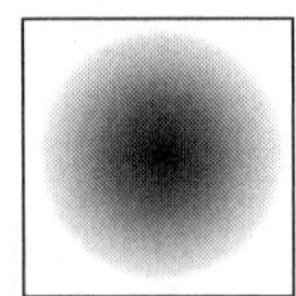

4 ***Radial** gradient.*

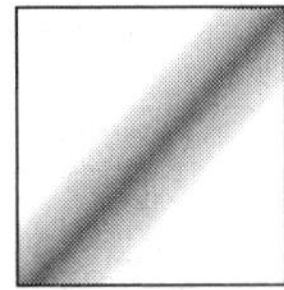

5 ***Reflected** gradient.*

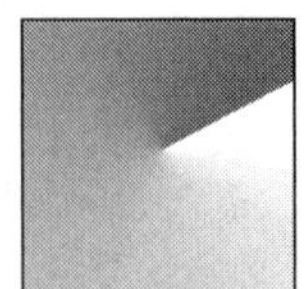

6 ***Angular** gradient.*

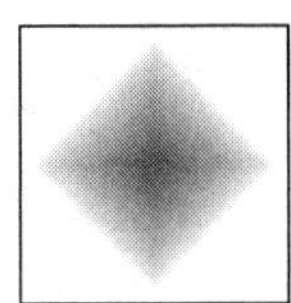

7 ***Diamond** gradient.*

1 *The left side of the **Gradient** tool **options bar**.*

2 *The right side of the **Gradient** tool **options bar**.*

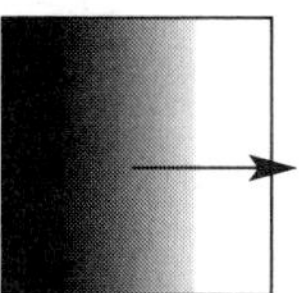

3 *The Gradient tool dragged from the middle to the right. This is a **Linear** gradient.*

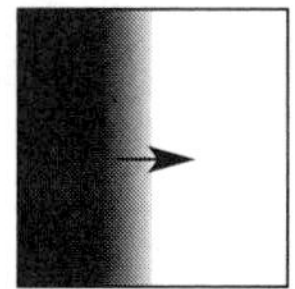

4 *The Gradient tool dragged a **short** distance in the middle using the same colors. The transitions are more abrupt.*

5 *The **gradient tool** was used in different directions to fill a rasterized type layer (**Lock transparent pixels** box checked).*

6.0!

Use the Gradient tool if you want to apply a gradient by dragging. Each time you drag with this tool, you will apply an additional gradient to the layer. Any additional gradient below full 100% opacity won't completely cover over the existing gradient. Unlike a gradient fill layer, once this type of gradient is applied, it can't be edited easily.

To apply a gradient using the Gradient tool:

1. Choose a layer or create a new layer.
2. *Optional:* Select an area of a layer. Otherwise, the gradient will fill the entire layer.
3. Choose the Gradient tool (it shares a pop-out palette with the Paint Bucket tool) (G or Shift-G).
4. On the Gradient options bar **1**–**2**:

   Click the first arrowhead, then click a **gradient preset** on the gradient picker.
   and
   Click a gradient style button: **Linear, Radial, Angular, Reflected,** or **Diamond**.
   and
   Choose a blending **Mode**.
   and
   Choose an **Opacity**.
5. Do any of the following optional steps:

   Check the **Reverse** box to reverse the order of colors in the gradient.

   Check the **Dither** box to minimize banding (stripes) in the gradient.

   Check the **Transparency** box to enable any transparency that was edited into the gradient (see page 217).
6. For a linear gradient, drag from one side or corner of the image or selection to the other. For any other gradient style, drag from a center point outward. Shift-drag to constrain the gradient to a multiple of 45°. To delete a Gradient tool fill, remove its state from the History palette.

   Drag a long distance to produce a subtle transition area or drag a short distance to produce an abrupt transition **3**–**5**. This works like the Scale slider in the Gradient Fill dialog box.

Gradient Tool

If you revise or delete a preset swatch, the actual gradient in the current gradient library isn't affected; you'll automatically be working on or deleting a copy of the preset.

To create or edit a gradient preset:

1. *Optional:* Open the Swatches palette if you're going to use it to choose colors for the gradient, and move it to the corner of your screen. Weirdly enough, you won't be able to move it around once the Gradient Editor is open.
2. Choose the Gradient tool (G or Shift-G), then click the Gradient thumbnail on the options bar to open the Gradient editor.
   or
   Double-click an existing Gradient Fill layer thumbnail on the Layers palette, then click the gradient thumbnail at the top of the Gradient Fill dialog box.
3. In the Gradient Editor, click the Presets swatch you want to create a variation of.
4. To choose a starting color, click the starting (left) color stop under the gradient bar **1**.
5. Click a color on the **Swatches** palette that you so conveniently stuck in a corner, or on the spectrum bar at the bottom of the **Color** palette, or in any open image window.
   or
   To create a gradient that will use the current **Foreground** or **Background** color, choose Foreground or Background from the Color pop-up menu at the bottom of the dialog box.
   or
   Click the **Color** swatch in the Gradient Editor, choose a color from the Color Picker, then click OK.
6. Click the ending (right) color stop under the gradient bar to set the ending color, then repeat step 5.
7. *Do any of these optional steps:*

   To **add** an intermediate color to the gradient, click below the gradient bar

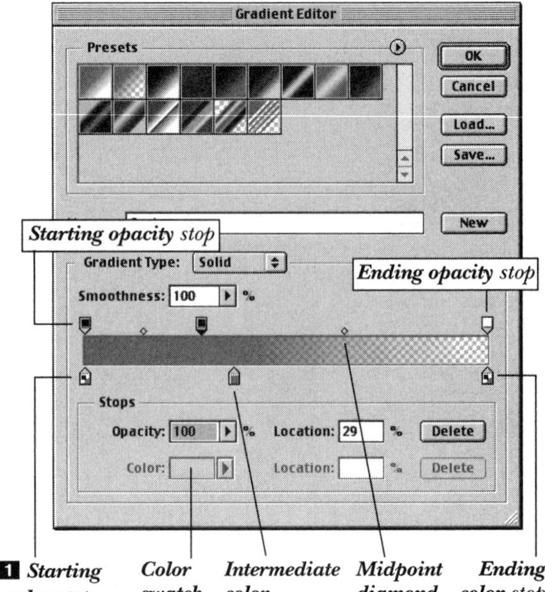

1 *Starting color stop*

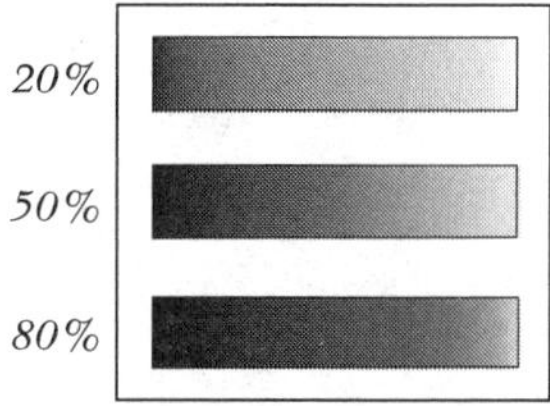

1 ***Location*** *settings*

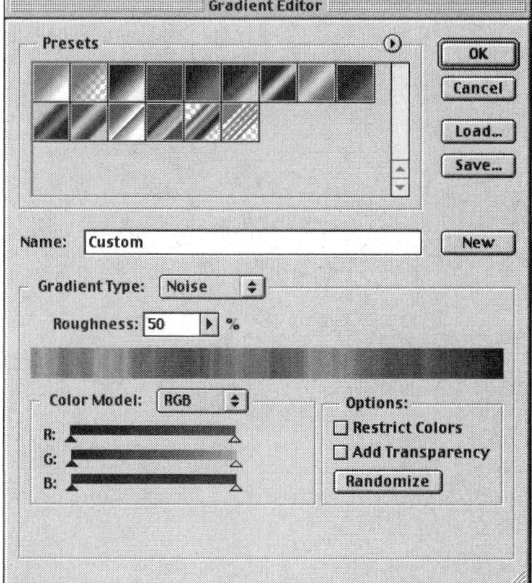

2 *Here's another option. From the* ***Gradient Type*** *pop-up, choose* ***Noise*** *to create a gradient composed of randomly chosen colors within the color range and Roughness you specify. The lower the* ***Roughness****, the smoother the color transitions. The color range is based on the model chosen on the* ***Color Model*** *pop-up menu.*

to create a new stop, then choose a color for the new stop as per step 5 on the previous page.

Move an intermediate color stop by dragging it.

To control the **abruptness** of a color transition, drag a midpoint diamond, which controls where the colors to the left and right of the diamond are of equal proportions (50% each), to a new position. Or click the diamond, then enter a percentage in the Location percentage field **1**. 0% is for the far left, 100% is for the far right.

Move the starting or ending stop, or enter a new value in the Location field for either one.

To **remove** a color, drag its stop downward off the bar.

Use Ctrl-Z/Cmd-Z to undo the previous operation.

8. Enter a name in the Name field, then click New. (Any time you edit a gradient, the Name changes to "Custom" automatically to ensure that you'll work on a copy of the gradient—not the original.)
9. Click OK. The new gradient preset is now available for use on the gradient picker.

   To save the presets currently on the gradient picker to a file for future use, see the instructions on the following page!

TIP To rename a swatch, double-click it, change the Name, then click OK.

TIP To delete a preset, Alt-click/Option-click on it.

6.0!

To save the current gradients to a separate file:

1. To open the Gradient Editor, choose the Gradient tool, then click the Gradient thumbnail on the options bar. Or double-click an existing Gradient Fill layer thumbnail on the Layers palette, then click the gradient thumbnail at the top of the Gradient Fill dialog box.
2. Click Save, enter a Name (keep the .grd extension), leave the default Adobe Photoshop 6 > Presets > Gradients folder as the location, then click Save. All the gradients currently displayed in the Presets panel will be saved to that separate file, and that file name will appear on the gradient picker menu after you relaunch Photoshop.
3. Click OK.

To use alternate gradient libraries:

1. Open the Gradient Editor (see step 1 in the previous set of instructions). Or click the gradient arrowhead to open the gradient picker.
2. Click the arrowhead in the circle at the top of the palette, then choose a gradient library from the bottom of the picker menu **1**. Custom libraries saved as per the previous set of instructions on this page will appear on this menu below the Adobe Photoshop default libraries.
3. Click Append to add the selected library to the bottom of the current presets.
   or
   Click OK to replace the current presets with the gradient library you chose.

6.0!

To restore the default gradients:

Choose **Reset Gradients** from the Gradient Editor palette menu, then click OK. Any newly created or newly modified presets will be removed!

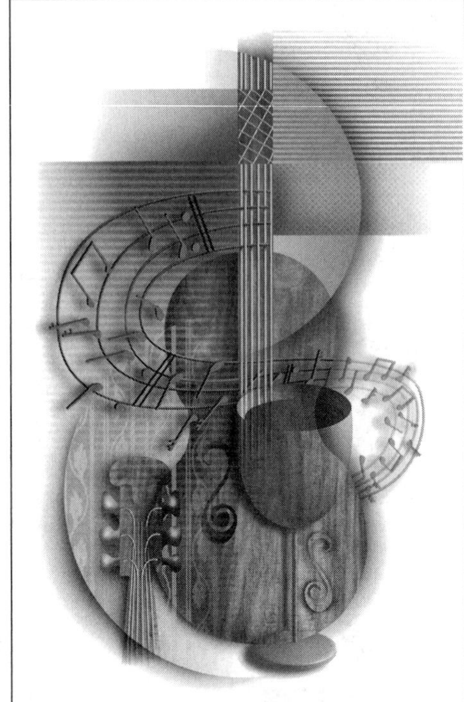

***Wendy Grossman** combined Photoshop gradients and Illustrator patterns to produce this **Guitar with Wine** image.*

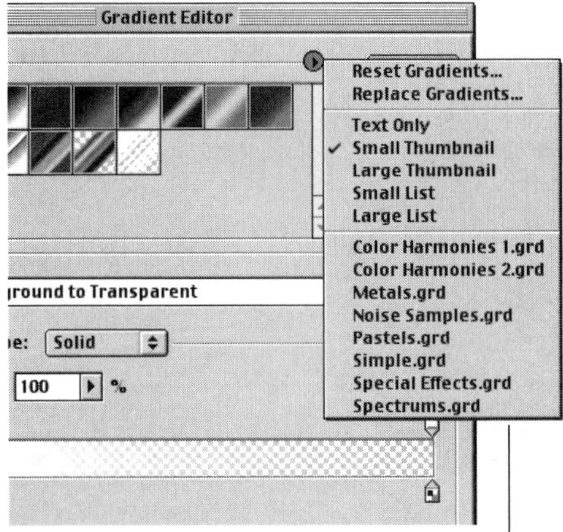

1 *Choose an alternate **gradient library** from the bottom of the pop-up menu in the **Gradient Editor**.*

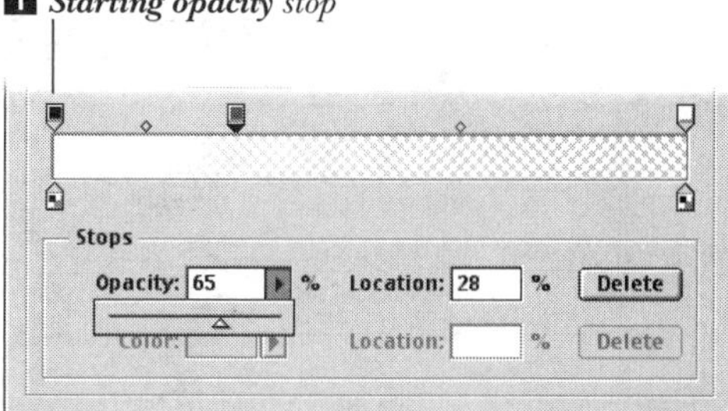

1 *Starting opacity stop*

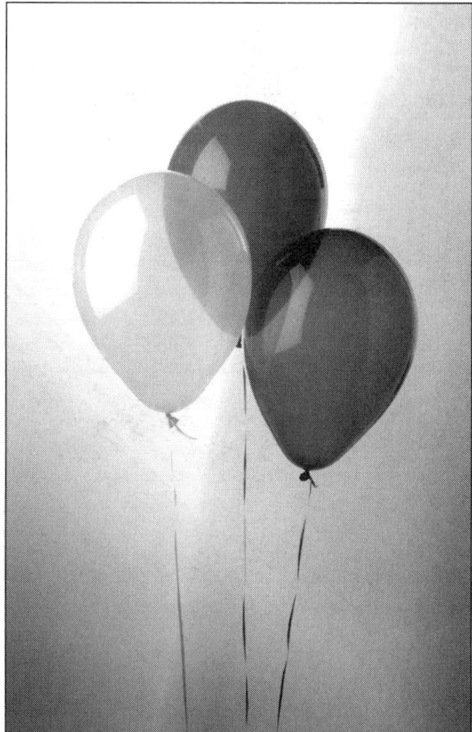

2 *Two gradients, on separate layers, were applied to this image. The middle of the gradients have a 20% opacity to allow the balloons to peek through.*

To change the opacity of gradient colors: 6.0!

1. Open the Gradient Editor, then click the gradient swatch you want to edit.
2. Click an opacity stop, located above the gradient bar **1**.
3. Choose an Opacity percentage (you can enter a percentage or use the slider). Look at the gradient bar to see a preview of the transparency effect.
4. *Do any of the following optional steps:*

   To add other opacity level stops, click just above the gradient bar, then choose an opacity percentage for each one.

   To delete a stop, drag it upward off the bar.

   To move a stop, drag it or change its Location percentage.

   To adjust the location of the midpoint opacity, drag one of the diamonds above the transparency bar or click a diamond, then change the Location percentage.
5. Enter a Name, then click New.
6. Click OK **2**. The exercise on the following page uses semi-transparent gradients on different layers.

6.0!

To create a multicolor wash:

1. Choose a layer.
2. *Optional:* Select an area of a layer.
3. Choose Gradient from the "Create new fill or adjustment layer" pop-up menu at the bottom of the Layers palette.
4. In the Gradient Fill dialog box, click the gradient thumbnail to open the Gradient Editor.
5. In the Gradient Editor, either choose an existing gradient preset that finishes with transparency or create a new gradient that fades to (finishes with) transparency, then click OK.
6. Choose a Style, Angle, and Scale for the gradient fill layer, then click OK.
7. Create another gradient fill layer, then repeat steps 4 and 5. Try out different Style, Angle, and Scale settings or drag the gradient in the image window 1–2.
8. *Optional:* Using the Layers palette, change the opacity or blending mode for, or restack, the gradient fill layers.

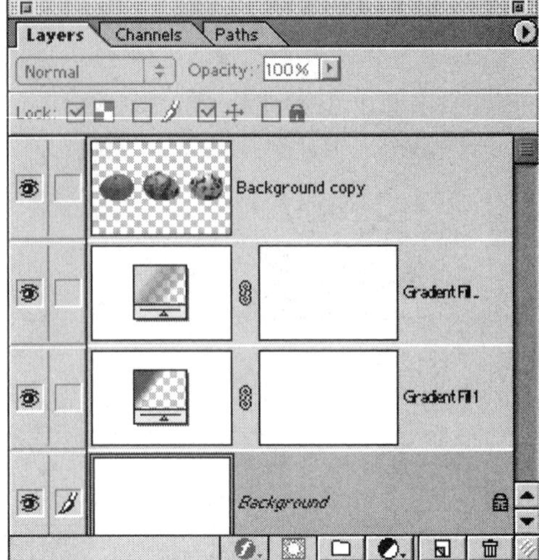

1 *Create a painterly effect by placing translucent gradient washes on separate* ***layers****.*

2 *A diamond gradient and a linear gradient.*

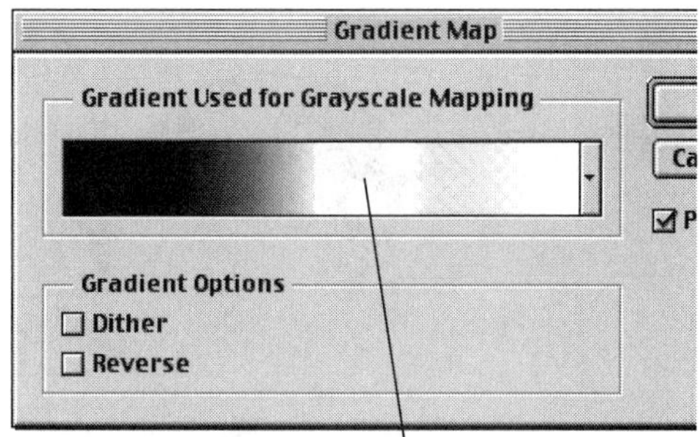

1 *Click the gradient* ***ramp*** *in the* ***Gradient Map*** *dialog box.*

6.0!

We saved the one of our favorite new features for last. The Gradient Map command applies (maps) a gradient based on luminosity levels (lights and darks) in the layer below it. This command can be used to colorize a grayscale image or re-render a color image in new tonalities, and the result can can anything from subtle to Day-glo. If you apply the Gradient Map via an adjustment layer, it will be fully reeditable.

The starting (left) color of the selected gradient is applied to the shadow areas of the layer. The ending (right) color of the gradient is applied to the highlight areas of the layer. Any color stops that are added to the gradient are applied to the midtone areas of the layer. The number of color transitions in the resulting layer will be based on the number of color stops in the selected gradient.

To apply a gradient map to a layer:

1. Choose a layer.
2. Choose Gradient Map from the "Create new fill or adjustment layer" pop-up menu at the bottom of the Layers palette.

   You can also apply the gradient map directly to a layer by choosing Image menu > Adjust > Gradient Map, but we prefer the adjustment layer approach because it offers more flexibility; a gradient map that is applied directly to an image layer can't be reedited or removed.
3. Click the Gradient arrowhead to open the gradient picker, click a preset gradient, then click the arrowhead again to close the picker, then click OK.
   or
   Click the gradient ramp to open the Gradient Editor **1**.
4. Change the starting and/or ending stop colors.
   and
   Add more color stops to the middle of the gradient ramp to add color to the

(Continued on the following page)

Gradient Map

midtone areas of the image. If your gradient contains four color stops, the layer will contain four major color transition areas.
and
Move the color stops to change the distribution of colors within the layer's tonal range, then click OK.

5. *Optional:* Check Dither to have random noise be added to color transitions in the layer to help prevent color banding.
6. *Optional:* Check Reverse to reverse the direction of the gradient colors. This will reverse the color distribution in the layer.
7. Click OK **2**–**4**. To reedit a gradient map at any time, double-click the gradient map layer thumbnail on the Layers palette.

TIP To heighten the contrast in the colors created using a gradient map adjustment layer, create an adjustment layer > Posterize using 4–6 levels, then restack the posterize layer between the image layer and the gradient map layer.

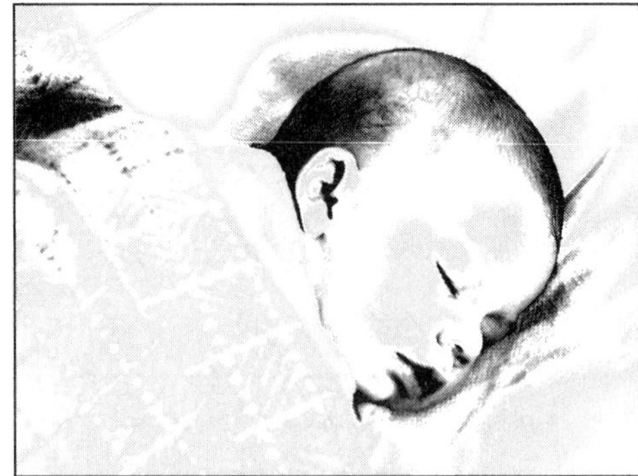

1 ***Gradient map*** *effect.*

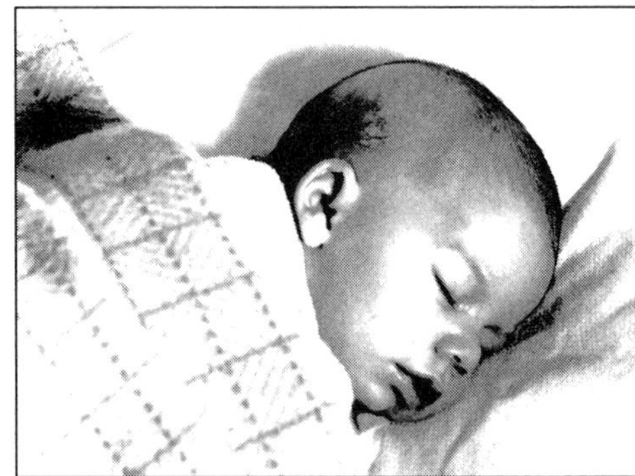

2 ***Gradient map*** *effect.*

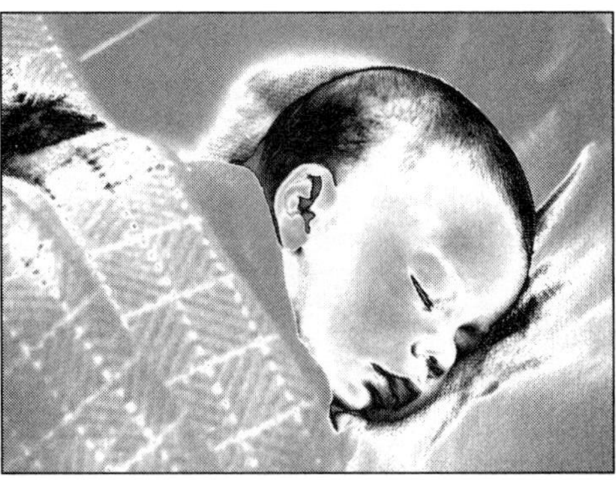

4 ***Gradient map*** *effect.*

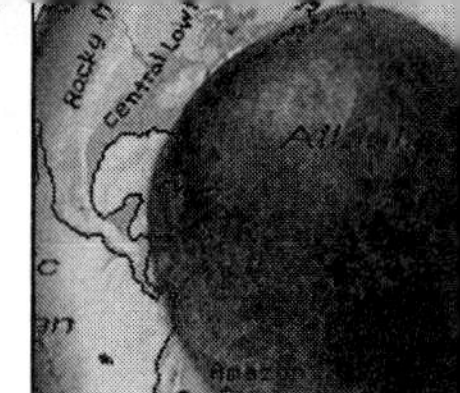

MORE LAYERS 14

Chapter topics

Change layer opacity
Apply layer effects
Blend pixels between layers
Create and use layer masks
Create a clipping group of layers
Link layers
Align and distribute layers

IN THIS CHAPTER you will learn about Photoshop's intermediate and advanced layers features. Be sure to read Chapter 7, Layers, to learn about basic layer operations first. (Adjustment layers are discussed on pages 152–155.)

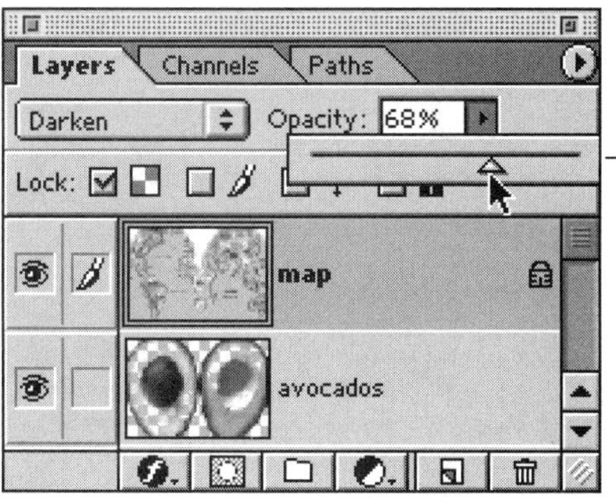

1 *Each layer can have a different **Opacity** level.*

Layer opacity

To change the opacity of a layer:

Choose an opacity from the Layers palette **1**. The lower the opacity, the more pixels from the layer below will show through the active layer **2**–**3**. The opacity of the Background cannot be changed.

or

Choose a tool other than a painting tool, then press 1 on the keyboard to change the opacity of an active layer to 10%, 2 to change the opacity to 20%, and so on. Or type both digits quickly (e.g., 15, for 15%).

TIP You can also choose an opacity for a layer using the Blending Options section of the Layer Style dialog box (see page 238).

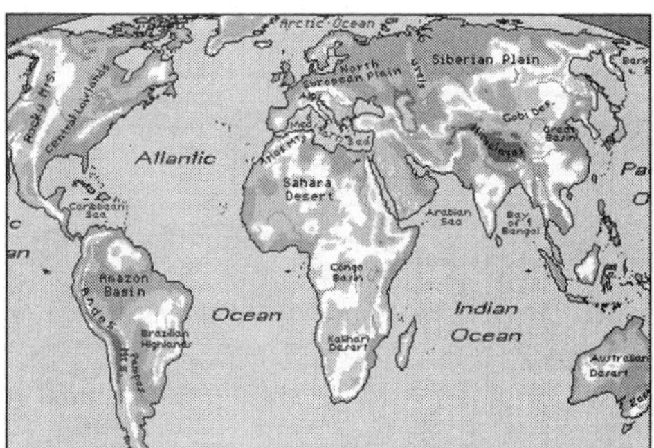

2 *The map layer, 100% Opacity, on top of the avocados layer.*

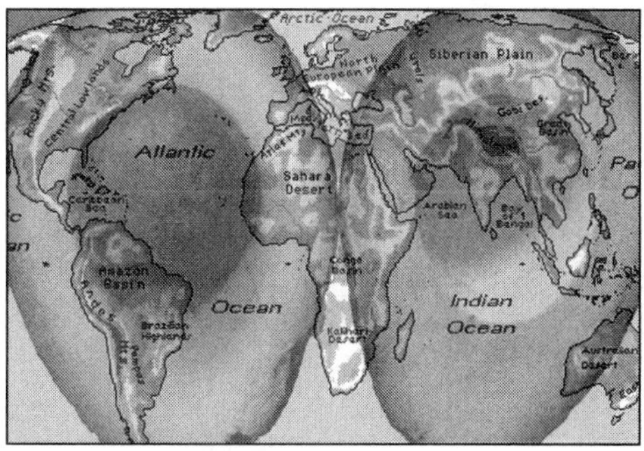

3 *The map layer opacity reduced to 68%.*

6.0!

Layer effects

Applying layer effects

The special effects that can be applied to a layer are as follows: Drop Shadow, Inner Shadow, Outer Glow, Inner Glow, Bevel and Emboss, Satin, Color Overlay, Gradient Overlay, Pattern Overlay, and Stroke. A layer effect (or effects) can be applied to any layer, even an editable type layer, and it can be turned on or off at any time. Layer effects automatically affect all opaque pixels on a layer, and will update if pixels are added, modified, or deleted from the layer.

TIP Don't confuse styles and effects. A style is simply a combination of one or more layer effects.

Effects are applied and edited from one central, chock-full dialog box (the **Layer Style** dialog box **2**), and they are displayed on the Layers palette as indented (nested) layers below the name of the layer to which they are applied. Effects are attached to, and move with, the main layer that they're applied to. Layer effects can't be applied to the Background of an image.

Before we get into specific effects, here are some general pointers:

- To **apply** an effect to a layer, double-click the layer name. In the Layer Style dialog box, click an effect name (don't just click the check box!), and choose settings for

*The "f" icon indicates that a **layer effect** is applied to that layer.*

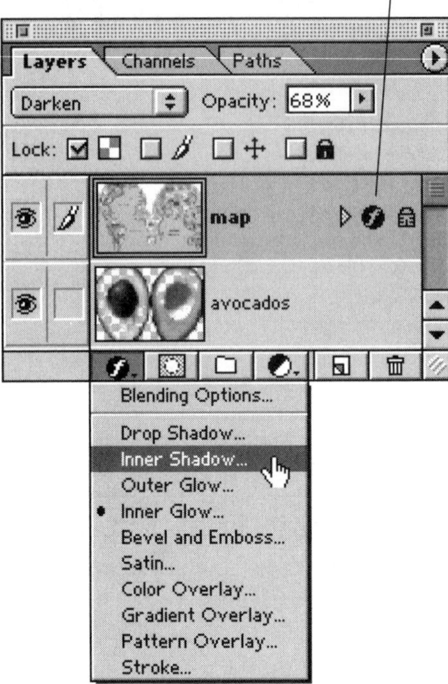

1 *Choose an effect name from the **Add layer style** pop-up menu. A bullet next to an effect signifies that that effect is currently applied to the active layer. The same effects can also be chosen from the **Layer** menu > **Layer Style** submenu.*

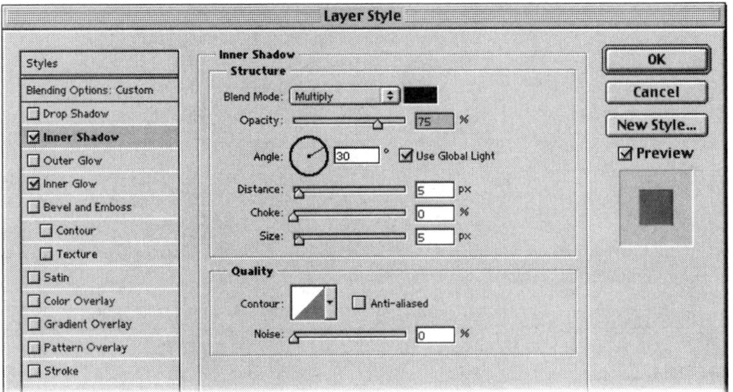

2 *The **Layer Style** dialog box is used to apply layer effects.*

Applying Layer Effects

Copy an effect from one layer to another

Choose a layer that contains an effect or effects, choose Layer menu > Layer Style > **Copy Layer Style**, choose another layer, then choose Layer menu > Layer Style > **Paste Layer Style**.

or

Expand the effects list for a layer, then **drag** an individual **effect name** over another layer name or over another layer's Effects bar.

or

To copy multiple effects from one layer to another, expand the effects list for a layer, then **drag** the **Effects** bar over another layer name or another layer's Effects bar. The duplicated effect(s) will replace any existing effects on the destination layer.

To ***hide*** *an effect from view temporarily, click the* ***eye*** *icon.*

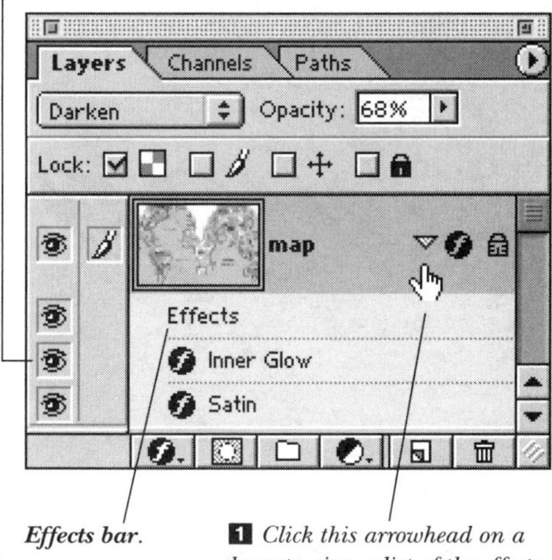

Effects bar.

1 *Click this arrowhead on a layer to view a list of the effects that are applied to that layer.*

the effect. More than one effect can be applied to the same layer. Check the **Preview** box to preview the effect in the image window. You can also apply an effect by choosing a layer, and then choosing an effect from the **Add layer style** pop-up menu at the bottom of the Layers palette.

- On the Layers palette, any layer to which a layer effect is currently applied will have an ƒ icon. Click the arrowhead next to the ƒ icon to view a list of the effects that are applied to that layer **1**. Each effect has its own hide/show eye icon.
- To **edit** an existing layer effect (or add another one), double-click the ƒ icon; or double-click the effect name nested under the layer name; or choose an effect from the ƒ (Add layer style) pop-up menu at the bottom of the Layers palette.
- To **hide** a layer effect, make sure the effects list for the layer in question is expanded, then click its eye icon. (Click in the same spot to redisplay the effect.)

  To temporarily **hide all** effects from all layers and speed performance, choose Layer menu > Layer Style > Hide All Effects. Choose Show All Effects to redisplay them.
- To **remove** an individual layer effect, double-click the layer name or the individual effect name on the Layers palette, then uncheck the box next to the effect name. Or drag the individual effect name over the Delete Layer (trash) button at the bottom of the Layers palette.

TIP If you recheck an effect that was turned off or deleted, the last-used options for that effect will redisplay.

TIP To **clear all** effects from the currently active layer, choose Layer menu > Layer Style > Clear Layer Style.

TIP Alt/Option click Reset to restore the Layer Style dialog box to the settings it had when it was opened.

6.0!

To apply the Drop Shadow or Inner Shadow effect:

1. Double-click a layer name.
2. Click on Drop Shadow.
3. Change any of the following settings: **1**

   Choose a **Blend Mode** from the pop-up menu.

   Click the color swatch to choose a different **shadow color** from the Color Picker (the new color will preview immediately), then click OK.

   Choose an **Opacity** percentage for the transparency of the shadow.

   Choose an **Angle** for the angle of the shadow relative to the original layer shapes. Check the Use Global Light box to use the angle that was entered in the Layer menu > Layer Style > Global Light dialog box. Uncheck this option if you want to use a unique angle setting for this particular effect. *Note:* If you readjust the Angle for an individual effect while Use Global Angle is checked, all effects that utilize the Global Angle option will also be modified. This option helps to make the lighting in multiple layer effects look more uniform.

   Choose a **Distance** for the distance (in pixels) of the drop shadow from the original layer shapes or for the width of an inner shadow **2**–**3**.

   TIP You can drag the actual shadow in the image window while the dialog box is open. Unfortunately, this will also move all effects that use the Global Light option.

   Choose a **Spread** (mask enlargement width before blurring) for the shadow. For Inner Shadow, choose a **Choke** (mask reduction) value for the shadow.

   Choose a **Size** for the blurriness (softness) of the shadow.

   In the Quality section, click the arrowhead to choose a preset **Contour** from the Contour picker for the edge profile of the shadow (see also page 230).

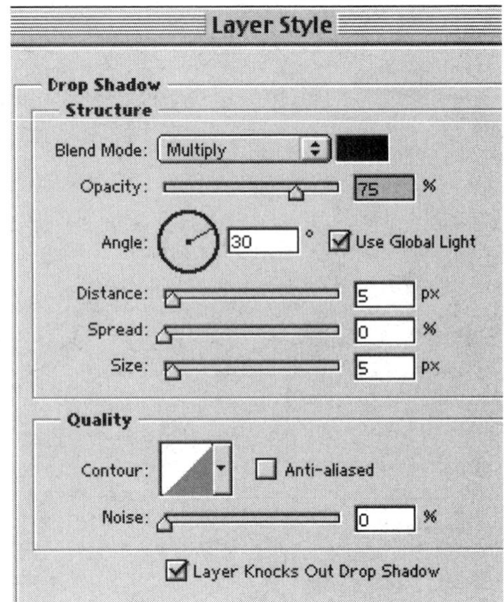

1

2 *Drop Shadow.*

3 *Inner Shadow (with a Drop Shadow, too).*

Drop Shadow; Inner Shadow

1 *The original layer with a* ***Drop Shadow****.*

2 *Choosing the new* ***Drop Shadow*** *layer.*

3 ***Distorting*** *the Drop Shadow.*

4 *The final image.*

Check the **Anti-aliased** box to soften the jagged edges between the shadow and other parts of the image.

Set the **Noise** level to adjust the amount of the edge speckling in the shadow.

Click the **Layer Knocks Out Drop Shadow** box to prevent the shadow from showing through any transparent parts of the layer. 6.0!

4. Click OK.

To transform a Drop Shadow:

1. Apply the Drop Shadow effect (instructions on the previous page) **1**, and keep the layer selected.
2. Choose Layer menu > Layer Style > Create Layer to transfer the shadow effect to its own layer.
3. Choose the new shadow layer **2**.
4. Choose Edit menu > Transform > Distort, then drag the handles of the bounding box to achieve the desired shape **3**–**4**.
5. *Optional:* Change the luminosity of the shadow via an adjustment layer or choose a different blending mode or opacity for the shadow layer. Check the "Lock transparent pixels" box on the Layers palette to limit any painting or fill changes to just the shadow shape.

TIP Link the shadow layer and its original object layer to move them in unison.

Note: To use a type mask selection for these steps, save the active selection to a channel first, and then load the channel as a selection. You can also save any active selection as a channel for later use.

To create a Drop Shadow without using an effect:

1. Create a selection to become the shadow shape. To select a silhouetted object, Ctrl-click/Cmd-click the object's layer.
2. Feather the selection (Ctrl-Alt-D/Cmd-Option-D).
3. Choose Select menu > Transform Selection or Right-click/Control-click and choose Transform Selection from the context menu, then transform and/or move the selection marquee.
4. Click the Create new layer button at the bottom of the Layers palette, then restack the new layer directly below the layer that contains the silhouetted object.
5. Choose Edit menu > Fill, choose Fill: Black, Mode: Normal, and Opacity: 75%, click OK, then deselect.
6. Move the shadow layer using the Move tool. You can also change its blending mode or opacity.

To apply an Outer or Inner Glow: 6.0!

1. Open the Swatches palette.
2. Double-click a layer name.
3. Click on Outer Glow or Inner Glow.
4. Choose **Structure** settings **1**:

   Choose a **Blend Mode** (see "Blending modes" on pages 30–32).

   To change the glow **color**, click the color swatch, choose a color from the Color Picker (or, while the Picker is open, from the Swatches palette). Choose a color that contrasts with the background color. It might be hard to see a light Outer Glow color against a light background color. The new color will preview on the images. Click OK.

   or

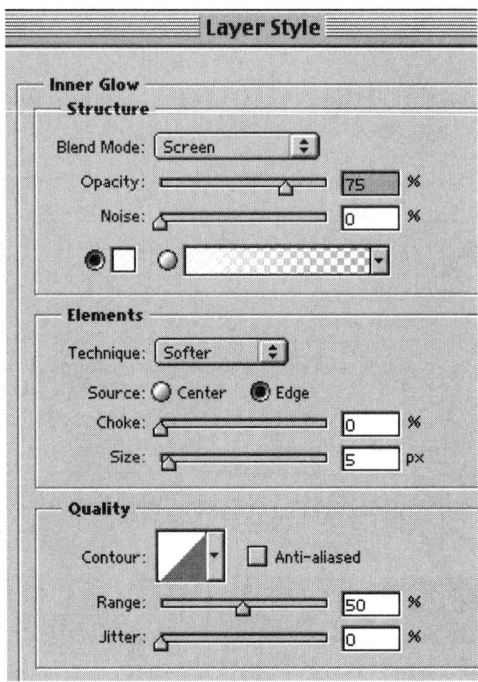

1 *Choose Structure, Elements, and Quality settings for an **Inner Glow** effect in the **Layer Style** dialog box.*

1 *Inner Glow (Center) (with a Drop Shadow).*

2 *Outer Glow.*

To create a glow with a **gradient**, click the arrowhead to choose a gradient from the Gradient picker; or click the gradient thumbnail to edit one of the presets or create a new gradient (see page 214).

Choose an **Opacity** for the transparency level of the glow.

Set the **Noise** level for the amount of speckling in the glow.

5. Choose **Elements** settings:

Choose Softer or Precise from the **Technique** pop-up menu to control how closely the mask follows the contours of areas that contain pixels.

For an Inner Glow, click **Center** to create a glow that spreads outward from the center of the layer pixels **1**. (Tip: Try this on type.) Click **Edge** to create a glow that spreads inward from the inside edges of the layer pixels.

For Outer Glow, set the **Spread** to define the width of the glow (a mask, actually) before it starts to blur **2**.

For Inner Glow, adjust the **Choke** to define the width of the glow before it starts to blur.

Choose a **Size** for the glow.

6. Choose **Quality** settings:

Click the arrowhead to choose a preset **Contour** from the Contour picker for the edge profile of the glow (see page 230).

Set the **Range** to control the placement of the contour effect along the width of the glow.

If the glow contains a gradient, set the **Jitter** to randomize the distribution of colors in the gradient.

7. Click OK.

TIP To apply a layer effect to type, make the type large and don't track it tightly.

6.0! The Bevel and Emboss command creates an illusion of depth by adding a highlight and a shadow to layer shapes.

To apply the Bevel or Emboss effect:

1. Open the Swatches palette.
2. Double-click a layer name on the Layers palette. It can be a type layer.
3. Click on Bevel and Emboss.
4. Choose **Structure** settings **1**:

   Choose a **Style**: Outer Bevel **2**, Inner Bevel **3**, Emboss or Pillow Emboss or Stroke Emboss (and **1**–**2** next page).

   Choose Smooth, Chisel Hard, or Chisel Soft from the **Technique** pop-up menu.

   Choose a **Depth** for the amount the highlight and shadow are offset from the layer shapes.

   Click the **Up** or **Down** button to switch the highlight and shadow positions.

   Choose a **Size** for the bevel or emboss effect.

   Raise the **Soften** value if you want to blur the sharp edges of the layer shape and thus soften the effect.
5. Choose **Shading** settings:

   Choose an **Angle** and an **Altitude** to change the location of the the light source. These settings will in turn affect the highlight and shadow. Check the Use Global Light box to use the current Angle and Altitude settings from the Layer menu > Layer Style > Global Light dialog box. Or uncheck this option to use a unique setting for this particular style. ***Beware!*** If you readjust an individual style's Angle or Altitude while the Use Global Light box is checked, all other styles that utilize the Global Light option will update, too.

   Click the **Gloss Contour** arrowhead, then choose from the Contour picker (see page 230).

   Choose a **Highlight Mode** and **Opacity** and a **Shadow Mode** and **Opacity** for

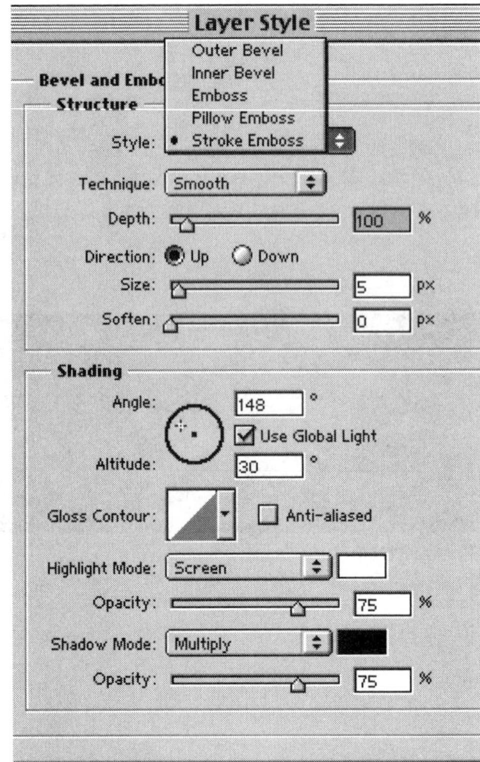

1 *Settings for the **Bevel and Emboss** layer effect.*

2 ***Outer Bevel.***

3 ***Inner Bevel** (with a Drop Shadow, too).*

EMBOSS

1 *Emboss (with a Drop Shadow, too).*

EMBOSS

2 *Pillow Emboss.*

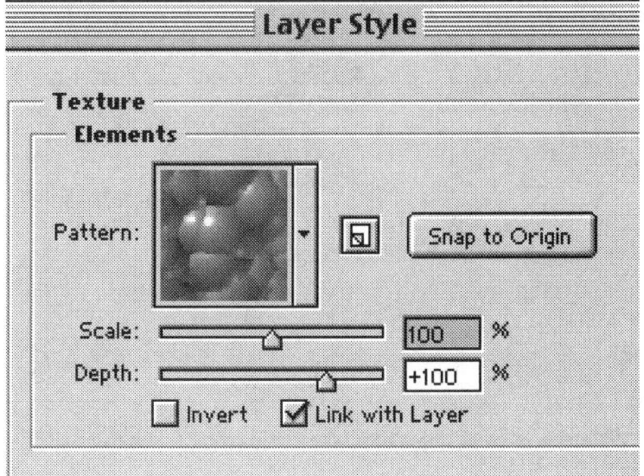

3 *The* ***Texture*** *options for the* ***Bevel and Emboss*** *layer effect.*

4 *Adobe's Tie Dye* ***texture*** *used with the* ***Bevel and Emboss*** *(Style: Emboss) layer effect.*

image highlight and shadow areas (see "Blending modes" on pages 30–32).

To change the highlight or shadow **color**, click either color swatch, then choose a color from the Color Picker (or, while the Picker is open, from the Swatches palette). The color will preview on the image. Then click OK.

6. To add a **Contour** to the bevel or emboss for the edge profile of the glow, click Contour at the left side of the dialog box box under Bevel and Emboss. Click the Contour arrowhead, then click a preset contour in the picker (see page 230). This feature can dramatically change the appearance of the effect.

Set the **Range** to determine the placement of the contour effect along the width of the glow. The Range option has no effect on the Emboss effect.

Check the **Anti-aliased** box to soften the hard edges between adjoining areas.

7. To add a texture to a bevel or emboss, click on **Texture** at the left side of the dialog box, click the Texture arrowhead, choose a pattern from the picker, then do any of the following **3**–**4**:

Adjust the **Scale** of the pattern.

Change the **Depth** to adjust the contrast of shadows and highlights in the pattern.

Check the **Invert** box to flip the shadows and highlights. This has the same effect as changing the Depth percentage from negative to positive, or vice versa.

Check the **Link with Layer** box to ensure that the texture and the layer will move in unison.

Drag in the image window to reposition the texture within the effect. Click **Snap to Origin** to realign the pattern to the upper left corner of the image.

If you have loaded in a custom pattern, click the Create new preset button to add it to the presets.

8. Click OK.

6.0! For all the layer effects except the Overlay effects and the Stroke effect, you can choose an edge style, called a contour. The contours control such elements as the fade on a drop shadow or a highlight on a bevel. Follow these steps if you want to modify the contour for an effect.

To change the profile of a contour:

1. Double-click a layer or effect name to open the Layer Style dialog box. For the Bevel and Emboss effect only, also click Contour at the left side of the dialog box.
2. Click the Contour thumbnail (not the arrowhead).
3. *Optional:* In the Contour Editor, choose a preset contour from the Preset pop-up menu to use as a starting point **2**.
4. Click on the graph to add points. Drag points to adjust the graph. The name "Custom" will automatically appear on the Preset pop-up menu.

   Check the Corner box to convert the currently selected point into a non-smooth corner point.
5. To save the custom graph as a file for reuse, click Save, enter a file name, then click Save again.
6. To save the custom graph as a preset contour, click New, enter a name, then click OK. The custom contour will be listed on the Contour picker.
7. Click OK to close the Contour Editor.

TIP To **delete** a contour, open the Contour picker, Alt-click/Option-click the contour you want to delete, then close the picker. *Note:* The contour will be deleted only from the current picker—not from the actual preset library.

TIP To **restore** the default contour library, open the Contour picker, choose Reset Contours from the Contour picker menu, then click OK. To choose a different library, choose a library name from the bottom of the Contour picker menu (click Append or click OK to replace).

Contour Editor

Picking from the picker

The profile thumbnails in the Contour picker illustrate different edge styles **1**. The gray areas in the profile represent opaque pixels; the white areas represent transparency. To close the picker, click the Contour arrowhead or click somewhere outside the picker in the Layer Style dialog box.

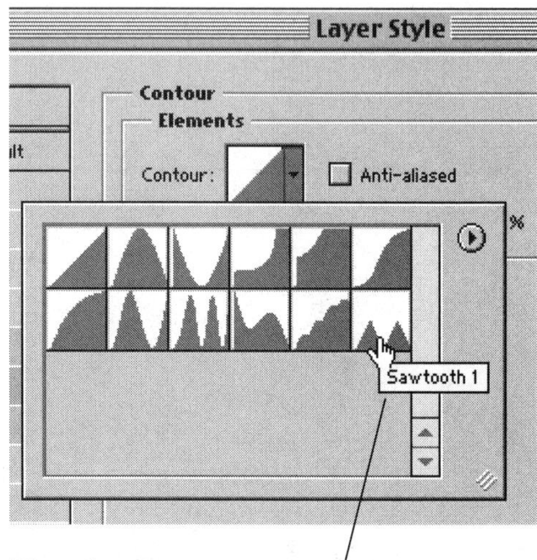

1 *You can use Tool Tips to learn the* ***names*** *of the various contours in the* ***Contour*** *picker.*

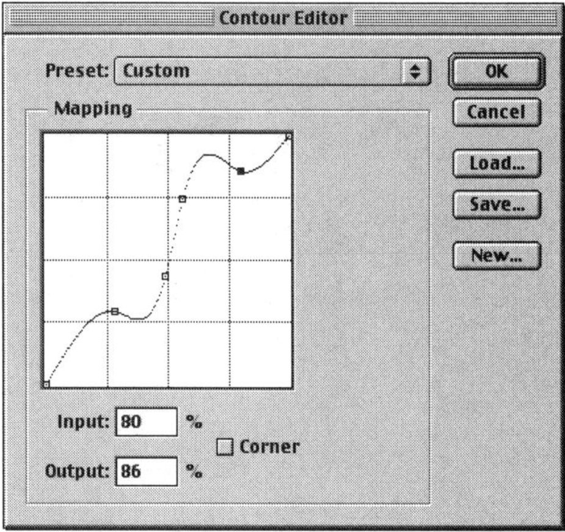

2 *Customize a contour using the* ***Contour Editor****.*

ILLUSTRATIONS
OF
ORNITHOLOGY

Walter Robertson

Walter Robertson

Wendy Grossman

Wendy Grossman

Wendy Grossman

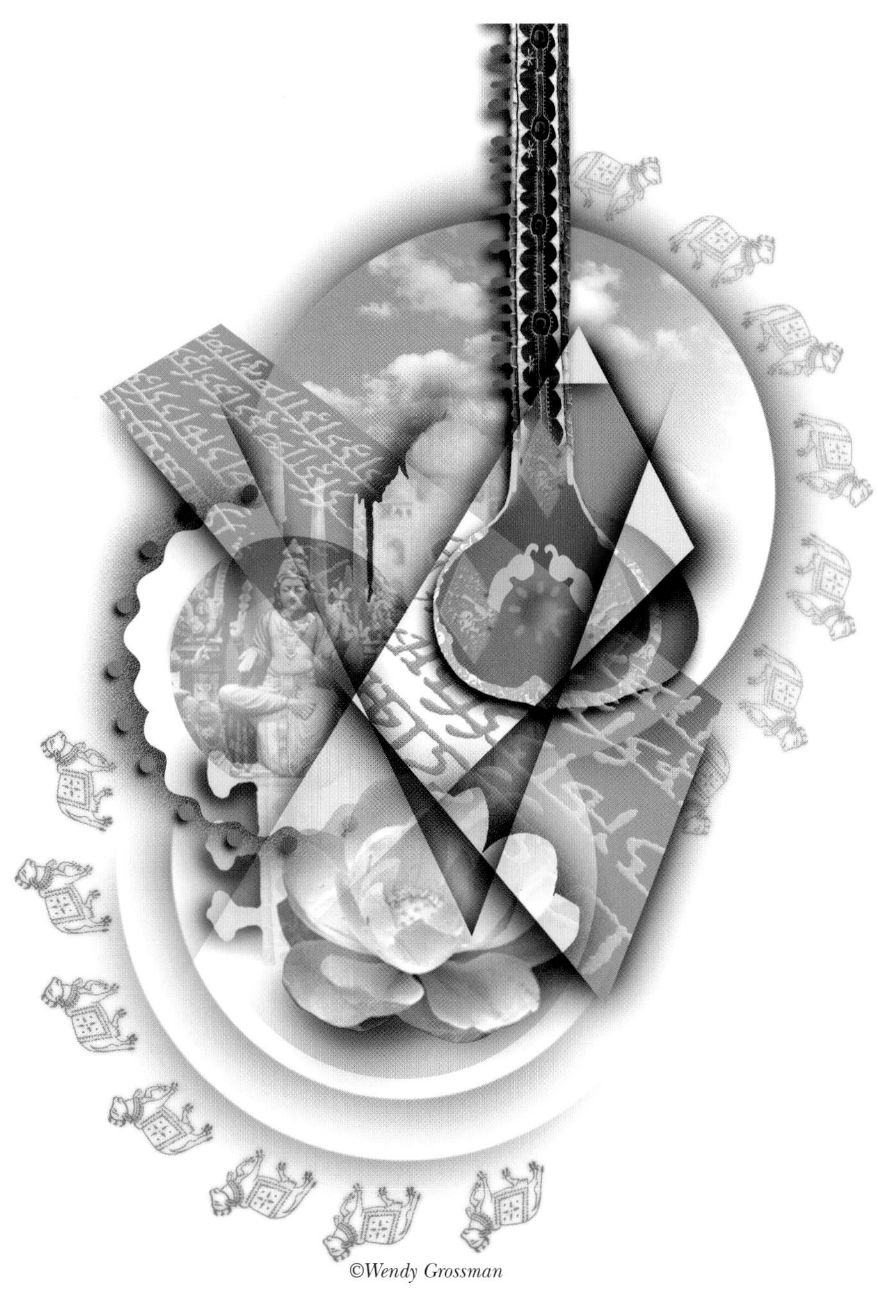

UNDER MY WINGS EVERY THING
STUDY AND CAREFULNESS EARN THIS REWARD
Naomi Shea

©Naomi Shea

David Wilkinson
Cutting Screw
NEW BEDFORD, MAS

Naomi Shea

©Naomi Shea

Naomi Shea

©Naomi Shea

Naomi Shea

Tropicus Cancri
Archipelago
NONDUM
COGNITA
COGNITA

©Naomi Shea

PAC
BELL
1
2 ABC
3 DEF
4 GHI
5 JKL
6 MNO
7 PRS
8 TUV
9 WXY
*
0 OPER
#

©Alan Mazzetti

Alan Mazzetti

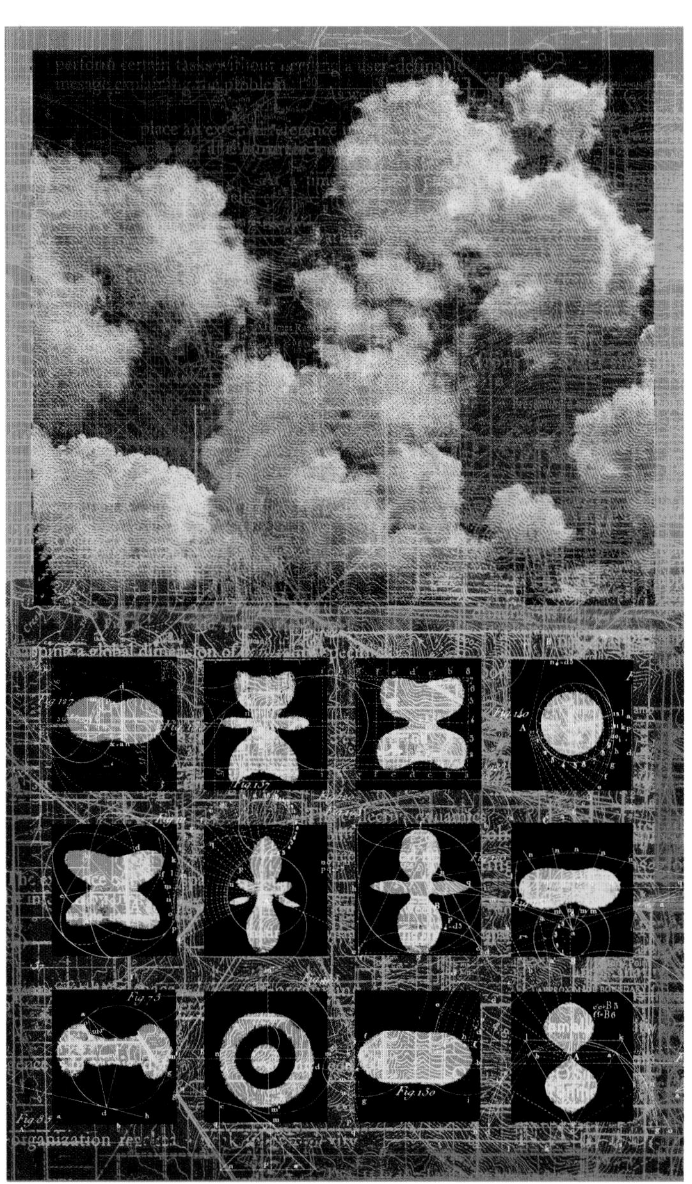

©Jeff Brice

Jeff Brice

MACH CONE
SMALL DISTURBANCE
FREESTREAM VELOCITY
22 October
October
home (m)
estimate
Damping ratio
Natural Frequency
Over damped
Time response curve of a second order system subjected
r = a sin 3θ
r = a cos 3θ
r = a cos 2θ

Jeff Brice

RANDOM
More people are signed into psychiatric services just after disturbances of the earth's magnetic field.
VISUAL
The Earth's magnetic field shows measurable effects on the metabolism of the pineal gland, (which produces melatonin and serotonin).
All the images, structures, sounds, social behavior, beliefs are cultural units.
spin I_i
spin I_f

Jeff Brice

DECLINATION (1950.0)
OUTPUT AXIS
PRECESSION
18 cm
23 cm
oviduct
ovary
uterus
seminal vesicle
bladder
urethra
clitoris
minus
majus
anus
vagina
glans
penis
WYOMING

Suling Wang

Suling Wang

Suling Wang

Alicia Buelow

Wings light quietly
warm landscapes, my skin
electrocuted, pores wide open
draw in hot
behind trails of gold
TOUCH
me

Alicia Buelow

from far away she looked like jesus
wild mane of hair
crown of thorns
from far away she looked like jesus
crucified, suffering
now close I can see
she is an angel
her disguise translucent as tissue paper
laid in wet strips over her breaking heart
the pain of her possession
how much she wants to have it
comfort comes only
in the shape of a lover
the size of the earth
who sees the beauty of sadness
who sees love inside fear
who pushes through her like the ocean
and changes the tide forever
this cocoon falls away
I can see what I've been seeing
hear what I've been hearing
touch what I've been touching
lavish heart
perfect beauty
turning everyone inside out
her music still resonating
within me
escape
within me
Fig.97
close I can see
is an angel

Alicia Buelow

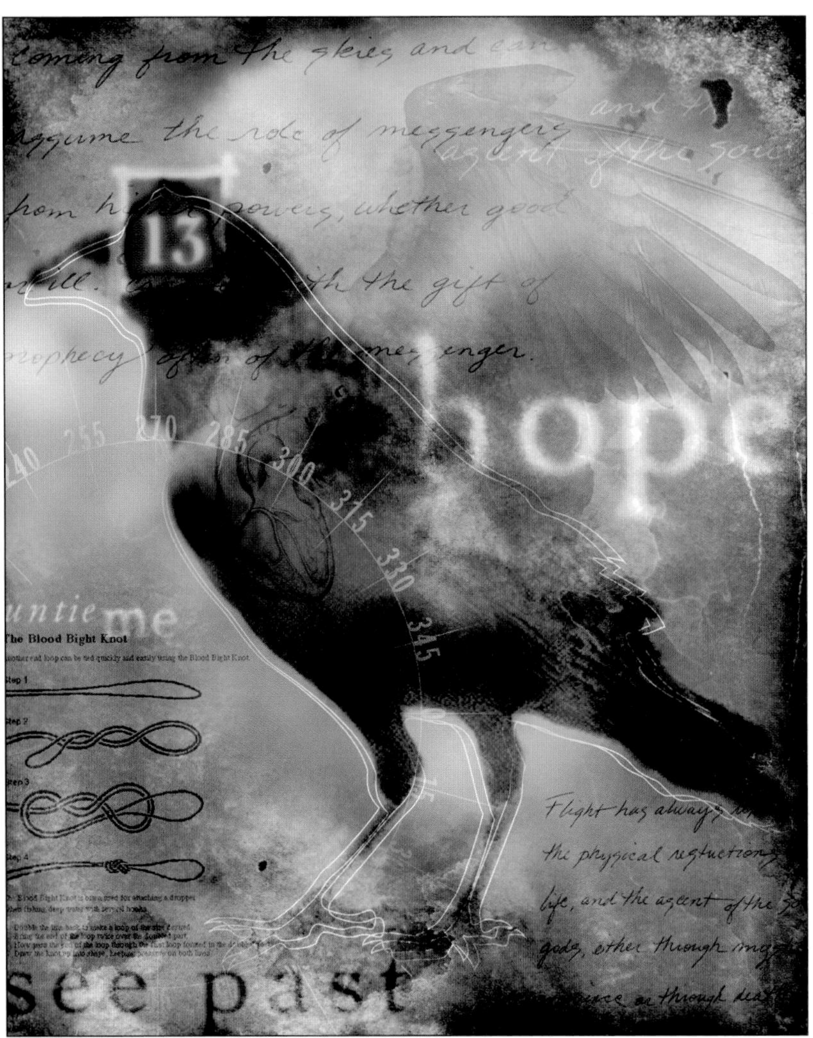
13
hope
untie me
The Blood Bight Knot
see past

GRATIAE
CHARITES

Soul
Sole
Foot leads eye, eye instructs foot, alternatingly.
Walking takes on the movement of soul
because, as the great philosopher Plotinus said,
the soul's motion is not direct

William Cook, a sailor in the US Navy, lies buried at the foot of Monkey Mountain in Vietnam. But he wasn't killed fighting the Viet Cong. He died in 1845, aboard the USS Constitution, during a good-will tour around the world. When the ship put into Da Nang Harbor for food and water, Cook was taken ashore, buried, and all but forgotten – until this year, when a group of Massachusetts veterans set out to find the grave of the first US serviceman buried on Vietnamese soil.
The search for
Seaman
Cook
By Peter Kneisel

THE COLISEUM, ROME.

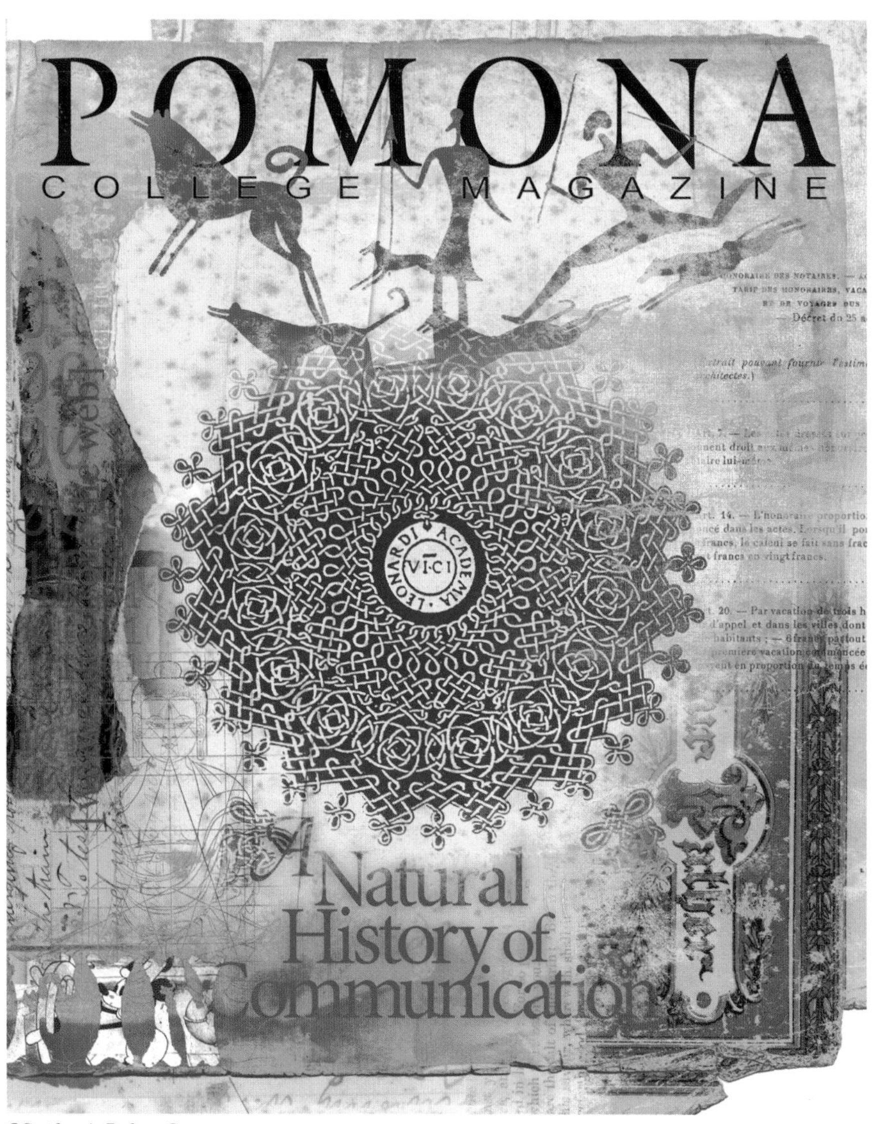
POMONA
COLLEGE MAGAZINE
A Natural History of Communication

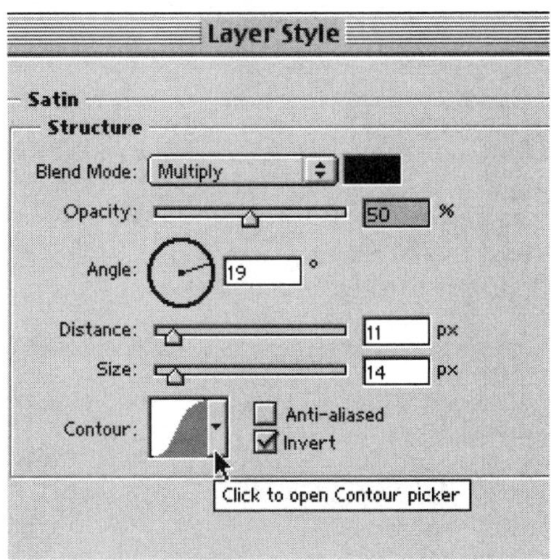

1 *Options for the* ***Satin*** *layer effect.*

2 *The* ***Satin*** *layer effect applied to editable type.*

3 *The* ***Satin*** *layer effect with the* ***Invert*** *box checked.*

To apply the Satin effect:

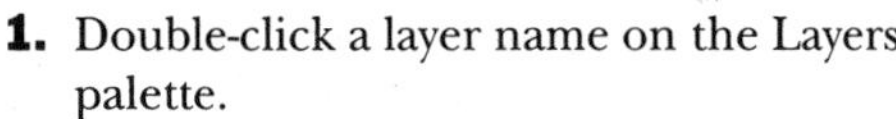

1. Double-click a layer name on the Layers palette.
2. Click on Satin.
3. Do any of the following **1**:

   Change the **Blend Mode** (see "Blending Modes" on pages 30–32).

   To change the overlay **color**, click the color swatch, then choose a color from the color picker.

   Adjust the **Opacity** of the effect.

   Change the **Angle** of the effect. This angle is independent of the Global Light settings.

   Set the **Distance** and the **Size** of the effect. You can also drag in the image window to adjust the distance.

   Click the **Contour** arrowhead, then choose from the Contour picker for the edge profile of the effect.

   Check the **Anti-aliased** box to soften the hard boundary between the effect and the underlying shape.

   Check the **Invert** box to swap the shadows and highlights.
4. Click OK **2**–**3**.

6.0!

To apply the Color Overlay effect:

1. Double-click a layer name on the Layers palette.
2. Click on Color Overlay.
3. Do any of the following **1**:

   Choose a **Blend Mode**.

   Click the color swatch, then choose a different **color** for the overlay.

   Adjust the **Opacity** of the overlay.
4. Click OK.

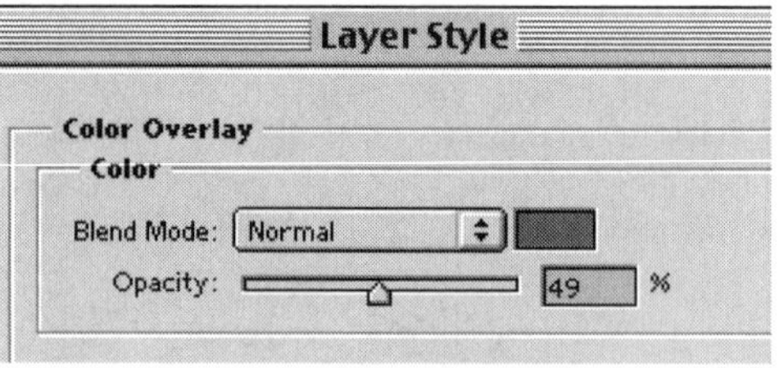

1 *Options for the **Color Overlay** layer effect.*

6.0!

To apply the Gradient Overlay effect:

1. Double-click the layer name on the Layers palette.
2. Click on Gradient Overlay.
3. Do any of the following **2**:

   Choose a **Blend Mode**.

   Adjust the **Opacity** of the overlay.

   Click the **Gradient** arrowhead, then choose a preset gradient from the Gradient picker.

   Check the **Reverse** box to change the direction of the gradient.

   Choose a **Style** (Linear, Radial, Angle, Reflected, or Diamond).

   Check the **Align with Layer** box to align the gradient with the shapes in the layer.

   Set the **Angle** of the gradient.

   Choose a **Scale** percentage for the placement of the midpoint of the gradient.

   You can also drag in the image window to **reposition** the gradient.
4. Click OK **3**. Read more about gradients on page 211.

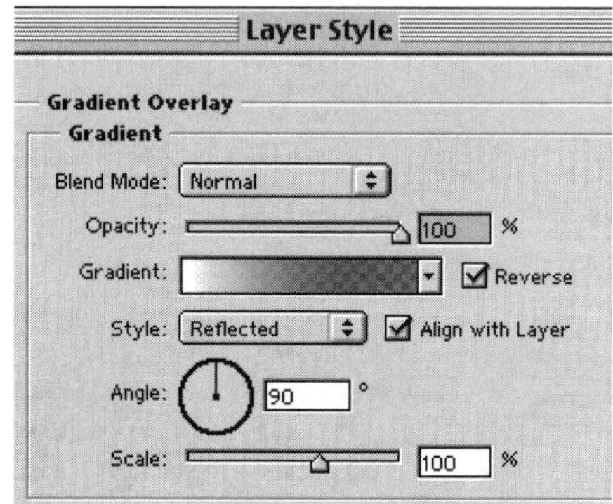

2 *Options for the **Gradient Overlay** layer effect.*

3 ***Gradient Overlay** (Style: Reflected, Reversed).*

Color Overlay; Gradient Overlay

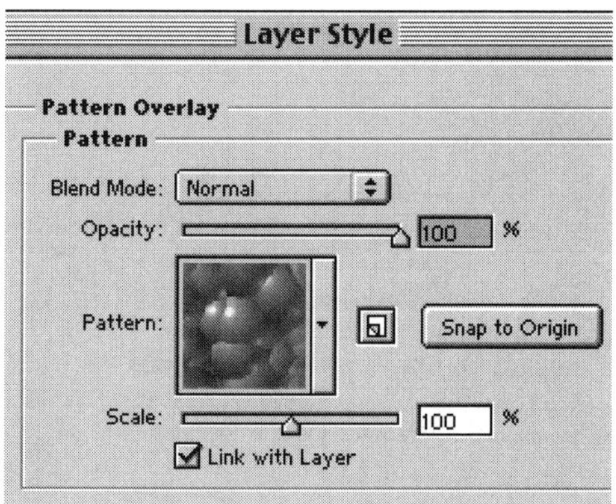

1 *Options for the* ***Pattern Overlay*** *layer effect.*

2 *The* ***Pattern Overlay*** *effect applied to a shape layer object.*

To apply the Pattern Overlay effect: 

1. Double-click a layer name on the Layers palette.
2. Click on Pattern Overlay.
3. Do any of the following **1**:

   Choose a **Blend Mode**.

   Adjust the **Opacity** of the overlay.

   Click the Pattern arrowhead, then choose a preset **pattern** from the picker.

   Click **Snap to Origin** to align the pattern with the upper left hand corner of the image. You can also drag in the image window to reposition the pattern.

   Choose a **Scale** percentage for pattern.

   Check the **Link with Layer** box to link the pattern to the layer.

   If you have loaded in a custom pattern, click the Create new preset button to make that pattern part of the presets.
4. Click OK **2**.

To apply a Stroke effect:

1. Double-click a layer name on the Layers palette.
2. Click on Stroke.
3. Do any of the following **1**:

   Choose a **Size** for the stroke.

   From the **Position** pop-up menu, choose whether you want the stroke to be Outside, Inside, or Centered on the edges of shapes in the layer.

   Choose a **Blend Mode**.

   Choose an **Opacity** percentage.

   Choose a **Fill Type** (Color, Gradient, or Pattern) and specify its details using the controls that become available. See Color Overlay and Gradient Overlay information on page 232; Pattern Overlay information on page 233.
4. Click OK **2**.

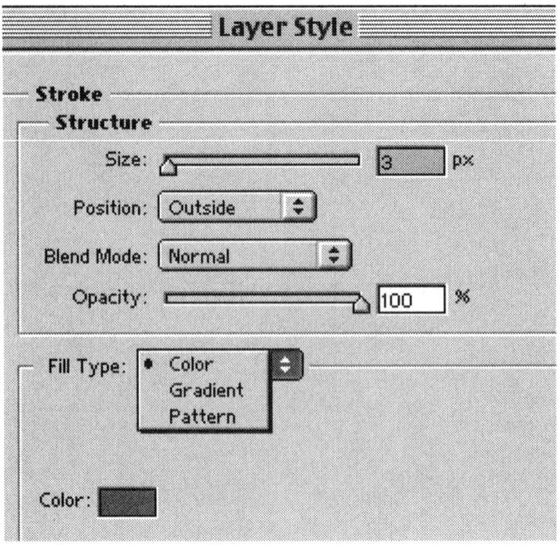

1 *Options for the* ***Stroke*** *layer effect.*

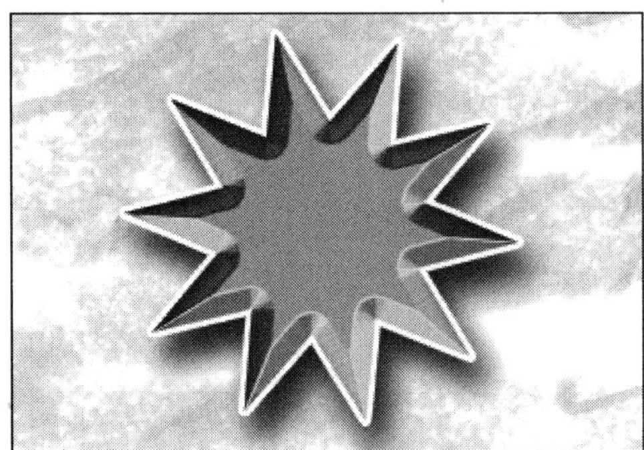

2 *The* ***Stroke*** *effect applied to a shape layer object.*

Stroke

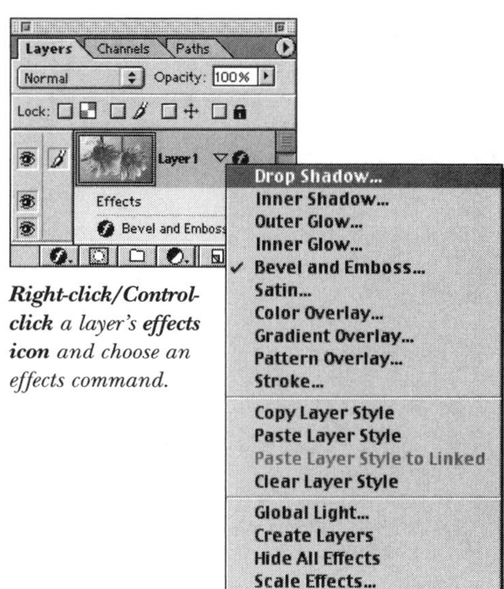

***Right-click/Control-click** a layer's **effects icon** and choose an effects command.*

Other effects commands 

The effects commands that are discussed in this section can be accessed either by Right-clicking/Control-clicking an existing effects icon for a layer on the Layers palette or via Layer menu > Layer Style.

Copy Layer Style copies all effects from a selected layer so they can be pasted into another layer.

Paste Layer Style pastes effects onto the current layer in the same document or in a different document; **Paste Layer Style to Linked** (layers) pastes effects onto any layers that are linked to the currently selected layer. In either case, a pasted effect will override an already applied effect only if they are both in the same category (e.g., a pasted Drop Shadow will replace an existing Drop Shadow).

Clear Layer Style eliminates all styles from the selected layer. It also restores the Blending Options to their default settings.

Global Light establishes a common Angle and Altitude for all current and future effects for which the Use Global Light option is turned on. And conversely, if you change the Angle or Altitude of any individual layer effect's when the Use Global Light option is on, all the other effects that have a Global Light option will update, as will the Angle and Altitude in the Global Light dialog box. Using a Global Light helps to unify lighting across multiple effects.

If more than one effect has been applied to a layer and you choose **Create Layers,** each effect will be placed on its own layer. The image won't look substantially different after this command is chosen, but the effects will no longer be editable via the Layer Style dialog box and they will no longer be associated with the layer that they were originally applied to. You may get a warning that effects may not completely carry over to layers. You don't have much choice if you want to keep the layers, though.

(Continued on the following page)

After applying the Create Layers command, any layer effect that is inside a shape (an inner glow, or a highlight or a shadow for a bevel or an inner emboss) will be placed on a new, separate layer, but it will be joined with the original shape layer in a clipping group; the original layer will be the base layer of the group. Any effect that is outside a shape (a drop shadow, an outer glow, or a shadow for a bevel or an outer emboss) will convert into separate layers below the original shape layer. Use Create Layer(s) to export a file to a multimedia program, such as Adobe After Effects or Adobe LiveMotion. The Create Layer(s) command cannot be applied to the Background of an image.

Hide All Effects temporarily hides layer effects for *all* layers in the document. To redisplay them, choose Layer menu > Layer Style > Show All Effects.

The **Scale Effects** opens a dialog box that allows you to increase or decrease the size of all the current effects on the selected layer. Only parameters defined in pixels (not those defined by a percentage) are affected.

Save it! 6.0!

Layer effects can be saved as a style on the **Styles palette** in ImageReady or Photoshop 6. See pages 471–472 to learn how to save effects as a style and how to apply a style to a layer.

1 *The original image.*

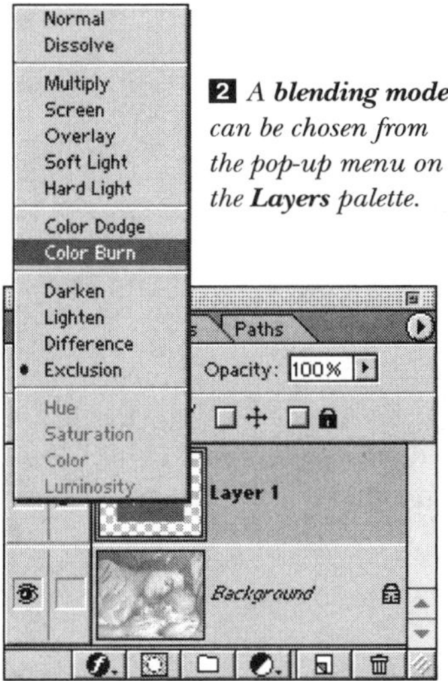

2 *A **blending mode** can be chosen from the pop-up menu on the **Layers** palette.*

3 *After **Color Burn** mode is chosen for the top layer.*

Blending layers

The layer blending modes

The layer blending mode you choose for a layer affects how that layer's pixels blend with pixels in the layer directly below it. Some modes produce subtle effects (e.g., Soft Light), while others produce dramatic color shifts (e.g., Difference). Normal is the default mode. The blending modes are discussed in detail on pages 30–32.

There are fours ways to choose a blending mode for a layer: 6.0!

- From the mode pop-up menu in the top left corner of the Layers palette **2**.
- Using the Shift + or Shift - shortcut. This cycles through the modes for the currently active layer (make sure a painting tool isn't selected when you do this!).
- By double-clicking the layer, then choosing Blending Options in the Layer Style dialog box.

TIP You can choose Behind mode for the Paintbrush, Airbrush, Paint Bucket, Pencil, History Brush, Clone Stamp, Pattern Stamp, or Gradient tool from the options bar, but not for a layer. In Behind mode, it will appear as if you're painting on the back of the current layer. And for the Paint Bucket tool, or any shape tool with the Create filled region button clicked, you can choose yet another mode, Clear, which works like an eraser. You must uncheck the "Lock image pixels" and "Lock transparent pixels" boxes on the Layers palette to access Behind and Clear modes.

6.0! You can control which pixels in the current layer will remain visible and which pixels from the underlying layer will show through the upper layer using the Blend If sliders in the Blending Options section of the Layer Style dialog box.

To fine tune the blending between two layers:

1. Double click a layer name on the Layers palette, then click Blending Options at the top left side of the dialog box.
   or
   Choose a layer, then choose Blending Options from the Layers palette menu.
2. *Optional:* In the **General Blending** section, modify the current layer's **Blend Mode** or **Opacity** **1**.
3. Check the Preview box.
4. In the **Advanced Blending** section, do any of the following:

   To control the opacity of the layer pixels (interior opacity) without affecting pixels in any layer effects that fall outside the edges of the layer (e.g., bevel, drop shadow, outer glow effect), adjust the **Fill Opacity**.

   Uncheck any **Channels** you want to exclude from blending with the underlying layer. To set the blend range for each channel one at a time, choose a channel from the Blend If pop-up menu; to work on all the channels simultaneously, leave Gray as the choice on the pop-up menu. The current image mode (e.g., RGB or CMYK) determines the available channels.

   Move the leftmost Blend If: **This Layer** slider to the right to remove shadow areas from the active layer.

   Move the rightmost **This Layer** slider to the left to remove highlights from the active layer.

   Move the leftmost **Underlying Layer** slider to the right to restore shadow areas from the layer directly below the active layer.

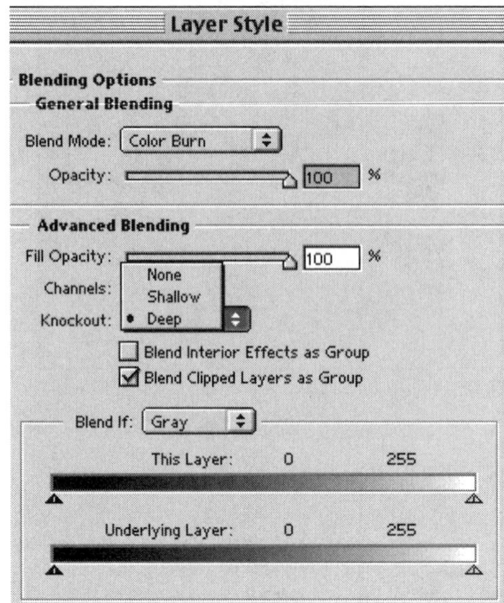

1 *The **Blending Options** settings in the **Layer Style** dialog box.*

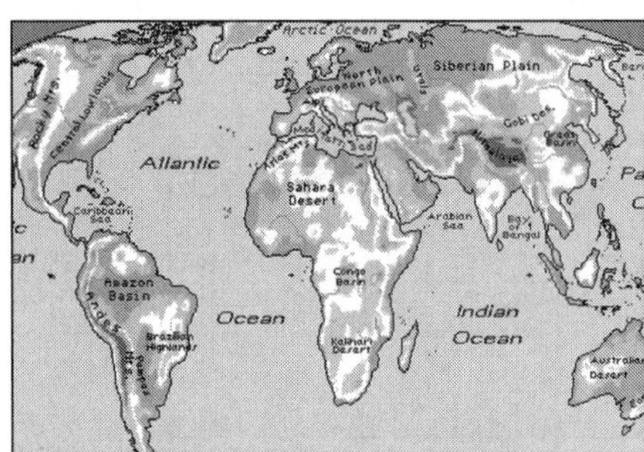

2 *The map layer is above an avocados layer.*

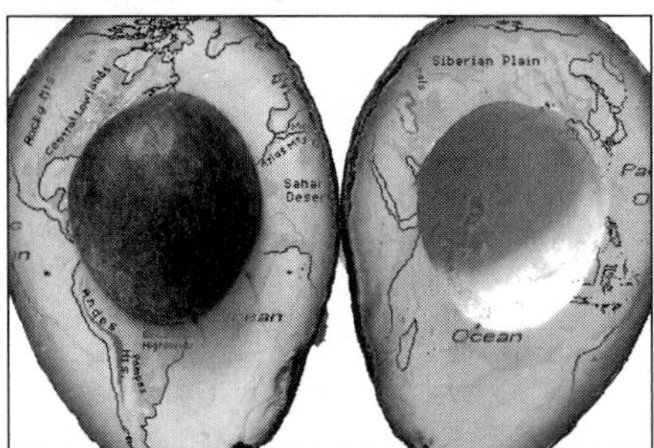

3 *The same image after dividing and moving the white **This Layer** slider and the black **Underlying** slider in the **Layer Style** dialog box.*

1 *The* ***Blend Clipped Layers as Group*** *box* ***checked****. The bottom layer of the clipping group (dune) controls the blending.*

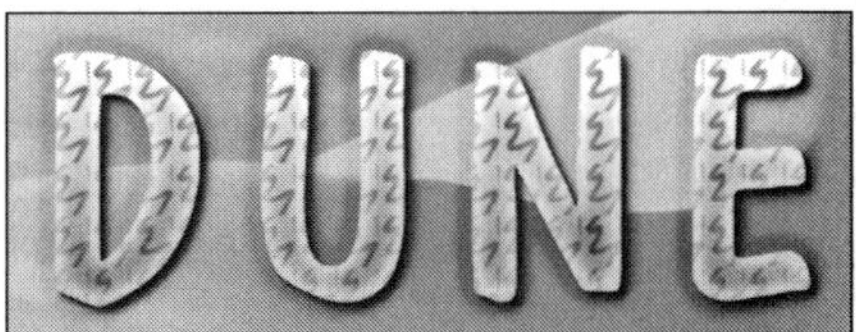

2 *The* ***Blend Clipped Layers as Group*** *box* ***unchecked****. The layer blending mode of the clipping group layer ("Pattern") is not controlled by the blending mode of the clipping group base layer.*

3 *The* ***Blend Interior Effect as Group*** *box* ***checked****. Here the inner glow and gradient overlay effects (seen in* **1** *above) are less visible.*

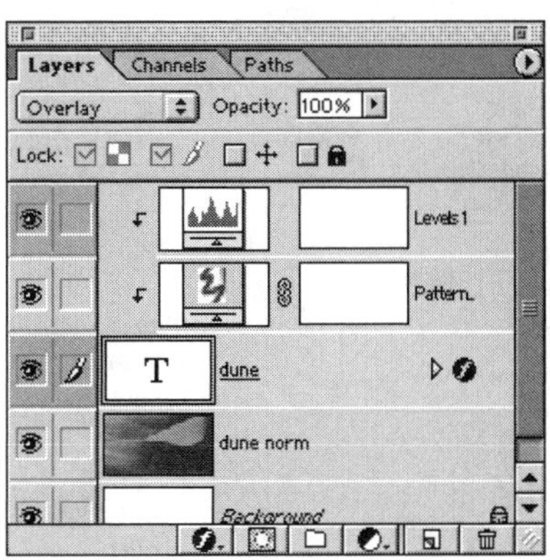

The ***clipping group*** *used in the above figures.*

Move the rightmost **Underlying Layer** slider to the left to restore highlights from the layer directly below the active layer.

5. Click OK (**2**–**3**, previous page).

TIP To adjust the midtones independently for either slider, Alt-drag/Option-drag the slider (it will divide in two).

6.0!

In the **Advanced Blending** section of the **Blending Options** (Layer Style dialog box) there are two check box options that control how clipping group layers, or single layers, blend with any underlying layers in an image (more about clipping groups on pages 247–248).

Blend clipped layers as a group

Double-click a base layer that has a Knockout setting of Shallow or Deep (see the next page). If the **Blend Clipped Layers as Group** box is checked (the default), the blending mode that's applied to the base layer of the clipping group controls how all the layers of the group as a whole blend with any underlying layers in the image **1**.

If the Blend Clipped Layers as Group box is unchecked, individual layers in a clipping group will blend with layers below the clipping group using each layer's own current blending mode, not the blending mode of the base layer **2**.

Blend interior effects as a group

Double-click a layer. If the **Blend Interior Effect as Group** box is unchecked (the default), the layer's interior effects (e.g., Inner Glow, Satin, Color Overlay, Pattern Overlay, or Gradient Overlay) will be used to blend the layer with underlying layers. The layer's blending mode (Layers palette) has less visual impact.

If the **Blend Interior Effect as Group** box is checked, the layer's interior effects will blend first with the layer's blending mode, then the whole blended collection of the layer will blend with underlying layers. The interior effects have less visual impact **3**.

6.0!

In Photoshop 6, you can control how many layers down a chosen layer will knockout (cut away underlying pixels)—all the way to the Background or down to a default stopping point among the layers below it.

To choose a knockout option for a layer:

1. Double-click a layer name on the Layers palette, then click Blending Options at the left side of the dialog box.
2. Make sure the Preview box is checked.
3. In the Advanced Blending area, choose from the Knockout pop-up menu **1**:

   None for no knockout.

   Shallow to knockout down to the default stopping point for a layer. The default stopping point will be one of two things: the layer directly below the layer set that the knockout layer is a part of, or, if the Blend Clipped Layers as Group box is checked, the bottommost layer in a clipping group.
   or
   Deep to knockout all the way down to the Background.
4. Click OK.

Knockout tips

- If the layer set that the knockout layer is a part of has a blending mode other than Pass Through, then the knockout will stop at the layer directly below the layer set, regardless of whether Shallow or Deep is chosen. The blending mode for other layer sets doesn't affect how a knockout layer and its layer set behave.
- If the knockout layer is in a clipping group within the layer set, then Shallow would stop at the bottommost layer of the clipping group, and Deep would knockout through the clipping group, but stop at the layer directly below the layer set.
- If the image contains no clipping groups or layer sets, then Shallow or Deep will knockout to the Background.

Knockout Options

None

Shallow

Deep

1 *In this example, the **sand** layer is part of a layer **set**. Therefore, **Shallow** knocks out to the layer below the set, whereas **Deep** knocks out all the way to the Background.*

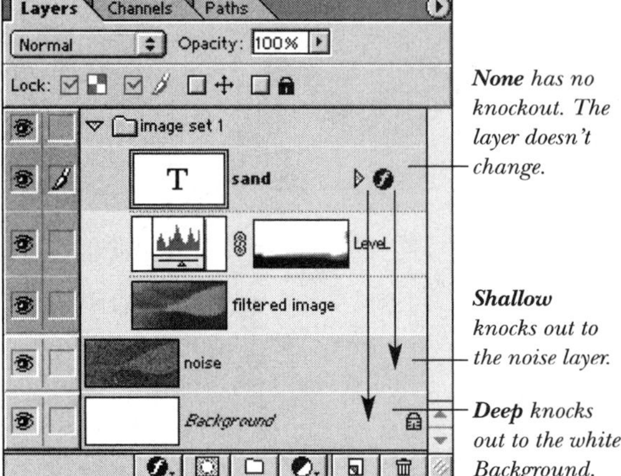

***None** has no knockout. The layer doesn't change.*

***Shallow** knocks out to the noise layer.*

***Deep** knocks out to the white Background.*

1 *The original image.*

2 *After applying the **Mezzotint** filter to the **duplicate** layer, then lowering the **opacity** of the duplicate layer.*

3 *A blended layer effect using the **Pointillize** filter.*

In these instructions, a filter is applied to a duplicate layer and then the original and duplicate layers are blended using Layers palette opacity and mode controls. Use this technique to soften the effect of an image editing command, like a filter, or to experiment with various blending modes or adjust commands. You can also use a layer mask to limit the area of the effect. If you don't like an effect, you can just delete the duplicate layer and start over.

To blend a modified layer with the original layer:

1. Choose a layer **1**.
2. Duplicate the layer by dragging it over the Create new layer button at the bottom of the Layers palette.
   or
   Choose Duplicate Layer from the Layers palette menu, then click OK.
3. Modify the duplicate layer (e.g., apply a filter or other image editing command).
4. On the Layers palette, adjust the Opacity to achieve the desired degree of transparency between the original layer and the modified, duplicate layer **2** and/or choose a different blending mode.
5. *Optional:* Create a layer mask to partially hide pixels on the top layer. Try adding a gradient to the layer mask to gradually fade the blend effect.

TIP To create a beautiful textural effect, duplicate the Background in a color image (preferably a Background that isn't solid white), highlight the new layer, and choose Image menu > Adjust > Desaturate (Ctrl-Shift-U/Cmd-Shift-U) to make it grayscale. Next, apply the Add Noise or Pointillize filter **3**. And finally, lower the opacity of, and try out different blending modes for, the new layer via the Layers palette.

TIP You could also click different channels in the Layer Style dialog box to control which channels in the duplicate layer will blend with the underlying layer.

Layer masks

A layer mask is an 8-bit grayscale channel that has white or black as its background color. By default, white areas on a layer mask permit pixels to be seen, black areas hide pixels, and gray areas partially mask pixels. You can use a mask to temporarily hide pixels on a layer so you can view the rest of the composite picture without them. Later, you can modify the mask, apply the mask effect to make it permanent, or discard the mask altogether.

An advantage of using a layer mask is that you can access it from both the Layers and Channels palettes. You'll see a thumbnail for the layer mask on the Layers palette and on the Channels palette when a layer that contains a mask is highlighted. Unlike an alpha channel selection, however, which can be loaded onto any layer, a layer mask can only be turned on or off for the layer or clipping group (group of layers) with which it's associated.

To create a layer mask:

1. Choose the layer you want to add a mask to.
2. *Optional:* Create a selection if you want to create a mask in that shape.
3. To create a white mask in which all the layer pixels are visible, choose Layer menu > Add Layer Mask > Reveal All or click the Add a mask button on the Layers palette **1**.
   or
   To create a black mask in which all the layer pixels are hidden, choose Layer menu > Add Layer Mask > Hide All or Alt-click/Option-click the Add a mask button on the Layers palette.
   or
   To reveal only layer pixels within an active selection, choose Layer menu > Add Layer Mask > Reveal Selection or click the Add a mask button at the bottom of the Layers palette.
   or

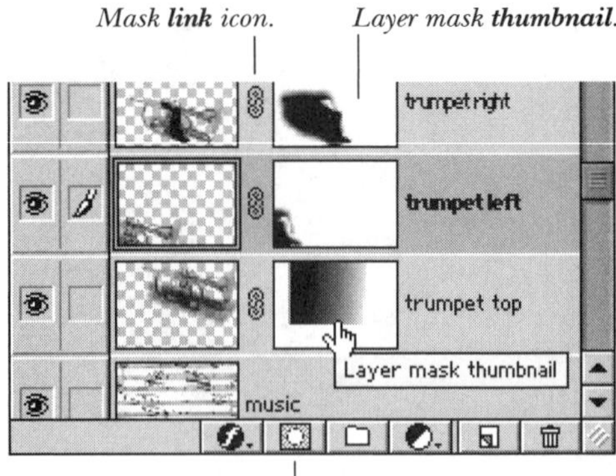

The Layers palette showing the three trumpet layers, each with its own ***layer mask****.*

2 *The trumpets* ***without layer masks****.*

3 *The trumpets* ***with layer masks****. The topmost trumpet fades out due to a gradient in its layer mask and portions of the middle and bottom trumpets are hidden via a black-and-white layer mask.*

Create Layer Mask

Other tools for modifying a mask

Try using the Eraser tool. The Burn, Dodge, Sponge, Sharpen, Blur, Smudge, Paint Bucket, and Gradient tools will all work as well. If you want to use any of the shape tools, you must first display the mask by itself (see step four at right).

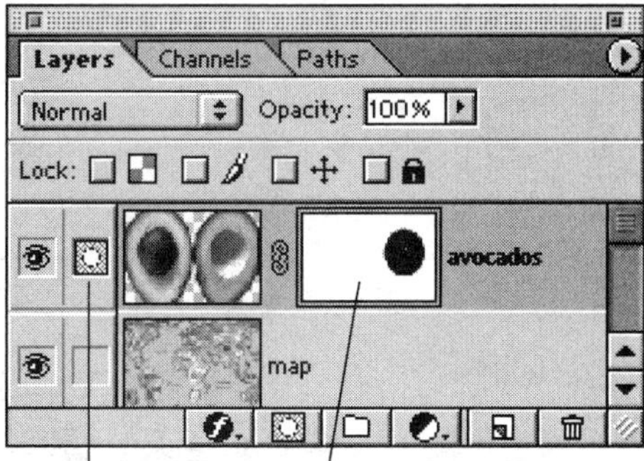

Mask icon **1** ***Layer mask thumbnail***

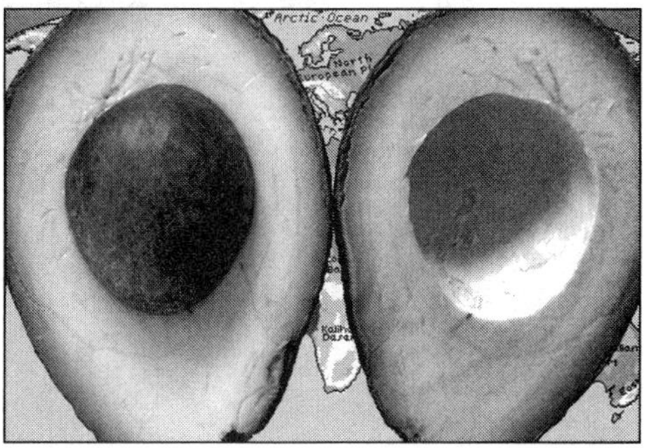

2 *The original image.*

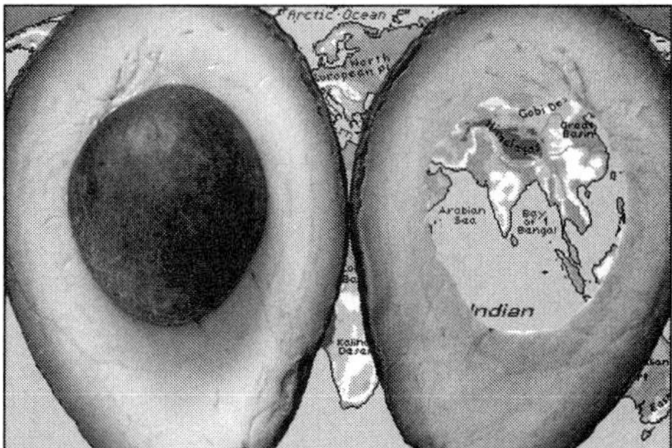

3 *The center of the avocado on the right is blocked by a* ***layer mask.***

To hide layer pixels within the selection, choose Layer menu > Add Layer Mask > Hide Selection or Alt-click/Option-click the Add a mask button at the bottom of the Layers palette.

To reshape a layer mask:

1. Choose the Paintbrush tool (B or Shift-B).
2. On the options bar, choose 100% Opacity (or a lower Opacity to partially hide layer pixels), choose Mode: Normal, and click a brush on the Brush picker.
3. To reshape the layer mask while viewing the layer pixels, click the layer mask thumbnail (not the layer name) on the Layers palette **1**. The thumbnail will have a dark border and a mask icon will appear for that layer.
   or
   To display the mask by itself in the image window, Alt-click/Option-click the layer mask thumbnail. (Alt-click/Option-click the layer mask thumbnail to redisplay the mask on the image.)
   or
   Alt-Shift-click/Option-Shift-click the layer mask thumbnail to display the mask overlay with the image. (Alt-Shift-click/Option-Shift-click the thumbnail again to restore the normal display.)
4. Paint on the picture with black as the Foreground color to enlarge the mask and hide pixels on the layer.
   and/or
   Paint with white as the Foreground color to reduce the mask and restore pixels on the layer.
   and/or
   Paint with gray as the Foreground color to partially hide pixels on the layer.
5. When you're finished modifying the layer mask, click the layer thumbnail **2**–**3**.

TIP To invert the effect of a layer mask, click the layer mask thumbnail, then choose Image menu > Adjust > Invert (Ctrl-I/Cmd-I). Hidden areas will be revealed, formerly visible areas will be hidden.

By default, a layer and its layer mask move in unison. Follow these steps to move layer pixels or a layer mask independently of one another.

To move a mask without moving its layer:

1. On the Layers palette, click the link icon between the layer thumbnail and the layer mask thumbnail **1**. The link icon will disappear.
2. Click the layer mask thumbnail.
3. Choose the Move tool (V).
4. Drag the layer mask in the image window.
5. Click again between the layer and layer mask thumbnails to re-link them.

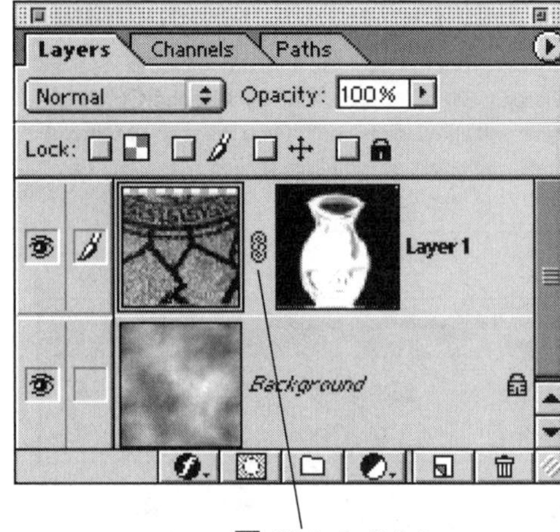

1 *Click the* ***link*** *icon.*

To duplicate a layer mask:

1. Choose the layer you want the duplicate mask to appear on.
2. From another layer, drag the thumbnail of the layer mask you want to duplicate over the Add layer mask button at the bottom of the palette.
   or
   To have the hidden and revealed areas be switched in the duplicate, Alt-drag/Option-drag the thumbnail of the layer mask you want to duplicate over the Add layer mask button.

   If you display the mask overlay with the image (see step 3 on the previous page), you can control the color and opacity of the mask overlay.

2

Move Mask; Duplicate Mask; Mask Display

To choose layer mask display options:

6.0!

1. Double-click a layer mask thumbnail.
2. Change the Overlay color and/or Opacity **2**, then click OK.

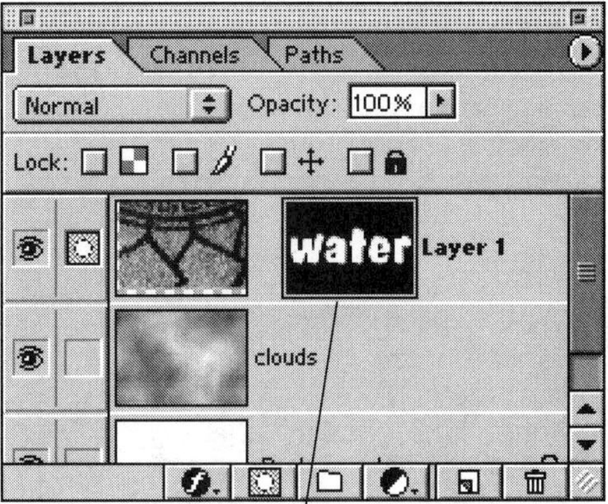

1 *The **layer mask thumbnail**. Layer 1 pixels are revealed through the **white** areas in the layer mask.*

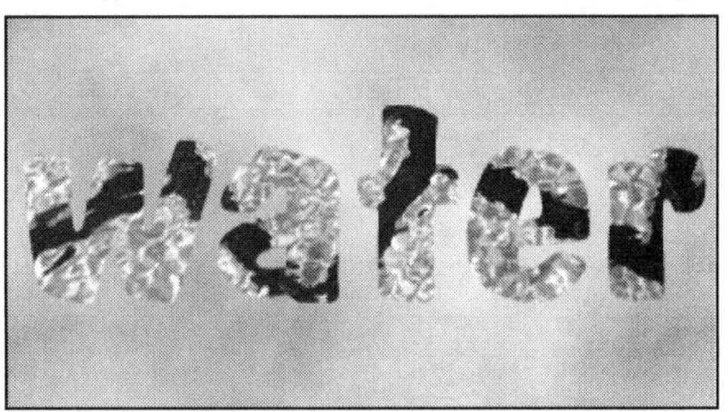

2 *In this image, the water layer is visible only through the letter shapes of the **layer mask**.*

To fill type with imagery using a layer mask: 6.0!

1. Activate a layer that contains non-transparent pixels (not the Background).
2. Choose the Type tool, then click the "Create a mask or selection button" on the options bar.
3. Choose a font and other type specifications, then click on the image. The image will temporarily display in QuickMask mode. Type the letters you want to appear. To turn the type into a selection, click the ✓ on the options bar, or click Enter (on the keypad), or choose any other tool.
4. Reposition the type selection using the Marquee tool. (Watch out! If you use the Move tool to move the selection, image pixels will be removed from the selection on the current layer.)
5. Choose Layer menu > Add Layer Mask > Reveal Selection to restrict layer pixels to the selection.
   or
   Choose Layer menu > Add Layer Mask > Hide Selection to hide layer pixels within the selection.
6. The type will now display as black or white pixels in the layer mask thumbnail **1**–**2**.

TIP To reposition the type area in the layer mask, first unlink the layer mask from the layer (click the link icon to make it disappear), then use the Move tool (V) to drag within the layer mask in the image window.

TIP To fill type with imagery using a layer clipping path (instead of a layer mask), see page 278.

To temporarily remove the effects of a layer mask:

Shift-click the layer mask thumbnail on the Layers palette (this won't select the layer mask thumbnail). A red "X" will appear over the thumbnail and the entire layer will be visible **1**. (Shift-click the layer mask thumbnail again to remove the "X" and restore the mask effect.)

Layer masks that are no longer needed should be discarded, because they take up storage space.

To apply or discard the effects of a layer mask:

1. On the Layers palette, click the thumbnail of the layer mask you want to apply or discard **2**.
2. Click the Delete Layer (trash) button. To make the mask effect permanent, click **Apply** **3** or to remove the mask without applying its effect, click **Discard**.
   or
   Choose Layer menu > Remove Layer Mask > Discard or Apply.

Clip it

Image layer pixels can also be masked using a layer **clipping path** that you create using the Pen tool or a shapes tool (see page 274).

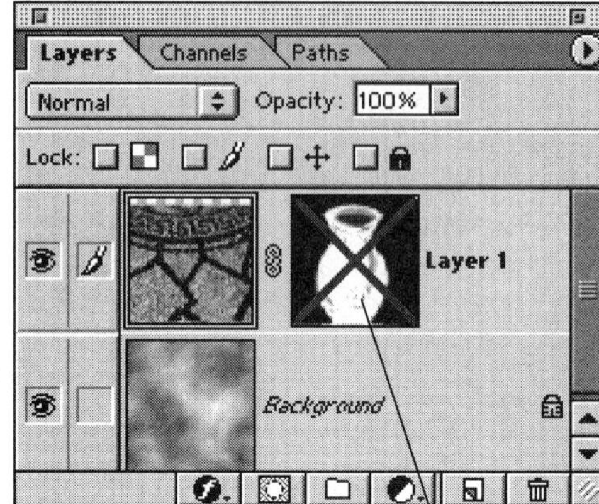

1 ***Shift-click** the **layer mask thumbnail.***

2 *Click the **layer mask** thumbnail.*

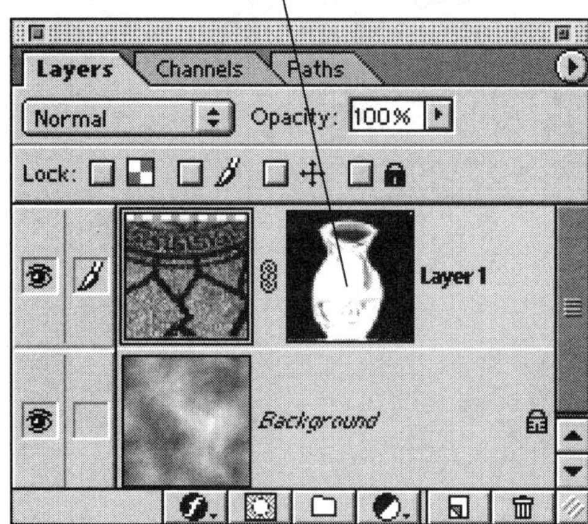

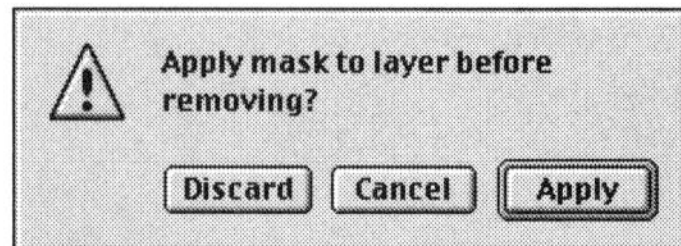

3 *Click **Apply** to make the mask effect permanent.*

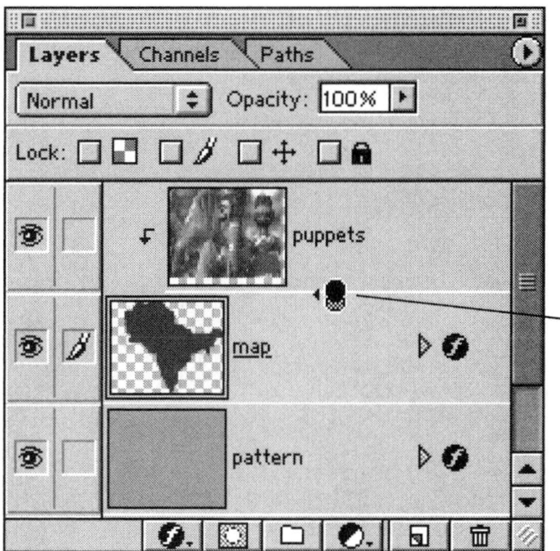

1 *Alt-click/Option-click between two layers to join them as a **clipping group**. A dotted line will appear, and the **base** layer will be underlined.*

2 *The map of India is **clipping** (limiting) the view of the puppets.*

Clipping groups

The bottommost layer of a clipping group of layers (the base layer) clips (limits) the display of pixels, and (by default) controls the mode and opacity of the layers above it. Only pixels within the grouped layers that overlap pixels on the base layer are visible.

To create a clipping group of layers:

1. Click a layer name.
2. Alt-click/Option-click the line between that layer name and the name just above it (the pointer will be two overlapping circles) **1–2**. (The layers you choose for a clipping group must be listed **consecutively** on the palette. Layers can be grouped with a layer set, but not with layers outside the set.)
3. *Optional:* Repeat the previous step to add more layers to the clipping group.

   The base layer name will be underlined, and the thumbnails for the other layers in the group will be indented.

TIP To create a clipping group from linked layers, choose Layer menu > Group Linked (Ctrl-G/Cmd-G).

TIP To fill type with imagery using a clipping group, see page 307.

TIP To learn how clipping group layers blend with underlying layers, see page 239.

When you remove (ungroup) a layer from a clipping group, any grouped layers above the layer you ungroup will also ungroup.

To remove a layer from a clipping group:

Alt-click/Option-click the line below the layer that you want to remove **1**. The layer will no longer be indented.

or

Click the name of the layer you want to remove, then choose Layer menu > Ungroup (Ctrl-Shift-G/Cmd-Shift-G).

To ungroup an entire clipping group:

1. Click the base layer in the group.
2. Choose Layer menu > Ungroup (Ctrl-Shift-G/Cmd-Shift-G) **2**.

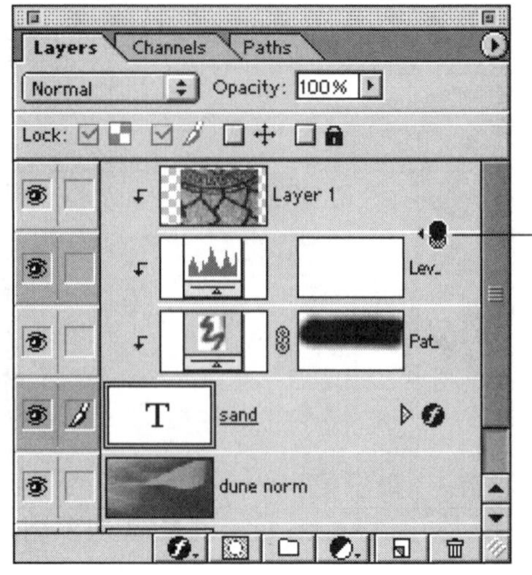

1 ***Alt-click/Option-click*** *below the layer to be removed from the clipping group.*

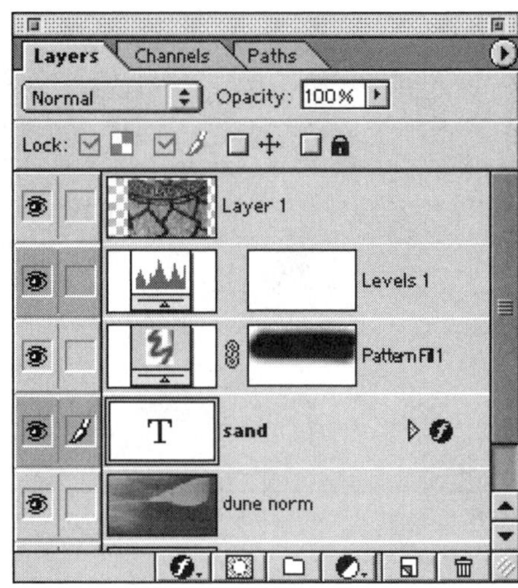

2 *Choose Layer menu >* ***Ungroup*** *to remove all layers from the clipping group.*

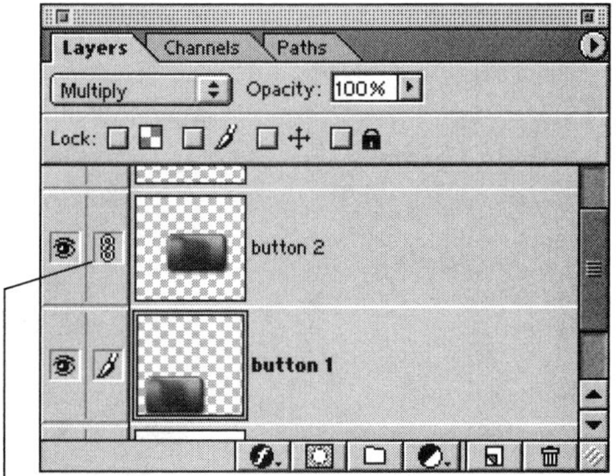

1 *Click to display the **link** icon in the second column on the Layers palette for any layers you want to link to the active layer. In this illustration, the "button 1" and "button 2" layers are linked.*

Linking layers

Linking is used to secure the position of multiple layers in relationship to one another. Once layers are linked together, they can be moved as a unit in the image window or drag-copied to another image, and they can be distributed or aligned.

Note: You can transform linked layers. In fact, you'll minimize image distortion due to resampling by transforming multiple layers all at once instead of one at a time.

To link layers (and move them as a unit):

1. On the Layers palette, click one of the layers that you want to link.
2. Click in the second column for any other layer you want to link to the layer you chose in the previous step. The layers you link **don't** have be consecutive. The link icon will appear next to any non-active, linked layers **1**.
3. *Optional:* Choose the Move tool (V), then press and drag the linked layers in the image window.

TIP To unlink a layer, click the link icon.

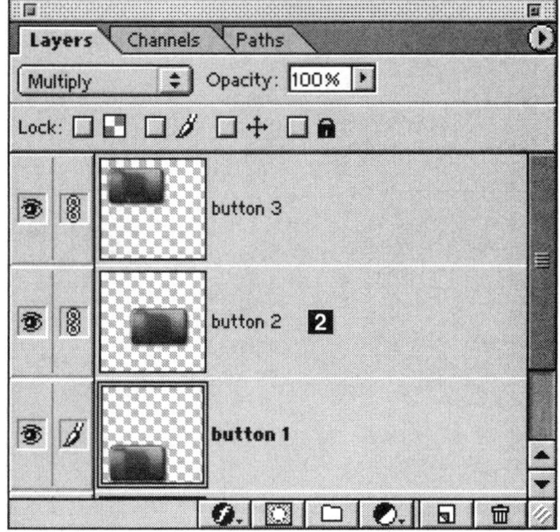

The Align Layers command is used to align the pixel edges of linked layers.

To align two or more linked layers:

1. Choose a layer that one or more other layers are linked to **2**. The layer you choose will be the reference position to which the other linked layers will align.
2. Choose Layer menu > Align Linked > Top Edges, Vertical Center, Bottom Edges, Left, Horizontal Center, or Right Edges **3** (and **1**–**2**, next page).
   or
   Click on the appropriate alignment button on the options bar.

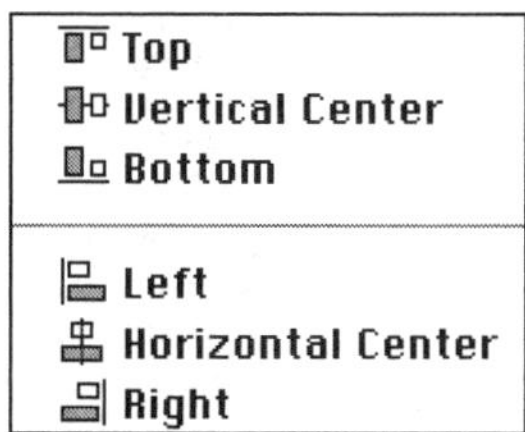

3 *Choose one of these options from the Layer menu > **Align Linked** or **Distribute Linked** submenu.*

Link Layers; Align Linked Layers

To align the pixel edge of a layer with a selection:

1. Create a selection.
2. Choose a layer to align with the selection.
3. Choose an align command from the Layer menu > Align To Selection submenu.
   or
   6.0! Click an alignment button on the options bar.

TIP Any layers linked to the chosen layer will also be aligned.

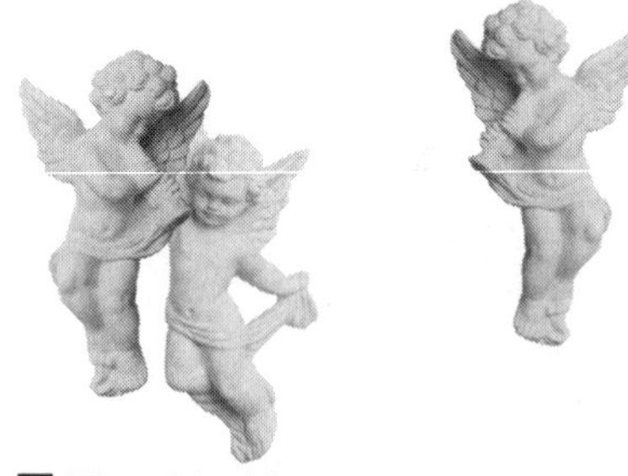

1 *The original image.*

You can distribute the pixel areas in linked layers using the Distribute Linked command.

To distribute three or more linked layers:

1. Choose a layer to which two or more other layers are linked.
2. *Optional:* Create a selection on that layer for the other layers to align to.
3. Choose Layer menu > Distribute Linked > Top Edges, Vertical Center, Bottom Edges, Left Edges, Horizontal Center, or Right Edges.
   or
   6.0! Click the appropriate distribute button on the options bar.
   The layers will be distributed evenly between the two layers that are furthest apart **2**–**3**.

TIP If you're not happy with the align or distribute option and you want to try a different one, undo the last option before using another distribute option.

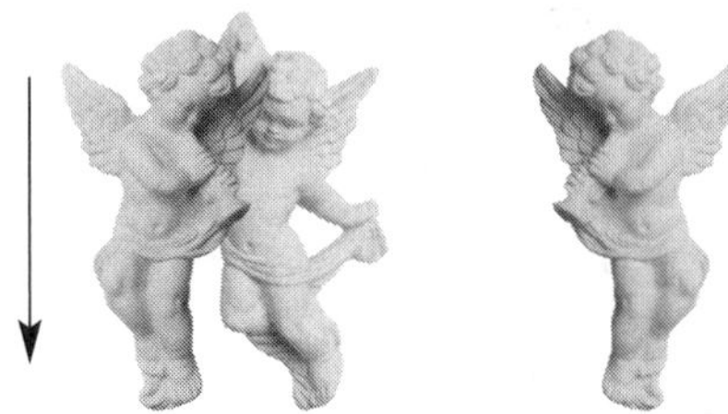

2 *The layers* ***aligned****: Bottom.*

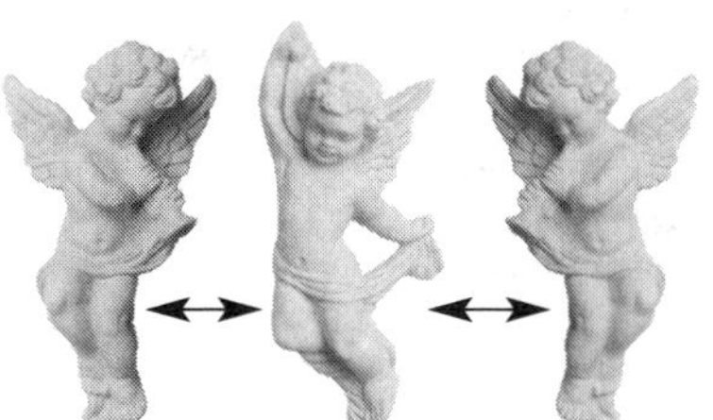

3 *The layers* ***distributed****: Horizontal Center.*

MASKS 15

*The active (selected) area is clear, the **Quick Mask** is semi-transparent.*

THIS CHAPTER COVERS two special methods for saving and reshaping a selection: alpha channels and Quick Mask mode.

If you save a selection to a specially created grayscale channel, called an **alpha channel**, you can load the selection onto the image at any time. A selection that has an irregular shape that would be difficult to reselect would be a logical candidate for this operation. A file can contain up to 24 channels, though from a practical standpoint, since each channel increases a picture's storage size (depending on the size of the selection area), you should be judicious when adding alpha channels. Alpha channels are accessed via the Channels palette **1**, and are saved or loaded onto an image via Select menu commands or the Channels palette. (To create a layer clipping path in place of an alpha channel to conserve file storage space, see page 274.)

Using Photoshop's **Quick Mask** mode, the selected or unselected areas of an image can be covered with a semi-transparent colored mask, which can then be reshaped using any editing or painting tool. Masked areas are protected from editing. Unlike an alpha channel, a Quick Mask cannot be saved, but when you return to Standard (non-Quick Mask) mode, the mask will turn into a selection, which can be saved.

Note: If you're unfamiliar with Photoshop's basic selection tools, read Chapter 5 before reading this chapter.

Layer masks are covered in Chapter 14.

*The **composite color channel***

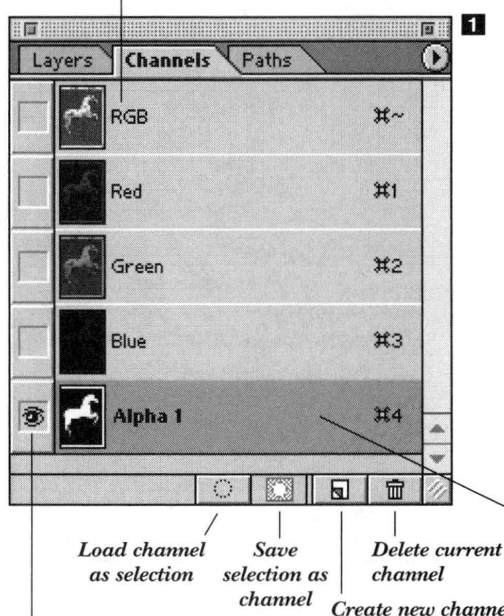

Load channel as selection

Save selection as channel

Delete current channel

Create new channel

*Click in the **eye** column to **show/hide** a channel.*

*Only the currently highlighted channel or channels can be edited. A non-color channel is called an **alpha channel**.*

Masks

A selection that is saved in an alpha channel can be loaded onto any image whenever it's needed.

Note: To convert an alpha channel into a spot color channel, see page 196.

To save a selection to a channel using the current options settings:

1. Create a selection **1**.
2. Click the Save selection as channel (second) button at the bottom of the Channels palette **2**.

1 *Select an area on a layer.*

To save a selection to a channel and choose options:

1. Create a selection **1**. *Optional:* Also choose a layer if you want to create a layer mask for it.
2. Choose Select menu > Save Selection.
3. *Do any of these optional steps:*

   Leave the Document setting as the current file or choose **Document**: New to save the selection to an alpha channel in a new, separate document **3**.

   Choose **Channel**: "[ ] Mask" to turn the selection into a layer mask for the current layer. Layer pixels will only be visible where the selection was.

   Enter a new **Name** for the selection.

   Choose an **Operation** option to combine a current selection with an existing alpha channel that you choose from the Channel pop-up menu. (The Operation options are illustrated on page 254.)

   Note: You can save an alpha channel with an image in the Photoshop, TIFF, Photoshop PDF, PICT, Pixar, or Targa format. To save a copy of a file without alpha channels, uncheck the Alpha Channels box in the Save As dialog box, if it's available.
4. Click OK. The selection will remain active.

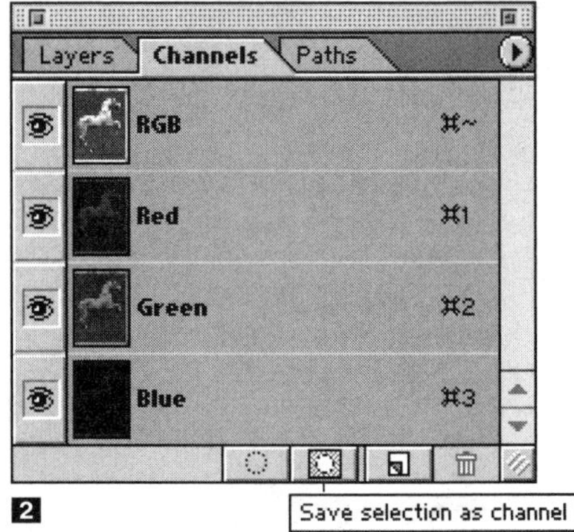

2

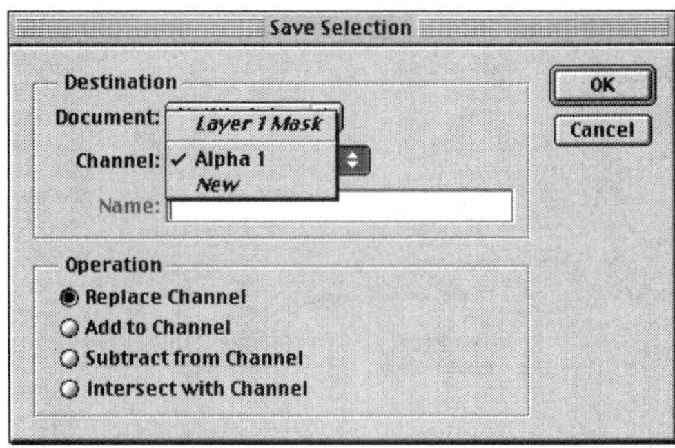

3 *Choose **Document, Channel,** and **Operation** options in the **Save Selection** dialog box.*

Save Selection to Channel

Load channel selection to another image

Make sure the source and destination images have the same dimensions and resolution, activate the destination image, then follow steps 2–6 at right, choosing the source document in the Load Selection dialog box. To load a layer mask selection, activate that layer first in the source image.

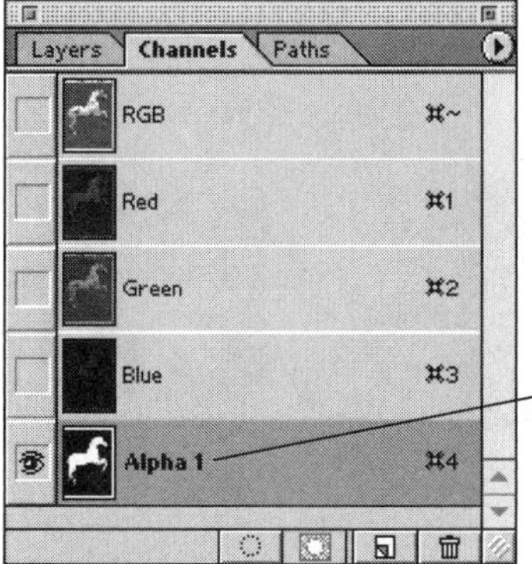

1 *Click an* ***alpha channel*** *name on the Channels palette.*

2 *An* ***alpha channel*** *displayed in the image window. The* ***selected*** *area is* ***white,*** *the* ***protected*** *area is* ***black.***

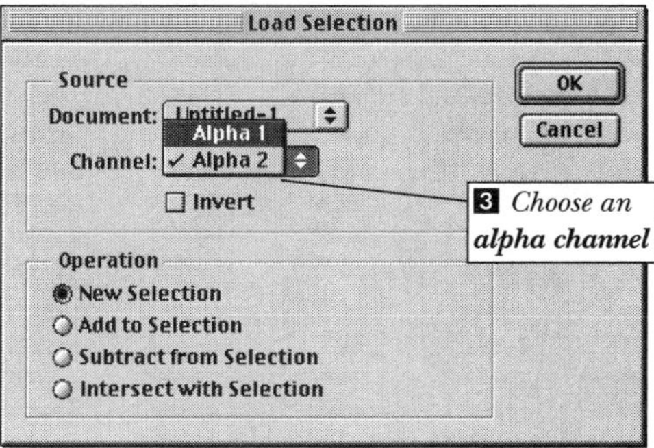

3 *Choose an* ***alpha channel***

An alpha channel can be displayed without loading it onto the image as a selection.

To display a channel selection:

1. Click an alpha channel name on the Channels palette **1**. The selected area will be white, the protected area black **2**.
2. To restore the normal image display, click the top (composite) channel name on the palette (Ctrl-~/Cmd-~).

TIP If the selection has a Feather radius, the faded area will be gray and will only be partially affected by editing.

TIP Reshape the mask with any painting tool using black, gray, or white "paint."

To load a channel selection onto an image using the current options:

On the Channels palette, Ctrl-click/Cmd-click the name of the alpha channel that you want to load.

To load a channel selection onto an image and choose options:

1. If the composite image isn't displayed, click the top channel name on the Channels palette. You can combine the channel selection with an existing selection in the image (see the next page).
2. Choose Select menu > Load Selection.
3. Choose the alpha channel name from the Channel pop-up menu **3**.
4. To combine the channel with an existing selection in the image, click an Operation option (see the next page).
5. *Optional:* Check the Invert box to switch the selected and unselected areas in the loaded selection.
6. Click OK.

TIP To select only non-transparent pixels on an active layer, choose Channel: [ ] Transparency in the Load Selection dialog box or Ctrl-click/Cmd-click the layer name on the Layers palette.

Save Selection Operations

When saving a selection, you can choose from these Operation options in the **Save Selection** dialog box:

New Channel saves the current selection in a new channel.

Shortcut: Click the Save selection as channel button on the Channels palette.

Channel and selection to be saved

Resulting channel

ADD

Add to Channel adds the new selection to the channel.

Channel and selection to be saved

Resulting channel

SUBTRACT

Subtract from Channel removes white or gray areas that overlap the new selection.

INTERSECT

Intersect with Channel preserves only white or gray areas that overlap the new selection.

Load Selection Operations

If a channel is loaded while an area of a layer is selected, you can choose from these Operation options in the **Load Selection** dialog box:

New Selection—the channel becomes the current selection.

Shortcut: Ctrl-click/Cmd-click the channel name or drag the channel name over the Load channel as selection button.

Selection and channel to be loaded

Resulting selection

ADD

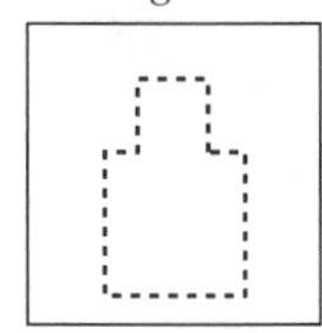

Add to Selection adds the channel selection to the current selection.

Shortcut: Ctrl-Shift-click/Cmd-Shift-click the channel name.

Selection and channel to be loaded

Resulting selection

SUBTRACT

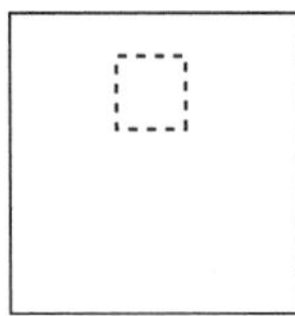

Subtract from Selection removes areas of the current selection that overlap the channel selection.

Shortcut: Ctrl-Alt-click/Cmd-Option-click the channel name.

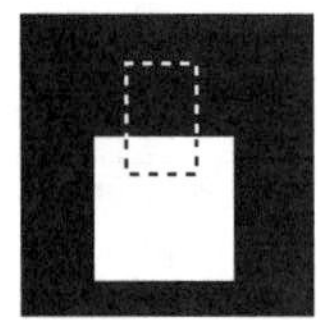

INTERSECT

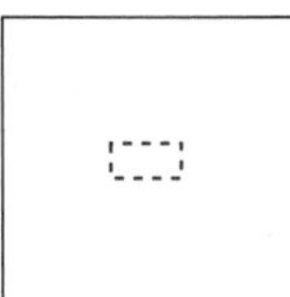

Intersect with Selection preserves only areas of the current selection that overlap the channel selection.

Shortcut: Ctrl-Alt-Shift-click/Cmd-Option-Shift-click the channel name.

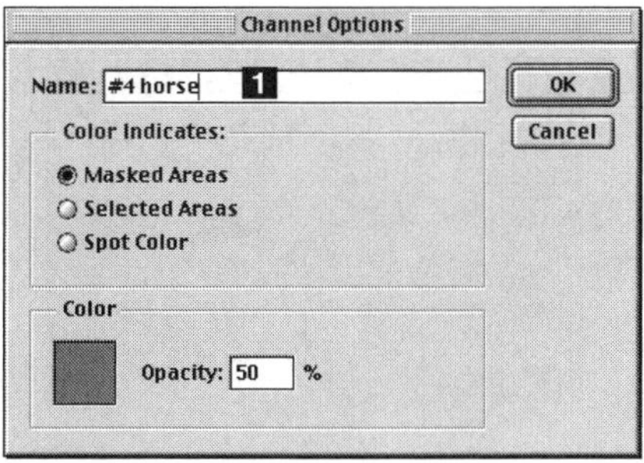

2 *The horse is the selected area.*

3 *The horse is still the selected area, but it is now* ***black*** *instead of white.*

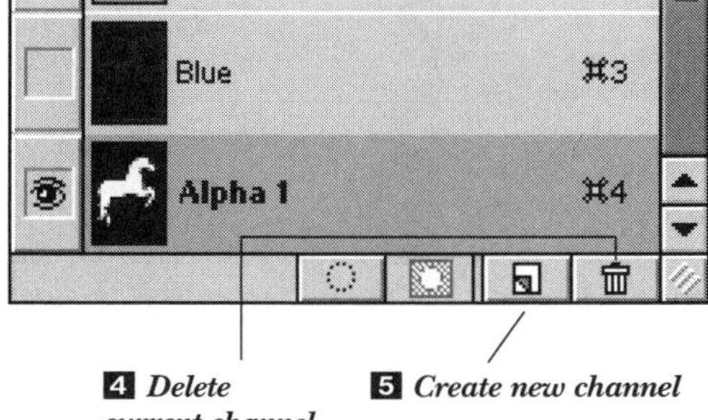

4 ***Delete current channel***

5 ***Create new channel***

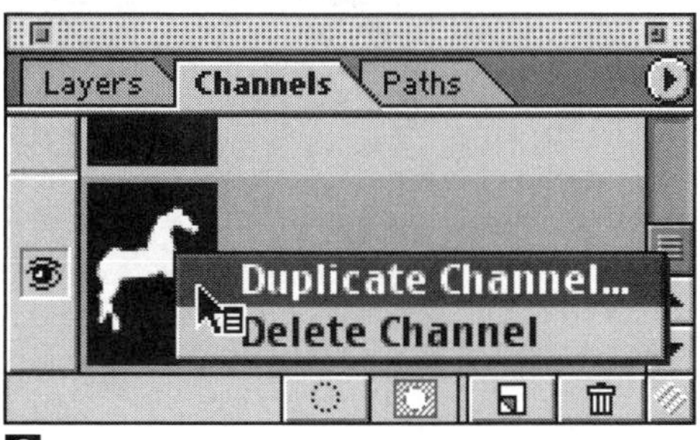

6

To choose channel options:

1. Double-click a channel name on the Channels palette.
   or
   Click a channel name, then choose Channel Options from the palette menu.
2. Type a new name in the Name field **1**.
   and/or
   Normally, the selected areas of an alpha channel are white and the protected areas are black or colored. To reverse these colors without changing which area is actually selected, click Color Indicates: Selected Areas **2**–**3**.
3. Click OK.

TIP To change the size of the channel thumbnails, choose Palette Options from the Channels palette menu, then click a different thumbnail size.

To delete a channel:

Drag the channel over the Delete current channel (trash) button.
or
Click the name of the channel that you want to delete on the Channels palette, click the Delete current channel button at the bottom of the palette **4**, then click Yes. Or Alt-click/Option-click the trash button to bypass the prompt.
or
Right-click/Control-click the Channel name, then choose Delete Channel from the context menu.

To duplicate a channel:

Drag the name of the channel you want to duplicate over the Create new channel button or into another image window **5**.
or
Right-click/Control-click the Channel name, choose Duplicate Channel from the context menu, change the name, if desired, then click OK **6**.

You can superimpose an alpha channel selection as a colored mask over an image, and then reshape the mask.

To reshape an alpha channel mask:

1. Make sure there is no selection on the image.
2. Click an alpha channel name on the Channels palette. An eye icon will appear next to it **1**.
3. Click in the left column at the top of the palette. An eye icon will appear. The alpha channel should be the only highlighted channel **2**.
4. Choose the Pencil or Paintbrush tool (B or Shift-B).
5. On the options bar:

   Click the Painting Brush arrowhead, then click a brush on the picker.
   and
   Choose Mode: Normal.
   and
   Choose 100% Opacity to create a full mask or a lower opacity to create a partial mask.
6. To enlarge the masked (protected) area, stroke on the cutout with black as the Foreground color **3**. You can click the Switch Colors button on the Toolbox (X) to swap the Foreground and Background colors **4**.

   To enlarge the unmasked area, stroke on the mask with white as the Foreground color **5**.
7. To hide the mask, click the alpha channel's eye icon or choose a layer on the Layers palette.

1 *Click the alpha channel name on the Channels palette.*

2 *Click in the left column at the top of the palette. Make sure the alpha channel name stays highlighted.*

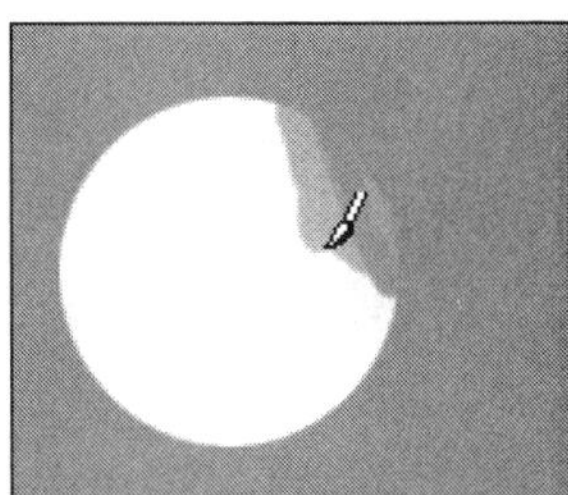

3 *Enlarge the **masked** area by stroking on the cutout with **black** as the Foreground color.*

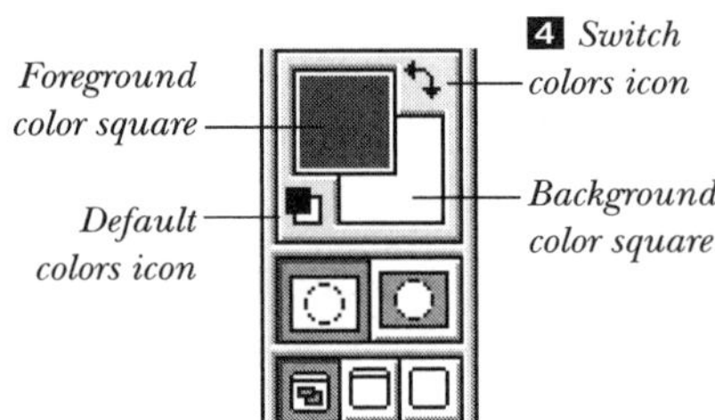

4 *Switch colors icon*

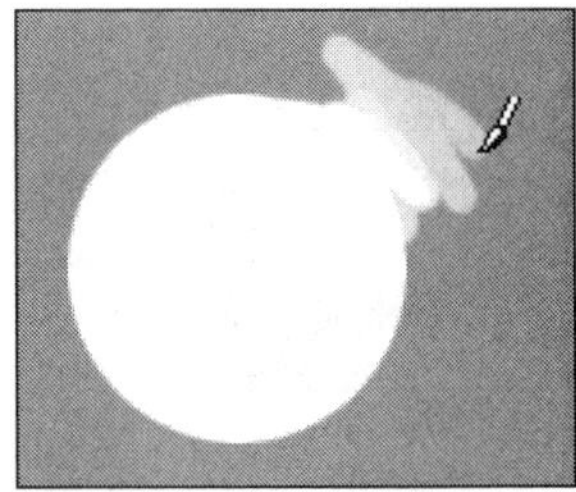

5 *Enlarge the **unmasked** area by stroking on the mask with **white** as the Foreground color.*

1 *Select an area on a layer.*

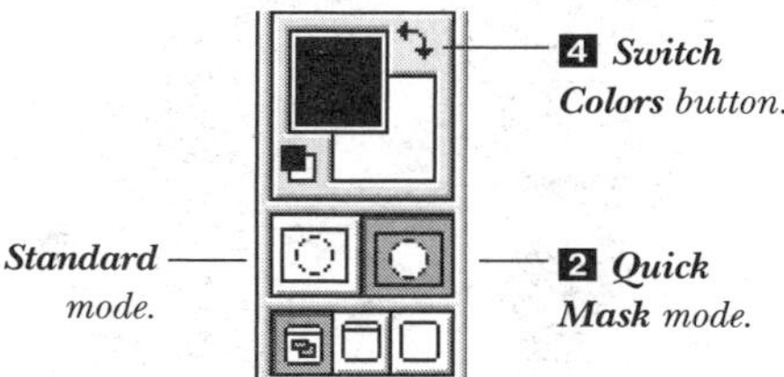

3 *The unselected area is covered with a* **mask**.

If you choose Quick Mask mode when an area of a layer is selected, a semi-transparent tinted mask will cover the unselected areas, and the selected areas will be revealed in a cutout. You'll still be able to see the image under the mask. The cutout (mask) can be reshaped using the Pencil, Airbrush, or Paintbrush tool.

Note: You can't save a Quick Mask to a channel (Select menu > Save Selection) while your image is in Quick Mask mode, but you can use Save Selection once you restore the standard screen display mode.

To reshape a selection using Quick Mask mode:

1. Select an area of a layer **1**.
2. Click the Quick Mask mode button on the Toolbox (Q) **2**. A mask will cover part of the picture **3**.
3. Choose the Pencil, Paintbrush, or Airbrush tool.
4. On the options bar:

   Click the Painting Brush arrowhead, then click a brush on the picker.
   and
   Choose Mode: Normal.
   and
   Move the Opacity slider to 100%.
   and
   Make sure the check box is unchecked (Auto Erase or Wet Edges).
5. Stroke on the cutout with black as the Foreground color to enlarge the masked (protected) area.
   or
   Stroke on the mask with white as the Foreground color to enlarge the cutout (unmasked area). You can click the Switch Colors button on the Toolbox (X) to swap the Foreground and Background colors **4**.
   or
   Stroke with gray or a brush with an opacity below 100% (options bar) to create a partial mask. When you edit the layer,

(Continued on the following page)

Quick Mask

that area will be partially affected by modifications.

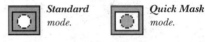

6. "Quick Mask" will be listed on the Channels palette and on the image window title bar while the image is in that mode. Click the Standard mode icon on the Toolbox (Q) when you're ready to turn off Quick Mask mode **1**. The nonmasked areas will turn into a selection.
7. Modify the layer. Only the unmasked (selected) area will be affected.

In these instructions, you'll create a mask without first creating a selection.

To create a Quick Mask without using a selection:

1. Choose the Pencil or Paintbrush tool, and choose options for the tool as per step 4 on the previous page.
2. Double-click the Quick Mask button on the Toolbox.
3. Click Selected Areas, then click OK.
4. Stroke with black on the layer **2**. The selected areas (not the protected areas) will be covered with a mask; you'll be creating what will become the selection. Press Q to return to standard mode.

The Quick Mask options only affect how a Quick Mask looks on screen—not how it functions.

To choose Quick Mask options:

1. Double-click "Quick Mask" on the Channels palette.
   or
   Double-click the Quick Mask mode button on the Toolbox.
2. Do any of the following: **3**

   Choose whether Color Indicates: Masked Areas or Selected Areas.

   Click the Color swatch, then choose a new Quick Mask color.

   Change the Opacity of the mask color.
3. Click OK.

Quick switch

To switch the mask color between the **selected** and **masked** areas without opening the Quick Mask Options dialog box, **Alt-click/Option-click** the Quick Mask mode button on the Toolbox.

Standard mode.

Quick Mask mode.

1 *The **Quick Mask** buttons on the **Toolbox**.*

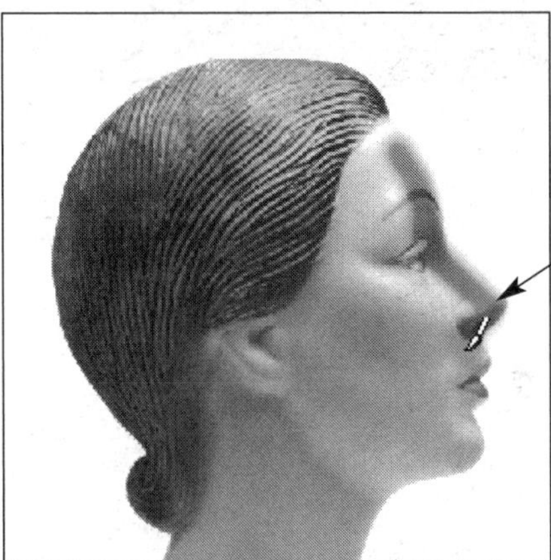

2 *Painting a mask on an image in **Quick Mask** mode.*

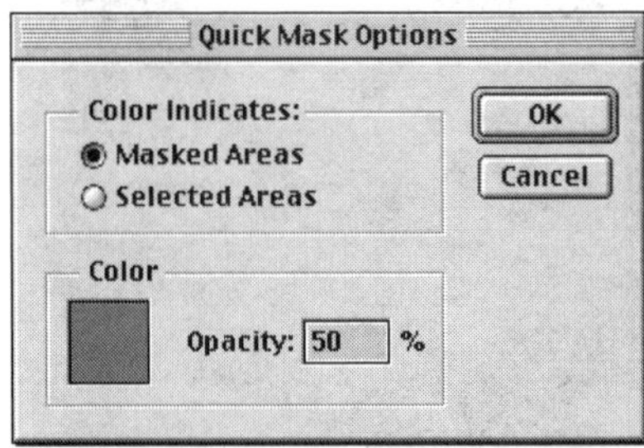

3 *In the **Quick Mask Options** dialog box, choose whether Color Indicates: **Masked Areas** or **Selected Areas**; click the **Color** swatch to choose a different mask color.*

Quick Mask

PATHS/SHAPES 16

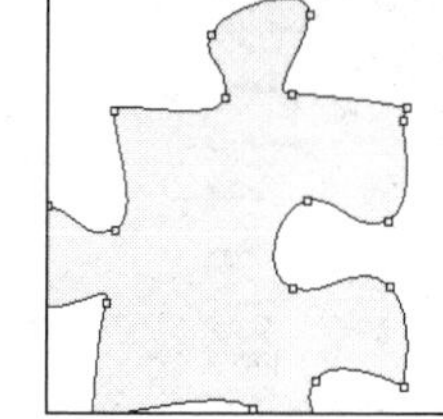

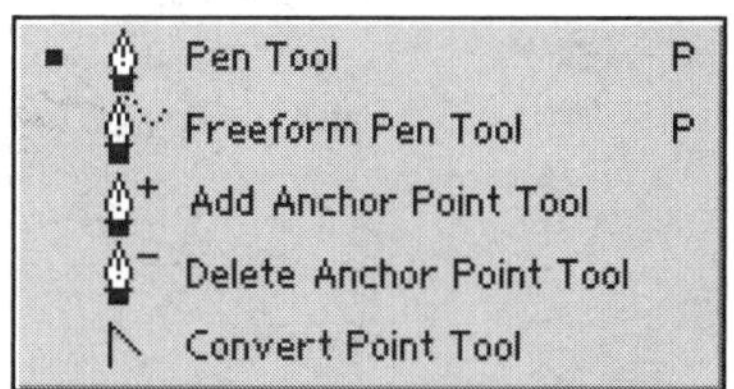

1 *The **pen** tools and path reshaping tools.*

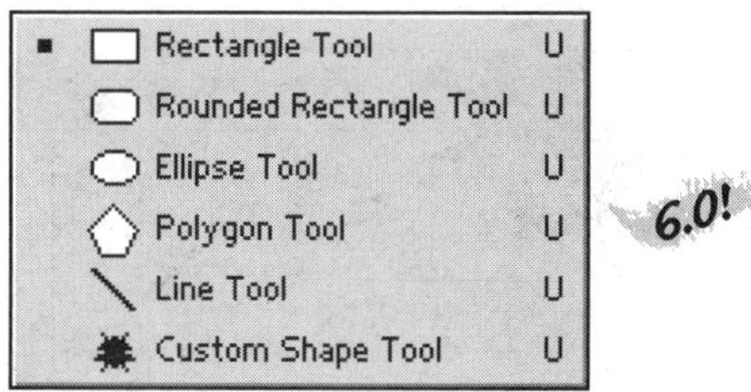

6.0!

2 *The **shape** tools.*

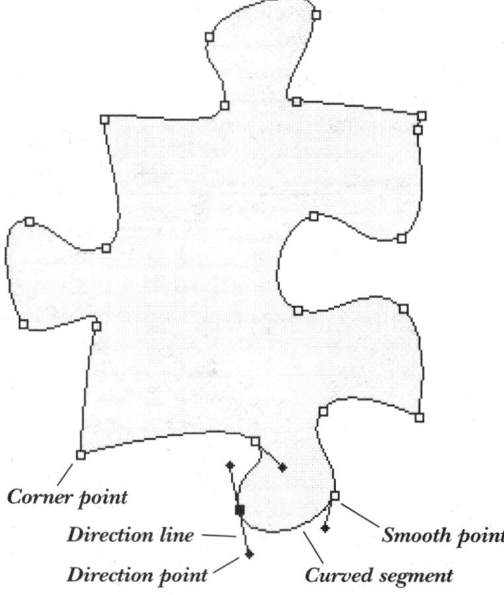

3 *A **path**. To reshape a path or shape, you can drag, add, or delete an **anchor point** or move a **segment**. A curved line segment can also be reshaped by adjusting its **direction lines**.*

PHOTOSHOP'S pen tools **1** and shape tools **2** create precise vector shapes, called paths, that consist of anchor points connected by curved or straight line segments **3**.

The pen tools can also be used to create **shape layers** whose visible areas are controlled by layer **clipping paths**. Shape layers contain editable fills and a layer clipping path that defines the shape's contour. Layer clipping paths are vector masks and work much like layer masks, but with an added bonus: they have sharp, precise path edges that occupy much less storage space than channels. A layer clipping path can be used on any fill or image layer.

6.0!

Paths created by the Pen tool and Freeform Pen tool are displayed, activated, deactivated, restacked, saved, and deleted using the **Paths** palette **4**. When a pen tool is chosen (and before a work path is created), you'll see two buttons on the options bar. Click the button on the left to create a **shape layer** or click the button on the right to create a **work path**.

4 *The **Paths** palette.*

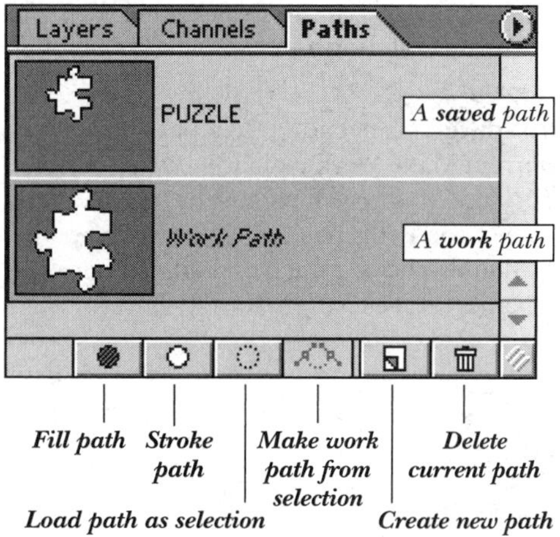

Paths and Shapes

Before we delve into the Pen tools, we'll show you how to create a path using a selection as a starting point. Once a selection has been converted into a path, you can precisely reshape it and then use it as a path or as a layer clipping path. You can also convert it back into a selection if you need to.

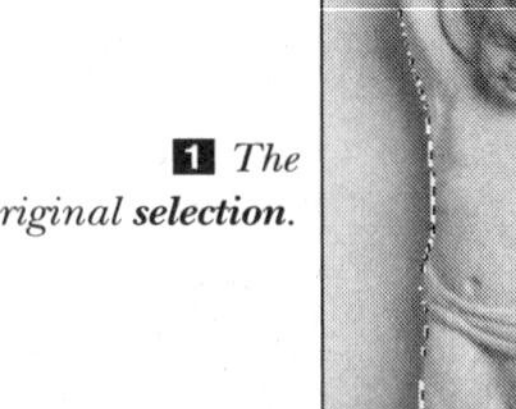

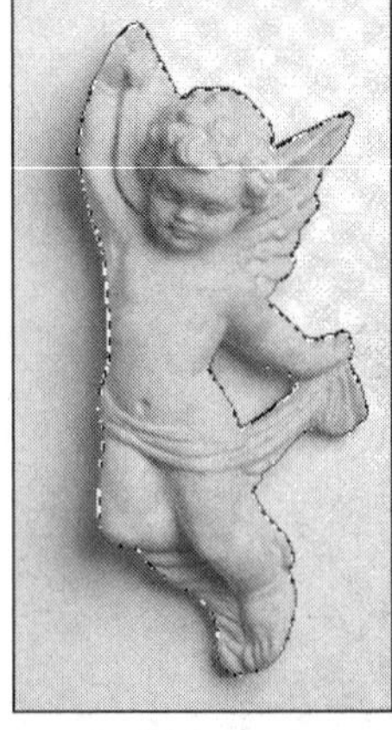

1 *The original* ***selection.***

To convert a selection into a path:

Method 1

1. Select an area of an image **1**.

   Note: Once you convert the selection into a path, any feathering on the selection will be removed.

2. Alt-click/Option-click the Make work path button at the bottom of the Paths palette **2**.
   or
   Choose Make Work Path from the Paths palette menu.

3. Enter a Tolerance value (0.5–10) **3**. At a low Tolerance value, many anchor points will be created and the path will conform precisely to the selection marquee, but a low Tolerance could cause a printing error. At a high Tolerance value, fewer anchor points will be created and the path will be smoother, but it will conform less precisely to the selection. Try 4 or 5.

4. Click OK **4**–**5**. The new work path name will appear on the Paths palette. Don't leave it as a work path, though! Save the path by double-clicking the path name, entering a name, then clicking OK.

Method 2

To convert a selection into a path using the current Make Work Path Tolerance setting, click the Make work path button at the bottom of the Paths palette. Now save the path by double-clicking the path name, entering a name, then clicking OK.

2 *Click the* ***Make work path*** *button on the* ***Paths*** *palette.*

3

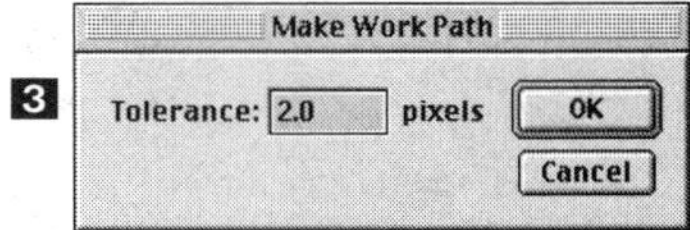

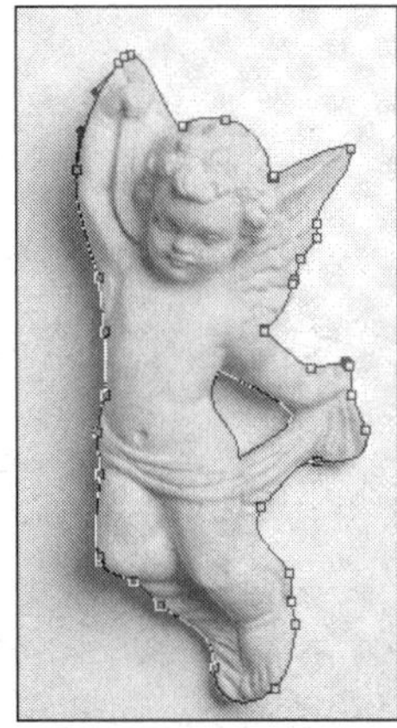

4 *The* ***selection*** *converted into a* ***path: Tolerance 2.***

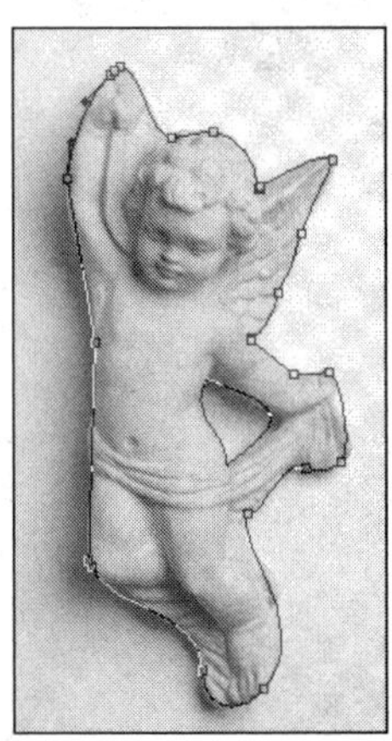

5 *The* ***selection*** *converted into a* ***path: Tolerance 6.***

1 ***Click** to create **straight** sides.*

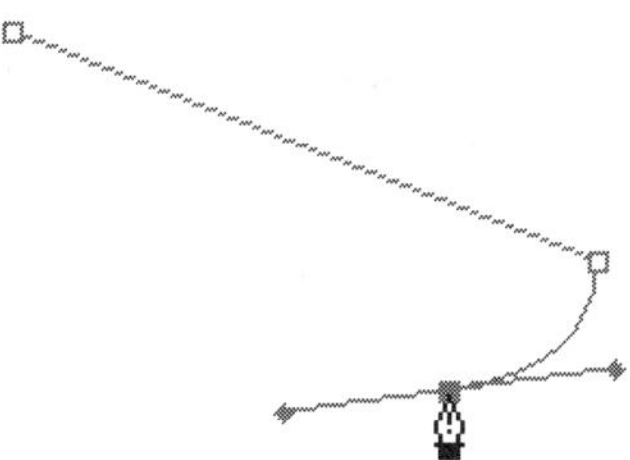

2 ***Drag** to create a **curved** segment.*

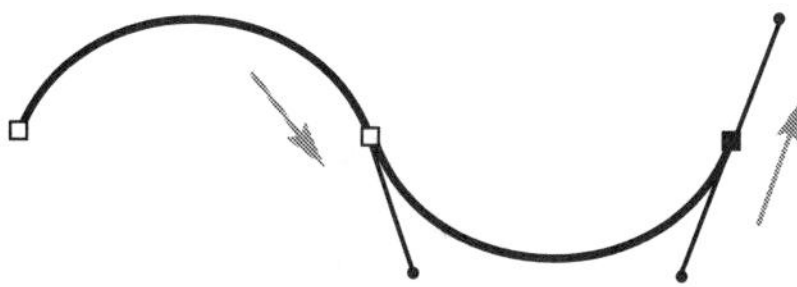

3 *Drag in the direction you want the curve to follow. Place anchor points at the **ends** of a curve, not at the height of a curve. The fewer the anchor points, the more graceful the curves.*

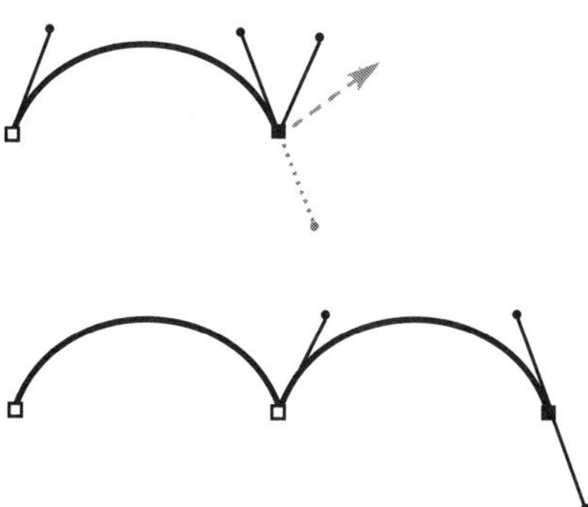

4 *To draw **non-continuous** curves, **Alt**-drag/ **Option**-drag from the last anchor point in the direction you want the next curve to follow. Both direction lines will be on the same side of the curve segment.*

To draw a path using the Pen tool:

1. Choose the Pen tool (P or Shift-P).
2. Make sure no paths are active on the Paths palette, then click the Create new work path button on the options bar. 6.0!
3. Check the Rubber Band box on the options bar to preview the line segments as you draw them.
4. Click in the image window, move the mouse, then click again to create a straight segment (Shift-click to draw the line at a multiple of 45°) **1**.
   or
   Drag to create a curved segment, then release the mouse. Direction lines will appear **2**–**3**.
   or
   To create a non-continuous curve, starting from on top of the last anchor point, Alt-drag/Option-drag in the direction you want the next curve to follow, release Alt/Option and the mouse, then drag in the direction of the new curve **4**.

   As you're drawing, press Delete once to erase the last created anchor point (or twice to delete the whole path).
5. Repeat the previous step as many times as necessary to complete the shape.
6. To end the path but leave it open, Ctrl-click/Cmd-click outside the path or click the Pen tool or any other tool. If you don't deselect the path name or the path, any additional paths you draw will be saved under the same name.
   or
   To close the path, click the starting point (a small circle icon will appear next to the pointer).
7. To save the new work path, double-click the path name, enter a name, then click OK. To reshape the path, see page 268.

TIP Choose a saved path before using the Pen to add the new path to the saved path name. Or to start with a saved path instead of a work path, click the Create new path button on the Paths palette.

Pen Tool

Like the Magnetic Lasso tool, when the Freeform Pen tool is used with its Magnetic option turned on, it creates a path automatically as you move or drag along areas of high contrast. The path will snap to the nearest distinct shade or color edge that defines a shape.

To draw a magnetic Freeform Pen path:

1. Hide any layers you don't want to trace.
2. Choose the Freeform Pen tool (P or Shift P).
3. Deslect all paths on the Paths palette. Then, on the Freeform Pen options bar, click the Create new work path button and check the Magnetic box.
4. Click the Magnetic Pen options button on the options bar, then choose settings on the Magnetic Options pop-up palette (see the next page).
5. Click to begin the path, then slowly move the mouse—with or without pressing the mouse button—along the edge of the shape that you want the path to describe **1**. As you move or drag, the path will snap to the edge of the shape. If you move or drag the mouse quickly, the tool might not keep pace with you.
6. If the path snaps to any neighboring shapes that you *don't* want to select, click on the edge of the shape that you *do* want to select to manually create an anchor point, and then continue to move or drag to finish the path.
7. To **close** the path **2**:

   Double-click anywhere over the shape to close with magnetic segments or Alt-double-click/Option-double-click to close with a straight segment.
   or
   Click on the starting point (a small circle will appear next to the Magnetic Pen tool pointer).
   or

1 *Click to start the path, then move the mouse around the object you want to select.*

2 *The completed* ***Magnetic Pen*** *path.*

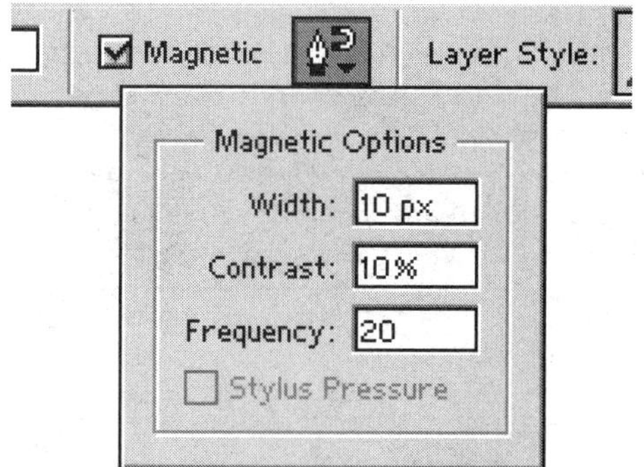

1 *When **Magnetic** is checked on the options bar for the **Freeform Pen** tool, you can then choose settings from the **Magentic Options** pop-up palette.*

Ctrl-click/Cmd-click anywhere over the shape.

To end the path but leave it **open**, press Enter/Return. You can then reposition the Pen tool and click to start another path for the same Work Path.

TIP To draw straight segments with a temporary Pen tool while the Freeform Pen is chosen, Alt-click/Option-click and continue clicking. Release Alt/Option to go back to the Freeform Pen.

TIP Press Esc to cancel a partial path.

The Magnetic Options pop-up palette 1

6.0!

The **Width** (1–40) is the width in pixels under the pointer that the tool considers when placing points. Use a wide Width for a high contrast image that has clear delineations between shapes. For a low contrast image with subtle gradations or closely-spaced shapes, use a narrow Width for more exact line placement.

TIP To have the Magnetic Freeform Pen pointer display as a circle in the current Width, click Other Cursors: Precise in File menu > Preferences > Display & Cursors. Or press Caps Lock to turn this option on temporarily.

TIP To decrease the Width incrementally while creating a path, press [. To increase the Width, press].

Contrast (0–100) is the degree of contrast needed between shapes for the tool to discern an edge. At a low Edge Contrast setting, even edges between low contrast areas will be discerned.

Frequency (5–40) controls how quickly fastening points are placed as you draw a path. The lower the Frequency, the faster fastening points will be placed and the more anchor points will be created.

The Freeform Pen tool creates a path by dragging. Anchor points will appear automatically when you release the mouse.

To draw a path using the Freeform Pen:

1. Choose the Freeform Pen tool (P or Shift-P). Deselect all paths on the Paths palette.
2. 6.0! On the Freeform Pen options bar, click the Create new work path button and uncheck the Magnetic box.
3. Draw a path in a freehand style. (To draw straight segments, Alt-click/Option-click; to resume freehand drawing, release Alt/Option when the mouse button is down.)
4. To **close** the path:

   Drag back over the starting point **1**–**2**. A small circle will display next to the Freeform Pen tool pointer.
   or
   Hold down Ctrl/Cmd and release the mouse to close the path with a final curved segment.

   To end the path but leave it **open**, just release the mouse.

TIP Enter a Curve Fit value (0.5–10 pixels) on the options bar to control how exactly your Freeform Pen path will match the movement of your mouse. The higher the Curve Fit, the fewer the points, and thus the smoother the shape.

To move a path:

1. On the Paths palette, click a path name.
2. 6.0! Choose the Path Component Selection tool (A or Shift-A). Then click the path in the image window to select it.
3. Drag the path in the image window **3**.

Freeform Pen

Beware!

As long as you don't click the blank area of the Paths palette, any additional paths you create will be part of the same Work Path. If you click the blank area and draw again without saving the existing work path, however, the new work path will **replace** the old one! To save a path so it's not replaced, see page 266.

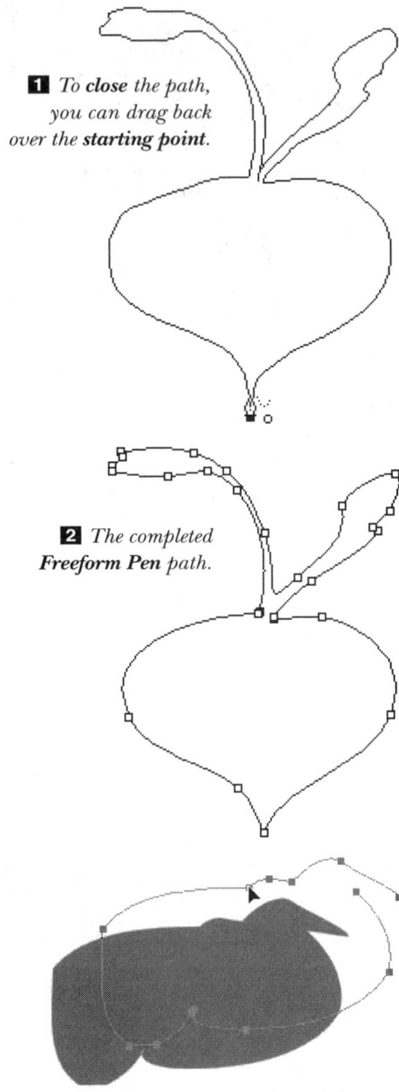

1 *To **close** the path, you can drag back over the **starting point**.*

2 *The completed **Freeform Pen** path.*

3 *A path is moved using the **Path Component Selection** tool.*

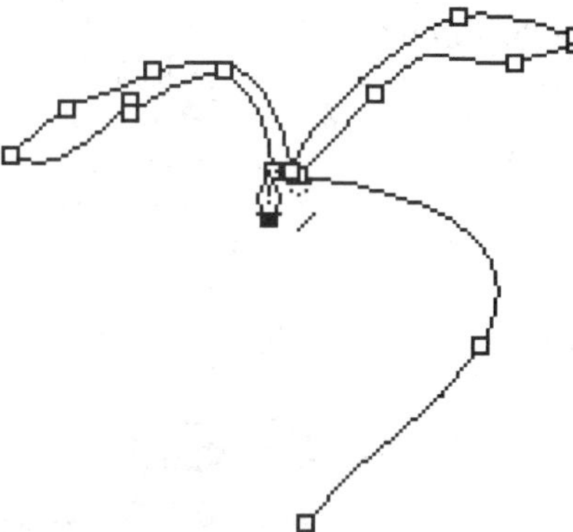

1 *To **add** to a path, drag from an **endpoint** using the Pen or Freeform Pen tool.*

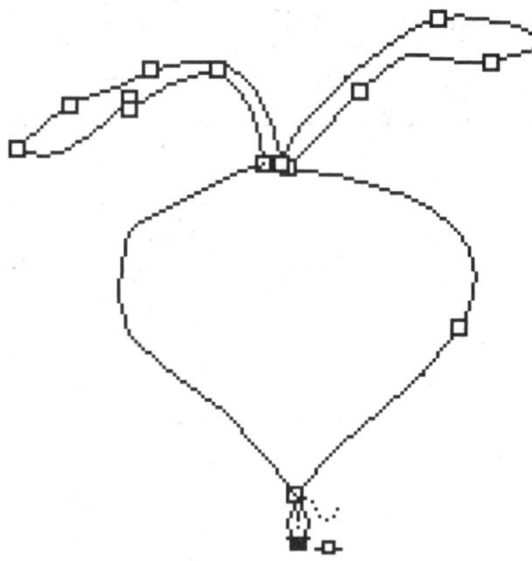

2 *Completing the addition.*

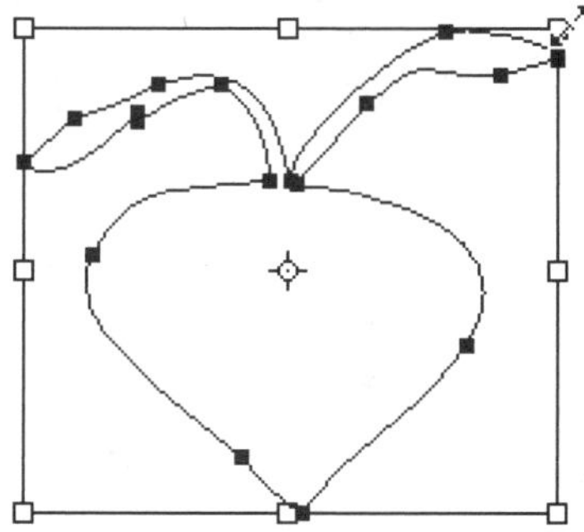

3 ***Scaling** a path.*

To add to an existing, open path:

1. Choose the Freeform Pen tool, or Pen tool (P or Shift-P).
2. Click the name of a saved open path or work path on the Paths palette.
3. Drag from either endpoint of the path **1**–**2**. To end the path, follow step 4 in the first set of instructions on the previous page.

To transform an entire path (or layer clipping path):

1. Choose the Path Component Selection tool (A or Shift-A).
2. Activate the path name on the Paths palette, then click inside the path in the image window. 6.0!
3. Choose Edit menu > Transform Path > Scale, Rotate, Skew, Distort, or Perspective; or choose Edit menu > Free Transform Path (Ctrl-T/Cmd-T).
4. Follow the instructions on pages 124–127 to perform the transformation.

TIP To repeat the transformation, choose Edit menu > Transform Points > Again or Edit menu > Transform Path > Again (Ctrl-Shift-T/Cmd-Shift-T).

TIP When the Path Component Selection tool is chosen, you have the option to check Show Bounding Box on the options bar. You can use the bounding box handles to transform a path as you would the handles on the Free Transform box. 6.0!

To transform points on a path:

1. Choose the Direct Selection tool (A), then select one or more individual points on a path (see page 267).
2. Choose Edit menu > Transform Points > Scale, Rotate, or Skew (the Distort and Perspective commands won't be available); or choose Edit menu > Free Transform Points (Ctrl-T/Cmd-T).
3. Follow the instructions on pages 124–127 to perform the transformation **3**.

Add to Path; Transform Path

To copy a path in the same image:

To make the copy a separate path name, on the Paths palette, Alt-drag/Option-drag the path name over the Create new path button at the bottom of the palette **1**, enter a name **2**, then click OK. (To copy the path without naming it, drag the path name without holding down Alt/Option.)

or

Choose the Path Component Selection tool, then Alt-drag/Option-drag the path in the image window. The two paths will have the same path name.

To drag-and-drop a path to another image:

1. Open the source and destination images, and click in the source image window.
2. Drag the path name from the Paths palette into the destination image window.

   or

   Choose the Path Component Selection tool (A), click the path, then drag it from the source image window into the destination image window.

   6.0!

   or

   Click the path name on the Paths palette, choose Edit menu > Copy (Ctrl-C/Cmd-C), click in the destination image window, then choose Edit menu > Paste (Ctrl-V/Cmd-V).

   Note: You can also copy and paste a layer clipping path that you've created for an image layer or shape layer.

A new path that's created with the Pen tool will be labeled "Work Path" automatically and it will save with the file. The next path you create, however, will replace the existing one. Follow these instructions to save a path so it won't be deleted by a new path. Once a path is saved, it's resaved automatically each time it's modified.

To save a work path:

Double-click the path name, enter a name **3**, then click OK.

Quick-save a work path

Drag the path name over the New Path button at the bottom of the Paths palette. Photoshop will assign it a default name. To rename it at any time, double-click the path name, then type a new name.

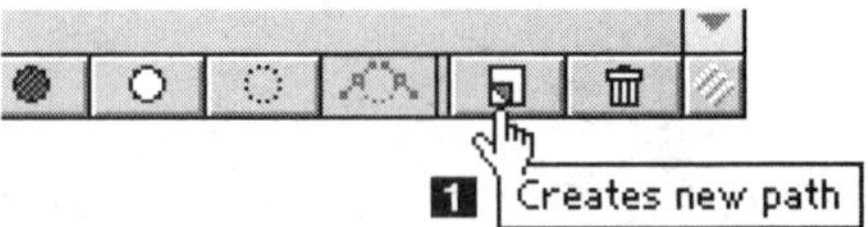

3 *Type a Name in the* ***Save Path*** *dialog box.*

Copy Path; Save Path

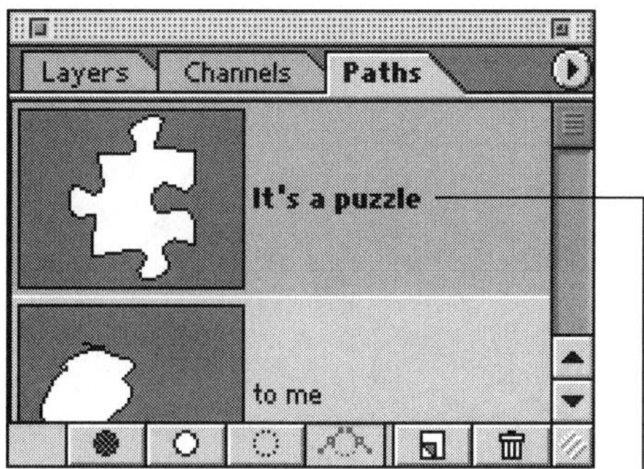

1 *To display a path, click its name on the* ***Paths*** *palette.*

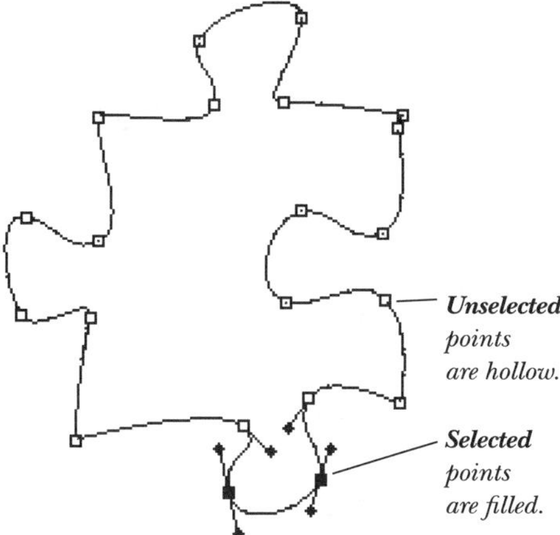

2 ***Click*** *with the* ***Direct Selection*** *tool to select* ***individual*** *points on a path.*

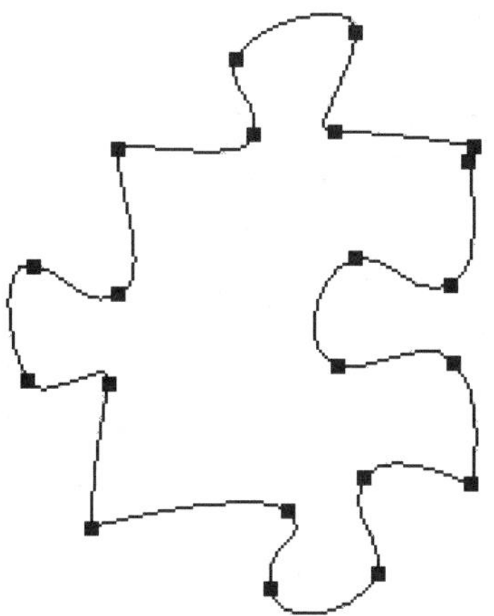

3 ***Click*** *with the* ***Path Component Selection*** *tool to select* ***all*** *the points on a path.*

To display a path:

Click the path name or thumbnail on the Paths palette **1**.

TIP To change the size of or turn off palette thumbnails, choose Palette Options from the Paths palette menu, then click a Thumbnail Size.

To hide a path:

Shift-click the path name on the Paths palette.

or

Click below the path names on the Paths palette.

To select anchor points on a path:

Method 1

1. Click a path name on the Paths palette.
2. Choose the Path Component Selection tool (A or Shift-A).
3. Click on the path in the image window or draw a marquee around it. All the anchor points on the path will be selected.

Method 2

1. Click a path name on the Paths palette.
2. Choose the Direct Selection tool (A or Shift-A).
3. Click on the path or subpath, then click on an anchor point **2**. Shift-click to select additional anchor points.

   or

   To select all the anchor points on the path, Alt-click/Option-click the path or subpath or draw a marquee around it **3**. An entire path can be moved when all its points are selected.

TIP To change the stacking position of a path, drag the path name up or down on the Paths palette.

TIP Hold down Ctrl/Cmd to use the Direct Selection tool while any Pen tool is chosen.

To reshape a path, you can move, add, or delete an anchor point or move a segment. To modify the shape of a curved line segment, move a direction line toward or away from its anchor point or rotate it around its anchor point.

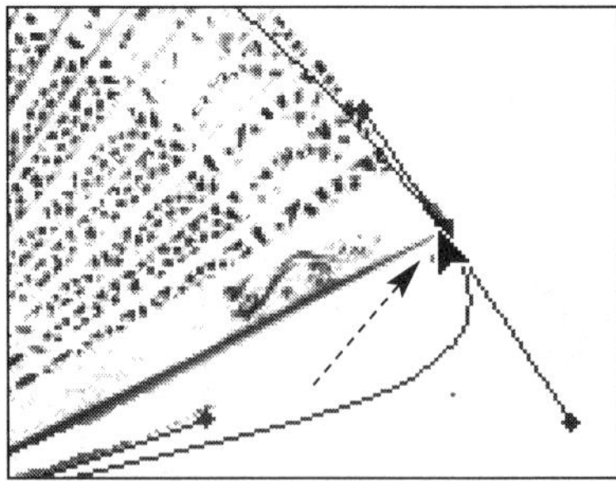
1 *Dragging an anchor point.*

To reshape a path:

1. On the Paths palette, click the name of the path you want to reshape.
2. Choose the Direct Selection tool (A or Shift-A). To access the Direct Selection tool when another pen tool is chosen, press Ctrl/Cmd.
3. Click on the path in the image window.
4. Do any of the following:

   Drag an anchor **point** or a **segment** **1**. To select a segment, drag a marquee that includes both of the segment's endpoints. Shift-drag to marquee additional segments (or subpaths).

   Drag or **rotate** a **direction line** **2**. If you move a direction line on a smooth point, the two segments that are connected to that point will also move. If you move a direction line on a corner point, on the other hand, only one curve segment will move.

   To **add** an anchor **point**, choose the Add Anchor Point tool, then click on a line segment (the pointer will be a pen icon with a plus sign when it's over a segment) **3**–**4**.

6.0! **TIP** If Auto Add/Delete is checked on the options bar, the Pen tool will turn into the Add Anchor Point tool when it's over a segment or the Delete Anchor Point tool when it's over a point. To turn this function off temporarily, hold down Shift.

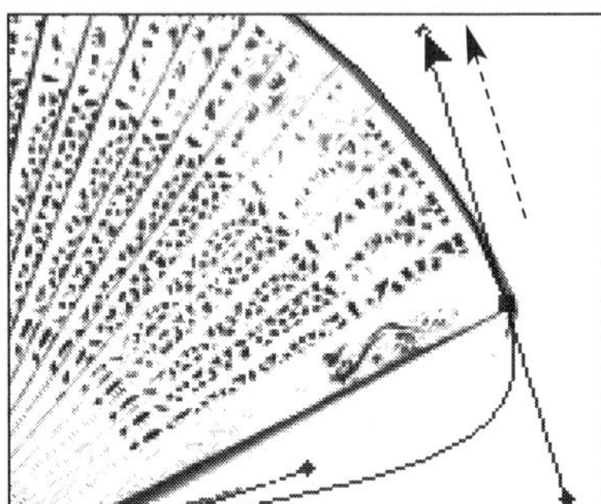
2 *Pulling a direction line.*

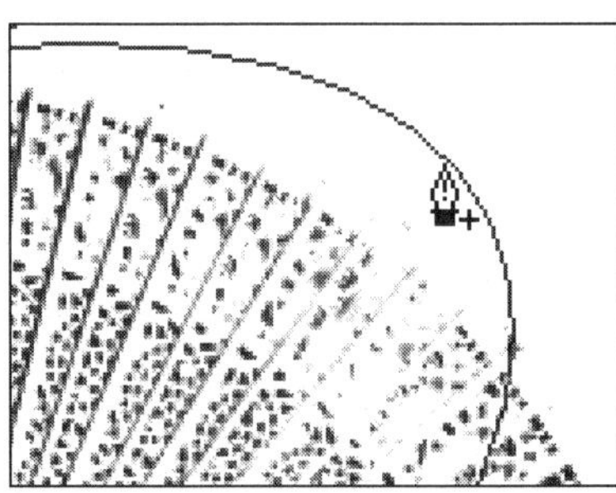
3 *Adding an anchor point.*

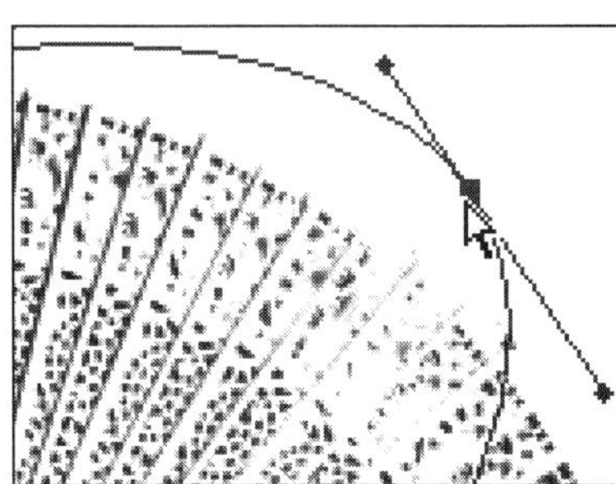
4 *The new anchor point.*

Reshape Path

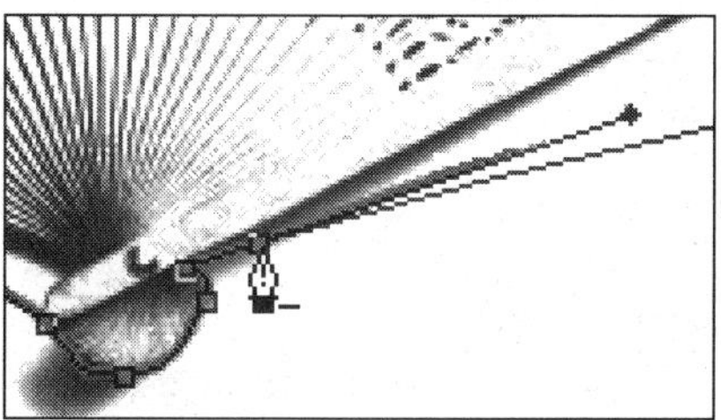

1 ***Deleting*** *an anchor pont.*

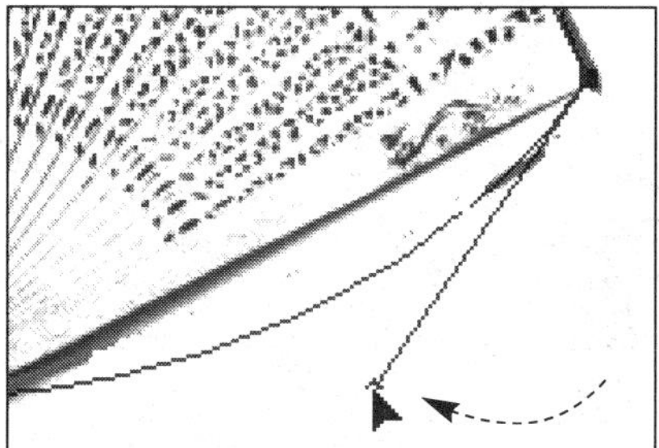

2 ***Converting*** *a* ***direction line.***

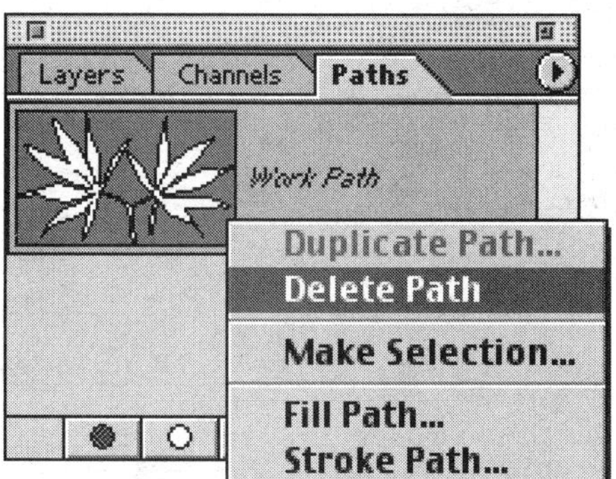

3 *To delete a path,* ***Right-click/Control-click*** *the path name, then choose* ***Delete Path*** *from the context menu.*

To **delete** an anchor **point**, choose the Delete Anchor Point tool, then click on the anchor point (the pointer will be a pen icon with a minus sign when it's over a point) **1**.

To **convert** a **smooth point** into a **corner point**, choose the Convert Point Tool (or hold down Ctrl-Alt/Cmd-Option if the Direct Selection tool is chosen or Alt/Option if a Pen tool is chosen), then click the anchor point (deselect the Convert Point tool by choosing another tool). To **convert** a **corner point** into a **smooth point**, choose the Convert Point tool, then drag away from the anchor point.

Use the Convert Point tool to rotate one direction line independently of the other direction line in the pair **2**. Once the Convert Point tool has been used on part of a direction line, you can use either the Convert Point tool or the Direct Selection tool to move its partner.

5. Click outside the path to deselect it.

Note: If the path you want to delete is a Work Path, simply drawing a new work path with the Pen tool will cause the original Work Path to be replaced.

To delete a path:

1. On the Paths palette, activate the path you want to delete.
2. Right-click/Control-click the path name, then choose Delete Path from the context menu **3**.
   or
   Alt-click/Option-click the Delete Path (trash) button on the Paths palette.
   or
   Click the Delete Path (trash) button, then click Yes.
   or
   Drag the path name over the Delete Path (trash) button.

6.0!

To deselect a path:

1. Choose the Direct Selection tool or the Path Component Selection tool (A or Shift-A).
2. Click outside the path in the image window. The path will still be visible in the image window, but its anchor points and direction lines will be hidden.

To convert a path into a selection:

1. *Optional:* Create a selection if you want to add, delete, or intersect the new path selection with it.
2. Ctrl-click/Cmd-click the name of the path you want to convert into a selection.
   or
   On the Paths palette, activate the name of the path you want to convert into a selection, then click the Loads path as selection button **1** at the bottom of the palette. The last used Make Selection settings will apply.

   To choose options as you load the path as a selection, Right-click/Control-click the path name and choose Make Selection from the context menu. You can apply a Feather Radius to the selection (enter a low number to soften the edge slightly) **2** or add, subtract, or intersect the path with an existing selection on the image (click an Operation option). The Operation shortcuts are listed in the sidebar on this page. Click OK. *Note:* If you turn on the Anti-aliased option, make the Feather Radius 0.
3. On the Layers palette, choose the layer you created the selection for.

Path-into-selection shortcuts

WINDOWS

Make path current selection	Ctrl-click path name
Add path to current selection	Ctrl-Shift-click path name
Subtract path from current selection	Ctrl-Alt-click path name
Intersect path with current selection	Ctrl-Alt-Shift-click path name

MACINTOSH

Make path current selection	Cmd-click path name
Add path to current selection	Cmd-Shift-click path name
Subtract path from current selection	Cmd-Option-click path name
Intersect path with current selection	Cmd-Option-Shift-path name

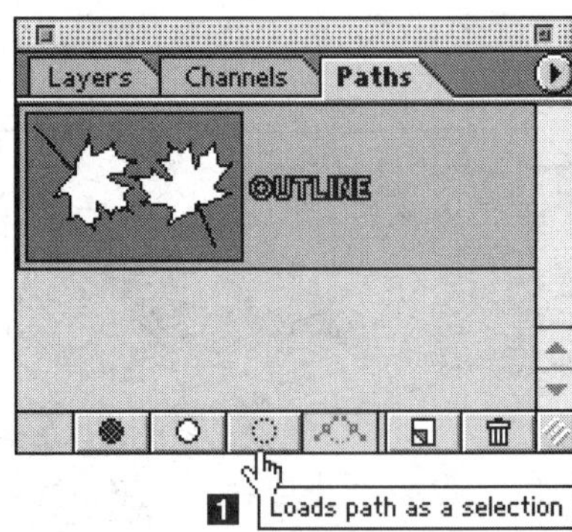

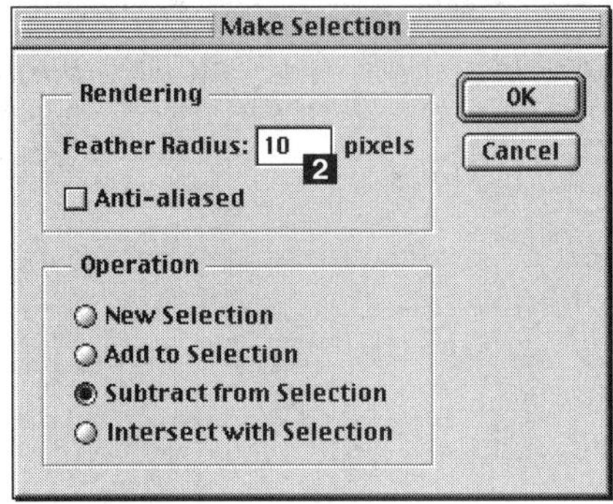

Deselect Path; Convert Path to Selection

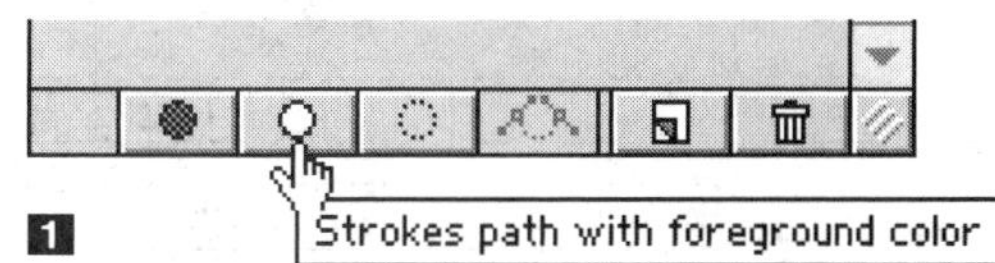

1

2 *The original image. (The path is shown in the thumbnail* **1** *on the previous page.)*

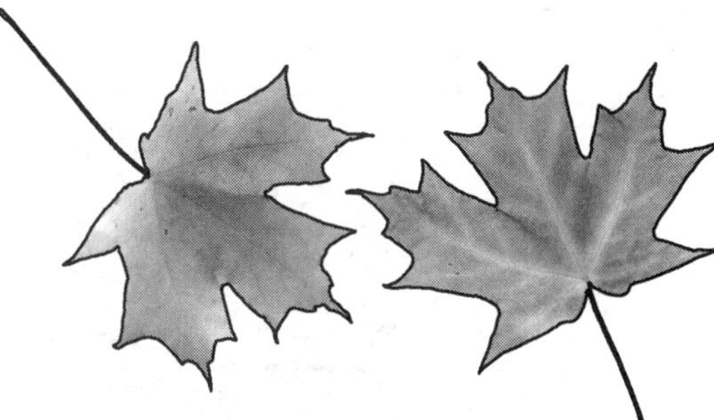

3 *A* ***Pencil*** *tool* ***Stroke*** *is applied to the* ***path****.*

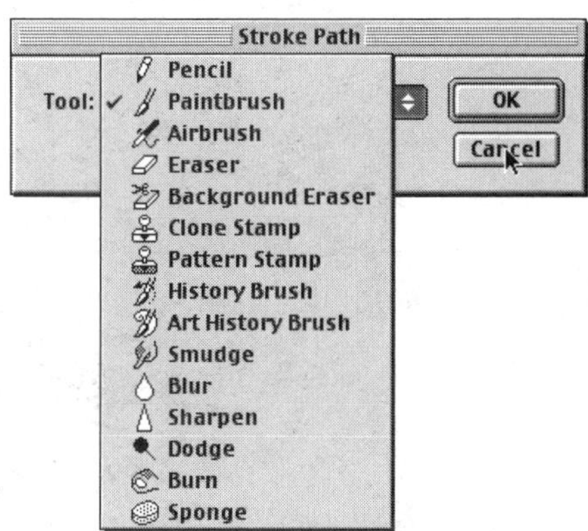

4 *You can* ***stroke*** *a path using any of these* ***tools****.*

When you apply color to (stroke) the edge of a path, the current tool and its current options bar attributes (e.g., Opacity and Mode) are used as the attributes for the stroke.

To stroke a path:

1. On the Paths palette, activate a closed or open path.
2. Using the Layers palette, activate the layer on which you want the stroke pixels to appear (not a shape layer).
3. Choose a tool. The tools that you can use are shown in figure **4**.
4. On the options bar: *6.0!*

   Choose a Mode.

   and

   Choose an Opacity (or Pressure).

   and

   Click the Painting Brush arrowhead, then click a brush on the picker. The stroke thickness will be the same as the diameter of the brush tip.
5. Choose a Foreground color.
6. Click the Strokes path (second) button at the bottom of the Paths palette **1**–**3**.

   If you want to switch tools, Alt-click/ Option-click the Strokes path button, choose from the Tool pop-up menu, then click OK **4**.

TIP You can apply an editable stroke effect to a layer clipping path using the Layer Style dialog box (see page 234).

Stroke Path

Use the Fill Path command to fill a path with a color, a pattern, or imagery.

To fill a path:

1. On the Paths palette, activate an open or closed path.
2. On the Layers palette, choose the layer you want the fill pixels to appear on.
3. To fill with a solid color other than white or black, choose a Foreground color.
   or
   To fill with imagery from a history state, move the History Brush icon to the state you want to use for the fill.

   (To fill with a pattern, you can use an existing preset.)
4. Alt-click/Option-click the Fills path (first) button at the bottom of the Paths palette **1**.
5. Choose from the Contents: Use pop-up menu **2**. For a pattern choose a pattern from the Custom Pattern picker.
   and
   Choose a Mode. Choose Clear mode to fill the path on a layer with transparency.
   and
   Enter an Opacity percentage.
6. *Optional:* If a layer (not the Background) is active, check the Preserve Transparency box to recolor only existing visible pixels on that layer, not any transparent areas.
7. *Optional:* Choose Rendering options (feathering and anti-aliasing).
8. Click OK **3**–**4**.

TIP To fill a path using the current Fill Path dialog box settings, click the path name, then click the Fills path button at the bottom of the Paths palette.

TIP You can apply an editable Color Overlay effect to a layer clipping path using the Layer Style dialog box (see page 232).

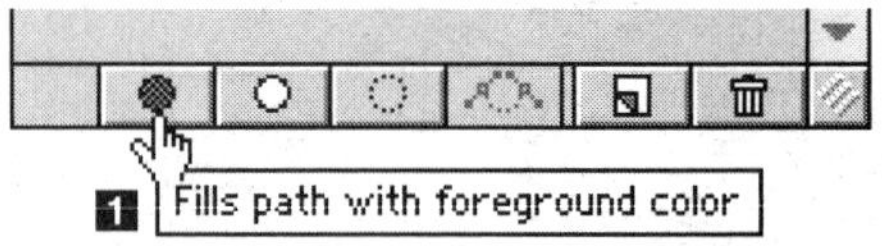

1

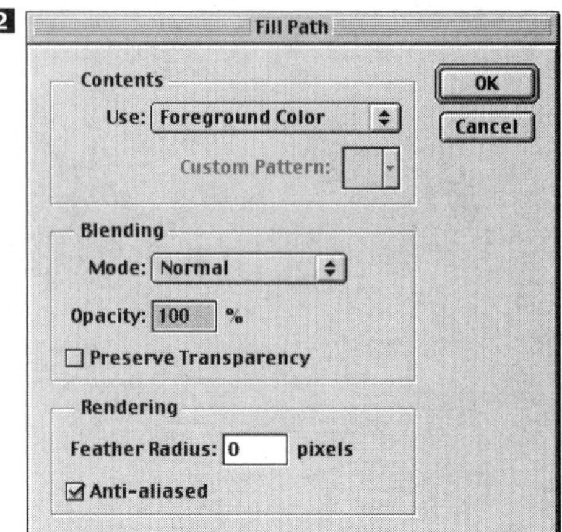

2

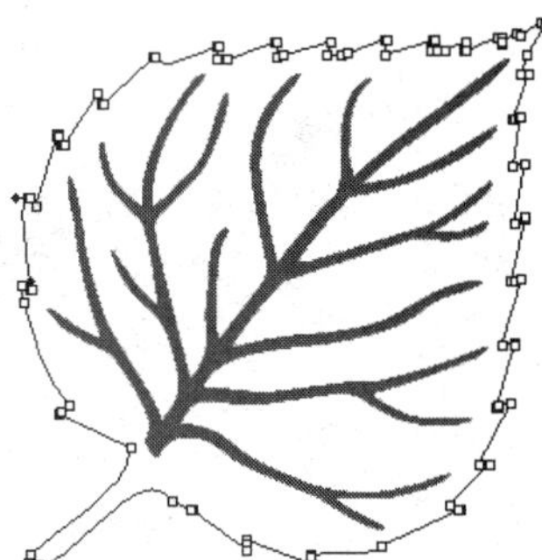

3 *The original path.*

4 *The path filled with a pattern, 50% opacity.*

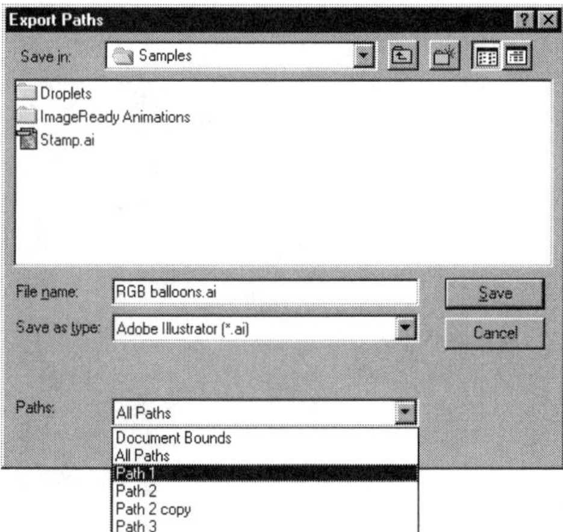

1 *Windows: Choose a path from the* ***Paths*** *drop-down menu.*

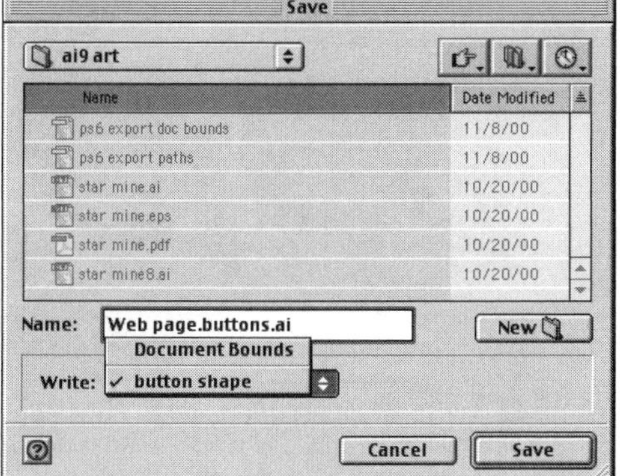

2 *Mac OS: Choose a path from the* ***Write*** *pop-up menu.*

You can create a path in Photoshop, export it to Adobe Illustrator or Macromedia FreeHand, and then use it as an editable path in that program. What's more, you can then place the same path back into Photoshop (see page 60).

Note: You could also use the Path Component Selection tool and the Clipboard to copy and paste or drag-and-drop an active path to another application (or to another open image in the same application).

To export a path to Illustrator or FreeHand:

1. Create and save a path. You can also use a shape layer's clipping path (see the next page). *Note:* To make a layer clipping path available on the Write pop-up menu, choose that layer before performing the next step.
2. Choose File menu > Export > Paths to Illustrator.
3. *Optional:* Change the name in the File Name (Win)/Name (Mac OS) field.
4. From the Paths (Win) **1**/Write (Mac) **2** pop-up menu:

   Choose an individual path name.

   or

   Choose All Paths to export all the paths in the image as one file. Document crop marks will be included in the export file.

   or

   Choose Document Bounds to export crop marks only for the current file.
5. Choose a location in which to save the path file.
6. Click Save. The path can be opened as an Adobe Illustrator document.

TIP To ensure that the path fits when you reimport it into Photoshop, don't alter its crop marks in Illustrator.

TIP You may have to choose Outline view in Illustrator to see the exported path, because it won't have a stroke.

6.0!

Layer clipping paths

A layer clipping path works like a layer mask, except the clipping path uses a vector path shape to delineate what is visible and what is masked in the current layer. The path can be created using the Pen tool, Freeform Pen tool, or a shape tool, or from a selection that is converted to a path. The layer clipping path produces a clean, sharp-edge shape that hides pixels on a layer. You can modify the path shape or discard the clipping path at any time.

A layer clipping path will display as a gray thumbnail on the Layers palette, and also on the Paths palette when the layer with the clipping path is selected. Like a layer mask, a layer clipping path is associated with only one layer.

To create a layer clipping path:

Method 1

1. On the Layers palette, choose the layer you want to add a clipping path to **1**.
2. To create a white mask in which all the layer pixels are visible, choose Layer menu > Add Layer Clipping Path > Reveal All or Ctrl-click/Cmd-click the Add a mask button on the Layers palette.
   or
   To create a gray mask in which all the layer pixels are hidden, choose Layer menu > Add Layer Clipping Path > Hide All or Ctrl-Alt-click/Cmd-Option-click the Add a mask button on the Layers palette.
3. Choose the Pen, Freeform Pen, or any shape tool and create a clipping path in the desired shape **2**–**3**. See page 261 for more info.

Method 2

1. On the Layers palette, choose the layer you want to add a clipping path to.
2. To reveal only layer pixels within a selected path, select a path on the Paths palette, then choose Layer menu > Add Layer Clipping Path > Current Path.

1 *A layer with strokes that will be clipped.*

2 *A layer clipping path is added,* ***Hide All,*** *and then the Pen tool is used to shape the path.*

3 *The effect of the* ***layer clipping path*** *on the layer imagery.*

Layer Clipping Path

EPS clipping paths—a new way

If you save a file containing a layer clipping path as a Photoshop EPS for import into another program (e.g., InDesign or QuarkXPress), the masking effect of the layer clipping path will be preserved in the other program. This method has an advantage over the Paths palette clipping path option because you are working directly with the image layer and can see how the image will be clipped before it's exported. Just be sure the Include Vector Data option stays checked in the EPS Options dialog box. *Note:* To import a Photoshop file that contains a layer clipping path into Illustrator 9, Place (uncheck Link) or Open the file in Illustrator 9 and choose to convert layers to objects.

1 *Using the Pen tool and the Add to shape area button, a second clipping path is added to a layer that already contains a layer clipping path.*

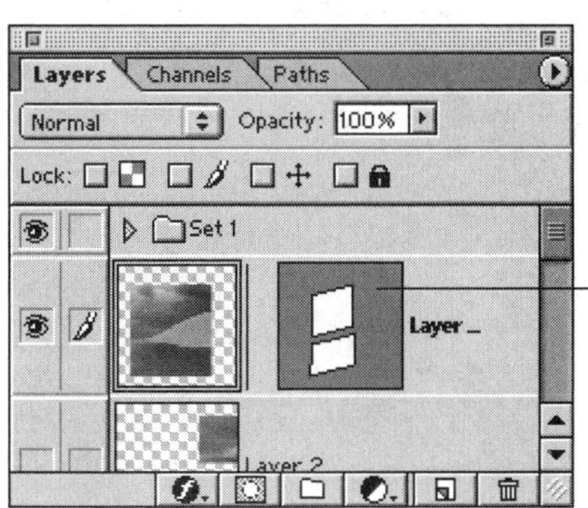

2 *The layer clipping path thumbnail now displays two clipping path shapes.*

The pathfinder operation buttons are used to create add-ons to, or cutouts from, an existing path or to create a separate path. 6.0!

To combine paths:

1. Click on a layer name for a layer that contains a layer clipping path. The clipping path thumbnail is now selected.
2. Choose a pen or shape tool.
3. On the options bar, click one of the four pathfinder operation buttons (add to shape area, subtract from shape area, intersect shape areas, exclude overlapping shape areas) and draw another path in the image window **1**–**2**.

If you reshape a layer clipping path, the masking effect in the image will change accordingly. 6.0!

To reshape a layer clipping path:

1. Choose the Direct Selection tool (A or Shift-A).
2. Click the clipping path in the image window to select it.
   or
   Click the layer name for the layer that has a layer clipping path. The clipping path thumbnail should be selected and the clipping path should be visible in the image window.
3. Click on the edge of the clipping path to reveal and select its anchor points.
4. Follow the steps on pages 268–269 to reshape the path.

A layer clipping path can be moved independently of its layer pixels at any time. It stays on its designated layer.

To reposition a layer clipping path:

1. Choose the Path Component Selection tool (A or Shift-A).
2. On the Layers palette, click the name of the layer that contains the clipping path.
or
Click on the clipping path in the image window.
3. Drag the clipping path to a new location. A different area of layer pixels will now be visible within the confines of the path **1**.

To duplicate a layer clipping path:

1. Choose the layer you want the duplicate to appear on.
2. From another layer, drag the layer clipping path thumbnail you want to duplicate over the Add a mask button **2**–**3**. The duplicate clipping path will appear on the active layer.

6.0!

To temporarily remove the effects of a layer clipping path:

Shift-click the layer clipping path thumbnail on the Layers palette. A red "X" will appear over the thumbnail and the entire layer will now be visible **4** (the layer clipping path thumbnail won't become selected).

(Shift-click the layer clipping path thumbnail again to remove the "X" and restore the clipping effect.)

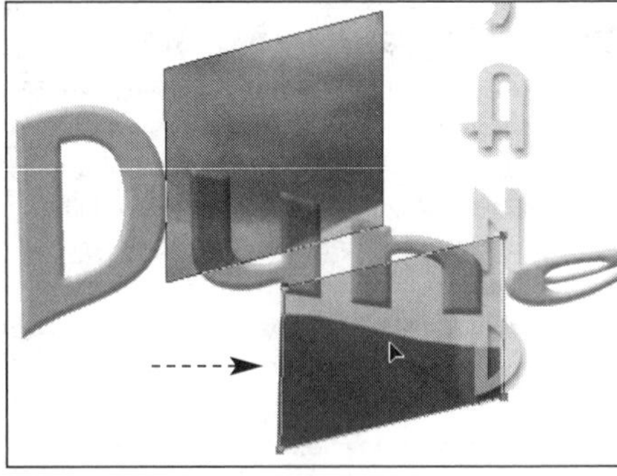

1 *The layer clipping path is* ***moved****, and now a different area of layer pixels is visible within it.*

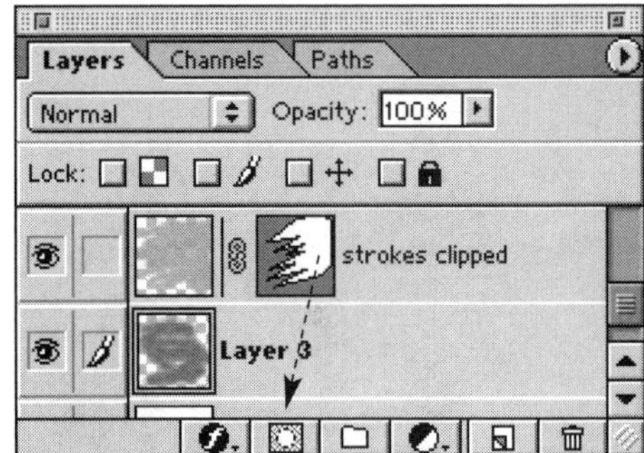

2 *Drag the layer clipping path thumbnail over the* ***Add a mask*** *button.*

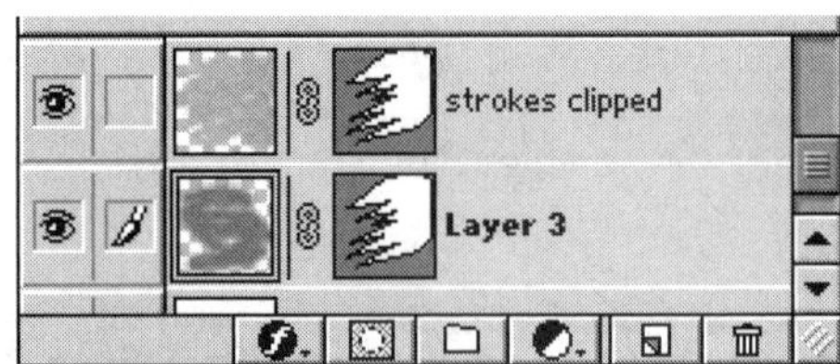

3 *A* ***copy*** *of the layer clipping path appears on the active layer (Layer 3).*

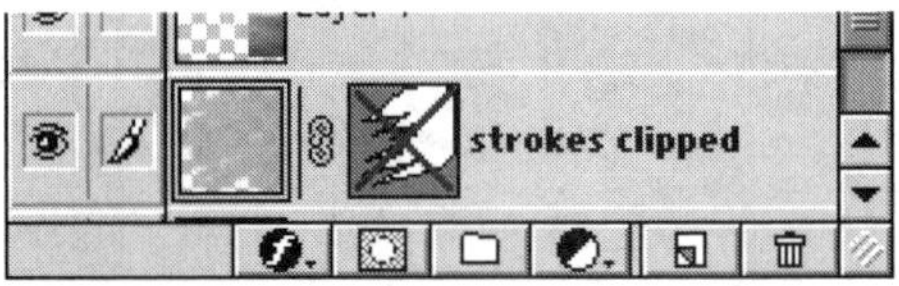

4 *The layer clipping path effect is* ***turned off temporarily.***

Reposition, Duplicate, Deactivate Clipping Path

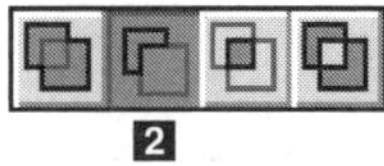

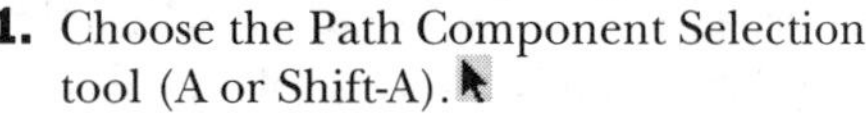

To reverse the revealed and hidden areas in a layer clipping path:

6.0!

1. Choose the Path Component Selection tool (A or Shift-A).
2. On the Layers palette, click the name of the layer that contains a clipping path, then click the clipping path in the image window.
   or
   Double-click the clipping path in the image window.

   With either method, the clipping path will first be highlighted, then its anchor points and segments will be selected **1**.
3. Click the Subtract from shape area (second) button on the options bar **2–3**, or press "-" (minus key).

   To switch the revealed and hidden areas again, click the first button (Add to shape area) on the options bar, or press "+".

You can delete any layer clipping paths that you no longer need, though you won't recoup any file storage space by doing so. 6.0!

To discard a layer clipping path:

1. On the Layers palette, click the thumbnail for the layer clipping path that you want to remove.
2. Click the Delete Layer (trash) button.
   or
   Drag the layer clipping path thumbnail over the Delete Layer button **4**.
   or
   Choose Layer menu > Delete Layer Clipping Path.
3. Click OK.

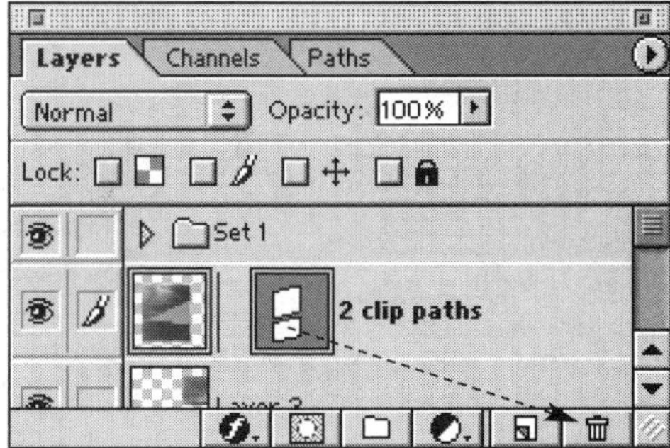

4 *Drag the layer clipping path thumbnail over the Delete Layer button.*

6.0!

To convert a layer mask into a layer clipping path:

1. Ctrl-click/Cmd-click a layer mask thumbnail on the Layers palette.
2. On the Paths palette, click the Makes work path button. Leave the path selected.
3. Choose Layer menu > Add Clipping Path > Current Path **1**.
4. *Optional:* Drag the layer mask thumbnail to the Delete Layer button on the Layers palette, then click Discard, or choose Layer menu > Remove Layer Mask > Discard, to remove the layer mask. The layer clipping path will remain.

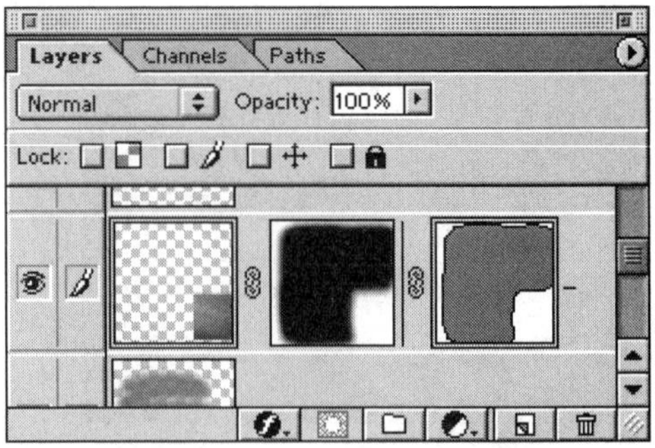

6.0!

To create an adjustment layer that uses a layer clipping path:

1. Create a new shape layer (see page 280).
2. Choose an adjustment layer command from the Layer menu > Change Layer Content submenu.
3. Make the desired adjustments in the dialog box, then click OK.

6.0!

You can fill type shapes with imagery using clipping paths.

To create a layer clipping path from type:

Method 1

1. Create a type layer (**1**, next page).
2. With the type layer selected, choose Layer menu > Type > Convert to Shape (**2**, next page).
3. From the Paths (yes Paths) palette menu, choose Save Path, then click OK.
4. Leave path selected in image. Back on the Layers palette, choose the image layer you want the new layer clipping path to appear on (not a layer with a clipping path).
5. Choose Layer menu > Add Layer Clipping Path > Current Path.
6. Delete or hide the type shape layer.

1 *The selection from a layer mask becomes the path for a layer clipping path. The layer now contains two mask thumbnails.*

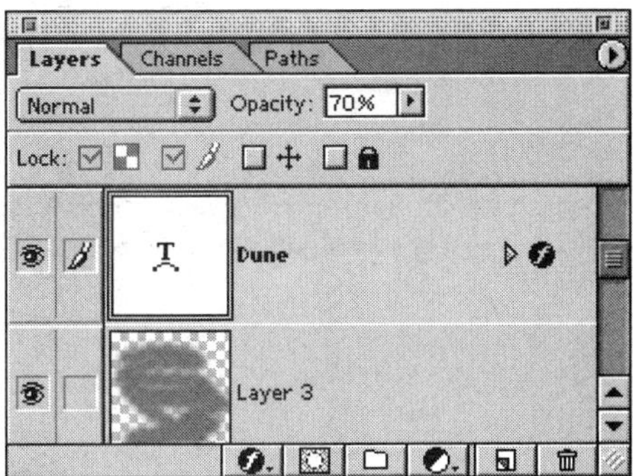

1 *Choose a **type** layer.*

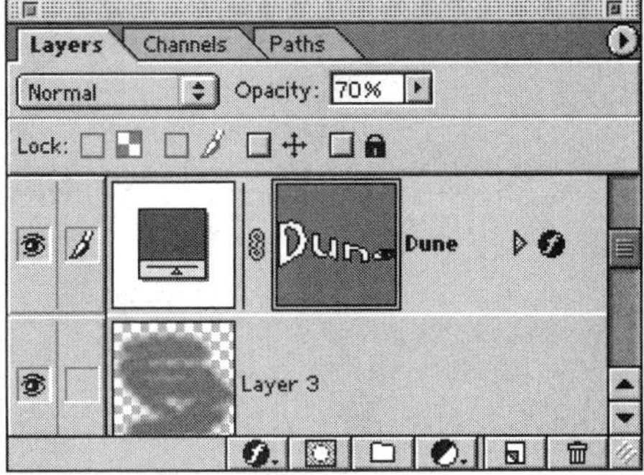

2 *Convert the type layer into a **shape** layer, then drag the **layer clipping path** thumbnail over the **Add a mask** button…*

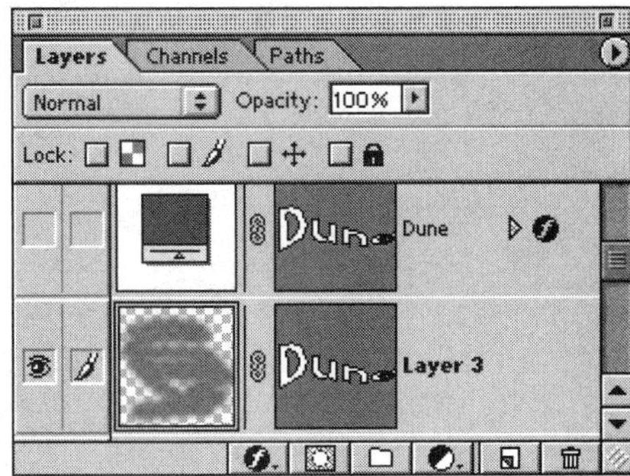

3 *…to copy the layer clipping path thumbnail to the selected layer (Layer 3 in this example). (Any layer effects on the original layer can also be copied by dragging them over the selected layer.)*

Method 2 6.0!

1. Create a type layer **1**.
2. Choose Layer menu > Type > Convert to Shape **2**.
3. Choose the layer you want the new layer clipping path to appear on (not a layer with a clipping path).
4. Drag the layer clipping path thumbnail that was created in step 2 over the Add a mask button on the Layers palette. A new layer clipping path will be created for the active layer **3**.
5. Delete or hide the type shape layer.

TIP For both Method 1 and Method 2, you can do any of the following:

Duplicate the original type layer before converting it so you'll have it available for future type edits, and thus future layer clipping paths. Hide the duplicate type layer.

Use the Path Component Selection tool to reposition the layer clipping paths within the layer at any time.

To reverse what is revealed and what is hidden on the layer, choose the Path Component Selection tool, Shift-click the clipping paths in the image, then click the Subtract from shape area (second) button (-) on the options bar.

6.0!

Shapes

A shape is a precise geometric or custom-shaped clipping path that reveals a solid color, gradient, or pattern fill within its contour and occupies its own layer **1**. A shape can be repositioned, transformed, or reshaped at any time; its fill content can be modified or changed to a different type at any time; and the usual layer styles, effects, blending modes and opacity settings can be applied to or chosen for it.

Unlike the main Photoshop image, which is a bitmap, shape layers are composed of vector data (think Adobe Illustrator or Macromedia Freehand). This means that shapes always look sharp and precise, whether they are printed on a PostScript printer, saved in PDF format or imported into a vector drawing program; in other words, they're resolution-independent.

Creating a shape layer involves drawing a vector path, just as you would in an illustration program.

To create a shape layer:

1. Choose a layer on the Layers palette. The new shape layer will be created above the layer you choose. *Note:* if the layer you choose has a layer clipping path, the shape will become part of the clipping path. To prevent this from happening, make sure the layer clipping path thumbnail is deselected.
2. Using the Color or Swatches palette, choose a Foreground color for the shape's color fill. (You'll learn how to fill a shape with a gradient or pattern later.)
3. Choose a shape tool on the Toolbox (U or Shift-U) **2**. Once a shape tool is selected, you can switch to a different shape tool by clicking one of the shape tool buttons on the options bar **3**.

Effects on a clipping path

Apply layer effects (Inner Glow, Bevel, etc.) to a shape layer or to a layer that has a clipping path to enhance edges, add a shadow, etc. If you apply the Stroke effect or any of the Overlay effects to stroke or fill the layer clipping path, you'll be able to modify the stroke or fill at any time.

1 *A star **shape** with a solid color fill.*

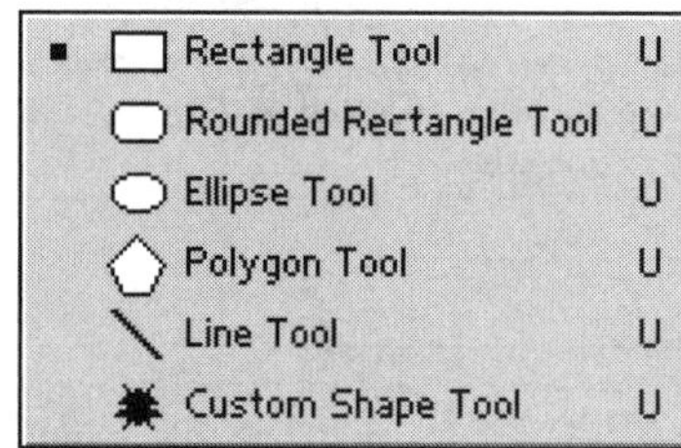

2 *The **shape** tools.*

3 *The **Custom shape** tool options bar.*

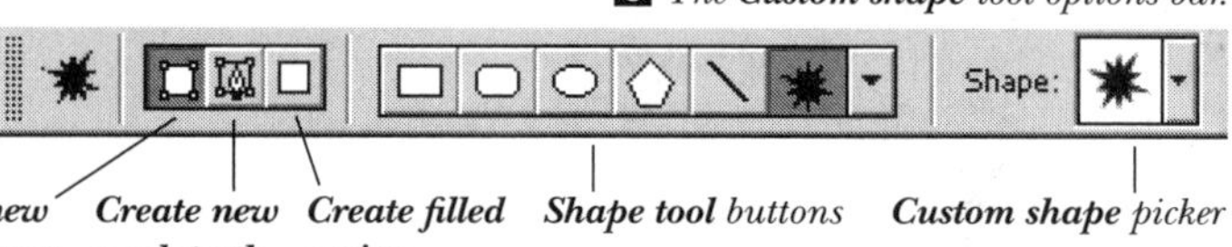

Photoshop versus ImageReady

The pen tools, Polygon tool, and Custom Shape tool are only available in Photoshop—not in ImageReady.

In Photoshop, multiple shapes can be drawn on the same shape layer and you can have them add to, subtract from, or intersect with each other by clicking the appropriate button on the options bar. In ImageReady, only one shape can be drawn per layer.

Shapes can be edited in Photoshop at any time. In ImageReady, shapes can only be transformed and moved, not edited.

1

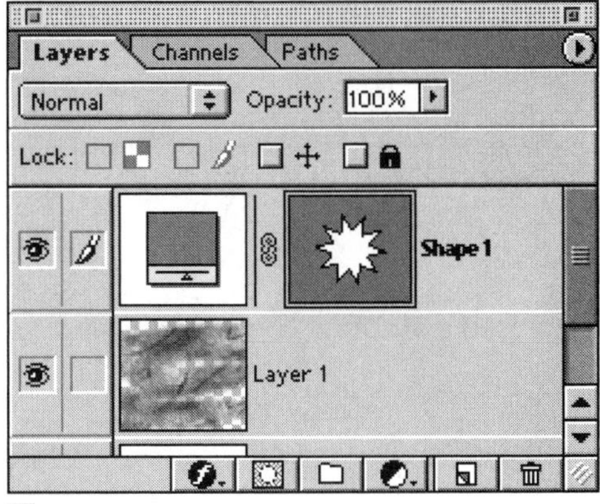

2

4. On the shape tool options bar:

   If you're using the Rounded Rectangle tool, choose a Radius value; for the Polygon tool, choose a number of Sides; for the Line tool, choose a Weight; and for the Custom Shape tool, choose a shape from the picker.
   and
   Click the Create new shape layer button. (If this button isn't available, it means an existing layer clipping path is selected; deselect that thumbnail first.)
   and
   Choose Layer Style, Mode and Opacity settings.

5. Drag in the image window to draw the shape. Alt-drag/Option-drag to draw from the shape's center. Shift-drag to constrain a rectangle to a square, an ellipse to a circle, or a line to a multiple of 45°. *Note:* In Windows, the draw-from-center function (Alt-dragging) may not work for the Custom Shape tool.

6. When the mouse is released, the shape will display **1**. A new Shape 1 layer will be listed on the Layers palette. It will have an adjustment layer icon thumbnail that controls its fill content and a layer clipping path thumbnail that controls its contour and location **2**.

The shapes tool can be used to create a temporary work path.

To create a work path:

1. Follow steps 1–4 starting on page 280.
2. Click the Create new work path button on the options bar **1**.
3. Drag in the image window to create the path shape **2**. Alt-drag/Option-drag to draw from the center. Shift-drag to constrain a rectangle to a square, an ellipse to a circle, or a line to a multiple of 45°.

   The new work path shape will be listed on the Paths palette **3**. To learn more about work paths, see page 260.

   Beware! Next time you use a shape tool with the Create new work option again, the existing work path will be replaced! To save the work path so it can't be replaced, double-click Work Path on the Paths palette, then click OK.

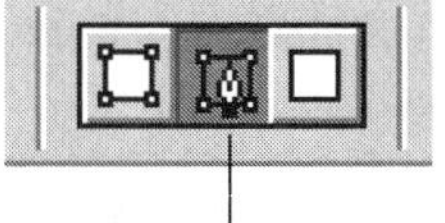

1 *Click the* ***Create new work path*** *button on the options bar.*

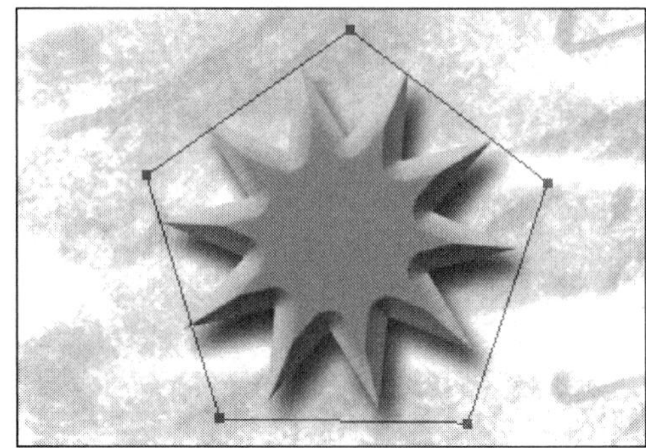

2 *A pentagonal* ***work path*** *is drawn.*

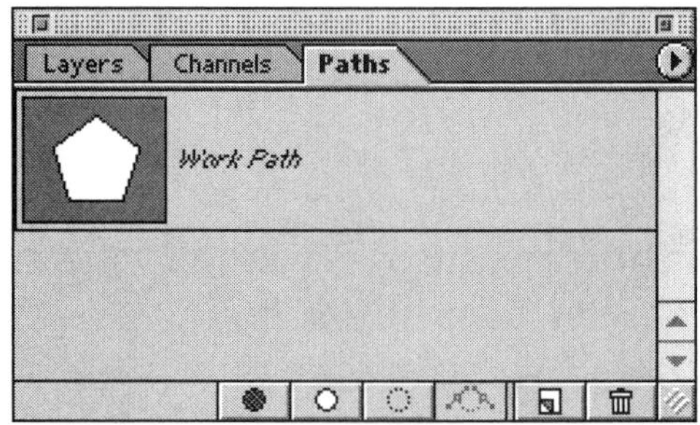

3 ***Work Path*** *appears on the Paths palette.*

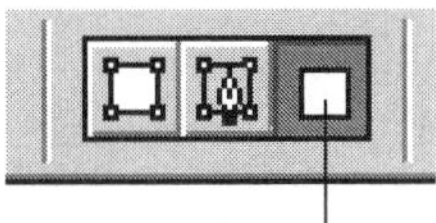

1 *Click the* ***Create filled region*** *button on the options bar.*

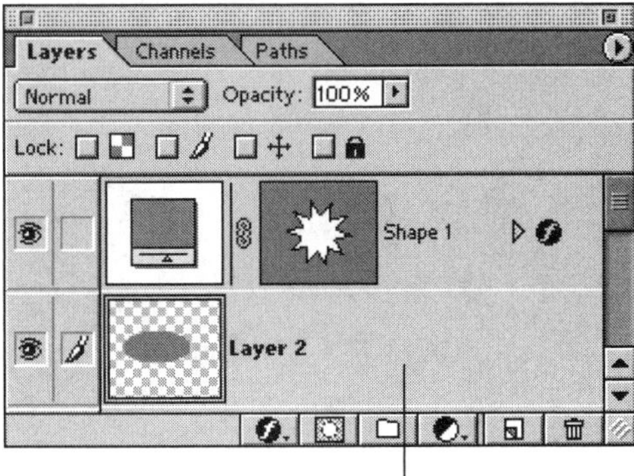

2 *On the Layers palette, the* ***Create filled region*** *shape displays as a normal rasterized layer, not as a shape layer.*

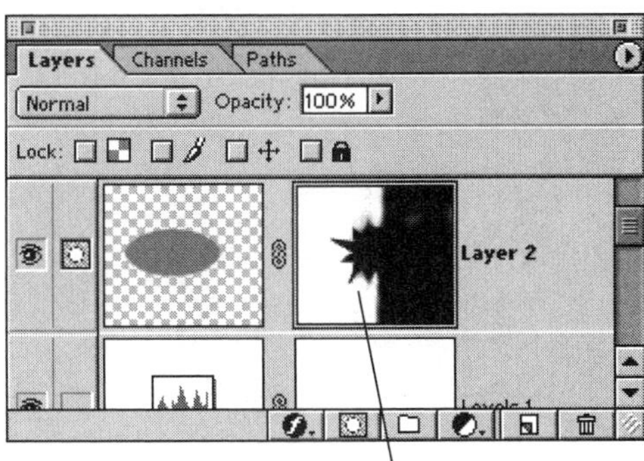

3 *Use the shape tool, with the Create Filled Region button clicked, to create a geometric area within an existing layer mask.*

6.0!

The shape tool can also be used to create a geometric pixel area on a layer. This is a quick way to produce a precise pixel shape without having to use a layer clipping path.

To create a geometric, rasterized pixel area:

1. Choose an image layer or create a new layer. A pixel shape cannot be created on a vector layer (shape or type layer).
2. Choose a Foreground color.
3. Choose a shape tool (U or Shift-U). Once a shape tool is chosen, you can then click a different shape tool button on the options bar.
4. On the options bar:

   Click the Create filled region button **1**.
   and
   If you're using the Rounded Rectangle tool, choose a Radius value; for the Polygon tool, choose a number of Sides; for the Line tool, choose a Weight; and for the Custom Shape tool, choose a shape from the picker.
   and
   Choose Layer Style, Mode and Opacity settings.
5. Drag across the image window to create the shape. A pixel area will be created **2**. Use brushes, editing tools, and filters, or whatever to modify the pixels.

TIP To create a geometric pixel area in a layer mask, click an existing layer mask thumbnail on the Layers palette, click the Create filled region button on the options bar, then drag **3**.

Geometric, Rasterized Pixel Area

6.0! This is how you can customize each shape tool so it behaves the way you want each time you use it.

To choose geometric options for a shape tool:

1. Choose a shape tool (U or Shift-U). If a shape tool is chosen, you can click a shape tool button on the options bar.
2. Click the Geometry Options arrowhead on the options bar **1**.
3. In the pop-up Options palette **2**, click Unconstrained, Square/Circle, Fixed Size, or Proportional. For Fixed Size or Proportional, enter a specific size in the W and H fields. Check From Center to have the tool draw from the center).
4. If you chose the Custom Shape tool, click the Custom Shape arrowhead **3**, then click a custom shape on the picker. Use the picker menu to load in other shape libraries.
5. Click the arrowhead again to close the Options palette or the picker.

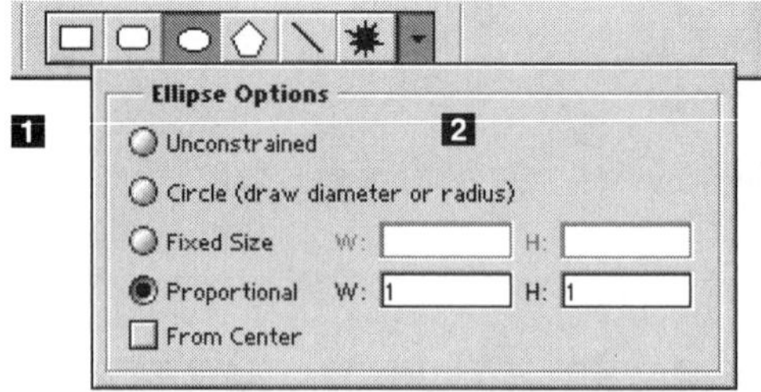

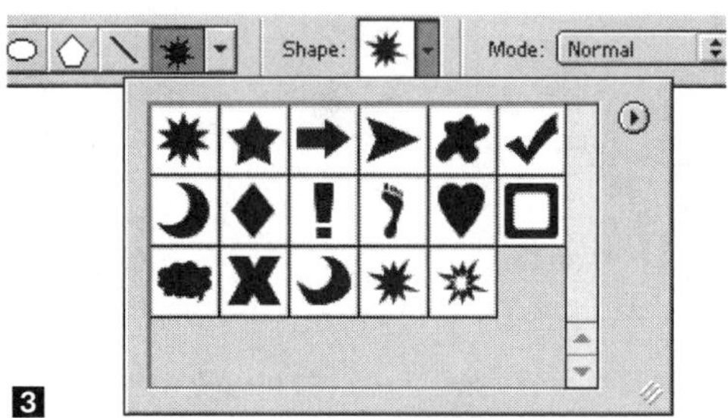

6.0! Since a shape layer contains vector data, you can modify the shape clipping path at any time; its crisp edge will stay crisp.

To reposition the layer clipping path of a shape layer:

1. Choose the Path Component Selection tool (A or Shift-A).
2. Click a shape in the image window.
   or
   Click a shape layer name on the Layers palette.
3. Drag the clipping path to a new location **4**. The layer clipping path thumbnail will update for the new position **5**.

TIP If you click a layer clipping path thumbnail on the Layers palette or even so much as pass the cursor over the thumbnail, the clipping path will become highlighted in the image window. The path won't be selected, though.

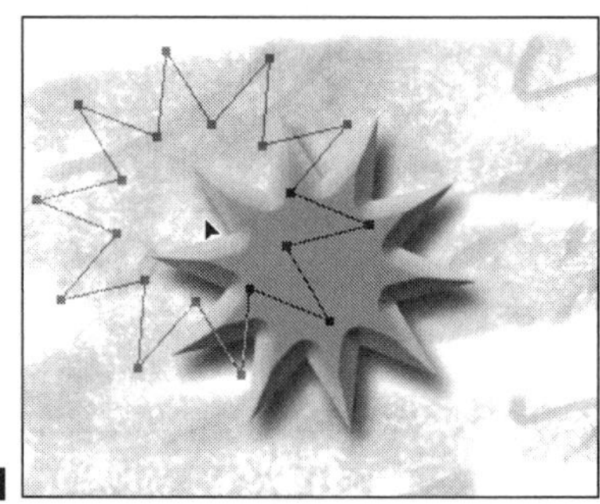

5 *The shape's layer clipping mask thumbnail reflects the new shape position. Compare with* **2** *on page 281.*

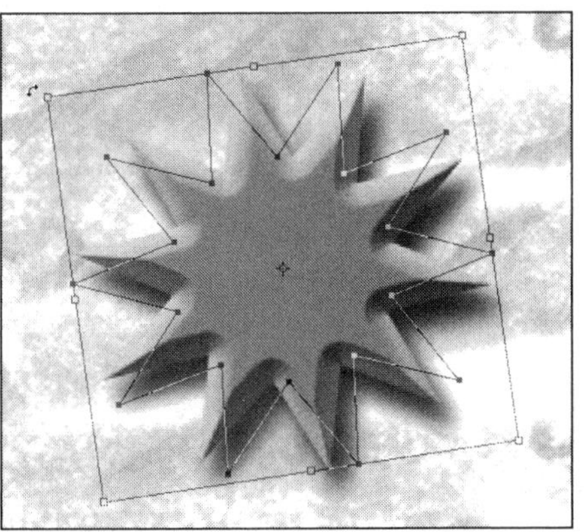

1 *Use the **Path Component Selection** tool (Show Bounding Box option checked) or the **Free Transform** command to display a layer clipping path's bounding box handles for a shape layer. Drag a handle to transform the shape's clipping path.*

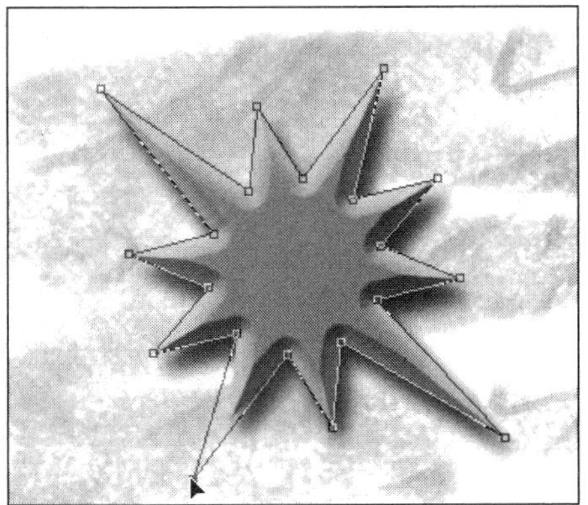

2 *Use the **Direct Selection** tool to drag an anchor point on the layer clipping path for a shape layer.*

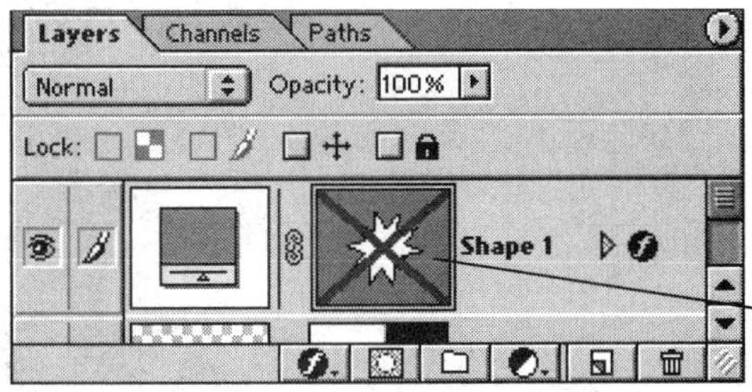

3 *This clipping path is temporarily **hidden**.*

To transform a shape layer: 6.0!

1. Choose the Path Component Selection tool (A or Shift-A).
2. Click a shape in the image window.
   or
   Click a shape layer name on the Layers palette.
3. Click the highlighted shape to display its anchor points (and its bounding box, too, if Show Bounding Box is checked on the options bar) **1**.
4. Follow the instructions on page 125 to transform the path.

To modify the contour of an existing shape layer: 6.0!

1. Choose the Direct Selection tool (A or Shift -A).
2. Click a shape in the image window.
   or
   Click a shape layer name on the Layers palette.
3. Click the edge of the highlighted shape to display its anchor points **2**.
4. Follow the instructions on pages 268–269 to reshape the path.

To temporarily hide the clipping path of a shape layer:

Shift-click the layer clipping path thumbnail on the shape layer (Layers palette). An "X" will appear over the thumbnail **3** and the entire layer's fill content will display. Shift-click the clipping path thumbnail again to remove the "X" and restore the clipping effect.

6.0!

To paste a path object from Illustrator into Photoshop as a shape layer:

1. In Illustrator, copy a vector object.
2. In Photoshop 6, choose Edit menu > Paste. In the Paste dialog box, click Shape Layer. Click OK **1**. The shape layer will be filled with the current foreground color, but it won't have a stroke. What you have pasted is the clipping path outline for the shape layer.

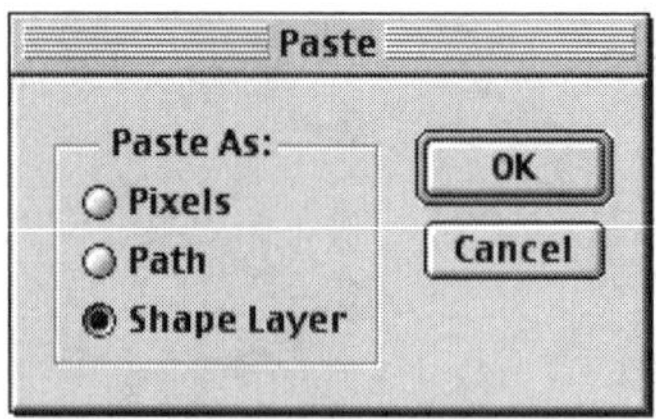

1

6.0!

To use the pathfinder options to add or subtract shapes from each other:

1. Create a shape layer.
2. Leave the layer clipping path for the new shape layer selected.
3. Make sure a shape tool is chosen.
4. Click one of the pathfinder buttons on the options bar (Add to shape area, Subtract from shape area, Intersect shape areas, Exclude overlapping shape areas) **2**.
5. Drag on top of the existing shape. A new shape path will be created that either extends or subtracts from the existing shape **3**.

TIP To reverse what is clipped and what is revealed by the clipping path, select the path with the Path Component Selection tool, then on the options bar, click the Subtract from shape area (second) button **4**–**5**. Click the Add to shape area (first) button to restore the original clipping setup.

2 *Click a* ***pathfinder*** *button. We chose Subtract from shape area.*

3 *The new shape path subtracts from (cuts out) the existing shape area.*

4

5

Solid color, pattern, or gradient

To change the fill contents of a shape to a gradient or pattern fill layer, or the command for an adjustment layer that uses the clipping path to define where the adjustment occurs, choose a command from the Layer menu > **Change Layer Contents** submenu.

1 *Create a **custom shape**.*

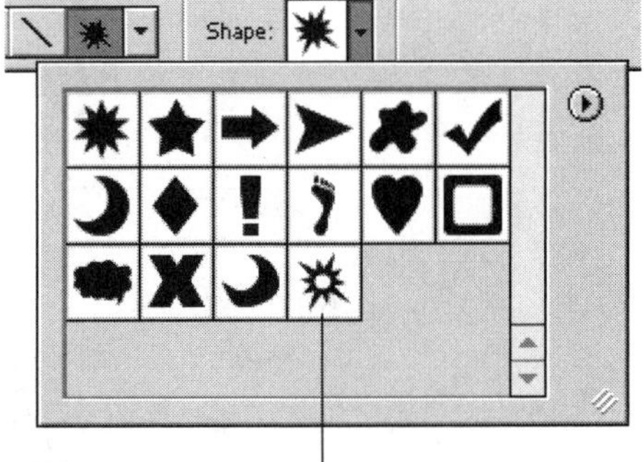

2 *The new shape appears on the **Custom Shape** picker.*

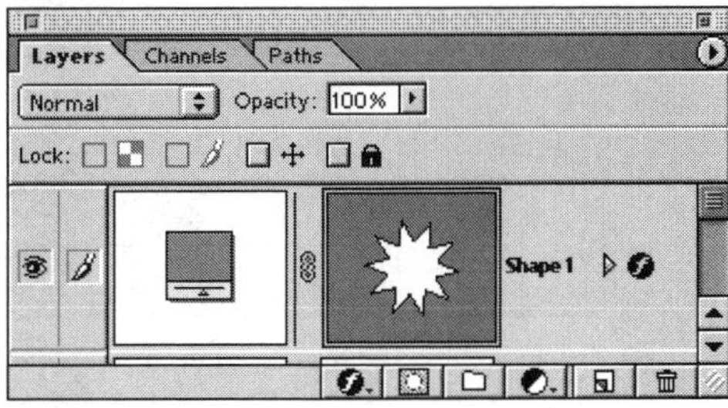

3 ***Shape layer** thumbnail.*

If you have altered the contour of a preset shape or pasted in a shape from Illustrator, you can then add that new shape to the custom shape picker so you can use it again. 6.0!

To add a shape to the custom shape picker:

1. Create a custom shape **1**.
   or
   Create a new shape layer from a pasted Illustrator object.
2. Click the shape layer name on the Layers palette.
3. Choose Edit menu > Define Custom Shape, enter a Name, then click OK.

   The new custom shape will appear on the custom shape picker **2**, and it will stay on the picker even if you exit/quit and relaunch Photoshop. It will be removed from the picker, however, if you load in a new library or reset the default custom shape library.

The fill contents of a shape layer can be changed at any time. 6.0!

To change the fill contents of a shape layer:

1. Double-click the shape layer thumbnail on the Layers palette (it has a slider icon) **3**.
   or
   Choose a shape layer, then choose Layer menu > Layer Contents Options.
2. Choose a new color from the Color Picker, then click OK.

In order to perform pixel edits on a shape layer, such as painting or a filter application, or to change a shape's clipping path into a (pixel) layer mask, it has to be rasterized first.

To rasterize a shape layer:

1. Choose a shape layer **1**.
2. Choose Layer menu > Rasterize:

   Shape to convert the shape layer into a filled pixel shape on a transparent layer, with no layer clipping path. Painting and editing can now occur on the layer **2**.

   Fill Content to convert the shape layer's fill content into a pixel area clipped by the existing layer clipping path. Painting and editing can now occur on the layer **3**.

   Layer Clipping Path to convert the layer clipping path into a pixel-based layer mask in the exact same shape and position. The fill content is still an editable solid color fill. The layer mask can be repositioned within the layer **4**.

   Layer produces the same results as the Shape option above **5**.

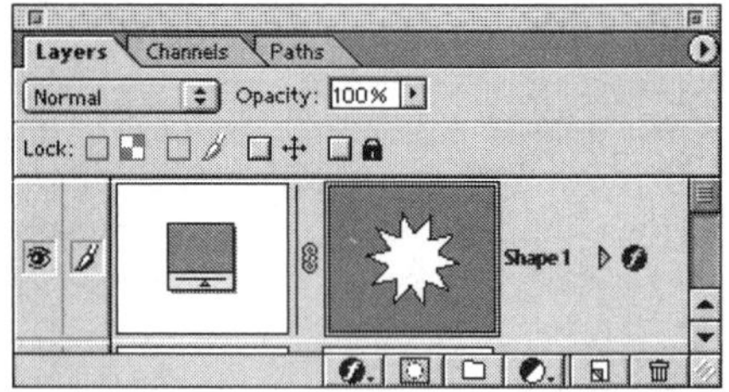

1 *The original shape layer on the Layers palette.*

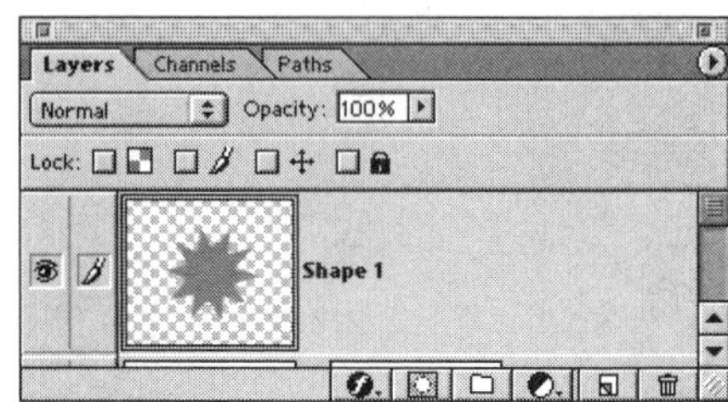

2 *The Rasterize > **Shape** command removes the clipping path.*

3 *The Rasterize > **Fill Content** command converts the adjustable fill into a normal pixel area.*

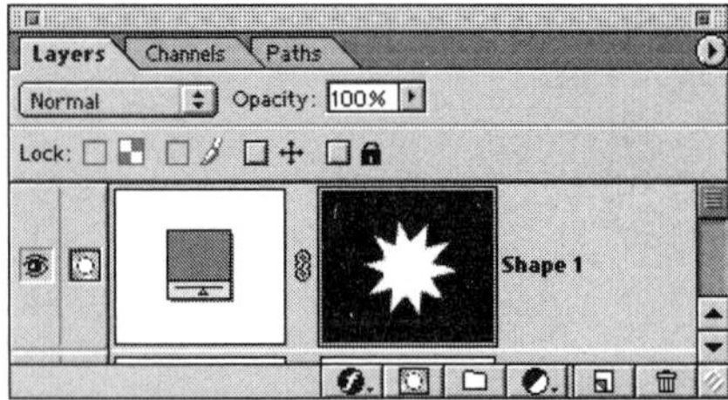

4 *The Rasterize > **Layer Clipping Path** command converts the layer clipping path into a layer mask.*

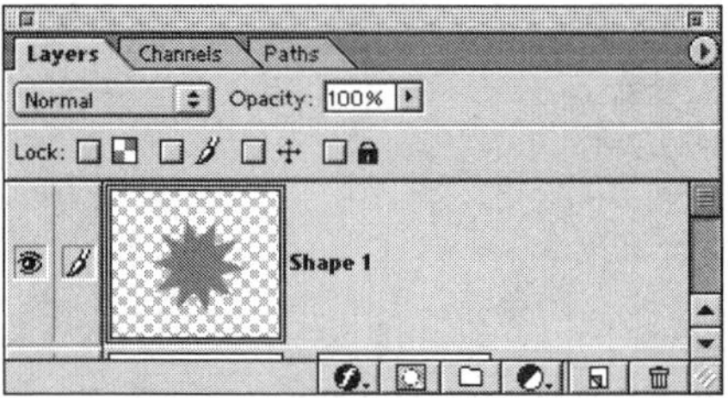

5 *The Rasterize > **Layer** command removes the clipping path (as in **2**, above).*

TYPE 17

IN THIS CHAPTER you'll learn how to create, transform, move, and warp an editable type layer; change its character and paragraph attributes; rasterize a type layer into pixels; screen back type or screen back an image behind type; fill type with imagery using Paste Into or a clipping group of layers; create fading type; create and use a type selection; add type to a spot color channel; and create a type mask for an adjustment layer.

Now it's vector! 6.0!

Type created in Photoshop 6 outputs with **crisp**, defined edges because the program uses the typeface's vector outlines when creating and modifying editable type—even though it still consists of pixels in the same resolution as the overall image. Photoshop 6 type output will always be sharp and resolution independent, whether printed to a PostScript printer or saved in PDF or EPS format.

What's more, in Photoshop 6 you can compose and edit type **directly** on the image, and each individual character can be assigned its own typographic attributes (e.g., font, size) either as you enter it or after it's created.

Creating type 6.0!

Different kinds of type

When type is created in Photoshop using the Type tool, it automatically appears on its own layer. Its attributes (e.g., font, style, point size, color, kerning, tracking, leading, alignment, and baseline shift) can be changed at any time. What's more, different attributes can be applied to different characters on the same **editable** type layer **1**. You can also transform it, apply layer effects to it, or change its blending mode or opacity.

What can't be done to an editable type layer? You can't apply filters or paint strokes to it or fill it with a gradient or a pattern. In order to apply those kinds of effects, you have to **rasterize** the type layer into pixels (Layer menu > Rasterize > Type) **2**. But you can't have your cake and eat it. Once type is rasterized, its typographic attributes (e.g., font, style) can't be changed. (Type placed from Adobe Illustrator into Photoshop is rasterized into pixels automatically.)

All type, editable and otherwise, is created using the Type tool, the Layer menu, the Character palette **3**, the Paragraph palette, and the options bar **4**.

Vector

1 *This is sharp, **editable**, vector type.*

2 *This type was **rasterized**, and then **filters** and **layer effects** were applied to it.*

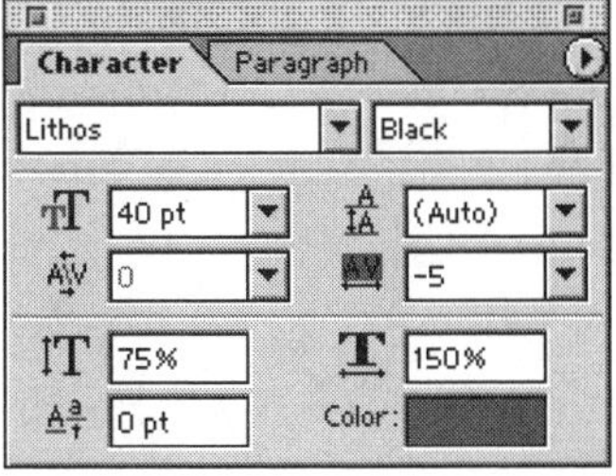

3 *Photoshop 6 introduces the **Character** and **Paragraph** palettes.*

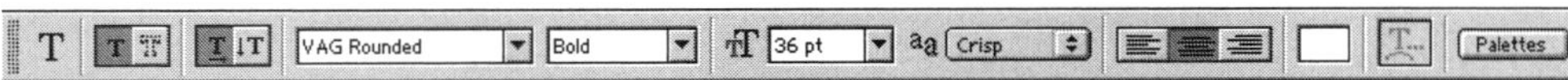

4 *The **options bar** for the **Type** tool.*

(Continued on the following page)

6.0!

You can also use the Type tool to create a **type selection** on the active layer. You can then convert the type selection into a **layer mask** (see page 242), or save it as an **alpha channel**, or save it as a **shape layer** for later use (see page 280).

Editable type (as opposed to type that is created as a selection on the active layer) automatically appears on its own layer, and it can be edited, moved, transformed, restacked, or otherwise modified without affecting any other layer. In Photoshop 6, you can be very casual about where you position type initially and which typographic attributes you choose for it since it's so easy to edit afterwards.

Note: Type that's created in a Bitmap, Indexed Color, or Multichannel image will appear on the Background, not on a layer, and it cannot be edited.

To create an editable type layer:

1. Choose the Type tool (T).
2. Click the "Create a text layer" button on the options bar **1**.
3. Click to define an insertion point for point type (see the sidebar at right).
   or
   Drag a marquee to define the boundaries of the bounding box for text to fit into for paragraph type.
4. On the options bar, do any of the following:

   Click the **Horizontally orient text** or **Vertically orient text** button.

   Choose a **font** family **2**.

   Choose a font **style**.

   Choose or enter a font **size**.

   Choose an **Anti-aliasing method**: Crisp (sharp edges), Strong (heavier edges), and Smooth (smoothest). Anti-aliasing gently smooths the edges of small to moderate size type by introducing partially transparent pixels along its edges.

Point or paragraph

When you click in the image window to create type using the Type tool, you are creating **point** type. This kind of type will keeps on going, disappearing off the edge of the image, until you type a return. Use point type if you want to control hyphenation and line breaks manually in a few lines of text.

When you drag in the image window with the Type tool to define an area for type to fit into, you are creating **paragraph** type. Paragraph type is designed for larger text blocks. You can choose between two algorithms for paragraph type—**Adobe Single-line Composer** and **Adobe Every-line Composer**—which control how Photoshop flows type to the next line when the type reaches the edge of the text bounding box. The differences between these two algorithms are subtle, but you may find them useful.

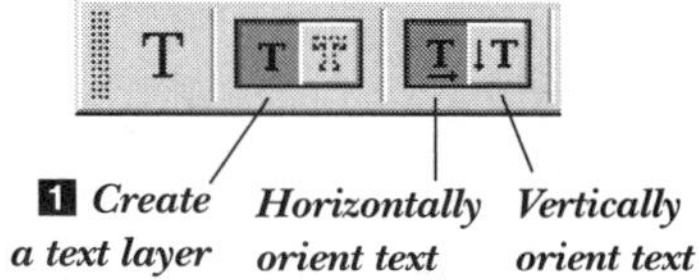

1 *Create a text layer*

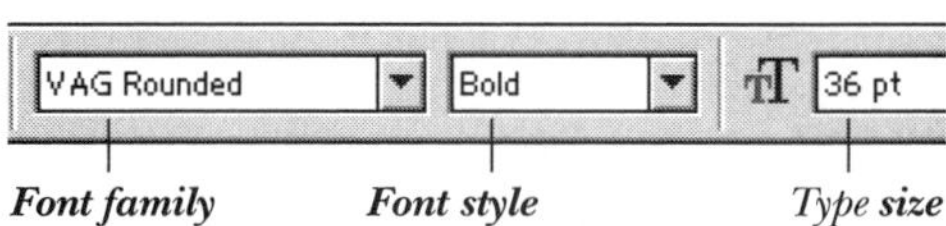

2 *The left side of the **Type** options bar.*

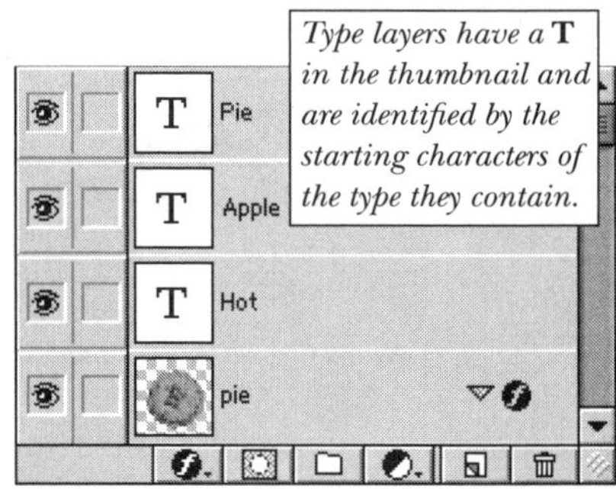

3 *For maximum flexibility, place individual words or characters on separate layers so they can be moved around independently.*

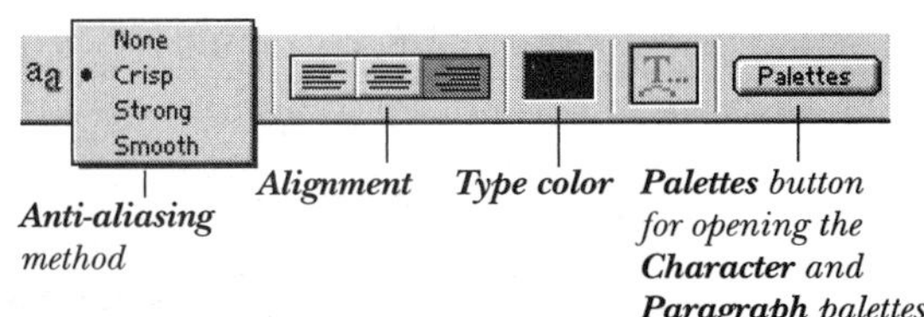

1 *The right side of the **Type** options bar.*

With anti-aliasing off (None), type will have jagged edges **1**–**5**.

Click an **alignment** button to align point type relative to its original insertion point or to align paragraph type to the left edge, right edge, or center of the text bounding box **6**.

Choose a **color** for the type by clicking the swatch on the options bar, then choosing a color from the Color Picker (or by using the Swatches palette or Colors palette).

Click the **Palettes** button to open the Character and Paragraph palettes and adjust those settings (you'll learn more about those palettes throughout this chapter).

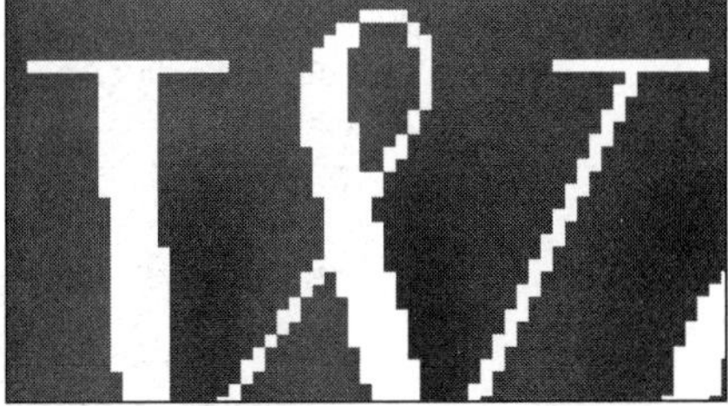

2 *Anti-aliased **None**.*

5. Type the text into the image window. *Beware!* The Save command is not available when the pointer is in a text block.
6. Press Enter (on the keypad) or click the ✓ on the options bar to accept the new text layer. (To cancel, press Esc or click the ✕.)

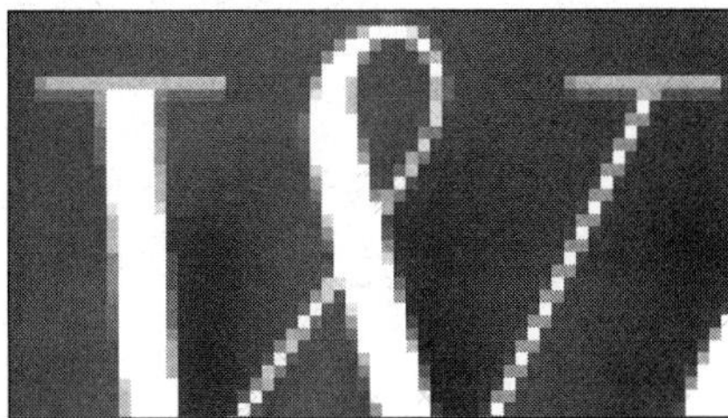

3 *Anti-aliased **Crisp**.*

TIP Photoshop initializes all the currently open fonts each time it's launched. If launching seems slow and you have a lot of fonts open, try closing some of the fonts you're not using—it should help speed things up.

TIP Each time you use the Type tool, a new layer is created. If you tend to create type by trial and error, keep this in mind; be sure to delete any type layers you don't need.

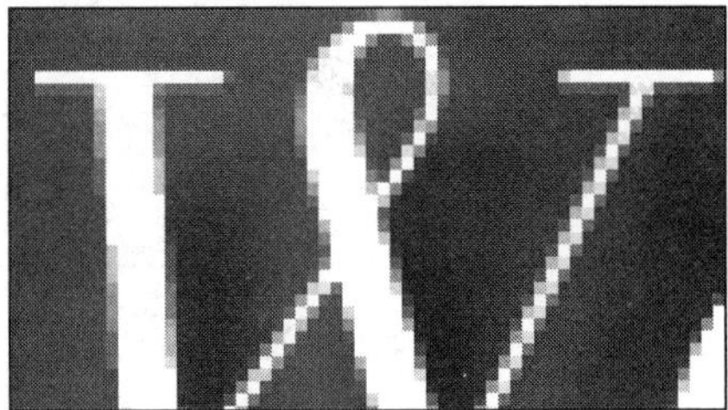

4 *Anti-aliased **Strong**.*

Align left

Align Right

Center

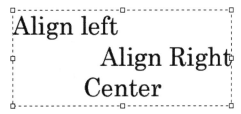

6 *The **alignment** buttons control where paragraph type is positioned within its bounding box (or where point type is positioned relative to the insertion point).*

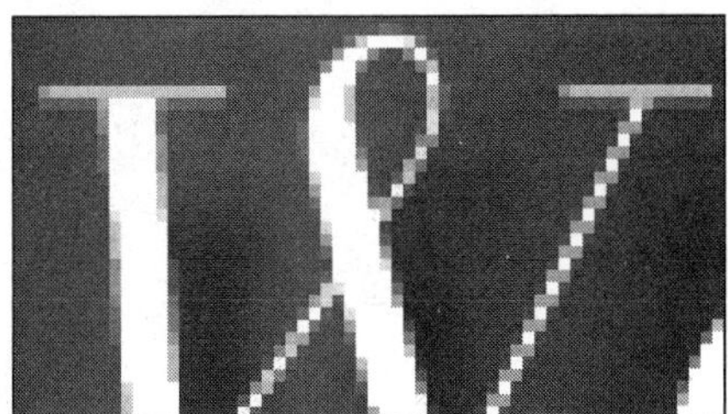

5 *Anti-aliased **Smooth**.*

6.0!

Editing text

To edit text, you need to select it. You can select a single character, a word, or all the characters on the same type layer. You can also select the bounding box for a whole block of text.

To select a whole block of text:

1. Choose the Move tool.
2. Check Show Bounding Box on the options bar.
3. Click the type layer name on the Layers palette. The text's bounding box will display.

TIP To transform text using its bounding box, see page 126.

To select all or some characters on a type layer:

Choose the Type tool (T), click in the type to create an insertion point, then drag across one or more characters to select them. Or double-click a word to select the whole word or triple-click a line of text to select the whole line.

or

With any tool selected, double-click the T icon for the type layer on the Layers palette. All the text on that layer will become selected and the Type tool will be chosen automatically.

Note: After performing the text edits, to take the text tool out of edit mode and commit to the editing changes, click the ☑ on the options bar; or press Enter on the keypad; or click any other tool; or choose a different layer.

(To cancel the editing changes, click the ☒ on the options bar or press Esc.)

TIP To apply layer effects to, or edit layer effects on, a type layer, double-click the layer name.

Selecting type with the Type tool

Select **text string**	Press and drag. Or click at beginning of the text string, then Shift-click at the end.
Select **word**	Double-click
Select **line**	Triple-click
Select **paragraph**	Quadruple-click
Select **all**	Ctrl-A/Cmd-A, quintuple-click in the text, or double-click the thumbnail in the Layers palette.

Selecting Text

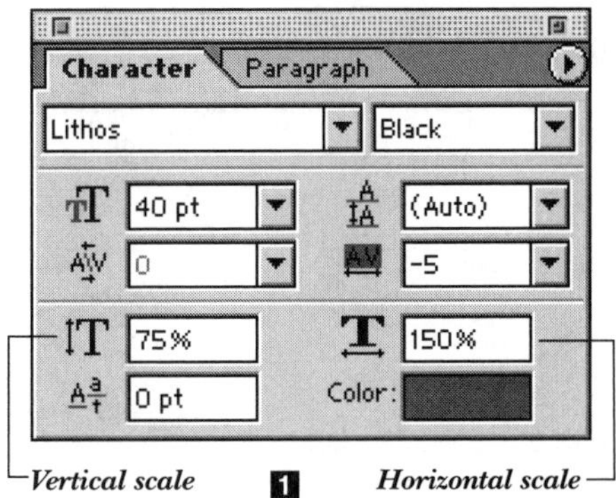

1

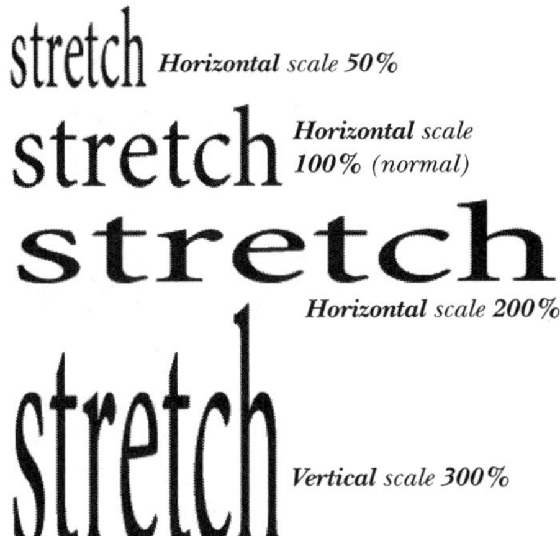

2 *Type can be* ***scaled*** *horizontally, vertically, or uniformly.*

Note: Use the Horizontal scale or Vertical scale commands (discussed below) only if you want to distort your characters (stretch or shorten them). To scale your characters uniformly, follow the second set of instructions on this page or select the characters you want to scale and change the font size using the Character palette. 6.0!

To scale selected characters:

1. On the Layers palette, click the layer that contains the text you want to scale.
2. Open the Character palette. You can do this via the Window menu or by choosing the Type tool (T) and then clicking the Palettes button on the options bar.
3. *Optional:* Choose the Type tool (T), then select the characters you want to scale. Otherwise, all the characters in the layer will be scaled.
4. Change the Vertical and/or Horizontal scale percentage on the Character palette **1**–**2**. If you didn't highlight any text for step 3 and you entered a value in either field (as opposed to choosing a value from either pop-up menu), press Enter/Return.

To scale all the text on a layer: 6.0!

1. Choose the Move tool.
2. Check Show Bounding box on the options bar.
3. Click the type layer name on the Layers palette.
4. Drag a corner handle to scale both the height and width or drag a side handle to scale just the height or width. Pause for redraw. Shift-drag to preserve the type's proportions.
5. To commit to the scale change, click the ☑ on the options bar or double-click the text block. The bounding box will remain visible.

   (To cancel the scale change, click the ☒ on the options bar or press Esc.)

Scaling Text

To adjust the spacing between a pair of characters (kern):

1. On the Layers palette, choose a text layer.
2. Click the Palettes button on the options bar to open the Character palette, if it isn't already open.
3. Choose Metrics from the Kerning pop-up menu to apply the font's built-in kerning (this is called Auto Kern in other applications). It's important to do this first, before applying manually kerning.
4. Choose the Type tool (T), then click to create an insertion point between two characters.
5. Choose a value from the Kerning pop-up menu or enter a value in the field **1**–**2** Use a negative value to move the characters closer together or a positive value to spread them apart.
   or
   Hold down Alt/Option and press the left or right arrow.

To adjust the spacing for a whole string of characters (track):

1. On the Layers palette, choose a text layer.
2. *Optional:* Choose the Type tool (T), then select the text you want to apply tracking to. Otherwise, tracking will affect all the type on the layer.
3. Click the Palettes button on the options bar to open the Character palette, if it isn't already open.
4. Choose a value from the Tracking pop-up menu or enter a value in the field **3**. Use a negative value to move the characters closer together or a positive value to spread them apart.

TIP If you use Alt/Option and the left or right arrow keys with the Move tool selected, you'll create copies of the whole text block.

TIP If you're creating type for the Web, don't track your letters too close together—it will be hard to read.

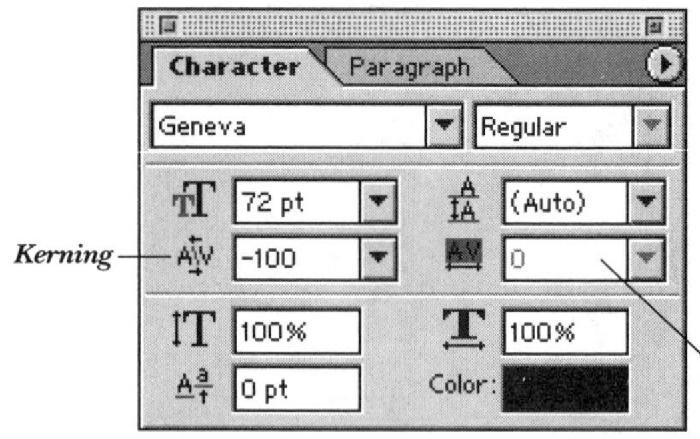

1 *The **Character** palette has some features that aren't found on the options bar.*

Kern

Kern

2 *Use a negative **kerning** value (-100, in this case) to tighten the **spacing between characters**.*

TRACKING TIPS

Tracking can help or impair readability, depending on how high the tracking values are. Try not to overdo it!

3 *We like to spread out little bits of text, as in the headline in this illustration, but not whole paragraphs.*

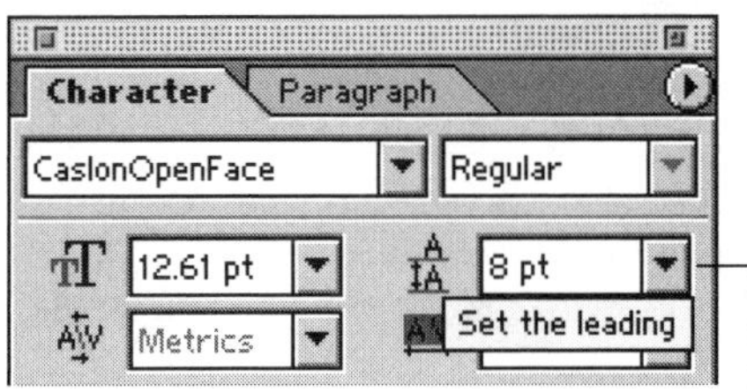

1 *The **Leading** area on the **Character** palette.*

It will be well, however, always to bear in mind, that cake of every sort is to be partaken of as a luxury, not eaten for a full meal. Those who attend evening parties several times a week, can hardly take too small a quantity of the sweet and rich preparations. Many a young lady loses her appetite bloom and health by indulgence in these tempting but pernicious delicacies; and dyspeptic complaints frequently are aggravated, if not originated, by the absurd fashion of making our evening circles places for eating and drinking, rather than social and mental enjoyment. They manage these things better in Paris. —*Sara Josepha Hale, 1841*

It will be well, however, always to bear in mind, that cake of every sort is to be partaken of as a luxury, not eaten for a full meal. Those who attend evening parties several times a week, can hardly take too small a quantity of the sweet and rich preparations. Many a young lady loses her appetite bloom and health by indulgence in these tempting but pernicious delicacies; and dyspeptic complaints frequently are aggravated, if not originated, by the absurd fashion of making our evening circles places for eating and drinking, rather than social and mental enjoyment. They manage these things better in Paris. —*Sara Josepha Hale, 1841*

2 *The type in boths paragraphs illustrated above has the same point size, but different **leading** values.*

6.0!

Leading is the space that separates each line of text from the one above it. Each character can have its own leading value; the highest value in a line controls that line. Consequently, if you apply different leading values to different lines of paragraph text and then edit the text in some way that causes it to reflow, the spacing between lines may change.

We can't guarantee that the text you're creating will be interesting, but using an adequate amount of leading between lines of text is essential for readability—even if it eats up more space on the page. Don't tire your reader before they've gleaned your pearls of wisdom!

Caution: It's too soon to tell whether large amounts of type will output properly from Photoshop. Do the bulky stuff in a layout or Web design program.

To adjust leading in horizontal type:

1. On the Layers palette, choose the layer that contains the text you want to apply leading values to.
2. *Optional:* Highlight the line or lines of text that you want to apply leading values to. To apply leading to point type, select the whole line. If you don't highlight text, the whole layer will be affected.
3. Choose or enter a Leading value on the Character palette **1**–**2**.

TIP Auto leading is calculated as a percentage of the font size. The ratio is set in the Justification dialog box which is opened from the Paragraph palette menu. The default value is 120% of the font size. The Auto leading amount for 30pt. type, for example, would be 36pt.

TIP To adjust the vertical spacing between characters in vertical type, highlight the characters you want to adjust, then change the Tracking value on the Character palette. It makes sense when you try it.

6.0!

To shift selected characters above or below the normal baseline:

1. On the Layers palette, click the layer that contains the text you want to shift.
2. *Optional:* Choose the Type tool (T), then select the characters you want to shift. Otherwise, all the characters on the layer will be shifted.
3. Open the Character palette.
4. Enter a value in the Baseline shift field **1** on the Character palette. Use a positive value to shift characters above the normal baseline; use a negative value to shift characters below the baseline **2**. If you didn't highlight any text for step 2, press Enter/Return.

6.0!

To use the controls on the Character palette menu:

1. Select the type to be modified or select a type layer to modify the whole layer.
2. From the Character palette menu **3**, choose any of the following:

   Faux Bold to simulate the bold style or **Faux Italic** to simulate the italic style. This is not available for warped text.

   All Caps or **Small Caps** to convert type set normally to those modes. Small Caps works only with uppercase/lowercase text.

   Superscript or **Subscript** to reduce the size of the type and raise or drop it relative to the normal baseline.

   Underline and/or **Strikethrough**.

   Ligatures or **Old Style** (applies only to OpenType font character sets that contain the selected characters).

   No Break (option checked) to have Photoshop keep the selected characters on a single line wherever possible.

   Fractional Widths to have Photoshop use fractions of pixels for type spacing for optimum appearance. Unchecking this option may improve readability for online applications that use small type. The Fractional Widths setting applies to the entire layer.

Ersatz

If you're using a font for which no actual bold (or italic) font is installed on your system and you turn on the **Faux Bold** (or **Faux Italic**) option, Photoshop whips up an ersatz bold (or italic) version of that font for you. Type purists (ourselves included) will notice that the shape or slant of the faux style doesn't quite match that of the authentic font.

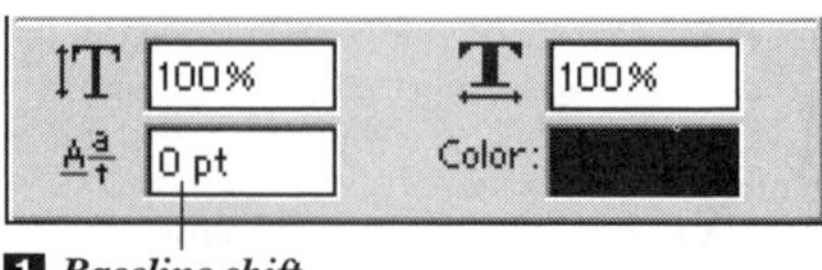

1 ***Baseline shift.***

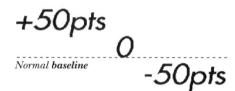

+50pts

0

Normal **baseline**

-50pts

2 *Use a positive or negative **Baseline** value to **shift** selected characters upward or downward.*

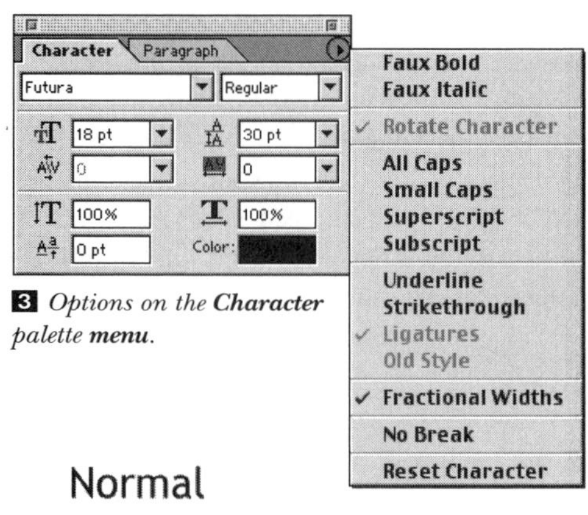

3 *Options on the **Character** palette **menu**.*

Normal

Faux Bold Superscript²

Faux Italic Subscript₃

ALL CAPS Underline

SMALL CAPS ~~Strikethrough~~

Use the Layer menu > Type > Horizontal or Vertical command to change the orientation of horizontal or vertical type.

To change type orientation:

1. On the Layers palette, choose the horizontal or vertical type layer whose orientation you want to change **1**.
2. Choose Layer menu > Type > Horizontal or Vertical **2**. You will probably need to reposition the type after applying either command.

TIP To rotate vertical type a different way, double-click its layer thumbnail, highlight the characters you want to rotate, then choose Rotate from the Character palette menu to check or uncheck the command **3**. This command is not available for horizontal type.

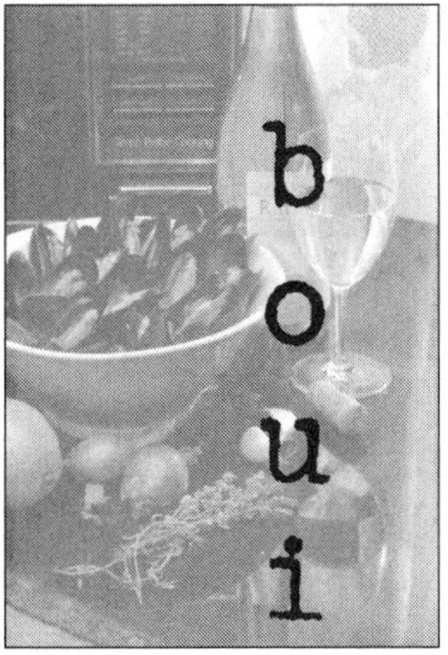

1 *The original* ***vertical*** *type.*

2 *The vertical type after choosing Layer menu > Type >* ***Horizontal****.*

3 *The original vertical type (figure* **1***) after choosing the* ***Rotate Character*** *command on the Character palette menu.*

6.0! Using paragraph settings

If you create text as paragraph type rather than point type, Photoshop offers you a variety of formatting options. When you forgo the manual control you have with point text, you get a pretty sophisticated automatic layout tool in exchange.

The Paragraph palette includes settings for justification and alignment as well as for indents and paragraph spacing. The palette menu allows you to fine tune those options.

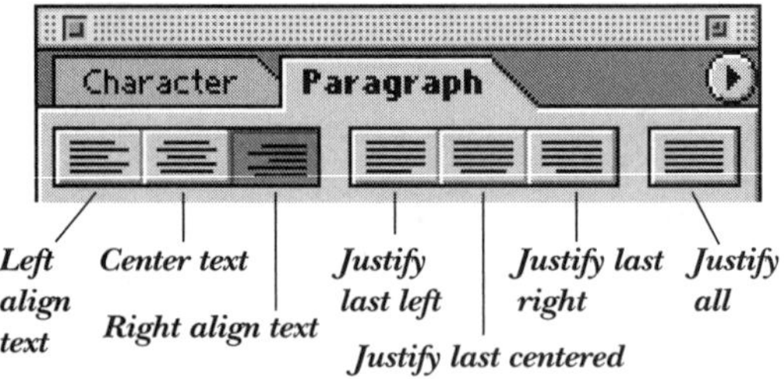

1 *The **alignment** and **justification** buttons at the top of the **Paragraph** palette.*

To set paragraph alignment and justification:

1. On the Layers palette, click the text layer you want to modify.
2. If you want to modify all the paragraphs in the layer, don't select any text.
   or
   To modify one or more paragraphs, choose the Type tool (T), then click in one paragraph or select a series of consecutive paragraphs.
3. If the Paragraph palette isn't open, click the Palettes button on the options bar, then click the Paragraph tab.
4. Click an alignment and/or justification button at the top of the palette **1**:

   The buttons in the first group, **Left align text, Center text,** and **Right align text,** align type to one edge of the text bounding box **2**.

   The second group of buttons, **Justify last left, Justify last centered,** and **Justify last right**, justifies the type, forcing all but the last line to fill the space between the margins **3**.

   The last button, **Justify all,** forces *all* the lines to fill the space, even the last line.
5. Check the Hyphenate box at the bottom of the palette to enable automatic hyphenation. This is essential for justified text, where it helps to eliminate large, unsightly gaps between words.

Left align text

Whoever you are holding me now in hand
Whoever you are holding me now in hand,
Without one thing all will be useless,
I give you fair warning before you attempt me further,
I am not what you supposed, but far different...

Center text

Whoever you are holding me now in hand
Whoever you are holding me now in hand,
Without one thing all will be useless,
I give you fair warning before you attempt me further,
I am not what you supposed, but far different..

Right align text

Whoever you are holding me now in hand
Whoever you are holding me now in hand,
Without one thing all will be useless,
I give you fair warning before you attempt me further,
I am not what you supposed, but far different..
Walt Whitman

2 *Paragraph **alignment** options.*

Justify last left — Civilization is the encouragement of differences. Civilization thus becomes a synonym of democracy. Force, violence, pressure, or compulsion with a view to conformity, is both uncivilized and undemocratic. —*Mohandas Gandhi*

Justify last centered — Civilization is the encouragement of differences. Civilization thus becomes a synonym of democracy. Force, violence, pressure, or compulsion with a view to conformity, is both uncivilized and undemocratic. —*Mohandas Gandhi*

Justify last right — Civilization is the encouragement of differences. Civilization thus becomes a synonym of democracy. Force, violence, pressure, or compulsion with a view to conformity, is both uncivilized and undemocratic. —*Mohandas Gandhi*

Justify all — Civilization is the encouragement of differences. Civilization thus becomes a synonym of democracy. Force, violence, pressure, or compulsion with a view to conformity, is both uncivilized and undemocratic. —*Mohandas Gandhi*

3 *Paragraph **justification** options.*

Good values

To enter a value in a non-default unit, type a unit after the value. Use **in** for inches, **pt** for points, **mm** for millimeters, **cm** for centimeters, **px** for pixels, and **pica** for picas. The value will be converted automatically to the current unit chosen in Edit menu > Preferences > Units & Rulers > Units: **Type**.

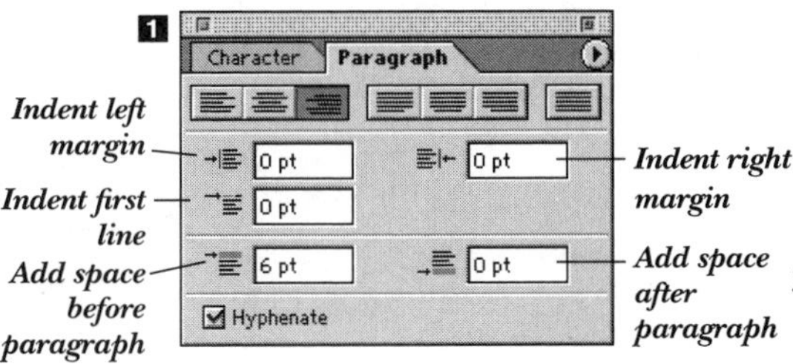

Civilization is the encouragement of differences. Civilization thus becomes a synonym of democracy. Force, violence, pressure, or compulsion with a view to conformity, is both uncivilized and undemocratic. —*Mohandas Gandhi*

2 *Indents of 0 (zero).*

Civilization is the encouragement of differences. Civilization thus becomes a synonym of democracy. Force, violence, pressure, or compulsion with a view to conformity, is both uncivilized and undemocratic. —*Mohandas Gandhi*

3 ***Indented** 2 picas **right** and **left**.*

Civilization is the encouragement of differences. Civilization thus becomes a synonym of democracy. Force, violence, pressure, or compulsion with a view to conformity, is both uncivilized and undemocratic. —*Mohandas Gandhi*

4 ***Indent** 1p4 **first line**.*

Civilization is the encouragement of differences.

Civilization thus becomes a synonym of democracy.

Force, violence, pressure, or compulsion with a view to conformity, is both uncivilized and undemocratic.

5 ***Add space before paragraph**.*

6.0!

The paragraph indent and space between paragraph controls let you shape your paragraphs for improved readability.

To adjust paragraph indents and spacing:

1. On the Layers palette, click the text layer you want to modify.
2. If you want to modify all the paragraphs in the layer, don't select any text.
   or
   To modify one or more paragraphs, choose the Type tool (T), then click in one paragraph or select a series of consecutive paragraphs.
3. If the Paragraph palette isn't open, click the Palettes button on the options bar, then click the Paragraph tab.
4. Change the **Indent left margin, Indent right margin 1–3**, or **Indent first line** value **4**. Use an Indent first line value to make text more readable if you don't have room to add space between paragraphs. Don't combine an Indent first line value above zero with added space between paragraphs—it looks unprofessional. Use a combination of left and right indentation values to make a pull quote or bulleted list stand out.
   and/or
   Enter **Add space before paragraph 5** and **Add space after paragraph** values.

TIP When the Type tool is active, the paragraph bounding box displays for paragraph type, which you can reshape by moving any of its handles. To reshape the text box and distort the type, Ctrl-drag/Cmd-drag any of the handles (temporary Move tool).

These are some of the settings that can make the difference between okay-looking type and professional-looking type.

To fine tune paragraph settings:

From the palette menu at the top right of the Paragraph palette, choose any of the following:

Roman Hanging Punctuation to have Photoshop move punctuation marks that fall at the ends of lines outside the type bounding box.

Justification and **Hyphenation** adjust the limits within which the Photoshop algorithms can operate as they adjust text to optimize its appearance **1**–**2**. (In the Justification dialog box, you can also set the Auto Leading value as a percentage of the type size.)

Note: Enter a Glyph Scaling value above the default 100% in the Justification dialog box to allow Photoshop to adjust the widths of the characters (glyphs) in a line to optimize how the text fits inside the bounding box.

Adobe Single-line Composer **3** and **Adobe Every-line Composer** **4** evaluate potential word breaks (hyphenation) in a paragraph, factoring in letter and word spacing values, in an attempt to minimize hyphenation. The Adobe Single-line Composer does this line by line; the Adobe Every-line Composer does it by evaluating the appearance of the paragraph as a whole. Every-line Composer can change word breaks at the beginning of a paragraph in order to create more visually appealing word breaks toward the end of the paragraph. We love Every-line Composer!

(Reset Paragraph resets the paragraph menu options to their default settings.)

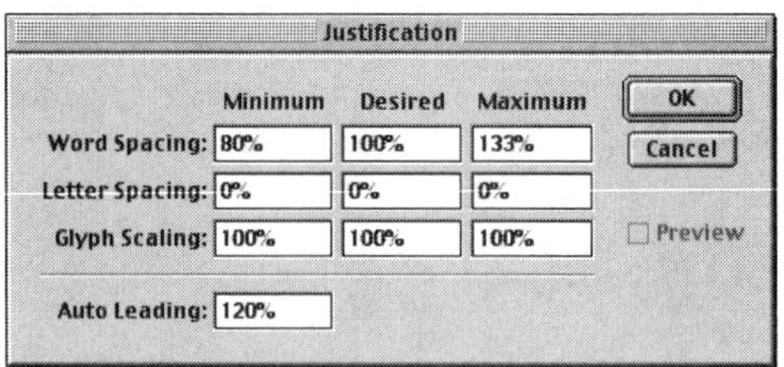

1 *In the **Justification** dialog box, choose **Minimum**, **Desired**, and **Maximum** values for adjusting line widths in justified text.*

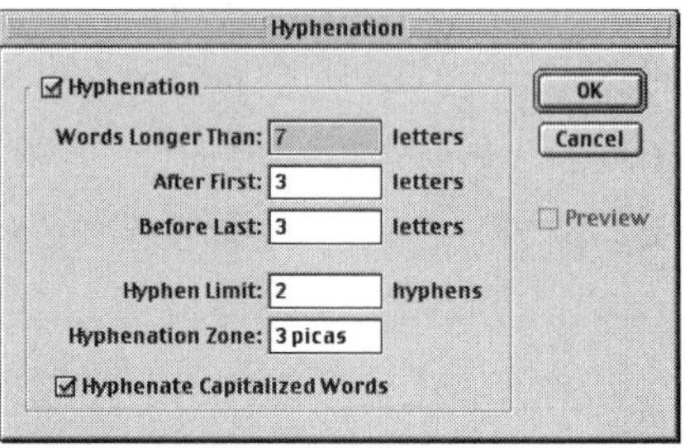

2 *In the **Hyphenation** dialog box, choose settings for breaks created in paragraph type.*

Civilization is the encouragement of differences. Civilization thus becomes a synonym of democracy. Force, violence, pressure, or compulsion with a view to conformity, is both uncivilized and undemocratic. — *Mohandas Gandhi*

3 ***Adobe Single-line Composer** goes through paragraphs line by line as it hyphenates words and adjusts the spacing between them.*

Civilization is the encouragement of differences. Civilization thus becomes a synonym of democracy. Force, violence, pressure, or compulsion with a view to conformity, is both uncivilized and undemocratic. —*Mohandas Gandhi*

4 ***Every-line Composer** considers the paragraph as a whole as it strives to optimize its appearance.*

The double sorwe of Troilus to tellen,
That was the king Priamus sone of Troye,
In lovinge, how his aventures fellen
Fro wo to wele, and after out of loye,

1 *The original type.*

The double sorwe of Troilus to tellen,
That was the king Priamus sone of Troye,
In lovinge, how his aventures fellen
Fro wo to wele, and after out of loye,

2 ***Scale.*** *Both the scale and skew transformations change the shape of the bounding box and* ***distort*** *the type itself. The type remains editable.*

3 ***Skew.***

4 ***Rotate.*** *Unlike scale and skew, the rotate transformation doesn't reshape the characters.*

The double sorwe
of Troilus to
tellen,
That was the king
Priamus sone of
Troye,

5 *The Type tool was used to transform the paragraph type* ***bounding box.*** *The characters don't change in shape or size.*

Special effects with type

First note a few restrictions. You can move, scale, rotate, and skew a paragraph bounding box on an editable type layer, but you have to rasterize a type layer in order to distort it or apply perspective commands to it. Second, you cannot transform a selection within a text layer. The Transform commands, discussed first, reshape the type as well as its bounding box.

A block of point or paragraph type can also be transformed using the Move tool (V). Check Show Bounding Box on the options bar, then choose a type layer on the Layers palette. The type's bounding box will display. Move any of the handles to transform the type using the same techniques as for Free Transform (see page 126).

And finally, a block of point or paragraph type can also be transformed by choosing the type layer on the Layers palette, then choosing Edit menu > Free Transform. Move the handles to transform the type. This method works with any tool selected (except the pen, shape, or path selection tools).

To transform a type bounding box and the type inside it:

Follow the instructions on page 126.

or

1. On the Layers palette, click the paragraph type layer you want to modify.
2. Choose the Type tool (T).
3. Click on the type in the image window.
4. Hold down Ctrl/Cmd and use the shortcuts for Free Transform (see page 126) **1**–**4**.

Follow these instructions if you want to modify the overall shape of a block of type without distorting the type characters.

To transform a type bounding box without transforming the type:

1. On the Layers palette, click the paragraph type layer you want to modify.

(Continued on the following page)

2. Choose the Type tool (T).
3. Click on the type in the image window.
4. Position the cursor over a handle, pause, then drag to scale the bounding box and reflow the type (5, previous page.)
   or
   Position the cursor outside one of the corners of the box (curved double-arrow pointer), then drag to rotate the box
   or
   Ctrl-drag/Cmd-drag in the box to move the whole type block.
5. To accept the changes, press Enter (keypad) or click the ✓ on the options bar. (To cancel, press Esc or click the ☒ on the options bar.)

6.0! Photoshop 6 also has a whole set of preset Warp Type transform functions that curve the bounding box and distort the type within it. Warped type remains editable.

To warp type on an editable layer:

1. On the Layers palette, click the text layer you want to warp.
2. To open the Warp Text dialog box 1:
   Choose Layer menu > Type > Warp Text.
   or
   Choose the Type tool (T), then click the Warp Text button on the options bar.
3. Choose from the Style pop-up menu.
4. Click Horizontal or Vertical as the basic orientation for the distortion.
5. Move the Bend, Horizontal Distortion, and Vertical Distortion sliders.
6. Click OK. The layer thumbnail will change to show that the text is warped 2–3.

TIP To scale or reshape warped type to make it fit into a specific area of a composition, choose the warped type layer, choose the Move tool (Show Bounding Box option checked), then reshape the bounding box.

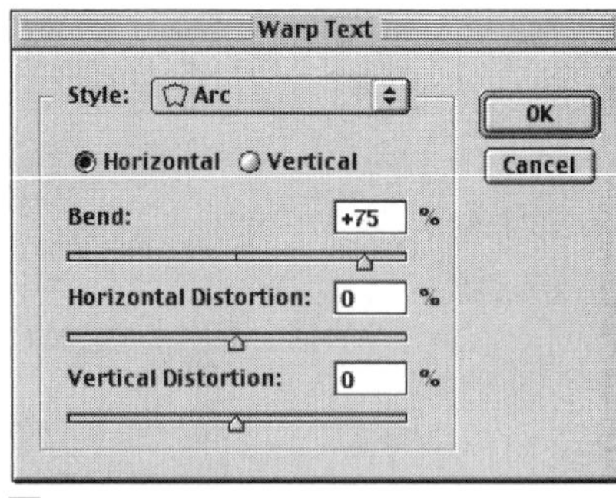

1 *The **Warp Text** dialog box.*

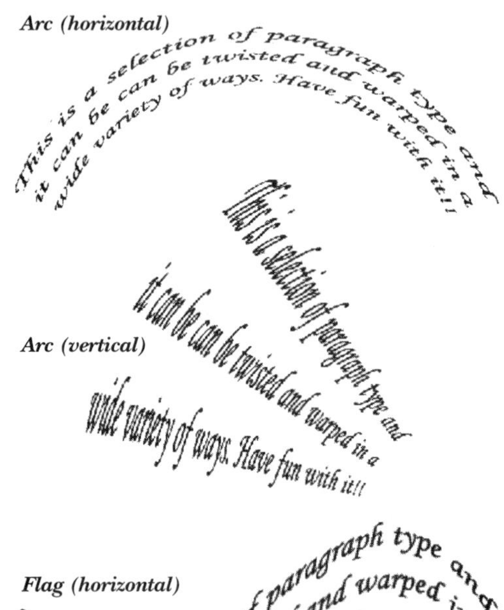

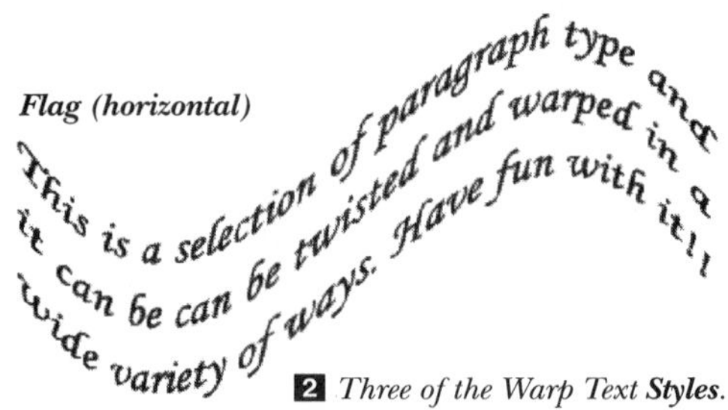

2 *Three of the Warp Text **Styles**.*

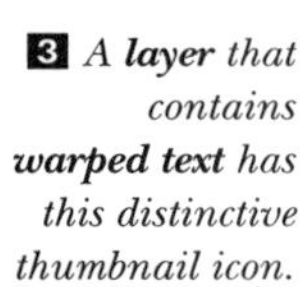

3 *A **layer** that contains **warped text** has this distinctive thumbnail icon.*

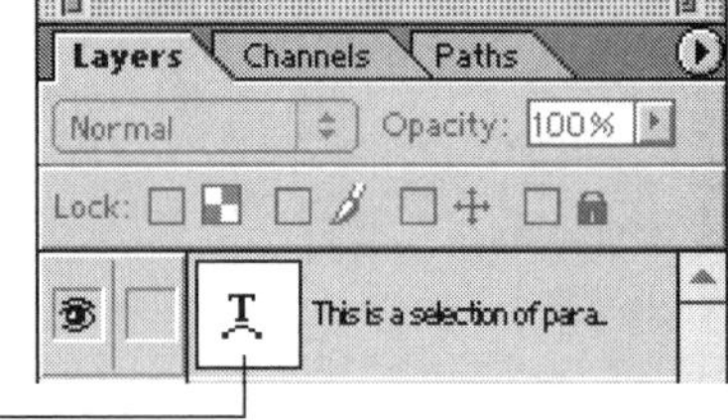

Missing fonts

If a font is missing (not available or installed) when you open a file that contains editable type and you then edit one of its type layers, an alert dialog box will appear **1**. If you click OK, font substitution will occur (an alert triangle will also display on the thumbnail of the offending layer on the Layer palette) **2**.

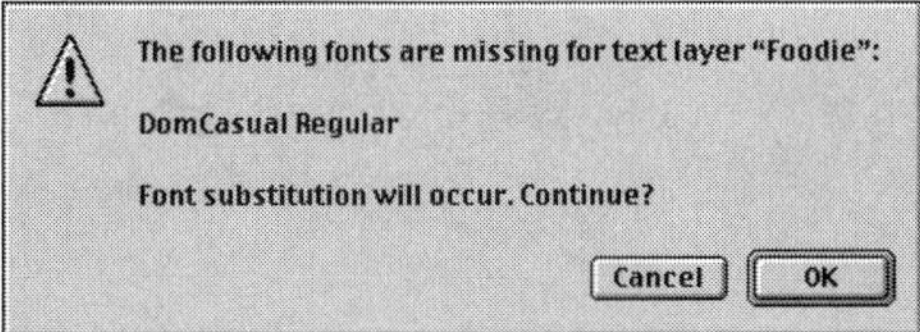

1 *The* ***missing fonts*** *alert dialog box.*

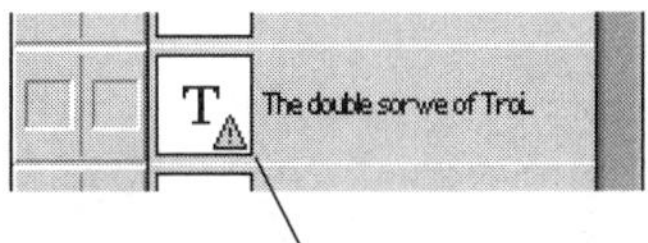

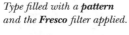

2 *The* ***missing fonts*** *alert triangle on the Layers palette.*

Type filled with a ***pattern***, ***Difference*** *mode.*

Type filled with a ***pattern*** *and the* ***Fresco*** *filter applied.*

Type filled with a ***pattern*** *and a* ***gradient***.

Type filled with a ***pattern*** *and the* ***Palette Knife*** *filter applied.*

To move a type layer:

Method 1

1. Choose the Move tool (V).
2. Right-click/Control-click the type in the image window and select the layer name from the context menu.
   or
   On the Layers palette, click the name of the layer you want to move.
3. Drag the type in the image window.
   or
   Press an arrow key.

Method 2 6.0!

1. Double-click the type layer thumbnail (the T).
2. Ctrl-drag/Cmd-drag the type in the image window.

To rework type shapes using a filter, or a tool such as the Paintbrush, Blur, Eraser, or Smudge, or the Transform > Distort or Perspective command, you must first convert the type into pixels, a process that's called rasterizing. You can't have your cake and eat it, though. Once type is converted to pixels, even though it remains on its own layer, its typographic attributes cannot be changed.

To rasterize type into pixels: 6.0!

1. On the Layers palette, choose the layer you want to rasterize. If you want to preserve the original, editable layer for later use, duplicate it and then rasterize the duplicate.
2. Choose Layer menu > Rasterize > Type. The ways in which rasterized type can be dressed up are almost limitless—just use your imagination. Here's just one little idea: Check "Lock transparent pixels" on the Layers palette, fill the rasterized type with a pattern, apply a filter to it, uncheck "Lock transparent pixels," then use the Smudge tool to smudge the edges of the type shapes.

(Continued on the following page)

To paint on rasterized type, choose the Paintbrush tool and a Foreground color, check the "Lock transparent pixels" box for the type layer, then draw brushstrokes in the image window. To paint behind the type, do it on the layer directly below the type layer **1**–**2**.

TIP If you apply the Color, Gradient, or Pattern Overlay effect, choose a blending Mode that allows the paint strokes to show through.

1

To screen back an image behind type:

1. Choose the background image on the Layers palette. You can use these instructions to lighten the background behind a Drop Shadow layer effect.
2. Choose Layer menu > New Adjustment Layer > Levels, then click OK.
   or
   6.0! Choose Levels from the "Create new fill or adjustment layer" pop-up menu at the bottom of the Layers palette.
3. Check the Preview box.
4. Move the gray Input slider a little to the left.
   and
   Move the black Output slider a little to the right.
5. Click OK **3**–**4**.

TIP To further adjust levels, try a different blending mode (try Screen or Overlay) or opacity for the Levels adjustment layer.

TIP To have the adjustment layer only affect the layer immediately below it, Alt-click/Option-click the line between the two layers on the Layers palette.

Rasterize without rasterizing

To make an editable type layer look painterly without rasterizing it into pixels, make the type layer the base layer in a **clipping group** (see page 247), and then draw brush strokes on the layer directly above the type layer. An advantage of using this method is that you can repaint the strokes or reposition them without affecting the type layer.

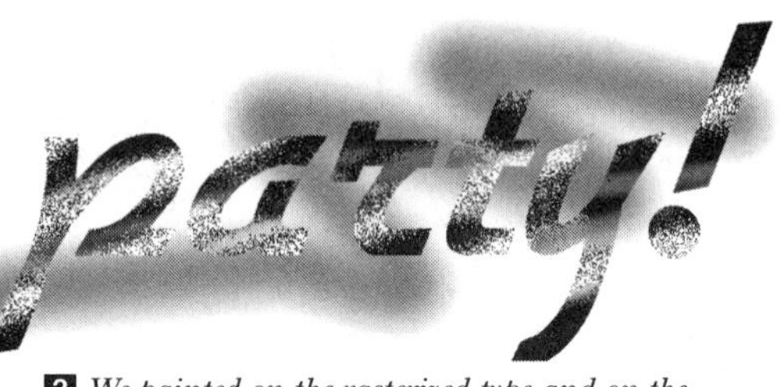

2 *We painted on the rasterized type and on the layer below it.*

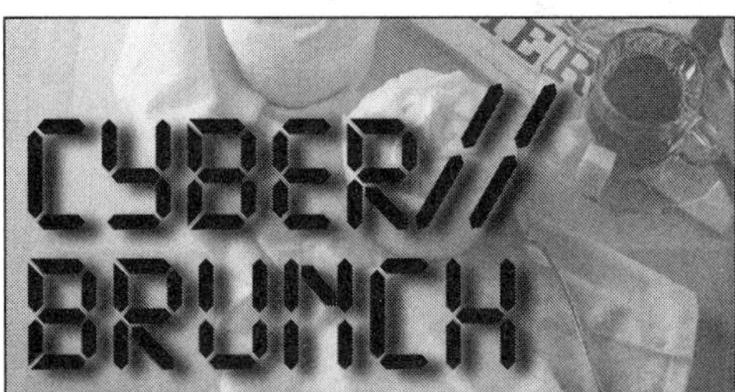

3 *After applying the **Levels** command to an adjustment layer over an image Background (Input Levels 0, .95, and 255, and Output Levels 92 and 255).*

4 *After filling the adjustment layer with a black-to-white **gradient** (upper right to lower left corner) to mask out the Levels effect in the upper right corner.*

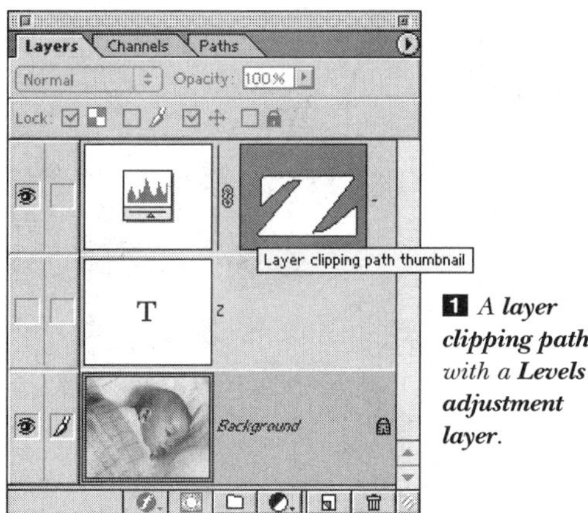

1 *A* ***layer clipping path*** *with a* ***Levels adjustment layer***.

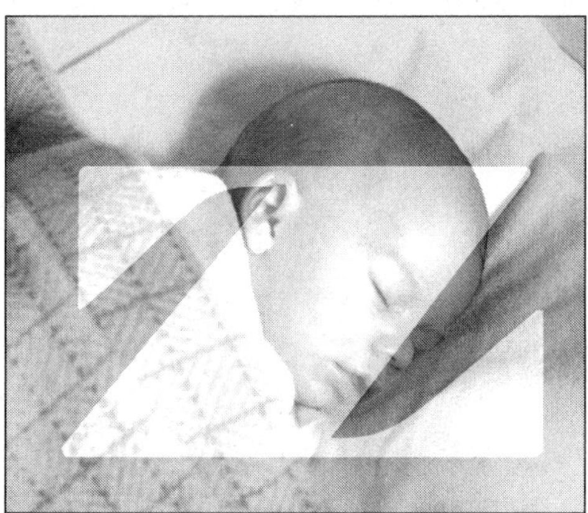

2 ***Screened back type***.

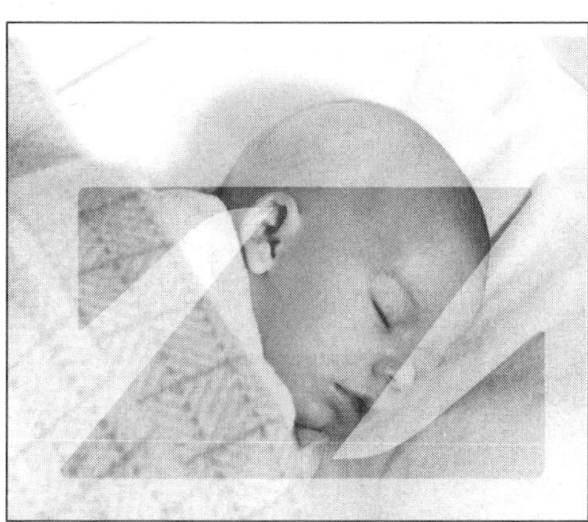

3 *A* ***screened back image*** *with type*.

To screen back type:

1. Create a type layer.
2. Duplicate the type layer by dragging it over the Create new layer button at the bottom of the Layers palette. Hide the original type layer (keep it for future type edits).
3. With the duplicate layer chosen, choose Layer menu > Type > Convert to Shape. **6.0!** The type layer will be converted into a shape layer with a layer clipping path. The original type shapes will be preserved, but its typographic attributes will no longer be editable.
4. Choose Layer menu > Change Layer Content > Levels **1**. **6.0!** The clipping effect won't be visible until you change the duplicate layer.
5. Move the gray Input (midtones) slider to the left to lighten the midtones in the type, then pause to preview. You can also move the Input highlights slider.
   and
   Move the Output shadows slider to the right to reduce the contrast in the type.
6. Click OK **2**. Click back on the background image layer.

TIP Change the blending mode for the adjustment layer or the base layer to restore some of the background color (try Overlay, Color Burn, or Hard Light mode). Lower the layer's opacity to lessen the Levels effect.

TIP To screen back an image with type, follow steps 1–4 above. For step 5, adjust the sliders to darken the type, remove any opacity or blending mode changes, then use an adjustment layer to lighten the imagery that's below the type layer **3**.

To fill type with imagery using Paste Into:

1. Create a type layer. It can be editable, converted to shape, or rasterized to pixels.
2. Activate a layer in the same file or in another file that contains the imagery you want to use to fill the type.
3. Choose Select menu > All or create a selection.
4. Choose Edit menu > Copy (Ctrl-C/Cmd-C).
5. Activate the image that contains the type layer, then Ctrl-click/Cmd-click the type layer name.
6. Choose Edit menu > Paste Into (Ctrl-Shift-V/Cmd-Shift-V) **1**–**2**. A new layer with a layer mask will be created automatically, and the pasted image will be revealed through the mask character shapes.
7. *Optional:* With the thumbnail for the new layer selected on the Layers palette, choose the Move tool (V), then drag to move the pasted image within the type shapes. Now click in the space between the layer thumbnail and the layer mask thumbnail to link the mask to the layer image. The position of the image inside the mask can't be changed while they remain linked. (Dragging with the Move tool now would move both the mask shape and the image inside it and expose the type layer underneath.)

TIP To move the type layer and the pasted image layer in unison, link the layer mask to the layer, then link the pasted image layer with the type layer.

TIP To fill type with imagery using a layer mask, see page 245; using a layer clipping path, see page 278.

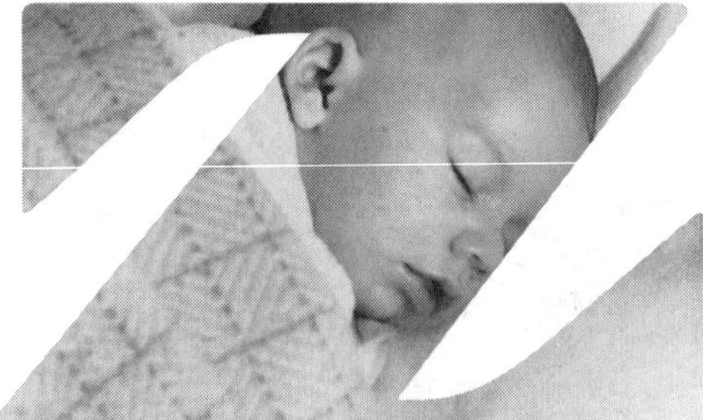

1 *Type filled with an image using the* ***Paste Into*** *command.*

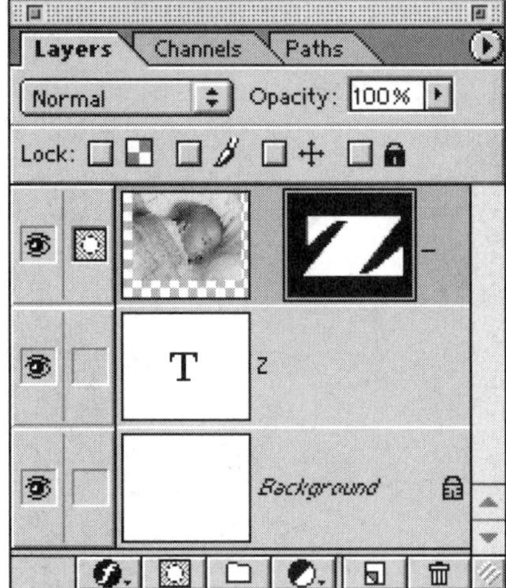

2 *The second layer is the original type layer; the topmost layer was created after pasting into the type selection.*

Letting go

To release a layer from a clipping group, **Alt-click/ Option-click** again on the line between an indented layer and the base layer.

1 *The separate layers before being joined in a clipping group.*

2 *The layers pulled apart so you can see their stacking order.*

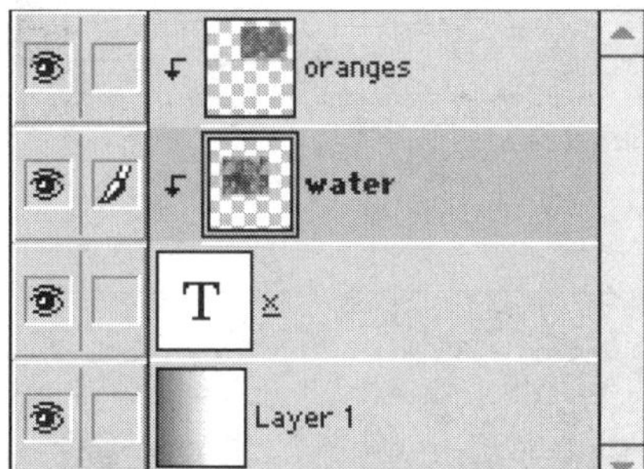

3 *The Layers palette after* ***Alt-clicking/ Option-clicking*** *the lines above the type layer. The type layer (the underlined name) is the* ***base*** *layer of the clipping group.*

To fill type with imagery using a clipping group of layers:

1. Create type using the Type or Vertical Type tool. It can be editable, converted to shape, or rasterized.
2. Move the type layer on the Layers palette just below the layer or layers that are to become the type fill **1**–**2**.
3. Alt-click/Option-click the line between the type layer name and the layer directly above it. The overlying layer will be indented with a down arrow to the left of the thumbnail and the base (bottom-most) layer of the clipping group will be underlined. Only pixels that overlap the letter shapes will be visible **3**–**4**.
4. *Optional:* Choose the type layer and use the Move tool to reposition the letters in the image window.
5. *Optional:* Alt-click/Option-click the lines between other layers that are directly above the clipping group to add them to the group.
6. *Optional:* Change the mode or opacity for any layer in the clipping group. By default, the blending mode of the base (underlined) layer affects the way the clipping group blends with layers below the group. Double-click the base layer name. Then in Layer Style, choose Blending Options and uncheck Advanced Blending: Blend Clipped Layers as Group to prevent the base layer from affecting the blending of indented layers with layers below the group.

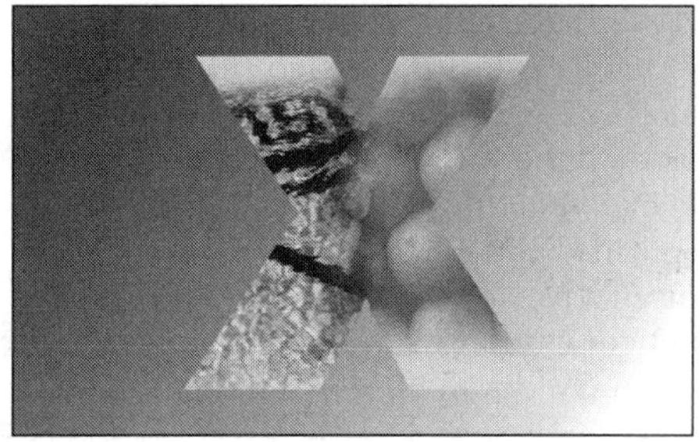

4 *Type filled with imagery using a* ***clipping group****.*

To create fading type:

1. Create type, and leave the type layer active. It can be editable or rasterized.
2. Click the Add a mask button at the bottom of the Layers palette. A layer mask thumbnail will appear next to the layer name **1**.
3. Choose the Gradient tool (G or Shift-G).
4. On the options bar: Click the Gradient arrowhead, then click the Foreground to Background swatch in the gradient picker; click the Linear gradient button; choose Mode: Normal; and choose Opacity: 100%.
5. Drag in the image window from top to bottom or right to left, at least halfway across the type. The type layer mask will fill with a white-to-black gradient. Type will be hidden where there is black in the layer mask **2**.

TIP Click the type layer thumbnail or name on the Layers palette to modify the layer; click the layer mask thumbnail to modify the layer mask. (Read more about layer masks in Chapter 14.)

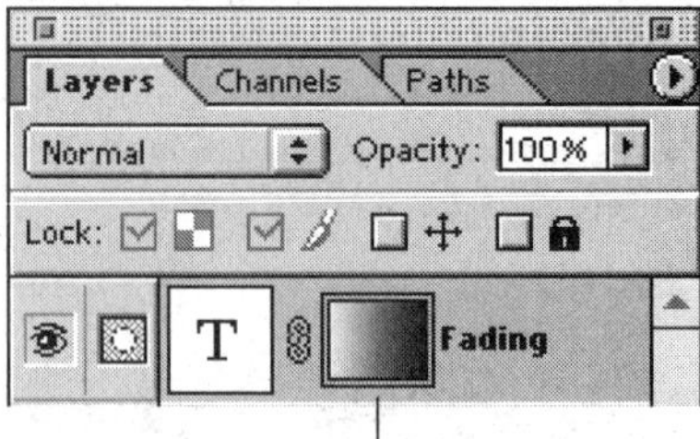

1 ***Layer mask*** *thumbnail.*

2 ***Fading*** *type.*

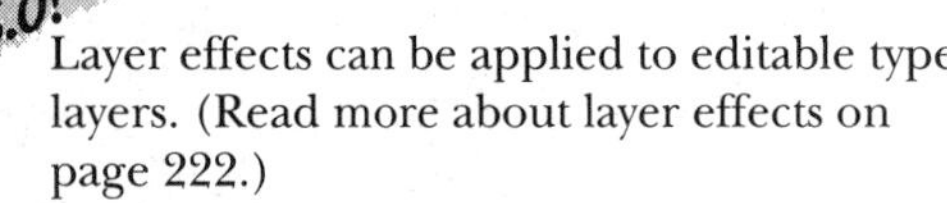

Layer effects can be applied to editable type layers. (Read more about layer effects on page 222.)

To apply layer effects to semi-transparent type:

1. Create type on an editable type layer.
2. Double-click the type layer name.
3. In Layer Style, click one or more of the layer effect names on the left side of the dialog box (e.g., Drop Shadow, Inner Shadow, Inner Glow, or Bevel & Emboss), and choose settings for each effect **3**–**4**. Apply the Satin effect to darken the contents of a type layer; use Color Overlay or Gradient Overlay to apply a tint; use Pattern Overlay to fill with a pattern.

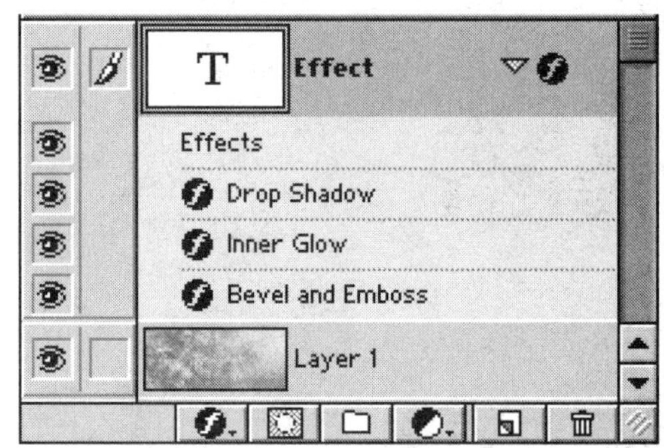

3 *The type layer shapes were used to create the mask for the* ***Paste Into*** *layer.*

4 ***Layer effects*** *applied to* ***type****.*

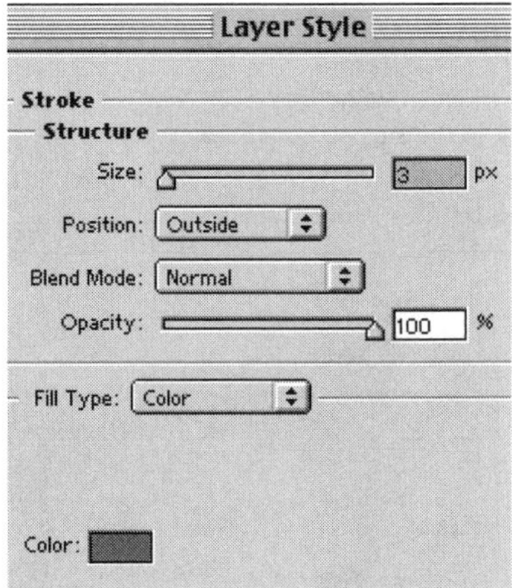

1 *Apply a **Stroke** to editable or rasterized type via the **Layer Style** dialog box.*

2 *A layer effect **Stroke** (Fill Type: Gradient) applied to editable type.*

3 *A **type mask selection**.*

4. Click Blending Options on the top left side of the Layer Style dialog box. For Advanced Blending, drag the Fill Opacity slider to 0%. Readjust any of the layer effects settings, if desired.
5. Click OK.

TIP To reposition the type with its effect, choose the type layer, choose the Move tool, then drag in the image window.

TIP To modify a layer effect, double-click the *f* icon or the layer name—the Layer Style dialog box will open.

To stroke a type layer: 6.0!

1. Double-click a type layer name on the Layers palette.
2. Click the word Stroke on the left side of the Layer Style dialog box and make sure the Preview box is checked.
3. Choose a stroke Size, Position (Outside, Inside, or Center), Blend Mode, Opacity, Fill Type, and Color **1**–**2**.
4. Click OK (Enter/Return).

The Type Mask tools create a selection in the shape of type characters. You might want to do this for a variety of reasons: to copy layer imagery in the shape of letters; to mask (limit) an adjustment layer effect to a type selection; or to add a layer mask using type characters for the mask shapes (Reveal Selection or Hide Selection).

To create a type selection: 6.0!

1. Activate the layer on which you want the type selection to appear (preferably not a type layer).
2. Choose the Type tool (T) and click the "Create a mask or selection" button on the options bar.
3. Click in the image window where you want the selection to appear. A Quick Mask will display temporarily.
4. Create and style the type. Click the ✓ on the options bar to accept the changes **3**.

(Continued on the following page)

Stroke Type; Type Selection

TIP Save a type selection to a new channel (click the Save selection as channel button at the bottom of the Channels palette) **1**. It can then be viewed on the Channels palette and loaded onto any layer or layer mask at any time.

To move a type selection:

6.0!

1. Choose the Rectangular Marquee tool (M) (not the Move tool!).
2. Click the New selection button on the options bar.
3. Drag from inside the selection in the image window.
   or
   Press an arrow key. Hold down Shift and press an arrow key to move the type selection 10 screen pixels at a time.

TIP If you drag a type selection using the Move tool, you'll cut away and move pixels inside the letter shapes from the active layer **2**.

TIP To deselect the selection, choose Select menu > Deselect (Ctrl-D/Cmd-D).

TIP To copy pixels from within a type selection, choose Edit menu > Copy to copy pixels only from the active layer or choose Edit menu > Copy Merged to copy pixels from all visible layers below the selection. Position the type selection over the desired pixels before using either copy command.

TIP To paste imagery into a type selection **3**, first select and copy an area of pixels from another layer or another image, create a type selection on the destination image, then choose Edit menu > Paste Into. The type selection will be deselected and a new layer will be created.

Line 'em up

To align or distribute multiple type layers, link them together (click in the second column on the Layers palette), then choose from the Layer menu > **Align Linked** or **Distribute Linked** submenu.

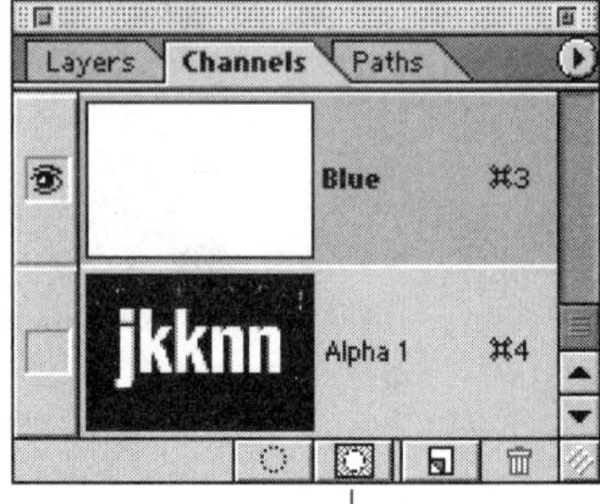

1 *To save a type mask selection to an alpha channel, click the* ***Save selection as channel*** *button on the* ***Channels*** *palette.*

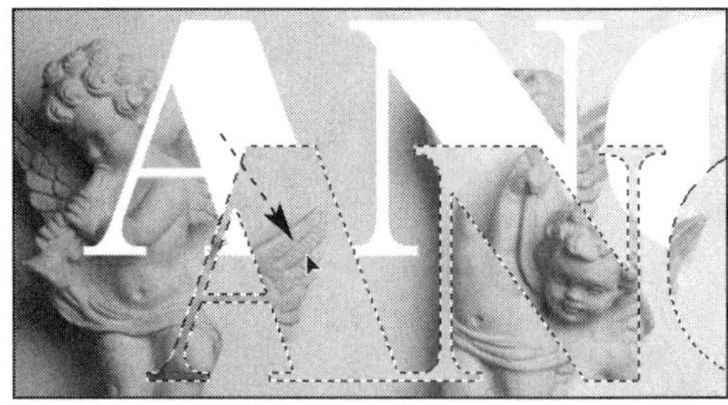

2 *When you use the Move tool to move a selection, the pixels in the selection move with the type outline.*

3 *Imagery pasted into a* ***type selection****.*

Move Type Selection

Don't lose your pixels

To deselect a selection, be sure to use Select menu > **Deselect** (Ctrl-D/Cmd-D). Don't press Delete or choose Edit menu > Clear—those commands will remove pixels from inside the selection!

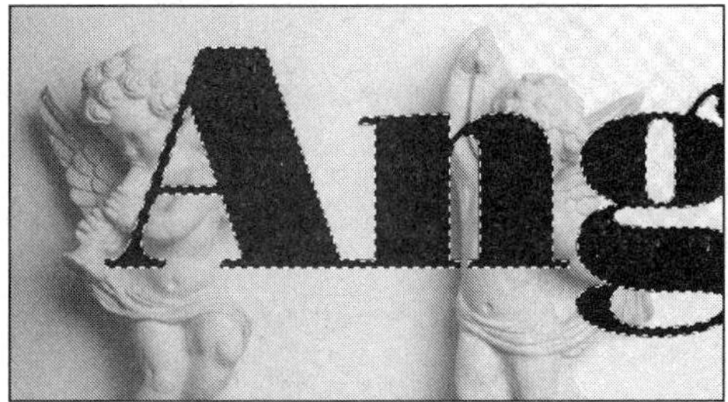

1 *Type in a spot channel.*

2 *A type mask selection in a spot channel displays on the image in the current* ***Ink Characteristics: Color*** *(see* **3***, below).*

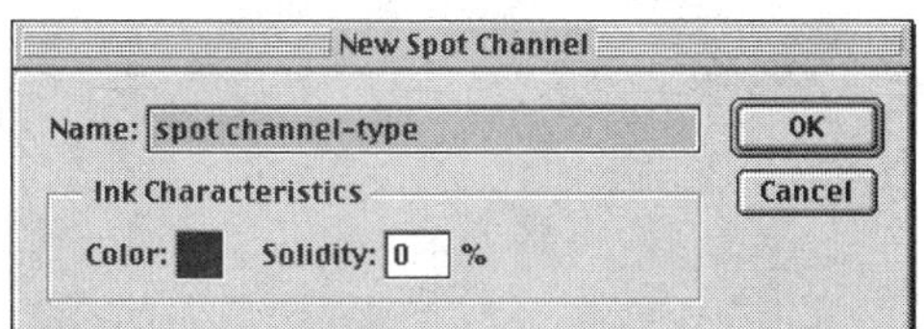

3 *You can change the* ***Solidity*** *value to view an on-screen-only simulation of the spot color ink tint. The Solidity value has no effect on the actual print output.*

To create type in a spot channel:

1. Create an editable type layer (Type tool) so you'll be able to modify it later on.
2. Follow steps 1–6 on page 193 to create a new spot channel.
3. Choose the type layer, then Ctrl-click/Cmd-click the type layer name to select only the visible parts of the layer (the character shapes).
4. On the Channels palette, choose the spot color channel name, and make sure its eye icon is showing.
5. Choose Edit menu > Fill, choose Use: Black, Normal mode, choose an Opacity value that will match the tint (density) value for the spot color ink, then click OK. The selection will fill with the spot channel color at 100%.
6. Choose Select menu > Deselect **1**–**3**.
7. *Optional:* Hide the type layer (click the eye icon on the Layers palette).

TIP To move the type in the spot color channel, choose that channel, choose the Move tool, then drag in the image window.

TIP To adjust the tint in a spot channel, see page 194.

You can't truly edit type in a spot channel. You have to remove the existing shapes from the channel and then add the revised text shapes to it.

To edit type in a spot channel:

1. On the Channels palette, choose the spot channel that contains the type.
2. Marquee the type, then press Delete to delete the type from the channel.
3. Choose Select menu > Deselect.
4. Double-click the original type layer thumbnail on the Layers palette, edit the type, then click ✓ on the options bar.
5. Follow steps 3–7 from the preceding set of instructions on this page. The spot color channel will now contain the revised type.

6.0!

To create a type mask for an adjustment layer:

1. Choose the Type tool (T), click the "Create a mask or selection" button on the options bar, then click in the image window where you want the type to appear.
2. Choose type attributes, enter characters, then click ✓ on the options bar. Leave the type selected.
3. Activate the layer above which you want the new adjustment layer to appear.
4. Choose an adjust command from the "Create new fill or adjustment layer" pop-up menu at the bottom of the Layers palette **1**. Choose adjustment options, then click OK. The type character shapes will become a mask for the adjustment layer. Only pixels directly below the character shapes will be affected by the adjustment **2**.

TIP You can also use an existing type layer to create a selection. First hide the type layer. Then select the type by Ctrl/Cmd-clicking the type layer thumbnail on the Layers palette. Finally, perform step 4, above.

TIP Alt-click/Option-click the layer mask thumbnail (thumbnail on the right) to display the mask alone. Alt-click/Option-click it again to restore the full image.

TIP With the adjustment layer selected, choose Image menu > Adjust > Invert (Ctrl-I/Cmd-I) to swap the black and white areas of the adjustment layer mask.

TIP Use the Move tool (its Auto Select Layer option unchecked) to reposition a type mask on a selected adjustment layer.

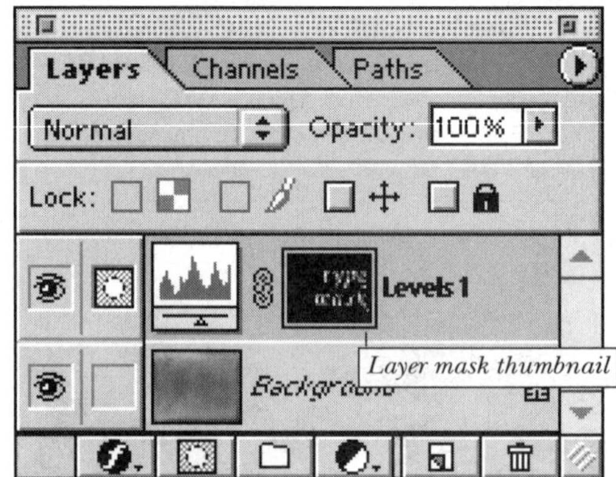

1 *The **type selection** functions as a **mask** for the **adjustment layer**.*

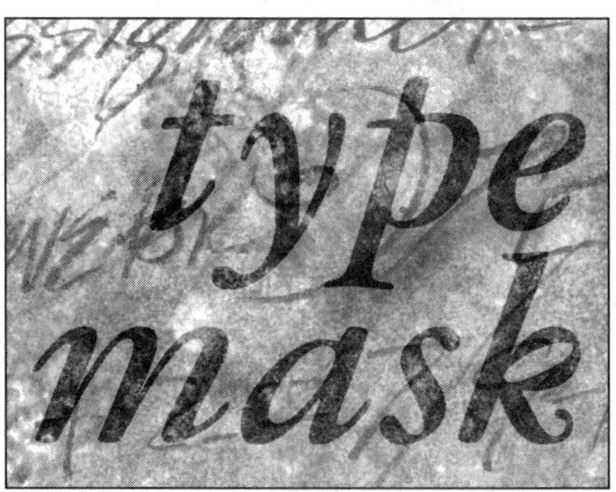

2 *Only pixels **below** the character shapes are affected by the **adjustment layer**.*

Type Mask for Adjustment Layer

FILTERS 18

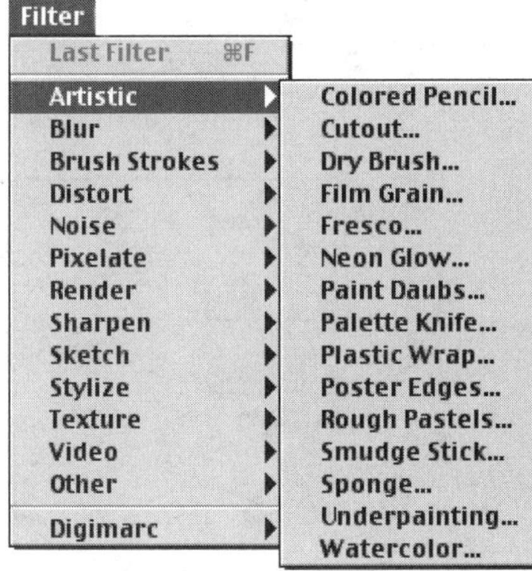

1 *Filters are grouped into submenu categories under the* ***Filter*** *menu.*

The ***Groucho*** *filter.*

PHOTOSHOP'S FILTERS can be used to produce a myriad of special effects, from slight sharpening to wild distortion. For example, a filter like Blur or Sharpen could be used for subtle retouching; the Color Halftone, Find Edges, Emboss, or Wind filter for more dramatic stylization; the Artistic, Brush Strokes, Sketch, or Texture filter to make imagery look hand-rendered; or the Lighting Effects filter to apply illumination.

This chapter has three components: techniques for applying filters; an illustrated compendium of all the Photoshop filters; and lastly, a handful of step-by-step exercises for using filters.

Filters are grouped into thirteen submenu categories under the Filter menu **1**. Third-party filters appear on their own submenus. (To install third-party filters, see Adobe Photoshop online Help.)

Filter basics

How filters are applied

A filter can be applied to a whole **layer** or to a **selection** on a layer. For a soft transition between the filtered and non-filtered areas, **feather** the selection before applying a filter.

Some filters are applied in one step (select it from a submenu). Other filters are applied via a dialog box in which one or more variables are specified. Choose Filter menu > **Last Filter (Ctrl-F/Cmd-F)** to reapply the last used filter using the same settings. Choose a filter from its submenu to choose different settings. To open the dialog box for the last used filter with its last used settings displayed, use the **Ctrl-Alt-F/Cmd-Option-F** shortcut.

All the filters are available for an image in RGB Color or Multichannel mode; not all filters are available for an image in CMYK,

(Continued on the following page)

Grayscale, or Lab Color mode. None of the filters are available for an image in Bitmap or Indexed Color mode, for an image that has 16 bits per channel.

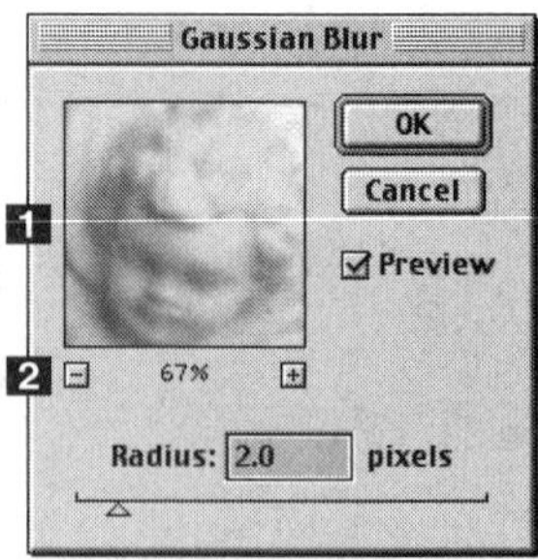

Using a filter dialog box

Most filter dialog boxes have a **preview window** 1. Drag in the preview window to move the image inside it. With some filter dialog boxes open, the pointer becomes a square when it's passed over the image window, in which case you can click to preview that area of the image. (Check the Preview box, if there is one, to preview the effect in the dialog box and the image window.)

Click the + button to zoom in on the image in the preview window, or click the – button to zoom out 2. A line will blink on and off below the preview percentage while a filter is rendering in the preview window.

TIP Press the up arrow on the keyboard to increase the value in a highlighted field by one unit (or .1 unit, if available); press the down arrow to reduce the value.

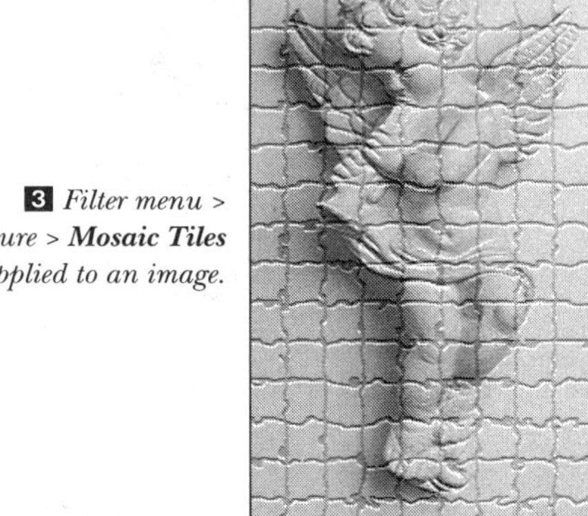

3 *Filter menu > Texture > **Mosaic Tiles** applied to an image.*

Lessening a filter's overall effect

6.0!

The **Fade** command can lessen a filter effect, an Image menu > Adjust, Extract, or Liquify command, or any paint, eraser, or editing tool stroke. After applying a filter, choose Edit menu > Fade [ ]... (Ctrl-Shift-F/Cmd-Shift-F), lower the Opacity, choose a blending Mode, then click OK 3–5.

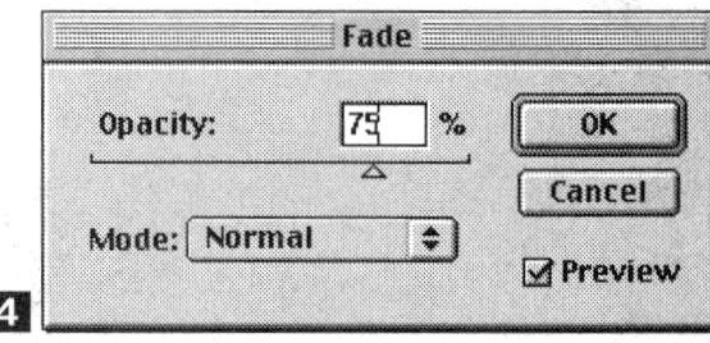

To lessen a filter's effect with the option to **test** different **blending modes**, do the following:

1. Duplicate the layer that you're going to apply the filter to.
2. Apply the filter to the duplicate layer.
3. On the Layers palette:

   Move the Opacity slider to the left to lessen (fade) the effect of the filter.

   and

   Choose a different blending mode (1–2, next page).

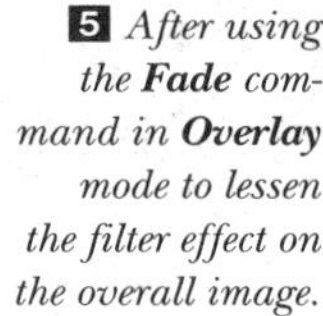

5 *After using the **Fade** command in **Overlay** mode to lessen the filter effect on the overall image.*

1 *The original image.*

2 *After applying the* ***Find Edges*** *filter to a* ***duplicate*** *of the original layer, lowering the* ***opacity*** *of the duplicate layer, and choosing Hard Light blending* ***mode*** *(also try Overlay, Color Dodge, or Difference).*

3 *After applying the* ***Poster Edges*** *filter to an image and then using the* ***History Brush*** *tool to restore the angel's face and tummy to its original state.*

Because the filter was applied to a copy of the original layer, later on you can change the blending mode or opacity of the filter effect layer to blend it differently with the original layer, or create a layer mask for the duplicate layer to hide or change the filter effect, or discard the filter layer entirely. When the image is finalized, merge the duplicate layer with the original layer.

Another way to soften a filter's effect is to modify pixels in only one of an image's color components. To do this, choose a layer, click a **channel** color name on the Channels palette, apply a filter (Add Noise is a nice one to experiment with), then click the top channel on the palette (Ctrl-~/Cmd-~) to redisplay the composite image.

You can selectively reduce a filter effect using the **History Brush**. Set the History Brush icon to a prior state on the History palette, and then draw strokes on the image **3**.

Restricting the area a filter affects

Create a **selection** first on a layer to have a filter affect only pixels within the selection. To create a soft-edged transition between the filtered and non-filtered areas, **feather** the selection before applying the filter.

You can also use a **layer mask** to limit the effect of a filter. The edge between the white and black areas of a layer mask can be soft, hard, or painterly, depending on the type of brush strokes you use to paint the black areas of the mask. By choosing Layer menu > Add Layer Mask > Reveal Selection when a selection is active and then applying a filter to the mask, the filter effect will be visible where the black and white areas of the layer mask meet (try Brush Strokes > Spatter; Pixelate > Pointillize; Stylize > Wind; or Distort > ZigZag or Ripple).

Or create a black-to-white **gradient** in the layer mask and then apply a filter to the layer image (not to the layer mask). The filter will apply fully to the image where the

(Continued on the following page)

mask is white and fade to nil in areas where the mask is black 1–3.

Making filter effects look less artificial

Apply **more than one** filter—the effect will look less canned. If the imagery you're creating lends itself to experimentation, try concocting your own formulas. And test different variables in a filter dialog box. If you come up with a sequence that you'd like to reuse, save it in an action.

Maximizing a filter's effect

Pumping up a layer's **brightness** and **contrast** values before applying a filter can help intensify the filter's effect (choose Image menu > Adjust > Levels, move the black Input slider to the right and the white Input slider slightly to the left, then click OK).

To **recolor** a layer after applying a filter that strips color (e.g., the Charcoal filter), use Image menu > Adjust > Hue/Saturation (check the Colorize box).

TIP The Sketch filters (with the exception of Water Paper) reduce a layer's colors to white and the current Foreground color, so choose a Foreground color before using any of those filters.

Texture mapping using a filter

And finally, for some filters (e.g., Conté Crayon, Displace, Glass, Lighting Effects, Rough Pastels, Texture Fill, and Texturizer), in lieu of using a preset pattern to create a texture effect, you can load in **another image** to use as the **pattern** for the texture effect. Lights and darks from the image you load in will be used to create peaks and valleys in the texture. The image you're using for the mapping must be saved in the Photoshop file format. In a filter dialog box that contains a Texture pop-up menu with a Load Texture option, select that option, locate a color or grayscale image file in the Photoshop format, then click OK.

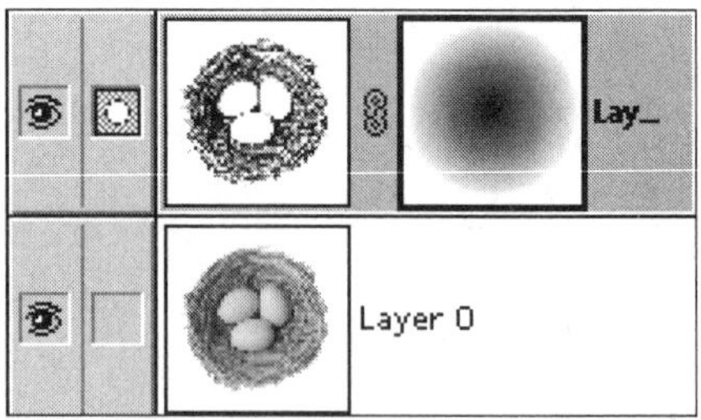

1 *A **radial gradient** in the **layer mask**...*

2 *...is diminishing the **Stamp** filter effect in the center of the nest.*

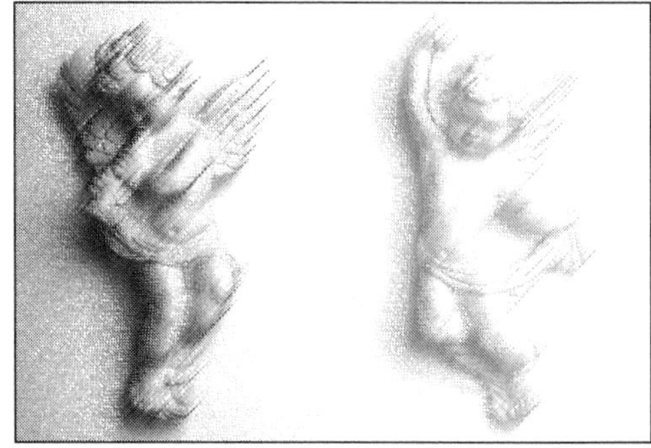

3 *The **Rough Pastels** filter is applied to the whole layer, but a **linear gradient** in the **layer mask** is diminishing the effect on the **right** side.*

All the filters illustrated

Artistic filters

Original image

Colored Pencil

Cutout

Dry Brush

Film Grain

Fresco

Neon Glow

Paint Daubs

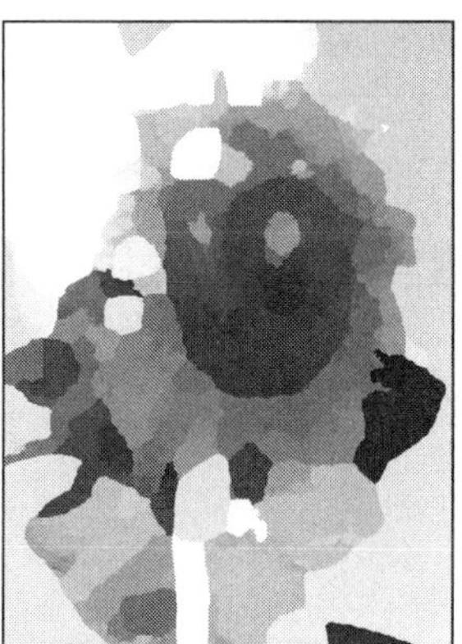
Palette Knife

Artistic filters

Original image

Plastic Wrap

Poster Edges

Rough Pastels

Smudge Stick

Sponge

Watercolor

Underpainting

Blur filters

Original image

Blur More

Gaussian Blur

Motion Blur

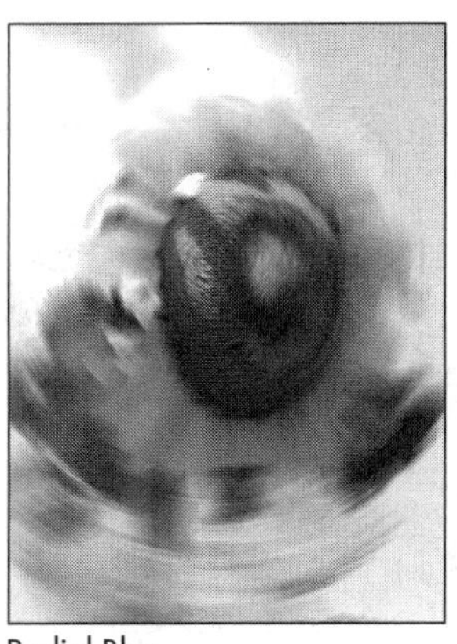
Radial Blur

Smart Blur (Normal)

Smart Blur (Edges Only)

Smart Blur (Overlay Edge)

Brush Strokes filters

Original image

Accented Edges

Angled Strokes

Crosshatch

Dark Strokes

Ink Outlines

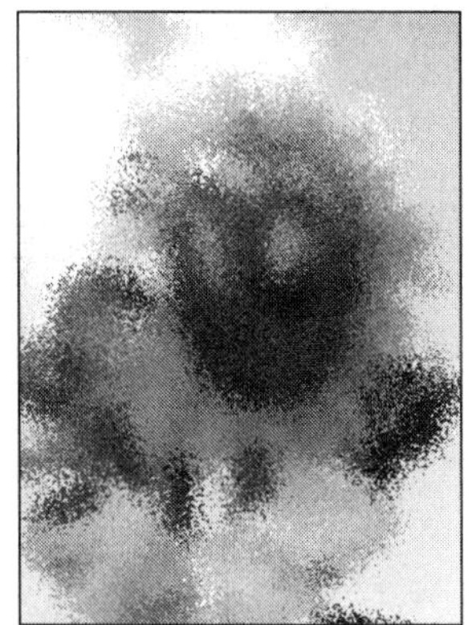
Spatter

Sprayed Strokes

Sumi-e

Distort filters

Original image

Diffuse Glow

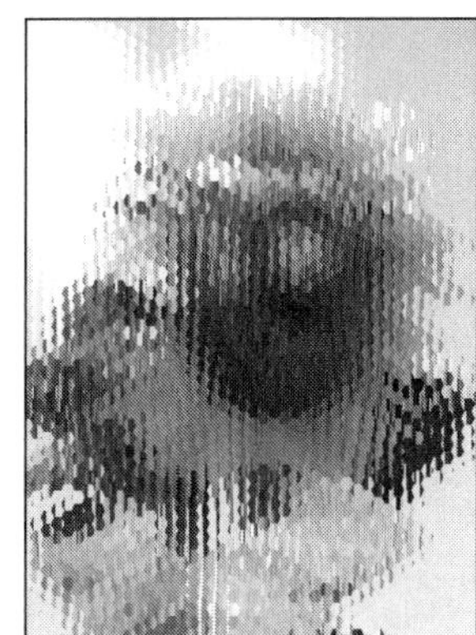
Displace

Glass

Ocean Ripple

Pinch

Polar Coordinates

Ripple

Shear

Distort filters

Spherize

Twirl

Wave (Type: Square)

Wave (Type: Sine)

ZigZag

Noise filters

Original image

Add Noise

Median

Pixelate filters

Original image

Color Halftone

Crystallize

Facet

Fragment

Mezzotint (Short Strokes)

Mezzotint (Medium Dots)

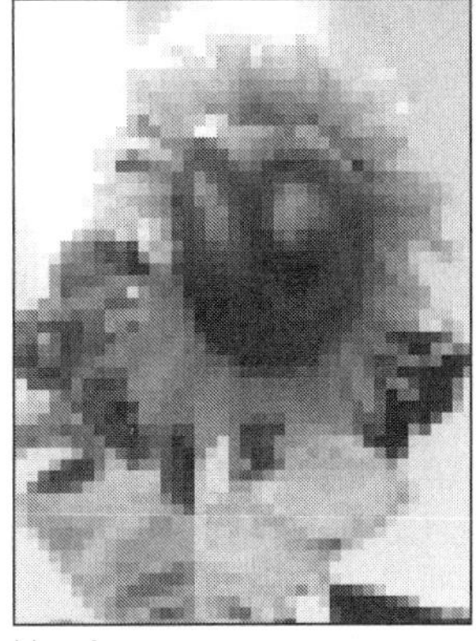
Mosaic

Pointillize

Render filters

Original image

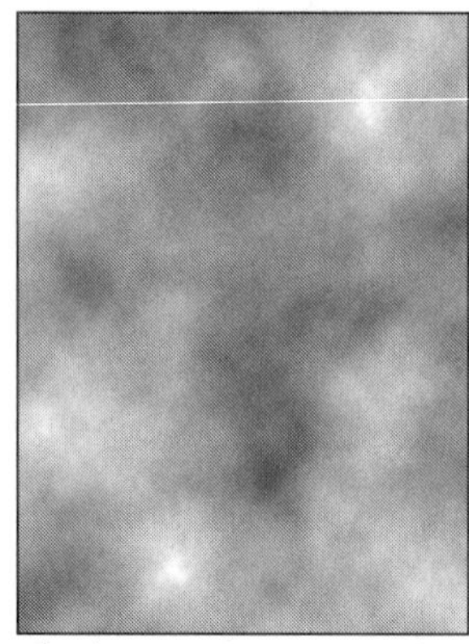
Clouds

Difference Clouds

Lens Flare

For the Lighting Effects filter, see pages 334–336.

Sharpen filters

Sharpen Edges

Sharpen More

Unsharp Mask

Sketch filters

Original image

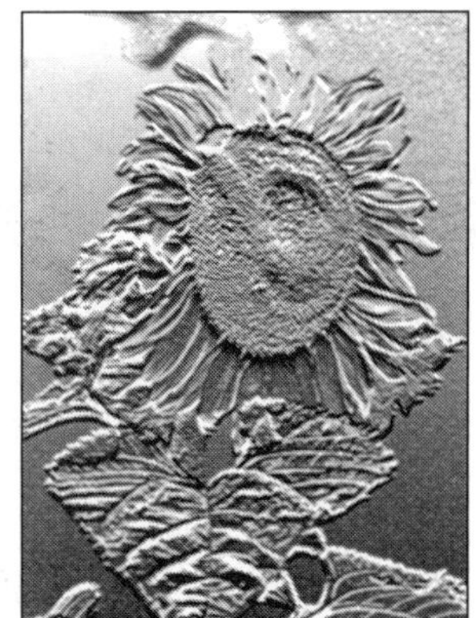
Bas Relief

Chalk & Charcoal

Charcoal

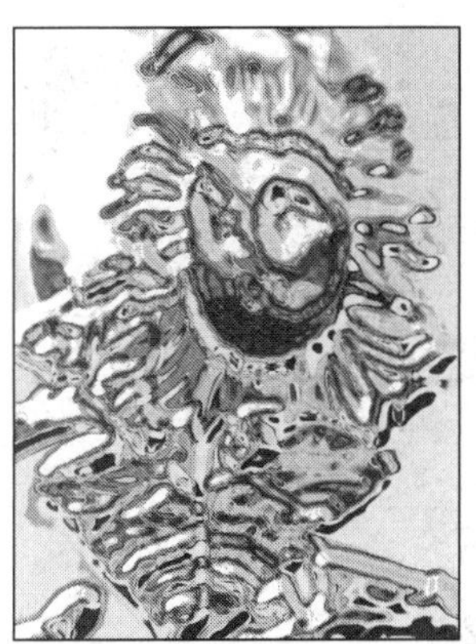
Chrome

Conté Crayon

Graphic Pen

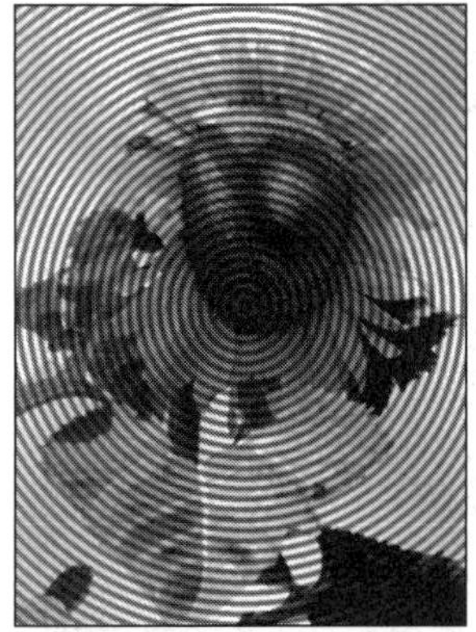
Halftone Pattern (Circle)

Halftone Pattern (Dot)

Sketch filters

Original image

Note Paper

Photocopy

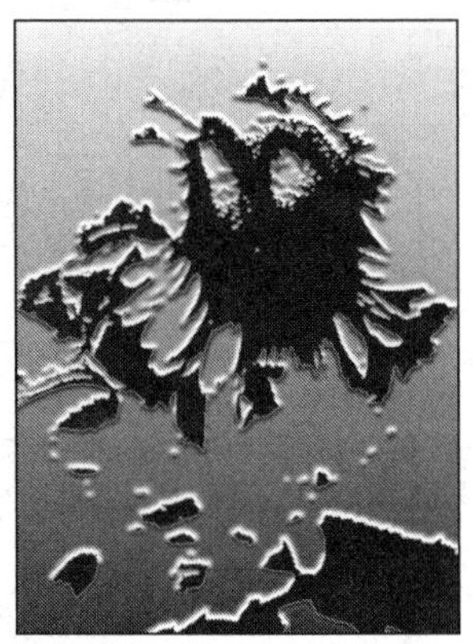
Plaster

Reticulation

Stamp

Torn Edges

Water Paper

Stylize filters

Original image

Diffuse

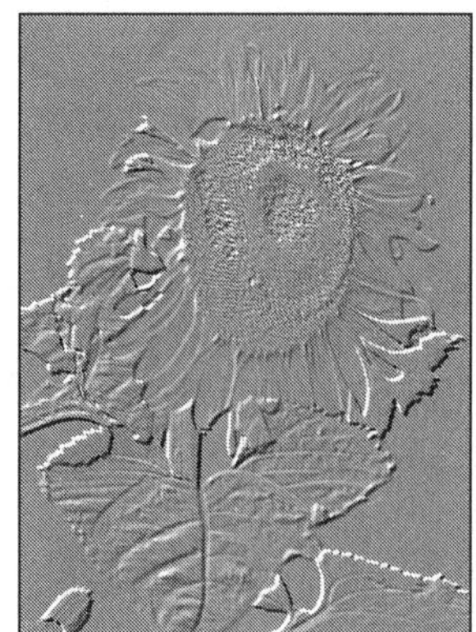
Emboss

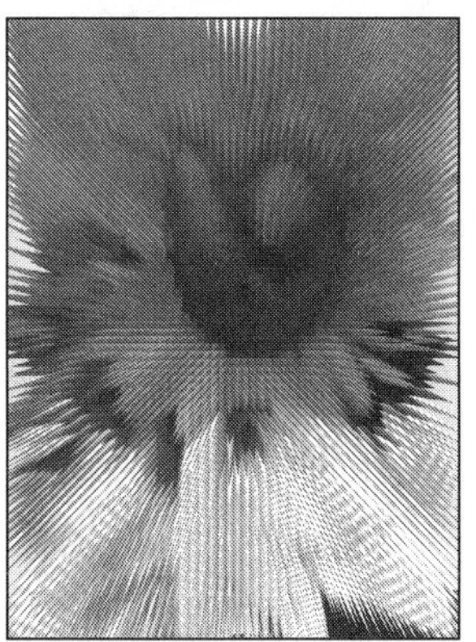
Extrude

Find Edges

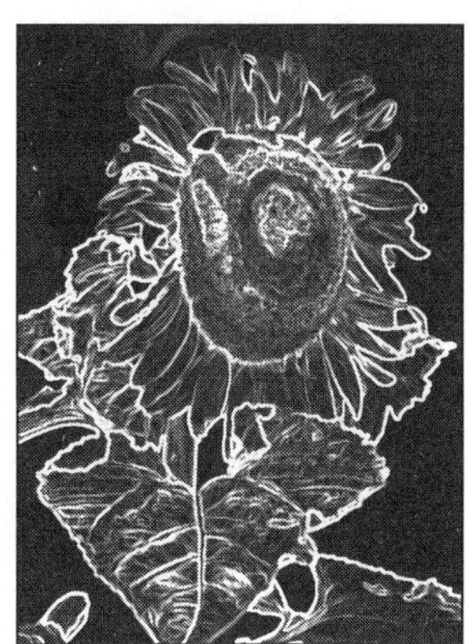
Glowing Edges

Solarize

Tiles

Tiles, then Fade (Overlay mode)

Stylize filters

Original image

Trace Contour

Wind

Texture filters

Craquelure

Grain (Horizontal)

Mosaic Tiles

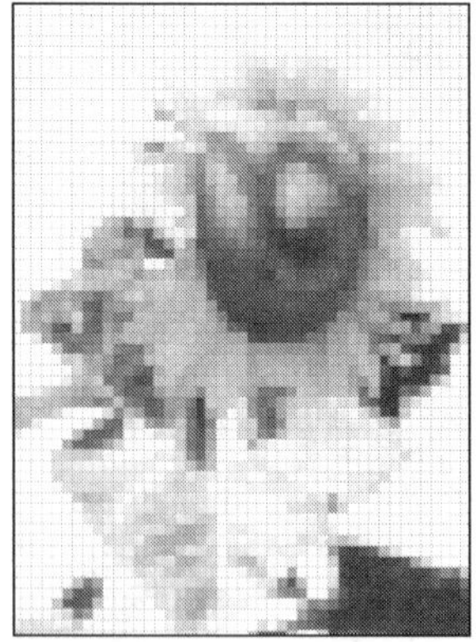
Patchwork

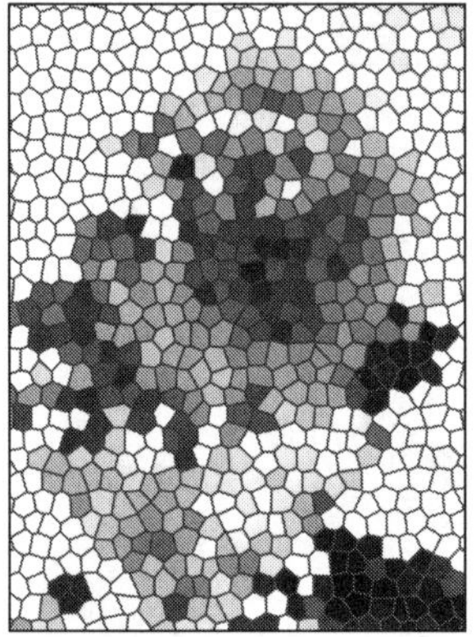
Stained Glass

Texturizer

1

PHOTO: PAUL PETROFF

2 *A wrinkled edge produced using the **Ripple** filter.*

A few filter exercises

Apply the Ripple, Twirl, or Zigzag filter to a target layer with a white border to produce a warped paper texture.

To create a wrinkled edge:

1. Choose white as the Background color.
2. Use Image menu > Canvas Size to add a border (use a one-layer image).
3. Choose the Rectangular Marquee tool (M or Shift-M).
4. Enter 8 in the Feather field on the Rectangular Marquee options bar.
5. Drag a selection marquee across approximately three quarters of the image (not the border).
6. Choose Select menu > Inverse (Ctrl-Shift-I/Cmd-Shift-I). The active selection will now include the added canvas area and part of the image 1.
7. Apply Filter menu > Distort > Ripple 2, Twirl, or Brush Strokes > Spatter, or a combination thereof. Move the preview in the filter dialog box to bring the edge of the image into the preview window.

Take the easy way out:

Use one of the "canned" frame effects from a third-party supplier, such as PhotoFrame from Extensis 3–4. You can apply more than one frame effect to the same image.

Artistic Edges and Frames

3 *A **Camera** edge from **Photoframe**.*

4 *A **Watercolor** edge from **Photoframe**.*

In these instructions, you will add a black or gray texture to a layer mask via a filter. Black areas in the layer mask will hide pixels in the layer, revealing imagery from the layer below it.

To apply a texture using a layer mask:

1. With an image open, create a new layer, and fill the new layer with white.
2. Create a layer mask for the new layer by clicking the Add layer mask button on the Layers palette, and leave the layer mask thumbnail active.
3. Apply Filter menu > Noise > Add Noise to the layer mask.
4. Apply another filter or series of filters to the layer mask 1–2. Try a Texture filter (Craquelure, Grain, Mosaic Tiles, Patchwork, and Texturizer). Or try Artistic > Dry Brush (small brush size), Palette Knife (small stroke size), Plastic Wrap (use Levels to increase contrast), Sponge, or Watercolor.
5. *Do any of the following optional steps:*

   To intensify a filter's effect, apply the Distort > Twirl or Ripple, or Stylize > Wind filter afterward.

   To fade a filter effect, use Edit menu > Fade.

   Adjust the opacity of the layer that has the layer mask; change blending modes (try Overlay, Soft Light, or Hue).

   To limit texture blending to some image channels, double-click the new layer name. In the Layer Style dialog box, click Blending Options, and in the Advanced Blending area, uncheck any channels you don't want to blend with the underlying image. You can also change the blending mode and opacity in this dialog box.

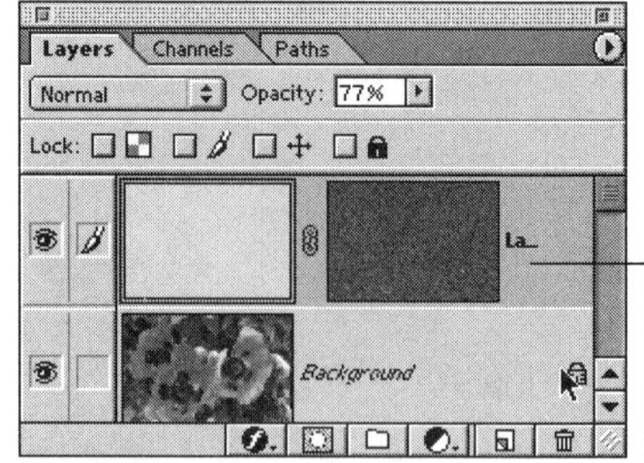

1 A ***filter*** *is applied to the* ***layer mask.***

2 *A filter applied via a* ***layer mask.***

3 *The original image.*

4 *The final image.*

Texture using Layer Mask

1 *The original image.*

2 *Theirs.*

3 *Ours.*

Turn a photograph into a painting or a drawing:

1. Open an image, choose Duplicate Layer from the Layers palette menu, then click OK.
2. Choose Filter menu > Stylize > Find Edges.
3. With the duplicate layer active, click the Add a mask button.
4. Paint with black at below 100% opacity on the layer mask to reveal parts of the layer below (**3**–**4**, previous page).
5. *Optional:* Lower the opacity of the duplicate layer.
6. *Optional:* For a dramatic effect of colors on a dark background, click the layer thumbnail, then choose Image menu > Adjust > Invert (Ctrl-I/Cmd-I).

TIP To produce a magic marker drawing, apply the Trace Contour filter, and apply Filter menu > Other > Minimum (Radius of 1 or 2) in lieu of step 2.

We've come up with a way to turn a photograph into a watercolor using the Median Noise and Minimum filters. Compare it to Photoshop's Watercolor filter. Here's an example of a way to apply a combination of filters to the same image.

Our watercolor filter:

1. Duplicate the layer that you want to turn into a watercolor.
2. With the duplicate layer active, choose Filter menu > Noise > Median.
3. Move the Radius slider to a number between 2 and 8.
4. Click OK.
5. Choose Filter menu > Other > Minimum.
6. Move the Radius slider to 1, 2, or 3.
7. Click OK **1**–**3**.
8. *Optional:* Apply Filter menu > Sharpen > Sharpen More.

In the following instructions, the Mosaic filter is applied using progressive values to a series of rectangular selections, so the mosaic tiles gradually enlarge as the effect travels across the image. (Using a gradient in a layer mask instead would gradually fade the Mosaic effect without changing the size of the mosaic tiles **1**.)

1 *This is the Mosaic filter applied using a **gradient** in a **layer mask**.*

To apply the Mosaic filter using graduated values:

1. Choose a layer.
2. Choose the Rectangular Marquee tool (M or Shift-M).
3. Marquee about one-quarter or one-fifth of the layer, where you want the mosaic tiles to begin.
4. Choose Filter menu > Pixelate > Mosaic.
5. Enter 6 in the Cell Size field **2**.
6. Click OK.
7. With the selection still active and the Rectangular Marquee tool still chosen, Shift-drag the marquee to the next adjacent quadrant **3**.
8. Repeat steps 4–7 until you've done the whole image, entering 12, then 24, then 30 in the Cell Size field. Or to create larger pixel blocks, enter higher numbers—like 8, 16, 28, and 34—in the Cell Size field.
9. Deselect (Ctrl-D/Cmd-D) **4**.

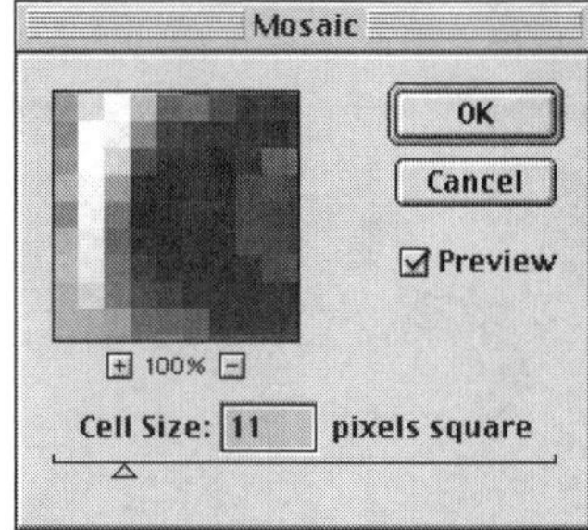

2 *Enter a number in the **Cell Size** field in the **Mosaic** dialog box. Enter progressively higher numbers each time you repeat step 5.*

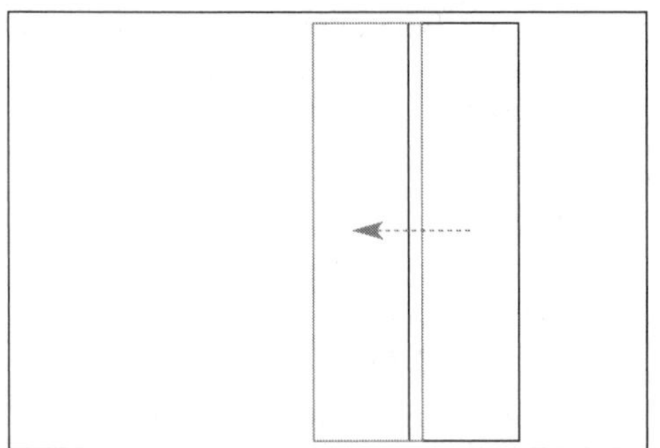

3 *Apply the Mosaic filter to a rectangular selection, move the marquee, then reapply the filter, and so on.*

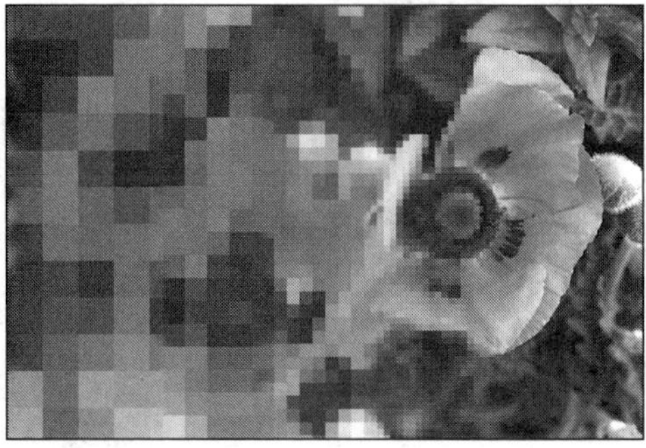

4 *A **graduated mosaic**.*

Mosaic Filter

1 *Select an object.*

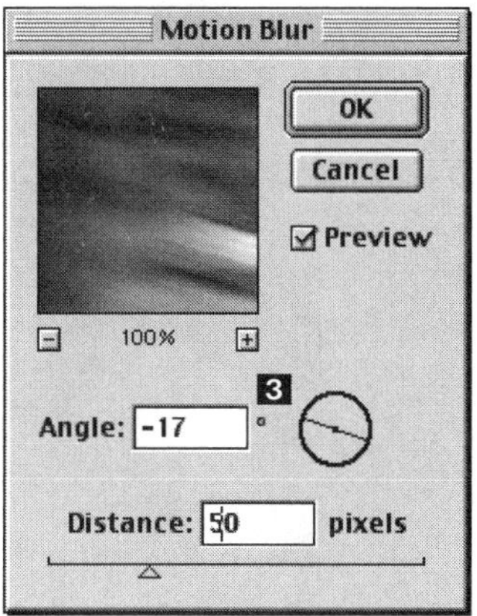

To create an illusion of motion, you will select an object that you want to remain stationary, copy it to a new layer, and then apply the Motion Blur filter to the original background.

To motion blur part of an image:

1. Select the imagery that you want to remain stationary **1**.
2. Choose Select menu > Feather (Ctrl-Alt-D/Cmd-Option-D).
3. Enter 5 in the Feather Radius field, then click OK.
4. Use the Ctrl-J/Cmd-J shortcut to copy the selection to a new layer **2**.
5. Choose the original layer that contains the background imagery.
6. Choose Filter menu > Blur > Motion Blur.
7. Choose an Angle between -360 and 360 **3**. (We entered -17 for our image.)
   and
   Choose a Distance (1–999) for the amount of blur. (We entered 50 for our image.)
   then
8. Click OK **4**.

4 *The completed* ***Motion Blur****.*

Motion Blur Part of an Image

The Lighting Effects filter produces a tremendous variety of lighting effects. You can place up to 16 light sources in your image, and you can assign a different color, intensity, and angle to each source.

Note: For optimal use of this filter, allocate a minimum of 50MB of RAM to Photoshop.

To cast a light on an image:

1. Make sure your image is in RGB Color mode **1**.
2. Choose a layer. *Optional:* Select an area on the layer to limit the filter effect.
3. Choose Filter menu > Render > Lighting Effects.
4. From the Style pop-up menu, choose Default or a preset lighting effect **2**.
5. ***For Light Type* 3:**

   Check the **On** box to preview the lighting effect in the dialog box.

   Choose from the **Light Type** pop-up menu. Choose Spotlight if you want the default light to be a narrow, elliptical, cone-shaped beam.

   Move the **Intensity** slider to adjust the brightness of the light. Full creates the brightest light **4**. Negative creates a black light effect.

   For the Spotlight Light Type, you can move the **Focus** slider to adjust the size of the beam of light that fills the ellipse shape (**5 a–b**, next page). The light source falls within the ellipse. Its highest intensity is located where the radius touches the edge of the ellipse.

   To change the **color** of the light, click on the color swatch, then choose a color from the Color Picker.
6. ***Do any of the following in the preview area:***

   Drag the center point to move the entire light.

1 *The **original** RGB image.*

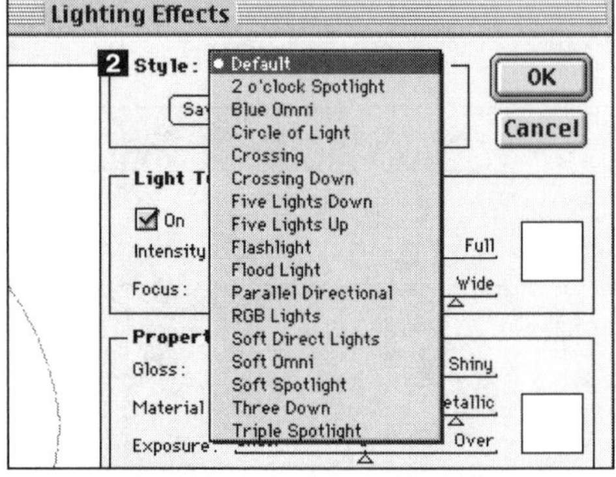

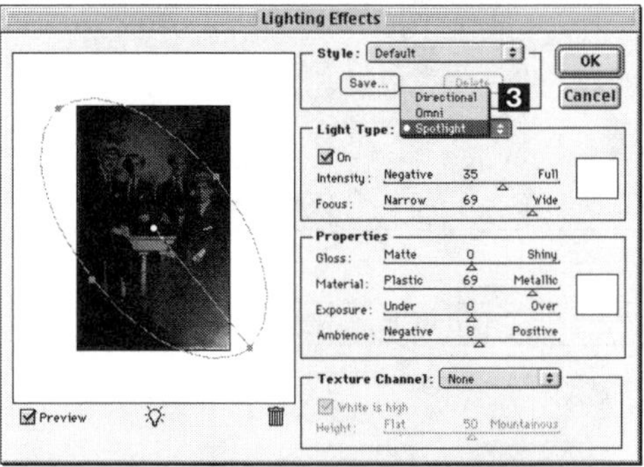

4 *The Default style spotlight ellipse at **Full Intensity**.*

5 *a The Default spotlight ellipse with a **Wide Focus**. The light is strongest at the sides of the ellipse.*

5 *b The Default spotlight ellipse with a **Narrow Focus**.*

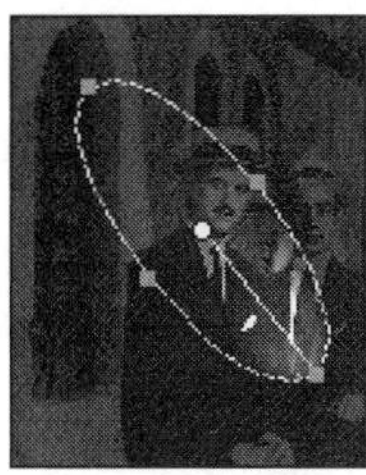

6 *The Default spotlight ellipse after dragging the **end and side points** inward to narrow the light beam.*

7 *a The spotlight ellipse **rotated** to the left by dragging a side point.*

7 *b The spotlight ellipse after dragging the **radius** inward to make the light beam more round.*

Drag either endpoint toward the center point to make the light more intense **6**.

For an ellipse, drag either side point to change the direction of the light or to widen or narrow it **7 a–b**.

7. ***Move the Properties sliders to adjust the surrounding light conditions on the active layer:***

Gloss controls the amount of surface reflectance on the lighted surfaces.

Material controls which parts of the image reflect the light source color—Plastic (the light source color is like a glare) or Metallic (the object surface glows).

Exposure lightens or darkens the whole layer **8 a–b**.

Ambience controls the balance between the light source and the overall light in the image **9 a–b**. Move this slider in small increments.

Click the Properties color swatch to choose a different **color** from the Color Picker for the ambient light around the spotlight.

8. *Do any of these optional steps:*

To add the current settings to the Style pop-up menu, click **Save**.

To **add** another light source, drag the light bulb icon into the preview window (**1**, next page).

(Continued on the following page)

8 *a The spotlight ellipse with the **Exposure Property** set to **Over**.*

8 *b The spotlight ellipse with the **Exposure Property** set to **Under**.*

9 *a The spotlight ellipse with a **Positive Ambience Property**.*

9 *b The spotlight ellipse with a **Negative Ambience Property**.*

To **delete** a light source, drag its center point over the trash icon.

To **duplicate** a light source, Alt-drag/Option-drag its center point.

9. Click OK.

Note: The last used settings of the Lighting Effects filter will remain in the dialog box until you change them or exit/quit Photoshop. To restore the default settings, choose a different style from the Style pop-up menu, then choose Default from the same menu. Click Delete to remove the currently selected style from the pop-up menu.

TIP To create a textured lighting effect, choose an existing alpha channel that contains a texture from the Texture Channel pop-up menu. Move the Height slider to adjust the height of the texture. This works best with the Spotlight Light Type.

TIP An Omni light creates a circular light source **2**. Drag an edge point to adjust its size.

TIP Shift-drag the side points on an ellipse to change the size of the ellipse, but keep its angle constant. Ctrl-drag/Cmd-drag the angle line to change the angle or direction of the ellipse, but keep its size constant.

TIP To create a pin spot, choose Light Type: Spotlight, move the Intensity slider to about 55, move the Focus slider to about 30, and drag the side points of the ellipse inward to narrow the ellipse. To cast light on a different part of the image, move the whole ellipse by dragging its center point.

TIP If the background of an image was darkened too much from a previous application of the Lighting Effects filter, apply the filter again to add another light to shine into the dark area and recover some detail. Move the Properties: Exposure and Ambience sliders a little to the right.

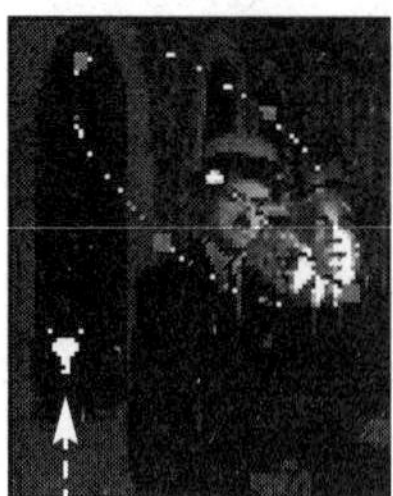

1 *Dragging a **new light source** onto the preview box.*

2 *The default **Omni** light is spherical, like a flashlight shining perpendicular to the image.*

Lighting effects by example

To produce **3**, we used a Spotlight with a wide Focus, rotated and reshaped the ellipse, moved the Exposure Property slider slightly toward Over to brighten the light source, and moved the Ambience Property slider slightly to the left to darken the background of the image. Then we Alt-dragged/Option-dragged the ellipse to duplicate the light and illuminate the face on the right. And finally, we created a new, low intensity light to illuminate the background **4**.

3 *The **final** image.*

4 *These three ellipses show the light source positions that were used to produce the image above.*

Lighting Effects Filter

LIQUIFY 19

1 *The **Liquify** dialog box, after applying the **Twirl Clockwise** tool to the Eiffel Tower.*

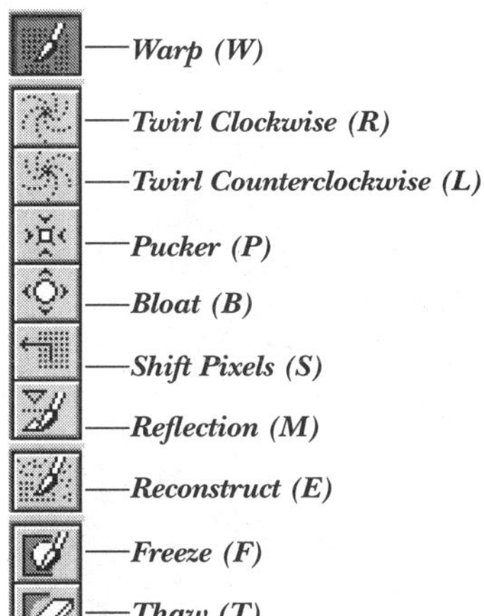

2 ***Tools** in the **Liquify** dialog box.*

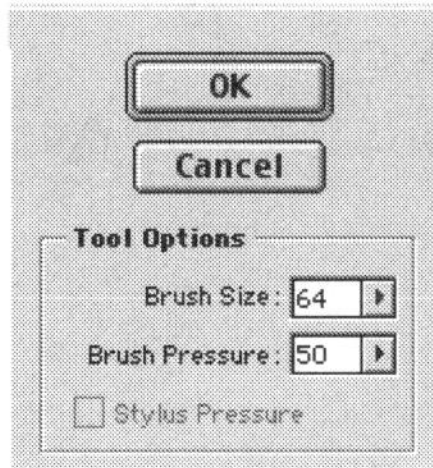

3 *The **Tool Options** portion of the Liquify dialog box.*

6.0!

ONE OF THE NEW FEATURES in Photoshop 6 is the Liquify command. This command lets you twist, warp, stretch, and otherwise distort an image layer. Like the Extract command, the Liquify command gives you a full-size preview right in the dialog box **1**. You apply the distortion (or reconstruction) with a brush, whose size and pressure are adjustable (like the brushes in the rest of Photoshop), and you can also use the brush to Freeze parts of the image to protect them from distortion, like masking. You can undo the havoc you have wrought, partially or completely, with the Reconstruct tool. The changes aren't permanent until you click the OK button to close the box.

To distort an image using the Liquify command:

Note: For safety's sake, work on a duplicate layer. You could also make a snapshot of the original image using the History palette.

1. Choose the layer whose contents you wish to liquify. Liquify will work only on a rasterized layer, not on an editable type or shape layer.
2. Choose Image menu > Liquify (Ctrl-Shift-X/Cmd–Shift-X). A full-screen, non-resizable dialog box will open.
3. You'll paint with one of the Liquify tools to apply distortion to your image **2**.

   First, in the Tool Options area, enter or choose a Brush Size (1–150 pixels), and a Brush Pressure (1–100%) for the rate at which distortion occurs on the image **3**. These two settings apply to all the Liquify tools. If you are using a graphics tablet, you can check the Stylus Pressure box to have the stylus determine the Brush Pressure.

(Continued on the following page)

4. *Optional:* Choose the **Freeze** tool (second from the bottom) (F) to mask parts of the image you want to protect.
and
Choose a color from the Freeze Color pop-up menu in the View Options area. The default is Red, the same color used for the Quick Mask feature.
and
Paint over the areas you wish to preserve in their current state. If you make a mistake, follow the next step.
5. *Optional:* To remove protection from frozen areas, choose the **Thaw** tool (T), then paint with the Thaw tool.
6. *Do any of the following optional steps:*

   To thaw all frozen areas and/or freeze all unfrozen areas, click the Freeze Area: **Invert** button.

   To thaw the entire image (make it all editable again), click the **Thaw All** button.

   To hide the mask created by the Freeze tool, uncheck the View Options: **Show Frozen Areas** box.

   Note: Even though frozen pixels won't be distorted by the Liquify tools, those tools can use patterns in the frozen imagery to distort non-frozen areas.
7. Choose any of these Liquify tools (type the shortcut to switch to the desired tool) and paint on the image in the dialog box:

   The **Warp** tool (W) pushes pixels in the direction you drag the brush **1**.

   The **Twirl Clockwise** (R) and **Twirl Counterclockwise** (L) tools rotate pixels as long as you hold down the mouse button or drag. The higher the Brush Pressure, the faster the rotation. (See **1** on the previous page.)

   The **Pucker** (P) and **Bloat** (B) tools push pixels toward or away from the center of the brush as long as you hold down the mouse button or drag **2**. The higher the Brush Pressure, the faster the pixels move.

1 *The result of applying the **Warp** tool. The arrow shows the direction of the brush stroke.*

2 *The result of applying the **Pucker** tool. The arrow shows the direction of the brush stroke.*

Liquify Command

1 *We used the **Reflect** tool to move the Seine closer to the Eiffel Tower to produce a lovely reflecting pool. It took two brush strokes to achieve this effect.*

2 *Alt-dragging/Option-dragging downward with the **Reflect** tool allowed part of the tower to float freely above the ground.*

The **Shift Pixels** tool (S) moves pixels at right angles to the direction of the brush's movement. By default, the pixels move to the left from the brush's direction. Alt-drag/Option-drag to move them to the right of the brush's direction.

The **Reflection** tool (M) copies pixels from the area to the right of your brush's direction and applies them, mirrored, to the area the brush passes over **1**. The tool picks up pixels on the right side of an upward stroke, the left side of a downward stroke. Alt-drag/Option-drag to copy pixels from the opposite side of the brush's position.

> **TIP** Try freezing the area whose pixels you want to reflect before using the Reflection tool.

8. To partially or completely undo the Liquify changes, read about the Reconstruction controls on page 341.
9. Click OK to accept your edits and return to the image window.

TIP To make the freeze mask conform to the shape of a selection, create a selection before choosing the Liquify command. Save the selection as an alpha channel, choose Image menu > Liquify, then choose that alpha channel from the Freeze Area: Channel pop-up menu. You can click Invert if you want to reverse the current frozen and unfrozen areas in the image.

6.0!

To help you keep track of the extent of your Liquify command edits, you can superimpose a mesh over the image. The mesh gridlines display the same pattern of distortion as the image itself. The mesh comes in handy if portions of your image lack a clear pattern, and is particularly useful when using the Reconstruct tool. You can adjust the size and color of the mesh.

To display the mesh using the View Options controls:

1. Check the Show Mesh box in the View Options area 1. A regularly-spaced set of grid lines will cover the image 2.
2. *Do any of the following optional steps:*

   Choose a relative size for the mesh from the **Mesh Size** pop-up menu.

   Choose a color for the mesh from the **Mesh Color** pop-up menu.

   If the Show Mesh box is checked and you want to hide the image, uncheck the **Show Image** box 3. You'll be able to see the distortion pattern in the mesh more clearly.

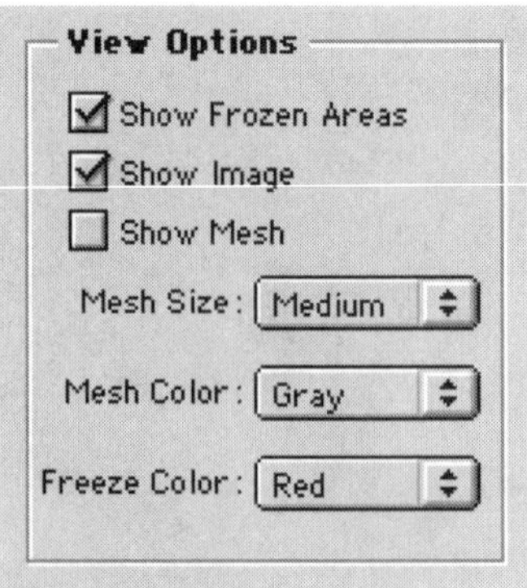

1 *The default **View Options** in the **Liquify** dialog box.*

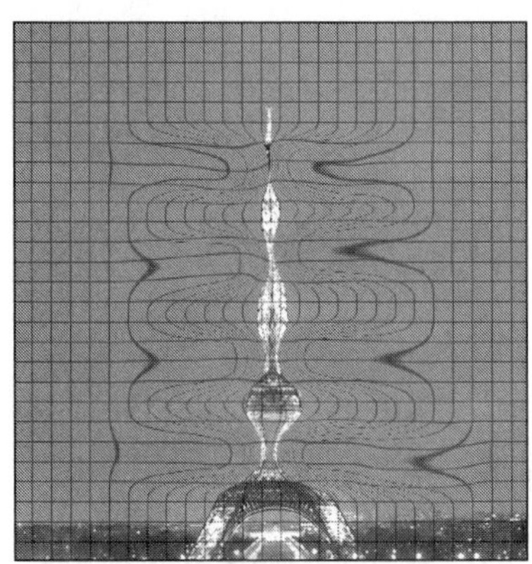

2 *A **Warped** Eiffel Tower, showing the image and the mesh...*

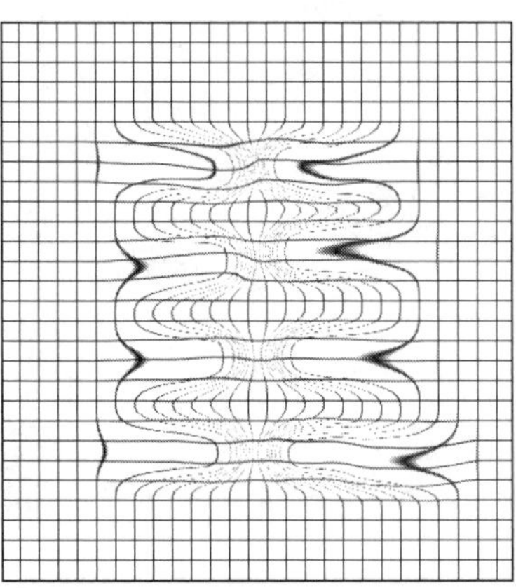

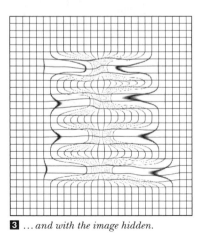

3 *...and with the image hidden.*

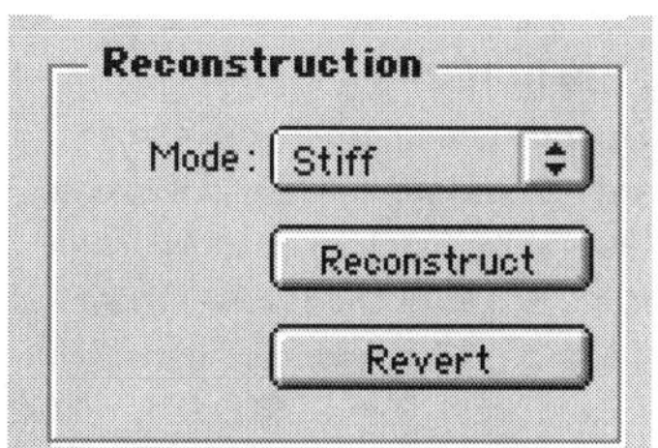

1 *The **Reconstruction** controls.*

Reconstruction 6.0!

After you've applied distortion to your image, you can use the Reconstruction controls **1** together with the Reconstruct tool to undo some or all of the distortion, or to extend the distortion into other areas of the image.

To remove all distortion from the preview image:

Click the Revert button in the Reconstruction area. The preview image (including frozen areas) will return to the state it was in when you opened the Liquify dialog box. (Don't confuse the Revert button with the Revert brush mode.)

To return all unfrozen areas to their initial state:

1. Choose Revert from the Reconstruction: Mode pop-up menu.
2. Click the Reconstruct button. The unfrozen parts of the preview image will return to the state they were in when you opened the Liquify dialog box. The frozen areas will be unaffected.

To return individual unfrozen areas to their initial state:

1. Choose Revert from the Reconstruction: Mode pop-up menu.
2. Choose the Reconstruct tool (E). Use the brush to paint the areas you want to restore. The restoration happens more quickly at the center of the brush.

6.0!

Perhaps as part of your use of the Liquify command you decide to freeze an area to which you have applied distortion. The Reconstruct tool allows you to extend that distortion from the frozen areas into unfrozen areas in interesting ways. You can also use the Reconstruct tool to sample a distortion from one part of the image and apply it elsewhere in the image.

To extend distortions from frozen areas into unfrozen areas:

1. Freeze one or more areas you have distorted. In this case, the borders of the image act as if they are frozen, too. Try reconstructing an area between two frozen areas.
2. Choose a reconstruction mode (other than Revert) from the Reconstruction Mode pop-up menu **1**.
3. Choose the Reconstruct tool (E) and paint on the image preview to restore unfrozen areas. Restoration occurs more quickly at the brush's center.

   or

   Click the Reconstruct button to reconstruct all unfrozen areas. The operation works by undoing your edits in reverse order, like a movie playing backwards. To stop the process, tap the Spacebar.

   Note (Mac OS only): Typing Esc. or Cmd-. [period] doesn't work to stop the reconstruction process, even though online help says it does. The online help is incorrect.

TIP To magnify and limit distortions to an area of the image, create a selection before choosing the Liquify command. The selected area will appear enlarged in the Liquify window. The View menu > Zoom in and Zoom out commands don't work for the Liquify dialog box.

TIP To undo all of your distortion and tool settings changes without closing the dialog box, Alt-click/Option-click the Cancel button to invoke the Reset command.

Deciphering the modes

The Rigid, Stiff, Smooth, and Loose Modes extend distortions of frozen areas into unfrozen areas, each in their own fashion. What results is part distortion and part restoration. **Smooth** and **Loose** produce more distortion, with a gradual boundary between frozen and non-frozen areas; **Rigid** and **Stiff** produce more restoration, with sharp boundaries between frozen and non-frozen areas. When you extend distortions, click the mouse or drag in one or two passes over the unfrozen areas.

The three choices at the bottom of the Mode pop-up menu allow you to copy various characteristics of the distortion at a specific point to other, unfrozen, parts of the image. **Displace** copies the displacement of the starting point to another point, moving imagery from one part of the image to another. **Amplitwist** takes displacement, rotation, and scaling from the starting point and copies them to other parts of the image. **Affine** copies all aspects of the distortion at the starting point to reconstructed areas, including displacement, rotation, horizontal scaling, vertical scaling, and skew.

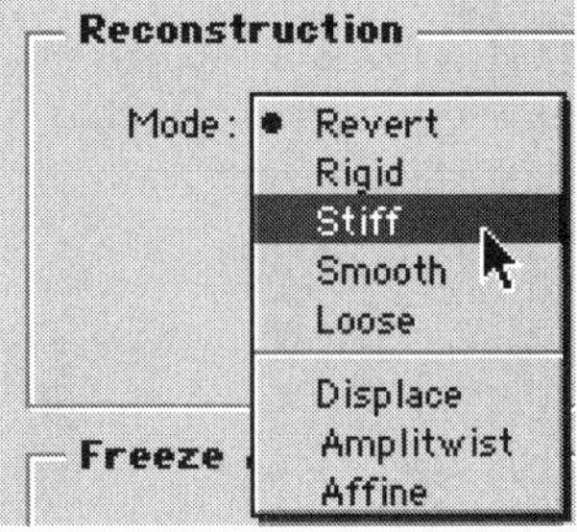

1 *The Reconstruction Mode pop-up menu.*

Frozen to Unfrozen

AUTOMATE 20

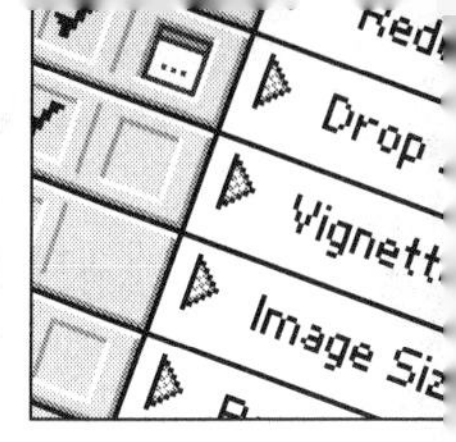

An **included** command has a black check mark; an excluded command has none. An **action**

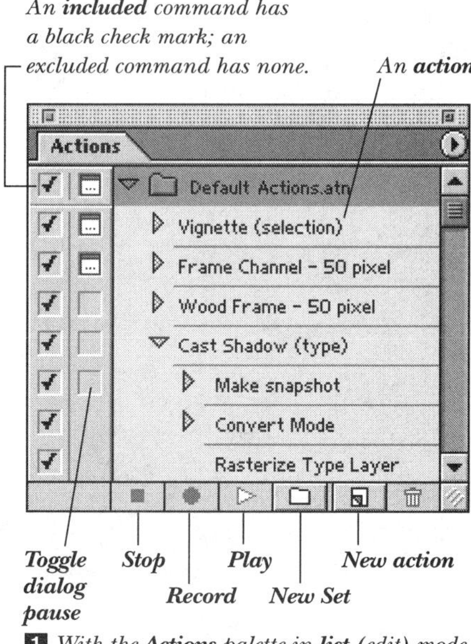

Toggle dialog pause **Stop** **Record** **Play** **New Set** **New action**

1 *With the* **Actions** *palette in* **list** *(edit) mode, you can exclude a command, toggle a dialog box pause on or off, rearrange the order of commands, record additional commands, rerecord a command, delete a command, or save actions and/or sets to an actions file. This is the default (start-up) mode.*

2 *The* **Actions** *palette in* **button mode**. *To turn Button mode on or off, choose Button Mode from the Actions palette command menu. The button colors and function keys chosen in the Action Options dialog box are displayed here.*

AN ACTION IS A recorded sequence of menu commands, tool operations, or other image editing functions that can be played back on a single file or on a group of files. Actions are especially useful for producing consistent editing results on multiple images. For example, you could use an action to apply a series of Adjust submenu commands or a sequence of filters. You could also save a sequence of concise steps into an action to prepare multiple images for print output or to convert multiple images to a different file format or image mode.

An action can be anything from a simple keyboard shortcut to an incredibly complex series of commands that trigger still other actions or that process a whole batch of images. Actions can help you can save seconds or hours of work time, depending on how they're used. Start by recording a few simple actions. You'll be programming more complex processes and boosting your productivity in no time.

6.0!

Actions can be created in Photoshop and ImageReady. The Actions palette is used to record, play back, edit, delete, save, and load actions **1**–**2**. Each action can be assigned its own keyboard shortcut for quick access. Actions can also be accessed via droplets—small applications created from actions. Draging a file or folder full of files onto a droplet icon activates the action.

TIP Make a snapshot of the image before running an action on it. That way, you can quickly revert, if necessary, to the pre-action state of the image, and you won't have to undo any action steps.

TIP With the Action Palette in list (edit) mode, Alt-click/Option-click a right pointing arrowhead to expand or collapse that action's entire list of steps.

Actions

Actions are saved in sets on the Actions palette. Sets are a convenient way of organizing task-related actions.

To create a new actions set:

1. Click the New Set button at the bottom of the Actions palette **1**.
2. Type a Name for the set **2**, then click OK.

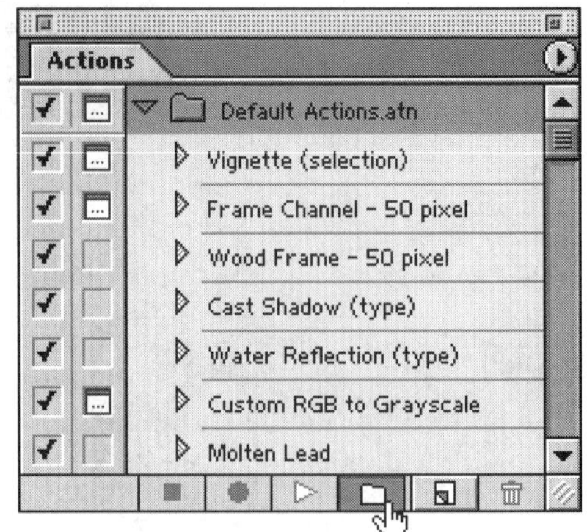

1 *New Action Set* button

As you create an action, the commands you use are recorded. When you're finished recording, the commands will appear as a list in indented (nested) format on the Actions palette.

Note: Some operations, such as Paintbrush tool strokes, can't be recorded.

To record an action:

1. Open an image or create a new one. Just to be safe, experiment by recording and playing back the action on a copy of the file.
2. Click the New Action button at the bottom of the Actions palette **3** or choose New Action from the Actions palette menu.
3. Enter a name for the action **4**.
4. *Optional:* Assign a keyboard shortcut Function Key and/or display Color to the action. The color you choose will only be displayed in button mode.
5. Click Record.
6. Execute the commands that you want to record as you would normally apply them to any image. When you enter values in a dialog box and then click OK, those settings will be recorded (except if you click Cancel).
7. Click the Stop button or press Esc to stop recording.
8. The action will now be listed on the Actions palette. Click the triangular button (list mode) to collapse the actions list.

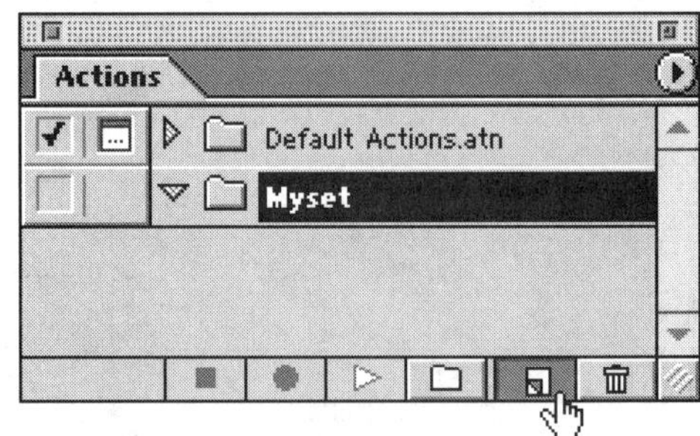

3 *New Action* button.

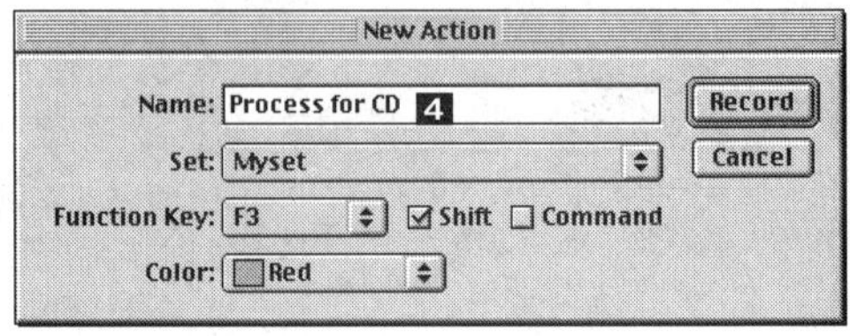

New Actions Set; Record Action

Newly recordable features 

The following is a list of commands, tools, and functions that can be incorporated into a recorded action. These items are in addition to those already supported by Photoshop 5.5:

Slice tool	Swatches palette
Magic Eraser	Color palette
Shape tool	Channels palette
Eyedropper tool	Styles palette
Choosing tool options	Setting some Preferences

It's all relative

The recording of any position-related operation (selection, slice, gradient, magic wand, path, or notes tools) is based on the current ruler units. The units can be **actual** (e.g., inches or picas) or **relative** (e.g., percent). An action that is recorded when an actual measurement unit is chosen cannot be played back on an image that is smaller than the original that was used for recording, whereas an action recorded when a relative unit is chosen will work in any other relative space and on an image of any dimensions.

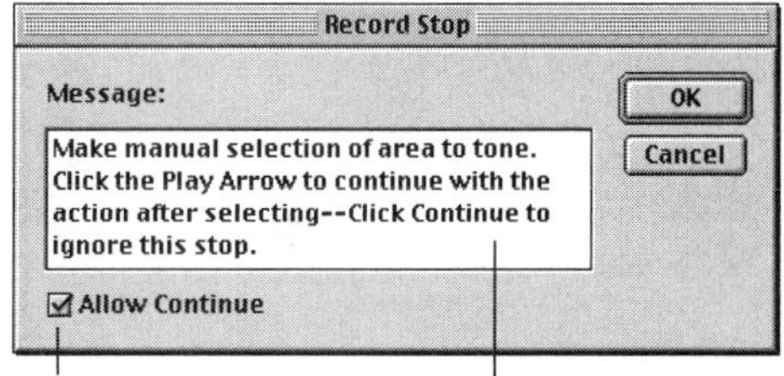

2 *Check the **Allow Continue** box to create a Continue button which the person replaying the action can press to bypass the stop command and resume playback.*

1 *Enter a **message** in the **Record Stop** dialog box to guide the user during playback.*

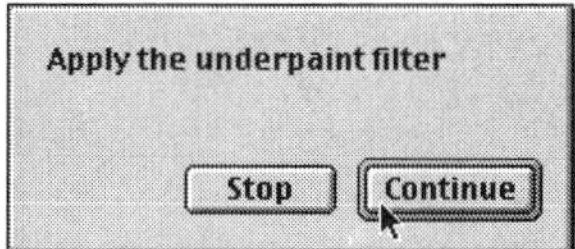

3 *The **Continue** button allows the user to continue the action wtihout performing manual tasks.*

TIP Double-click an action name on the palette to open the Action Options dialog box, where you can rename the action or reset its shortcut key or color.

TIP Include the Save command in an action with caution. When using the Save As command, be sure not to change the file name. You may want to make the action pause at the Save dialog box to prevent existing files from being overwritten (see below). To delete a Save or any other command from an action, see page 350.

You can insert a stop into an action that will interrupt the playback, at which point you can manually perform a non-recordable operation, such as drawing brushstrokes or spotting dust specs. When the manual operation is finished, you resume the playback by clicking on the play button a second time. A stop can also be used to display an informative alert message at the pause.

To insert a stop in an action:

1. As you're creating an action, pause at the point at which you want the stop to appear. For an existing action, click the command name after which you want the stop to appear.
2. Choose Insert Stop from the Actions palette menu.
3. Type an instructional or an alert message for the person who's going to replay the action **1**. It's a good idea to specify in your stop message that after performing a manual step, the user should click the Play button on the Actions palette to resume playback. The message will only appear while the stop dialog box is open.
4. *Optional:* Check the Allow Continue box **2** to include a Continue button in the stop alert box **3**. This allows the user to choose to continue the action without performing any manual tasks. *Note:* With Allow Continue unchecked, you will still be able to click Stop at that point in the action playback and then

(Continued on the following page)

Insert a Stop

click the Play button on the palette to resume the action playback.

5. Click OK.
6. The stop will be inserted below the command you highlighted in step 1 **1**.

TIP If an action is replayed while the Actions palette is in button mode, the Play button won't be accessible for resuming the playback after a stop. Click the action name again (the Play button will be red) to resume play instead. Choose list mode for the palette when you're using stops.

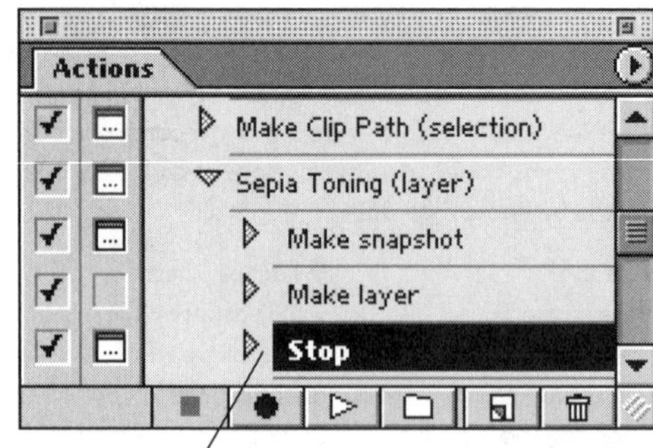

1 *A* ***Stop*** *command.*

To exclude or include a command from playback:

1. Make sure the Actions palette is in list—not button—mode. (In button mode, you can only execute an entire action, and any previously excluded commands won't play back.)
2. On the Actions palette, click the right-pointing triangle next to an action name to expand the list, if it isn't already expanded.
3. Click in the leftmost column to remove the check mark and exclude that command from playback **2**. (Click in the same spot again to restore the check mark and include the command.)

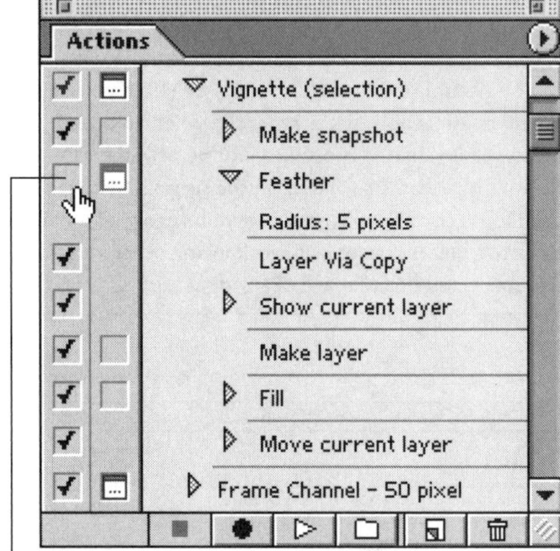

2 *The "Vignette" action is* ***expanded*** *on the Actions palette. The Feather step is unchecked to* ***exclude*** *it from playback.*

To play back an action on an image:

1. Open the image that you want to play back the action on.
2. Choose list mode for the Actions palette (uncheck button mode).
3. Click an action name on the palette.
4. Click the Play button on the palette **3**.
   or
   Create a droplet from the desired action, then drag files onto the droplet icon (see page 349 on how to make your own droplets).

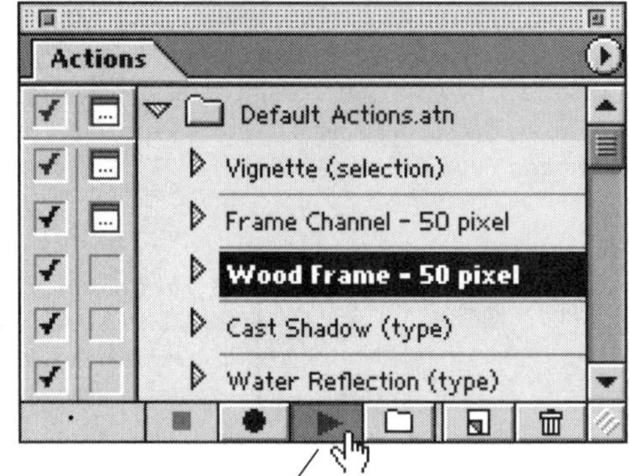

3 *Click the* ***Play*** *button on the palette.*

Playback options

Four options for playback control are available on the Actions palette menu—but only when the palette is in list mode.

Accelerated: The fastest option.

Step by Step: When this option is chosen, the action's list expands on the Actions palette. Each step applies to the image as the commands on the action list highlight and execute.

Pause for [ ] seconds: This option works like Step by Step, but with an additional user-defined pause inserted at each step.

Pause for Audio Annotation: This option allows the pausing of the playback until the audio note has completed.

More playback options

- To play an action starting from a specific command within the action, click that command name, then click the Play button or choose Play from the Actions palette menu.
- To play one command in a multi-command action, click the command name, then Ctrl-click/Cmd-click the Play button or Ctrl/Cmd double-click the command.

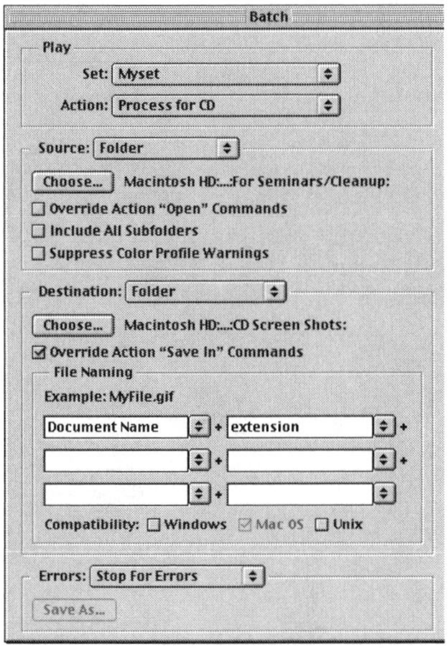

The ability to replay an action using the Batch command is one of the most powerful features of actions.

Note: Batch processing will end at a stop command in an action. You should remove any inserted stops from an action if you're going to use it for batch playback.

To replay an action on a batch of images: 6.0!

1. Make sure all the files for batch processing are located in the same folder.
2. Choose File menu > Automate > Batch.
3. Choose a set from the Set pop-up menu and choose an action from the Action pop-up menu **1**.
4. Choose Source: Folder.
   and
   Click Choose, then locate the folder that contains the files you want to process.
5. Choose Destination: None to leave the files open after processing; or choose Save and Close to save the files over their originals; or choose Folder to save the files to a new folder (click Choose to specify the destination folder).
6. *Optional:* If you chose Folder for the previous steps and checked the Override Action "Save In" Commands box, the image will save to the folder designated in step 5 during playback when a Save command occurs in the action.
7. Click OK. The batch processing will begin.

TIP For efficient batching, organize your files and folders ahead of time. Make sure all your source files are in the same folder—and make sure the destination folder exists!

TIP For efficient memory management, set the History States in the Preferences Dialog to 1 before batching. You can even include the setting and resetting of the History States inside the action itself!

1

6.0!

If Folder is chosen as the Destination for batch files, there are many options for the resultant file names. For example, the files can be named sequentially using serial numbers or letters so they don't replace each other in the new folder. There are also options for ensuring that the file names are compatible with various operating systems.

To choose batch naming options:

1. Choose File menu > Automate > Batch.
2. Choose Destination: Folder.
3. Choose options from the pop-up menus in the File Naming area **1** or simply type in any text you want to include in the name.
4. Verify that the naming convention chosen is what you want via the *Example* name.
5. Check any of the boxes for file name Compatibility: Windows, Mac OS, or Unix.

   Note: The files being processed by the Batch command are always saved in their original format. To force them to save to another format, when creating the action, record the Save As command (leave the name alone), then continue the action with the Close command. When choosing batch settings, be sure to check the Override Action "Save In" Commands box.
5. *Optional:* By default, Photoshop will stop the batch process when it encounters an error message. You can choose to have the Batch play through and just keep track of the error messages in a text file by choosing Log Errors to File from the Errors menu. If this option is chosen and errors are encountered, a message will appear after processing. In order to see the logged error messages, click Save As and give the error log file a name.

TIP It's a good idea to create the folder for saving the processed files *before* using the Batch command.

1

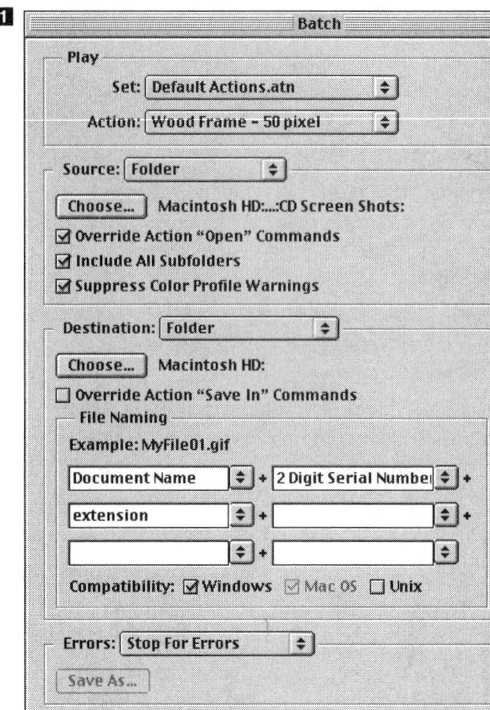

Batch Naming Options

Back and forth

To make a droplet that was created in Windows useable on Mac OS (Mac OS ready), drag the droplet onto the Photoshop 6 **application** icon. To make a Mac-made droplet useable on Windows, add the extention **.exe** at the end of the droplet name.

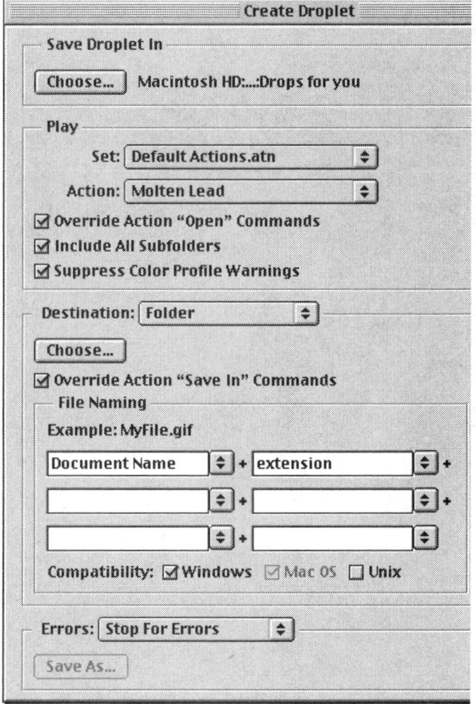

1

*This is what a **droplet** icon looks like.*

6.0!

Photoshop 6 adds the ability to turn an action into its own little application called a droplet. The droplet can sit out on the desktop or in a folder waiting for some "action." If you drag a file or a folder full of files onto the droplet icon, the droplet will cause the file to be processed automatically.

Once a droplet is created it can be given to other users or used on other computers, since it's a standalone "action." Photoshop 6 will launch in order to let the droplet do its work, just in case the program isn't open when any graphic files are dragged onto the droplet icon.

To create a droplet from an action:

1. Choose File menu > Automate > Create Droplet.
2. Click Choose, then choose the location where you want to save the droplet **1**.
3. Choose a set from the Set pop-up menu and choose an action from the Action pop-up menu.
4. Check any play options you want to be included in the droplet.
5. Choose Destination options (see steps 5 and 6 on page 348).
6. Click OK to have Photoshop create a mini application droplet.

TIP In ImageReady, you can create a droplet simply by dragging an action to the Desktop.

Droplets

Note: A command that's available only under certain conditions (e.g., the Feather command requires an active selection) can't be added to an action unless you also set up or add in that condition.

To add commands to an action:

1. On the Actions palette, click the right-pointing triangle next to an action's name to expand the list, if it's not already expanded, then click the command name after which you want the new command to appear.
2. Choose Start Recording from the Actions palette menu or click the Record button **1**.
3. Perform the steps to record the command(s) that you want to add.
4. Click the Stop button **2** to stop recording.

TIP To copy a command from one action to another, expand both action lists, then Alt-drag/Option-drag the command you want to copy from one list to the other. If you don't hold down Alt/Option while dragging, you'll cut the command from the original action. Be careful if you copy any Save commands—they may contain info that's specific to the original action.

Beware! To save the current list of actions as a set for later use, follow the instructions on page 353 **before** you clear any items from the Actions palette.

To delete a command from an action:

1. Click the name of the command that you want to delete **3**. Shift-click to highlight additional commands, if desired.
2. Click the Delete (trash) button at the bottom of the Actions palette, then click OK.
   or
   Drag the command to the Delete button.

Record redux?

A command can be inserted into an existing action using **Insert Menu Item**. Dialog box settings, however, won't be recorded using this command. Instead, the action will open the dialog box, wait for user input, and then resume. We recommend following the first set of instructions for adding a command (on this page) as a means to insert a controllable pause for any dialog box.

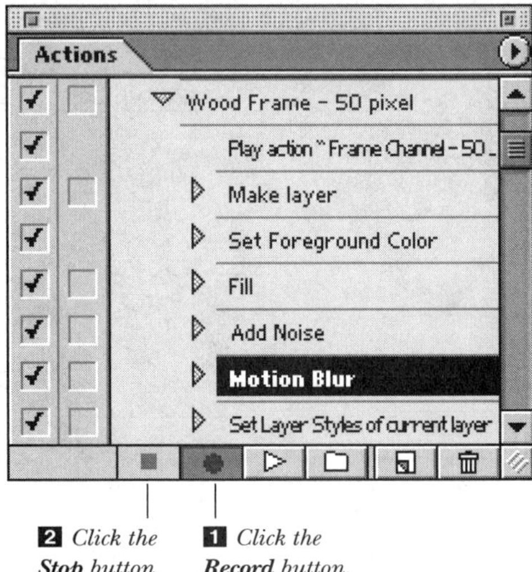

2 *Click the* ***Stop*** *button.* **1** *Click the* ***Record*** *button.*

3 *Click the command that you want to delete, then click the* ***Delete*** *button.*

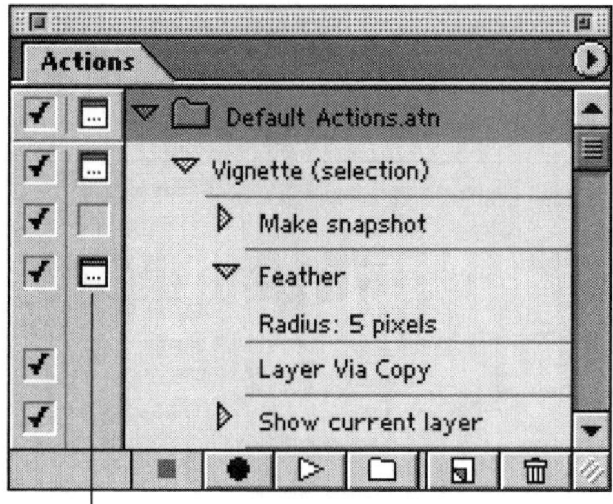

1 *The **dialog box** icon*

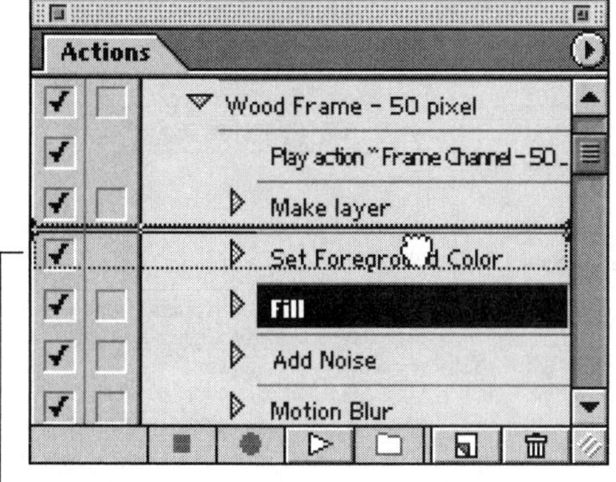

2 *The Fill command being **moved upward** on the list.*

A modal control is a pause in an action. A modal control can be turned on for any command that uses a dialog box or tool that requires pressing Enter/Return to apply the effect. If you encounter a modal control upon playing back an action, you can either enter different settings in the dialog box or click OK to proceed with the settings that were originally recorded for the action.

To activate/deactivate a modal control in an action:

1. Make sure the Actions palette is in list mode (not button mode).
2. On the Actions palette, click the right-pointing triangle (list toggle button) next to the action name to expand the list, if it's not already expanded.
3. Click in the second column from the left to display the dialog box icon **1**. (Click again in the same spot if you want to remove the modal control.) The action will pause and display this command's dialog box when the modal control is encountered, at which point you can enter new values, or accept the existing values, or cancel. The playback will resume after you close the dialog box.

Beware! Changing the order of commands in an action may cause a different overall effect to occur in any images it is played back on.

To change the order of commands:

1. On the Actions palette, click the right-pointing triangle next to an action name to expand the list, if it's not already expanded.
2. Drag a command upward or downward on the list **2**.

To rerecord an entire action using different dialog box settings:

1. Click the name of the action that you want to revise.
2. Choose Record Again from the Actions palette menu. The action will play back,

(Continued on the following page)

stopping at commands that use dialog boxes.

3. When each dialog box opens, enter new settings, if desired, then click OK. When the dialog box closes, the rerecording will continue.
4. To stop the rerecording, click Cancel in a dialog box or click the Stop button at the bottom of the Actions palette.

To rerecord a single command in an action:

1. On the Actions palette, double-click the command you want to rerecord **1**.
2. Enter new settings.
3. Click OK. Click Cancel to have any revisions be disregarded.

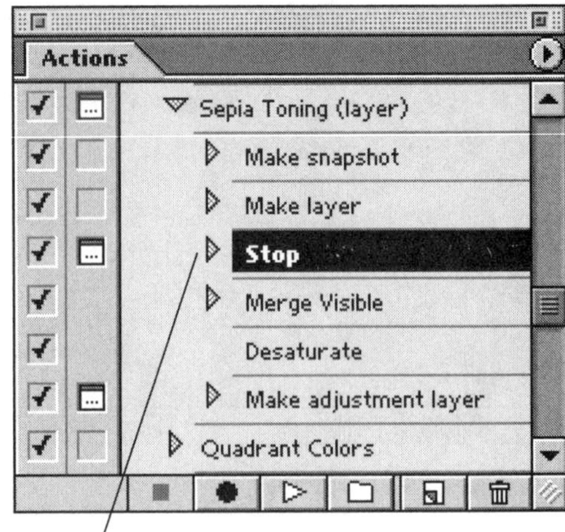

1 ***Double-click*** *the command you want to* ***rerecord****.*

If you want to experiment with an action or add to it without messing around with the original, work on a duplicate.

To duplicate an action:

Click the name of the action you want to duplicate, then choose Duplicate from the Actions palette menu.

or

Drag the name of the action you want to duplicate over the "Create new action" button at the bottom of the Actions palette **2**.

TIP To duplicate a command in an action, click the command name, then choose Duplicate from the palette menu. Or drag the command over the "Create new action" button at the bottom of the Actions palette.

2 *To* ***duplicate*** *an action, drag the action name over the* ***Create new action*** *button.*

To delete an entire action:

1. Highlight the name of the action you want to delete.
2. Click the Delete (trash) button at the bottom of the Actions palette, then click OK.

   or

   Alt-click/Option-click the Delete button.

Rerecord, Duplicate, Delete Action

Where are actions stored?

All actions that are visible on the Actions palette list are stored in the **Actions Palette.psp** (Win) or **Actions Palette** (Mac OS) file in the System Folder > Preferences > Adobe Photoshop 6 Settings folder. They live there until they are replaced or the file is trashed. To keep a set from being inadvertently removed, save it as a separate file!

For easy access, save your Actions Sets in the Adobe Photoshop 6 > Presets > **Photoshop Actions** folder. Then they will appear at the bottom of the Actions palette menu.

Actions and AppleScript

Mac OS: An action can be controlled from another scriptable application, such as AppleScript. AppleScript is a relatively easy scripting language to learn. A scriptable application like InDesign, Filemaker Pro, QuarkXPress, or Hypercard lets you drive actions externally using the AppleScript do-script command.

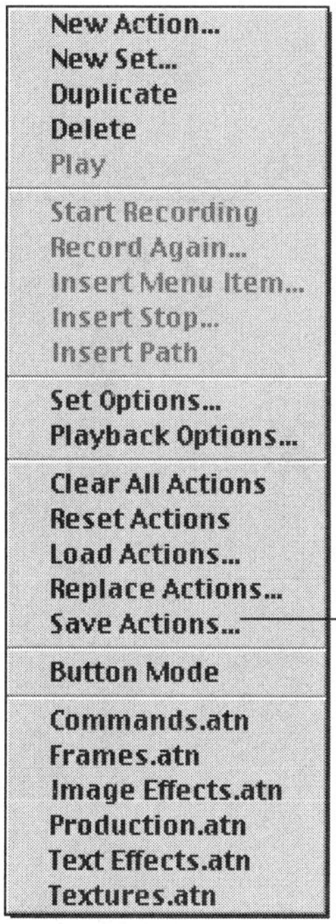

New Action...
New Set...
Duplicate
Delete
Play
Start Recording
Record Again...
Insert Menu Item...
Insert Stop...
Insert Path
Set Options...
Playback Options...
Clear All Actions
Reset Actions
Load Actions...
Replace Actions...
Save Actions...
Button Mode
Commands.atn
Frames.atn
Image Effects.atn
Production.atn
Text Effects.atn
Textures.atn

1 *Choose **Save Actions** from the Actions palette menu. (To load an actions set, choose **Load Actions**.)*

Actions are stored automatically in actions sets (a set can contain one or more actions). Follow these instructions to save an actions set to a file for use on another computer or as a backup to prevent accidental or inadvertent loss.

To save an actions set to a file:

1. Click the actions set you want to save.
2. Choose Save Actions from the Actions palette menu **1**.
3. Type a Name for the actions set file.
4. Choose a location in which to save the actions set file.
5. Click Save. The new file will be regarded as one set, regardless of the number of actions it contains.

TIP If you Alt-drag/Option-drag an action into another actions set, it will copy automatically.

To load an additional actions set onto the Actions palette:

1. Click the set name that you want the loaded set to appear below.
2. Choose Load Actions from the Actions palette menu **1**.
3. Locate and highlight the actions set file you want to append.
4. Click Load/Open.
   or
   Choose an actions set name from the bottom of the palette menu. (These sets are stored in the Adobe Photoshop > Presets > Photoshop Actions folder.)

To replace the current actions set with a different actions set:

1. Choose Replace Actions from the Actions palette menu.
2. Locate and highlight the actions set file that you want to replace the existing sets with.
3. Click Load/Open.

You can make an action run within another action.

Beware! The action that will be added to another action will run through all of its commands, and thus will affect the currently open image. So, make sure that you perform this recording on a duplicate image!

To run one action in another action:

1. Open a file.
2. On the Actions palette, click the right-pointing triangle (list toggle button) next to the action name to expand the list, if it's not already expanded, then select the command after which you want the added action to appear **1**.
3. Click Record **2**.
4. Choose the action to be added **3**.
5. Click the Play Button **4** to record it into the other action (you can't double-click the action). The added action will run through its commands. The new command on the actions list will have this name: "Play Action [action name] of set [set name]."
6. Click the Stop button when the original action is finished **5**.

TIP An action can include multiple actions, but be careful, planning ahead is essential. An action may have been moved or modified or may be unavailable the next time you call upon it. Spend some time organizing your actions and sets, and back up often.

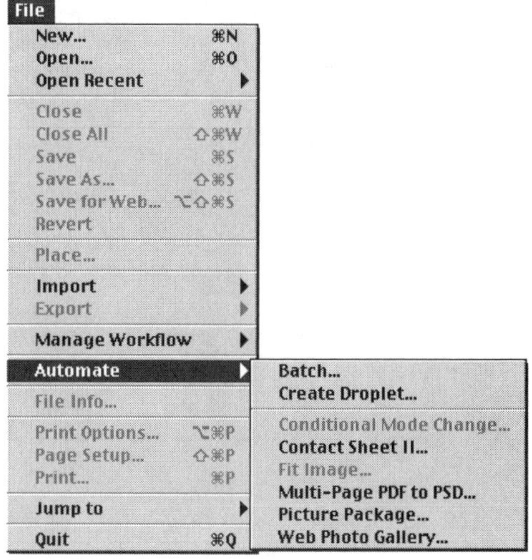

1 *The **Automate** commands under the File menu.*

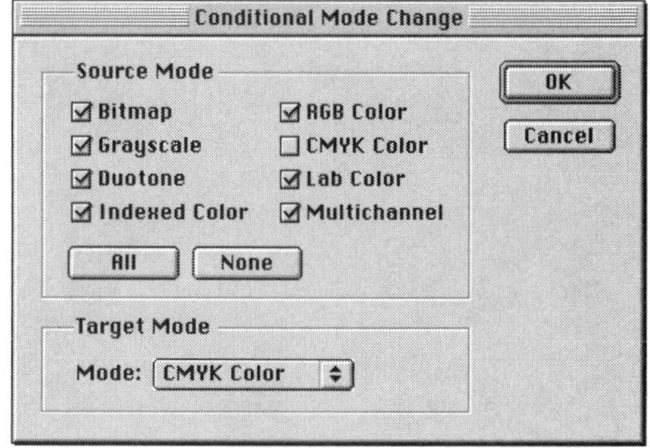

2 *Choose the **Source Mode** and **Target Mode** in the **Condition Mode Change** dialog box.*

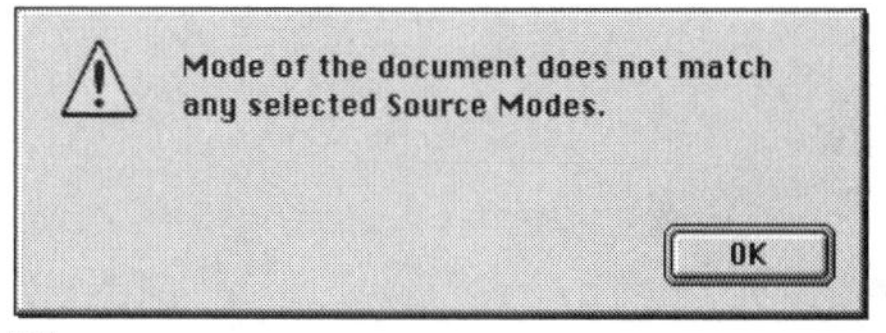

3

Other automate commands

In addition to the Batch and Create Droplet commands on the Automate submenu, there are six other commands that work like actions on steroids: Conditional Mode Change, Contact Sheet II, Fit Image, Multi-Page PDF to PSD, Picture Package, and Web Photo Gallery **1**. These commands combine many complex command sequences into one dialog box setting. Adobe will more than likely offer more of these pumped-up actions in the future and surely third-party developers will supply even more. It's a computer doing what a computer does best.

By adding this command to an action, you can ensure that all the files being processed will have the desired image mode.

To perform a conditional image mode change:

1. Choose File menu > Automate > Conditional Mode Change.
2. Select the source file image mode that you want to convert **2**.
3. Choose the desired image mode from the Target Mode: Mode drop-down menu. If the image mode of the processed file doesn't match any of the selected Source Modes, an alert dialog box will appear (click OK) **3**.
4. Click OK.

A contact sheet is an arrangement of image thumbnails on a page, all with the same size bounding box—with or without file name captions.

To create a contact sheet:

1. Move all the images you want to appear on the contact sheet or sheets into one folder or nest them in subdirectories/subfolders of that folder. Also make sure all the files you want to appear on a contact sheet or sheets are saved in a format that Photoshop can read. And finally, make sure the files aren't open.
2. Choose File menu > Automate > Contact Sheet II.
3. Click Choose, locate the folder that contains the images for the contact sheet, then click "Select [folder name]." **1**

   Optional: Check the Include All Subdirectories/Subfolders box if you want to include images in any subdirectories/subfolders inside the designated folder—not just files on the top level of the source directory/folder.
4. Choose a measurement unit from the Document: Width and Height pop-up menus, then enter a Width and Height for the contact sheet.
5. Choose a Resolution for the sheet.
6. Choose a Mode for the contact sheet.
7. In the Thumbnails area of the dialog box, choose a Place option to specify the direction in which the images are to be arranged: in horizontal or vertical rows.
   and
   Enter the number of Columns and Rows to appear on the contact sheet. The contact sheet layout will preview on the right side of the dialog box.
8. *Optional:* Check the Use Filename As Caption box to have a caption with the file's name appear under each thumbnail. If you use this option, choose a Font and Font Size for the captions.
9. Click OK **2**.

1

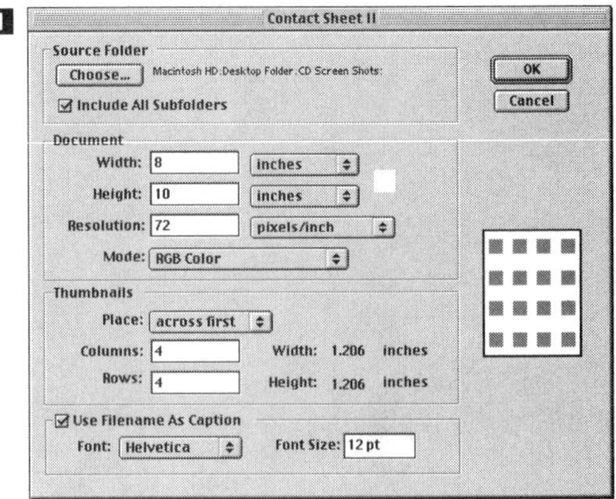

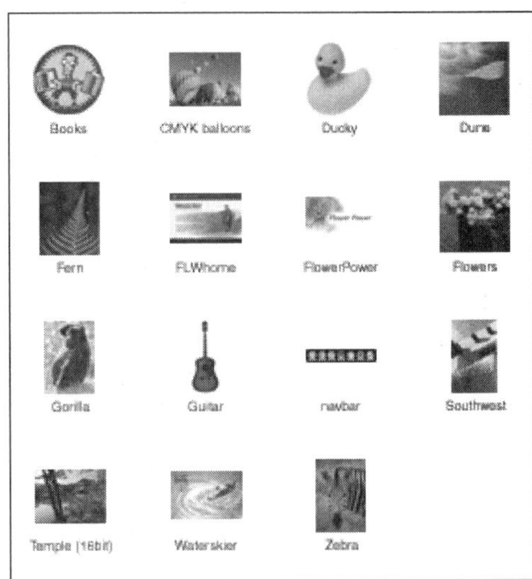

2 *A contact sheet with filename captions.*

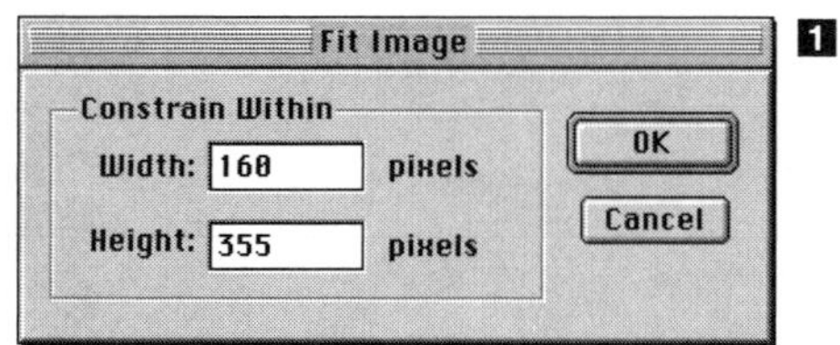

1

Note: Be forewarned, the Fit Image changes an image's dimensions via resampling (by adding or deleting pixels). The image resolution will remain constant.

To fit an image to width and/or height dimensions:

1. Open a file.
2. Choose File menu > Automate > Fit Image.
3. Enter the desired Constrain Within: Width and Height dimensions.

   The smaller of the numbers will be used for the fit. For example, say your source image is 210 x 237 and you enter 275 in the Height field and 1500 in the Width field. The image will be fit to the 275 dimension at the original aspect ratio (with a long dimension of 310).
4. Click OK.

A multi-page Acrobat PDF file can be imported into Photoshop. See pages 58 and 62 to learn more about PDF. ("PSD" is the extension for the Photoshop file format.)

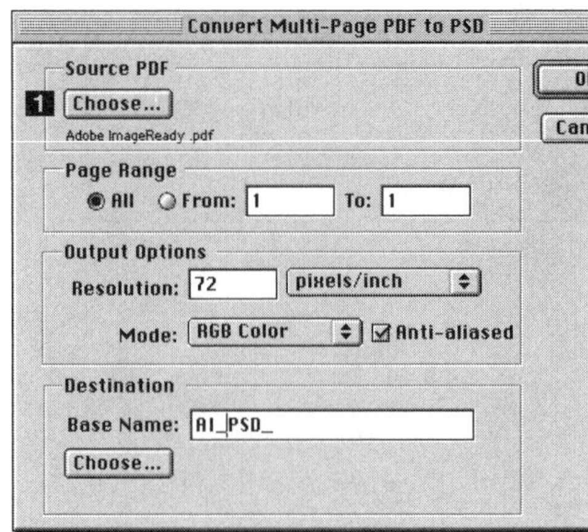

To convert a multi-page PDF to Photoshop format:

1. Choose File menu > Automate > Multi-Page PDF to PSD.
2. Under Source PDF, click Choose, then locate and select the PDF file you want to convert **1**.
3. Click a Page Range: All or click From and enter a page range. It's a good idea to be familiar with the source file, because you won't see a preview of the PDF file.
4. In the Output Options area, enter a Resolution. For a PDF that contains type for print output, enter a minimum Resolution of 250 ppi so the type will rasterize well. 72 ppi is sufficient for a PDF for Web output.
5. Choose a Mode (you can change the image mode later in Photoshop).

   Checking the Anti-aliased option slightly softens the edges of type characters, but it also makes them slightly thinner.
6. Under Destination, leave the Base Name as is or enter a new name for the converted file. The name will be followed by 0001.psd, 0002.psd, and so on, to identify the source pages.
7. Click Choose, then locate and select a destination folder for the converted files.
8. Click OK. Image windows will quickly display and close on screen while the conversion process is happening. When it's completed, all the converted files will be located in the folder you designated in the previous step, and they can be opened and edited like any other Photoshop files.

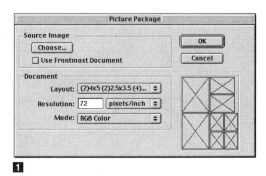

The Picture Package plug-in arranges multiple sizes of one image on the same sheet, like the layouts produced by traditional photo studios. You can choose from a variety of preset sizes and configurations.

To create a picture package:

1. Choose File menu > Automate > Picture Package.
2. Click Choose **1**, locate the image you want to use, then click Select.
   or
   Check the Use Frontmost Document box to use the currently open, active image.
3. In the Document area of the dialog box, choose a Layout option for the size (in inches) of the images that will appear on the page. The layout will preview on the right side of the dialog box.
   and
   Choose a Resolution for the picture package file.
   and
   Choose a color Mode for the picture package file.
4. Click OK or press Enter/Return. Sit there and do nothing while the Picture Package command does the work for you (watch what happens on the History palette) **2**.
5. Save the new file in the desired format.

TIP Press Esc to stop the command during processing.

TIP To create your own custom layouts, see "Customizing picture package layouts" in Adobe Photoshop on-line Help.

2 *This is the (2) 4 x 5 & (2) 2.5 x 3.5 & (4) 2 x 2.5* ***Picture Package Layout****. Many other layout options are available.*

6.0!

Using the Web Photo Gallery command, you can export multiple images directly as a Web site. Photoshop does all the work for you. You'll get, automatically: a gallery homepage with its index.htm file, which can be opened in any Web browser for previewing the photo gallery; individual JPEG image pages inside an images subfolder; HTML page files inside a pages subfolder; and JPEG thumbnail images inside a thumbnails subfolder.

Note: When you're ready to upload your Web gallery to a server, ask your Internet service provider (ISP) which file and folder naming conventions to use, and also ask for uploading instructions.

To create a Web gallery:

1. Make sure the images you want to use for the gallery are contained or nested in one folder.
2. Choose File menu > Automate > Web Photo Gallery.
3. Choose a layout style from the Styles menu for the website: Horizontal Frame, Simple, Table, or Vertical Frame. Note the dialog box preview for each style.
4. Choose an Options pop-up menu setting for text information, image size and resolution, fonts used, file naming conventions, and link colors:

   Choose **Banner**, then enter the information you want to appear on every page of the gallery **1**. Type the Site Name, Photographer, and Date, and choose the Font and Font Size for the banner text.

   Choose **Gallery Images** to choose quality, size, and border settings for the images used on every gallery page **2**. The size of the border around each image is measured in pixels. If you check the Resize Images box, Photoshop will resize the source images for placement on individual image pages for you; with this box unchecked, Photoshop will leave the source image size alone.

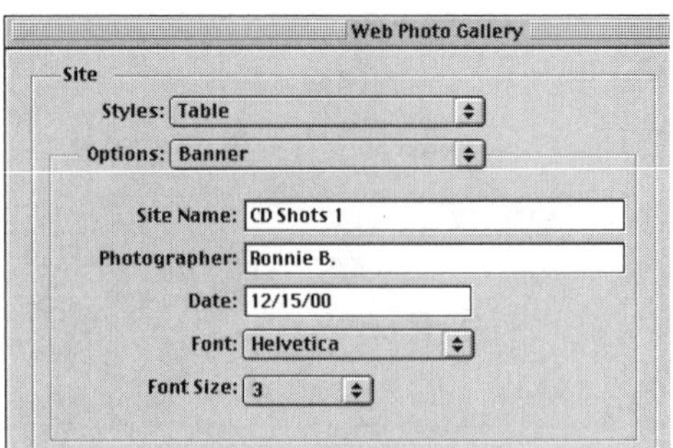

1 *The Web Photo Gallery dialog box with* ***Banner*** *chosen on the Options pop-up menu.*

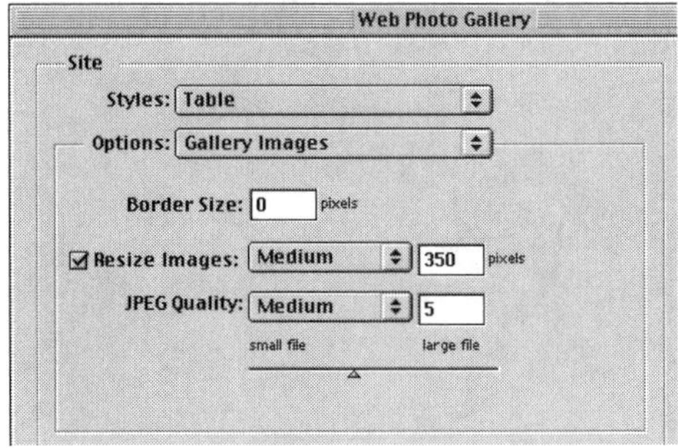

2 *The Web PhotoGallery dialog box with* ***Gallery Images*** *chosen on the Options pop-up menu.*

Web Photo Gallery

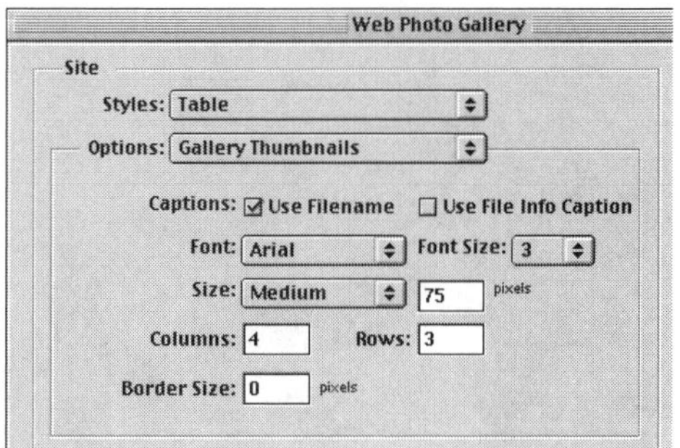

1 *The Web Photo Gallery dialog box with* ***Gallery Thumbnails*** *chosen on the Options pop-up menu.*

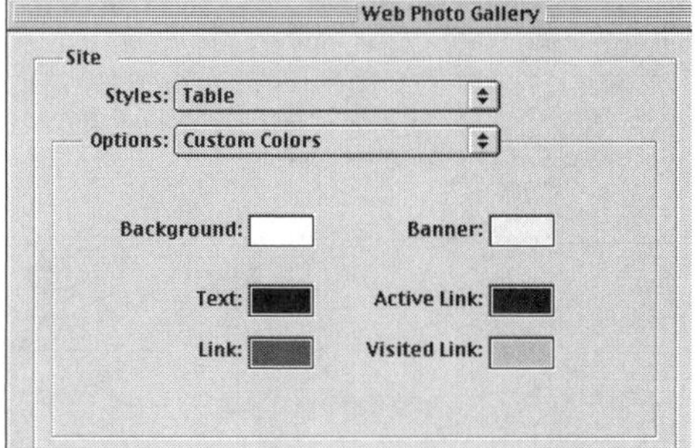

2 *The Web Photo Gallery dialog box with* ***Custom Colors*** *chosen on the Options pop-up menu.*

If you chose Gallery Images, also choose a rough size from the Resize Images pop-up menu or enter a specific resize percentage, and choose a JPEG Quality (0–12). The higher the JPEG Quality, the larger the file size. You can also move the slider; as you do so, watch how the selection on the JPEG Quality pop-up menu changes.

Choose **Gallery Thumbnails** to set options for the home page of the web gallery **1**. Check the Use Filename As Caption box to have a caption with the file's name appear under each thumbnail. Check the Use File Info Caption to use the text from the file's File menu > File Info dialog box. Also choose Font settings for the text; choose the thumbnail image Size; and choose thumbnail layout settings (Columns, Rows, and Border Size fields).

Choose Custom Colors to choose colors for Background, Banner Text, and Links spaces **2**. Click a color swatch to change it via the Color Picker (remember to use Web Safe colors if possible).

5. Click Source, locate the folder that contains the images you want to use, then click Select.

   Optional: Check the Include All Subdirectories/Subfolders box if you want to include images in any subdirectories/subfolders inside the designated folder—not just files on the top level of the source directory/folder.

6. Click Destination, locate the folder that you want to save the resulting HTML files in, then click Select.

7. Click OK. Photoshop will create the following files: at least one home page named index.htm; JPEG files for the images and thumbnails; and HTML files for the other pages of the site.

(Continued on the following page)

TIP Keep all the gallery files and folders within one folder in order to preserve the links.

TIP If you click on a thumbnail or caption in a Web browser, an enlarged view of that image will appear. You may also get navigation arrows to enable the viewer to navigate to the previous picture, next picture, or home page **1**.

TIP The navigation arrows will be saved as individual files in the "Images" folder in your chosen destination folder, under the names home.gif, previous.gif, and next.gif. You can open any of these images in ImageReady and edit them, or replace them with your own images. If you do so, choose File menu > Save Optimized and save with the same name to the same location. Answer yes to any alert dialog boxes.

TIP To change the grayscale palette of the original navigation arrow file to a color palette, on the ImageReady Optimize palette, change the GIF palette setting from Custom to another type. Then use Image menu > Adjust > Hue/Saturation to colorize the existing arrow or drag-and-drop another image into the ImageReady main window to use it as a substitute for the default navigation arrow.

TIP See "Customizing and creating web photo gallery styles" in the Adobe Photoshop on-line Help for more ideas and options regarding this feature.

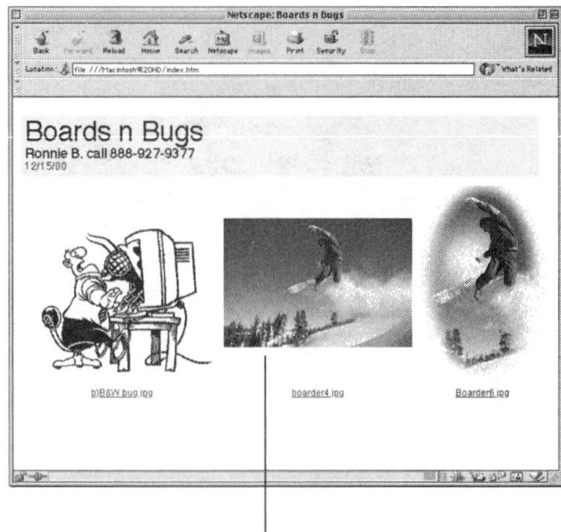

1 *The finished* ***Web Photo Gallery*** *homepage. Clicking a thumbnail image or name here on the homepage links you to an enlarged image view page, complete with navigation arrows.*

PREFERENCES 21

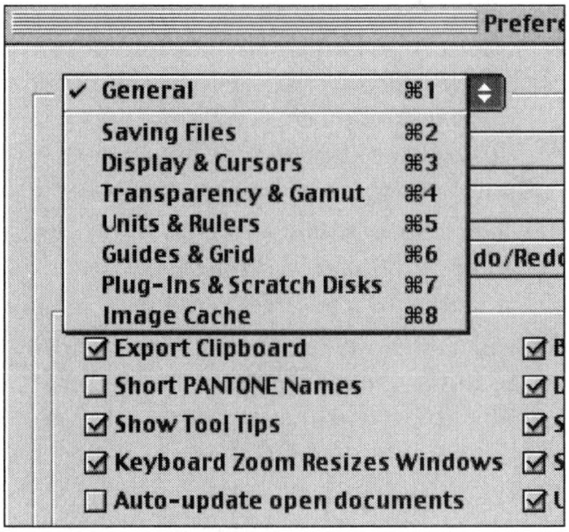

*To access the preferences dialog boxes quickly, use the **Ctrl-K/Cmd-K** shortcut to open the General Preferences dialog box, then use any of the shortcuts illustrated above to access other dialog boxes, or click **Next** or **Prev** on the right side of the dialog box to cycle through them.*

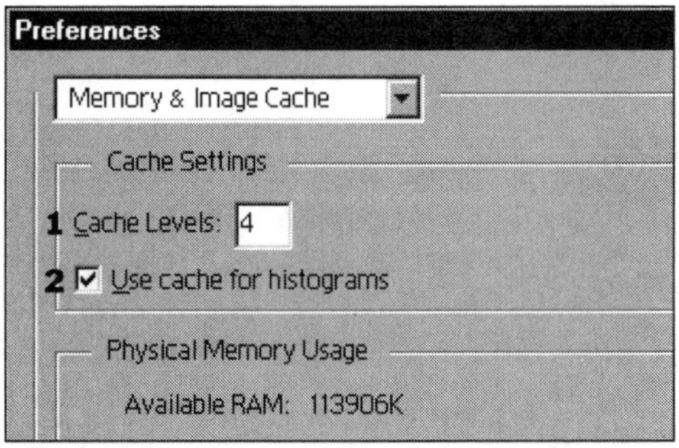

Windows: Memory & Image Cache Preferences

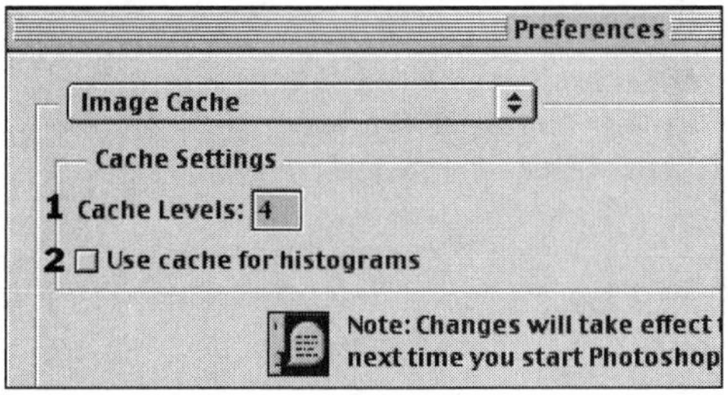

Mac OS: Image Cache Preferences

PREFERENCES ARE settings that apply to the application as a whole, such as which ruler units are used, or if channels display in color. Most preference changes take effect immediately; a few take effect on re-launching (we've noted those exceptions). All are saved when you exit/quit Photoshop. To access the preferences dialog boxes the fast-and-easy way, see the illustration at left. Or use the Edit menu > Preferences submenu.

To reset all the preferences to their default values:

Hold down Ctrl-Alt-Shift (Win)/Cmd-Option-Shift (Mac OS) at Startup. Click Yes to delete the Photoshop settings file. Do the same thing at startup for ImageReady.

Memory & Image Cache Preferences (Win)
Image Cache Preferences (Mac OS)

1 The image cache is designed to help speed up screen redraw when you're editing or color adjusting high resolution images. Low-resolution versions of the image are saved in individual cache buffers and are used to update the on-screen image. The higher the **Cache Levels** value (1–8), the more buffers are used, and the speedier the redraw.

2 Check **Use cache for histograms** for faster, but slightly less accurate, histogram display in the Levels and Histogram dialog boxes.

General Preferences

1 Choose the Adobe **Color Picker** to access the application's own Color Picker. If you're trying to mix a color in Photoshop to match a color in a browser, use the Windows or Apple Color Picker.

2 Choose an **Interpolation** option for reinterpretation of an image as a result of resampling or transforming. Bicubic is slowest, but highest quality. Nearest Neighbor is fastest, but poorest quality.

3 Choose the shortcut key for Redo from the **Redo Key** pop-up menu. 6.0!

4 Enter the maximum number of **History States** that can be listed on the History palette at one time (1–100). 6.0!

5 Check **Export Clipboard** to have the current Clipboard contents stay on the Clipboard when you exit/quit Photoshop.

6 Check **Short PANTONE Names** if your image contains Pantone colors and you are exporting it to another application.

7 Check **Show Tool Tips** to see an on-screen display of the name of the tool or icon currently under the pointer.

8 With **Keyboard Zoom Resizes Windows** unchecked, the illustration window won't resize when the view size is changed using Ctrl/Cmd- + or -.

9 Check **Auto-update open documents** to have documents save automatically when jumping between Photoshop and ImageReady. Documents update after jumping, whether this option is on or off.

10 Check **Show Asian Text Options** to view and set options for Chinese, Japanese, and Korean type. 6.0!

11 Check **Beep When Done** to have a beep sound when any command that takes time to process (has a progress bar) is done processing.

12 With **Dynamic Color Sliders** checked, colors above the sliders on the Color palette will update as the sliders are moved. Turn this option off to speed performance.

13 With **Save Palette Locations** checked, palettes that are open when you exit/quit Photoshop will appear in their same location when you re-launch.

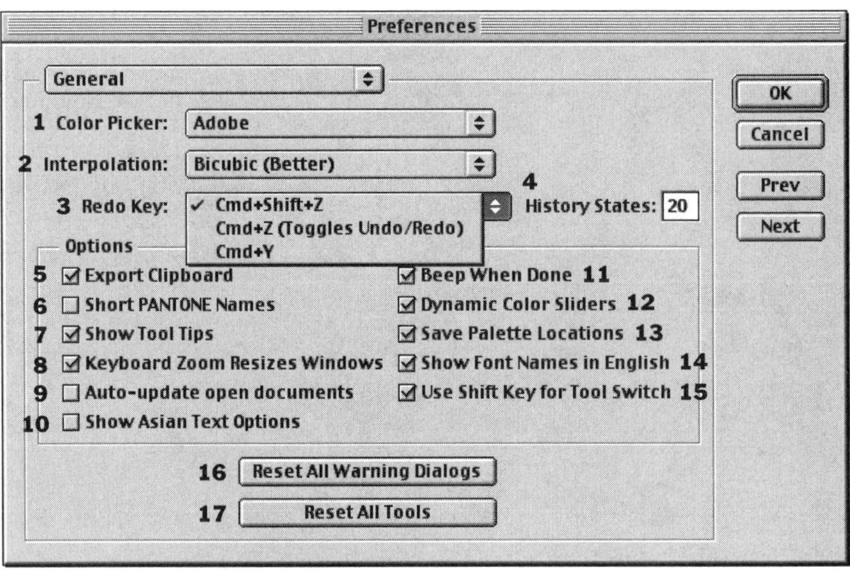

General Preferences

14 With **Show Font Names in English** checked, font names on the Font pop-up menu will display in English, not in the native language.

15 With **Use Shift Key for Tool Switch** checked, hidden tools can be accessed using Shift and the letter assigned to a tool (e.g., Shift-R cycles through the Blur, Sharpen, and Smudge tools).

16 Click **Reset All Warning Dialogs** to reenable all warning prompt messages that have been disabled by selecting the Don't Show Again option in individual message dialog boxes.

17 Click **Reset All Tools** to reset all tools to their default settings and their default position in the Toolbox.

Saving Files Preferences

1 Choose **Image Previews: Never Save** to save files without previews, choose **Always Save** to save files with the specified previews, or choose **Ask When Saving** to assign previews for each individual file when it's saved for the first time.

Mac OS: Click **Icon** to display a thumbnail of the image in its file icon on the desktop. Click **Full Size** to include a 72-ppi PICT preview for applications which require this option when importing a non-EPS file. Click **Macintosh Thumbnail** and/or **Windows Thumbnail** to display a thumbnail of an image when its name is highlighted in the Open dialog box.

2 *Mac OS:* Choose **Append File Extension: Always** or **Ask When Saving** to include a three-letter abbreviation of the file format type (i.e., "tif" for TIFF) when you save a Macintosh file. This is helpful when converting to Windows.

Win and Mac: Choose/check **Use Lower Case** if you want the extension to appear in lowercase characters.

3 Check **File Compatibility: Maximize backwards compability in Photoshop format** to maximize file compatibility with previous versions of Photoshop and other programs (e.g., a rasterized version of each layer is saved for programs that don't support vector data). This option produces larger file sizes and causes files to save more slowly.

Check **Enable advanced TIFF save options** to enable the TIFF format (for saving layers and annotations) and to use JPEG or ZIP compression.

4 In the **Recent file list contains [ ] files** field, enter the maximum number of files that can be listed on the File menu > Open Recent submenu (0–30).

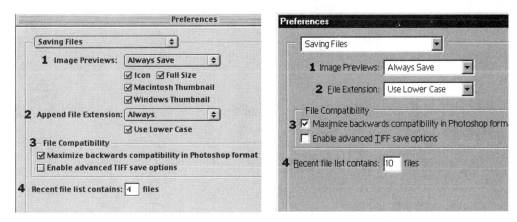

Preferences
Saving Files
1 Image Previews: Always Save
☑ Icon ☑ Full Size
☑ Macintosh Thumbnail
☑ Windows Thumbnail
2 Append File Extension: Always
☑ Use Lower Case
3 File Compatibility
☑ Maximize backwards compatibility in Photoshop format
☐ Enable advanced TIFF save options
4 Recent file list contains: 4 files

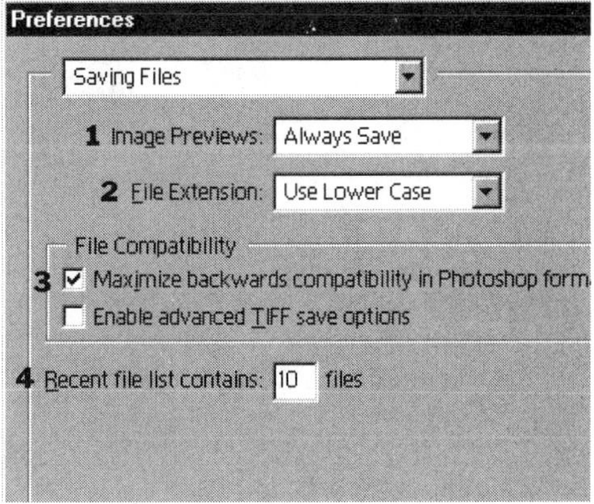

Display & Cursors Preferences

1. Check **Color Channels in Color** to display individual RGB or CMYK channels in color on the Channels palette in the image window. Otherwise, channels will display as grayscale.
2. Check **Use Diffusion Dither**, when using a monitor set to 8-bit color, to have Photoshop use a dithering method to improve color simulation.
3. Check **Use Pixel Doubling** to speed up preview redraws by showing a low res preview first. This doesn't affect actual pixels—it's just for redrawing. 6.0!
4. For the **Painting Cursors** (Gradient, Line, Eraser, Pencil, Airbrush, Paintbrush, Rubber Stamp, Pattern Stamp, Smudge, Blur, Sharpen, Dodge, Burn, and Sponge tools) click **Standard** to see the icon of the tool being used, or click **Precise** to see a crosshair icon, or click **Brush Size** to see a round icon the exact size of the brush tip (up to 999 pixels).
5. For the non-painting tools (Marquee, Lasso, Polygon Lasso, Magic Wand, Crop, Eyedropper, Pen, Gradient, Line, Paint Bucket, Magnetic Lasso, Magnetic Pen, Measure, and Color Sampler), click **Other Cursors: Standard** or **Precise**.

TIP Depending on the current Preferences setting, depressing the Caps Lock key will turn Standard cursors to Precise, Precise to Brush Size, or Brush Size to Precise.

Standard *cursor*

Precise *cursor*

Brush Size *cursor*

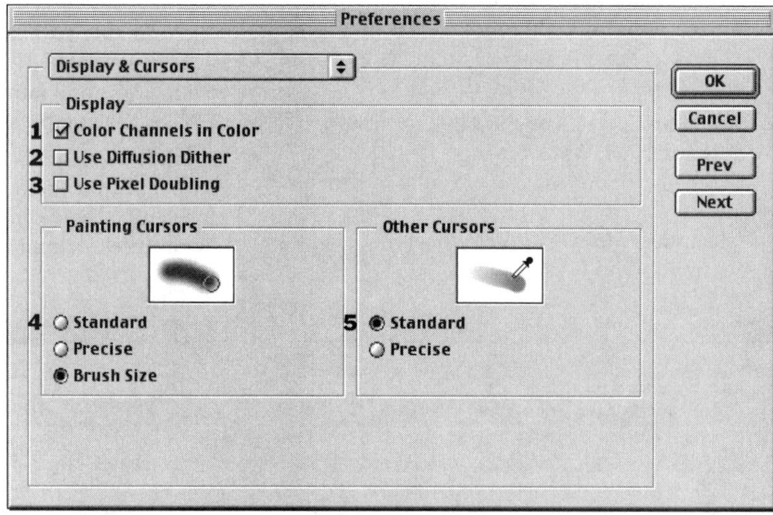

Transparency & Gamut Preferences

1 A checkerboard grid is used to represent transparent areas on a layer (areas that don't contain opaque pixels). You can choose a different **Grid Size**.

2 Change the **Grid Colors** for the transparency checkerboard by choosing Light, Medium, Dark, Red, Orange, Green, Blue, or Purple. Or choose Custom to choose your own colors.

3 Check **Use video alpha (requires hardware support)** if you use a 32-bit video card that allows chroma keying for video editing. You will be able to see through certain parts of the video image.

4 To change the color used to mark out-of-gamut colors on an image if you're using the **Gamut Warning** command, click the **Color** square, then choose a color from the Color Picker. You can lower the Gamut Warning color **Opacity** to make it easier to see the image color underneath.

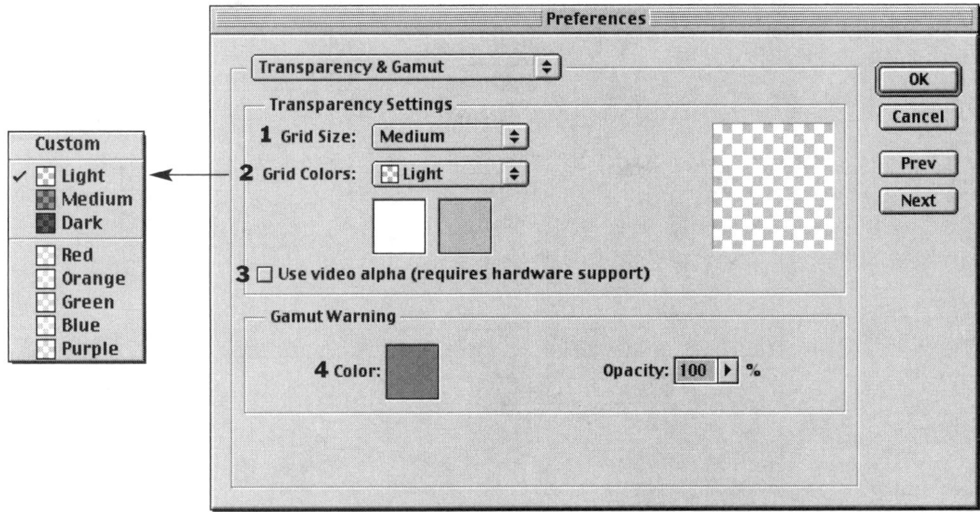

***Grid Size**: Large; Grid Colors: Medium*

Units & Rulers Preferences

1 Choose a unit of measure from the **Units: Rulers** pop-up menu for the horizontal and vertical rulers that display in the image window. (Choose View menu > Show Rulers to display the rulers.)

6.0! Choose the same or a different unit for **Type** from the Type pop-up menu.

TIP If you change the measurement units for the Info palette **1**, the ruler units will change in this dialog box also, and vice versa.

TIP You can also open this dialog box by double-clicking either ruler in the image window.

2 Enter **Column Size: Width** and **Gutter** values to help the Image Size and Canvas Size commands fit images for the appropriate column width in a layout program.

3 For **Point/Pica Size**, click **PostScript** (the default) to have Photoshop use the newfangled method for calculating the points-to-inch ratio, or click **Traditional** to use the pre-desktop publishing ratio.

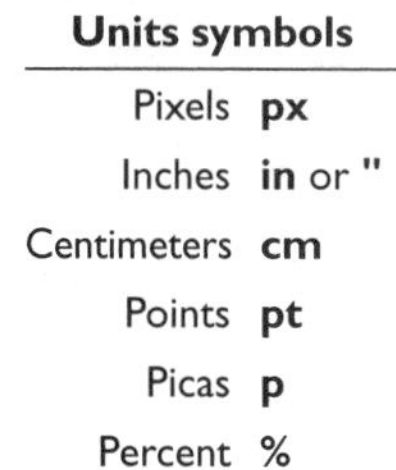

Units symbols	
Pixels	**px**
Inches	**in** or "
Centimeters	**cm**
Points	**pt**
Picas	**p**
Percent	%

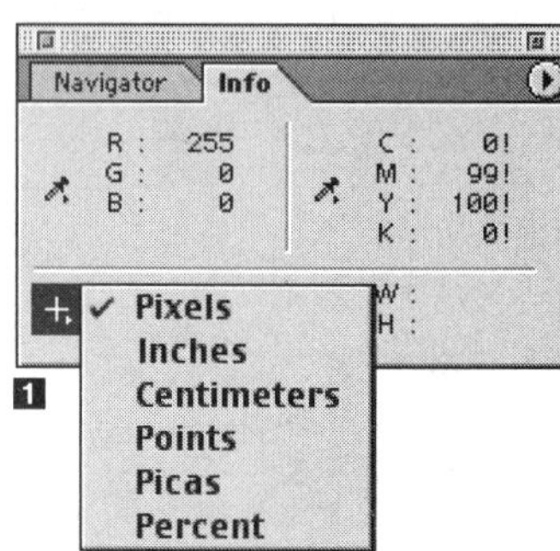

1

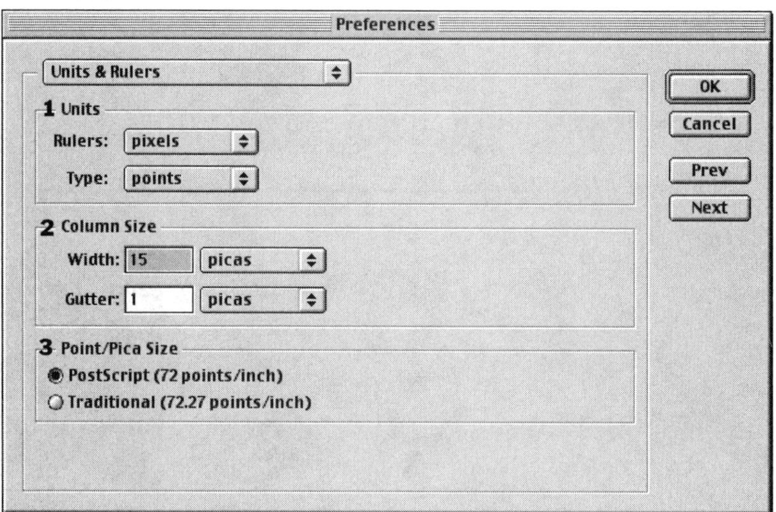

Guides & Grid Preferences

Note: Changes in this dialog preview immediately in the image window.

1 Choose a preset color for the removable ruler **Guides** from the **Color** pop-up menu. Click the color square to choose a color from the Color Picker.

2 Choose Lines or Dashed Lines for the **Guides Style**.

3 Choose a preset color for the non-printing **Grid** from the **Color** pop-up menu. Click the color square to choose a color from the Color Picker.

4 Choose Lines, Dashed Lines, or Dots for the **Grid Style**.

5 To have grid lines appear at specific unit-of-measure intervals, choose a unit of measurement from the drop-down menu, then enter a new value in the **Gridline every** field. If you choose **percent** from the drop-down menu, grid lines will appear at those percentage intervals, starting from the left edge of the image.

6 To add grid lines between the thicker grid line increments chosen in the Gridline every field, enter a number in the **Subdivisions** field.

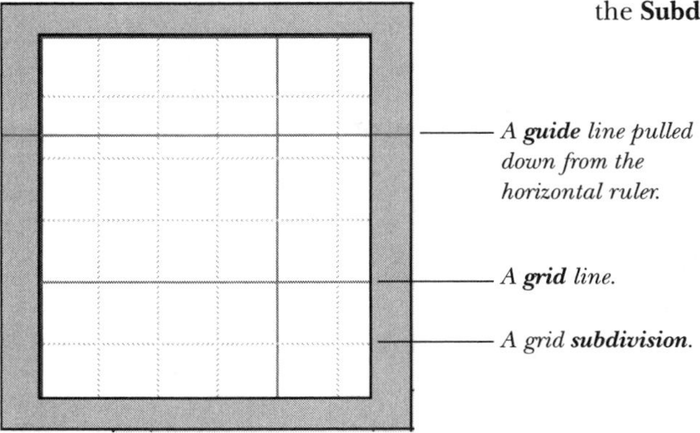

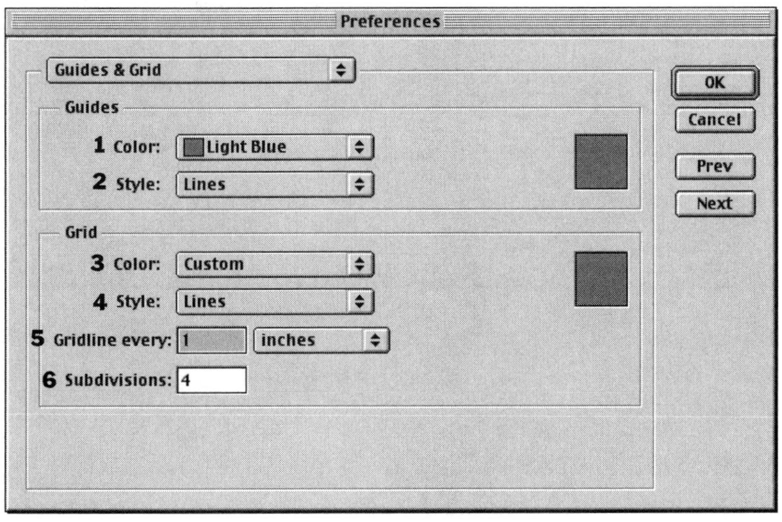

Plug-ins & Scratch Disk Preferences

Note: For changes made in this dialog box to take effect, you must exit/quit and relaunch Photoshop.

1 Click **Additional Plug-Ins Folder**, then click Choose if you need to relocate or use another plug-ins folder. Photoshop needs to know where to find this folder in order to access the plug-in contents of third-party plug-ins. Photoshop's internal Plug-Ins module shouldn't be moved out of the Photoshop folder unless you have a specific reason for doing so. Moving it could inhibit access to filters, the Import-Export and Effects commands, and some file formats under the save commands.

2 The **First** (and optional Second, Third, or Fourth) **Scratch Disk** is used when available RAM is insufficient for processing or storage. Choose an available hard drive from the First pop-up menu. Startup is the default.

As an optional step, choose an alternative **Second, Third,** or **Fourth** hard drive to be used as extra work space when necessary. If you have only one hard drive, of course you'll have only one scratch disk.

TIP *Mac OS:* Hold down Cmd-Option to open the Plug-Ins folder dialog box when launching Photoshop. Continue to hold down these keys, and the Scratch Disk Preferences dialog box will open.

TIP If your scratch disk is a removable cartridge, removing the cartridge while Photoshop is running may cause the program to crash.

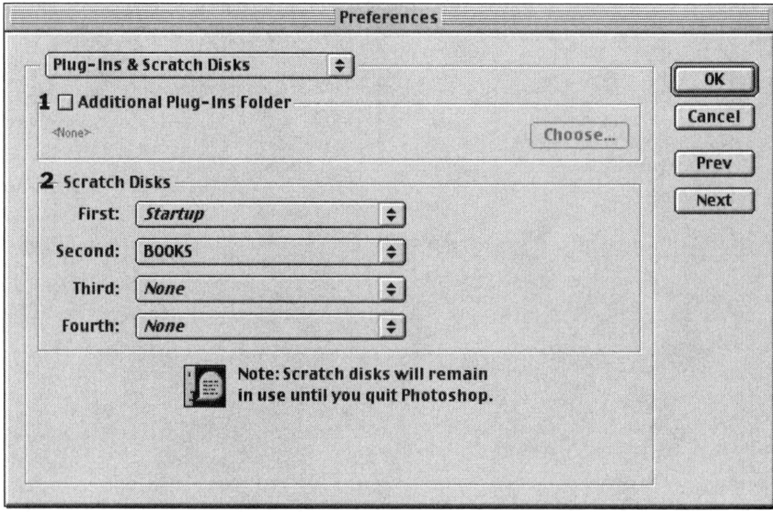

Plug-ins & Scratch Disk Preferences

Directions to the library

Each **preset** library type has its own file extension and default folder which is located in the Adobe Photoshop 6 > **Presets** folder.

The **default preset** libraries are not listed on the picker menu or the Preset Manager menu. In Mac OS, these libraries are located in System Folder > Preferences > **Adobe Photoshop 6 Settings** under their respective file names. In Windows, the libraries are located in **Windows/Application Data/Adobe/Photoshop/6.0/Adobe Photoshop 6 Settings**.

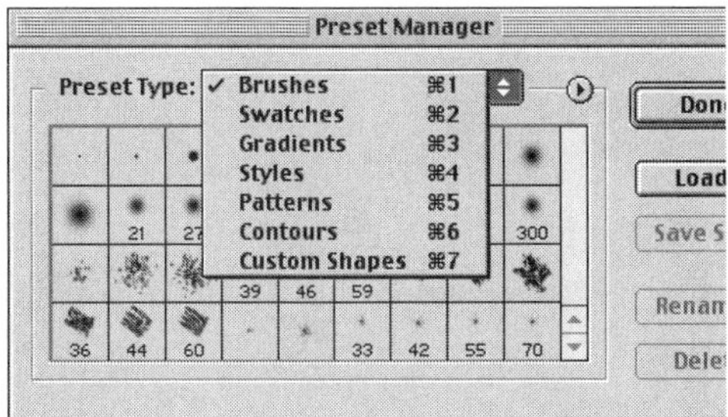

1 *Start by choosing a category from the* ***Preset Type*** *pop-up menu in the* ***Preset Manager****.*

6.0!

No doubt you've already become acquainted with many of the **pickers** that were introduced in Photoshop 6, such as the brush tip and gradient pickers. The Swatches palette also functions as a picker. Each picker item is called a **preset**, and each collection of presets is called a **library**.

The Preset Manager is used to organize, append, replace, and reset which items are loaded onto each of the pickers; those same changes can also be made in individual pickers. Changes made to a picker will be reflected in the Preset Manager, and vice versa.

To use the Preset Manager:

1. Choose Edit menu > Preset Manager.
2. *Optional:* Click the arrowhead in the circle at the top of the dialog box and choose a different view for the Preset Manager: Text Only, Small Thumbnail, Large Thumbnail, Small List, or Large List.
3. Choose a category of presets from the Preset Type pop-up menu **1**.
4. *Do any of the following:*

   Click the arrowhead in the circle and choose a library name from the bottom of the menu. Click **Append** to **add** the new library to the current library or click **OK** to **replace** the current library with the new library.

   Click **Load** to have the new library append to the current library.

   Click or Shift-click the presets you want to delete, then click **Delete** (you can't Shift-click color Swatches). The default presets can be deleted, and they can be restored at any time.
5. Click Done. The picker you edited will update.

TIP Preset library files can be shared among Photoshop users.

6.0!

To reset or replace a preset:

1. Choose Edit menu > Preset Manager.
2. From the Preset Type pop-up menu, choose the preset type you want to reset or replace.
3. *Optional:* Since any new and unsaved presets on the list will be deleted, we recommend saving the current library before resetting or replacing.
4. From the Preset Manager menu (the arrowhead in the circle) **1**:

   Click **Reset** [preset type] to restore the default library for the chosen type, then click Append to append the default presets to the current library or click OK to replace the current library with the default preset (click Cancel if you change your mind).
   or
   Click **Replace** [preset type] to replace the current library with another library.

TIP You can also reset or replace a library from any of the pickers.

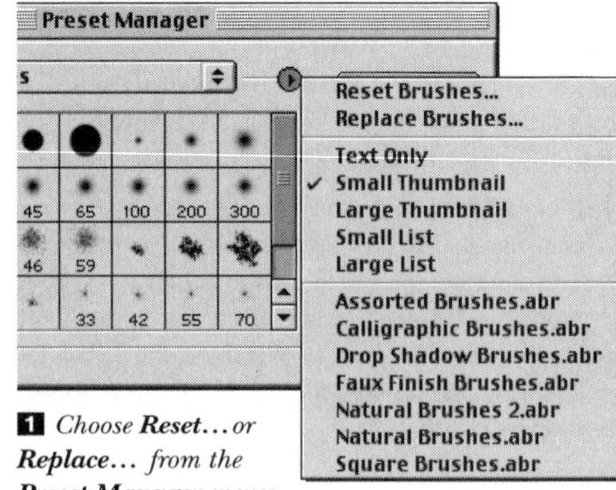

1 *Choose* ***Reset...*** *or* ***Replace...*** *from the* ***Preset Manager*** *menu.*

Preset Manager

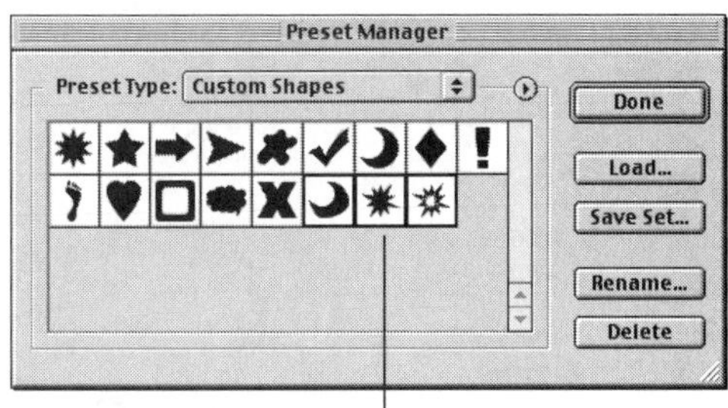

1 *Shift-click the presets you want to save in a* ***subset****.*

6.0!

The Preset Manager can also be used for copying a subset of selected presets in a currently open library into a new library.

To save a subset of items in their own library:

1. Choose Edit menu > Preset Manager.
2. From the Preset Type pop-up menu, choose the preset type you want to save as a subset.
3. Shift-click the presets you want to save in a subset **1**. (Shift-clicking doesn't work on the Swatches palette.)
4. Click Save Set, leave the location as the default preset folder, then enter a Name for the new library.
5. Click OK.

TIP To rename a preset in a library, double-click the preset item/swatch or click the preset, click Rename, enter a new name for the brush, swatch, or whatever, then click OK. If you selected multiple presets, you will be prompted to enter multiple names.

TIP You can select multiple presets in the Preset Manager, but you can only select one preset in an actual picker.

6.0!

If you define a new brush, pattern, or custom shape via the Edit menu, add a new swatch to the Swatches palette, add a new style to the Styles palette, create a new gradient in the Gradient Editor dialog box, or create a new contour in any Contour picker, that new preset item will display on the appropriate tool's picker on the options bar. The new item will also display for the chosen Preset Type in the Preset Manager.

The new item will be saved in the Adobe Photoshop Preferences file temporarily and it will display in the picker even after you exit/quit and relaunch Photoshop—as long as you don't open another library in the same category (e.g., another brush library), or reset the picker, or reset the picker category in the Preset Manager. If you do any of those things, the new item will be discarded. Here's how to save it.

To save a new picker item to a new library:

1. Create a new item for the current options bar or dialog box picker.
2. On the picker menu, choose Save [preset type] **1**
   or
   Choose Edit menu > Preset Manager, choose the appropriate Preset Type, click or Shift-click on the item(s) to be saved, then click Save Set.

   Note: We recommend using the Preset Manager approach because you can limit via selection which item(s) will go into the new library. Also, we think it's simpler, visually, to append a few items rather than a whole, large library.
3. Enter a name, leave the default extension and location as is, then click Save.

TIP In order for a newly created library name to appear on the picker menu and on the Preset Type pop-up menu in the Preset Manager, you must exit/quit and relaunch Photoshop **2**.

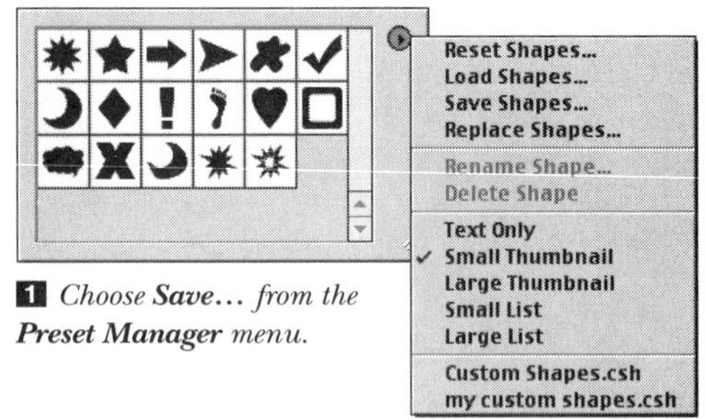

1 *Choose* ***Save...*** *from the* ***Preset Manager*** *menu.*

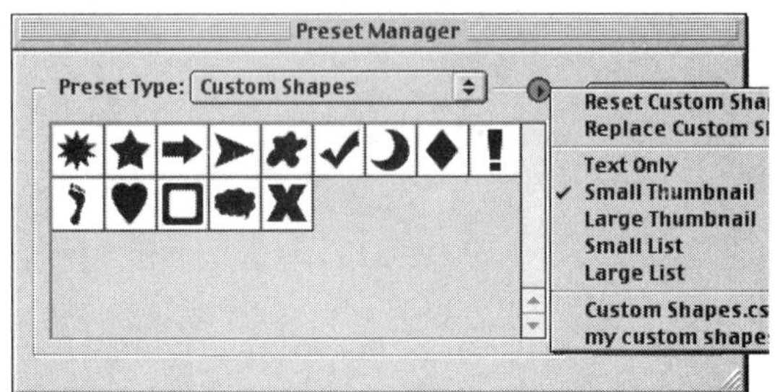

2 *The new* ***library*** *appears on the* ***Preset Manager*** *menu and on the* ***Preset Type*** *pop-up menu.*

PRINT 22

Resolution of output devices

Hewlett Packard LaserJet	600 or 1200 dpi
Hewlett Packard DeskJet	600 x 300/2400 x 1200 dpi
IRIS SmartJet	300 dpi (looks like 1600 dpi)
3M Rainbow	300 dpi
Canon Color Laser/Fiery	400-600 dpi
Epson Stylus Color/Photo ink-jet	1440 x 720 dpi
Linotronic imagesetter	1200–4000 dpi

AN IMAGE CAN be printed from Photoshop to a laser printer, to a color printer (e.g., ink-jet, dye sublimation), or to an imagesetter. A Photoshop image can also be imported into and then printed from a drawing application, like FreeHand or Illustrator; a layout application, like QuarkXPress or InDesign; a multimedia application, like Director or After Effects; or prepared for viewing online. (For online output, see the next chapter.)

This chapter contains instructions for outputting to various types of printers, applying trapping, preparing an image for another application, saving a file in the EPS, DCS, TIFF, BMP, or PICT format, creating a duotone, and creating a percentage tint of a Pantone color. The last part of the chapter is devoted to color reproduction basics. To print a spot color channel, see page 195.

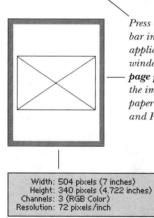

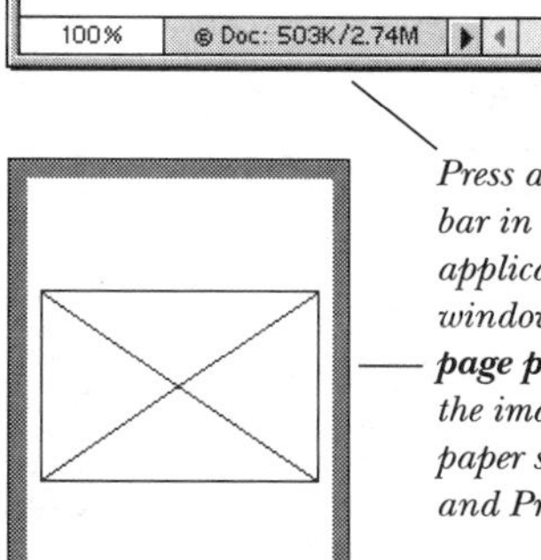

Press and hold on the ***Status*** *bar in the lower left corner of the application window (Win)/image window (Mac) to display the* ***page preview****—a thumbnail of the image in relationship to the paper size and other Page Setup and Print Options specifications.*

Width: 504 pixels (7 inches)
Height: 340 pixels (4.722 inches)
Channels: 3 (RGB Color)
Resolution: 72 pixels/inch

Alt-press/Option-press and hold on the Status bar to display ***file information****.*

Print

Printing from Photoshop

Note: Only currently visible layers and channels will print.

To print to a black-and-white laser printer in Windows:

1. Choose File menu > Print (Ctrl-P).
2. 6.0! Choose your Source Space **1**. The **Document** option uses the color profile of your image (for the specifics of color management, see Chapter 2). The **Proof Setup** option uses the color profile of your proof which you selected in the View menu > Proof Setup.
3. Choose your Print Space **2**. For the Profile option, choose **Same As Source** to print using the profile you selected for your Source Space in the previous step. If you want to print using the color profile of another color space, offset press, monitor, or printer, choose that profile from the pop-up menu.
4. If the Intent option is available, leave it at the default setting of **Relative Colorimetric**. Intent determines how the color conversion will render when sent to any profile other than Same as Source.
5. In Print dialog box, make sure the **Print to File** box is unchecked.
6. Click OK.

TIP To print only a portion of an image, select that area with the Rectangular Marquee tool. Then, in the Print dialog box, click Print Range: Selection.

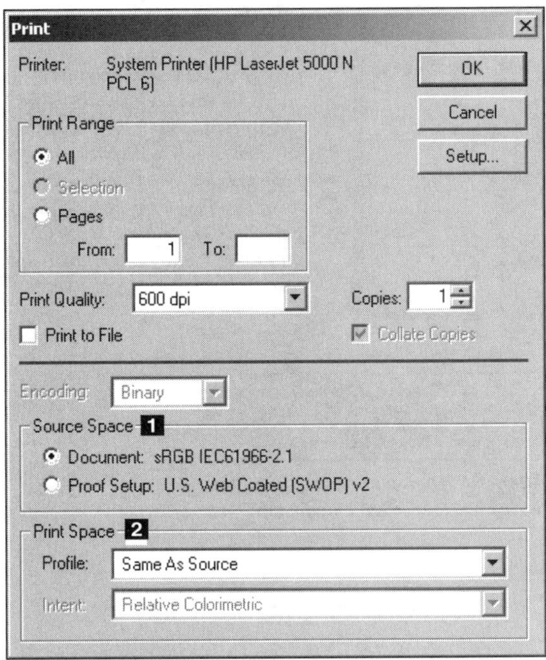

Resolution overkill?

If your image resolution is greater than two and a half times the screen frequency (which is way higher than you need) you'll get a warning prompt when you send the image to print. If this occurs, copy the file using File menu > Save As with the As a Copy option checked, then lower the image resolution using Image menu > Image Size.

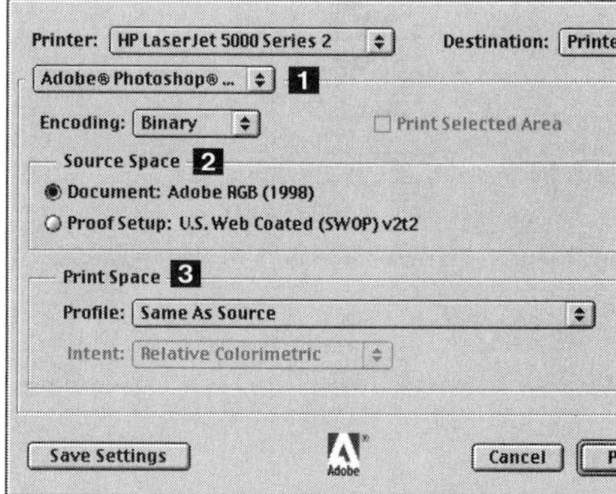

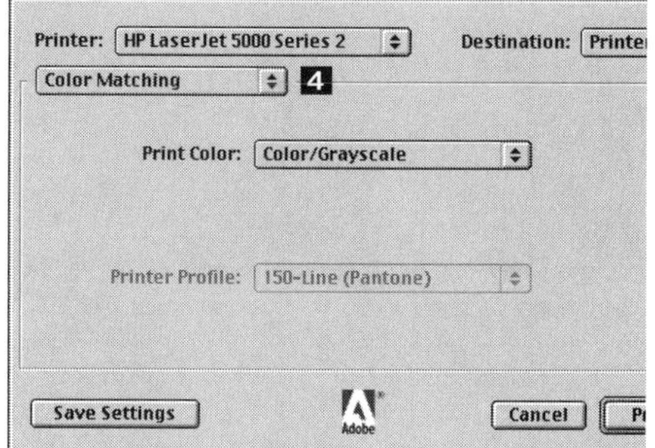

*Click **Save Settings** in the Print dialog box to save the current settings. They'll become the new default settings.*

Note: Only currently visible layers and channels will print.

To print to a black-and-white laser printer on Mac OS:

1. Choose File menu > Print (Cmd-P).
2. Choose **Adobe Photoshop 6.0** from the second pop-up menu **1**.
3. Choose Encoding: **Binary**.
4. Choose a Source Space **2**. **Document** uses the color profile embedded or assigned to your image (for the specifics of color management, see Chapter 2). **Proof Setup** uses the color profile of your output device that you selected in the View menu > Proof Setup. 6.0!
5. Choose your Print Space **3**. For the Profile option, choose **Same As Source** to print using the profile you selected for your Source Space in the previous step. If you want to print using the color profile of another color space, offset press, monitor, or printer, choose that profile from the pop-up menu.
6. If the **Intent** option is available, leave it at the default setting of Relative Colorimetric. Intent determines how the color conversion will render when sent to any profile other than Same as Source.
7. Choose **Color Matching** from the second pop-up menu **4**. Then choose Print Color: **Color/Grayscale**.
8. Make sure Destination: **Printer** is chosen.
9. Click Print.

TIP If your image doesn't print and you have a print spooler or a file that contains JPEG-encoding, try printing with ASCII Encoding. (ASCII printing takes longer, so it shouldn't be your first choice.)

TIP To print only a portion of an image, make a rectangular selection first. Then in the Print dialog box, choose Adobe Photoshop 6.0 from the pop-up menu and check Print Selected Area.

To print to a PostScript color printer:

1. To print to a PostScript Level 2 or higher printer, choose the appropriate Color Settings for your output device (CMYK, in this example). Choose Image menu > Mode > CMYK Color so you will be able to see the results on screen.
2. *Windows*: Choose File menu > Page Setup (Ctrl-Shift-P).

   Choose the correct color printer option from the Name/Format For drop-down menu. (A printer driver must be installed in your system for its name to appear on this menu.) Click OK.
3. Choose File menu > Print (Ctrl-P/Cmd-P).
4. *Mac OS:* Choose Adobe Photoshop 6.0 from the second pop-up menu.
5. Click **Document** for your Source Space. *6.0!* It will probably say U.S. Web Coated, or Untagged CMYK unless you have selected a different CMYK color space in your Color Settings dialog box.
6. From the Print Space: Profile pop-up menu:

   Choose **Same As Source** to print using the Source Space profile. There will be no color conversion during the printing process.
   or
   Consider choosing **PostScript Color Management** if you cannot find your printer's profile in the list of Profiles. This option will send all of the file's color information along with the Source Space profile to the printer; the printer (rather than Photoshop) will manage the color conversion process.

   TIP The only way to determine which is the best Print Space setting is to run multiple test prints. Try the various color space settings and decide which space gives you the best print results.
7. Choose **Relative Colormetric** for the rendering Intent, if that pop-up menu is

Screens

For a PostScript Level 2 printer, click **Screens** in the Page Setup dialog box (on Mac OS, it's available for the Adobe Photoshop 6.0 menu option), uncheck Use Printer's Default Screens, then check **Use Accurate Screens** **1**, but don't change the Ink angles. The Halftone Screens options will take effect if you print from Photoshop or save the file in the EPS or DCS 2 format and then print to a PostScript printer.

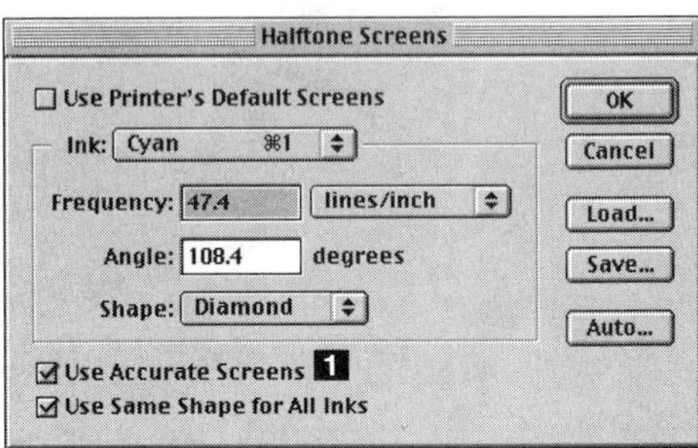

available. As noted in the previous section, Intent determines how the color conversion will render when sent to any Print profile other than Same as Source.

8. *Windows:* Click Setup, click Properties, choose Color, then click OK.

Mac OS: Choose Color Matching from the pop-up menu that now says "Adobe Photoshop 6.0," then choose Print Color: Color/Grayscale.

9. Click Print.

TIP To print an individual layer or channel, make that the sole visible layer or channel before choosing File menu > Print.

TIP Our service bureau advises us to not choose Lab color for the image mode or for the profile from the Print Space Profile menu. The reasons: Very few people calibrate their monitors or edit images in Lab mode. Also, our service bureau claims that printouts sent to both dye sublimation and IRIS printers show banding and color shifts when sent as Lab mode. When sent as CMYK color mode, the printouts produced better results. Ask your service bureau or print shop for their opinion.

Note: Before printing your file, save your image at the resolution that your prepress house says is appropriate for the color printer or imagesetter you're going to use.

To prepare a file for an IRIS or dye sublimation printer or an imagesetter:

1. To print on a PostScript Level 2 printer, choose File menu > Page Setup, (Mac OS: choose Adobe Photoshop 6.0 from the second pop-up menu), click Screen, uncheck Use Printer's Default Screens, check the Use Accurate Screens box, then click OK twice. Be sure to choose Image menu > Mode > CMYK Color before saving as EPS.
2. Choose File menu > Save As and check the As a Copy option (Ctrl-Shift-S/Cmd-Option-S).
3. Choose a location in which to save the file.
4. Choose Format: **Photoshop EPS**, then click Save.
5. Choose a **Preview** option **1**–**2** and choose **Encoding: Binary**.
6. If you've changed the screen settings in the Halftone Screens dialog box (as per your service bureau's instructions), then check the **Include Halftone Screen** box.
7. Click OK.

Color separation basics

Convert the image to **CMYK Color** mode, then choose File menu > **Print** (Mac OS: choose Adobe Photoshop 6.0 from the pop-up menu). Under Source Space, choose **Document**. It should say U.S. Web Coated (SWOP) v2 unless you have selected a different option in your Color Setting dialog box. Under Print Space, choose **Separations** for the Profile, then click **Print**.

TIP In the Print Options dialog box, check the calibration bars, registration marks, corner cropmarks, center cropmarks, or labels option. Some of these options may not be available on a non-PostScript printer.

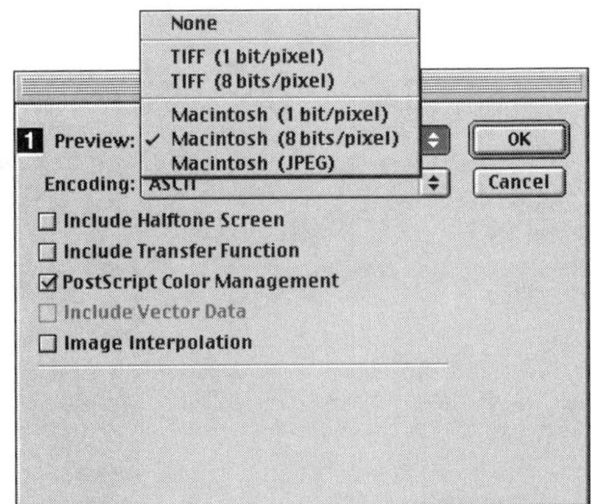

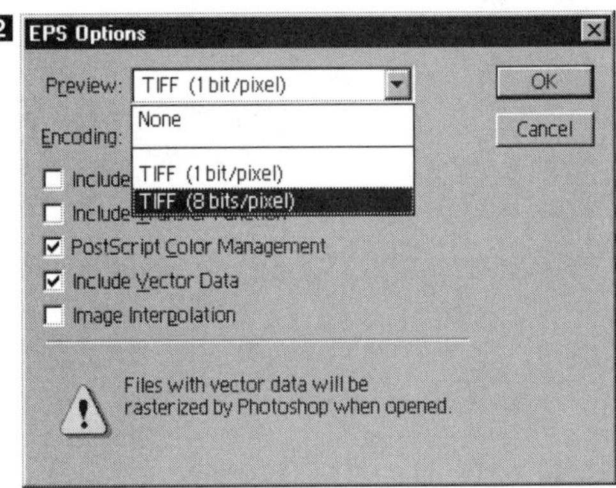

IRIS, Dye Sub, Imagesetter

6.0!

The Print Options dialog box

1. Check the **Center Image** box to position your image in the center of the page or uncheck Center Image and enter new top and left values to move image on the page.
2. Change the Scaled Print Size: **Scale** percentage or enter specific values in the Height and Width boxes to reduce or enlarge the image for printing purposes only. *Note:* The Scale, Height and Width options are linked; changing any one option will affect the other two.
3. Check the **Scale to Fit Media** box to have the image be adjusted to fit on the paper size selected in File menu > Page Setup.
4. Check the **Show Bounding Box** option to have a box be placed around your image to show the image boundary. Pull a handle or side of the box to scale your image for printing purposes only.
5. If a rectangular selection is currently active in the image, check the **Print Selected Area** option to print only that selected portion.
6. Check the **Show More Options** box to display Color Management and Output settings (accessed via the pop-up menu). All of these options are also found in the Page Setup and Print dialog boxes and are discussed in those particular sections. Note that both the Print and Page Setup dialog boxes can be quickly accessed by clicking either button in the top right of the Print Options dialog box.
7. Under Show More Options, for Output, check the **Include Vector Data** box to have Photoshop print the edges of vector objects (type and shapes) at the printer's full resolution.
8. Click OK.

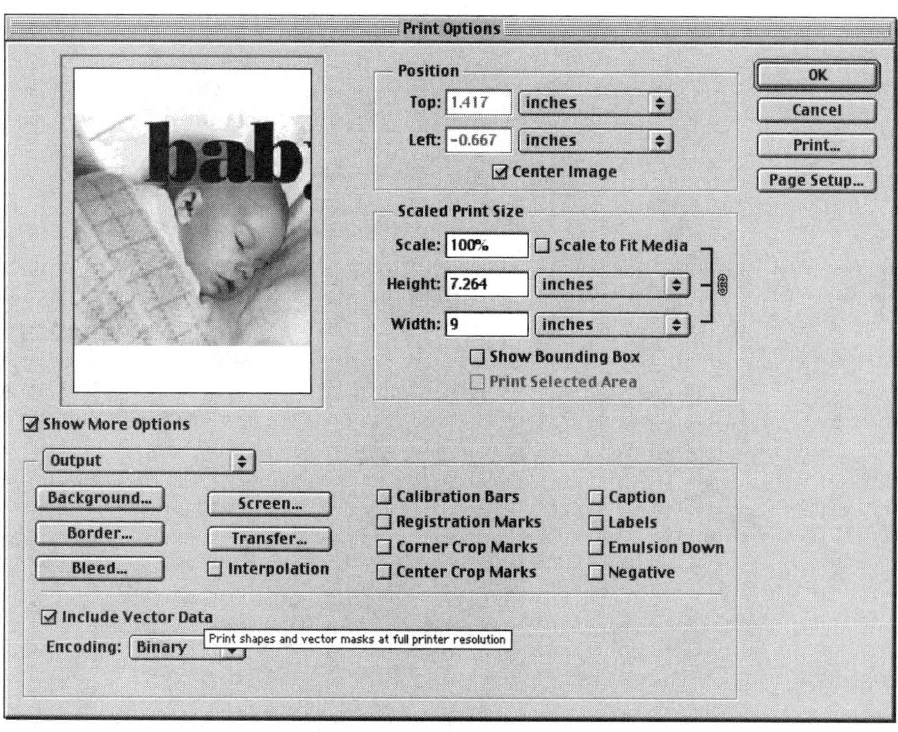

Print Options

The Page Setup dialog box

Mac OS: Choose Adobe Photoshop 6.0 from the pop-up menu to access the following options.

1 To print a colored background around the image, click **Background**, then choose a color.

2 To print a black border around an image, click **Border**, choose a measurement unit, then enter a Width (maximum is 10 pts).

3 **Bleed** prints crop marks inside the image at a specified distance (Width) from the edge of the image (maximum is 9.01 pts).

4 **Caption** prints text, that was entered into the File menu > File Info box, outside the image area.

5 **Calibration Bars** creates a grayscale and/or color calibration strip outside the image area.

6 **Registration Marks** creates marks that a print shop uses to align color separations.

7 **Corner Crop Marks** and **Center Crop Marks** create short little lines that a print shop uses to trim the final printed page.

8 **Labels** prints the image's title and the names of its channels.

9 For film output, ask your print shop whether you should choose **Negative** or **Emulsion Down**.

10 **Interpolation** reduces jaggies when outputting to some PostScript Level 2 (or higher) printers.

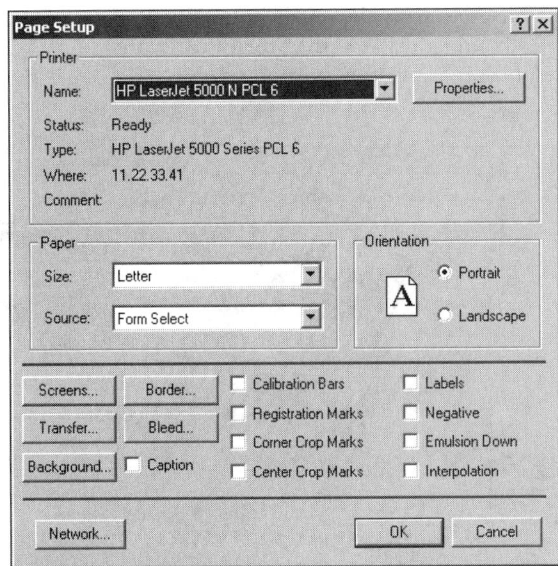

1 *Page Setup in Windows.*

2 *Page Setup in Mac OS.*

Page Setup

The Page Setup options illustrated

Photoshop's Trap command slightly overlaps solid color areas in an image to help prevent gaps that may occur due to plate misregistration or paper shift. Trapping is only necessary when two distinct, adjacent color areas share less than two of the four process colors. You don't need to trap a continuous-tone or photographic image.

Note: Photoshop's Trap command flattens all layers and it uses only the spread technique, unlike other applications which may also use the choke method. Consult with your press shop before using this command, and apply it to a copy of your image; store your original image without traps.

To apply trapping:

1. Open the image to which you want to apply trapping, and make sure it's in CMYK Color mode.
2. Choose Image menu > Trap.
3. If a prompt appears, click OK.
4. Enter the Width that your press shop recommends **1**.
5. Click OK.

1 *Choose a **Trap Width**.*

Preparing files for other applications

Photoshop to QuarkXPress

To color separate a Photoshop image in QuarkXPress, convert it to CMYK Color mode before importing it into QuarkXPress. Different imagesetters require different formats, so ask your prepress house whether to save your image in the TIFF (see page 390) or EPS file format (see page 387) or in either of the two DCS formats (see page 389). Use the TIFF format if you're going to apply color management features to the image in QuarkXPress 4.

Photoshop to InDesign

InDesign can separate Photoshop PDFs (RGB or CMYK), and it can import PSD files directly. It can also read any ICC profile embedded in a Photoshop file.

Photoshop to a film recorder

Color transparencies, also called chromes, are widely used as a source for high quality images in the publishing industry. A Photoshop file can be output to a film recorder to produce a chrome. Though the output settings for each film recorder may vary, to output to any film recorder, the pixel count for the height and width of the image file must conform to the pixel count the film recorder requires for each line it images. If the image originates as a scan, the pixel count should be taken into consideration when setting the scan's resolution, dimensions, and file storage size.

For example, let's say you need to produce a 4 x 5-inch chrome on a Solitaire film recorder. Your service bureau advises you that to output on the Solitaire, you have the choice of a 4K image at 4096 pixels x 3276 pixels for a resolution of 819 dpi; an 8K image at 8192 pixels x 6553 pixels for a resolution of 1638 dpi; or a 16K image at 16,384 pixels x 13,107 pixels for a resolution of 3276 dpi. (Other film recorders may require different resolutions.) Choose File menu > New, enter

Keeping a background transparent

To import a Photoshop image into a drawing or page layout application and maintain its transparent background, save the image with a **layer clipping path** (see page 274).

Check your preferences

Before saving a file for use in another application, find out if the target application requires the **Maximize Backwards Compatibility** box to be checked in Photoshop's Saving Files Preferences in order to open a Photoshop format file **1**. This option saves a composited image for preview along with the layered version for applications that don't support layers. It also saves a rasterized copy of any vector art for those applications that don't support vector data. Note that checking this option will result in lengthier saving times and larger file sizes. Some applications also require the **Image Previews** options to be checked **2**. For a Web file, however, uncheck Image Previews to save a few extra bytes of storage size and speed up the transfer time.

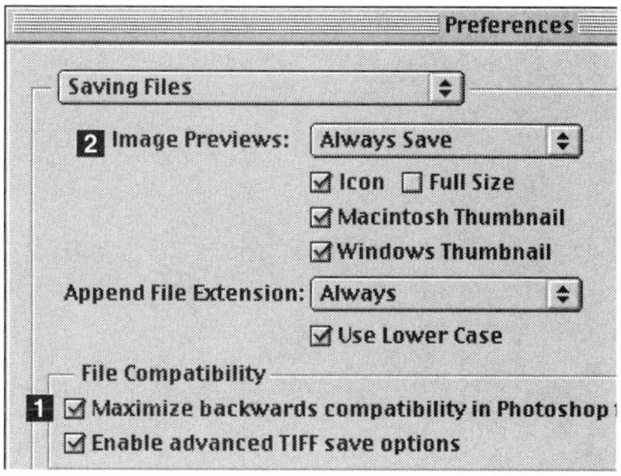

Preferences
Saving Files
2 Image Previews: Always Save
Icon Full Size
Macintosh Thumbnail
Windows Thumbnail
Append File Extension: Always
Use Lower Case
File Compatibility
1 Maximize backwards compatibility in Photoshop
Enable advanced TIFF save options

the desired dimensions and resolution, and choose RGB Color Mode. Click OK to produce the image entirely within Photoshop. Or note the resolution and dimensions and ask your prepress shop to match those values when they scan your image.

Photoshop to Illustrator 6.0!

Compatibility between Photoshop 6 and Illustrator 9 has been greatly maximized. If you drag-and-drop a Photoshop selection or layer into Illustrator, the image will appear on the Layers palette in Illustrator as a group containing a generic clipping path and the image. Any opacity, blending modes, masking, or clipping of the image will be ignored.

You can use the Path Component Selection tool to drag-and-drop a layer clipping path from Photoshop into Illustrator. Or you can use Photoshop's File menu > Export Paths to Illustrator command to export a saved path, then open the saved path file in Illustrator. In either case, the path will become an editable vector object in Illustrator, with no fill or stroke.

If you copy and paste a layer from Photoshop into Illustrator, any layer mask or layer clipping path will be ignored.

If you place a Photoshop image with the Link box checked in Illustator's Place dialog box, it will appear on the Layers palette as one image sublayer. The image will be properly masked but certain blend modes may produce strange effects.

If you embed a Photoshop image as you place it (uncheck the Link box) or open the image in Illustrator, you can choose whether to convert layers into objects or into one flattened layer. If you opt to convert Photoshop layers into objects, each object will appear on its own nested layer within an image sublayer. The Background will also be a separate, opaque layer. It can be deleted or modified in Illustrator. All transparency values and blending modes will be preserved and listed as editable appearances

(Continued on the following page)

in Illustrator. Layer masks and layer clipping paths will become opacity masks. Any Paths palette clipping path saved with the Photoshop file will remain in effect. Shape layers, though, will become image layers, not vector objects. Each separate layer will have a bounding box the size of the original Photoshop image.

If you opt to flatten Photoshop layers into one image layer, all transparency, blending modes, and layer mask effects will be preserved visually, but they won't be editable in Illustrator. Any Paths palette clipping path in the Photoshop file will remain in effect.

The resolution of any Photoshop TIF, EPS, or PSD image that's opened or placed in Illustrator will remain intact, but the Photoshop image will take on the color mode of the Illustrator file. Illustrator raster filters, raster effects, and certain vector effects can be applied to the imported image.

Photoshop to CorelDRAW

Windows version 9/Mac OS version 8: Save the file as EPS, TIFF, JPEG, BMP, or PSD (Photoshop format), and in RGB Color or CMYK Color mode. In CorelDRAW, use File menu > Import to open the file. Alternatively, you could drag-and-drop a layer or copy-and-paste a layer or a selection from Photoshop into a CorelDRAW window. CorelDRAW 9 can read a layered Photoshop image, with each layer becoming a separate object. You can use the Export Paths to Illustrator command to export a Photoshop path to a file, and then open that file in CorelDRAW.

Once it's imported into CorelDRAW, the bitmap image can be moved around; you can perform some bitmap edits on it; you can convert it to a different color mode or color depth; and you can resample it by changing its image size and/or resolution. You can also create a color mask in CorelDRAW in order to mask out portions of the bitmap image.

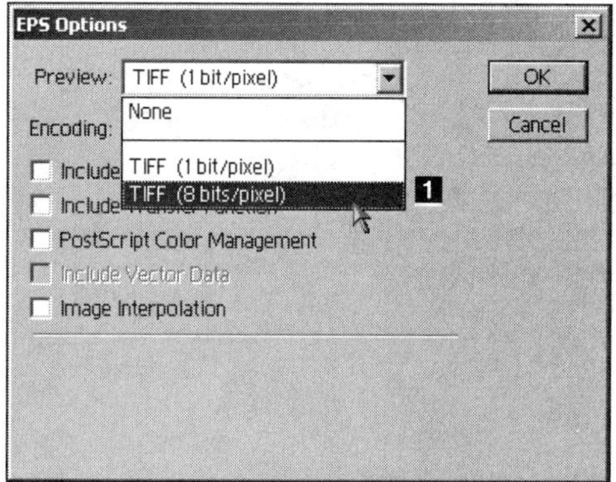

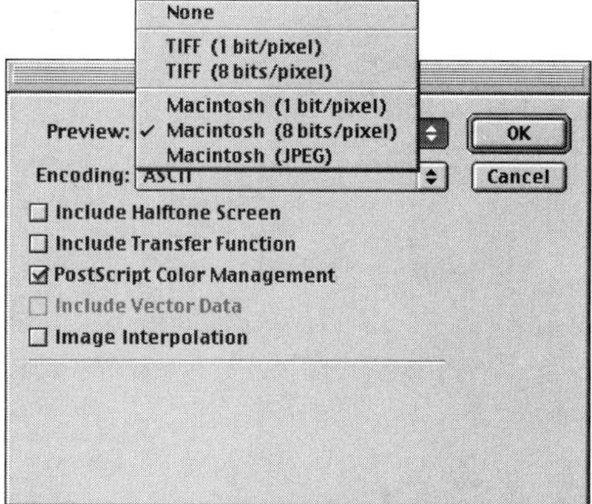

2 *The* ***EPS*** *format is available for an image in any image mode except Multichannel. Alpha channels and spot channels are discarded when you save in this format.*

The EPS format is a good choice for importing a Photoshop image into an Illustration program or into a page layout program (e.g., QuarkXPress, PageMaker, or InDesign). Printing an EPS file requires a PostScript or PostScript emulation printer.

To save an image as an EPS:

1. If the image is going to be color separated by another application, choose Image menu > Mode > CMYK Color.
2. Choose File menu > Save As (Ctrl-Shift-S/Cmd-Shift-S).
3. Enter a name and choose a location in which to save the file.
4. Choose Format: **Photoshop EPS**.
5. *Optional:* Check **Embed Color Profile** to have Photoshop embed a color profile that tags the image with your working color space. Or you can check **Use Proof Setup** above it. Checking this option will include a "soft proof" with your file—an onscreen preview of how your image will look when it is printed on a certain type of printer. For more on color management, see Chapter 2.

   Click Save. Note that any layers will be flattened.
6. From the Preview pop-up menu, choose a 1-bit/pixel option to save the file with a black and white preview or choose an 8-bits/pixel option to save the file with a grayscale or color preview (Win) **1**/(Mac) **2**.

   Mac OS: Choose either TIFF preview option if you're planning to open the file in a Windows application.
7. For most purposes, you should choose Encoding: **Binary**, since Binary encoded files are smaller and process more quickly than ASCII files. However, for some applications, PostScript clone printers, or printing utilities that cannot handle Binary files, you'll have to choose ASCII. JPEG is the fastest

(Continued on the following page)

Save as EPS

encoding method, but it causes some data loss. A JPEG file can only print on PostScript Level 2 or higher printer.

8. If you've changed the frequency, angle, or dot shape settings in the Halftone Screens dialog box, then check the Include Halftone Screen box.
9. The PostScript Color Management Option will convert the file's color data to the printer's color space. Don't select this option if you are going to import the file into another color managed application—unpredictable color shifts may occur!
10. If you have vector elements on your page (shapes or type), check Include Vector Data. Note that saved vector data in EPS files is available to other applications, but when you reopen the file in Photoshop, the vector data will be rasterized.
11. Check Image Interpolation if the image is low resolution and you want it to be anti-aliased.
12. Click OK.

Multichannel

You can save a **Multichannel mode** image in the **Photoshop DCS 2.0** format as a single file or multiple files. The DCS 2.0 format preserves channels. A Multichannel image cannot be saved as a Photoshop EPS for composite (single-page) printing. Converting an image to Multichannel mode flattens all layers and converts the channels to spot color channels.

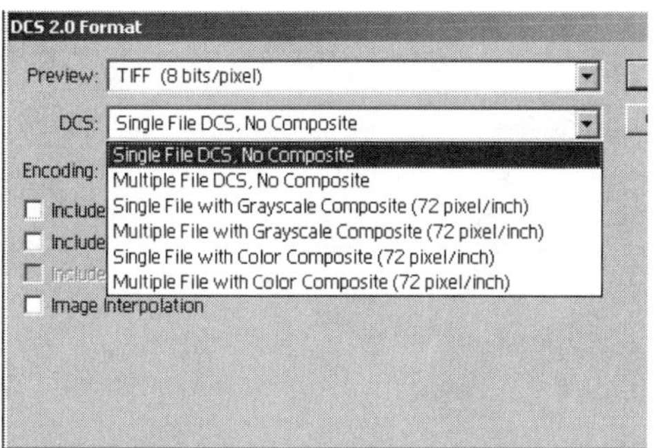

1 *Choose a **DCS** option in the **DCS 2.0 Format** dialog box (Windows).*

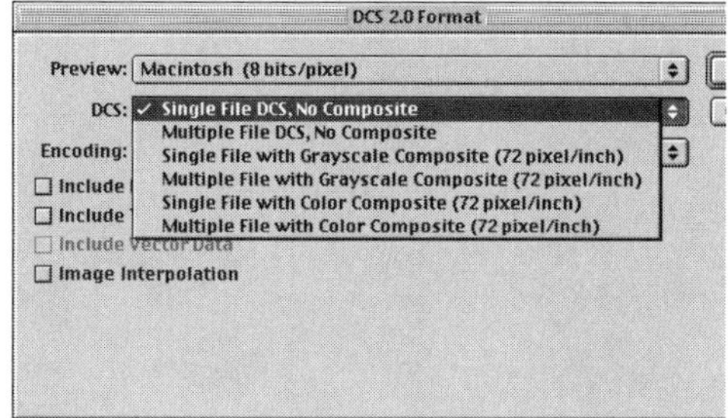

2 *Choose a **DCS** option in the **DCS 2.0 Format** dialog box (Mac OS).*

The DCS formats are relatives of the EPS format. The DCS 1.0 (Desktop Color Separation) format preseparates the image in Photoshop, and it produces five related files, one for each CMYK channel and one for the combined, composite CMYK channel. The newer DCS 2.0 format preserves any alpha and spot color channels along with the color channels, and also offers the option to save the combined channels into one file or as multiple files. A DCS file can be printed only on a PostScript printer.

To save an image as a DCS 2.0:

1. Choose Image menu > Mode > CMYK Color, choose File menu > Save As (Ctrl-Shift-S/Cmd-Shift-S), enter a name and choose a location in which to save the file, then choose Format: **Photoshop DCS 2.0**.
2. *Optional:* Check Embed Color Profile or Use Proof Setup. For details see step 5 on page 387. Click Save.
3. From the Preview pop-up menu, choose a **1 bit/pixel** option to save the file with a black and white preview or choose an **8 bits/pixel** option to save the file with a grayscale or color preview.
4. Choose a DCS option: **Single File** (all the separations together in one file) or **Multiple File** (one file for each separation), and with No Composite, a Grayscale Composite, or a Color Composite preview **1** (Win)/**2** (Mac).
5. Choose an **Encoding** option: Binary, ASCII, or JPEG (with compression).
6. Leave the Include Halftone Screen and Include Transfer Function boxes unchecked. Let your prepress shop choose settings for these options.
7. Check **Include Vector Data** if you have any vector graphics (shapes or type).
8. Check **Image Interpolation** if the image is low resolution you want it anti-aliased.
9. Click OK.

A TIFF file can be imported by most applications, including QuarkXPress, PageMaker, and InDesign. Color profiles are recognized by, and color management options are available for, this format. QuarkXPress, PageMaker and InDesign can color separate a CMYK TIFF.

Photoshop 6.0 allows for saving layers in TIFF format. Check the Layers option to preserve the layers in your file. You can also choose to save any spot color channels and annotations in your file. To access any of these advanced TIFF settings, choose Edit menu > Preferences > Saving Files, and check the **Enable advanced TIFF save options** box.

6.0!

Beware! Few image or layout programs can currently work with a layered TIFF, in which case the TIFF will be flattened on import!

To save an image as a TIFF:

1. Choose Image menu > Mode > CMYK Color, choose File menu > Save As (Ctrl-Shift-S/Cmd-Shift-S), enter a name, and choose a location for the file.
2. Choose Format: **TIFF**.
3. *Optional:* Not all programs can import a TIFF with an alpha channel. If your target application does not do so, uncheck the Alpha Channels box to discard any alpha channels. For Advanced TIFF, check or uncheck any Save: options.
4. *Optional:* Check the Embed Color Profile option to have Photoshop include the current embedded color profile in the TIFF file. For more on color management, see Chapter 2.
5. Click Save.
6. For Advanced TIFF, choose a **Compression** method **1**. All compression methods reduce a file's storage size. However, some programs cannot open TIFF saved with JPEG or ZIP compression. In this case, LZW compression is recommended; no image data will be lost.

   Note: If you're ultimately going to color separate your file, service bureaus recommend using no compression at all.

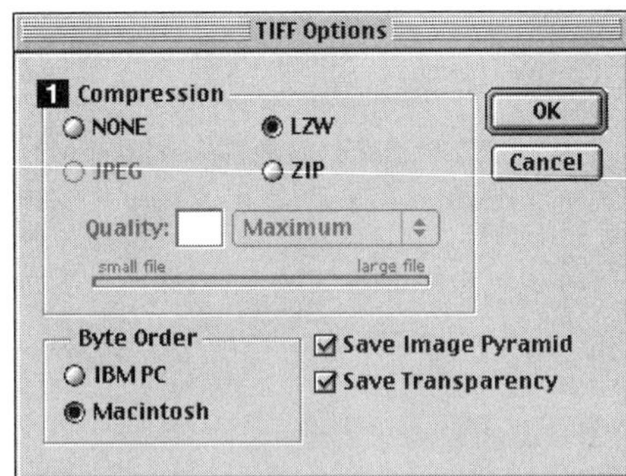

Save as TIFF

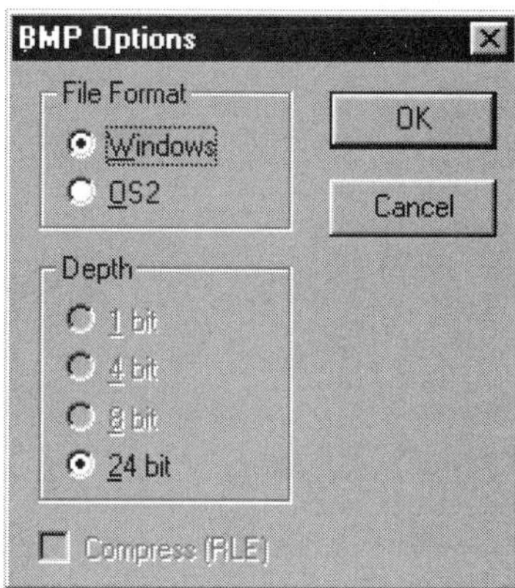

1 *Windows: Choose a **File Format** option and a **Depth** option.*

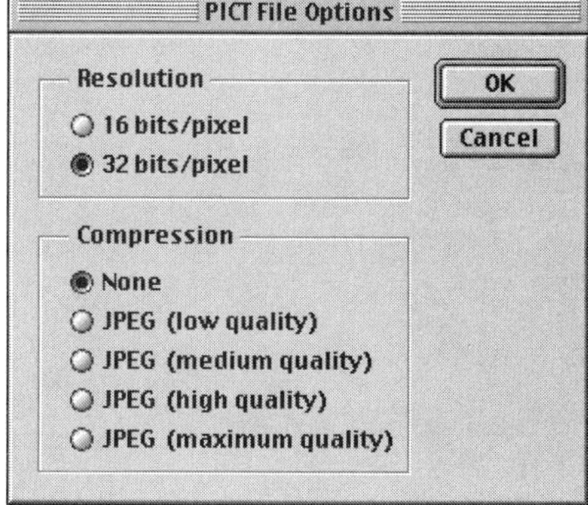

2 *Mac OS.*

7. Choose **IBM PC** or **Macintosh** for the platform the file will be exported to.
8. For Advanced TIFF, check the **Save Image Pyramid** box to create a file that contains multiple resolutions of your image. Photoshop does not currently offer options for opening image pyramids; InDesign does.

   Check the **Save Transparency** box if you have any transparency in your file.
9. Click OK.

   Note: Photoshop can't save transparent areas (Transparency) without also saving Layers, so be sure to check both options.

A BMP or PICT file can be opened or placed as a bitmap image in Adobe Illustrator. Both of these file types can also be imported into most multimedia applications.

Mac OS: The PICT format is not available for an image in CMYK Color mode.

To save an RGB image as a BMP or PICT:

1. Choose File menu > Save As.
2. Enter a name and choose a location in which to save the file.
3. *Windows:* Choose Format: BMP, click Save, then choose a File Format.

   Mac OS: Choose Format: PICT File, then click Save.
4. *Windows:* Click a Depth option **1**.

   Mac OS: Click a Resolution option**2**. (For an image in Grayscale mode, check 4 bits/pixel or 8 bits/pixel.)
5. Choose a Compression setting. The JPEG compression options are available only for an image that has a 32-bit resolution. The lower the quality setting, the greater the compression. If the image is going to be output to a multimedia application, click Resolution: 16 bits/pixel.
6. Click OK.

Producing duotones

Only about 50 shades of an ink color can be printed from one plate, so print shops are sometimes asked to print a grayscale image using two or more plates instead of one, adding midtones or highlights to extend an image's tonal range. The additional plates can be gray or a color tint. You can convert an image to Duotone mode in Photoshop to create a duotone (two plates), tritone (three plates), or quadtone (four plates).

Note: Duotone printing is tricky, so ask your print shop for advice. A duotone effect can't be proofed on a PostScript color printer; only a press proof is reliable. If you're a novice at duotones, try using one of the duotone (or tritone or quadtone) curves presets provided by Photoshop. You can load them in to use as is or adapt them for your own needs (click Load in the Duotone Options box, then open Adobe Photoshop > Presets > Duotone folder).

To produce a duotone:

1. Choose Image menu > Mode > Grayscale. An image with good contrast will work best.
2. Choose Image menu > Mode > Duotone.
3. Check Preview to see your color and curves changes immediately.
4. Choose Type: Duotone **1**.
5. Click the Ink 2 color square **2**. (Ink 1 will be the darkest ink; the highest ink number should be the lightest ink.)
6. To choose a matching system color, like a Pantone color, choose from the Book pop-up menu, then type a color number or click a swatch. Subtle colors usually look better in a duotone than bright colors.
   or
   To choose a process color, click Picker, then enter C, M, Y, and K percentages.
7. Click OK.
8. For a process color, enter a name next to the color square. For a custom color, leave the name as is.

Threes and fours

Printing a **tritone** (three inks) or a **quadtone** (four inks) requires specifying the order in which the inks will print on press. You can use the Overprint Colors dialog box to adjust the on-screen representation of various ink printing orders, but these settings won't affect how the image actually prints. Ask your print shop for advice about printing.

Back to square one

The Duotone dialog box opens with the last-used settings. If you change the duotone Type and then want to restore the last-used settings, hold down Alt/Option and click **Reset**.

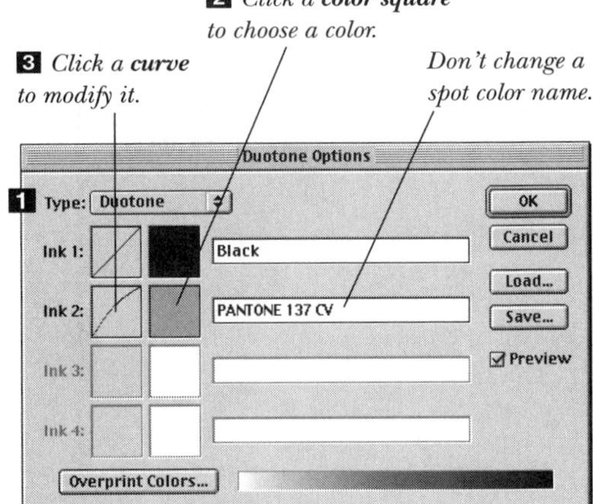

In the ***Duotone Options*** *dialog box, choose Type:* ***Duotone****, then click the* ***Ink 2*** *color square.*

Nice curves

Reshaping the duotone curve for an ink color affects how that color is distributed among an image's highlights, midtones, and shadows. With the curve shape shown in the screenshot above, Ink 2 will tint the image's midtones. To produce a pleasing duotone, try to distribute Ink 1 and Ink 2 in different tonal ranges.

Here's an example. Use black as Ink 1 in the shadow areas, somewhat in the midtones, and a little bit in the highlights. Then use an Ink 2 color in the remaining tonal ranges—more in the midtones and light areas and less in the darks.

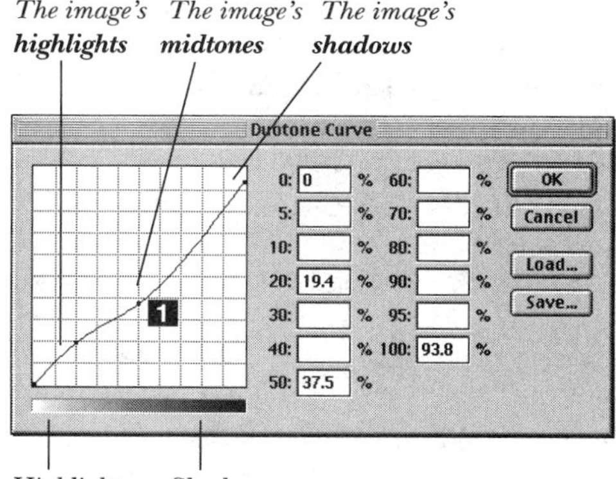

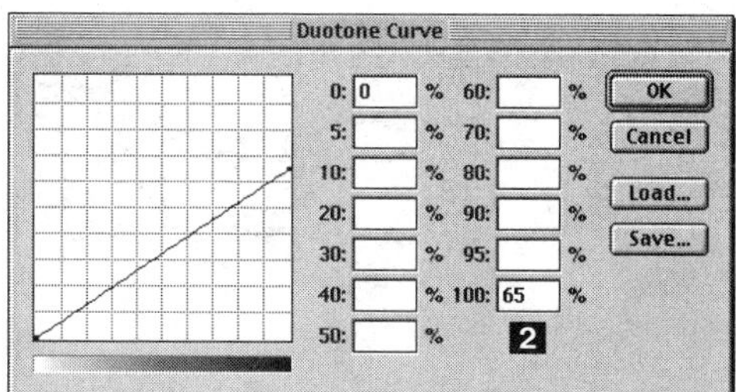

*This is the **Duotone Curve** dialog box for a monotone print. The 100% field value has been lowered to the desired PANTONE tint percentage.*

9. Click the Ink 2 curve (3 previous page).
10. Drag the curve upward or downward in the Duotone Curve dialog box 1. To produce a pleasing duotone, the Ink 1 curve should be different from the Ink 2 curve.
11. Click OK.
12. Click the Ink 1 curve, then repeat steps 10 and 11.
13. *Optional:* Click Save to save the current settings to use with other images.
14. Click OK to close the dialog box.
15. Save the file in the EPS format.

TIP To reduce black ink in the highlights, for the black ink (Ink 1) curve, enter 0 in the 5% box. To reduce color in the shadows, for the color ink (Ink 2) curve, enter 85 in the 100% box.

TIP If you're using a Pantone color and you're going to output the image from an illustration or page layout program, turn on Short PANTONE Names in Edit menu > Preferences > General.

Here's a low-budget—but effective—way to expand the tonal range of a grayscale image. It's printed as a monotone (using one plate).

To print a grayscale image using a Pantone tint:

1. Open a grayscale image.
2. Choose Image menu > Mode > Duotone.
3. Choose Monotone from the Type drop-down menu.
4. Click the Ink 1 color square, then click Custom, choose the desired Pantone color, then click OK.
5. In the Duotone Options dialog box, click on the Ink 1 curve.
6. In the 100% field, enter the desired tint percentage value 2. Leave the 0% field at 0 and all other fields blank. Click OK.
7. Click OK to close the dialog box.
8. Save the file in EPS format.

Color reproduction basics

A computer monitor displays additive colors by projecting red, green, and blue (RGB) light, whereas an offset press prints subtractive colors using CMYK or spot color inks. Obtaining good CMYK color reproduction on an offset press is a real art. The output image will resemble the on-screen image only if the monitor is carefully calibrated for that output device. *Note:* In this section we're discussing offset press output. For online imaging issues, see the next chapter!

Photoshop determines how to convert an RGB image to CMYK mode and how to display a CMYK mode preview based on the current settings in the Edit menu > Color Settings dialog boxes. Some of these dialogs are discussed on the following pages.

These are the major steps in color separation:

- Choose Color Settings
- Obtain a color proof using those settings
- Match the on-screen preview to the proof

To enter custom CMYK settings: 6.0!

1. Choose Edit menu > Color Settings.
2. From the Working Spaces: CMYK pop-up menu, choose one of the default U.S. prepress defaults that matches your chosen press and paper type (unless you're printing your file in Japan or Europe).
3. If you want control over the various CMYK settings, then choose Working Spaces: **Custom CMYK**. Name your setting and choose or enter the Ink Options for the offset press **1**, such as the **Ink Colors** and **Dot Gain**. Ask your print shop about these settings.

   Other characteristics of the offset press are entered in the **Separation Options** area **2**, but since these settings are particular to each press, you must ask your print shop for this information. In short, the **Separation Type** tells Photoshop about the type of press used: Does the press use the **GCR** (gray component

Ask your print shop at the outset

As we said a second ago, color separating is an art. Start by asking your print shop the following questions so you'll be able to choose the correct scan resolution and settings in the Custom CMYK dialog box:

What lines-per-inch setting is going to be used on the press for my job? This will help you choose the appropriate scanning resolution.

What is the dot gain for my choice of paper stock on that press? Allowances for dot gain can be made using the Custom CMYK dialog box.

Which printing method will be used on press—UCR or GCR? GCR produces better color printing and is the default choice in the Custom CMYK dialog box. (GCR stands for Gray Component Replacement, UCR stands for Undercolor Removal.)

What is the total ink limit and the black ink limit for the press? These values can also be adjusted in the Custom CMYK dialog box.

Note: Change the dot gain, GCR or UCR method, and ink limits before you convert your image from RGB Color mode to CMYK Color mode. If you change any of these values after conversion, you must convert the image back to RGB Color mode, readjust the values, then reconvert to CMYK Color mode.

In which file format should the file be saved? Ask the print shop what file format it needs.

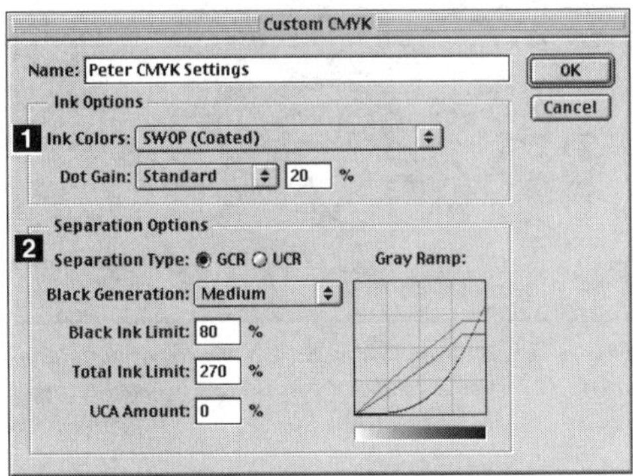

*In this screenshot of the **Custom CMYK** dialog box, the Black Ink Limit and the Total Ink Limit values have been changed to values suggested by a print shop. The graph maps the current values.*

Total readout

To display total ink coverage percentages on the Info palette for the pixels currently under the pointer, choose **Total Ink** from the pop-up menu next to the leftmost eyedropper on the palette **3**. This readout is based on the current CMYK settings.

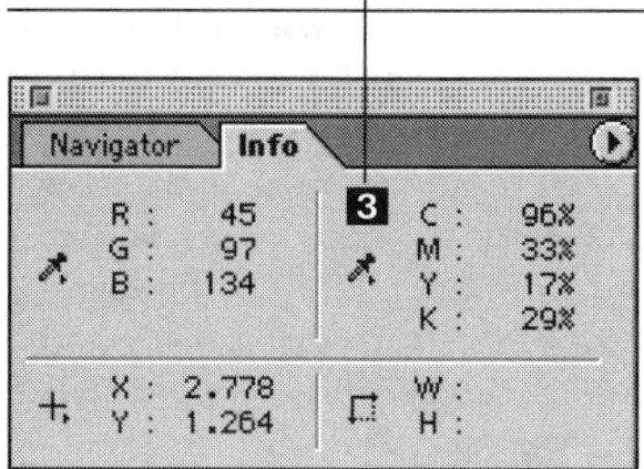

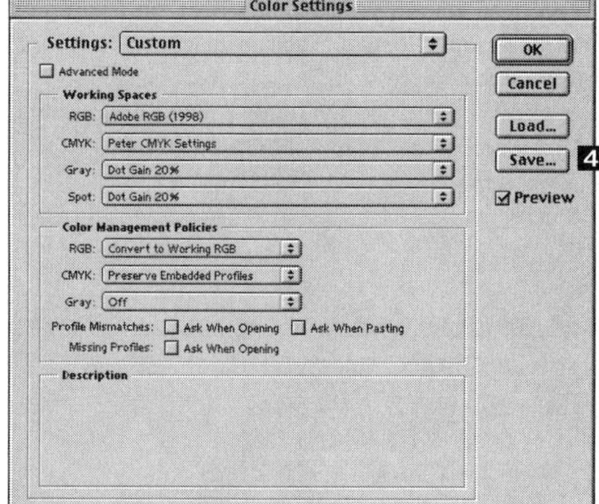

*In the **Color Settings** dialog box, click **Save**, to save your custom settings with the specific CMYK settings.*

Another option

To save your custom CMYK settings as just a profile, not as a full color setting, from the CMYK pop-up menu in the Working Spaces area of the Color Settings dialog box, choose Save CMYK. Leave the name and extension and file location as is, then click Save. The new profile can now be accessed by clicking Load on the same CMYK: menu.

replacement) or **UCR** (undercolor removal) method, and how does the print shop handle black ink?

The **Black Generation** amount controls how much black ink is used when the RGB components of light are translated into CMY inks. Black is substituted for a percentage of CMY inks to prevent inks from becoming muddy when they're mixed together. How much black is substituted is determined by the Black Generation amount.

Finally, each press shop uses its own amount of ink coverage on each separation plate. Some shops use less than 100% maximum ink coverage for each plate. Ask your press shop for its **Total Ink Limit** percentage settings.

Continue with the steps below.

Instead of reentering this information every time you need to do an RGB-to-CMYK conversion, you can save your Custom CMYK settings, and all other settings, as a preset.

To save the custom CMYK settings as a preset:

6.0!

1. Once you've entered your CMYK settings in the Custom CMYK dialog box, enter a name, then click OK.
2. Click Save **4**. Name the file, leave the default location of the Settings folder, then click Save again.
3. Enter any notes in the Color Settings Comment dialog box and click OK twice. The next time you output in that particular press situation, open the Color Settings dialog box, and from the Settings pop-up menu, choose the preset you just saved for that press. *Note:* These settings affect the conversion from RGB to CMYK color mode. If you subsequently readjust any settings in the Custom CMYK dialog box, you will have to reconvert your image from RGB to CMYK mode again using the new settings. Always keep a copy of your image in RGB Color mode for reconverting.

The Proof Colors and Proof Setup commands provide a way to soft proof an image by using the custom CMYK profile you set up in the previous steps, or by using the color profile for output devices available in your system. Soft proofs provide a fairly accurate preview of how an image will look when printed to that specific output device.

6.0!

To create a custom proof setup:

1. Choose View menu > Proof Setup > Custom.
2. From the Profile pop-up menu, choose the custom CMYK profile you created on the previous pages **1**. If Color Settings has been set to the custom CMYK profile (as explained on the previous pages), then the profile should be the current Working CMYK space on the list. Otherwise, look near the bottom of the menu list to locate your custom CMYK profile.
3. Choose an Intent. Ask your printshop for advice on this. See page 40 for more on Intents.
4. Click the Save button, and enter a name. Leave the location and extension as is. Click Save, then click OK.
5. Choose View menu > Proof Colors (Ctrl-Y/Cmd-Y) to turn on the soft proofing feature (it should now have a check mark). The saved proofing profile will be listed at the bottom of View menu > Proof Setup submenu.

TIP When Proof Colors is on (checked), the name of the proofing profile being used will be listed on the document's title bar.

TIP Proof Colors needs to be turned on for each opened image. The soft proof of each RGB mode image can now reflect the profile chosen on the Proof Setup submenu (in this case, the custom CMYK settings profile), but the actual image information will be changed only if the image is converted to CMYK Color mode using the current Color Settings.

File compression

To reduce the storage size of an image, use a compression program like WinZip or PKZip (Win) or DiskDoubler or Stuffit (Mac). Compression using this kind of software is non-lossy, which means the compression doesn't cause data loss.

If you don't have compression software, choose File menu > Save As, and choose TIFF from the Format pop-up menu. If you want to save the file without alpha channels, also uncheck the Alpha Channels box. Click Save. Check the LZW or Zip Compression box in the TIFF Options dialog box. LZW and Zip compression is non-lossy. Not all applications will import an LZW or Zip TIFF, though. And some applications will import an LZW or Zip TIFF only if it doesn't contain any alpha channels. JPEG compression is not recommended. See below.

If you're saving an image for print output, we don't recommend using the JPEG file format, since JPEG compression is lossy, and additional image data is lost with each compression. The data loss may not be noticeable on screen, but it may be quite noticeable on high resolution output. JPEG is more suitable for Web output.

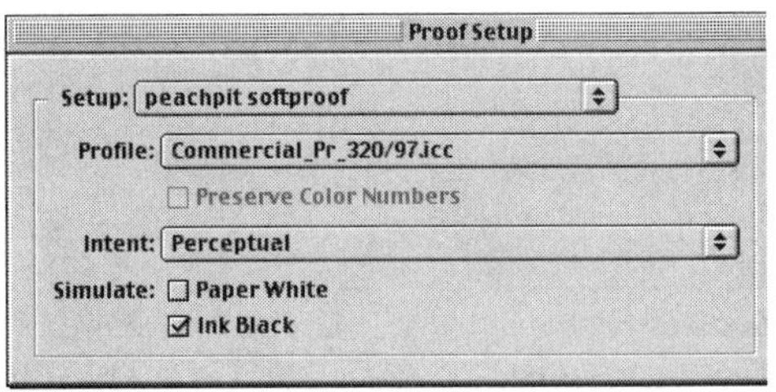

1 *Choose View menu > **Proof Setup** > **Custom** to open this dialog box.*

Custom Proof Setup

Desaturate another way

You can use Image menu > Adjust > **Hue/Saturation** instead of the Sponge tool to correct out-of-gamut colors in individual color categories. Move the Saturation slider to the left to desaturate.

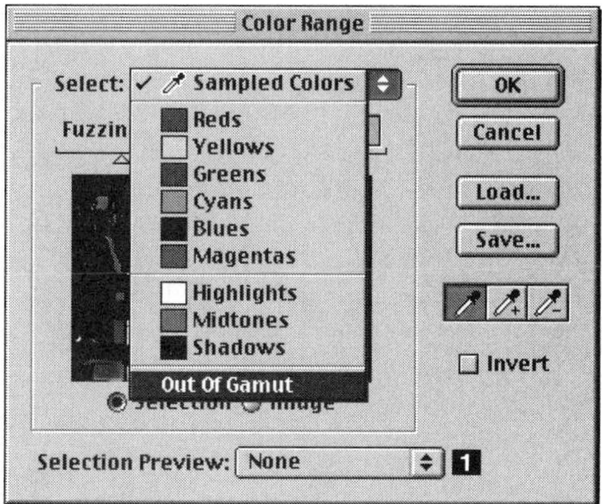

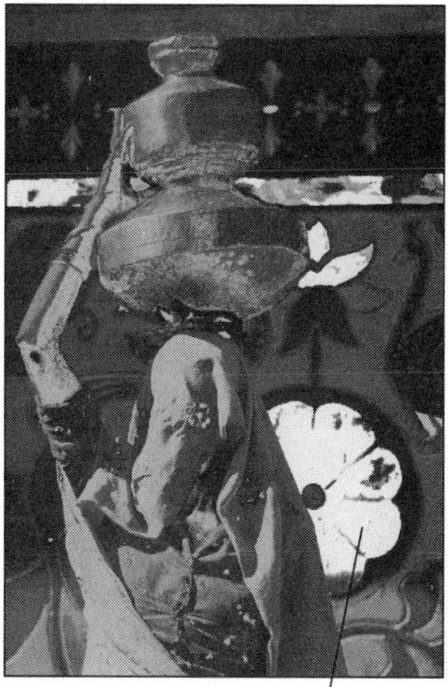

2 *For illustration purposes,* ***out-of-gamut*** *colors in this image are shown in white instead of the usual gray.*

If you convert an image to CMYK Color mode, its colors are automatically forced into printable gamut. In certain cases, however, you may want to see which areas are out-of-gamut (non-printable) in RGB first, and then change some of them manually. Use the steps below to display out-of-gamut colors and bring them into printable gamut.

Note: CMYK color equivalents are generated based on the current CMYK settings in the Color Settings dialog box, so adjust those settings first (see page 394).

To correct out-of-gamut colors:

1. Open your RGB Color image.
2. Choose View menu > Gamut Warning.
3. *Optional:* To select and restrict color changes to only the out-of-gamut areas, choose Select menu > Color Range, choose Select: Out Of Gamut **1**, then click OK.
4. Choose the Sponge tool (O or Shift-O).
5. On the Sponge options bar, choose Desaturate from the Mode pop-up menu, choose a Pressure percentage, and choose a tip from the Brush picker.
6. Choose a layer.
7. Drag across the gray, out-of-gamut areas **2**. As they become desaturated, they will redisplay in color. Don't desaturate colors too much, though, or they'll become dull.

TIP To preview the image in CMYK, choose View menu > Gamut Warning again to uncheck the command. Next, make make sure Working CMYK is chosen on the View menu > Proof Setup submenu. This should reflect your CMYK settings in the Color Settings dialog box. Finally, choose View menu > Proof Colors.

TIP When the pointer is over an out-of-gamut pixel, exclamation points will appear next to the CMYK readout on the Info palette.

Color correction: First glance

Such a complex topic as color correction is beyond the scope of this QuickStart Guide. It involves using many commands, including Levels, Curves, Color Balance, and Unsharp Mask. You can get some assistance from the resources listed in the sidebar at right. Just by way of introduction, though, these are the basic steps in the color correction process:

- Calibrate your monitor.
- Scan or acquire a PhotoCD image into Photoshop.
- Limit tonal values to determine where the darkest shadow and lightest highlight areas are in the image, and then limit the highest and lowest tonal values to the range that your print shop specifies. (Areas outside this range won't print well.)
- Color balance to correct any undesirable color cast in the image. You can correct the overall color balance or the neutral gray component of the image.
- Unsharp Mask to resharpen the image.
- Print a CMYK proof, and then analyze the proof with color-reading instruments to determine the exact color characteristics of the output.
- Readjust the Photoshop image, then print and analyze another proof.

On-screen output: Do all your color correction in RGB Color mode. Proof it by viewing it on other monitors or through a browser.

Print output: If you're working with a CMYK scan, do all your correction in CMYK Color mode. For an image that's going to be color separated, Adobe recommends using RGB Color mode and then converting the image to CMYK Color mode using the proper Color Settings options.

TIP Use adjustment layers for your color adjustments so you'll be able to easily readjust the image on a non-flattened copy of the image later on.

Continue your studies

Real World Photoshop 6
by David Blatner and Bruce Fraser

Production Essentials, 2nd edition
by Bruce Fraser

Real World Scanning and Halftones, 2nd edition
by David Blatner, Glenn Fleishman, and Steve Roth

Proof it 6.0!

To fine-tune your settings, it's a good idea to print a CMYK proof. Use the CMYK test image called Olé No Moire (Testpict.jpg for Windows) that Photoshop provides for this purpose. It's on the CD, in Goodies > Calibrate (Win) or Goodies > Calibration (Mac OS). Before opening it, however, choose Edit menu > Color Settings, and for Profile Mismatches:, check Ask When Opening. Open the image. If the Missing Profile alert box opens, click Leave as is (don't color manage), then click OK.

Web/ImageReady 23

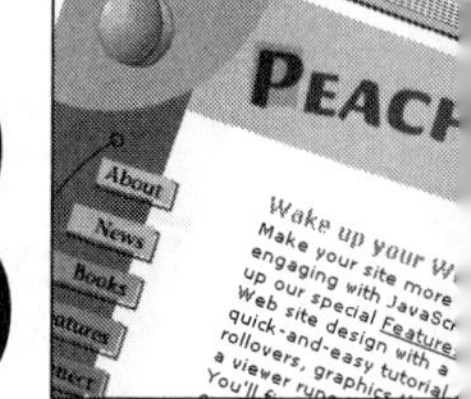

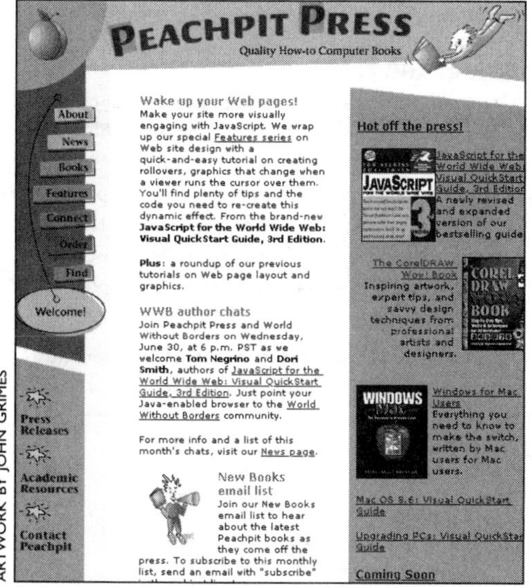

ARTWORK BY JOHN GRIMES

Visit Peachpit Press's web site: http://www.peachpit.com.

This chapter covers the preparation of Photoshop images for use in multimedia (on screen) and on the World Wide Web (online). Conversion to **Indexed Color** mode is covered first, then using Photoshop images in Adobe **LiveMotion** and **After Effects**, and finally, preparing images for viewing on the Web using Adobe **ImageReady**.

Since Web graphics are viewed on screen, this chapter includes a brief introduction to preparing graphics for presentation on monitors in general. When you're preparing graphics to be viewed on screen (as opposed to print), issues of storage and transmission of data become particularly important. We'll start with the conversion of images to Indexed Color mode, a technique that helps to shrink file sizes while preserving as much color information as possible.

Once the groundwork is laid, you'll be ready to dive right in to the real Web stuff. Ready to dive in right now? Then skip ahead to page 409, *Photoshop to the Web*.

Note: You'll be jumping back and forth between ImageReady and Photoshop for the instructions in this chapter.

Indexed color

Some multimedia and video programs and some computer systems will not import a Photoshop image that contains more than 256 colors (8-bit color). By converting an image to Indexed Color mode, you can reduce the number of colors in its color table. (For industrial-strength optimization features, read our section on ImageReady.)

Note: Converting a multi-layer image to Indexed Color mode will cause its layers to be flattened. Use the Save As command to work on a copy of the image.

To convert an image to Indexed Color mode:

1. Make sure the image is in RGB Color mode.
2. Choose Image menu > Mode > Indexed Color, then click OK.
3. Check the Preview box, if desired, then choose a Palette **1**:

   You can choose Exact if the image contains 256 or fewer colors. No colors will be eliminated.

   Choose System (Mac OS) if the file is going to be exported to an application that only accepts the Mac default palette.

   Choose System (Windows) if you're going to export the image to the Windows platform.

   Choose Web if the image is intended for Web viewing. This option limits the Color Table to only those colors that are available in the most popular Web browsers.

   Choose Uniform to create a table of colors evenly chosen from the spectrum. The color table will not shift to include the predominant areas of image color.

   Choose Local (Perceptual, Selective, or Adaptive) to create a table of colors based solely on the colors in the current image.

   6.0! Choose Master (Perceptual, Selective, or Adaptive) to use a master table of colors that you previously created from a set

Painting in Indexed Color mode

In Indexed Color mode, the Pencil, Airbrush, and Paintbrush tools produce only fully opaque strokes. For those tools, leave the Opacity slider on the options bar at 100%. Dissolve is the only tool mode that produces a different stroke at a lower opacity.

Beyond the Forced

If you want to have more control over which colors will be chosen for the palette beyond what the Forced option offers, create a selection (or selections) that contains the colors you want to appear on the palette before converting your image to Indexed Color mode, then choose Palette: Local (Perceptual), Local (Selective), or Local (Adaptive) for step 3, at left.

You can also use the Master palette option to control the colors in the image (see page 403).

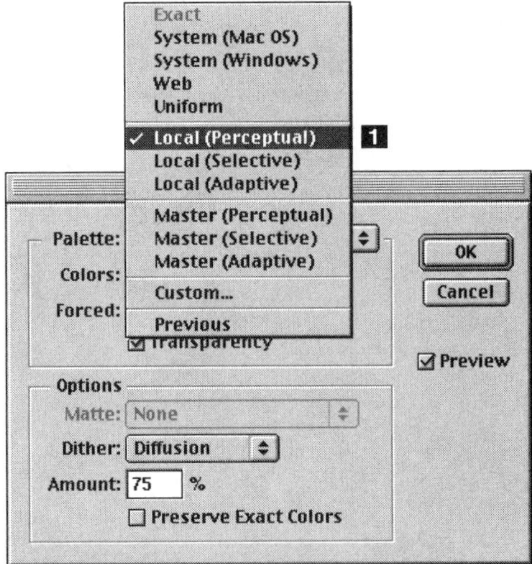

Indexed Color Mode

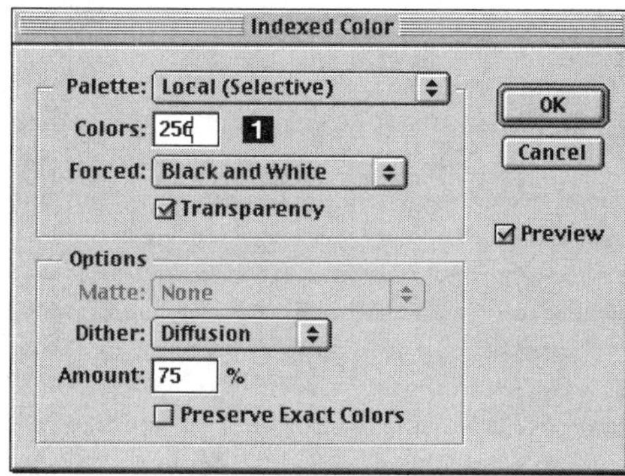

of images. (For information on creating master palettes, see page 403.)

Choose Perceptual, Selective, or Adaptive based on which colors you want preserved in the index conversion. See page 417 for details about the three palettes.

To create your own palette, choose Custom, edit the Color Table, if desired, then click OK. (Click Save if you want to save the table for later use. Click Load to load in a previously saved table.) Click OK and skip the remaining steps.

Choose Previous to use the custom palette used in the previous conversion, if any.

4. If you chose the Local or Master Uniform, Perceptual, Selective, or Adaptive palette, enter the number of Colors for the table **1**. The fewer the number of colors in the image, the smaller the file size will be, but the more dithered it will be.

5. Choose a Forced option to add specific colors to the color table. Choose Black and White to add pure black and pure white; Primaries to add red, green blue, cyan, magenta, yellow, black, and white; Web to add the 216 Web-safe colors (and leave the remaining number of colors as Selective colors); or Custom to pick your own colors.

6. Check the Transparency box to preserve transparent areas of the image. Uncheck this option to have transparent areas fill with the Matte color or fill with white if the Matte color is set to None.

   If the image has transparency, choose a Matte color to fill partially transparent pixels along the edge of the image.

7. Choose Dither: None, Diffusion, Pattern, or Noise. Dithering simulates additional colors that are not in the table. Choosing None will cause areas with sharp color transitions to look posterized, so use this with flat-color images. Diffusion may

(Continued on the following page)

produce the closest color substitutions, but it can also produce a dotty effect. The Pattern option adds pixels in a more structured arrangement. Noise produces a subtle dotty effect where colors meet.

8. If you chose Dither: Diffusion, you can enter an Amount of dither to control what percentage of colors will be dithered. If you choose this option, check the Preserve Exact Colors box. Dithering will then be turned off for any color in the image that exactly matches a color on the color palette. Don't try to proof this on screen, though—you probably won't see it.
9. Click OK.

To edit the color table in an Indexed Color image:

1. Choose Image menu > Mode > Color Table. All the picture's colors will display in the Color Table.
2. Click on a color to be replaced **1**.
   or
   Select a bunch of colors by dragging across them.
3. Move the slider up or down on the vertical bar to choose a hue **2**, then click a variation of that hue in the big square **3**.
4. *Optional:* To choose only Web-safe colors, check the Only Web Colors box **4**. If this option is off and you choose a non-Web safe color, the non-Web color alert icon will appear next to the color swatch **5**. If you then click this icon, Photoshop will substitute the closest Web-safe color.
5. Click OK. If you selected more than one color for step 2, choose a second color now, then click OK.
6. Click OK.

TIP To add arbitrary color to a Grayscale picture, convert it directly to Indexed Color mode and then modify its color table. Try the Black Body or Spectrum table.

Shrink it down

To reduce an Indexed Color table to two colors and the shades between them, first, choose Image menu > Mode > Color Table. Drag across the Color Table from the first swatch in the upper left corner to the last swatch in the lower right corner. Next, choose a first color from the Color Picker: Move the slider up or down on the vertical bar to choose a hue **2**, click a variation of that hue in the large rectangle **3**, then click OK. Next, choose a last color from the Color Picker. For the best results, choose a warm first color and a cool last color, or vice versa. Click OK to exit the Color Picker, then click OK again.

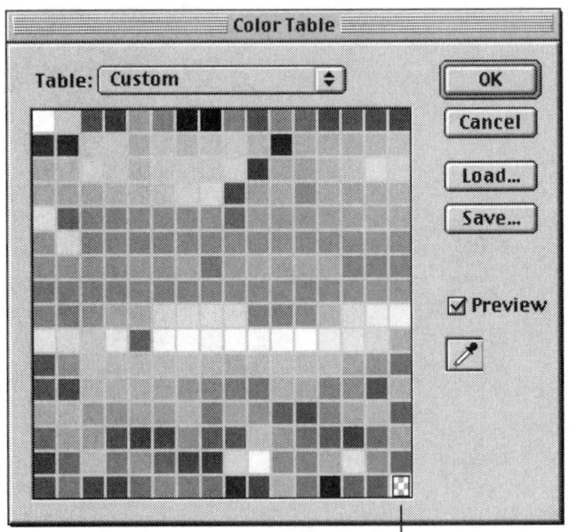

1 *Click a color or drag across a series of colors in the* ***Color Table*** *dialog box.*

This ***transparency*** *swatch displays if the Transparency box is checked in the Indexed Color dialog box.*

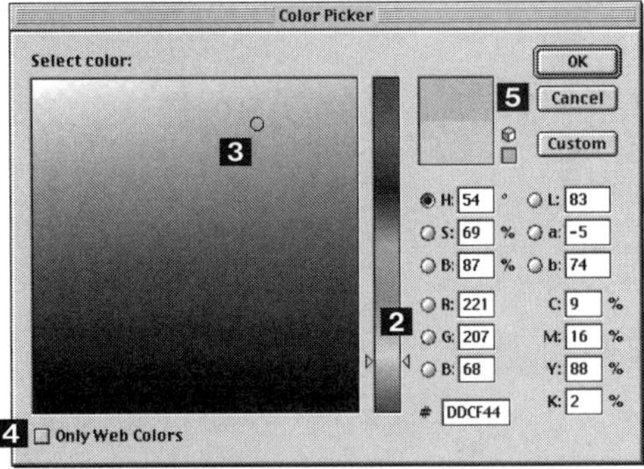

Indexed Color Table

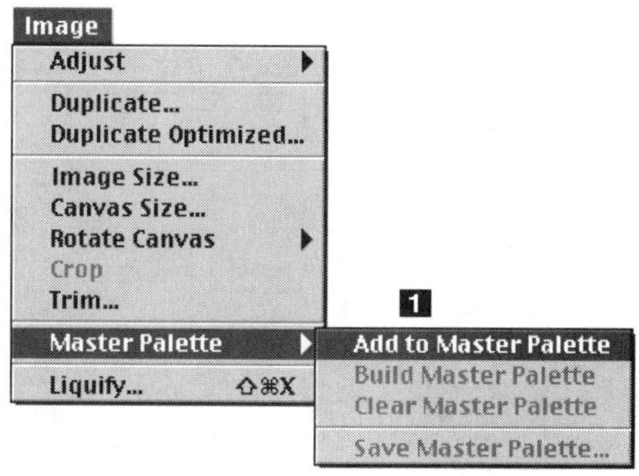

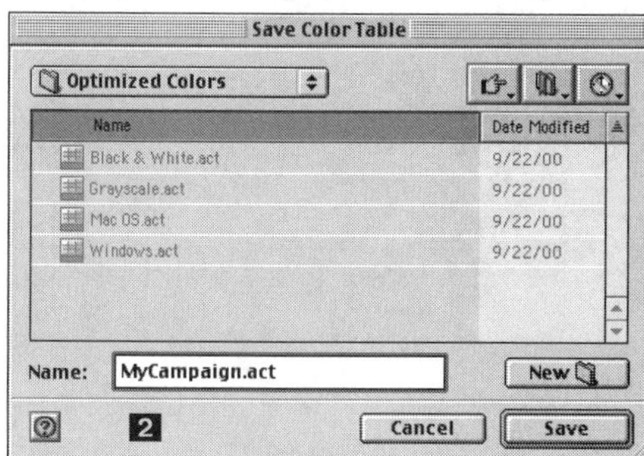

6.0!

ImageReady's master palettes offer a way to make sure that every image in a group uses an identical palette. Master palettes can help you save space on an image-packed CD-ROM or, for example, ensure that a Web site's GIFs use the same colors as those of a corporate logo.

You create a master palette by first adding colors from one or more images and then saving and naming the palette. The master palette can then be applied to other images that need to match the image group.

To create an ImageReady master palette for indexed images:

1. If you've previously created a master palette, clear it by choosing Image menu > Master Palette > Clear Master Palette.
2. Open an image whose colors you want to use in building a master palette.
3. Choose Image menu > Master Palette > Add to Master Palette **1**.
4. Repeat steps 2 and 3 to add the colors of any other images to the master palette.
5. Once you've added all the desired images, choose Image > Master Palette > Build Master Palette.
6. Finally, choose Image > Master Palette > Save Master Palette.
7. By default, the new master palette will be saved in the Optimized Colors folder within Photoshop 6's Presets folder and given the .act (Adobe Color Table) extension **2**. Give the palette a descriptive name and click Save. The palette now will be available for applying to other images.

6.0!

To apply a master palette to other images:

1. Open an image within ImageReady.
2. On the Optimize palette, choose the master palette from the Color reduction algorithm pop-up menu that you want to use **1**. The image's colors will be remapped to the master palette, which you can see by clicking the image window's Optimized tab.

TIP To use a palette created in another application, choose Load Color Table from the Color Table palette menu. You can then navigate to the folder that contains the palette you want to use.

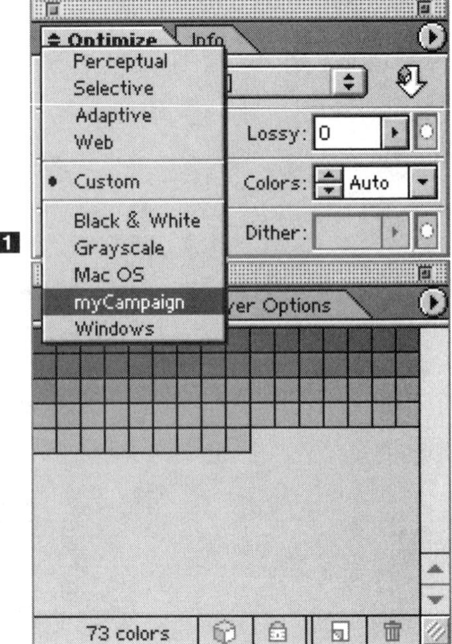

1

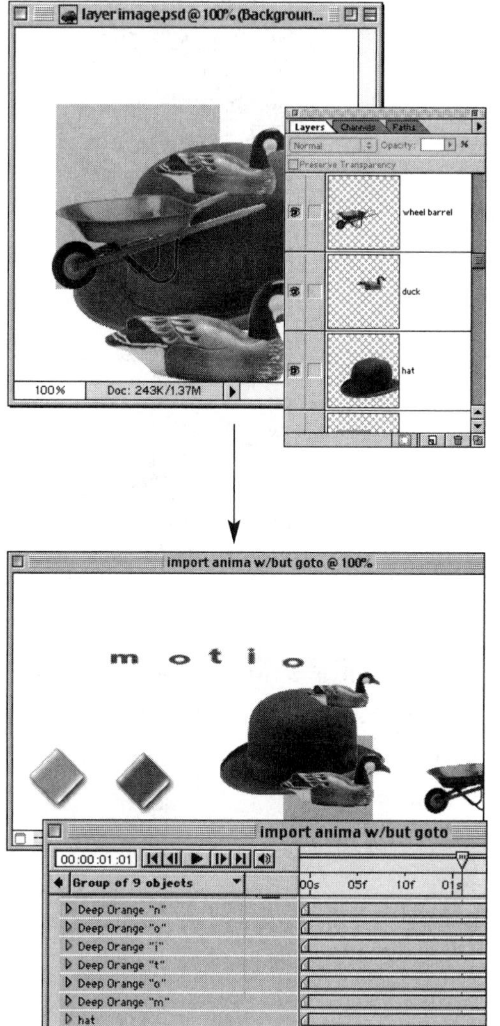

1 *A layered Photoshop file was placed into LiveMotion. The placed layers were then converted into individual objects. The "layer" objects can be animated like any LiveMotion object.*

Photoshop to LiveMotion

A layered Photoshop file can be used as the building blocks for an animation in LiveMotion, Adobe's Web animation application. You can use Photoshop's Layers palette like a storyboard to develop an image sequence. Hide and show picture elements on individual layers to preview object appearances, move layers in the image window using the Move tool to test animated motion, then place the file into LiveMotion.

One way to get a Photoshop file that contains multiple layers into LiveMotion is via LiveMotion's Place command. Another way is to drag-and-drop a layer from Photoshop into a LiveMotion composition.

A multi-layered Photoshop file will be flattened into a one-layer object when it's placed in LiveMotion. Once it's placed, though, you can use the Object menu > Convert Layers Into command to convert the layers either into separate objects on separate layers, or into a sequence of frames on one object layer. Any of the individual objects that result from such a conversion can then be selected in LiveMotion's Timeline editor and styled **1**.

To top it all off, using LiveMotion's Edit Original command, any Photoshop object that's been placed or dropped into LiveMotion can be opened and edited back in Photoshop (actually, you'll be working off a copy of the original file). When the newly edited copy is saved in Photoshop, it will update automatically in LiveMotion. This means that you have all the professional Photoshop tools at your disposal to revise a LiveMotion animation quickly.

Photoshop layers that are converted in LiveMotion into separate objects keep their stacking order from Photoshop (**1**–**3**, next page). The lowest (backmost) layer will become the lowest object on the Timeline editor list in LiveMotion. You'll need to think ahead, though: Restack layers before you place them.

Before placing a layered Photoshop file into LiveMotion

To simplify placing a Photoshop image into LiveMotion, do the following in Photoshop:

- Make sure the image has a non-transparent Background layer, not a Layer 0. When possible, leave the Background layer blank. When the image is placed and converted in LiveMotion, the Background will become a solid color object, which you can delete, if desired.
- Create an alpha channel if you want to silhouette any shapes in LiveMotion. Make sure the alpha channel has a black background and a white silhouette.
- Rasterize all vector, new fill, or shape layers in Photoshop. This will cause all layer clipping paths to be converted into layer masks. Layer masks will place into LiveMotion and mask the layer contents. Layer masks are accessed via LiveMotion's Properties palette, and are called alpha channels.

  Gradient layers will only place successfully into LiveMotion if they have been rasterized and any layer masks applied or discarded.
- Convert the file to RGB Color mode.
- When a layered Photoshop file is placed into LiveMotion as a composite, one-layer object, all opacity, adjustment layer, layer effect, and blending mode effects are preserved. If you then apply any Convert Layers Into command to the placed file, however, those effects will be nullified. If you need to preserve effects on a placed image, leave the object as one layer in LiveMotion—don't convert it into separate objects. You'll have more flexibility if you apply effects in LiveMotion rather than in Photoshop (e.g., opacity changes, opacity masks, shadows, 3D).
- If you want to work with editable text, enter text in LiveMotion, as Photoshop text will become imagery.

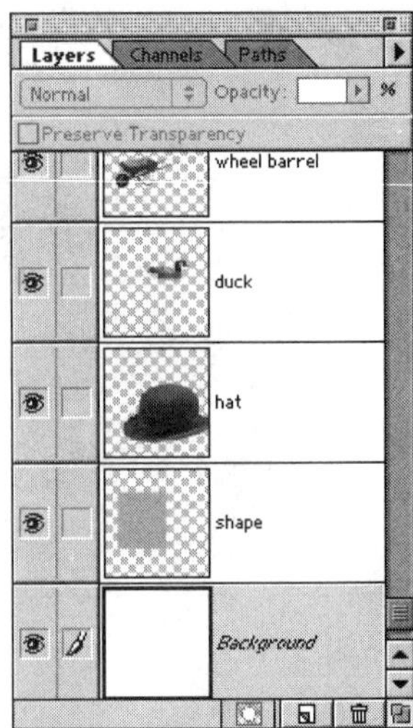

1 *The Layers palette in **Photoshop** showing the individual layers, including the Background.*

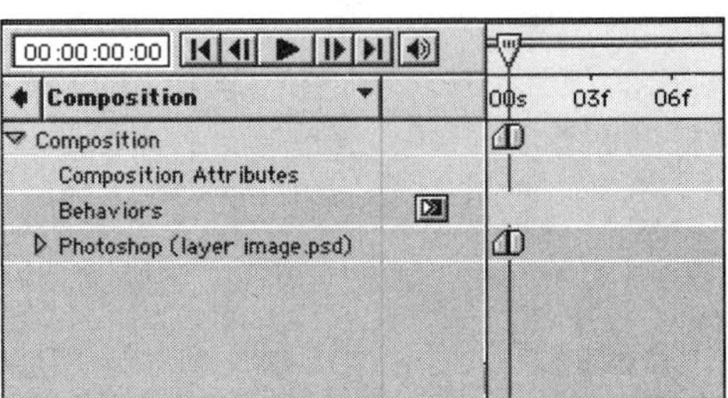

2 *This is how the LiveMotion **Timeline** looks after a layered Photoshop file is **placed**.*

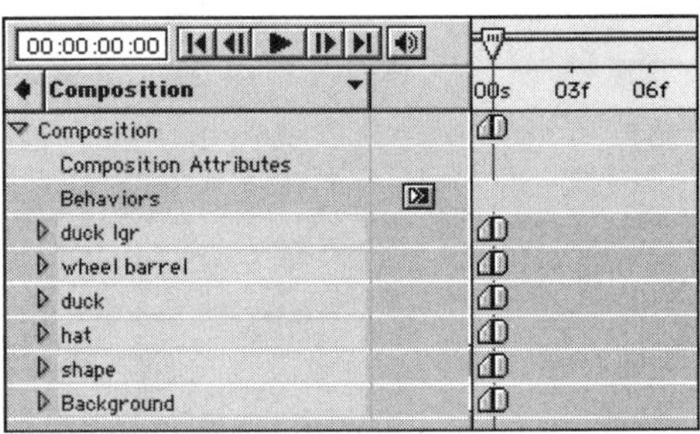

3 *After choosing Object menu > Convert Layers Into > **Objects**.*

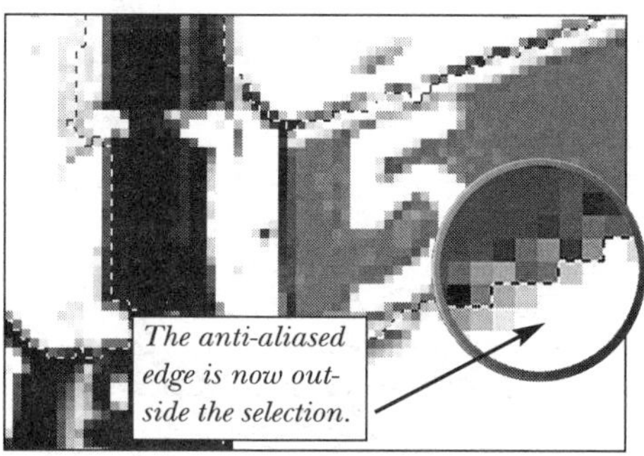

The anti-aliased edge is now outside the selection.

1 *After using the Magic Wand tool to select the white background around the signpost and then inversing the selection, some of the original anti-aliased edge remained. Select menu > Modify >* ***Contract*** *(by one pixel) was used to shrink the selection inward.*

2 *These two pixel images were pasted into another program. The object on the left was copied without contracting the selection in Photoshop. The object on the right was copied after contracting the selection in Photoshop to remove its* ***halo****.*

- Filters can be applied either in Photoshop or LiveMotion. Photoshop has more filters than LiveMotion, but in LiveMotion you'll have the power to hide or remove individual filter effects.

Avoiding halos when copying anti-aliased objects to other programs

In order to create smooth shape transitions, Photoshop adds pixels to object edges (this is called anti-aliasing). These added pixels fade gradually from opaque to transparent. Thus when the object is selected, because the object's edge includes semitransparent pixels, some background pixels also wind up being included in the selection.

If you paste a Photoshop selection into a composition in another program that has a different background color, the selection may have a small, but noticeable (and undesirable) halo around it. The halo effect will also be visible if the object is used in an animation in which it moves across a background that isn't uniform or that gradually changes.

To prevent halos, start by selecting an object in Photoshop without its anti-aliased edge. Ctrl-click/Cmd-click a layer name to select the object, then zoom in to at least 200% view so you can see the object's edge clearly. Choose Select menu > Modify > Contract and contract the selection by 1 or 2 pixels to remove the anti-aliased edge **1**–**2**. Finally, copy the object selection and paste it into the other program.

TIP For another approach to reducing problems with anti-aliased selections, see pages 421.

Photoshop to After Effects

You can import a layered Photoshop image into Adobe After Effects 4.1 and position it in the Time Layout window to create animated effects over time for Video or QuickTime output. A layered Photoshop file can be imported as an After Effects composition file. Individual layers and groups will remain intact.

6.0! Alternatively, a layered Photoshop image can be imported and merged into After Effects as a pre-composited image. To keep the Photoshop layers, adjustment layers, layer effects, blending modes, and alpha channels intact when you import the image, use After Effects' File menu > Import > Photoshop as Comp. Editable type layers will render correctly in After Effects (you don't need to render them first). Layer masks will also import into, and render correctly in, After Effects.

A Photoshop clipping group will import into After Effects as a pre-composition. As such, it can be placed and manipulated as a unit. If you double-click a clipping group composition in the After Effects Project window, the separate layers of the clipping group will display in the Time Layout window.

An alpha channel in a Photoshop file will be available for matting using After Effects' Set Matte Effect command. Any other channels will be ignored.

Sometimes the same image is used in both a print-related project (in which 250 ppi or higher resolution is commonplace) and an After Effects project. Don't use the hi-res file in After Effects. Instead, downsample a copy of it to the correct dimension and resolution for that application using File menu > Image Size in Photoshop.

Matching colors between Photoshop and other applications

If you try to mix a color in Photoshop using the same RGB values as a specific color used in Macromedia Director or Netscape Navigator, you probably won't be able to achieve an exact match, because Director and Navigator use the Windows Color Picker or Apple Color Picker (depending on your platform) to determine RGB color values (the number that's attached to each R, G, and B component), whereas Photoshop, by default, uses its own color picker.

If you use the Windows/Apple color picker instead of the Photoshop color picker, the colors you mix using the RGB sliders on the Color palette in Photoshop will match the colors used in Director. To switch pickers, choose Edit menu > Preferences > General, choose Color Picker: Windows/Apple, then click OK. Remember to reset this preference to the Photoshop color picker when you're finished.

Photoshop to video

If you're using an Avid video production system, use these image dimensions: 720 x 486 pixels (D-1 NTSC). For a QuickTime movie, the image can have any dimensions. For both Avid and QuickTime, the recommended image resolution is 72 ppi. Don't bother using a higher resolution than that.

Golden rules for creating Web images

- Let the content of the image—whether it's flat color or continuous-tone—determine which file format you use.
- Use an image as low in pixel size as is practical, balancing the file size with image quality. And remember this fail-safe option for flat-color images for viewing on both Windows and Mac browsers: Use the Web color sliders and the Web Safe color ramp on the Color palette, and Web-shift any existing flat-color areas.
- Try to reduce the number of colors in the image's Color Table.
- View your Web image through a Web browser on computers other than your own so you can see how quickly it actually downloads and how good (or bad) it looks.

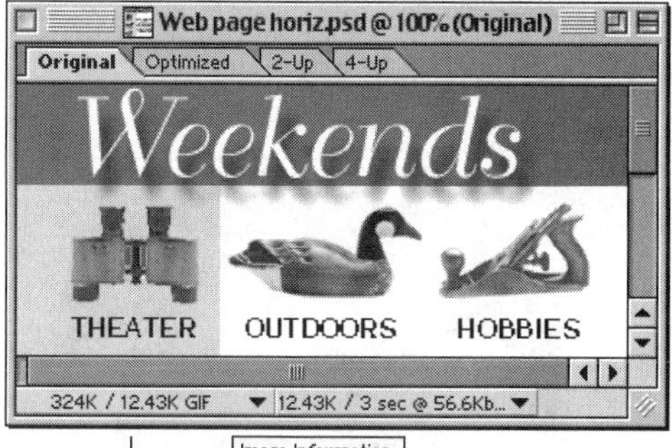

1 *Choose **Original/Optimized File Sizes** from ImageReady's **Image Information** pop-up menu to view a size readout for the file.*

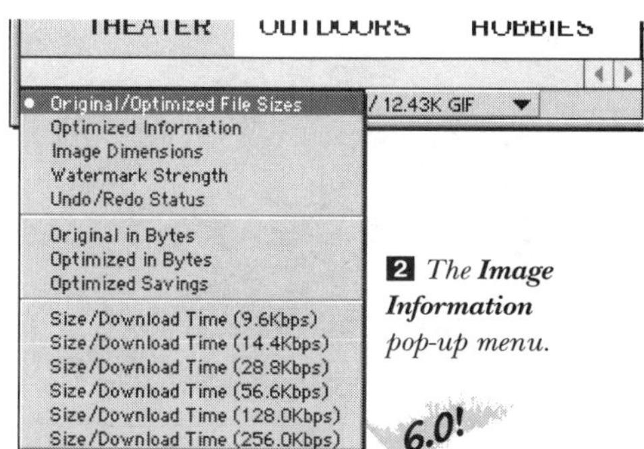

2 *The **Image Information** pop-up menu.*

Photoshop to the Web

The basic formula for outputting a Photoshop image for on-line viewing may seem straightforward: Design the image in RGB mode and save it, then Jump to ImageReady 3.0 and optimize the file for Web output. But if an image looks overly dithered (grainy and dotty), or was subject to unexpected color substitutions, or takes too long to view on a Web page, it means your onscreen design is not outputting well.

Four important issues you'll need to address for on-line output are discussed on the following pages: The pixel size of the image, the color palette, the color depth, and the file format (GIF or JPEG).

Image size

In order to calculate the appropriate image size, you must know the monitor size and the modem speed of your intended viewers beforehand. In most cases, you should be designing your image for a 800 x 600-pixel viewing area, the most common monitor size, and a 56 Kbps modem, the most common modem speed.

The Web browser window will display within these parameters, so your maximum image size will occupy only a portion of the browser window—about 10 inches wide (740 pixels) by 7.5 inches high (550 pixels). The image resolution needs to be only 72 ppi.

To determine the file storage size of an image, don't rely on Photoshop's Document Sizes reading on the image window status bar. Instead, Jump to ImageReady (click on the bottom of the Photoshop Toolbox), optimize the file, make sure Original/Optimized File Sizes is chosen from the Image Information pop-up menu at the bottom of the main window, and note the file size information **1**–**2**. Saving a file in the GIF or JPEG file format reduces its storage size significantly, because these formats have built-in compression schemes.

(Continued on the following page)

To determine a file's actual storage size:

Windows: Right-click the file in Windows Explorer and choose Properties from the pop-up menu.

Mac OS: Highlight the file name in the Finder, then choose File menu > Get Info.

If you know the exact file size of the compressed image, you can then calculate how long it will take to transmit over the Web. Better still, choose Size/Download Time from ImageReady's Image Information pop-up menu for various modem speeds and look at the readouts **1**.

The degree to which the GIF or JPEG file format compresses depends on how compressible the image is **2**. Both formats cause a small reduction in image quality, but it's worth the size-reduction tradeoff, because your image will download faster on the Web. ImageReady 3 now offers weighted optimization, which helps finesse that tradeoff by letting you selectively compress different areas of an image (see page 421).

A file size of about 50K traveling on a 56 Kbps modem will take about 9 seconds to download.

- A document with a flat background color and a few flat-color shapes will compress a great deal (expect a file size in the range of 20 to 50K).
- A large document (over 100K) with many color areas, textures, or patterns (e.g., an Add Noise texture covering most of the image) won't compress nearly as much.
- Continuous-tone, photographic images may compress less than flat-color images when you use the GIF format. If you posterize a continuous-tone image down to somewhere between four and eight levels, the resulting file size will be similar to that of a flat-color image, but you will have lost the continuous color transitions in the bargain. JPEG is the better format choice for a photographic-type image.

To summarize, if an image must be large (500 x 400 pixels or larger), ideally it should

Create a browser window layer

Take a screen shot of your browser window, open the file in Photoshop, and paste it into a document as your bottommost layer. Now you can design your layout for that specific browser window's dimensions.

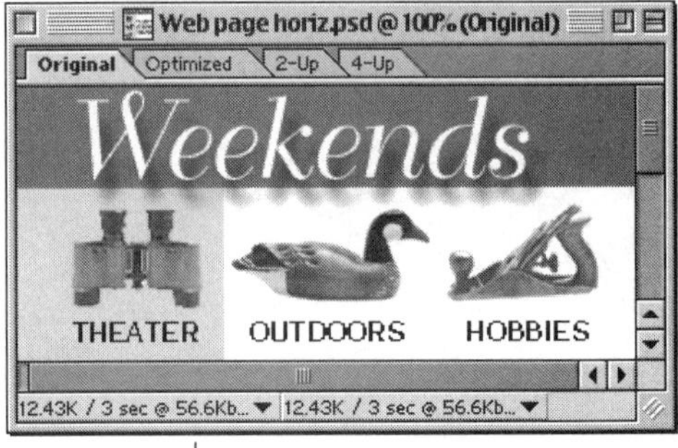

1 *Choose* ***Size/Download Time*** *from ImageReady's* ***Image Information*** *pop-up menu.*

2 *Size comparisons of* ***GIFs****.*

20K GIF*, from a* ***5-level posterized*** *image.*

120K GIF*, from a* ***continuous-tone*** *image.*

*GIF is a suitable optimization format for this image, because it has **flat-color** shapes.*

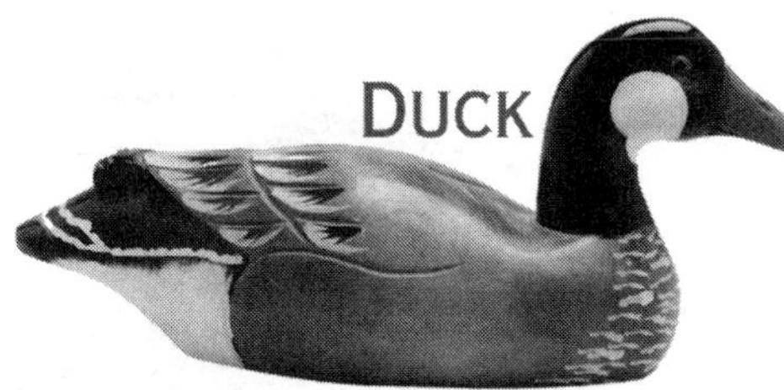

***GIF** optimization is also a good choice for this **hybrid** image, which contains both sharp-edged (type) and continuous-tone (ducky) elements.*

contain only a handful of large, flat-color shapes. For an image that has intricate shapes and colors, try to restrict its size to only a portion of the Web browser window.

TIP Patterned imagery that completely fills the background of the browser window is usually created using a tiling method in a Web-page creation program or using HTML code. ImageReady can also be used to create the code for, and generate, a background tile effect (see pages 473–475).

GIF

GIF is an 8-bit file format, which means a GIF image can contain a maximum of 256 colors. GIF is the standard format, though, because a majority of Web users have 8-bit monitors which can display a maximum of 256 colors—not the thousands or millions of colors that make images look pleasing to the eye. It's a good choice for images that contain flat-color areas and shapes with well-defined edges, such as type.

To save an image in the GIF format and to see how it will actually look when it's viewed via the browser, use File menu > Save for Web in Photoshop or optimize and save it in ImageReady (see page 418).

Your color choices for a GIF image should be based on what a Web browser palette can realistically display. Most browser palettes are 8-bit, which means they can display only 256 colors. Colors that aren't on the palette are simulated by dithering, a display technique that intermixes color pixels to simulate other colors.

To prevent unexpected dithering, consider optimizing your image using ImageReady's Web palette. Or Web Snap most of the colors in the image in ImageReady and manually Web-shift critical areas of flat color. More about these methods later in the book. Color substitutions will be particularly noticeable in flat-color areas. The new weighted optimization feature can be used to fine tune dithering and color reductions (see page 421).

TIP If you want to apply a gradient fill to a large area of an image and you're going to use the GIF format, create a top-to-bottom gradient. Top-to-bottom gradients produce smaller file sizes than left-to-right or diagonal gradients.

Color depth

If you lower an image's color depth, you will reduce the actual number of colors it contains, which will in turn reduce its file size and speed up its download time on the Web. Color reduction may produce dithered edges and duller colors, but you'll get the reduction in file size that you need.

You can reduce the number of colors in an 8-bit image to fewer than the 256 colors it originally contained using Photoshop's Indexed Color dialog box (the old-fashioned way), Photoshop 6's Save for Web dialog box (better), or ImageReady's Optimize palette (best). Photoshop 6's Save for Web dialog box and ImageReady's Optimize palette both provide several features that will give you the opportunity to preview how an image will look with fewer available colors.

TIP Always preview an image at 100% view to evaluate color quality.

Color depth

Number of colors	Bit depth
256	8
128	7
64	6
32	5
16	4
8	3
4	2
2	1

JPEG

The JPEG format may be a better choice for preserving color fidelity if your image is continuous tone (contains gradations of color or is photographic) and your viewers have 24-bit monitors (which have the capacity to display millions of colors).

A JPEG plus: It can take a 24-bit image and make it as small as the GIF format can make an 8-bit image.

JPEG shortcomings: First, a JPEG file has to be decompressed when it's downloaded for viewing on a Web page, which takes time.

Secondly, JPEG is not a good choice for flat-color images or type, because its compression methods tend to produce artifacts along the well-defined edges of these kinds of images.

*JPEG optimization is suitable for this **continuous-tone** image.*

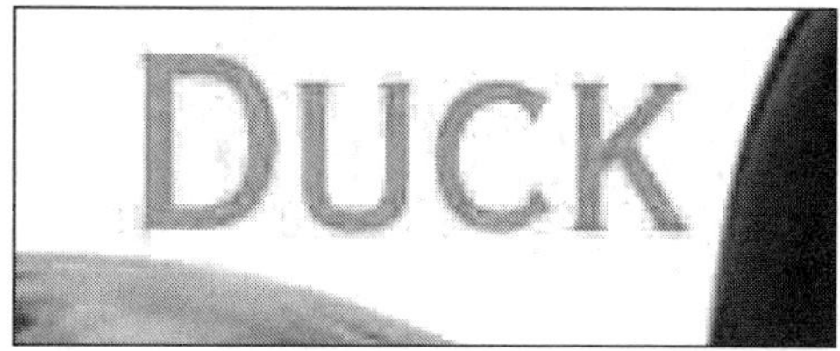

*JPEG isn't a great choice for optimizing **sharp-edged** imagery. Note the artifacts around the type.*

*The word "duck" looks crisper in this **GIF**.*

And third, not all Web users have 24-bit monitors. A JPEG image will be dithered on an 8-bit monitor, though dithering in a continuous-tone image will be less noticeable than in an image that contains flat colors. You can lower your monitor's setting to 8-bit to preview what the image will look like in an 8-bit setting, or simply use View menu > Preview > Browser Dither in ImageReady. If it doesn't contain type or objects with sharp edges, the JPEG image will probably survive the conversion to 8-bit.

JPEG format files can also be optimized as Progressive JPEG, which is supported by both the Netscape Navigator and Internet Explorer browsers (versions 4 and up). A Progressive JPEG displays in increasing detail as it downloads onto a Web page.

If you choose JPEG as your output format, you can experiment in ImageReady or in Photoshop's Save for Web dialog box by optimizing an image, then using the 4–Up option to preview several versions of the image in varying degrees of compression. Decide which degree of compression is acceptable by weighing the file size versus diminished image quality. In ImageReady, you can save the optimized file separately and leave the original file intact to preserve it for potential future revision.

Each time an image is optimized using the JPEG format, some image data is lost. The greater the degree of compression, the greater the data loss. To prevent such data loss, first edit and save your image in Photoshop. Then Jump to ImageReady; perform further edits, if desired; optimize the file; and finally use File menu > Save Optimized to output the file in the JPEG format.

Dithering

Dithering is the intermixing of two palette colors to create the impression of a third color. It's used to make images that contain a limited number of colors (256 or fewer)

(Continued on the following page)

appear to have a greater range of colors and shades. Dithering is usually applied to continuous-tone images to increase their tonal range, but—argh, life is full of compromises—it can also make them look a bit dotty.

Dithering usually doesn't produce aesthetically pleasing results in flat-color images. This is because the browser palette will dither pixels to recreate any color that the palette doesn't contain. For a flat-color image, it's better to create colors in Photoshop or ImageReady using the Web Color sliders and the Web Safe color ramp on the Color palette. Existing flat-color areas should also be selected and Web-shifted to make them Web safe.

Continuous-tone imagery is, in a way, already dithered. Some continuous-tone imagery looks fine on a Web page with no dithering and 256 colors. The fewer the colors in the palette of a non-dithered continuous-tone image, the more banding will occur in its color transitions. A Dither value is chosen in ImageReady or in Photoshop's Save for Web dialog box. The higher the Dither value, the more seamless the color transitions will appear, but the image may also look more dotty. You can decide which of these two evils appears lesser to your eye.

One more consideration: Dithering adds noise and additional colors to the file, so compression is less effective when dithering is turned on than when it's off. So, with dithering enabled, you may not be able to achieve your desired degree of file compression. As is the case with most Web output, you'll have to strike an acceptable balance between aesthetics and file size.

Anti-aliasing

Anti-aliasing blends the edge of an object with its background. It achieves this blending by adding pixels with progressively less opacity along an object's edge. When imagery is composited or montaged in Photoshop, anti-aliasing helps to smooth the transitions between shapes. With anti-aliasing turned

Select without the anti-aliasing

To select imagery on a layer without selecting semi-transparent pixels on its anti-aliased edge, Ctrl-click/Cmd-click the layer name. Then use Select menu > Modify > Contract, and contract by 1 pixel.

*A closeup of an image with a **small** amount of **dithering**.*

*The same image with a **lot** of **dithering**.*

Photoshop 6's Save for Web

Many of Photoshop's file optimization features are combined in the File menu > **Save for Web** dialog box **1**. There you'll find Original, Optimized, 2-Up, and 4-Up preview tabs at the top of the main window; a Color Table palette; and format, matte, quality, and other options. You'll also find the Preview menu and Preview in [browser] button in this dialog box. In this chapter, we focus on optimization in ImageReady, but you can apply the same learning steps to any of the equivalent features that are found in Photoshop's Save for Web dialog box. The details of the Save for Web dialog box are pictured on page 476.

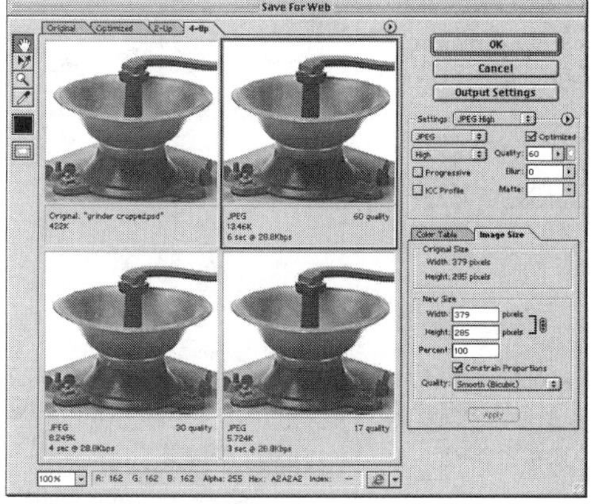

1 ***Photoshop's Save for Web*** *dialog box.*

sharp because its edge pixels won't be blended with the background color.

If you create a selection using a tool with anti-aliasing turned on, though, a fringe of pixels may be picked up in the selection from the background of the original image. If you copy and paste this type of shape onto a flat-color background, the fringe may become painfully visible. To prevent this from happening, before creating your selection, uncheck the Anti-aliased box on the options bar for your marquee, lasso, or Magic Wand tool.

You can also use the Matte option on ImageReady's Optimize palette to control how partially transparent pixels (the kind of pixels that are created by anti-aliasing) are treated in GIFs and JPEGs. Photoshop 6 and ImageReady both provide options for controlling the amount of anti-aliasing on type. This option can be chosen in, and transferred between, the two programs. The new matting and anti-aliasing controls help to eliminate unwanted halos.

PNG-8 and PNG-24

The two PNG formats can save partially transparent pixels (e.g., soft, feathered-edges) using a method called alpha transparency. With alpha transparency, a pixel can have any one of 256 levels of opacity, from totally transparent to totally opaque. The PNG-8 format is limited to a maximum of 256 colors in the optimized image, and is similar to the GIF format. The PNG-24 format allows for millions of colors in the optimized image and is similar to the JPEG format. The PNG formats use a lossless compression method (no data is lost).

Are there any drawbacks to using PNG? For one thing, animation cannot be done in the PNG format (animation *can* be done in the GIF format) and PNG-24 files have larger file sizes than equivalent JPEGs. More importantly, PNG is not yet supported directly by the two major Web browsers.

(Continued on the following page)

Internet Explorer versions 4.0 and later directly support PNG, as does Netscape Navigator 6 and later. Earlier versions of Explorer and Navigator require a plug-in, like PNG Live, in order to display this format. What's wrong with a plug-in? Viewers may be reluctant to spend time downloading a plug-in, but your site will not display at its full potential without it.

The ImageReady toolbox

6.0! The ImageReady toolbox looks similar to Photoshop's, but it contains a few extra Web-related tools **1** for creating image maps, viewing image maps, viewing slices, previewing rollover effects, and switching to a Web browser. Its Jump To button jumps to Photoshop.

Like Photoshop, ImageReady now includes a context-sensitive tool options bar, which changes depending on which tool is currently chosen **2**–**3**. Drag the bar's left edge to move it anywhere on the desktop. To collapse the bar, double-click the left edge **4** (ImageReady only).

We mean ImageReady 3.0 too!

We're using the 6.0! icon to mark both Photoshop 6 and ImageReady version 3.0 features.

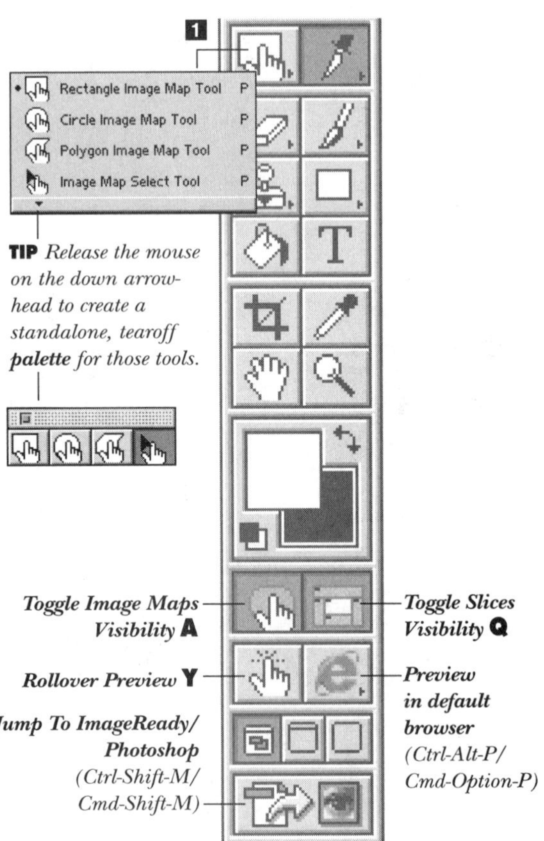

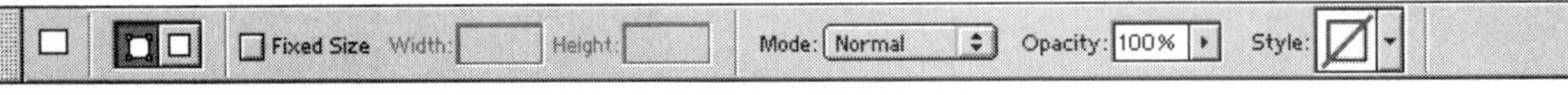

2 *The options bar with the* ***Rectangle shape*** *tool chosen.*

3 *The options bar with* ***Type*** *tool chosen.*

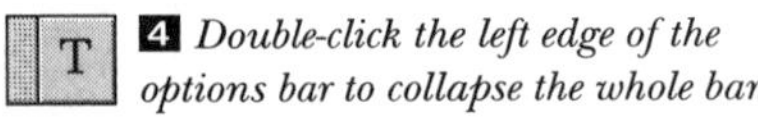

4 *Double-click the left edge of the options bar to collapse the whole bar.*

Four of the GIF color palettes

Note: What Web designers commonly refer to as "color palettes," ImageReady tool tips calls "color reduction algorithms" (huh?).

Perceptual
Generates a color table based on the colors currently in the image, with particular attention to how people actually perceive colors. This table's strength is in preserving overall color integrity.

Selective
Generates a color table based on the colors currently in the image. The Perceptual and Selective options are similar, but the Selective option leans more toward preserving flat colors and Web-safe colors.

Adaptive
Generates a color table based on the part of the color spectrum that represents most of the color in the image. This choice produces a slightly larger optimized file.

TIP If you switch among the Perceptual, Selective, or Adaptive options, any Web-safe colors that are currently on the Color Table palette are preserved.

Web
Generates a color table by shifting image colors to colors that are available in the standard Web-safe palette. (In order to create a palette that works on both platforms, since the Windows and Mac browser palettes share only 216 out of 256 possible colors, the palette contains only 216 colors.) This choice produces the least number of colors and thus the smallest file size, but not necessarily the best image quality.

Optimizing images for the Web using ImageReady

Optimization is the process by which file format, storage size, and color parameters are chosen for an image in order to maximize its quality, yet still enable it to download quickly on the Web. While an image can be optimized in Photoshop 6 via the File menu > Save for Web command (a one-stop optimize dialog box), we think the better approach is to Jump to ImageReady and use the various palettes in ImageReady for optimization, because they offer more options.

Note: As we explained in the sidebar on the previous page, if you learn how to use ImageReady, you'll also be learning about the options in Photoshop 6's Save for Web dialog box, because they're almost identical. The Save for Web dialog box is pictured on page 476.

ImageReady provides many choices and options for optimization. In this section you will learn the basic steps. Always remember your overall goal is to reduce the file size until the image quality reaches its reduction limit (starts to degrade). Keep this goal in mind as you choose palette settings.

GIF and JPEG are the two most commonly used file formats for displaying graphics on the Web. GIF is recommended for images that contain elements with sharp edges, such as flat-color areas, line art, and text. The PNG-8 format, which is similar to GIF, uses the same Optimize palette options as GIF, and the optimize results are practically the same. An optimized GIF or PNG-8 file can contain up to 256 colors.

Photoshop 6's Save a Copy command can also be used to save copies of a file in the GIF or JPEG format, but we believe ImageReady offers superior GIF and JPEG saving options because of all of its optimization variables and preview features. For this reason, in this book we've decided to focus on optimizing GIFs and JPEGs in ImageReady.

To optimize an image in the GIF or PNG-8 format:

1. If you're working in Photoshop 6, save your file, then click the Jump to button at the bottom of the Toolbox (Ctrl-Shift-M/Cmd-Shift-M). ImageReady will launch, if it isn't already open, and the image will open in that application.
   or
   In ImageReady, choose File menu > Open, locate an image, then click Open.
2. Click the 2-Up tab at the top of the image window to display both the original and optimized previews of the image simultaneously **1**.
3. Display the Optimize palette (Window menu > Show Optimize).
4. Choose a named, preset combination of optimize settings from the Settings pop-up menu **2**. Leave the preset as is, and save your file.
   or
   Follow the remaining steps to choose custom optimization settings.
5. Choose GIF or PNG-8 from the file format pop-up menu.
6. Choose a **palette** option (color reduction algorithm) from the next pop-up menu (see the sidebar on the previous page). The GIF and PNG-8 formats permit a maximum of only 256 colors.

   Perceptual, Selective, **3** and Adaptive render the optimized image using colors from the original image.

   Web shifts all the image colors to Web-safe colors **4**. This is not generally the best choice if the image contains continuous-tone areas, blends, or gradients.

   Custom optimizes image color based on a palette you have previously saved in Photoshop or ImageReady.

   Mac OS and Windows optimize image color based on the Standard palette for that particular operating system.

1 *2-Up view in **ImageReady**.*

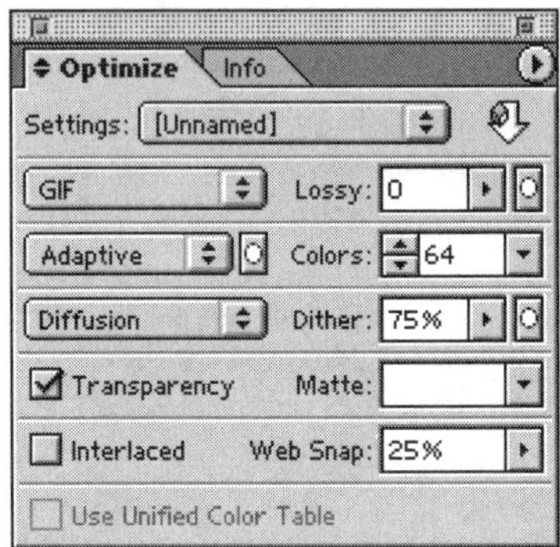

2 ***ImageReady's Optimize** palette.*

3 *The **Selective** palette produces a **smoother** optimization.*

4 *The **Web** palette produces a **dithered** optimization.*

Fading away

Transparent GIFs and JPEGs cannot show soft-edged shapes against transparency. If you want your image to fade into a flat-color background (as in a Drop Shadow or Outer Glow Effect), create two layers in your Photoshop or ImageReady document: a lower layer that contains a flat color filled with the Web-safe color that will be used on the Web page; and an upper layer that contains the image element with a soft, feathered edge or an Effect such as Drop Shadow.

1 ***Selective*** *palette with a* ***high Dither*** *value.*

2 *The* ***Web*** *palette with a* ***high Dither*** *value produces, as one would expect, a lot of* ***dithering****.*

3 *A GIF image with Transparency checked and* ***Matte*** *set to* ***a color****. This results in a thin line of color along the edge of each shape.*

7. From the next pop-up menu, choose a **Dither** method: No Dither, Diffusion, Pattern, or Noise. Dither simulates image colors for 8-bit display (you won't be able to see this on the palette). Dither increases a file's size. Diffusion produces the most subtle effect with the least increase in file size.

   Choose a Dither percentage **1**–**2**. A high Dither value will produce more color simulation, but will also result in a larger file size. To modify dithering using a channel, see page 421.
8. Choose the maximum number of **Colors** to be generated in the color table. Choose a standard setting from the drop-down menu or enter an exact number in the field. For the Web, Mac, and Windows palettes, this field defaults to Auto. Auto sets the number of colors in the color table automatically to either the number of colors used in the image or to 256, whichever is lower. You can choose or enter a Colors number to override the Auto setting.
9. Check the **Transparency** box to have ImageReady preserve any transparent pixels in the image (areas of a layer where the checkerboard pattern shows). The GIF format doesn't allow for partially transparent pixels; the PNG-8 format does. (See the sidebar on this page.) Transparency permits the creation of non-rectangular image borders. With Transparency unchecked, transparent pixels will be filled with the current Matte color.
10. To control how partially transparent pixels along the edge of an image blend with the background of a Web page (as on the edges of anti-aliased elements), choose a **Matte** option. Set the Matte color to the color of the Web page background, if you happen to know what that color is **3**. If the backgound

(Continued on the following page)

Optimize as GIF or PNG-8

color is unknown, set Matte to None, which will result in a hard, jagged edge **1**. Both options eliminate halo effects along the edge of an image when it's displayed on the Web. Any soft-edged effect (such as a Drop Shadow) on top of transparency will fill with the current Matte color.

11. Check the **Interlaced** box to have the GIF or PNG image display in successively greater detail as it downloads on the Web page. This option causes the file size to increase slightly.
12. Choose or enter a **Web Snap** percentage to establish the range of colors that will automatically snap to their Web-safe equivalents. The higher the Web Snap, the fewer the number of colors in the image and the smaller the file size, but the more dithered or posterized the image will become **2**.
13. *Optional:* For a GIF only, you can adjust the **Lossy** value to further reduce the file size of the optimized image. As the name "Lossy" implies, some image data will be discarded, but the slight reduction in image quality may be justified by the savings in file size. (To modify lossiness using a channel, see page 421.)
14. Save the file. See pages 430–431.

TIP To save a current [Unnamed] set of palette options, choose Save Settings from the palette menu. Enter a name (*Windows:* Use the .irs extension), locate and open the Adobe Photoshop 6 > Presets > Optimize Settings folder (the default), then click Save. Your saved set will display on the Settings pop-up menu in ImageReady and also in the Save for Web dialog box in Photoshop 6.

6.0!

To guard against losing your current settings, save them as a "Temp" set. Replace the former temp file each time with the new one.

How to treat a hybrid

For a hybrid image that contains flat areas of color or type and photographic imagery, the best choice may be the GIF format using the Perceptual, Selective, or Adaptive palette (not the Web palette). This combination will strike a good balance between keeping the flat-color areas Web safe and rendering the continuous-tone areas reasonably well.

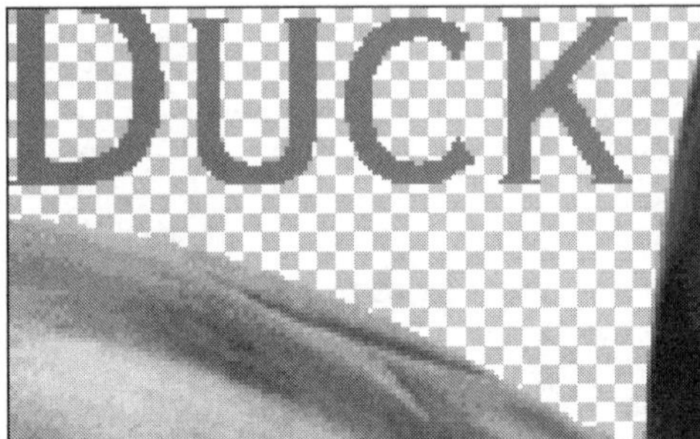

1 *A GIF image with Transparency checked and* ***Matte*** *set to* ***None****. There's a hard edge along each shape.*

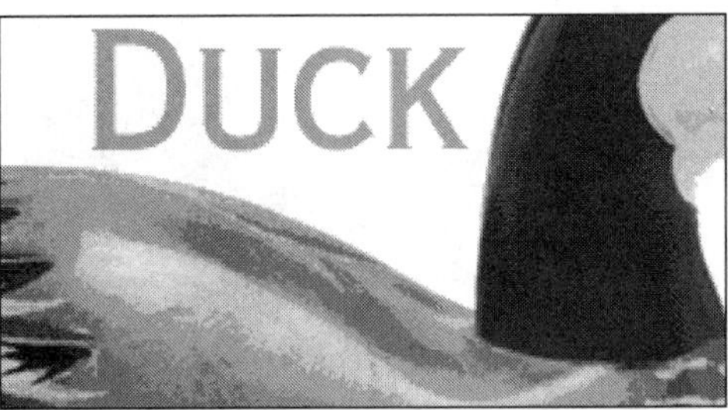

2 *The* ***Selective*** *palette with a* ***high Web Snap*** *value produces* ***posterization****.*

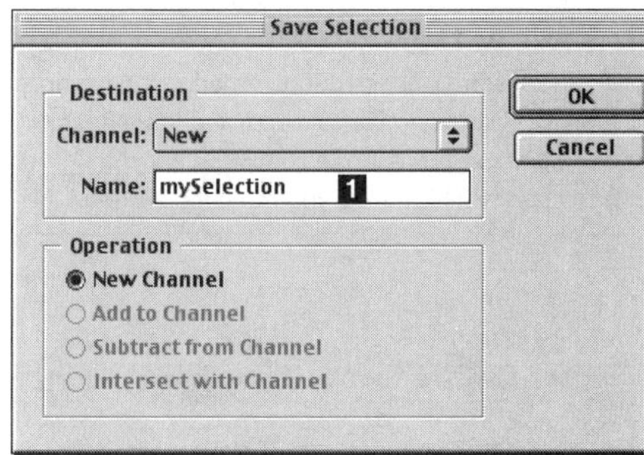

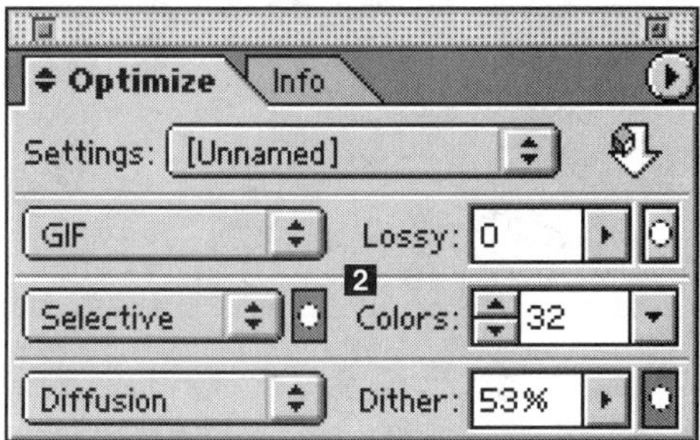

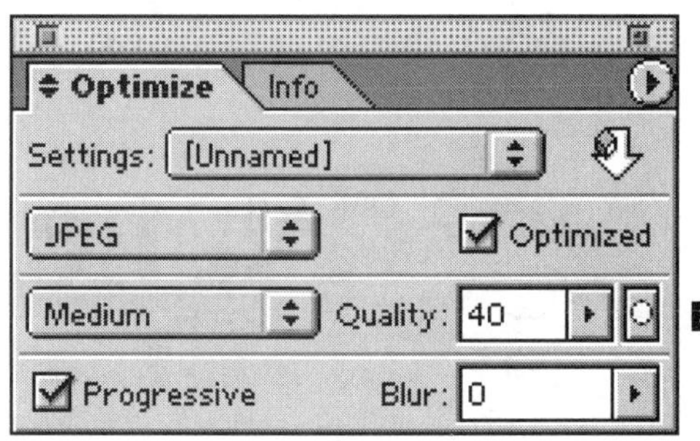

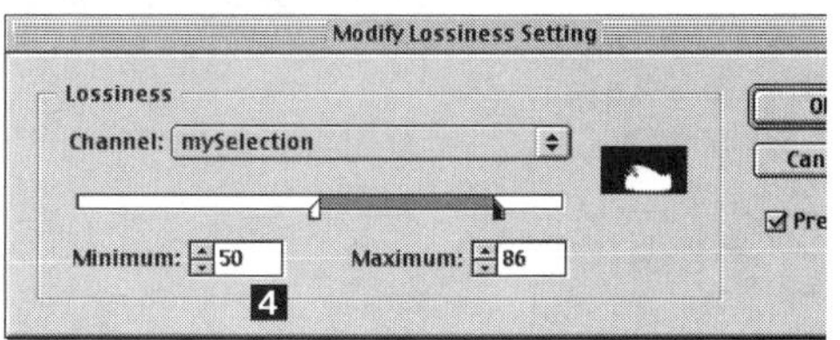

6.0!

Weighted optimization, a new feature in ImageReady 3, lets you set maximum and minimum quality limits for compressing GIF, PNG, and JPEG images. By creating and saving a selection channel, the maximum limits will be applied to the channel's white area (the area inside the original selection); minimum limits applied to the black areas (areas outside the selection). Color reduction and dithering limits can be set for GIFs and PNG-8s, lossy value limits for GIFs, and overall quality limits for JPEGs.

To use weighted optimization:

1. Create a channel by selecting an area in the image and choosing Select menu > Save Selection.
2. Leave the Channel pop-up menu set to New, enter a name in the Name field, then click OK **1**.
3. On the Optimize palette, click any one of the Channel buttons (next to the color reduction pop-up menu **2** or the Lossy and Dithering text boxes for a GIF or PNG; next to the Quality text box **3** for a JPEG).
4. From the Channel pop-up menu, choose your selection's channel. Also set the Minimum and Maximum values **4** with the sliders, arrows, or text windows, then click OK.

TIP You can also choose a channel that was created in Photoshop for step 3.

To use the ImageReady previews:

Click the 4-Up tab on the main window to see an original view and three previews simultaneously. ImageReady will use the current Optimize palette settings to generate the first preview, and then automatically generate ("autopopulate") the two other previews as variations on the current optimization settings. You can click on any preview and change the Optimize palette settings for **just that preview**.

(Continued on the following page)

Weighted Optimization; Previews

The Optimized preview(s) will update every time a value or setting is changed on the Optimize palette. To stop the preview from updating, click the Stop button on the main window progress bar **1**. A halted preview icon (triangle with an exclamation point) will display in the lower right corner of any halted preview **2**. If you change a setting on the Optimize palette or click the alert triangle, the preview will update automatically.

TIP When you use the Save Optimized command, the settings for the currently selected Optimized preview (not the Original preview) are saved. Keep track of this if you use the 4-Up preview.

Jump To

Leave both Photoshop and ImageReady open so you can quickly make changes to the same open file in either program. Use the **Jump to** command or button to jump back and forth (**Ctrl-Shift-M/Cmd-Shift-M**).

The two programs are very much in sync with each other. A file can be open simultaneously in both programs, and changes made to the file in one program will automatically be reflected in the other **3**. If you start working on an image in ImageReady, jump to Photoshop to perform some edits, then jump back to ImageReady, the Photoshop edits will be identified on the **History** palette in ImageReady as a single history state named **Update From Photoshop**. Photoshop's History palette will list an **Update from ImageReady** history state for any changes made in ImageReady. You can click an earlier state at any time to undo the other program's edits.

6.0!

Revert is a state

The Revert command is now recorded as a state on the History palette in Photoshop 6 and ImageReady, and using this command does not wipe out the existing states. This means you can undo a Revert.

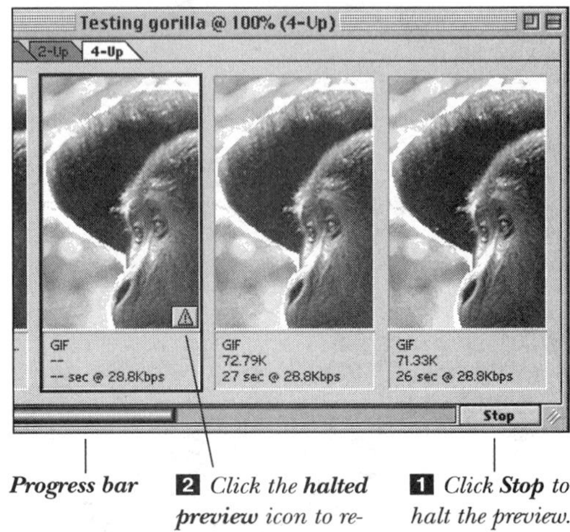

Progress bar

2 *Click the* ***halted preview*** *icon to re-generate the preview.*

1 *Click* ***Stop*** *to halt the preview.*

3 *This* ***Update*** *progress bar will appear if you open a file in ImageReady, edit it in Photoshop, and then Jump back to Image Ready.* ***Tip:*** *regardless of whether you check or uncheck* ***Auto-Update Files*** *in General Preferences in ImageReady or* ***Auto-update open documents*** *in Photoshop, files will automatically update between the two programs.*

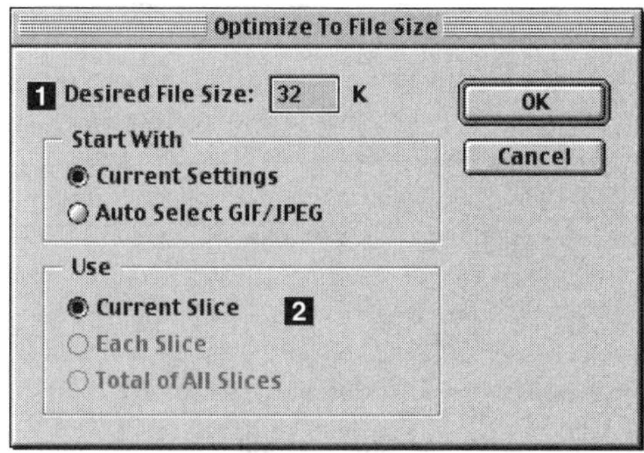

Why not let ImageReady make all the decisions for you? All you need to decide is how large you want the optimized image to be.

To quick-optimize:

1. Choose Optimize to File Size from the Optimize palette menu.
2. Enter a value in the Desired File Size field for the final optimized file size. 1
3. Click Start With: Current Settings to use the current settings on the palette.
   or
   Click Auto Select GIF/JPEG to let ImageReady pick the optimize method.
4. If the image has multiple slices, you can click Use Current Slice, Each Slice, or Total of All Slices. 2
5. Click OK. Presto—ImageReady will choose all Optimize palette settings for you and generate an optimized file to your designated file size requirements.

3 *Click the **Droplet** icon on the **Optimize** palette, or drag it to the Desktop.*

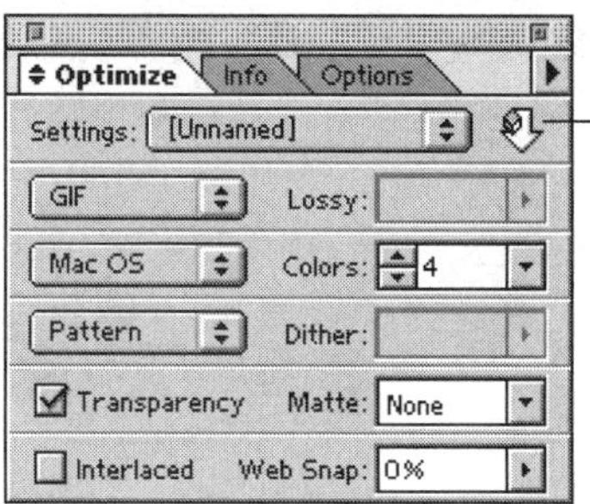

A droplet is a tiny but powerful application that holds and applies the Optimize palette settings that were in effect when the droplet was created.

To create and apply a droplet:

1. Click the Droplet icon on the Optimize palette 3, choose a location in which to save it, then click Save.
   or
   Drag the Droplet icon from the Optimize palette to the Desktop.
2. To optimize a file or a whole folder of files using the Optimize palette settings in the droplet, drag the file or folder icon over the Desktop droplet icon. An optimized version of the file(s) will be saved in the same location as the droplet.

   Note! ImageReady and/or Photoshop must be launched for a droplet to work!

TIP Double-click the droplet 4, then double-click the Batch Options command 5 to access the Batch Options dialog box.

*A **droplet** icon on a Mac Desktop.*

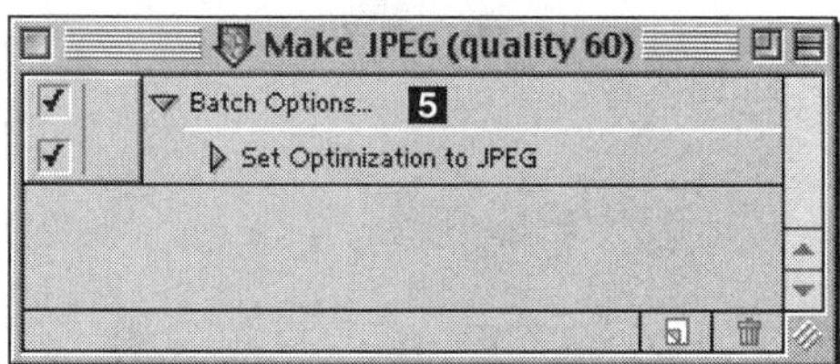

Quick-Optimize; Droplets

JPEG is the format of choice for optimizing continuous-tone imagery for display on the Web (photographs, paintings, gradients, or blends). If you optimize to JPEG, the file's 24-bit color depth will be preserved, and these colors will be seen and enjoyed by any Web viewer whose monitor is set to millions of colors (24-bit depth). Keep in mind, however, that JPEGs are optimized using a compression method that is lossy, which means it causes image data to be eliminated.

The PNG-24 format is similar to JPEG, except that PNG allows for multiple levels of transparency along edges and employs a lossless method of compression. PNG-24 files are larger than equivalent JPEGs.

To optimize an image in the JPEG or PNG-24 format:

1. If you're working in Photoshop 6, save your file, then click the Jump to button at the bottom of the Toolbox. ImageReady will launch, if it isn't already open.
   or
   In ImageReady, choose File menu > Open, locate the image, then click Open.
2. Click the 2-Up tab at the top of the main window to display the original and optimized previews of the image simultaneously.
3. Display the Optimize palette (Window menu > Show Optimize) **1**.
4. From the **Settings** pop-up menu, choose JPEG High **2**, JPEG Low, JPEG Medium, or PNG-24, leave this preset setting as is, then save your file.
   or
   Follow the remaining steps to choose custom settings.
5. Choose **JPEG** as the format from the next pop-up menu.
6. From next pop-up menu, choose Low, Medium, High, or Maximum as the compression quality for the optimized image (**1**–**2**, next page).
   or

JPEGs and Web-safe colors

JPEG compression adds compression artifacts to an image. Because of this, Web-safe colors in a JPEG image are rendered un-Web-safe after compression. This is acceptable because the JPEG format is usually used to optimize continuous-tone images, and on these type of images, browser dither isn't objectionable. Don't try to match a color area in a JPEG file to a color area in a GIF file or on the background of a Web page, though, because the JPEG color will shift and dither when the image is compressed.

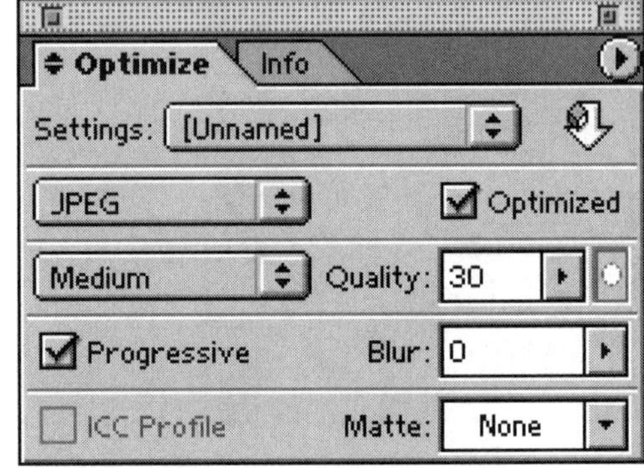

1 *The **ImageReady Optimize** palette.*

2 *A **JPEG** optimized with **High** Quality.*

Check your profiles

An embedded profile will slightly increase a file's size. As of this writing, Internet Explorer for Mac versions 4.01 and later support profiles. On the Mac, ColorSync makes sure the browser and the operating system know the viewer's monitor profile. This helps to ensure consistent color between the monitor and JPEG files. As color management support and profile automation improve, and as soon as Navigator supports embedded profiles, embedded profiles will become standard. Windows has a bit of catching up to do in this area. For the moment, use your own judgment.

1 *A JPEG optimized with* ***Medium*** *quality.*

2 *A JPEG optimized with* ***Low*** *quality. Note how pixelated the image has become.*

Move the **Quality** pop-up slider to an exact level of compression. Watch the adjacent compression pop-up menu setting change when you change the Quality value. (To vary compression using a selection channel, see page 421.)

Always remember, the lower the compression (or the higher the quality), the larger the file size.

7. Check the **Progressive** box to make the optimized image display on the Web page in successively greater detail.
8. Increase the **Blur** value to lessen the visibility of JPEG artifacts that arise from JPEG's compression method and also reduce the file size. Be careful not to over-blur the image, though, or your details will soften too much. The Blur setting can be lowered later to reclaim image sharpness.
9. *Optional:* Check the ICC Profile box to embed an ICC Profile in the optimized image. To utilize this option, the original image must have had a profile embedded into it in Photoshop. See the sidebar on this page.
10. Choose a **Matte** color to be used for areas of transparency found in the original image. If you choose "None," transparent areas will appear as white.

    Note: The JPEG format doesn't support transparency. To have the Matte color simulate transparency, use the same solid color as the background of the Web page, if that color is known.
11. *Optional:* Check the Optimized box to produce the smallest file size. ***Beware!*** Older browsers (version 3.0 or earlier) may not be able to read a JPEG that's saved with this option.
12. Save the file (see pages 430–431).

TIP To save the current settings as a named preset, see page 420.

Optimize as JPEG or PNG-24

Let's say you have an image that you're going to optimize in the GIF format using the Perceptual, Selective, or Adaptive palette, but the image has flat-color areas that aren't Web safe. Before outputting that image online, you can make the flat-color areas Web safe.

To make flat-color areas Web safe:

1. Open the image in ImageReady, and optimize it in the GIF format.
2. Choose the Eyedropper tool.
3. Click on a flat-color area to be made Web safe **1**.
4. Open the Color Table palette. The color you just clicked on will now be the highlighted swatch **2**.
5. Click the Web Snap button at the bottom of the palette. A diamond will display on the selected swatch to signify that the color was shifted to a Web-safe equivalent.
6. *Optional:* Click the Lock Color button to preserve the currently selected swatch even if the number of colors in the GIF palette is reduced.

TIP Shift-click with the Eyedropper tool on other areas in the image to select more than one color, then Web-shift all the selected colors at once. Or use the Magic Wand tool or a lasso or marquee tool to make a selection or selections in the image, choose the Select All From Selection command from the Color Table palette menu, then click the Web Snap button at the bottom of the palette.

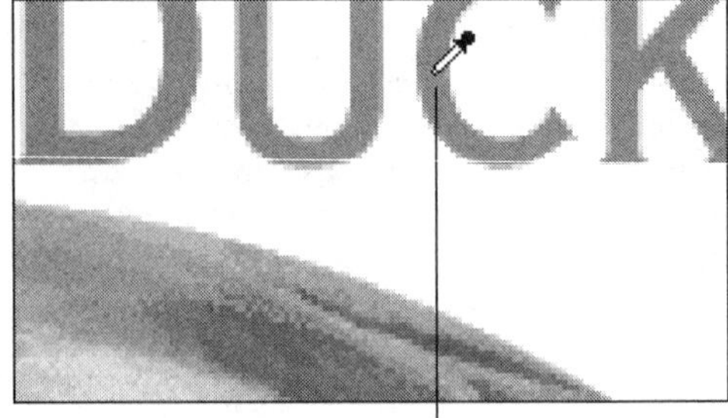

1 *Click on a **flat-color** area with the **Eyedropper** tool.*

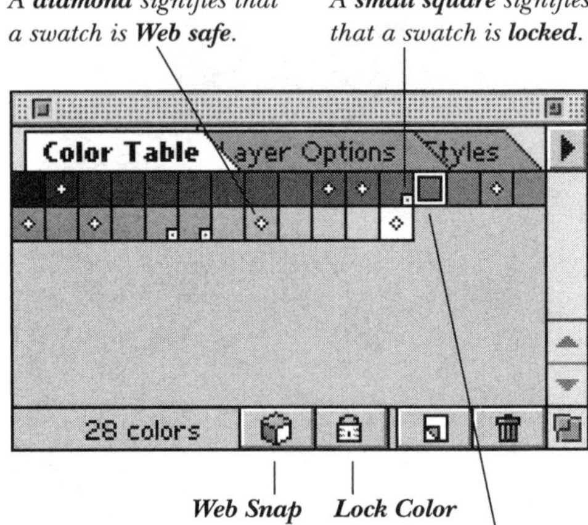

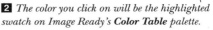

2 *The color you click on will be the highlighted swatch on Image Ready's **Color Table** palette.*

Make Flat-Color Areas Web Safe

1 *An image optimized as a JPEG in ImageReady with* ***Browser Dither*** *turned* ***off****.*

2 *The same image optimized as a JPEG, but with Preview >* ***Browser Dither*** *turned* ***on****. The image's millions of colors are reduced to the browser's 8-bit color palette (and the Web viewer's 8-bit monitor).*

Using various preview methods in ImageReady, you can get a pretty reliable idea of how optimized images will look when they're viewed online. This will help you choose appropriate settings as you optimize your images.

According to Websnapshot.com, about 10% of Web viewers use an 8-bit monitor, which displays a maximum of 256 colors. Macintosh and Windows browsers, on the other hand, use a color palette of 216 colors. Dithering is used to recreate any colors in an image that are not on the browser's palette.

To preview potential browser dither in an optimized image:

1. Open the image in ImageReady, and show at least one optimized preview in the main window.
2. Choose View menu > Preview > Browser Dither (Ctrl-Shift-Y/Cmd-Shift-Y) **1**–**2**.

Controlling dithering

When you use ImageReady to optimize an image, the application applies dithering to simulate colors that were in the original image but won't appear in the optimized image's color palette. You can control the amount of this type of dithering via the Dither field on the Optimize palette. If you raise the Dither value, the optimized image will more closely color-match the original—but at the expense of a slightly larger file size.

The Web Snap value on the Optimize palette also affects the amount of browser dither in an image. The higher the Web Snap, the less the optimized image will be dithered, and the smaller will be its file size. The more the optimize image colors match the browser's 8-bit palette, the less dramatically the optimized image will change if the Browser Dither option is turned on. Some degree of dithering is acceptable in continuous-tone imagery, though, and it's more pleasing than the color banding that a high Web Snap value can cause.

Since the Windows operating system uses a higher gamma value than the Macintosh operating system, an image will appear darker on Windows and lighter on a Mac. When you create Web graphics for cross-platform use, it's important to preview and adjust your image for both platforms.

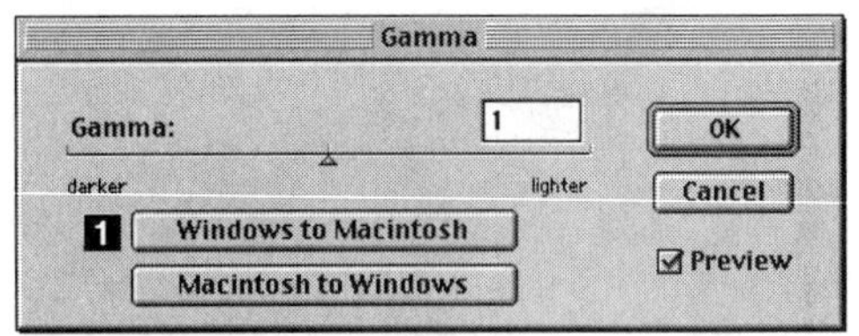

To preview Windows and Mac gamma values:

With an optimized preview showing in ImageReady, choose View menu > Preview > Standard Macintosh Color to simulate the Mac gamma value or Standard Windows Color to simulate the Windows gamma value.

Choose View menu > Preview > Uncompensated Color to view the preview with no gamma compensation. Choose Embedded Color Profile to match the ImageReady preview (based on monitor RGB) with the profile assigned to, or embedded in, the image in Photoshop. This option will be grayed out if the image lacks a profile. 6.0!

TIP The Ctrl-Alt-Y/Cmd-Option-Y shortcut cycles through the four Preview options (but it's hard to keep track of which preview is currently showing).

2 *An image after clicking the* ***Windows to Macintosh*** *button. The lower gamma value has caused the image to look darker.*

To change the gamma for an optimized file:

1. With an image with an optimized preview showing in ImageReady, choose Image menu > Adjust > Gamma.
2. Click "Windows to Macintosh" to change the gamma to the Mac gamma value. The image will look darker on a Mac **1**–**2**.

   or

   Click "Macintosh to Windows" to change the gamma to the Windows gamma value. The image will look lighter on a Mac **3**.

   Either choice will compensate for the other platform's tendency to darken or lighten.
3. Click OK.

TIP You can also use the slider to manually choose a gamma value in between the

3 *The same image after clicking the* ***Macintosh to Windows*** *button. The image looks lighter.*

Keep the code

There are two methods for copying source code from ImageReady into an HTML-editing program. One, you can click and drag through the source code diplayed at the bottom of the browser window to select it **2**, then copy and paste it into the HTML-editing or Web-page creation program. Or, two, in ImageReady you can use Edit menu > Copy HTML Code > For All Slices for the current file, then paste the source code into an HTML-editing or Web-page creation program.

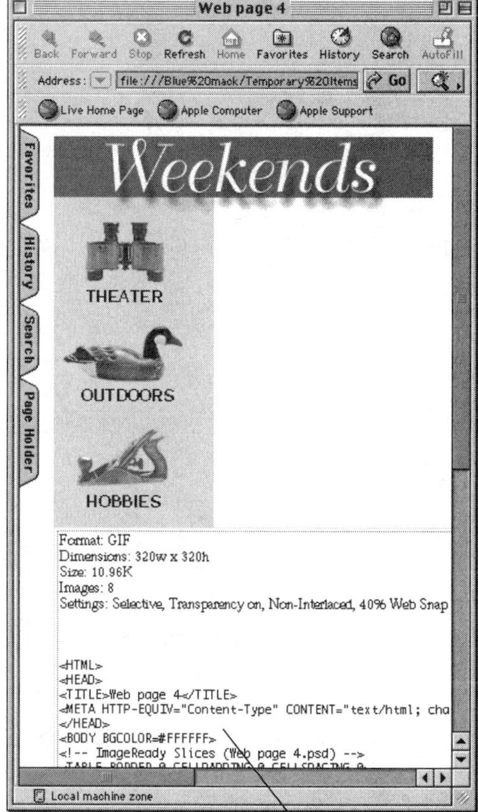

1 *An image being viewed in Microsoft's* ***Internet Explorer****.*

2 *This is the* ***HTML source code*** *from ImageReady.*

button choices or to set a gamma value for another platform. The gamma setting is a relative setting. If you set a value, close the dialog box, then reopen the dialog box, the setting will be back at 1.

For a more definitive simulation of online viewing for an optimized image, use ImageReady's Preview in Browser button. You can choose from any browsers currently installed in your system. *Note:* This preview feature won't test the actual download time for an image over an actual Web connection, and it will display a preview for your monitor type only—not for another monitor type. Nevertheless, it's very useful.

To preview an optimized image in a browser on your system:

6.0!

1. With an optimized image opened in ImageReady, click the Toolbox Preview in Browser button, or press the button and choose a browser from the submenu.
2. The browser will launch and the image will load into the browser window **1**. Any GIF animations or rollovers created in ImageReady will also preview.
3. Quit out of the browser, if desired, then click back on any ImageReady palette or window to switch back to ImageReady.

   Note: Be sure to preview your final files by actually uploading them to the Web. Do this on both computer platforms and a spectrum of monitor types.

TIP If your monitor color depth is set to higher than 8 bit and you want to see how an image will look in an 8-bit browser, set your system to 256 colors first, then launch your browser. We've seen only minor differences between this method and setting ImageReady to preview Browser Dither.

To save a file in ImageReady:

1. Make sure you're in ImageReady and the file you want to save is open, then choose File menu > Save (Ctrl-S/Cmd-S).
2. Enter a file name and leave the file extension as is **1**. Choose a location, then click Save. The file will save in the Photoshop format automatically. The saved file doesn't contain optimization settings.

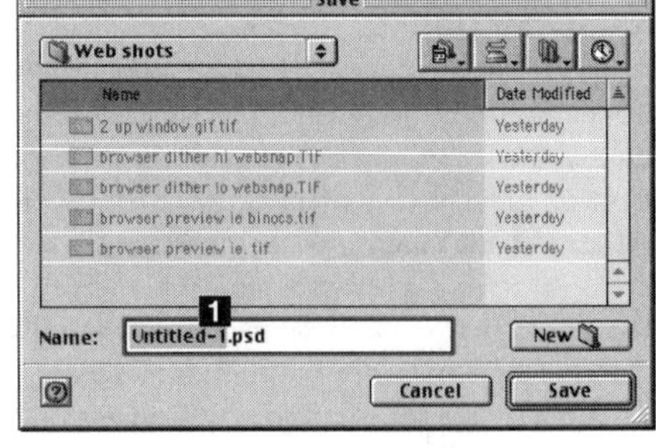

6.0! Follow these instructions to save a file as an optimized file according to the settings currently chosen on the Optimize palette.

To save an optimized file in ImageReady:

1. Choose File menu > Save Optimized (Ctrl-Alt-S/Cmd-Option-S).
2. To control how the file will be saved, choose one of the following from the Format pop-up menu: **2**

   HTML and Images to create an HTML file and save the image slices as a separate file.

   Images Only to save just the image slices.

   HTML Only to create an HTML file without saving the image files. A separate HTML file will automatically be assigned the .htm or .html extension and it will be saved in the same location as the optimized file.
3. Check the Include GoLive Code box if you want your HTML or Javascript to be editable from within Adobe GoLive.
4. *Optional:* Click Output Settings, then choose HTML in the pop-up menu to choose HTML preferences for formatting and coding **3**. Use these options to establish consistency between the HTML in ImageReady and that of other HTML-editing applications.

   Click OK now, or follow the next step before clicking OK.

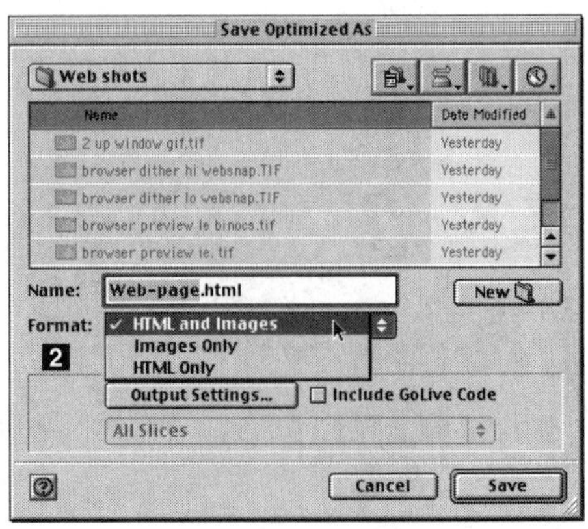

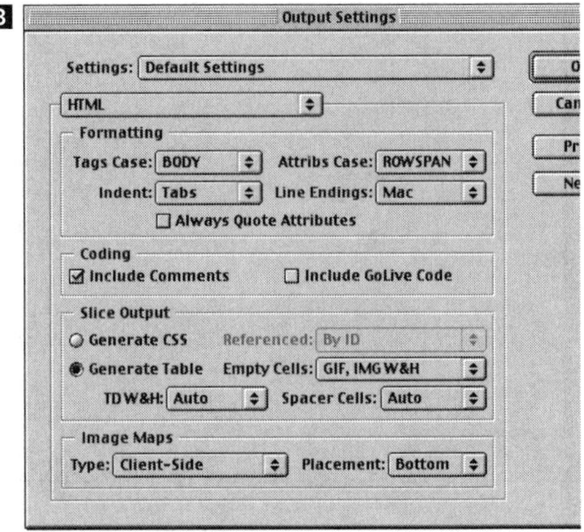

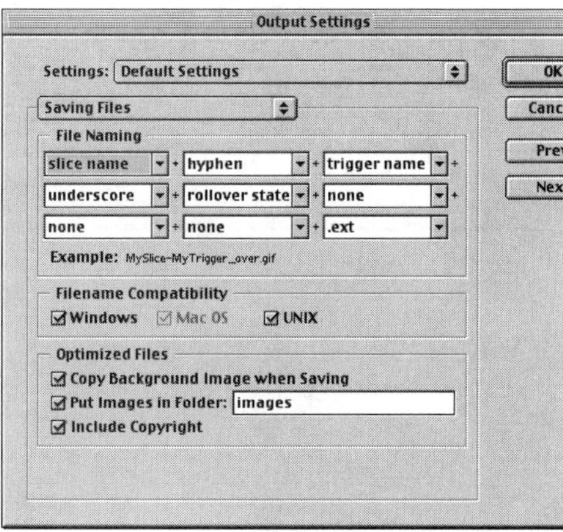

1

5. Choose Saving Files from the second pop-up menu to choose File Naming conventions for any autogenerated files, such as slices and rollover frames, to be saved with the optimized file and used in the HTML page **1**. Work with your HTML specialist before making changes in these fields. Choose naming options for each field from the various pop-up menus in the File Naming area. If the naming convention seems confusing, leave the default settings as is.

Turn on any platform **Filename Compatibility** options.

Turn on any **Optimized Files** options. Choose the folder you want to save the autogenerated files in.

6. Click OK to exit the Output Settings dialog box.

7. Type a file name, choose a location, then click Save.

TIP Use the Save As or Save Optimized As command to save another version of a file under a different name.

TIP To attach a URL or an Alt tag to an image, use the Slice palette (see page 447).

To update an existing HTML file:

If you have modified an optimized file and you want to update the HTML file that's associated with it, choose File menu > Update HTML, locate the HTML file for that image, click Open, then click OK when the update is finished. Any HTML code generated for the optimized file will be updated, even if that code is already copied and pasted into a larger HTML file, and *even* if that larger file contains other tables from other image files.

Using the Image Info dialog box, you can modify the browser window page title for, or embed copyright information into, an HTML file.

To change a Web page title or embed copyright information:

1. With the image open in ImageReady, choose File menu > Image Info (Ctrl-Shift-K/Cmd-Shift-K).
2. Change the page title in the Page Title field **1**. The page title is the text that displays on the browser window title bar (the text between the HTML <TITLE> tags). The default title is the title of the current file for the image.
   and/or
   Enter information in the Copyright field to embed pertinent copyright information into the HTML file.
3. Click OK.

Layer effects in Image Ready

Layer effects also exist in and can be applied in ImageReady. They are a great way to apply special effects to type because they're so flexible and easy to modify. You can even drag an effect (or effects) from the Layers palette to the Styles palette to save the effect(s) as a style (see page 472), and then apply that style to other layers. Drag an individual effect name or drag the whole effects bar to drag a combination of effects. Wow.

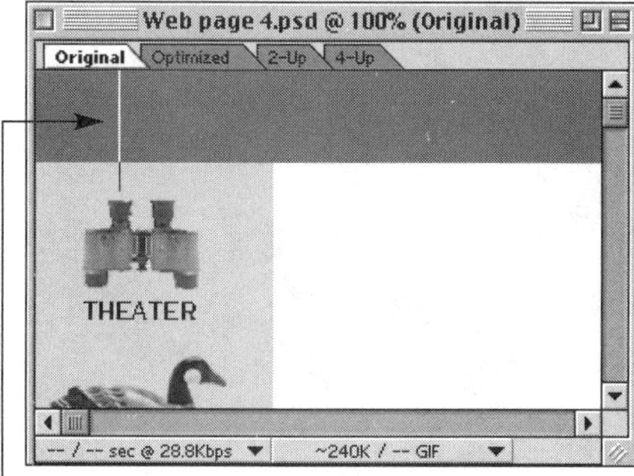

1 *Click with the **Type** tool to create an insertion point, then start typing.*

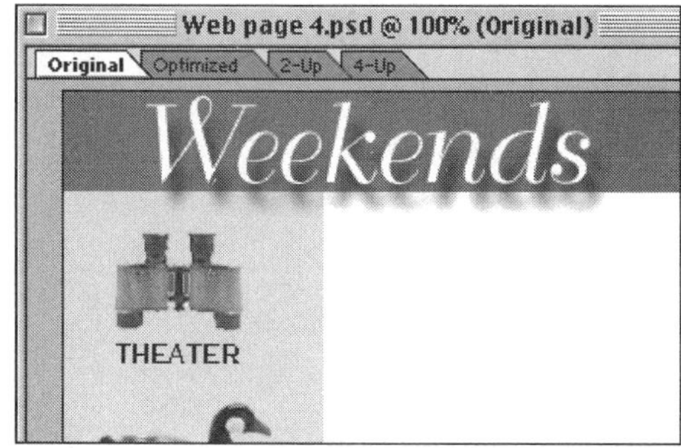

2 *The type is entered.*

You create and style type in ImageReady the same way that you do in Photoshop 6. As in Photoshop, type in ImageReady is entered directly on the image and it can be styled using the options bar, the Character palette, or the Paragraph palette. In this respect, ImageReady 3 and Photoshop 6 also resemble Adobe Illustrator. To learn how to create type in ImageReady, read chapter 17, Type. 6.0!

Furthermore, in ImageReady, as in Photoshop, type automatically appears on its own layer and it remains editable until or unless you render the layer into bitmap type. You can apply any layer effect or style to editable type and it will remain editable. When type is optimized in ImageReady, whether it's rendered or not, it becomes bitmapped, like the overall image.

Some significant differences should be noted: Unlike type in Photoshop, type in ImageReady cannot be created as a selection, converted to a work path, or converted to shapes.

To enter type in ImageReady:

1. Make sure the Original view is chosen for image in the main window.
2. Choose the Type tool or the Vertical Type tool (T or Shift-T).
3. Click in the image window where you want the type to start. A flashing insertion marker will appear **1**.
4. Follow the steps on page 289 to create point or paragraph type **2**.

Tips for creating online text

- All type layer attributes and anti-aliasing options are preserved, for editable or rendered type, when jumping a file between Photoshop and ImageReady.
- Type in Photoshop or ImageReady can be anit-aliased. Since anti-aliasing works by adding colors to type edges, it also adds colors to a file's Color Table and slightly increases its file storage size.

(Continued on the following page)

Type in ImageReady

- Some people believe small type should be anti-aliased if it's being created for on-screen output. We believe the opposite—that small-sized type looks better when it's aliased. Use ImageReady's preview features to decide for yourself.
- When you create type for online viewing, use a larger point size than you would normally choose for print output. This will help make the type legible on screen.

  Note: The same type size on a Web page will display differently on a Mac screen than on a Windows screen due to the ppi resolution difference between Macintosh and Windows monitors (72 for the former, 96 for the latter). Be sure to test your page or site on both platforms.
- You can toggle the Faux Bold or Faux Italic style on or off on ImageReady's Character palette menu. These type styles are designed for use with font families that lack a true bold or italic style. There's also an Underline option for producing the Web convention of underlined text links (not the actual links, though!).
- Remember to make type colors Web safe to prevent dithering. To make a color Web safe in ImageReady, choose the Eyedropper tool, click on a type character, then Web-shift the color using the Color Table palette (see page 426).

  6.0! To make a non-Web-safe color Web-safe in Photoshop 6, double-click the T thumbnail on the type layer, then click the Color swatch on the options bar or the Character palette. In the Color Picker, either click the non-Web color alert icon to substitute the closest Web-safe equivalent or check Only Web Colors, then click OK.

Mixed optimization

Hybrid images, which contain both continuous-tone imagery and flat areas of color (like type), pose a special challenge **1**. You can use Photoshop's or ImageReady's slicing feature to frame off different areas of a hybrid image and then apply a different optimization to each area. To facilitate slicing for mixed optimization, whenever possible position type so it doesn't overlap any continuous-tone areas. Optimize type slices as GIF and continuous-tone areas as JPEG. (See pages 435–447 for more information about slicing.)

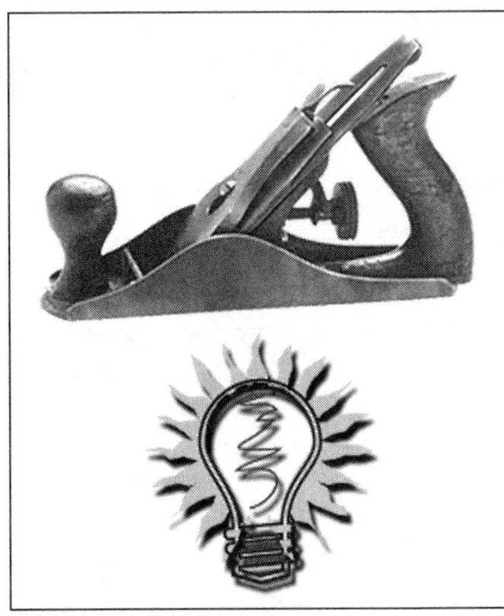

1 *This is a hybrid image. It contains both* ***continuous-tone*** *imagery and* ***flat*** *color areas.*

Behind the scenes

In HTML, a table can be used as a grid system that controls the layout of graphics and text on a Web page. Table cells can be coded to display separate images and data or portions of a large, sliced graphic. Frames function like separate windows within the larger browser window. A frame can display an HTML graphic, page, or site independently from the other frames on the same Web page. To learn more about HTML tables and frames, see Lynda Weinman's ***Designing Web Graphics.3*** or ***Creative HTML Design*** (both New Riders Publishing); ***HTML 4 for the World Wide Web*** by Elizabeth Castro (Peachpit Press); or ***HTML: The Definitive Guide*** by Chuck Musciano and Bill Kennedy (O'Reilly & Associates).

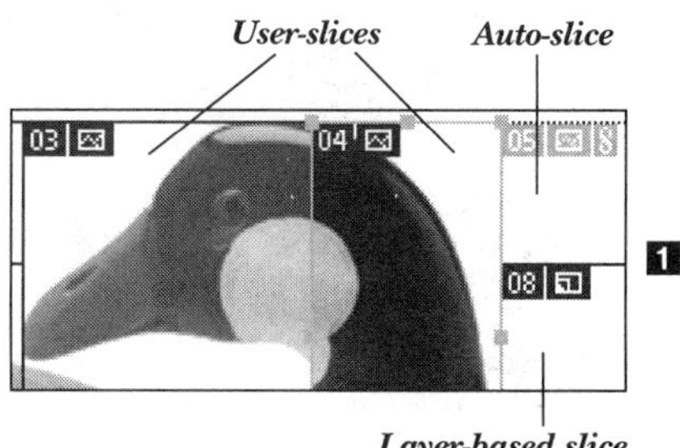

1

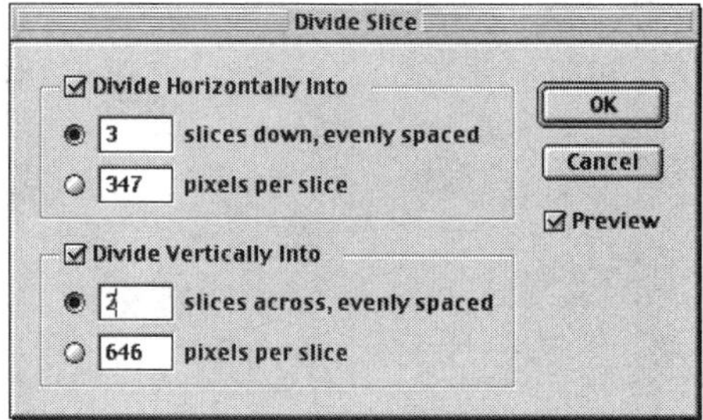

2

Slicing

Slicing is a process by which an image is divided into distinct **zones**. One purpose of slicing is to divide up a large image to enable it to download faster. A group of small slices downloads more quickly than a single large image does. The browser assembles the slices into the overall image in sequence using HTML tables and frames.

Slices created using the **Slice** tool (next page) are called "**user-slices**," **1**. **Layer-based slices** (page 437) automatically size themselves to include all visible pixels within a selected layer. Whether you create user-slices or layer-based slices, ImageReady generates "auto-slices" for the rest of the image. **Auto-slices** have gray labels.

Slices can be created, selected, edited, and displayed in both Photoshop and ImageReady. We prefer to use ImageReady, since it has more slice options. To show the Slice palette in ImageReady, choose Window menu > **Show Slice** or click **Slice Palette** on the Slice Select tool options bar. (In Photoshop, click Slice Options on the Slice Select tool options bar to view the Slice Options dialog box.) The palette and the dialog box have the same features.

To slice an image using commands:

1. Choose Slices menu > Promote to User-slice, then choose Slices menu > Divide Slice. Check the Preview box.
2. Check the Divide Horizontally Into box to create horizontal slices **2**, then enter the desired number of slices in the "slices down, evenly spaced" field or enter the desired number of "pixels per slice" for the height of each horizontal slice.
   and/or
   Check the Divide Vertically Into box to create vertical slices, then enter the desired number of slices in the "slices across, evenly spaced" field or enter the desired number of pixels per slice for the width of each vertical slice.

(Continued on the following page)

Auto Slicing

3. Click OK **1**. A label will appear in the upper left corner of each slice to identify that slice number. Numbering begins at 01 and proceeds from left to right, top to bottom.

TIP After the Divide command is used, all the slices will be selected. To highlight only one slice, choose the Slice Select tool (K or Shift-K), then click on that slice zone.

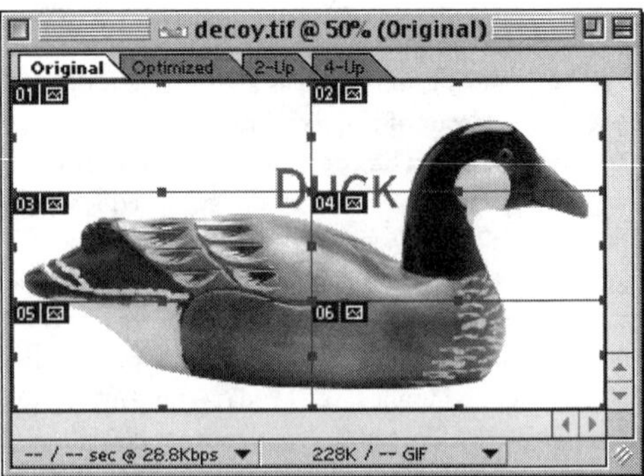

1 *An image divided into* ***six slices****.*

Using the Slice tool, you can control manually where the slice divisions occur. You can resize, reposition, or restack a user-slice—but not an auto-slice.

To slice an image manually:

1. Choose the Slice tool (K or Shift-K).
2. Drag diagonally across part of the image to designate the first slice **2**–**3**. A label with a number will appear in the upper left corner of the slice zone and a thin highlight frame with resizing handles will appear around the new slice. ImageReady will divide the rest of the image into auto-slices.
3. *Optional:* Draw additional user-slices with the Slice tool. Each new slice will be assigned a label and a number, and ImageReady will continue to redivide and renumber the rest of the image into auto-slices.
4. *Optional:* To divide a slice into smaller user-slices, choose the Slice Select tool (K or Shift-K), click on a user-slice or auto-slice to highlight it, choose Slices menu > Divide Slice, then click OK. Each new slice will be assigned its own number.

TIP A selected slice will display normally; a non-selected slice will be dimmed. In ImageReady, to adjust how light or dark a slice looks when it's highlighted, choose a different percentage for User-slices and/or Auto-slices in the Color Adjustments area of the Edit menu > Preferences > Slices dialog box **4**.

2 *Drag to create a* ***slice*** *using the* ***Slice*** *tool.*

3 *A* ***new slice*** *is created.*

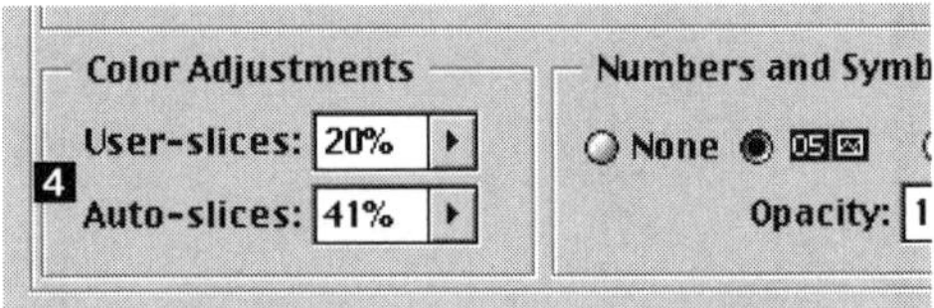

Plot your slices

To plot out your slice areas before creating them, display the rulers (Ctrl-R/Cmd-R), drag guides from the rulers and release them where you want slice borders to occur, then choose Slices menu > **Create Slices from Guides**. *Beware!* This command deletes all previous slices. Also, since guides always extend from edge to edge, you will be able to produce a checkerboard of similarly-sized slices, but not a more irregular arrangement. You can resize the resulting slices by dragging the slice border handles or combine two or more selected slices by choosing Slices menu > Combine Slices, but this could be more laborious than using the Slice tool would have been to begin with.

Layer-based slices automatically update the slice borders whenever you transform, move, or add layer effects to, the related layer. They are especially useful when creating rollovers that contain different effects (like a drop shadow) that enlarge the layer.

To create a layer-based slice:

Choose a layer on the Layers palette, then choose Layer menu > New Layer Based Slice.

To convert an auto-slice or a layer-based slice into a user-slice:

1. Choose the Slice Select tool (K or Shift-K).
2. Click on the slice you want to convert.
3. Choose Slices menu > Promote to User-slice.

To delete slices:

1. Choose the Slice Select tool (K or Shift-K).
2. To delete one slice, click on it; to delete multiple slices, Shift-click all the slices you want to delete. Then choose Delete Slice(s) from the Slices menu or the Slice palette menu, or simply press Backspace/Delete.
   or
   To delete all the slices in an image, choose Slices menu > Delete All.

If you make a user-slice smaller, ImageReady automatically generates and renumbers auto-slices to fill in the exposed gaps.

If a slice is enlarged, it may cover slices behind it. You can manually remove any of the hidden slices. Don't worry, though—saving an optimized file will eliminate any overlapping slice frames or table cells. To see what's hiding behind a slice, use any of the arrange buttons on the Slice Select tool option bar to assist you.

To resize user-slices:

1. Choose the Slice Select tool. Slice borders will automatically display.
2. Click on the user-slice you want to resize.
3. Drag a side handle to resize along one axis or drag a corner handle to resize along two axes 2–3.

Hide/show slice borders and labels

Click the Slice Visibility button on the Toolbox 1 or press "Q" to toggle between hiding and showing slices. In Photoshop, show or hide slices using the View menu > Show > Slices command.

TIP Every document starts out with a default auto slice that is the size of the entire image. It has a light gray label and is numbered "01."

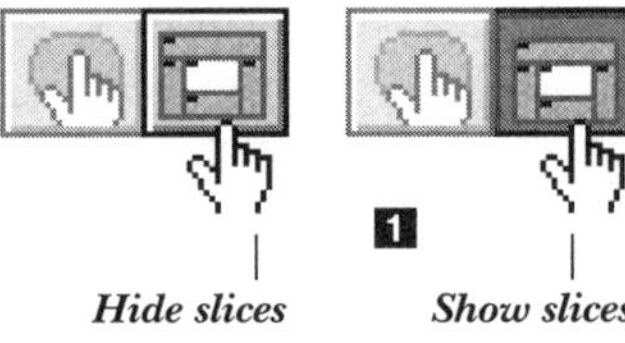

2 *To* ***resize*** *a user-slice, drag a handle with the* ***Slice Select*** *tool.*

3 *The* ***auto-slices*** *around the resized slice will reconfigure* ***automatically****.*

Resize User-Slices

Join forces

To combine multiple auto- or user-slices into one larger slice, select two or more slices, then choose Slices menu > **Combine Slices**. The resulting single user-slice will have the dimensions of the smallest rectangle that could surround all the selected slices.

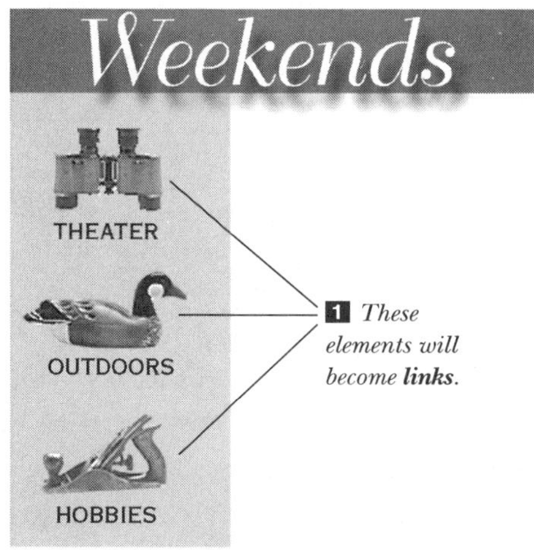

1 *These elements will become* ***links****.*

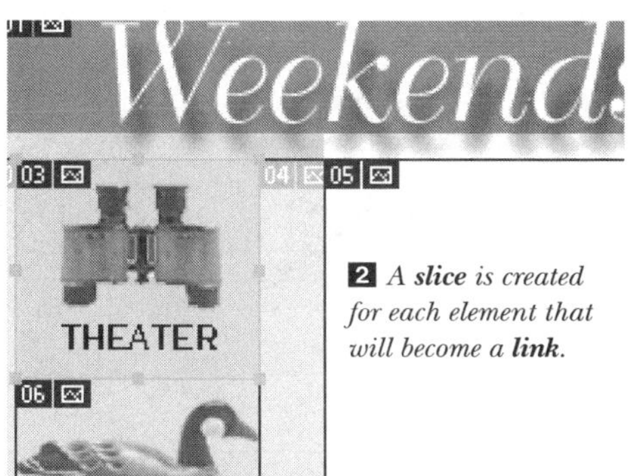

2 *A* ***slice*** *is created for each element that will become a* ***link****.*

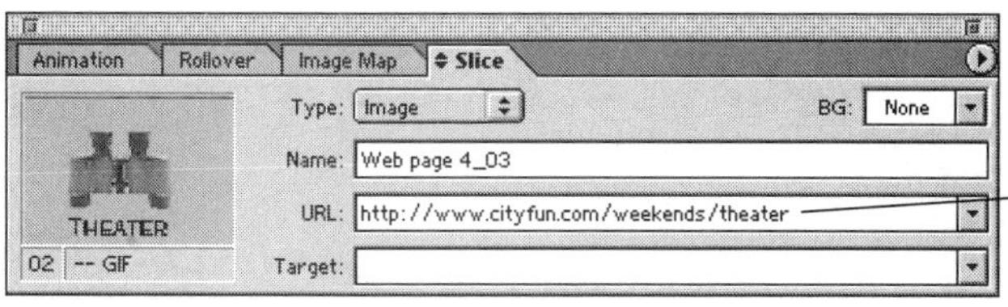

3 *Enter the destination Web address in the* ***URL*** *field.*

You can attach a URL link to a slice on a Web page. When that slice is clicked on by a Web viewer, the viewer is taken automatically to the Web page that's associated with that URL address. Slices with links are usually created over obvious graphic elements (buttons, words, or icons) so the viewer can identify them easily.

In ImageReady, you can create multiple slices in a single image, and you can assign a different URL address to each slice. Using slices to define all the links on one image eliminates the need to create, align, or resize multiple image layers.

To slice an image into multiple links:

1. Open or create an image that contains imagery to be used as links. Commonly used link elements include buttons, thumbnails, or icons **1**. A series of links arranged in a column or row is called a "navigation bar."
2. Choose the Slice tool (K or Shift-K).
3. Drag diagonally to create a slice over each individual portion of the image that you want to become a link **2**.
4. Choose the Slice Select tool (K or Shift-K).
5. Click on a slice. The selected slice will display as a thumbnail on the Slice palette. (Choose Window menu > Show Slice if the palette isn't displayed.)
6. Enter the destination Web address in the URL field **3**.
7. *Optional:* The Target info tells the browser which HTML frame to load the link contents into and which existing HTML frames to preserve. The Target field becomes available when information is entered into the URL field. Press

(Continued on the following page)

Tab to move to this area of the palette, then choose one of the following from the drop-down menu: _blank opens a new browser window for the link contents; _self loads the new link contents into the HTML frame for the current slice; _parent replaces the current HTML frames with the new link contents; and _top loads the new link contents into the entire browser window (this is similar to the _parent option).

8. Repeat steps 5–7 for any other slices you want to designate as links.

TIP If the image has only one slice (the default auto-slice for the image), you can use the URL field on the Slice palette to attach a link address to the entire image.

Overlapping slices are displayed and numbered based on the order in which they were created. You can rearrange the stacking order of user-slices and layer-based slices at any time.

To arrange the slice stacking order:

1. Choose the Slice Select tool (K or Shift-K) and click on the slice whose order you want to change **1**. 6.0!
2. Click the desired stacking order tool in the options bar (unavailable stacking options will be dimmed) **2**. The slice stacking order will be changed **3**.

By aligning user-slices along a common edge or distributing them evenly along the same axis, it's possible to create smaller, faster-to-download HTML files. You cannot align or distribute layer-based slices, since their position is tied to the layers.

To align user-slices along a common edge:

1. Choose the Slice select tool, then Shift-click the slices you want to align.
2. Click one of the six alignment icons in the options bar **4**. 6.0!

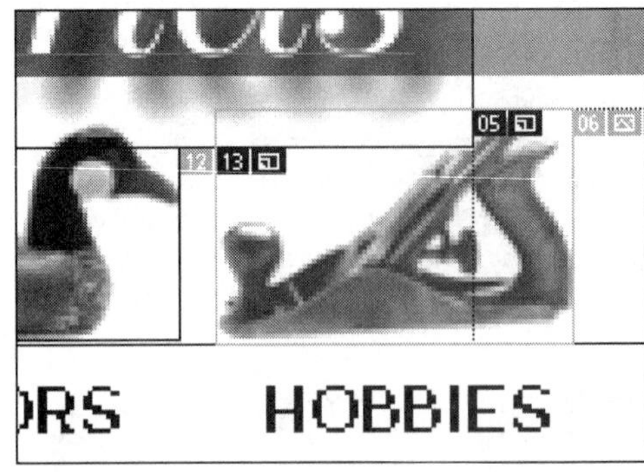

1 *Slice #13 is behind other slices.*

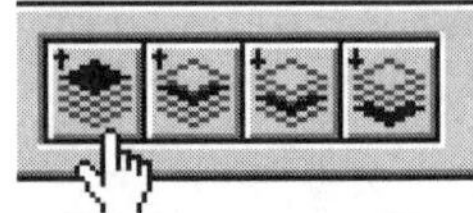

2 *The **Bring Slice to Front** button is clicked (options bar).*

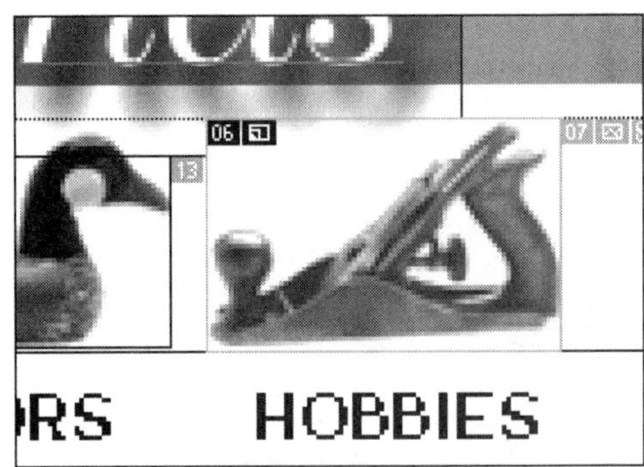

3 *Slice #13 has now become slice #06 and is now in front of the slices around it.*

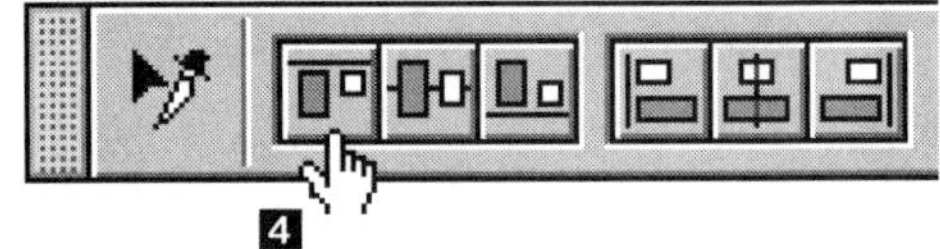

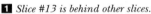

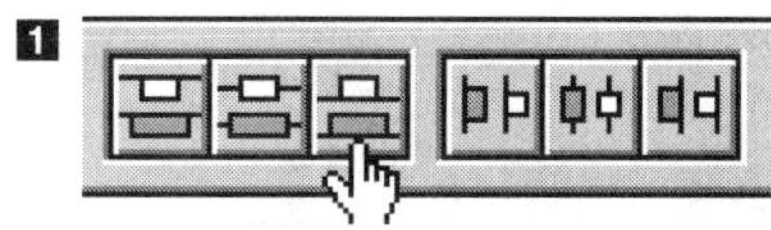

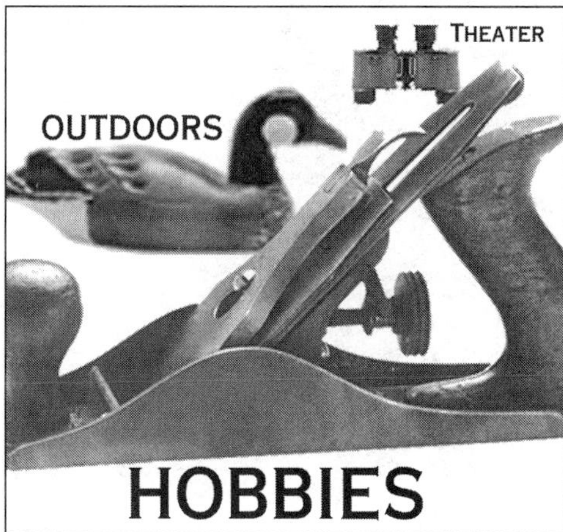

2 *This image, because it contains overlapping elements, is a good candidate for coding as an* ***image map*** *using the Layer Options palette.*

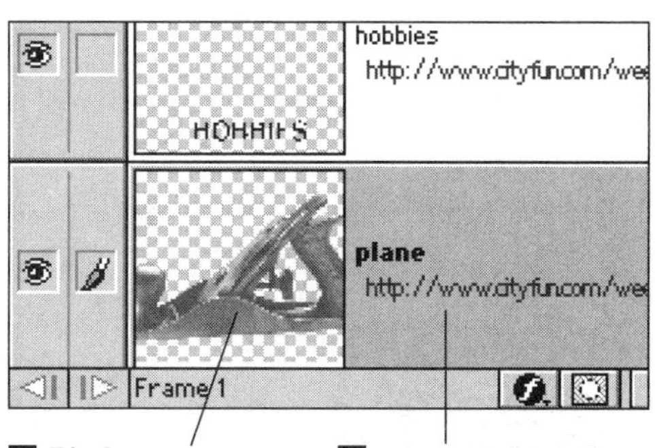

3 ***Pixel areas*** *(not transparent areas) will become* ***hotspots*** *for the* ***image map.***

6 *After the* ***URL*** *address is entered on the Image Map palette, it appears below the layer name.*

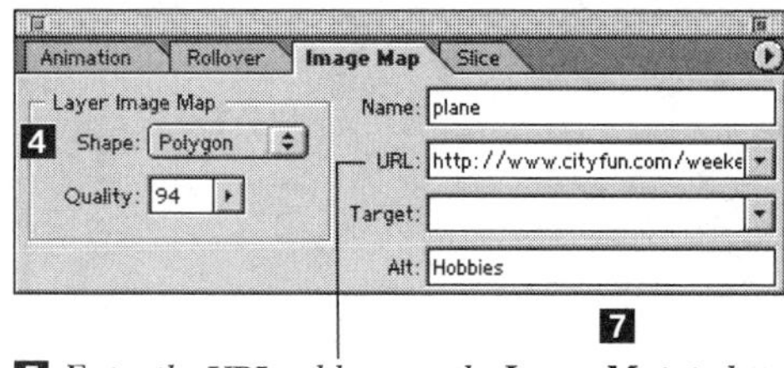

5 *Enter the* ***URL*** *address on the* ***Image Map*** *palette.*

To evenly distribute user-slices along a common axis:

1. Choose the Slice Select tool (K or Shift-K), then Shift-click the slices you want to distribute.
2. Click one of the six distribution icons in the options bar **1**. 6.0!

An image map is an image that contains designated hotspots, each with its own URL link **2**. Use this method if you have a non-rectangular hotspot shape or when you'd rather have a single image file instead of multiple files for slices.

ImageReady lets you create layer-based or tool-based image maps. A layer-based map, which includes any non-transparent pixel areas in a layer, is automatically updated whenever you edit that layer. Tool-based maps can be aligned to a common edge or distributed along a common axis. You can also duplicate a tool-based map's dimensions and settings. It's easy to change a layer-based map to a tool-based one. 6.0!

To create a layer-based image map:

1. On the Layers palette, choose a layer that has transparent areas **3**.
2. Choose Layer menu > New Layer Based Image Map Area. A rectangular image map will surround the layer's non-transparent areas.
3. Choose a shape for the hotspot (Rectangle, Circle, or Polygon) from the Shape pop-up menu on the Image Map palette **4**.
4. Enter a URL address (including the "http://" prefix) **5**. The URL address will appear below the layer name on the Layers palette **6**.
5. *Optional:* The Target info tells which HTML frame to load the link contents into and which existing HTML frames to preserve. The Target field is only available once you enter a URL.

(Continued on the following page)

6. *Optional:* In the Alt field enter the word or words you want to appear if the user's Web browser does not display images (**7**, previous page) (see page 447).
7. Repeat steps 1–6 for any other layers.

TIP You can change the image map's shape by choosing the Image Map Select tool (P or Shift-P), then choosing from the Shape pop-up menu on the Image Map palette.

TIP When using a Polygon, the Quality field or slider lets you adjust how tightly the image map follows the image's outline.

Note: ImageReady codes an image map in HTML as client-side or server-side. To choose between these two options, click Output Settings in the Save Optimized dialog box, then choose from the Image Maps Type pop-up menu.

6.0!

To create a tool-based image map:

1. Choose the Rectangle Image Map, Circle Image Map, or Polygon Image Map tool (P or Shift-P).
2. Draw a rectangle or circle over an area in the image window. Shift-drag to create a square. Alt-drag/Option-drag to draw a rectangle or circle from its center.
   or
   Create a straight-sided polygon by clicking on a starting point, then clicking for each subsequent corner until you surround the area. Double-click anywhere to close the selection automatically **1**.
3. Enter a URL address (including the "http://" prefix) on the Image Map palette.
4. *Optional:* The Image Map palette's Target field identifies into which HTML frame the link contents will be loaded and which existing HTML frames will be preserved (see page 439). The Target field is only available once you enter a URL.
5. *Optional:* In the Image Map palette's Alt field, enter the word or words you want

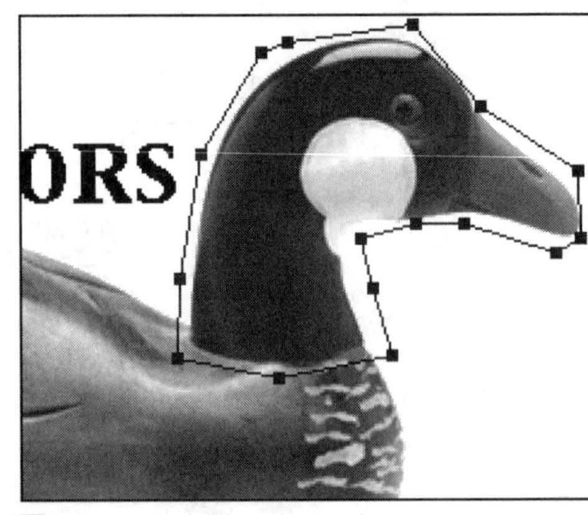

1

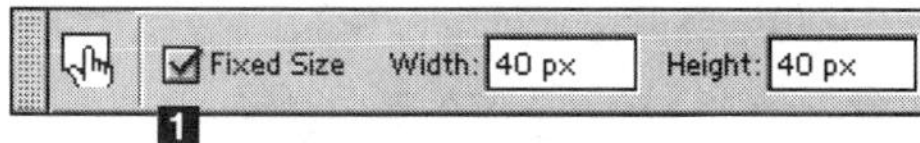

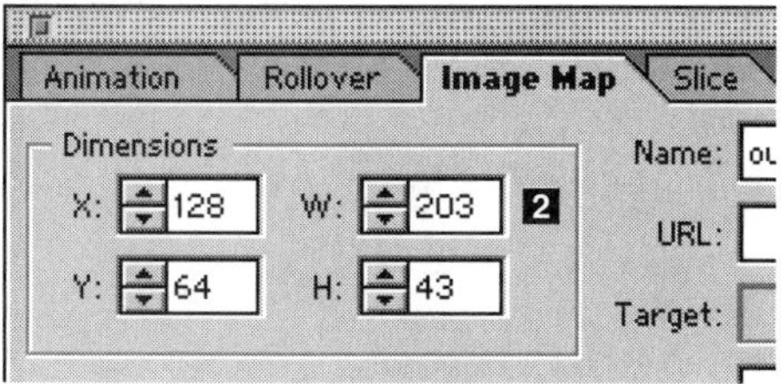

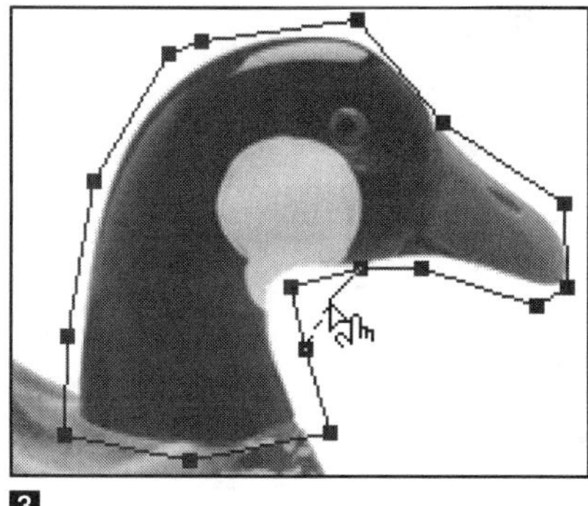

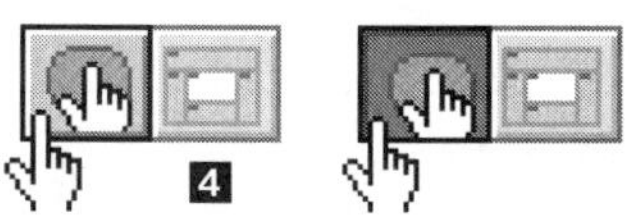

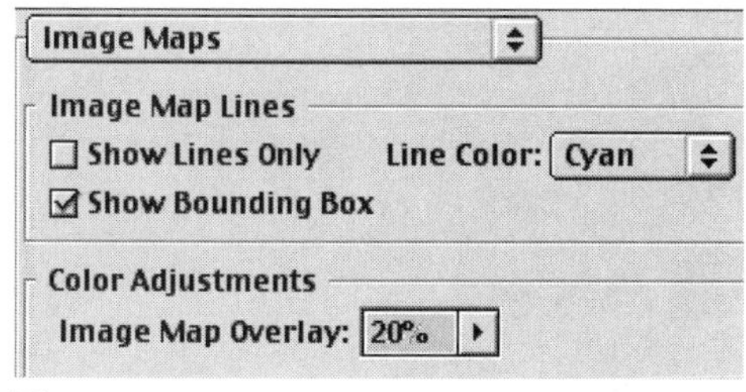

to appear if the user's Web browser does not display images.

6. Repeat steps 1–6 for any other image maps you want to create.

TIP To specify the exact dimensions of a rectangle or circle before you draw it, check Fixed Size on the options bar and enter Width and Height values **1**.

TIP To precisely reposition or resize a rectangle or circle after you draw it, use the Image Map palette's X and Y fields or W and H fields **2**. Or choose the Image Map Select tool, then click and drag any one of the map's handles **3**.

To change an image map from layer based to tool based: 6.0!

1. Choose the Image Map Select tool (P or Shift-P), then click on the layer-based image map you want to convert.
2. Choose Promote Layer Based Image Map Area from the Image Map palette menu.

To hide/show image maps: 6.0!

Click the Image Map visibility button on the Toolbox or press "A" to toggle between the two **4**.

or

Choose View menu > Show > Image Maps.

TIP You can adjust how image maps are displayed (color, lines, and bounding box opacity) in the Edit menu > Preferences > Image Maps dialog box in ImageReady **5**.

6.0!

To select an image map:

1. Make sure the image maps are visible and choose the Image Map Select tool (P or Shift-P).
2. Click an image map in the image window (Shift-click to select more than one image map).

6.0!

To delete an image map:

Select an image map, then press Enter/ Return.

or

Choose Delete Image Map Area from the Image Map palette menu.

6.0!

By aligning tool-based image maps along a common edge or distributing them evenly along the same axis, it's possible to create smaller HTML files that will download more quickly. You cannot align or distribute layer-based image maps, since their position is tied to their layers.

To align tool-based image maps along a common edge:

1. Choose the Image Map Select tool (P or Shift-P), then Shift-click the image maps you want to align.
2. Click one of the six alignment icons on the options bar.

6.0!

To evenly distribute tool-based image maps along a common axis:

1. Choose the Image Map Select tool (P or Shift-P), then Shift-click the image maps you want to distribute.
2. Click one of the six distribution icons on the options bar **1**.

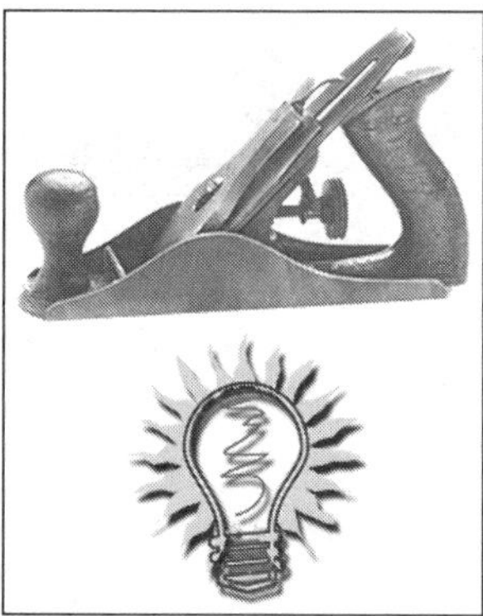

1 *The continuous-tone element (the plane) in this* ***hybrid*** *image should be optimized as a* ***JPEG****; the vector element (light bulb) should be optimized as a* ***GIF****.*

If the image you're working with is a hybrid, meaning it contains both sharp-edged elements (e.g., type or linework) and continuous-tone areas, try to draw a slice around each of those areas. Then you can optimize each slice separately using settings that are appropriate for that type of imagery **1**.

To optimize an individual slice:

1. Choose the Slice Select tool (K or Shift-K).
2. Click on a slice.
3. Choose Optimize palette settings. Use the GIF format to optimize sharp-edged areas; use the JPEG format to optimize continuous-tone areas.

TIP If you select two or more slices that have different Optimize palette settings, the palette will display only the settings that are shared by the selected slices. If you change any of the available settings, however, the new settings will apply to all the currently selected slices.

TIP If you later decide you want to optimize all the slices the same way, choose the Slice Select tool, choose Select menu > All Slices, then choose settings on the Optimize palette. If you choose Select menu > Deselect Slices, the Optimize palette will go blank.

This technique for copying optimization settings is speedy and efficient.

To copy optimization settings from one slice to another:

1. Choose the Slice Select tool (K or Shift-K).
2. Click on a slice that has the desired optimization settings.
3. Drag the droplet icon from the Optimize palette over any unselected slice; the current palette settings will be applied to that slice **2**.

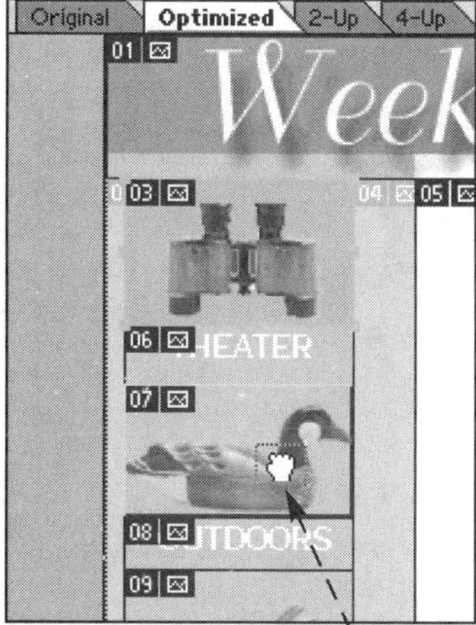

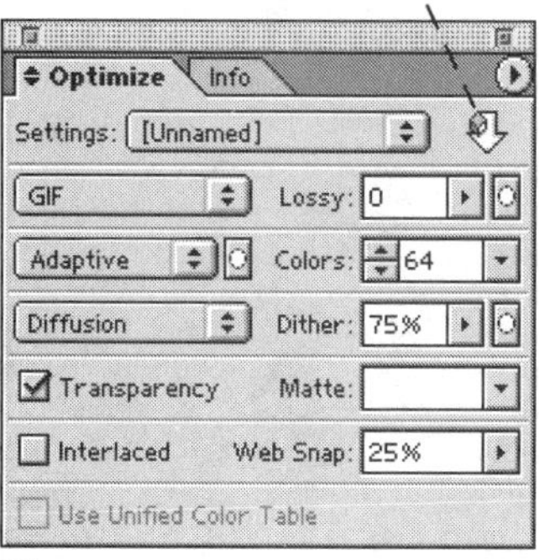

2 *Drag the* ***Droplet*** *icon from the* ***Optimize*** *palette over an unselected slice.*

When user-slices are linked, they automatically share the same optimization settings. Linked slices that are optimized in the GIF format also share the same Color Table and dither pattern, which helps to disguise edge seams.

To link slices:

1. Choose the Slice Select tool (K or Shift-K).
2. Click a slice, then Shift-click one or more additional slices **1**.
3. Choose Slices menu > Link Slices. The linked slices will now have their own label color **2**.

TIP To add a slice to an already linked set, select the slice you want to add, plus all the slices in the set, then choose Slices menu > Link Slices.

To unlink slices:

To unlink one slice, click on it with the Slice Select tool (K or Shift-K), then choose Slices menu > Unlink Slice.

or

To unlink a set of slices, click one of the slices in the set with the Slice Select tool, then choose Slices menu > Unlink Set.

or

To unlink all the slices in an image, choose Slices menu > Unlink All.

Note: Auto-slices created by ImageReady are already linked. If you unlink an auto-slice, it will become a user-slice.

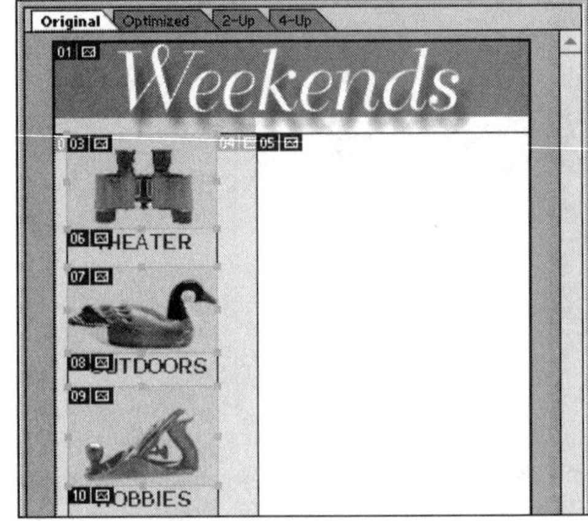

1 *Three slices are **selected**.*

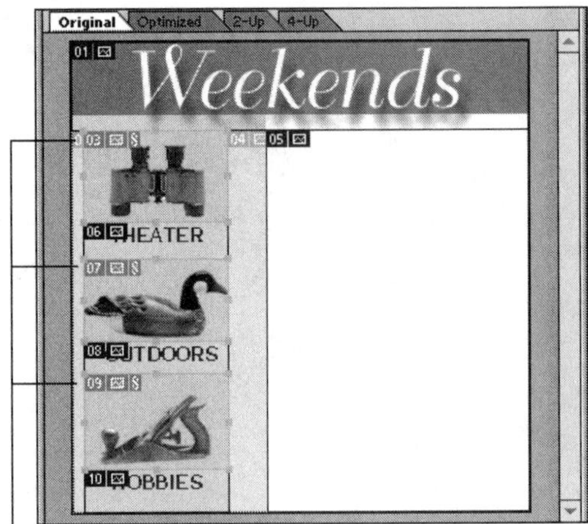

2 *The **linked** slices share the same label color.*

Older, non-graphic Web browsers (or any browser for which the Show Pictures preference is turned off) will display text, but no Web graphics. In order to display an image as a generic icon with text for browsers that can't or won't display graphics, Web designers attach a unique HTML Alt tag to each graphic. Alt tags also help visually impaired people use text browsers that "speak" the link. Here's how to attach an Alt tag in ImageReady.

To attach an Alt tag to a slice or to an entire image:

1. Show the Slice palette. If the expanded palette isn't displayed, double-click the Slice palette Tab.
2. *Optional:* Click on a slice using the Slice Select tool.
3. In the Alt field on the Slice palette, enter the word or words that you want to substitute for the image **1**.

TIP Even if the image displays in the browser only as the Alt tag text, any attached URL links will still link the viewer to the designated site.

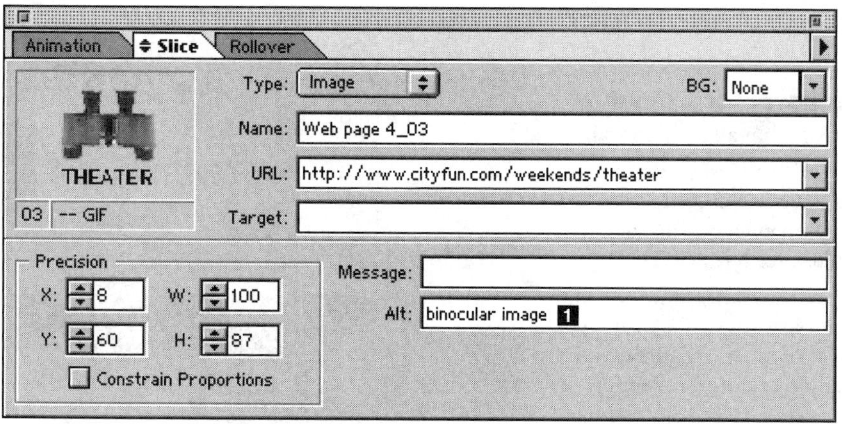

Rollovers

Now that you understand something about slices, you're ready to create another kind of hotspot: a **rollover**. A rollover is a screen event that occurs when the mouse is moved over or clicks on an area of a Web page that has a built-in modification. Three basic types of rollovers can be created: a change in an image area (e.g., color change, layer effect); the substitution of one image for another; or text or a secondary graphic that appears in another area of the browser window (when the mouse is over a button, keyword, or icon). Rollovers are like the voice of a Web page. They identify the key areas of a Web page that the viewer should pass their mouse over or click on, and they make a Web page more entertaining.

To create a rollover, you first need to divide the image into slices. (So go back and read the slice section first—no cheating!) In ImageReady, rollovers are created using the Rollover palette, and by displaying and hiding layers on the Layers palette. In ImageReady, that's all a rollover really does—it turns Layers palette layers on or off as per your built-in instructions. (To create a rollover using a layer effect, see page 451. To create a secondary rollover, see page 453.)

To create a rollover for a slice:

1. Open an image that already contains slices, and display the Slice palette.
2. Choose the Slice Select tool (K or Shift-K), then click on the slice that you want to use for a rollover.
3. If the imagery you want to use for the rollover is not already on its own layer, choose Select menu > Create Selection from Slice, then choose Layer menu > New > Layer via Copy (Ctrl-J/Cmd-J).
   or
   If the imagery in the slice is already on a separate layer, duplicate that layer now via the Layers palette.

Three basic rollovers

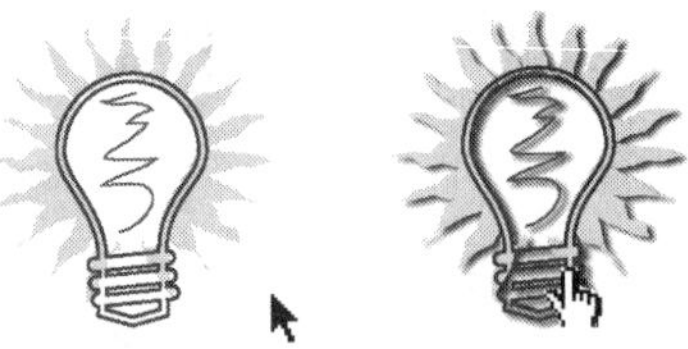

*The image itself **changes** (here a Drop Shadow layer effect was added).*

*A new image is **substituted** for the current image.*

***Secondary** text (or an image) appears in another area of the image.*

The new **rollover thumbnail.**

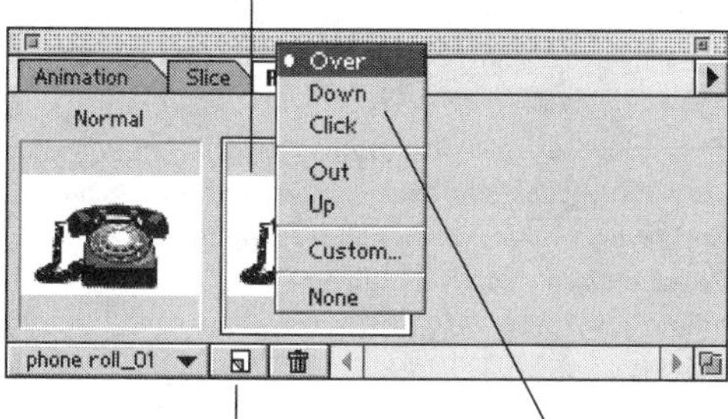

1 *To create a rollover, first click the* ***Create new rollover state*** *button.*

2 *Then choose* ***Over, Down,*** *or* ***Click*** *from the pop-up menu.*

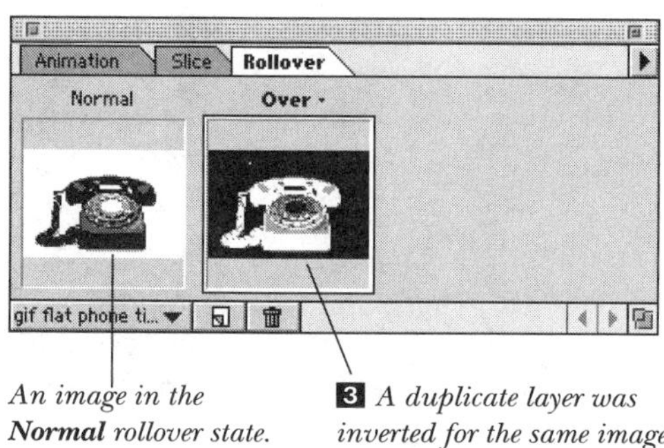

An image in the ***Normal*** *rollover state.*

3 *A duplicate layer was inverted for the same image in the* ***Over*** *rollover state.*

4 *When the* ***Over*** *thumbnail is selected, the* ***inverted*** *layer becomes* ***visible*** *and the* ***normal*** *layer is* ***hidden.***

4. Click the Rollover tab to display the Rollover palette. The current slice will appear as a thumbnail on the palette.
5. Click the "Create new rollover state" button at the bottom of the Rollover palette **1**. A copy of the current slice will appear as a new thumbnail on the palette.
6. ImageReady automatically assigns a rollover state to thumbnails in this default sequence: Over, Down, Click. If you want to override this default, from the pop-up menu above the new rollover thumbnail, choose the rollover state (triggering event) that you want to be the initiator for the rollover you'll create in the remaining steps **2**.

   Over: The mouse must be over the slice area, but not pressed down.

   Down: The mouse button must be down when it's over the slice. Some Web designers like to display a special graphic for the mouse button down.

   Click: The mouse must be clicked (button pressed and released) when it's over the slice. A Click will cause the browser to attempt to link to any URL that's attached to the slice.
7. Modify the imagery on the separate or duplicate layer (from step 3) to make it look different from the original layer. Suggestions: Invert the layer's color or luminosity (Image menu > Adjust > Invert) **3**; apply a texture or distort filter to the layer (see the sidebar on the next page); or change the layer's hue or saturation. You could also substitute a new rollover image for, or in addition to, the existing imagery in the slice. The imagery on the original layer won't change.
8. On the Layers palette, show the duplicate layer and hide the original layer from which the duplicate was created **4**.
9. Switch between the Normal and rollover thumbnails on the Rollover palette, and

(Continued on the following page)

compare them in the main window. The Rollover palette tracks the changes on the Layers palette as each rollover thumbnail is selected. Use File menu > Preview in [browser], of course, for a more realistic preview. Or try ImageReady's new preview function (see page 452).

Beware! Always take note of which Rollover palette thumbnail is currently selected as you modify a layer. Each thumbnail should produce a different look.

TIP The total number of layers in the overall image remains the same, regardless of which type of rollover you're currently working on. When you create a layer for one state, that layer is copied automatically to the other states. In order to make each rollover state thumbnail look different, you'll need to hide or show the different layers or layer effects.

TIP You can create a separate image for each rollover state (e.g., one icon for the Over state and a different icon for the Click state). Just remember to create a separate layer or layer effect for each state.

TIP Double-click the gray background on the Rollover palette (or choose Palette Options from the Rollover palette menu) to choose a Thumbnail Size for the Rollover palette. Large thumbnails make for easier viewing. The Animation and Slice palettes have their own thumbnail sizes.

TIP To create a rollover in which new imagery is added to the existing image, create new imagery on a duplicate or additional layer, making sure to match the size and location of the imagery on the original layer 4–5. In this case, the original layer should always be visible.

More rollover ideas

Here are some further suggestions for modifying a **duplicate** layer (step 7 on page 449):

To produce an enlarging/contracting rollover effect, scale the duplicate layer up a little using Edit menu > Transform > Scale, or use Filter menu > Blur > Radial Blur to stretch the shape 1–2, or use Filter menu > Distort > Pinch (with a negative Amount) to bulge it out 3.

To make a button or image area look like it's flipping, use Edit menu > Transform > Flip Horizontal or Flip Vertical (see the ducky on page 448).

1 *The **original** button.*

2 *After applying the **Radial Blur** filter.*

Since this button changes sizes for a rollover, it is a good choice for a layer based slice! The slice will size itself to the largest pixel area of the layer.

3 *After applying the **Pinch** filter to the original image (negative Amount).*

4 *An image in the **Normal** rollover state.*

5 *The same image in the **Over** rollover state. A layer with a hand-drawn glow effect is visible below the bulb layer.*

The image in the ***Normal*** *rollover state.*

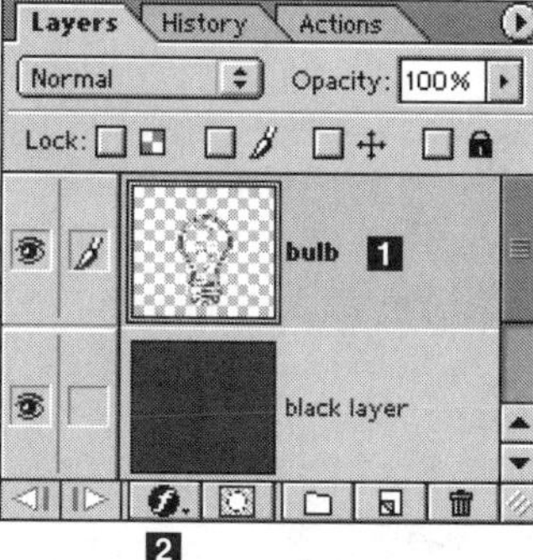

2

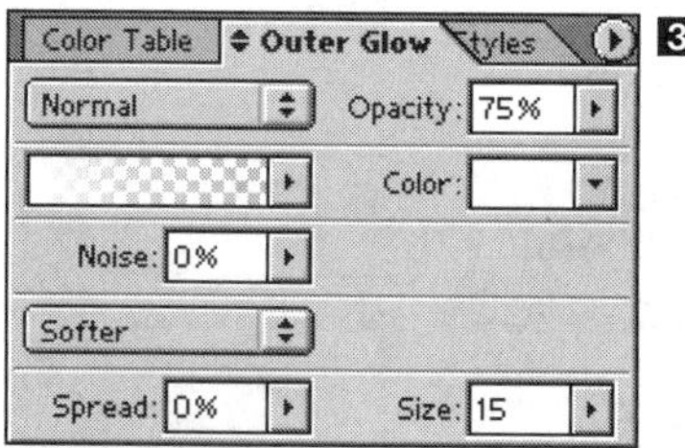

3

The image in the ***Over*** *rollover state. An Outer Glow* ***effect*** *was added to the layer.*

A great advantage to using layer effects is that you don't have to duplicate a layer to achieve a visible change between rollover states, since different layer effects can be applied to (or turned off for) the same layer for each different rollover state.

To create a rollover using a layer effect:

1. Choose the Slice Select tool, then click on a slice.
2. Click the "Create new rollover state" button at the bottom of the Rollover palette.
3. From the pop-up menu, choose a rollover state for the new rollover thumbnail.
4. Display the Layer Options palette.
5. Choose a layer that has transparency **1**.
6. Choose an effect from the "Add layer effects" pop-up menu at the bottom of the Layers palette **2**. Try Inner Shadow to recolor the inner edges of the layer image or Outer Glow to recolor the area behind the layer imagery **3**.
7. The Layer Options palette will now show options for the layer effect you just chose. To intensify an effect, raise the Size, Distance, Depth, or Intensity. If you're using Bevel and Emboss to make a button look convex, click the opposite option on the Effects palette (e.g., Up versus Down) to reverse the lighting direction and make the rollover version look concave. (See page 228.) Try the Color Fill effect at a low opacity to apply a tint and enhance a concave effect.
8. Preview the rollover (instructions on the next page).

TIP The ImageReady Styles palette contains predefined layer effects or combinations of effects that you can use (see page 471).

TIP A layer effect will only be visible on the Layers palette **4** (and on the image) when the rollover state thumbnail that it's assigned to is selected.

TIP To remove an effect (or effects), see page 223.

You can now preview a rollover within ImageReady or, if you prefer, stick with the tried-and-true Web browser-based preview.

6.0!

To preview a rollover in ImageReady:

1. Click the Rollover Preview button on the Toolbox (Y).
   or
   Click the Preview button on the Rollover palette.
2. Move your cursor over the image within the image window to see the rollover action. To stop the action, click the Preview or Play button again.

To preview a rollover in a Web browser:

1. Save your ImageReady file.
2. Choose a currently installed browser from the File menu > Preview in submenu.
   or
   Click the Preview in Default Browser button on the Toolbox (Ctrl-Alt-P/Cmd-Option-P).
3. In the browser, roll the mouse over (Over), press the mouse down on (Down), or click on (Click) the area of the image that contains the rollover.

   Note: You can verify a URL address even if you're not currently online. Pass the mouse over the slice area—the attached URL address will appear at the bottom of the browser window.

   Note: You will not be able to preview the Down state in any pre-4.0 browser version of Navigator or Explorer. In these earlier browser versions, the mouse action will open a browser context menu instead.

1 *When the* ***Over*** *thumbnail is selected...*

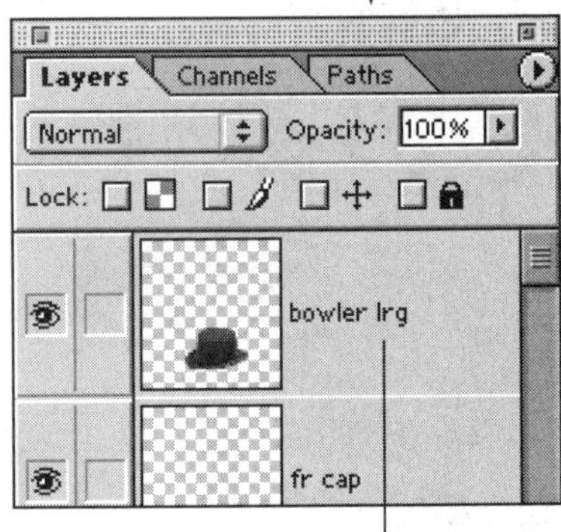

2 *...the "bowler lrg" layer becomes* ***visible****.*

Preview Rollover

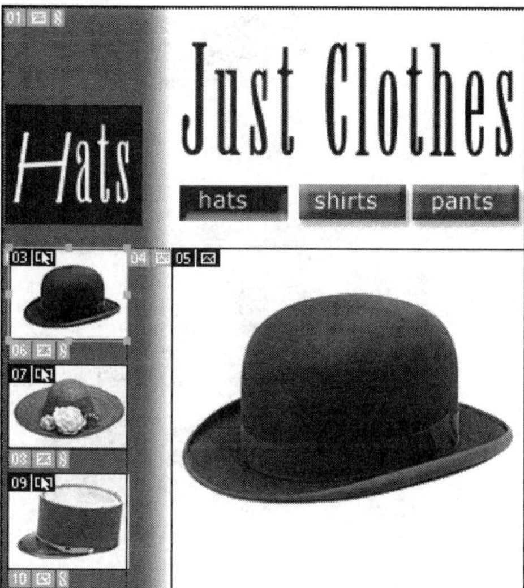

3 *For this layout, we created a column of small images and then sliced each of them individually. A larger version of each slice image was used as a separate secondary rollover image.*

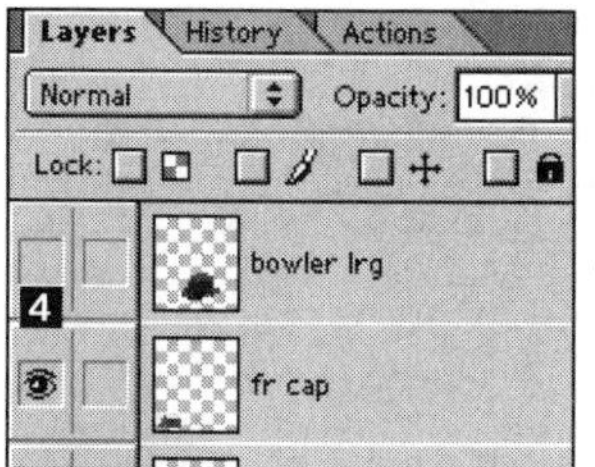

4 *When the* ***Normal*** *thumbnail is selected, the "bowler lrg" layer is* ***hidden****.*

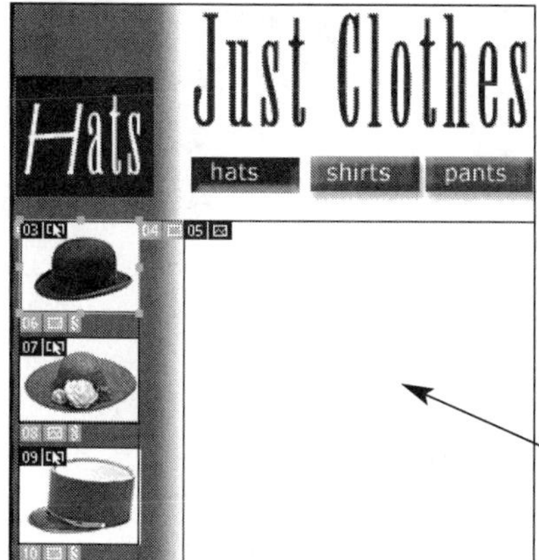

5 *The* ***rollover image*** *is* ***hidden*** *for the* ***Normal*** *state.*

The ***final*** *layout.*

In a secondary rollover, as the viewer moves the mouse over a keyword, image, or icon, supplementary text, or a supplementary image appears. When the viewer moves the mouse away from the key word or image, the supplementary info disappears. Using secondary rollovers helps to reduce visual clutter, because it reduces how much text or how many images initially appear on a Web page.

To create a secondary rollover:

1. Choose the Slice tool (K or Shift-K).
2. Draw a new slice over part of an image to become the Normal rollover state. The slice will appear as a new thumbnail on both the Slice and Rollover palettes.
3. Click the "Create new rollover state" button at the bottom of the Rollover palette. A copy of the current slice will appear as a new thumbnail on the palette.
4. Choose the Over state from the pop-up menu above the new thumbnail (**1**, previous page).
5. Create a new layer, then create the supplementary image or text on that layer (**2**, previous page).
   or
   Use Copy and Paste or drag-and-drop to create a new layer, then edit the image on that new layer.
6. Choose the Move tool, then drag the layer to the correct location relative to the overall image (**3**, previous page).
7. Click the Normal rollover state thumbnail, and make sure the new layer is hidden for that state **4**–**5**. **Don't** hide the layer that contains the original slice zone the mouse will be rolling over.

Secondary Rollover

To create a button for a Web page:

1. Click the Normal state on the Rollover palette.
2. Choose a shape tool: Rectangle, Rounded Rectangle, or Ellipse (U or Shift-U).
3. On the shape tool options bar, click the Create New Shape Layer button.
4. Choose a Foreground color, then drag diagonally to draw a shape **1**. The shape will appear on its own layer automatically.
5. *Optional:* To quickly apply a predefined layer effect to the button, display the Styles palette, then drag a style name or swatch from the Styles palette over the button layer on the Layers palette or over the shape in the main window **2**. (Or select the shape, then click the style on the Styles palette.)

   TIP If you apply a predefined layer effect that already has rollover states, a slice will be applied automatically to your shape.
6. Choose the Slice tool, then draw a slice around the new button for the Normal rollover state. The new slice will appear as a thumbnail on both the Slice and Rollover palettes.
7. Follow steps 3–9, starting on page 448, to create a rollover with the button **3**.

1 *The new* ***shape****.*

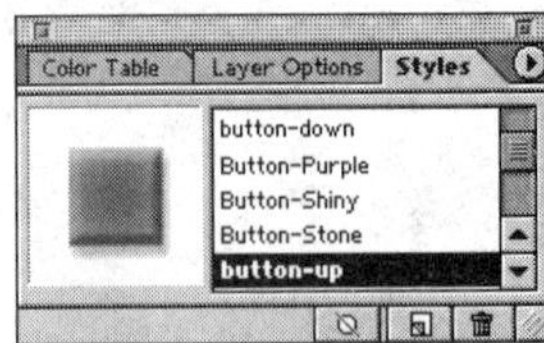

2 *The* ***button-up Style****.*

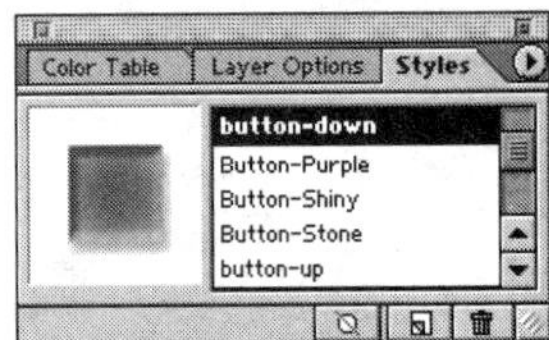

3 *After creating and selecting the Over rollover thumbnail, the* ***button-down Style*** *is applied to the shape layer.*

Button

GIF animations

In a GIF animation, multiple image frames play back in a user-specified sequence. Animated effects that you can create for a Web page include text or graphics that move, fade in or out, or change in some other way.

To produce an animation in ImageReady, you'll create multiple image frames via the Animation palette. Then you'll modify individual layers via the Layers palette for each frame (each frame has its own unique Layers palette setup). And finally, you'll save the sequence of frames as a single GIF file—ready for online viewing.

In this QuickStart Guide, we provide the instructions for creating two basic animation effects: moving a layer element and fading a layer element in or out. Once you've mastered the basics, you'll be ready to try more complex animation projects.

6.0!

The Animation palette

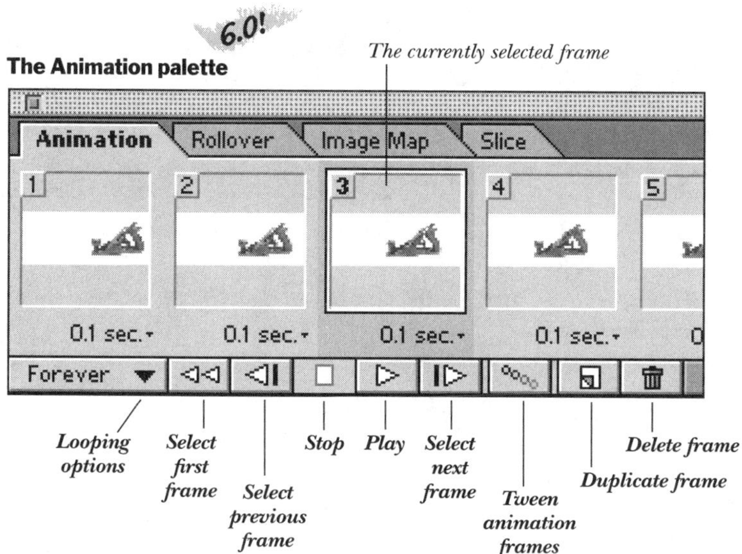

GIF Animations

To move layer imagery across an image via animation:

1. Open or create an image that has a background layer and a layer with imagery silhouetted on transparency (see pages 98 and 205–209) **1**.
2. Display the Animation palette by clicking the Animation tab or by choosing Window menu > Show Animation.
3. Choose a layer on the Layers palette.
4. Choose the Move tool and drag the layer element to one side of the main window **2**. The current thumbnail on the Animation palette will update to reflect the new position.
5. Click the "Duplicate current frame" button at the bottom of the Animation palette. The Duplicate frame is now selected.
6. The layer chosen for step 3 should still be selected.
7. Choose the Move tool (V), then drag the layer element to the opposite side of the main window **3**. The current thumbnail on the Animation palette will update to reflect this change **4**. Leave this layer selected!
8. Click the Tween button on the Animation palette. (Tweening adds frames in between selected frames.) 6.0!
9. Click Layers: **All Layers** to copy pixels from all layers to the new frames—even layers that were not modified (**1**, next page). (Also choose this option to record changes that occur simultaneously in two or more layers.) Or click **Selected Layer** to copy only pixels from the currently selected layer to the new frames. All other layers will be hidden.
   and
   Check which layer **Parameters** the in-between frames will modify: Position, Opacity, and/or effects (more about effects on pages 222–235).
   and

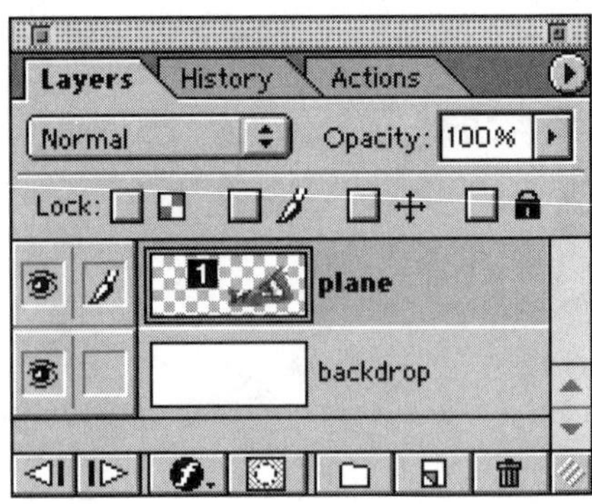

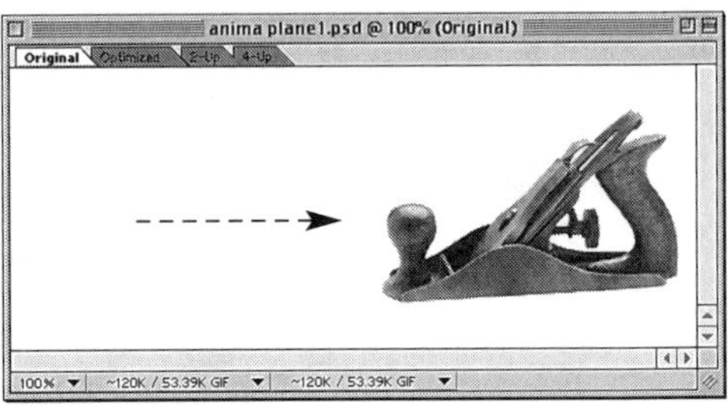

2 *Drag the layer element to one* ***side*** *of the main window.*

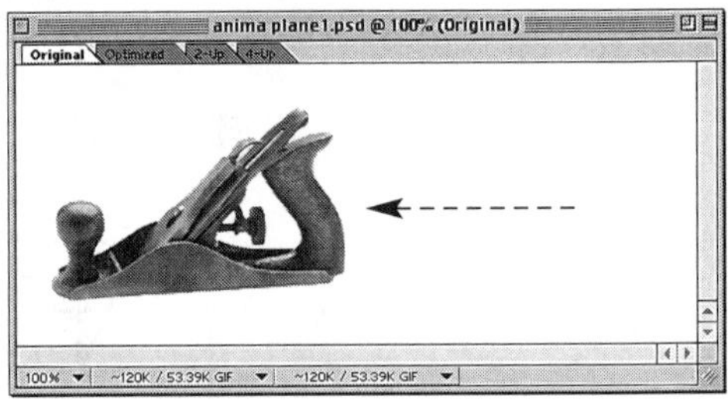

3 *Drag the same layer element to the* ***opposite*** *side of the main window for the* ***duplicate*** *animation frame.*

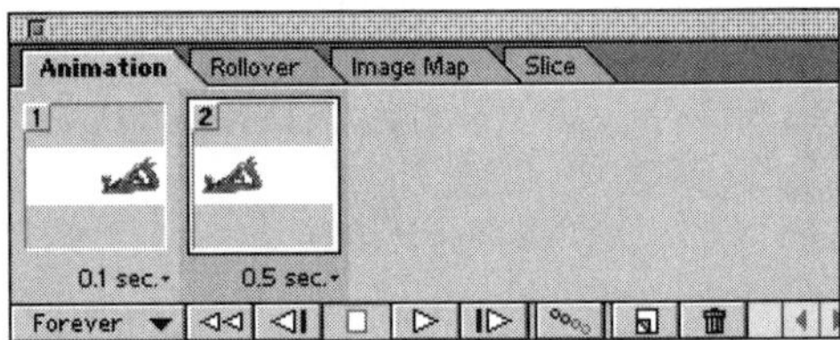

4 *The* ***original*** *(start) and* ***duplicate*** *(end) frames.*

More animation options

- Click, then Shift-click, to **select** a range of frames. Drag to **move** one frame or a selected range of frames.
- To flatten each frame into a layer, choose Animation palette menu > **Flatten Frames into Layers**. Any pre-existing layers will remain.
- Choose Animation palette menu > **Reverse Frames** to reverse the frame sequence. This is the equivalent of playing the animation backwards

Tween it again

To redo a tween, Shift-click to select all the frames that were added by the tween, drag them to the palette Delete button, modify one of the two remaining frames, then use the Tween command again..

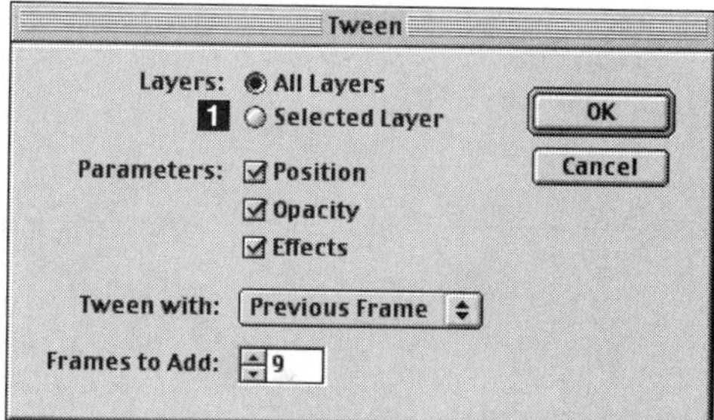

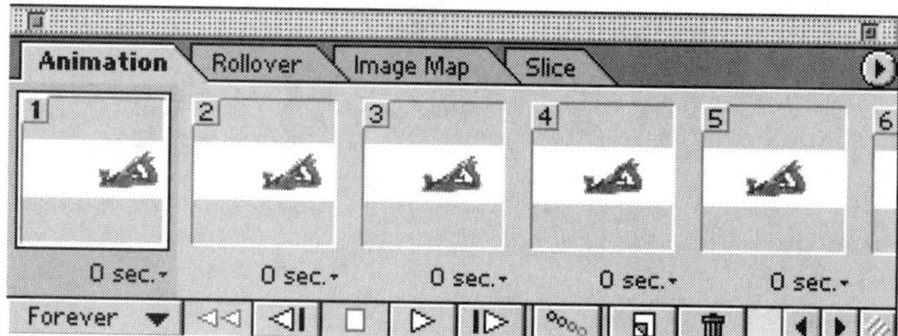

2 *The Animation palette after tweening. When the animation is played back, the layer element now moves smoothly from one side of the main window to the other.*

From the **Tween with** pop-up menu, choose to add the in-between frames between the currently selected frame and the Previous Frame. (*Note:* If you select two or more frames before opening the Tween dialog box, only the Selection option will be available on the "Tween with" pop-up menu.)
and
Via the **Frames to Add** arrows or field, specify how many frames are to be added in total (1–100). The greater the number of frames, the smoother (less choppy) the animation, but also the larger the file size and the longer the download time.

10. Click OK **2**. Now preview the animation (see page 459).

TIP You can use a type layer for an animation, and it need not be rendered. You can make type fade in or out or move across the image or use it in any other layer animation effect.

TIP If you want your animations to download and play back quickly, keep them small in pixel size (approximately 200 x 200 pixels or less).

To make imagery fade in or out:

In order to make stationary or moving imagery fade in or out on a Web page, you'll need to adjust the opacity of the imagery instead of, or in addition to, its position. Follow the instructions starting on page 456, but choose the desired starting layer Opacity value **1** (and position, if desired) for step 4, then choose the desired ending layer Opacity value **2** (and position, if desired) for step 7. Make sure the Opacity box is checked in the Tween dialog box (step 9) **3**.

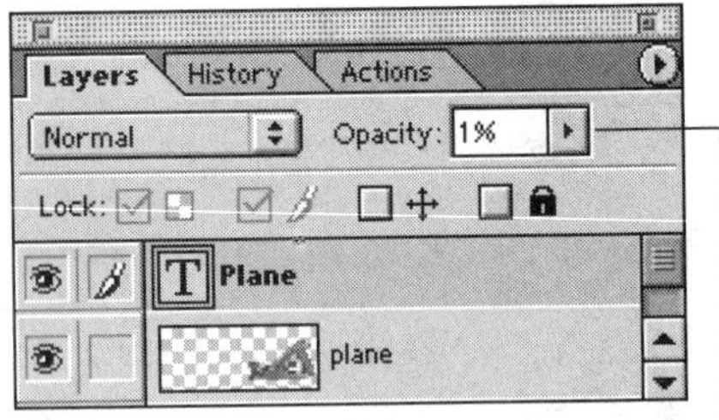

1 *The Layers palette for the* ***first*** *animation frame. Note the* ***Opacity*** *setting.*

2 *The Layers palette for the* ***second*** *animation frame.*

To remove frames from an animation:

To remove one frame from an animation, click on the frame, then choose Delete Frame from the Animation palette menu or drag the frame over the palette Delete button (this can be undone).

or

To delete the entire animation except for the first frame, choose Delete Animation from the Animation palette menu, then click Delete.

3 *After tweening, the tool* ***moves*** *to the left and the word "Plane"* ***fades*** *in.*

To choose options for animation playback:

Beware! Don't jump to or click on another program or choose Preview in [browser] while an animation is playing. If you do so, the animation will continue to play in the background and will steal processing time from the application you clicked on or jumped to.

Choose a **Looping** option from the pop-up menu on the lower left corner of the Animation palette to specify whether the animation will play back Once or Forever (loop continuously) (**4**, next page). Or choose Other and enter the specific number of playback times for the animation, then click OK. Resist creating an endlessly looping animation—it can be a real turn-off for Web viewers.

To specify how long an individual, selected frame will be displayed during playback,

What you can tween

An animation can include a change in a layer element's **position** (as in the steps on pages 456–457), a change in layer **opacity**, or a transition from one layer **effect** to another (except for the Gradient/Pattern effect, which cannot be used with the Tween command). Or you can simply tween between a layer effect that's turned **on** and the same effect turned **off** (layer effects are discussed on pages 222–235). Since these types of modifications are created via Layers palette options, they don't affect actual layer pixel values. (The animation effect discussed on the next page does actually change layer pixels.)

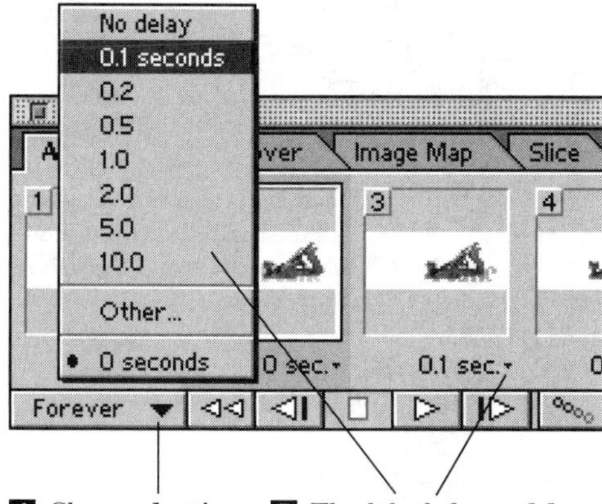

4 *Choose a **looping** option for the animation (**Once** or **Forever**).*

5 *The default **frame delay time** is **No delay** (0 seconds). You can choose a different delay time for any individual frame in the animation from the pop-up menu under the frame. A delay time of 0.1 seconds will be slightly slower than the default.*

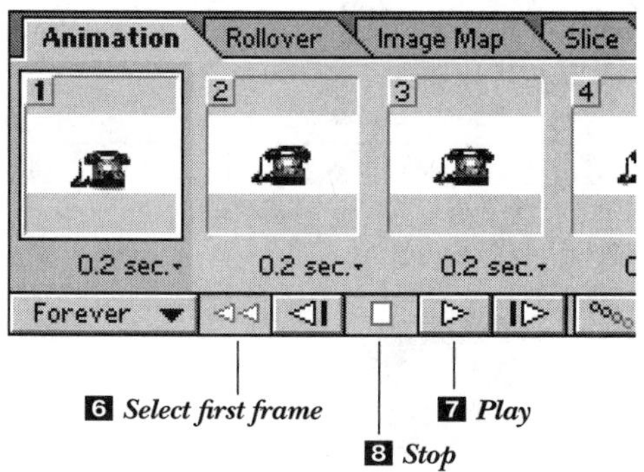

6 *Select first frame* **8** *Stop* **7** *Play*

choose a **delay value** from the Select frame delay time pop-up menu below the frame on the Animation palette **5**. Each frame can have a different delay setting. The "No delay" option is the equivalent of 0 seconds. You can also choose Other, enter a custom delay time (0–240), then click OK.

The looping and frame delay settings will save with the file and control the animation playback when the Web page is viewed in a browser.

To preview an animation:

1. Click the Original or Optimized tab in the main window.
2. If the first frame isn't selected, click the Select first frame button at the bottom of the Animation palette **6**.
3. Click the Play button **7**. The animation will play back at a slower-than-normal pace. (The ImageReady preview is slower than the realistic Preview in [browser]).
4. Click the square Stop button to stop the animation **8**.
5. Save the file, then click the Preview in Default Browser button on the Toolbox. Click back in ImageReady when you're finished previewing. If the animation won't play in the browser, see page 463.

In these instructions, you'll learn how to make a layer element rock back and forth. This type of animation modifies actual pixel values and is copied to all the existing frames. You'll be creating a duplicate layer for each incremental stage (rocking position) of the layer modification.

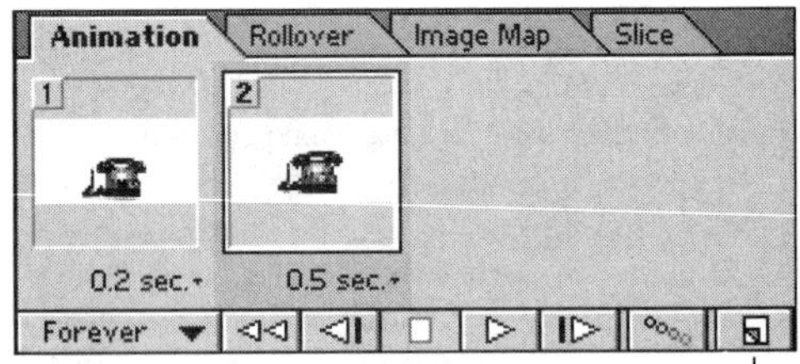

1 *Duplicate current frame*

To create a rocking animation:

1. Open an image, and open the Animation palette.
2. Click the Duplicate current frame button at the bottom of the Animation palette **1**. The Duplicate frame will now be selected.
3. Click the Tween button on the Animation palette, click Layers: All Layers, enter the desired number of Frames to Add to complete the animation, then click OK.
4. Click on the animation frame where you want the rocking effect to start.
5. On the Layers palette, duplicate the layer that is to be animated.
6. On the duplicate layer, edit actual pixels (e.g., rotate the layer slightly, apply brushstrokes, make color or tonal adjustments, or perform other transformations) **2**. Hide the original layer so you can see the change **3**. The change will display inside the selected frame on the Animation palette.
7. Click on the next animation frame (or click the Next frame button at the bottom of the Layers palette) **4**. Show the original layer **5** and hide the duplicate, modified layer **6**.
8. Click on the next consecutive frame. Show the duplicate, modified layer and hide the original, unmodified layer.
9. Continue to alternately hide, then show, the two layers for the remaining frames in the animation.

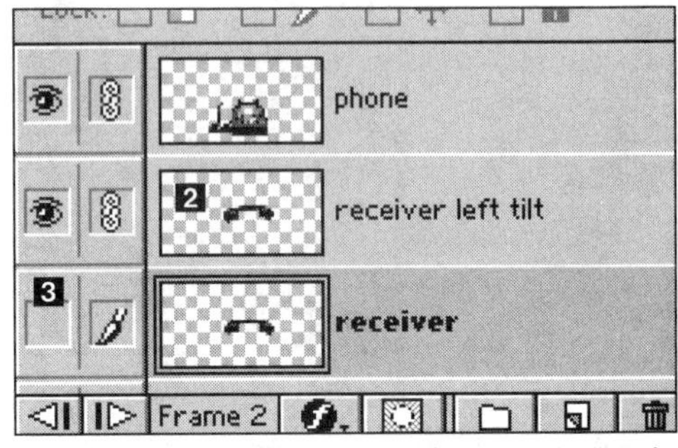

*The "**receiver left tilt**" layer is **visible** and the "**receiver**" layer is **hidden**. The handle rotates to the left.*

*Now the "**receiver**" layer is **visible** and the "**receiver left tilt**" layer is **hidden**.*

Re-editing

If you want to make an additional pixel edit (e.g., another transformation) to the original layer element, make yet another duplicate of that layer, and perform the edit on the new duplicate. Then, for one animation frame, show the original layer and hide the duplicates. For the next animation frame, show the first duplicate layer and hide the original and second duplicate. For the next animation frame, show the second duplicate layer and hide the original and first duplicate, and so on **1**.

"Receiver left tilt" shows.

"Receiver" shows.

"Receiver right tilt" shows.

1 *For this animation sequence, we created three layers and made each layer visible in the order pictured.*

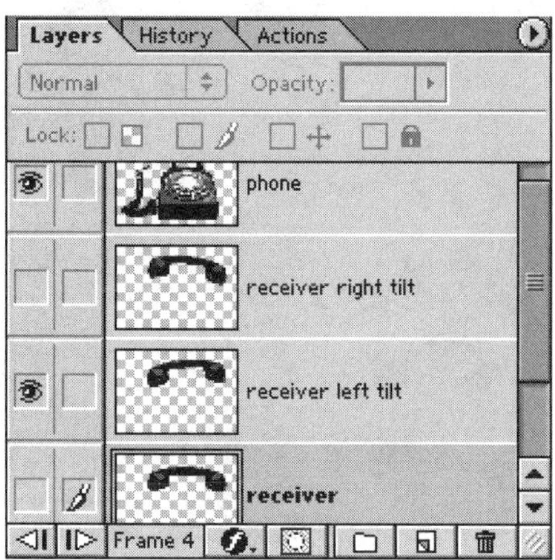

To edit an animation:

If you go back and change pixels on a layer (e.g., paint, adjust color or luminosity, perform a transformation), those modifications will be copied automatically to *all* the animation frames in which that layer is visible.

If you hide or show a layer; change a layer element's position, opacity, or blending mode; or change a layer effect for one frame, these changes will *not* be copied to any other frames. This is because these types of edits are achieved via the Layers palette and don't actualy change pixel values. To copy this type of layer edit to all the frames, choose **Match Layer Across Frames** from the Animation palette menu.

Since some of the Layers palette edits fall into the categories of the Parameters in the Tween dialog box (Position, Opacity, and Effects), you can manually change those Parameters for individual frames at any time without affecting any other frames.

Note: The Match Layer Across Frames command **removes** any changes on the currently selected layer that were achieved through tweening. If you can't afford to lose such changes, edit your animation using the method described on the next page instead.

In these instructions, an animation is expanded by adding all or a part of the same animation in reverse. During playback, the animation will play forward and then backwards in a smooth loop.

To make an existing animation reverse itself to the first frame:

1. Click the last frame on the Animation palette.
2. Click the Tween button on the Animation palette.
3. Click Layers: All Layers; check all the Parameter boxes; choose Tween with: First Frame; then enter the desired number of Frames to Add.
4. Click OK.

Follow these steps if you have created an animation effect for a layer and have now decided you want to add another animation effect to a different layer.

To apply a second animation effect to an existing animation:

1. Choose or create the layer that you want to apply the second animation to.
2. On the Animation palette, click on the frame where you want the new animation effect to start **1**.
3. For the start of this layer's animation sequence, position the layer imagery exactly where you want it, and adjust its opacity or effect(s), if desired **2**.
4. Click the frame where you want the new animation sequence to end.
5. For the end of this layer's animation sequence, modify the layer element's position or opacity, or remove or adjust any layer effects. Keep the layer selected!
6. If you chose the first and last animation frames for steps 2 and 4, respectively, choose Select All Frames from the Animation palette menu.

   or

   If you did *not* choose the first and last animation frames for steps 2 and 4, click the frame you chose for step 2, then Shift-click the frame you chose for step 4. A range of frames is now selected.
7. Click the Tween button on the Animation palette to tween immediately.

   6.0! *or*

   Choose Tween from the Animation palette menu, click Layers: Selected Layer, check the Parameters you've just modified (Position, Opacity, or Effects), then click OK **3**.

   The secondary animation effect will develop incrementally within the range of frames you selected for step 6. Any preexisting layer animation effects will be preserved.

1 *The **starting** frame for the second animation effect.*

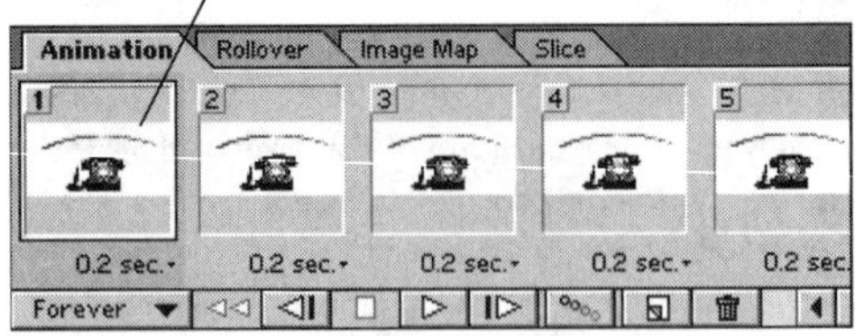

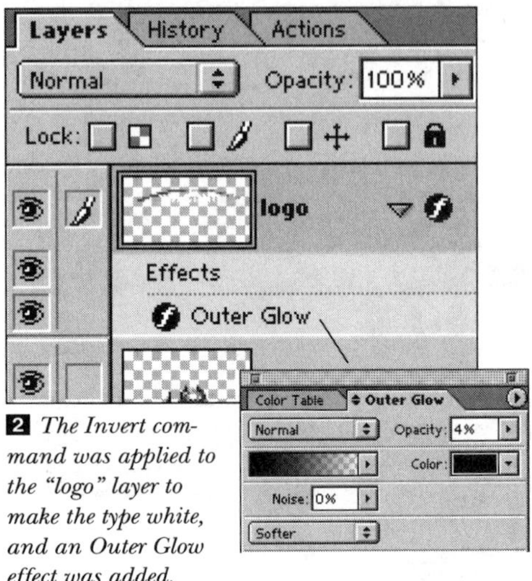

2 *The Invert command was applied to the "logo" layer to make the type white, and an Outer Glow effect was added.*

Outer Glow, 4% Opacity.

A tweened frame in the middle.

3 *The completed **animation**.*

Outer Glow, 100% Opacity.

Apply a Second Animation

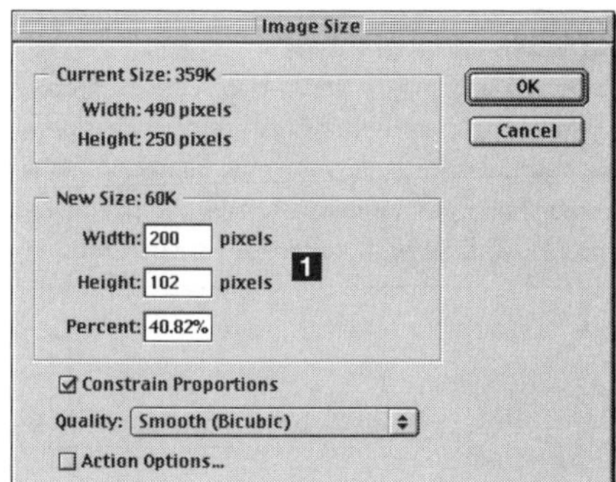

2 *This is the original animation (not easy to illustrate on paper!).*

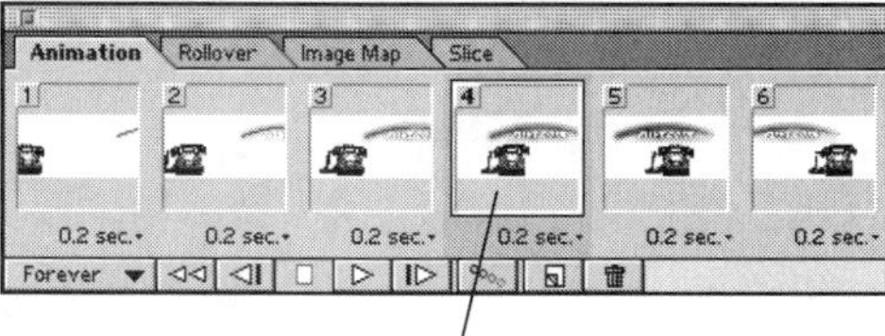

3 *Click a frame somewhere around the* ***middle*** *of the animation sequence.*

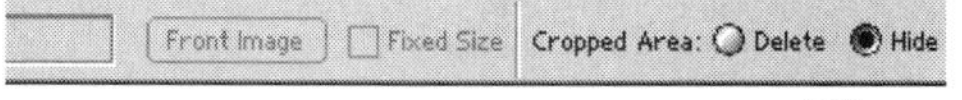

4

If the animation you've created is too large or unwieldly to be played back in the browser or takes too long to download, here are two remedies. Either lower its file size using the Image Size command or lower its file size by cropping. Regardless of which method you use, be sure to work on a copy of the file (use File menu > Save As).

To reduce the image size:

1. Choose Image menu > Image Size.
2. Lower the Width and Height to 200 by 200 (or 150 x 300) pixels or smaller **1**.
3. Make sure the Quality is set to Smooth (Bicubic).
4. Click OK.

To crop the image:

1. If the animation moves **across** the main window, click a frame somewhere in the middle of the animation sequence on the Animation palette **2**–**3**.
   or
   If the animation stays **centered** in the main window, click any frame.
2. Display the Info palette, and drag its tab to tear it away from its group.
3. Choose the Crop tool (C).
4. On the Crop options bar, choose which Cropped Area option will be used for cropping: **4** 6.0!

   Delete to permanently remove any pixels that extend beyond the crop boundary.
   or
   Hide to preserve any pixels that extend beyond the crop boundary. Choose this option if layer elements move across the image in the animation or if a background layer element moves behind a smaller object on a foreground layer. When the animation is played back, the hidden areas will enter from beyond the edge of the new crop boundary. You can use the Move tool at a later time to manually adjust where a layer is positioned within the crop boundary.

(Continued on the following page)

5. Drag the Crop tool diagonally to define the smaller image size **1**, watching the W and H (crop boundary dimension) readouts on the Info palette. Move the crop boundary handles, if necessary, to achieve the exact desired crop size. Reduce the size to approximately 200 x 200 pixels (or 150 x 300) pixels or less (see the first tip on this page).
6. To apply the crop effect, double-click inside the crop boundary or press Enter/Return.
7. Preview the animation to see how it looks (see page 459) **2**.

TIP 200 x 200 (or 150 x 300) pixels is merely a suggested crop size. If you want to experiment with different crop sizes, click on the file's pre-crop state on the History palette between attempts. Be sure to test each crop size in ImageReady using File menu > Preview in [browser]. And for real playback results, of course, upload your page for viewing on the Internet.

TIP The speed at which an animation plays back in a browser is partially determined by the speed of the Web viewer's CPU, as well as such factors as the browser version and the amount of RAM currently allocated to the browser.

Other ways to slim down

In addition to cropping, you can also reduce a file's size by lowering the number of layers or animation frames it contains, or by lowering the number of colors in its color table. Remember, a smaller file size makes for faster downloading. (Did we say that before?)

1 *Draw a **crop** marquee on the image.*

2 *After cropping, the animation elements emerge from, and disappear outside, the edge of the main window.*

Crop Image

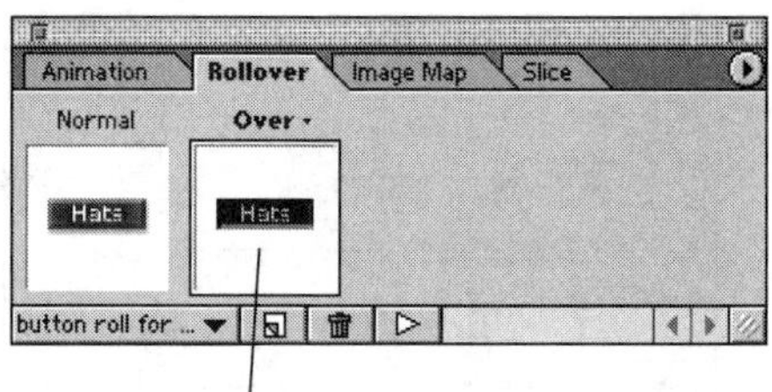

1 *Create a* ***new rollover*** *thumbnail for a slice. (We changed the "button-up" Style to the "button-down" Style for the Over state.)*

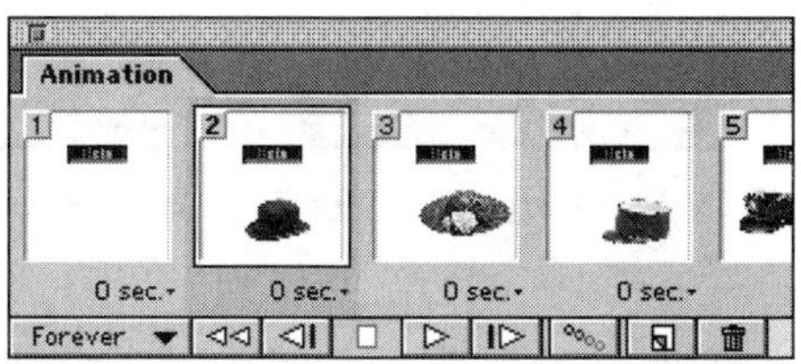

2 ***Add frames*** *to the animation via the* ***Animation*** *palette.*

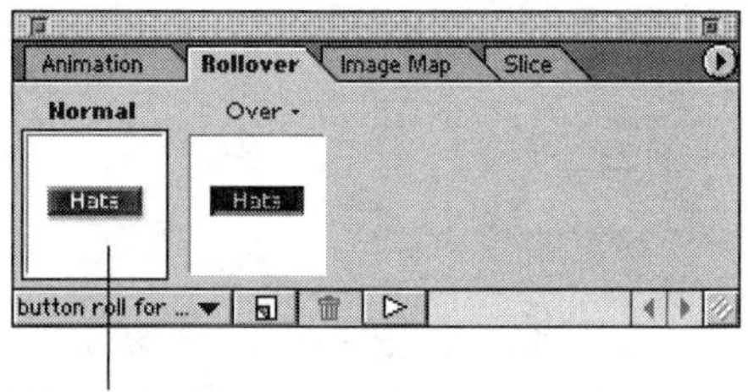

3 *Click the* ***Normal*** *rollover thumbnail.*

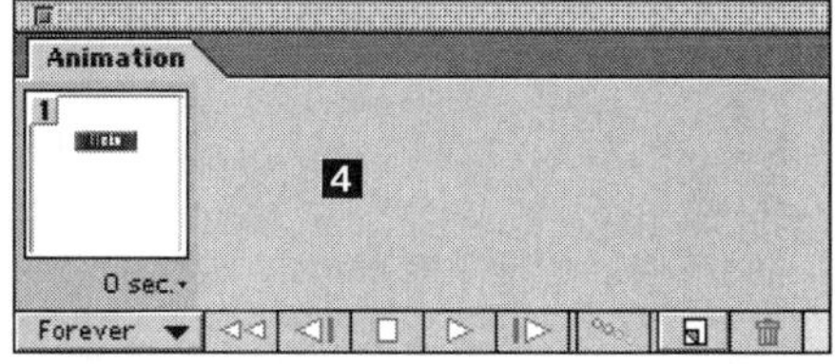

It's easy to program a secondary rollover so it triggers an animation sequence—and it makes for a lively and entertaining Web page. To achieve this effect, you'll combine the new rollover and animation skills you've acquired.

To make a rollover trigger an animation sequence:

1. On the Rollover palette, create a new rollover thumbnail for a selected slice in an image, preferably using the Over state (see page 449) **1**.
2. Drag the Animation tab out of its palette group to display it separately.
3. With the new rollover thumbnail selected on the Rollover palette (not the Normal rollover thumbnail), click on the Animation palette and create frames and events for the animation (see pages 456–457) **2**.
4. Click the Normal rollover thumbnail **3**. All the frames except the first frame will temporarily disappear from the Animation palette **4**.
5. Save the file and preview it using File menu > Preview in [browser].

6.0! The new type warp feature, which lets you apply any of 14 distortions, makes it easy to create text animations.

To create a type warp animation:

1. Open or create an image that has a background layer and a layer with editable type silhouetted on transparency.
2. Choose the type layer on the Layers palette **1**.
3. Display the Animation palette, click the first frame, then click the "Duplicate current frame" button.
4. With the Type tool still selected, click the Warp button on the Type options bar **2**.
5. In the Warp Text dialog box:

   Choose a warp style from the Style pop-up menu **3**.
   and
   Click Horizontal or Vertical to control the direction of the warp.
   and
   Use the Bend, Horizontal Distortion, and Vertical Distortion sliders or fields to achieve the desired "warpage." Use the main document window to preview your adjustments.
6. Click OK **4**.
7. The current frame in the Animation palette will update to display the warp. With the second frame still selected, click the Tween button on the Animation palette. Click Layers: All Layers, enter the desired number of Frames to Add, then click OK.
8. Choose a delay value for the frames and click the Play button on the Animation palette to run the animation.

TIP Not all the animation features may be available for warped vertical text.

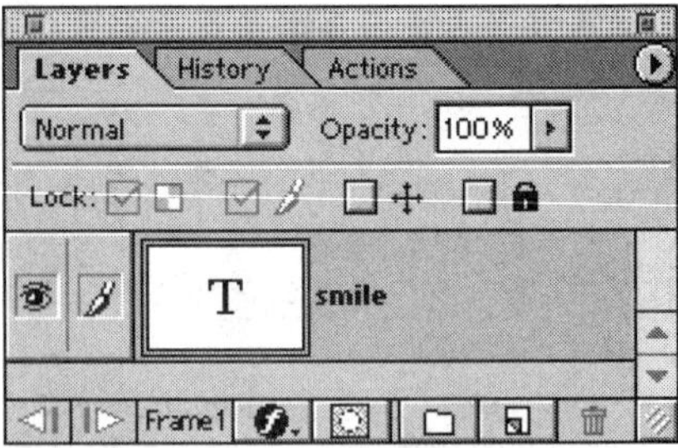

1 *Start with a normal* ***editable type layer****.*

2 *Click the* ***Warp*** *button on the Type options bar.*

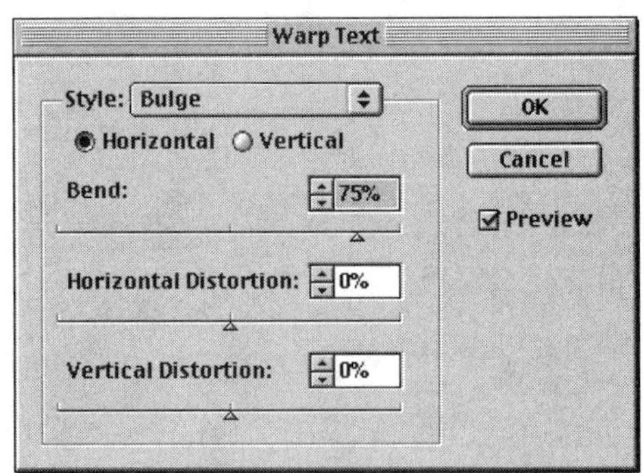

3 *Adjust the* ***Style*** *and* ***Bend*** *parameters in the* ***Warp Text*** *dialog box.*

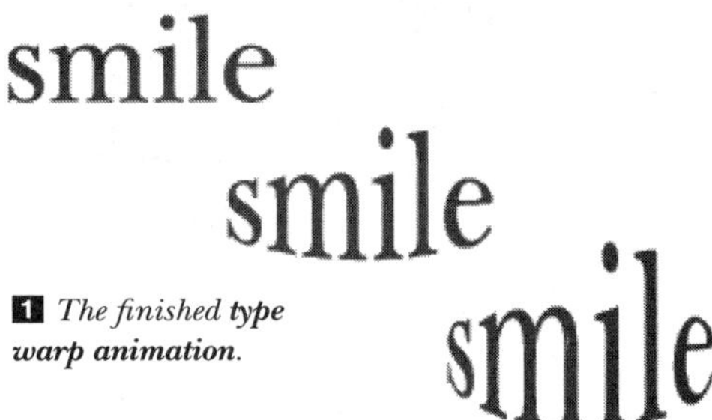

1 *The finished* ***type warp animation****.*

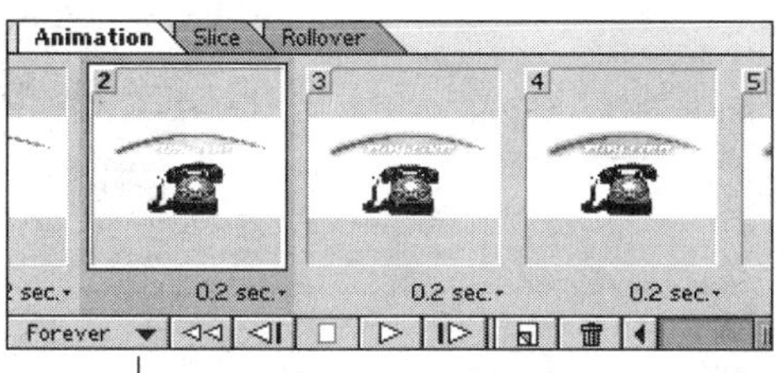

1 *As long as the file stays in the* ***Photoshop*** *format, each animation element stays on a* ***separate layer***.

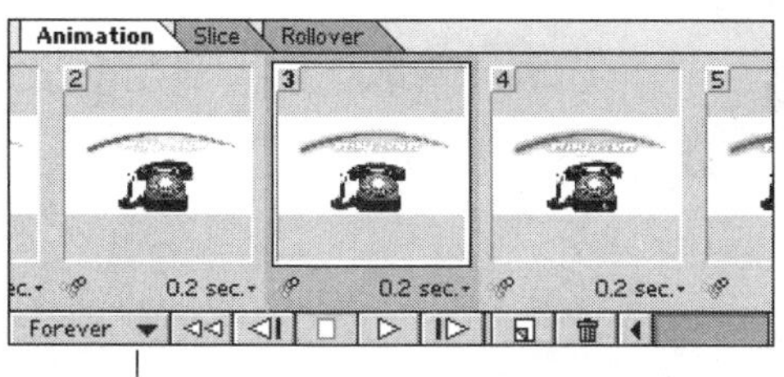

2 *In the* ***Save Optimized*** *format, the animation frames are unchanged, but now each layer* ***matches*** *a* ***specific frame*** *in the* ***animation***.

To remove or adjust a type warp: 6.0!

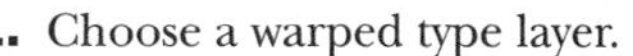

1. Choose a warped type layer.
2. Click the Type tool and click the Warp button 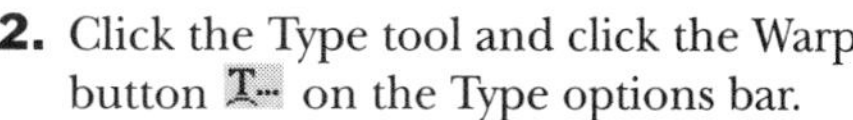 on the Type options bar.
3. To remove the warp, from the Style pop-up menu, choose None.
   or
   To adjust the warp, choose a different Style, or click the opposite orientation button, or adjust the Bend, Horizontal Distortion, or Vertical Distortion settings.

TIP You can also select any frame on the Animation Palette, then click the Warp button and adjust the warp for just that frame.

To save a GIF animation:

Use File menu > **Save** to save an animation as a Photoshop file; the GIF settings currently on the Optimize palette will be stored in the file. Choose the Perceptual, Selective, or Adaptive palette from the Optimize palette, and whichever Dither method you think will help to smooth the transitions between frames. The Save command has no effect on the Layers palette (compare this with the Save Optimized command, which is discussed next) **1**. This is the file to keep for future editing.

When you use File menu > **Save Optimized** (Ctrl-Option-S/Cmd-Option-S), the format is automatically set to GIF—not Photoshop. There is one exception to this: If the file contains a rollover that triggers an animation, the format will automatically be HTML instead of GIF. The Save Optimized command has a dramatic effect on layers. Instead of preserving the separate layer elements that make up the animation, Save Optimized matches each layer to a specific frame in the animation **2**. Watch what happens on the Layers palette when you reopen the Save Optimized file. Read more about the Save Optimized command on page 430.

The only benefit to opening a GIF format animation that we can think of is to apply or modify the optimization settings for the file.

To open a GIF format animation:

1. Choose File menu > Open (Ctrl-O/Cmd-O).
2. Locate and click on the .gif file.
3. Click Open. The animation frames will be preserved. The Layers palette, however, will now show a succession of layers, one layer for each animation frame. Individual layer elements can no longer be edited independently!

To optimize an animation:

1. Choose Optimize Animation from the Animation palette menu.
2. Check Optimize By: **Bounding Box** to save the initial frame as well as only the areas that are modified from one frame to the next **1**. This will reduce the file size, but it also may limit which GIF editors besides ImageReady can edit it.
   and/or
   Check **Redundant Pixel Removal** to remove any pixels in an object or a background that doesn't change and thus would be repetitive (redundant) when each new frame loads. This also helps to reduce the file size.

   Note: Neither option will change the way the animation actually looks—it all happens behind the scenes.

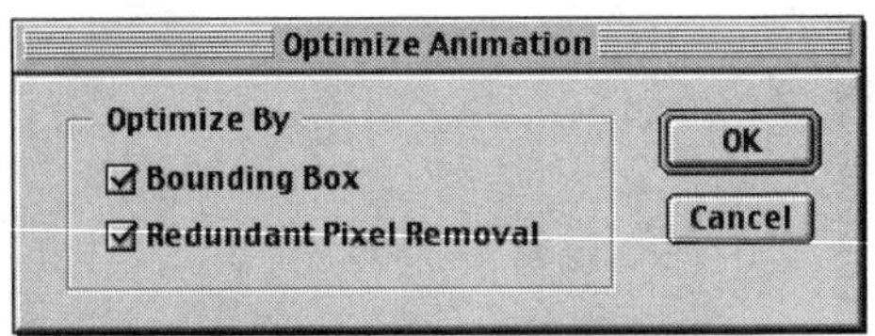

1 *Click **Optimize By** options in the **Optimize Animation** dialog box.*

Soft-edged effects

Most of the layer effects produce soft-edged shadows and colors. Soft edges don't always optimize well in the GIF format, but GIF is the only format that can be used for animations. Keep this in mind as you create animations, and be sure to preview them using File menu > Preview in [browser].

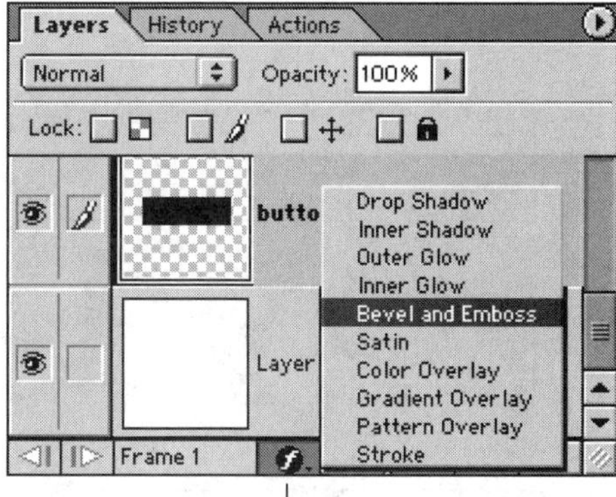

1 ***Add layer effect*** *pop-up menu.*

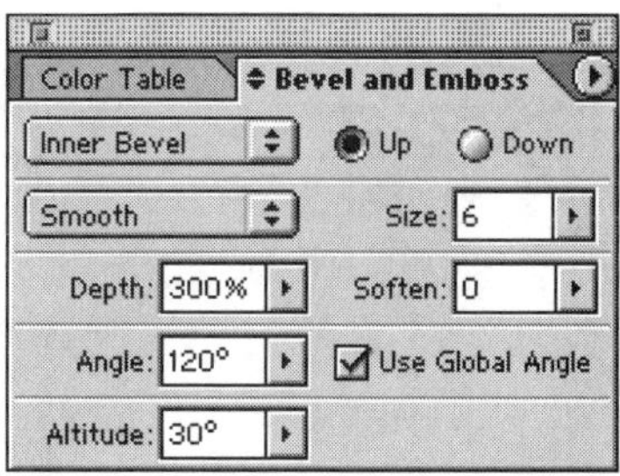

2 *Choose **separate** settings for each **effect**.*

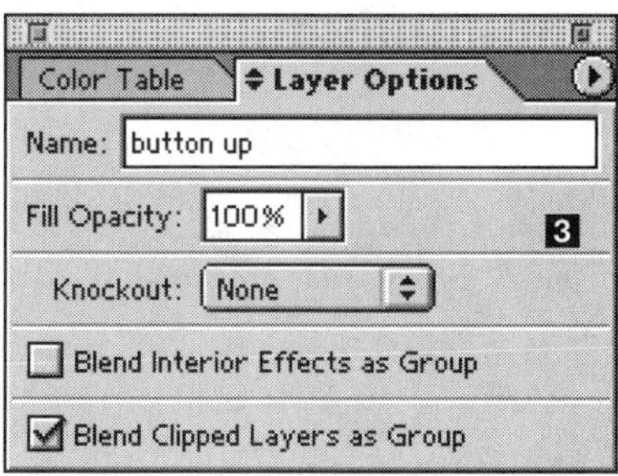

Layer effects

ImageReady offers the same layer effects as Photoshop (see page 222). While Photoshop controls layer options through the Layer Style dialog box, ImageReady handles them with a contextual Layer Options palette.

As in Photoshop, ImageReady effects have the same Layers palette features: they are listed below the name of the layer to which they are applied; move with that layer; include a right-side expand/collapse arrow for listing the effects; and each effect has its own hide/show icon. 6.0!

To apply layer effects in ImageReady:

1. Choose a layer.
2. Choose an effect from the Layer menu > Layer Style submenu.
   or
   Choose from the "Add layer effect" pop-up menu at the bottom of the Layers palette **1**.
3. Choose options for the effect from the Layer Options palette (the Options palette will show different options for each effect) **2**.
4. *Optional:* Apply additional effects to the same layer.
5. Click on any layer name to bring back the general Layer Options palette **3**. See page 237 for information on these features. If these general options aren't visible on the Layer Options palette, choose Show Options from the palette menu.

TIP You can copy one effect by dragging it to another layer. Or drag the layer's main Effects bar over another layer to copy all the effects under the bar.

TIP Click the up/down arrowhead on the Options palette tab to show more options (e.g., the Contour options) for each effect. Check out the full set of options for Bevel and Emboss! 6.0!

(Continued on the following page)

Layer Effects in ImageReady

TIP To display an applicable context menu for layers or effects, Right-click/Control click a layer name, an effect layer name, or the layer's main Effects bar **1**.

To remove a layer effect:

To remove one effect, drag it over the palette Delete layer (trash) button.
or
To remove all the effects under a layer, drag the layer's main Effects bar over the palette Delete layer button **2**.

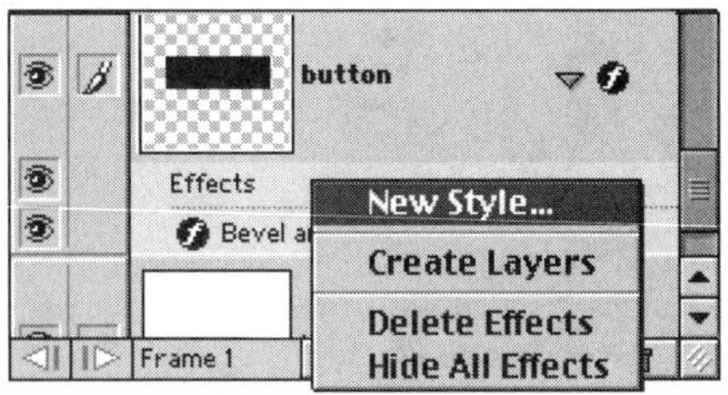

1 *This* ***context menu*** *will open if you Right-click/Control-click an* ***Effects bar****.*

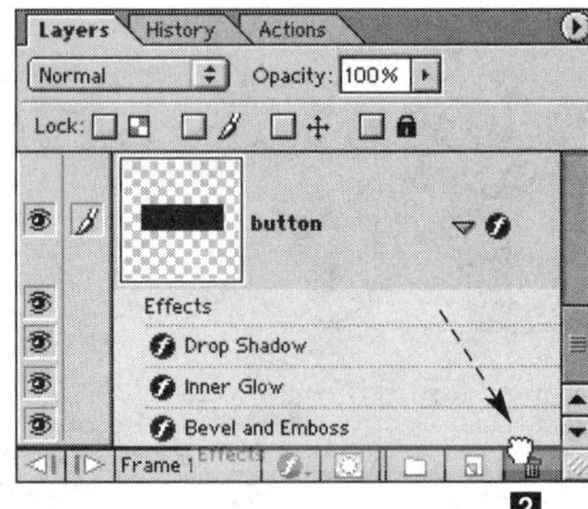

2

Other layer features in ImageReady

- Here's an easy way to remember which image edits apply automatically to animation frames and which do not: changes that are made via the Layers palette don't alter actual pixel values and thus **don't** automatically appear on new animation frames or rollover states. These changes include choosing a different blending mode, adjusting the layer opacity, hiding or showing the layer, applying or adjusting an effect, or moving layer elements. (Okay, okay, moving imagery isn't strictly a Layers palette thing.) Non-Layers palette modifications **do** apply automatically to animation frames.
- To help you navigate through frames on the Animation palette, you can use the Current frame number readout, Previous frame button, or Next frame button on the Layers palette **3**.
- To align image elements (e.g., navigation buttons) on a Web page layout, link those layers, then choose Layer menu > Align Linked (see page 249).
- 6.0! To organize layers and effects, you now can create layer sets, which can be shown or hidden as needed (see pages 131 and 122).
- To protect layers and layer sets, ImageReady has an expanded set of layer locks (see pages 131 and 133).

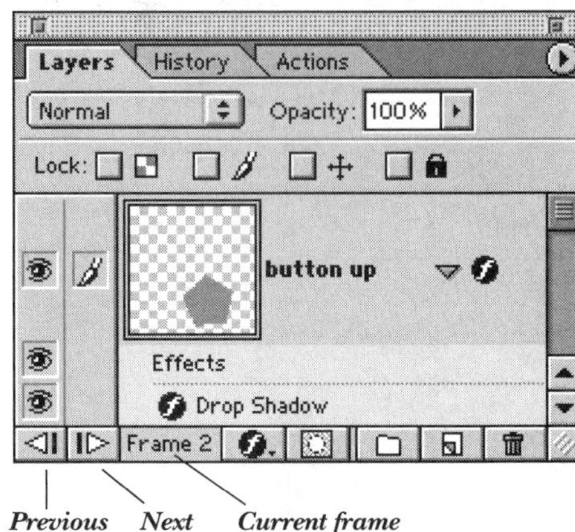

3 *Use these buttons on the* ***Layers*** *palette to navigate through frames on the* ***Animation*** *palette.*

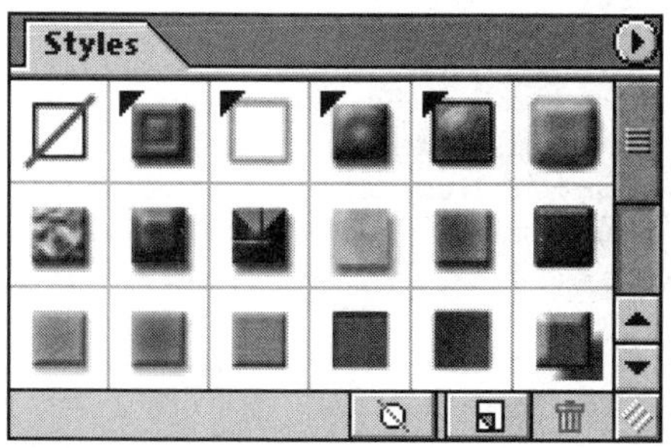

1 *The **Small Thumbnail** display mode on the **Styles** palette. Styles that contain rollovers have a triangle in the upper left corner. See next page.*

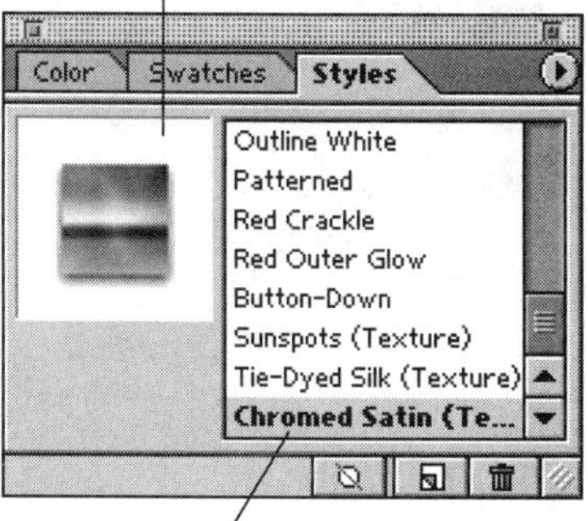

2 *The **Large Thumbnail** display mode (in ImageReady) on the **Styles** palette. (In Photoshop, Large Thumbnail mode shows only large thumbnails, with no text list.)*

3 *First choose a layer, then **double-click** a swatch or swatch name on the **Styles** palette.*

The Styles palette is a convenient place to store individual effects or combinations of effects. Once it's saved on the Styles palette, an effect or effects combo can be applied to any layer with a flick of the mouse. The same styles are available in both ImageReady and Photoshop 6 (they are stored in the Adobe Photoshop 6 > Presets > Styles directory/folder.)

6.0!

In ImageReady, choose from three display modes for the Styles palette from its option menu: Small Thumbnail **1**, Small List or Large Thumbnail (name and swatch) **2**.

(To save an effect as a style, see the following page.)

To apply a style to a layer:

Choose a layer, then click a style on the Styles palette **3**.

or

Drag a Style name or swatch over any selected or unselected layer on the Layers palette **4**.

or

Drag a Style name or swatch over an image shape in the image window.

Note: Normally, when you apply a style to a layer, any currently applied effects are replaced by the effects in the style. If you hold down Shift as you double-click or drag a style name, that style's effects will be *added* to, rather than replace, any existing effects. Effects in the style *will* replace any existing effect with the same name, however (e.g., a Drop Shadow effect in the style will replace a Drop Shadow effect already applied to the layer).

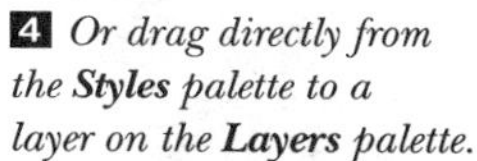

4 *Or drag directly from the **Styles** palette to a layer on the **Layers** palette.*

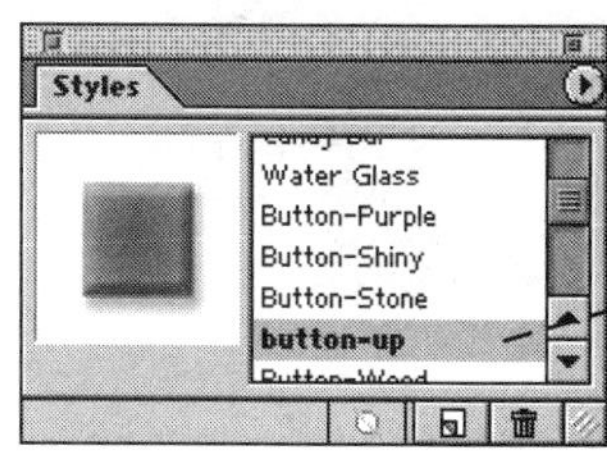

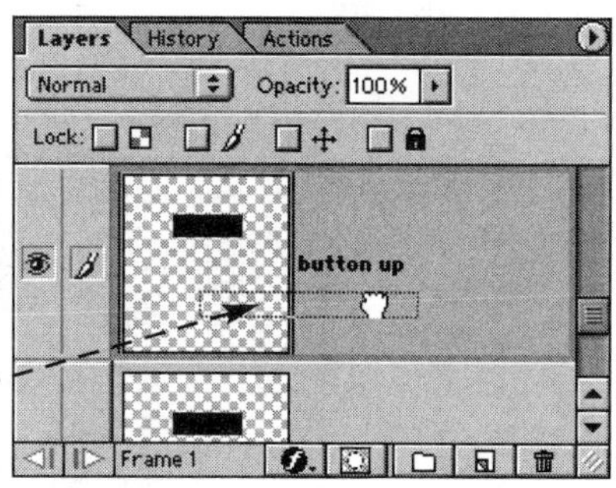

6.0!

To preserve a layer effect as a style:

1. In Photoshop or ImageReady, display the Styles palette.
2. Drag one nested Effect layer onto the Styles palette.
   or
   To preserve a combination of effects, drag the nested Effects bar from the Layers palette onto the Styles palette **1**.
   Regardless of which method you use, a New Style 1 will be created.
3. With the new style still selected, choose Style Options from the Styles palette menu, rename the style, then click OK **2**.

Rollover styles 6.0!

Rollover states can now be stored in a style, along with layer effects. Create a layer-based slice for an ImageReady layer. Then create a rollover for that layer. Drag the layer name or the layer shape over the Styles palette, or, select the layer name and choose New Style from the Styles palette menu. Be sure to check the Include Rollover States option in Style Options **2**. Click OK.

Now you can drag the rollover style thumbnail (designated by the triangle in the upper left corner) from the Styles palette over a layer name or layer shape in the image window to apply that rollover. Or click the thumbnail to apply it to the currently active layer.

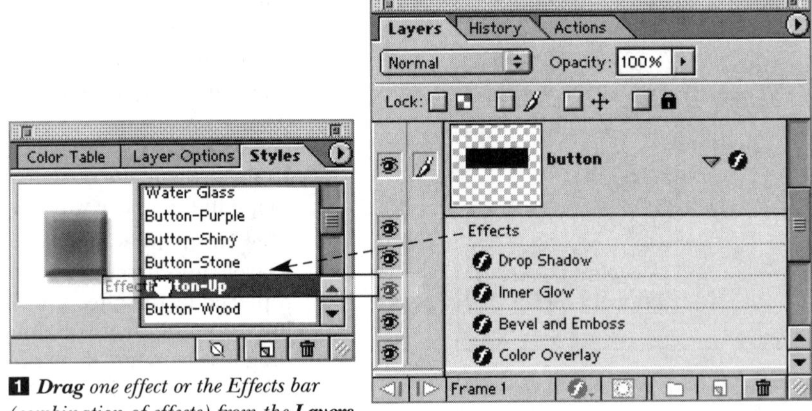

1 ***Drag*** *one effect or the Effects bar (combination of effects) from the* ***Layers*** *palette to the* ***Styles*** *palette.*

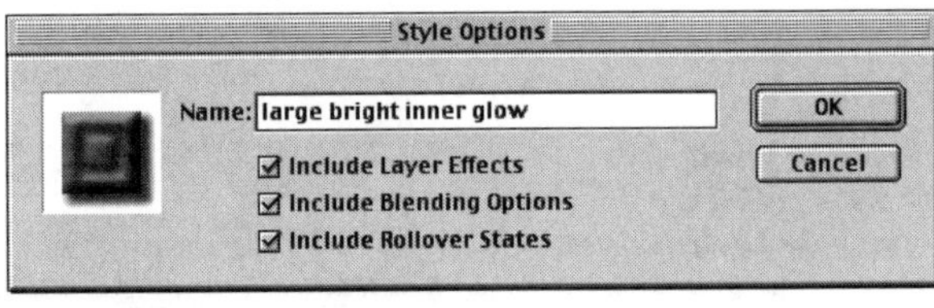

2 *Then* ***rename*** *the new style.*

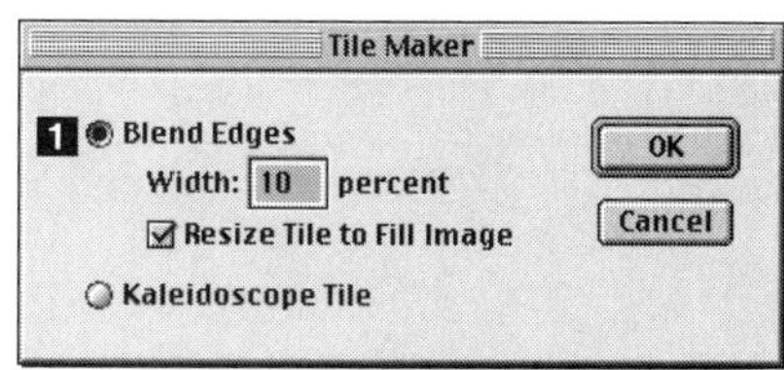

2 *This image was tiled using the **Blend Edges**, Width 10, and Resize options. The tile edges **overlap**.*

3 *This image was tiled **without** applying the Tile Maker filter. The tile edges **don't overlap**.*

Background tiling

Tiling produces a repetition of the same image in a checkerboard pattern. It's a frequently used method for filling (and decorating) the background of a Web page. Why use tiling rather than one large image for this purpose? First, because a small tile file will download more quickly than a large image will. And second, a tiled image will always fill the viewer's entire browser window—regardless of the window size.

You can use ImageReady to convert an image into an HTML tile file and then attach that HTML tile file as a background to a particular image (instructions on the next page). The background will display when the file is previewed in a browser. You could also assign a color instead of a tiled image to fill the background of a Web page.

To create a tile for an HTML background:

1. In ImageReady, open a file to become the tiled image. Use a low-contrast image with close color values, if possible, so the imagery and type that download on top of it will be readable. If there are any slices, choose Slices menu > Delete All.
2. Crop the image if you want to use only part of it.
3. Choose Filter menu > Other > Tile Maker **1**–**2**.
4. Click Blend Edges to make each tile edge blend (overlap) with the next tile. Enter a Width percentage (1–20) for the amount of blend (overlap) **1**.
5. Check the Resize Tile to Fill Image box to make the tile size match the current image size. With this option unchecked, the tile will be reduced in size by the current Width amount (e.g., a Width of 10 will reduce the tile size by 10 percent).
   or

(Continued on the following page)

Click Kaleidoscope Tile to have the filter generate an abstract image from the original.

6. Click OK.
7. Choose File menu > Save Optimized (Ctrl-Alt-S/Cmd-Option-S), change the default name, choose a location in which to save it, then click Save.

6.0!

To preview an image as a tiled background:

1. Open an image in ImageReady.
2. Delete all slices.
3. Choose File menu > Output Settings > Background.
4. Click View As: Background.
5. Click OK.
6. To preview the background, click the Preview in Default Browser button on the Toolbox or press the button and choose from the available browsers.

TIP In the File menu > Save Optimized (or Save Optimized As) dialog box, click the Output Settings button to access the output settings dialog box, choose Background from the second pop-up menu, then follow steps 3–4 above.

Take a road more traveled

While ImageReady is capable of producing HTML background tiling, you may find reason to attach a tiled background to your Web page in a Web-page creation program like Adobe GoLive or Macromedia Dreamweaver. Ask your Web programmer or layout specialist which program to use to code background tiling into the overall Web-page code.

Tiling tips

- An image will be repeated, if necessary, to fit to the size of the browser window. If you don't want the background image to repeat at all, use a large optimized image (around 800 x 800 pixels, containing very few colors and shapes).
- If the file you've chosen for the background image contains an animation, the animation will automatically play back repetitively across the browser page. Visually overwhelming, yes, but maybe just the kind of effect you're looking for.

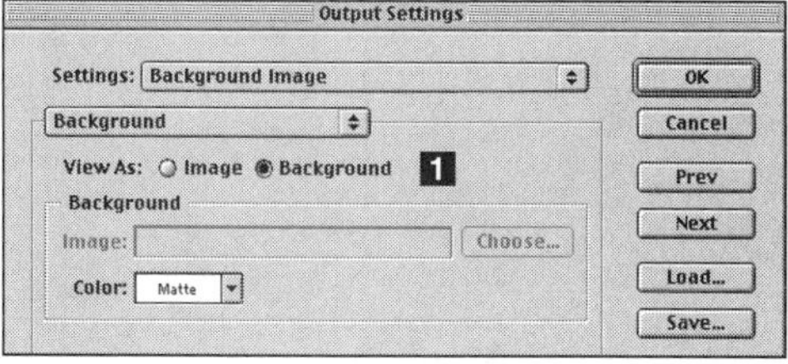

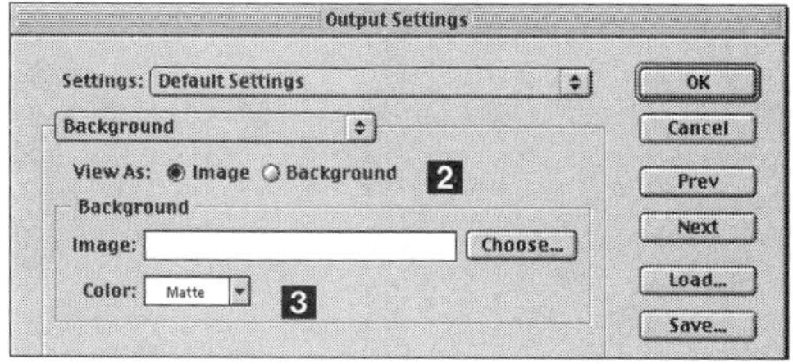

To attach an HTML tile file as a background for an image: 6.0!

1. Open the image.
2. Choose File menu > Output Settings > Background.
3. Choose View As: Image (if available) **2**.
4. Click Choose, locate the optimized file, then click Open.
   and/or
   To choose a solid color for the background, choose a color from the Color pop-up menu next to the Color swatch **3** or click the Color swatch and choose a color from the color picker (check the Only Web Colors box). This color will display while any imagery is downloading and through any transparent areas in the main image or tile.
5. Click OK.
6. To preview the background, click the Preview in Default Browser button on the Toolbox or press the button and choose from the available browsers.

To remove an HTML tile background or solid color from an image:

1. Open the image, then choose File menu > Output Settings > Background.
2. Delete the file name from the Image field.
   or
   Choose None from the Color pop-up menu.
3. Click OK.

To use Photoshop's Save for Web dialog box:

We would feel a nagging sense of guilt if we didn't at least show you what the Photoshop Save for Web dialog box looks like. As we mentioned earlier in this chapter, Save for Web is like ImageReady Lite. ImageReady has all of the same optimizing features as the Save for Web dialog box—and much, much more. If you want to learn more about the Save for Web optimizing features, just use the page numbers in the callouts in the illustration below to direct you to the equivalent information about ImageReady.

TIP The shortcut for opening the Save for Web dialog box is Ctrl-Shift-Alt-S/ Cmd-Option-Shift-S.

Preview tabs (top left corner of the dialog box), see pages 421–422.

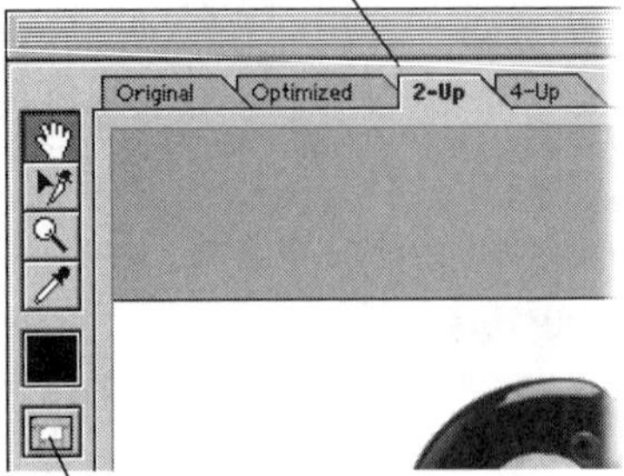

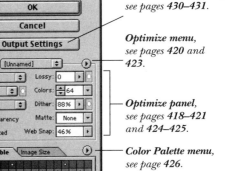

Slice Visibility, see page 438.

6.0!

Preview menu, see pages 427–428.

6.0!

Output Settings menu, see pages 430–431.

Optimize menu, see pages 420 and 423.

Optimize panel, see pages 418–421 and 424–425.

Color Palette menu, see page 426.

Color Table panel, see page 426.

Optimization info area, see pages 409 and 410.

Preview in [browser], see page 429.

SHORTCUTS A

GENERAL SHORTCUTS	Windows 98/NT	Mac OS
Show/hide all palettes, including Toolbox	Tab	Tab
Show/hide all but Toolbox	Shift + Tab	Shift + Tab
Undo	Ctrl + Z	⌘ + Z
Accept crop, transform, or any dialog	Enter	Return or Enter
Toggle Cancel to Reset in dialog	Alt	Opt
Cancel crop, transform, or any dialog	Esc or Ctrl + . (period)	Esc or ⌘ + . (period)
Exit type dialog from keyboard	Enter (on numeric keypad)	Enter
Activate button in alert dialog	First letter of button (e.g., N = No)	First letter of button (e.g., N = No)
Increase value in highlighted field by 1 (or .1)	Up Arrow	Up Arrow
Increase value in highlighted field by 10 (or 1)	Shift + Up Arrow	Shift + Up Arrow
Decrease value in highlighted field by 1 (or .1)	Down Arrow	Down Arrow
Decrease value in highlighted field by 10 (or 1)	Shift + Down Arrow	Shift + Down Arrow
Adjust angle in 15° increments	Shift + drag in angle wheel	Shift + drag in angle wheel
Cancel out of pop-up slider (mouse button up)	Esc	Esc
Commits edit in pop-up slider (mouse button up)	Enter	Return or Enter
Reset pop-up slider to prev (mouse button down)	Hold Alt and move cursor outside slider rectangle	Hold Opt and move cursor outside slider rectangle
Help	F1	Help
Access Adobe Online	Click on identifier icon on Toolbox	Click on identifier icon on Toolbox

	Windows 98/NT	Mac OS
PALETTES		
Show/hide Color	F6	F6
Show/hide Layers	F7	F7
Show/hide Info	F8	F8
Show/hide Actions	F9	F9
TOOLS		
Choose a tool		
Rectangular Marquee	M	M
Move	V	V
Lasso	L	L
Magic Wand	W	W
Crop	C	C
Slice	K	K
Airbrush	J	J
Paintbrush/Pencil	B	B
Rubber Stamp	S	S
History Brush	Y	Y
Eraser	E	E
Blur	R	R
Dodge	O	O
Pen	P	P
Add-anchor-point	+ (plus)	+ (plus)
Delete-anchor-point	- (minus)	- (minus)
Direct-selection	A	A
Type	T	T
Measure	U	U
Gradient/Paint Bucket	G	G
Notes	N	N
Eyedropper	I	I
Hand	H	H
Zoom	Z	Z

	Windows 98/NT	Mac OS
Cycle through tools		
Marquee tools	Shift + M	Shift + M
Lasso tools	Shift + L	Shift + L
Rubber Stamp tools	Shift + S	Shift + S
Blur, Sharpen, and Smudge tools	Shift + R	Shift + R
Toning tools	Shift + O	Shift + O
Pen tools	Shift + P	Shift + P
Type tools	Shift + T	Shift + T
Eyedropper tools	Shift + I	Shift + I
Cycle through above tools	Alt + click in tool slot	Option + click in tool slot
Toggle tools		
Move tool	Ctrl	⌘
Precise cursors	Caps Lock	Caps Lock
Pencil to Eyedropper	Alt	Option
Line to Eyedropper	Alt	Option
Paint Bucket to Eyedropper	Alt	Option
Blur to Sharpen; Sharpen to Blur	Alt	Option
Dodge/Burn tool	Alt	Option

TOOL BEHAVIOR

Change brush opacity in 10% increments	Number keys (2 = 20%, 3 = 30%)	Number keys (2 = 20%, 3 = 30%)
Constrain tools		
Constrain to horizontal or vertical axis (Eraser, Paintbrush, Pencil, Blur, Sharpen, Smudge, Dodge, or Burn tool)	Shift + drag	Shift+ drag
Draw, erase, etc. in straight lines (Eraser, Paintbrush, Pencil, Blur, Sharpen, Smudge, Dodge, or Burn tool)	Shift + click	Shift + click
Constrain to 45° axis (Line, Gradients, (or Convert-point tool)	Shift + drag	Shift + drag
Crop tool		
Rotate crop marquee	Drag outside crop marquee	Drag outside crop marquee
Move crop marquee	Drag inside crop marquee	Drag inside crop marquee
Resize crop marquee	Drag crop handles	Drag crop handles
Maintain aspect ratio of crop box	Shift + drag corner handles	Shift + drag corner handles

	Windows 98/NT	Mac OS
Resize crop from center	Alt + drag handles	Option + drag handles
Constrain crop from center	Alt + Shift + drag handles	Option + Shift + drag handles
Apply crop	Enter	Enter/Return
Slice tool		
Toggle between slice and slice selection tool	Ctrl	⌘
Draw square slice	Shift + drag	Shift + drag
Draw from center outward	Alt + drag	Option + drag
Draw square slice from center outward	Alt + Shift + drag	Option + Shift + drag
Reposition slice while creating	Spacebar + drag	Spacebar + drag
Toggle Snap to Slices on and off	Ctrl key while drawing	Ctrl key while drawing
Move tool		
Move constrained to 45°	Shift + drag	Shift + drag
Copy selection or layer	Alt + drag	Option + drag
Nudge layer/selection 1 pixel	Ctrl + arrow key	⌘ + arrow key
Nudge layer/selection 10 pixels	Ctrl + Shift + arrow key	⌘ + Shift + arrow key
Lasso tool		
Add to selection	Shift + click, then draw	Shift + click, then draw
Delete from selection	Alt + click, then draw	Option + click, then draw
Intersect with selection	Alt + Shift + click, then draw	Option + Shift + click, then draw
Draw using Polygonal Lasso	Click, then Alt-drag	Click, then Option-drag
Polygonal Lasso tool		
Add to selection	Shift + click, then draw	Shift + click, then draw
Delete from selection	Alt + click, then draw	Option + click, then draw
Intersect with selection	Alt + Shift + click, then draw	Option + Shift + click, then draw
Draw using Lasso	Alt + drag	Option + drag
Constrain to 45° while drawing	Shift + drag	Shift + drag
Magnetic Lasso tool		
Add to selection	Shift + click, then draw	Shift + click, then draw
Delete from selection	Alt + click, then draw	Option + click, then draw
Intersect with selection	Alt + Shift + click, then draw	Option + Shift + click, then draw

	Windows 98/NT	Mac OS
Add point	Single click	Single click
Remove last point	Backspace or Delete	Delete key
Close path	Double-click or Enter	Double-click or Enter or Return
Close path over start point	Click on start point	Click on start point
Close path using straight line segment	Alt + double-click	Option + double-click
Switch to Lasso	Alt + drag	Option + drag
Switch to Polygonal Lasso	Alt + click	Option + click
Eraser tool		
Erase to History	Alt + drag	Option + drag
Smudge tool		
Smudge using Foreground color	Alt	Option
Burn and Dodge tools		
Set Burn or Dodge to Shadows	Alt + Shift + W	Option + Shift + W
Set Burn or Dodge to Midtones	Alt + Shift + V	Option + Shift + V
Set Burn or Dodge to Highlights	Alt + Shift + Z	Option + Shift + Z
Sponge tool		
Desaturate setting	Alt + Shift + J	Option + Shift + J
Saturate setting	Alt + Shift + A	Option + Shift + A
Measure tool		
Measure constrained to 45° axis	Shift + drag	Shift + drag
Create protractor	Alt + click + drag on end point	Option + click + drag on end point
Paint Bucket tool		
Change color of area around canvas	Shift + click outside canvas	Shift + click outside canvas
Eyedropper tool		
Choose Background color	Alt + click	Option + click
Toggle to Color Sampler tool	Shift	Shift
Delete sampler	Alt + Shift + click on sampler	Option + Shift + click on sampler
Color Sampler tool		
Delete sampler	Alt + click on sampler	Option + click on sampler

	Windows 98/NT	Mac OS

DISPLAY

Change view size

	Windows 98/NT	Mac OS
Zoom in	Ctrl + Spacebar + click or drag or Ctrl + Alt + + (plus)	⌘ + Spacebar + click or drag or ⌘ + + (plus)
Zoom out	Ctrl + Alt + Spacebar + click or Ctrl + Alt + - (minus)	⌘ + Option + Spacebar + click or ⌘ + - (minus)
Zoom to 100%	Double-click Zoom tool	Double-click Zoom tool
Zoom to fit in window	Double-click Hand tool	Double-click Hand tool
Fit on screen	Ctrl + 0	⌘ + 0
Actual pixels	Ctrl + Alt + 0	⌘ + Option + 0
Zoom in without changing window size	Ctrl + + (plus)	⌘ + Option + + (plus)
Zoom out without changing window size	Ctrl + - (minus)	⌘ + Option + - (minus)

Hand tool

	Windows 98/NT	Mac OS
Toggle to zoom in	Ctrl	Z
Toggle to zoom out	Alt	Option
Fit image on screen	Double-click tool slot	Double-click tool slot

Zoom tool

	Windows 98/NT	Mac OS
Zoom out	Alt + click	Option + click
Actual size	Double-click tool slot	Double-click tool slot

Show/hide

	Windows 98/NT	Mac OS
Show/hide Edges	Ctrl + H	⌘ + H
Show/hide Path	Ctrl + Shift + H	⌘ + Shift + H
Show/hide Rulers	Ctrl + R	⌘ + R
Show/hide Guides	Ctrl + " (quote)	⌘ + " (quote)

Grid and guides

	Windows 98/NT	Mac OS
Snap to Guides	Shift + Ctrl + ; (semicolon)	Shift + ⌘ + ; (semicolon)
Lock Guides	Alt + Ctrl + ; (semicolon)	Option + ⌘ + ; (semicolon)
Snap guide to ruler	Shift + drag guide	Shift + drag guide
Toggle guide orientation (H/V)	Alt + drag guide	Option + drag guide

Move image in window

	Windows 98/NT	Mac OS
Scroll up one screen	Page up	Page up
Scroll up 10 units	Shift + page up	Shift + page up
Scroll down one screen	Page down	Page down

	Windows 98/NT	Mac OS
Scroll down 10 units	Shift + page down	Shift + page down
Scroll left one screen	Ctrl + page up	⌘ + page up
Scroll left 10 units	Ctrl + Shift + page up	⌘ + Shift + page up
Scroll right one screen	Ctrl + page down	⌘ + page down
Scroll right 10 units	Ctrl + Shift + page down	⌘ + Shift + page down
Move view to left	Home key	Home key
Move view to right	End key	End key

Navigator palette

Scroll viewable area of image	Drag view proxy	Drag view proxy
Move view to new portion of image	Click in preview area	Click in preview area
View new portion of image	Ctrl + drag in preview area	⌘ + drag in preview area

Screen modes

Toggle Standard/Full Screen with Menu/Full Screen modes	F	F
Toggle menu when in Full Screen with Menu mode	Shift + F	Shift + F

View

Preview > CMYK	Ctrl + Y	⌘ + Y
Gamut Warning	Ctrl + Shift + Y	⌘ + Shift + Y

FILE MENU

New	Ctrl + N	⌘ + N
Open	Ctrl + O	⌘ + O
Open As	Ctrl + Alt + O	⌘ + Option + O
Close	Ctrl + W	⌘ + W
Save	Ctrl + S	⌘ + S
Save As	Ctrl + Shift + S	⌘ + Shift + S
Save A Copy	Ctrl + Alt + S	⌘ + Option + S
Revert	F12	F12
Page Setup	Ctrl + Shift + P	⌘ + Shift + P
Print	Ctrl + P	⌘ + P
Preferences > General	Ctrl + K	⌘ + K
Saving Files	Ctrl + 2	⌘ + 2
Display & Cursors	Ctrl + 3	⌘ + 3
Transparency & Gamut	Ctrl + 4	⌘ + 4

	Windows 98/NT	Mac OS
Units & Ruler	Ctrl + 5	⌘ + 5
Guides & Grid	Ctrl + 6	⌘ + 6
Plug-Ins & Scratch Disks	Ctrl + 7	⌘ + 7
Memory & Image Cache	Ctrl + 8	⌘ + 8
Exit/Quit	Ctrl + Q	⌘ + Q
New with default settings	Ctrl + Alt + N	⌘ + Option + N
Preferences with last settings	Ctrl + Alt + K	⌘ + Option + K

CLIPBOARD

Cut	Ctrl + X	⌘ + X
Copy	Ctrl + C	⌘ + C
Copy Merged	Ctrl + Shift + C	⌘ + Shift + C
Paste	Ctrl + V	⌘ + V
Paste Into	Ctrl + Shift + V	⌘ + Shift + V

BLENDING MODES

Layer blending modes

Set layer to next blend mode	Shift + + (plus)	Shift + + (plus)
Set layer to previous blend mode	Shift + - (minus)	Shift + - (minus)

Blending mode for brush or layer

Normal	Alt + Shift + N	Option + Shift + N
Dissolve	Alt + Shift + I	Option + Shift + I
Multiply	Alt + Shift + M	Option + Shift + M
Screen	Alt + Shift + S	Option + Shift + S
Overlay	Alt + Shift + O	Option + Shift + O
Soft Light	Alt + Shift + F	Option + Shift + F
Hard Light	Alt + Shift + H	Option + Shift + H
Color Dodge	Alt + Shift + D	Option + Shift + D
Color Burn	Alt + Shift + B	Option + Shift + B
Darken	Alt + Shift + K	Option + Shift + K
Lighten	Alt + Shift + G	Option + Shift + G
Difference	Alt + Shift + E	Option + Shift + E
Exclusion	Alt + Shift + X	Option + Shift + X
Hue	Alt + Shift + U	Option + Shift + U
Saturation	Alt + Shift + T	Option + Shift + T

	Windows 98/NT	Mac OS
Color	Alt + Shift + C	Option + Shift + C
Luminosity	Alt + Shift + Y	Option + Shift + Y
Threshold (Bitmap mode)	Alt + Shift + L	Option + Shift + L
Behind	Alt + Shift + Q	Option + Shift + Q

COLOR

Colors

Swap Foreground/Background colors	X	X
Reset to default colors	D	D

Fill

Open Fill dialog	Shift + Backspace	Shift + Delete
Fill with Foreground color	Alt + Delete/Backspace	Option + Delete
Fill with Foreground color, Preserve Transparency on	Shift + Alt + Delete/Backspace	Shift + Option + Delete
Fill with Background color	Ctrl + Delete/Backspace	⌘ + Delete
Fill with Background color, Preserve Transparency on	Shift + Ctrl + Delete/Backspace	Shift + ⌘ + Delete
Fill from History	Ctrl + Alt + Backspace	⌘ + Option + Delete

Color palette

Cycle through color bars	Shift + click on color bar	Shift + click on color bar
Choose specific color bar	Right-click on color bar	Control + click on color bar

Swatches palette

Add Foreground color as a new swatch	Click in empty slot	Click in empty slot
Insert new swatch color	Shift + Alt + click in palette	Shift + Option + click in palette
Replace swatch color with Foreground color	Shift + click	Shift + click
Delete swatch	Ctrl + click on swatch	⌘ + click on swatch
Choose swatch as Foreground color	Click on swatch	Click on swatch
Choose swatch as Background color	Alt + click on swatch	Option + click on swatch

BRUSHES

Brushes palette

Select first brush	Shift + [	Shift + [
Select previous brush	[	[
Select next brush	]	]
Select last brush	Shift +]	Shift +]

	Windows 98/NT	Mac OS
Delete brush	Alt + click	Option + click
Edit brush name	Double-click on brush	Double-click on brush

SELECTIONS

All	Ctrl + A	⌘ + A
Deselect	Ctrl + D	⌘ + D
Reselect	Ctrl + Shift + D	⌘ + Shift + D
Inverse	Ctrl + Shift + I	⌘ + Shift + I
Feather	Ctrl + Alt + D	⌘ + Option + D
Nudge selection marquee 1 pixel	Arrow key	Arrow key
Nudge selection marquee 10 pixels	Shift + arrow key	Shift + arrow key

FILTERS

Reapply last filter	Ctrl + F	⌘ + F
Fade last filter	Ctrl + Shift + F	⌘ + Shift + F
Reapply filter with the last settings	Ctrl + Alt + F	⌘ + Option + F

Lighting Effects dialog

Clone light in preview area	Alt + drag light	Option + drag light
Delete light in preview area	Delete key	Delete key
Adjust light footprint without affecting angle	Shift + drag handle	Shift + drag handle
Adjust light angle without changing footprint	Ctrl + drag handle	⌘ + drag handle

LAYERS

Layer menu

New > Layer	Ctrl + Shift + N	⌘ + Shift + N
New Layer without dialog	Ctrl + Alt + Shift + N	⌘ + Option + Shift + N
Layer via Copy	Ctrl + J	⌘ + J
Layer via Cut	Ctrl + Shift + J	⌘ + Shift + J
Group with previous	Ctrl + G	⌘ + G
Ungroup	Ctrl + Shift + G	⌘ + Shift + G
Merge Down/Linked/Group	Ctrl + E	⌘ + E
Merge Visible	Shift + Ctrl + E	Shift + ⌘ + E

	Windows 98/NT	Mac OS
Layers palette		
Show/hide layer	Click in eye icon area	Click in eye icon area
Toggle show all layers/show just this layer	Alt + click on eye icon area	Option + click on eye icon area
Show/hide multiple layers	Click + drag thru eye icon area	Click + drag thru eye icon area
Link layer to current target layer	Click in link icon area	Click in link icon area
Turn on/off linking for multiple layers	Click + drag thru link icon area	Click + drag thru link icon area
Create new, empty layer	Click Create new layer button	Click Create new layer button
Create new, empty layers with Layer Options dialog	Alt + click Create new layer button	Option + click Create new layer button
Duplicate layer	Drag layer to Create new layer button	Drag layer to Create new layer button
Delete layer using warning alert	Click Delete current layer button	Click Delete current layer button
Delete layer, bypass warning alert	Alt + click Delete current layer button	Option + click Delete current layer button
Change layer opacity in 10% increments	Number keys (2 = 20%, 3 = 30%)	Number keys (2 = 20%, 3 = 30%)
Toggle preserve transparency for target layer	/ (forward slash)	/ (forward slash)
Load layer pixels as selection	Ctrl + click layer thumbnail	⌘ + click layer thumbnail
Add layer pixels to selection	Ctrl + Shift + click layer thumbnail	⌘ + Shift + click layer thumbnail
Subtract layer pixels from selection	Ctrl + Alt + click layer thumbnail	⌘ + Option + click layer thumbnail
Intersect layer pixels with selection	Ctrl + Alt + Shift + click layer thumbnail	⌘ + Option + Shift + click layer thumbnail
Activate top layer	Shift + Alt +]	Shift + Option +]
Activate next layer (up)	Alt +]	Option+]
Activate previous layer (down)	Alt + [	Option + [
Activate bottom layer	Shift + Alt + [	Shift + Option + [
Edit Layer Options	Double-click layer name	Double-click layer name
Layer Effects		
Toggle effects without dialog on or off	Alt + menu item	Option + menu item
Edit Layer Effect Options (last edited)	Double-click layer effect icon	Double-click layer effect icon
Clear each effect on layer one at a time	Alt + double-click effect icon	Option + double-click effect icon
Move effect	Drag in image	Drag in image
Move effect constrained to 45° axis	Shift + drag in image	Shift + drag in image

	Windows 98/NT	Mac OS
In Layer Effects dialog		
Drop shadow	Ctrl + 1	[⌘] + 1
Inner shadow	Ctrl + 2	[⌘] + 2
Outer glow	Ctrl + 3	[⌘] + 3
Inner glow	Ctrl + 4	[⌘] + 4
Bevel and emboss	Ctrl + 5	[⌘] + 5
Adjustment layers		
New adjustment layer	Ctrl + click Create new layer button	[⌘] + click Create new layer button
Edit adjustment layer	Click adjustment icon	Click adjustment icon
Layer masks		
Create layer mask with Reveal All/ Reveal Selection	Click on mask button	Click on mask button
Create layer mask with Hide All/ Hide Selection	Alt + click on mask button	Option + click on mask button
Link/unlink layer and layer mask	Click Lock layer mask icon	Click Lock layer mask icon
Open Layer Mask Options dialog	Double-click layer mask thumbnail	Double-click layer mask thumbnail
Toggle layer mask on/off	Shift + click layer mask thumbnail	Shift + click layer mask thumbnail
Toggle rubylith mode on/off	\	\
Toggle viewing layer mask/composite	Alt + click layer mask thumbnail	Option + click layer mask thumbnail
Toggle Group/Ungroup with previous	Alt + click line between layers	Option + click line between layers
Merge layers		
Merge down a copy of current layer into layer below	Alt + Merge Down	Option + Merge Down
Merge a copy of all visible layers into current layer	Alt + Merge Visible	Option + Merge Visible
Merge a copy of linked layers into layer below	Alt + Merge Linked	Option + Merge Linked
Arrange layers		
Bring to Front	Ctrl + Shift +]	[⌘] + Shift +]
Bring Forward	Ctrl +]	[⌘] +]
Send to Back	Ctrl + Shift + [	[⌘] + Shift + [
Send Backward	Ctrl + [	[⌘] + [

CHANNELS PALETTE

	Windows 98/NT	Mac OS
Target individual channels	Ctrl + [1–9]	⌘ + [1–9]
Target composite channel	Ctrl + ~ (tilde)	⌘ + ~ (tilde)
Show or hide channel	Click in eye icon area	Click in eye icon area
Add/remove channel to targeted channels	Shift + click on channel	Shift + click on channel
Create new channel	Click on New Channel button	Click on New Channel button
Create new channel with Channel Options dialog	Alt + click New Channel button	Option + click New Channel button
Duplicate channel	Drag channel to New Channel button	Drag channel to New Channel button
Delete channel using warning alert	Click Delete Channel button	Click Delete Channel button
Delete channel bypassing warning alert	Alt + click Delete Channel button	Option + click Delete Channel button
Create new spot color channel	Ctrl + click New Channel button	⌘ + click New Channel button
Create new channel from selection	Click on Save Selection button	Click on Save Selection button
Create new channel from selection with Channel Options	Alt + click Save Selection button	Option + click Save Selection button
Load channel as selection	Click Load Selection button or Ctrl + click channel thumbnail	Click Load Selection button or ⌘ + click channel thumbnail
Add channel to selection	Shift + click Load Selection button or Ctrl + Shift + click channel thumbnail	Shift + click Load Selection button or ⌘ + Shift + click channel thumbnail
Subtract channel from selection	Alt + click Load Selection button or Ctrl + Alt + click channel thumbnail	Option + click Load Selection button or ⌘ + Option + click channel thumbnail
Intersect channel with selection	Alt + Shift + click Load Selection button or Ctrl + Alt + Shift + click thumbnail	Option + Shift + click Load Selection button or ⌘ + Option + Shift + click thumbnail
Edit Channel Options	Double-click channel name	Double-click channel name

QUICK MASK

Toggle Quick Mask on/off	Q	Q
Invert Quick Mask mode	Alt + click Quick Mask button	Option + click Quick Mask button
Open Quick Mask Options dialog	Double-click Quick Mask button	Double-click Quick Mask button

PATHS

Paths palette

Create new path	Click New Path button	Click New Path button
Create new path with New Path dialog	Alt + click New Path button	Option + click New Path button

	Windows 98/NT	Mac OS
Duplicate path	Drag path to New Path button	Drag path to New Path button
Delete path using warning alert	Click Delete Path button	Click Delete Path button
Delete path, bypass warning alert	Alt + click Delete Path button	Option + click Delete Path button
Save work path into path item	Drag Work Path onto New Path button	Drag Work Path onto New Path button
Convert selection into work path	Click Make Work Path button	Click Make Work Path button
Convert selection into work path with Work Path dialog	Alt + click Make Work Path button	Option + click Make Work Path button
Convert path into selection	Click Load Selection button	Click Load Selection button
Convert path into selection with Make Selection dialog	Alt + click Load Selection button	Option + click Load Selection button
Stroke/fill path		
Stroke path with Foreground color	Click Stroke Path button	Click Stroke Path button
Stroke path using Stroke Path dialog	Alt + click Stroke Path button	Option + click Stroke Path button
Fill path with Foreground color	Click Fill Path button	Click Fill Path button
Fill path using Fill Path dialog	Alt + click Fill Path button	Option + click Fill Path button
Paths and selections		
Load path as selection	Ctrl + click path thumbnail	⌘ + click path thumbnail
Add path to selection	Ctrl + Shift + click path thumbnail	⌘ + Shift + click path thumbnail
Subtract path from selection	Ctrl + Alt + click path thumbnail	⌘ + Option + click path thumbnail
Intersect path with selection	Ctrl + Alt + Shift + click thumbnail	⌘ + Option + Shift + click thumbnail

HISTORY

History palette		
Toggle back/forward one step	Ctrl + Z	⌘ + Z
Step forward	Shift + Ctrl + Z	⌘ + Shift + Z
Step backward	Alt + Ctrl + Z	⌘ + Option + Z
Duplicate history state (other than current)	Alt + click state	Option + click state
Create new snapshot	Click Create new snapshot button	Click Create new snapshot button
Create new document from state/snapshot	Click Create new document button	Click Create new document but- ton
History brush tool		
Constrain to horizontal or vertical axis	Shift + drag	Shift + drag
Paint straight lines	Shift + click	Shift + click

TRANSFORM

	Windows 98/NT	Mac OS
Free Transform	Ctrl + T	⌘ + T
Transform > Again	Ctrl + Shift + T	⌘ + Shift + T
Free Transform with duplication	Ctrl + Alt + T	⌘ + Option + T
Transform Again with duplication	Ctrl + Alt + Shift + T	⌘ + Option + Shift + T
Scale using center point (free transform)	Alt + drag corner handles	Option + drag corner handles
Skew using center point (free transform)	Ctrl + Alt + Shift + drag side handles	⌘ + Option + Shift + drag side handles

ADJUST DIALOGS

	Windows 98/NT	Mac OS
Levels	Ctrl + L	⌘ + L
Auto Levels	Ctrl + Shift + L	⌘ + Shift + L
Curves	Ctrl + M	⌘ + M
Color Balance	Ctrl + B	⌘ + B
Hue/Saturation	Ctrl + U	⌘ + U
Desaturate	Ctrl + Shift + U	⌘ + Shift + U
Invert	Ctrl + I	⌘ + I

Reopen dialog

	Windows 98/NT	Mac OS
Levels with last settings	Ctrl + Alt + L	⌘ + Option + L
Curves with last settings	Ctrl + Alt + M	⌘ + Option + M
Color Balance with last settings	Ctrl + Alt + B	⌘ + Option + B
Hue/Saturation with last settings	Ctrl + Alt + U	⌘ + Option + U

TYPE

Type tool

	Windows 98/NT	Mac OS
Designate type origin	Click or click + drag	Click or click + drag
Re-edit existing type	Click on type in image	Click on type in image

Type Tool dialog

	Windows 98/NT	Mac OS
Zoom in on image	Ctrl + + (plus)	⌘ + + (plus)
Zoom out of image	Ctrl + - (minus)	⌘ + - (minus)

Alignment

	Windows 98/NT	Mac OS
Left/Top	Ctrl + Shift + L	⌘ + Shift + L
Center	Ctrl + Shift + C	⌘ + Shift + C
Right/Bottom	Ctrl + Shift + R	⌘ + Shift + R

	Windows 98/NT	Mac OS
Size		
Increase point size by 2 pts.	Ctrl + Shift + >	⌘ + Shift + >
Increase point size by 10 pts.	Ctrl + Alt + Shift + >	⌘ + Option + Shift + >
Decrease point size by 2 pts.	Ctrl + Shift + <	⌘ + Shift + <
Decrease point size by 10 pts.	Ctrl + Alt + Shift + <	⌘ + Option + Shift + <
Leading		
Increase leading by 2 pts.	Alt + Down Arrow	Option + Down Arrow
Increase leading by 10 pts.	Ctrl + Alt + Down Arrow	⌘ + Option + Down Arrow
Decrease leading by 2 pts.	Alt + Up Arrow	Option + Up Arrow
Decrease leading by 10 pts.	Ctrl + Alt + Up Arrow	⌘ + Option + Up Arrow
Kerning/tracking		
Increase kern/track 20/1000 em space	Alt + Right Arrow	Option + Right Arrow
Increase kern/track 100/1000 em space	Ctrl + Alt + Right Arrow	⌘ + Option + Right Arrow
Decrease kern/track 20/1000 em space	Alt + Left Arrow	Option + Left Arrow
Decrease kern/track 100/1000 em space	Ctrl + Alt + Left Arrow	⌘ + Option + Left Arrow
Baseline shift		
Increase baseline shift by 2 pts.	Alt + Shift + Up Arrow	Option + Shift + Up Arrow
Increase baseline shift by 10 pts.	Ctrl + Alt + Shift + Up Arrow	⌘ + Option + Shift + Up Arrow
Decrease baseline shift by 2 pts.	Alt + Shift + Down + Arrow	Option + Shift + Down + Arrow
Decrease baseline shift by 10 pts.	Ctrl + Alt + Shift + Down Arrow	⌘ + Option + Shift + Down Arrow
Move insertion point		
Move to the right one character	Right arrow	Right arrow
Move to the left one character	Left arrow	Left arrow
Move up one line	Up arrow	Up arrow
Move down one line	Down arrow	Down arrow
Move to the right one word	Ctrl + Right Arrow	⌘ + Right Arrow
Move to the left one word	Ctrl + Left Arrow	⌘ + Left Arrow
Select		
Select word	Double-click	Double-click
Select one character to the right	Shift + Right Arrow	Shift + Right Arrow
Select one character to the left	Shift + Left Arrow	Shift + Left Arrow
Select one word to the right	Ctrl + Shift + Right Arrow	⌘ + Shift + Right Arrow
Select one word to the left	Ctrl + Shift + Left Arrow	⌘ + Shift + Left Arrow

	Windows 98/NT	Mac OS
Select one line above	Shift + Up Arrow	Shift + Up Arrow
Select one line below	Shift + Down Arrow	Shift + Down Arrow
Select all characters	Ctrl + A	⌘ + A
Select characters from insertion point	Shift + click	Shift + click

Type Mask and Vertical Type Mask tools

Add to selection	Shift + click, then draw	Shift + click, then draw
Delete from selection	Alt + click, then draw	Option + click, then draw
Intersect with selection	Alt + Shift + click, then draw	Option + Shift + click, then draw
Designate type origin	Click + drag	Click + drag

CURVES DIALOG

Add color as new point on curve	Ctrl + click in image	⌘ + click in image
Add color as individual points for each curve	Ctrl + Shift + click	⌘ + Shift + click
Move points	Arrow keys	Arrow keys
Move points in multiples of 10	Shift + arrow keys	Shift + arrow keys
Add point	Click in grid	Click in grid
Delete point	Ctrl + click on point	⌘ + click on point
Deselect all points	Ctrl + D	⌘ + D
Toggle grid between fine/coarse	Alt + click in grid	Option + click in grid
Select next control point	Ctrl + Tab	⌘ + Ctrl + Tab
Select previous control point	Ctrl + Shift + Tab	⌘ + Ctrl + Shift + Tab
Select multiple control points	Shift + click	Shift + click

HUE/SATURATION DIALOG

Move range to new location	Click in image	Click in image
Add to range	Shift + click/drag in image	Shift + click/drag in image
Subtract from range	Alt + click/drag in image	Option + click/drag in image
Edit master	Ctrl + tilde	⌘ + tilde
Edit individual colors	Ctrl + 1–6	⌘ + 1–6

3D TRANSFORM DIALOG

Select tool	V	V
Direct-selection tool	A	A
Cube tool	M	M
Sphere tool	N	N

	Windows 98/NT	Mac OS
Cylinder tool	C	C
Add-anchor-point tool	+ (plus)	+ (plus)
Delete-anchor-point tool	- (minus)	- (minus)
Pan Camera tool	E	E
Trackball tool	R	R
Hand tool	H	H
Zoom tool	Z	Z
Toggle Select/Direct-selection tools	Ctrl + Tab	⌘ + Tab
Pan image	Spacebar + drag	Spacebar + drag
Zoom in	Ctrl + Spacebar + drag/click	⌘ + Spacebar + drag/click
Zoom out	Ctrl + Alt + Spacebar + click	⌘ + Option + Spacebar + click

INDEX

Index

C

D

E

Q

R

S

T

U

V

W

©Alan Mazzetti, Repair Ripoffs

one above the
have a fine
gradually until
The summer
and cool,
of an
calculated
its wonderful

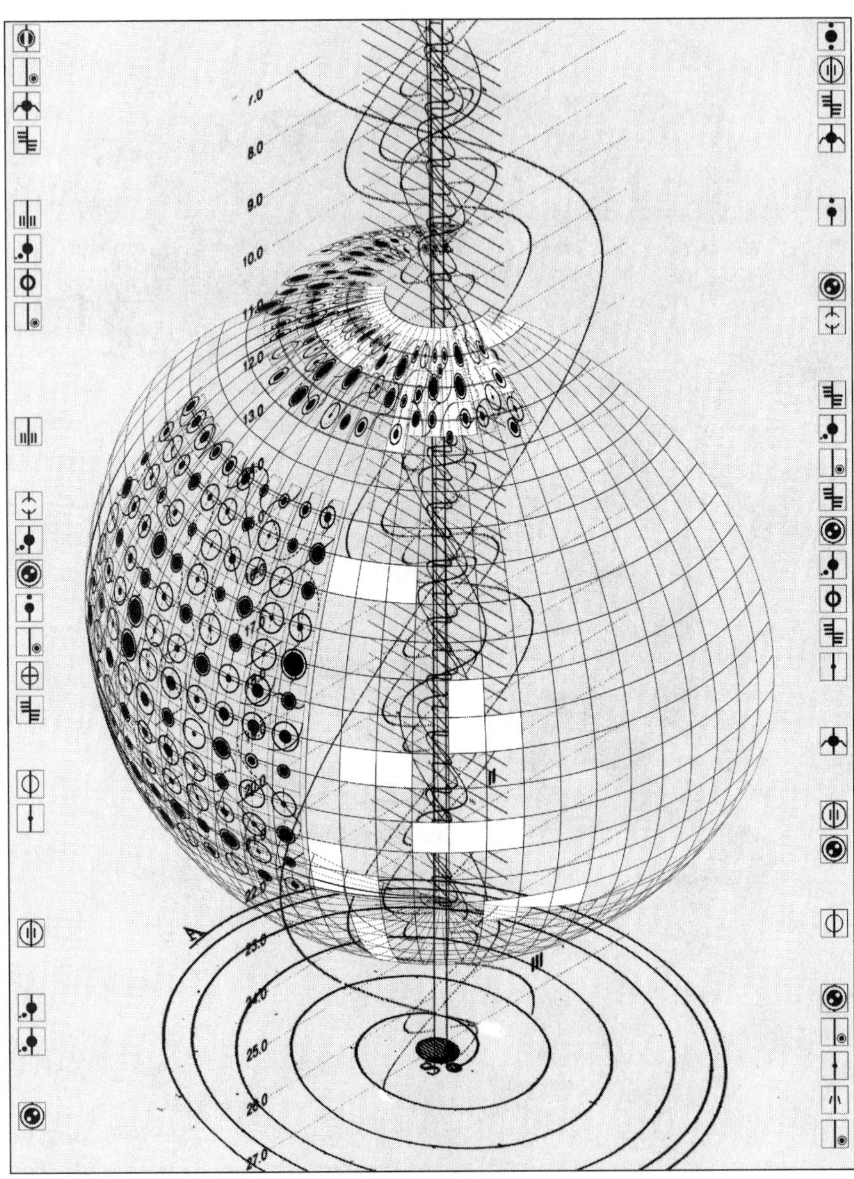
7.0
8.0
9.0
10.0
11.0
12.0
13.0
14.0
17.0
20.0
22.0
23.0
24.0
25.0
26.0
27.0

©Jeff Brice

New from Peachpit Press

VISUAL QUICKSTART ONLINE LIBRARY!

FREE TRIAL OFFER

25 top Web and Graphics QuickStarts, just $49.95 a year!

Our new **Visual QuickStart Online Library** offers you

- Easy access to the most current information on Web design and graphics via the Web–wherever you are, 24 hours a day, 7 days a week
- Powerful, advanced search features that enable you to find just the topics you want across multiple books, ranked by relevance
- Updates to new editions of the books as they become available
- Easy ways to bookmark, make notes, and send email alerts to colleagues
- Complete access to 25 bestselling books for only $49.95 (that's more than $450 worth of books for less than the price of three *Visual QuickStart Guides*!)

You'll find all your favorite *Visual QuickStart Guides,* as well as those you want to read next, including:

HTML 4 for the World Wide Web
Photoshop for Macintosh and Windows
Illustrator for Windows and Macintosh
Perl and CGI for the World Wide Web
Flash for Windows and Macintosh

Free Trial Offer!

Check it out! We invite you to sample a FREE trial subscription to Peachpit's new Visual QuickStart Online Library for one week. Just go to **www.quickstartonline.com** and sign up for your free trial today! You'll have complete access to the Library for one week, absolutely free.

www.quickstartonline.com

Quick search... Quick find... QuickStart!

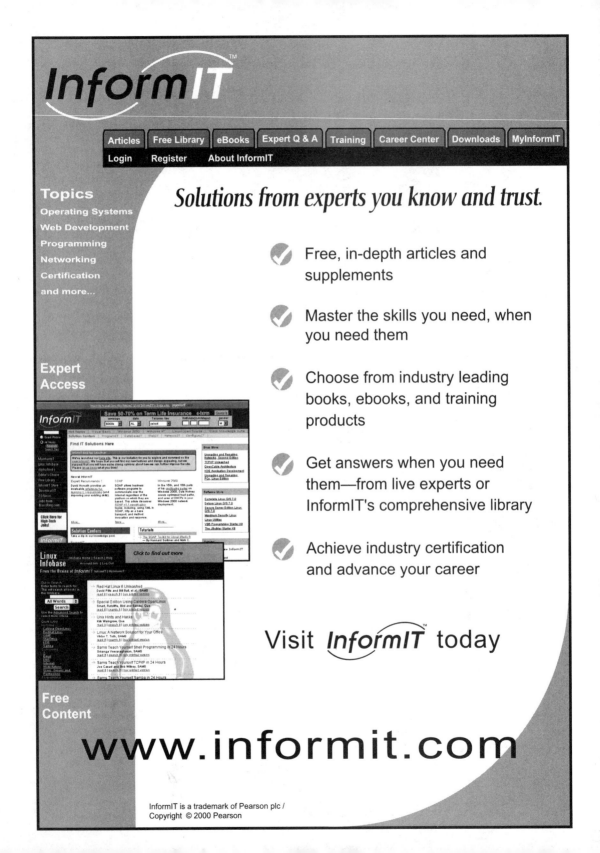